RENEWALS 458-4574

DATE DUE

| | | | |
|---|---|---|---|
| | | | |
| OCT 6 | | | |
| OCT 1 8 | | | |
| | | | |
| | | | |
| | | | |
| | | | |
| | | | |
| | | | |
| | | | |
| | | | |
| | | | |
| | | | |
| | | | |
| | | | |
| GAYLORD | | | PRINTED IN U.S.A. |

# Terrorism, Asymmetric Warfare, and Weapons of Mass Destruction

WITHDRAWN
UTSA LIBRARIES

# Terrorism, Asymmetric Warfare, and Weapons of Mass Destruction

## Defending the U.S. Homeland

ANTHONY H. CORDESMAN

Published in cooperation with the
Center for Strategic and International Studies,
Washington, D.C.

**Westport, Connecticut**
**London**

**Library of Congress Cataloging-in-Publication Data**

Cordesman, Anthony H.
   Terrorism, asymmetric warfare, and weapons of mass destruction : defending the U.S.
homeland / by Anthony H. Cordesman.
    p.  cm.
  ISBN 0–275–97427–8 (alk. paper)
  1. United States—Defenses.  2. United States—Military policy.  3. Terrorism—United
States—Prevention.  4. Asymmetric warfare—United States.  5. Weapons of mass
destruction.  I. Title.
  UA23.C67   2002
  355′.033073—dc21         2001036313
British Library Cataloguing in Publication Data is available.

Copyright © 2002 by Center for Strategic and International Studies

All rights reserved. No portion of this book may be
reproduced, by any process or technique, without the
express written consent of the publisher.

Library of Congress Catalog Card Number: 2001036313
ISBN: 0–275–97427–8

First published in 2002

Praeger Publishers, 88 Post Road West, Westport, CT 06881
An imprint of Greenwood Publishing Group, Inc.
www.praeger.com

Printed in the United States of America

The paper used in this book complies with the
Permanent Paper Standard issued by the National
Information Standards Organization (Z39.48–1984).

10  9  8  7  6  5  4  3

Library
University of Texas

# Contents

# Acknowledgments

The author would like to thank Linnea Raine, Andrew Li, Preston Golson, and Aviva Roller for their assistance in researching and editing this book.

*Chapter 1*

# The Changing Face
# of Asymmetric Warfare
# and Terrorism

The tragic attacks on the World Trade Center and the Pentagon on September 11, 2001 have made it all too clear that wars do not have to be declared and threats do not have to be overt. It is brutally clear there is a wide spectrum of potential threats to the U.S. homeland that do not involve the threat of overt attacks by states using long-range missiles or conventional military forces. Such threats can range from the acts of individual extremists to state-sponsored asymmetric warfare. They can include covert attacks by state actors, state use of proxies, and independent terrorist groups. They can include attacks by foreign individuals and residents of the United States whose motives can range from religion to efforts at extortion. Motives can range from well-defined political and strategic goals, to religion and political ideology, crime and sabotage, or acts by the psychologically disturbed. The means of attack can vary from token uses of explosives, cyber-terrorism, car and truck bombs, and passenger airliners to the use of weapons of mass destruction (WMD).

We have already experienced some devastating attacks, but no pattern of attacks on U.S. territory has yet emerged that provides a clear basis for predicting how serious any given form of attack will be in the future, what means of attack will be used, or how lethal new forms of attack will be if they are successful. As a result, there is a major, ongoing debate over the range of threats that need to be considered, the seriousness of such threats, and how the U.S. government should react. Years before the attacks of September 2001, a Government Accounting Office (GAO) report on terrorism summarizes the various views within the U.S. government regarding these uncertainties as follows:

There are three schools of thought on the terrorist threat: (1) some believe the threat and likelihood of terrorist attack is very low and does not pose a serious risk; (2) others believe the threat and likelihood of terrorist attack is high and could seriously disrupt the U.S. national and economic security; and (3) still others believe assessments of the threat and vulnerability to terrorist attack need to be accompanied by risk assessments to rationally guide the allocation of resources and attention. The expert further stated that such risk assessments would include analyses of vulnerability and susceptibility to terrorist attack and the severity of potential damage. According to U.S. intelligence agencies, conventional explosives continue to be the weapon of choice for terrorists. Although the probability of their use may increase over time, chemical and biological materials are less likely terrorist weapons because they are more difficult to weaponize and the results are unpredictable. Agency officials also noted that terrorist's use of nuclear weapons is the least likely scenario, although the consequences could be disastrous.[1]

We now know all too well how vulnerable we really are, but it is difficult to predict how such threats will evolve in the future, and the extent to which states and their proxies will use unconventional methods of attack as distinguished from terrorists. Potential foreign attackers have good reason to fear American military power, and most are still unlikely to launch such attacks without considering the risks. At the same time, it is painfully clear that America's very strengths create an incentive to attack it using asymmetric forms of warfare. Waging asymmetric warfare against the United States offers the greatest chance of success and the least risk of retaliation, and some key technologies are evolving in ways that aid the attacker. For example, biological and information warfare will inevitably make the potential threat from foreign and domestic attackers more serious over time.

The National Intelligence Council (NIC) provided the following estimate of this emerging threat in its December 2000 analysis of global trends through the year 2015, and its forecasts of future trends make an important contrast to the GAO's estimate of the current threat:

> Regions, countries, and groups feeling left behind will face deepening economic stagnation, political instability, and cultural alienation. They will foster political, ethnic, ideological, and religious extremism, along with the violence that often accompanies it. They will force the United States and other developed countries to remain focused on "old-world" challenges while concentrating on the implications of "new-world" technologies at the same time. States with ineffective and incompetent governance not only will fail to benefit from globalization, but in some instances will spawn conflicts at home and abroad, ensuring an even wider gap between regional winners and losers than exists today.
>
> . . . The United States will face three types of threats:
>
> • Asymmetric threats in which state and nonstate adversaries avoid direct engagements with the U.S. military but devise strategies, tactics, and

weapons—some improved by "sidewise" technology—to minimize U.S. strengths and exploit perceived weaknesses;

- Strategic WMD threats, including nuclear missile threats, in which (barring significant political or economic changes) Russia, China, most likely North Korea, probably Iran, and possibly Iraq have the capability to strike the United States, and the potential for unconventional delivery of WMD by both state or nonstate actors also will grow; and

- Regional military threats in which a few countries maintain large military forces with a mix of Cold War and post–Cold War concepts and technologies.

. . . The potential for conflict will arise from rivalries in Asia, ranging from India-Pakistan to China-Taiwan, as well as among the antagonists in the Middle East. Their potential lethality will grow, driven by the availability of WMD, longer-range missile delivery systems, and other technologies.

Internal conflicts stemming from religious, ethnic, economic, or political disputes will remain at current levels or even increase in number. The United Nations and regional organizations will be called on to manage such conflicts because major states—stressed by domestic concerns, perceived risk of failure, lack of political will, or tight resources—will minimize their direct involvement.

Export control regimes and sanctions will be less effective because of the diffusion of technology, porous borders, defense industry consolidations, and reliance on foreign markets to maintain profitability. Arms and weapons technology transfers will be more difficult to control.

Prospects will grow that more sophisticated weaponry, including weapons of mass destruction—indigenously produced or externally acquired—will get into the hands of state and nonstate belligerents, some hostile to the United States. The likelihood will increase over this period that WMD will be used either against the United States or its forces, facilities, and interests overseas. . . . Rapid advances and diffusion of biotechnology, nanotechnology, and the materials sciences, moreover, will add to the capabilities of our adversaries to engage in biological warfare or bio-terrorism.

. . . Most adversaries will recognize the information advantage and military superiority of the United States in 2015. Rather than acquiesce to any potential U.S. military domination, they will try to circumvent or minimize U.S. strengths and exploit perceived weaknesses. IT-driven globalization will significantly increase interaction among terrorists, narcotraffickers, weapons proliferators, and organized criminals, who in a networked world will have greater access to information, to technology, to finance, to sophisticated deception-and-denial techniques and to each other. Such asymmetric approaches—whether undertaken by state or nonstate actors—will become the dominant characteristic of most threats to the U.S. homeland.

. . . They will be a defining challenge for U.S. strategy, operations, and force development, and they will require that strategy to maintain focus on traditional, low-technology threats as well as the capacity of potential adversaries to harness elements of proliferating advanced technologies. At the same time, we do not know the extent to which adversaries, state and nonstate, might be influenced or deterred by other geopolitical, economic, technological, or diplomatic factors in 2015.

. . . Over the next 15 years, transnational criminal organizations will become increasingly adept at exploiting the global diffusion of sophisticated information, financial, and transportation networks. Criminal organizations and networks based in North America, Western Europe, China, Colombia, Israel, Japan, Mexico, Nigeria, and Russia will expand the scale and scope of their activities. They will form loose alliances with one another, with smaller criminal entrepreneurs, and with insurgent movements for specific operations. They will corrupt leaders of unstable, economically fragile, or failing states; insinuate themselves into troubled banks and businesses; and cooperate with insurgent political movements to control substantial geographic areas. Their income will come from narcotics trafficking; alien smuggling; trafficking in women and children; smuggling toxic materials, hazardous wastes, illicit arms, military technologies, and other contraband; financial fraud; and racketeering. . . . The risk will increase that organized criminal groups will traffic in nuclear, biological, or chemical weapons. The degree of risk depends on whether governments with WMD capabilities can or will control such weapons and materials.

. . . Estimates of the number of distinct ethnic-linguistic groups at the beginning of the twenty-first century run from 2,000 to 5,000, ranging from small bands living in isolated areas to larger groups living in ancestral homelands or in diasporas. Most of the world's 191 states are ethnically heterogeneous, and many contain ethnic populations with co-ethnics in neighboring states. By 2015, ethnic heterogeneity will increase in almost all states, as a result of international migration and divergent birthrates of migrant and native populations. . . . States with poor governance; ethnic, cultural, or religious tensions; weak economies; and porous borders will be prime breeding grounds for terrorism. In such states, domestic groups will challenge the entrenched government and transnational networks seeking safehavens.

. . . At the same time, the trend away from state-supported political terrorism and toward more diverse, free-wheeling, transnational networks— enabled by information technology—will continue. Some of the states that actively sponsor terrorism or terrorist groups today may decrease or even cease their support by 2015 as a result of regime changes, rapprochement with neighbors, or the conclusion that terrorism has become counterproductive. But weak states also could drift toward cooperation with terrorists, creating defacto new state supporters. . . . Between now and 2015 terrorist tactics will become increasingly sophisticated and designed to achieve mass casualties. We expect the trend toward greater lethality in terrorist attacks to continue.

. . . Many potential adversaries, as reflected in doctrinal writings and statements, see U.S. military concepts, together with technology, as giving the United States the ability to expand its lead in conventional war-fighting capabilities. . . . This perception among present and potential adversaries will continue to generate the pursuit of asymmetric capabilities against U.S. forces and interests abroad as well as the territory of the United States. U.S. opponents—state and such nonstate actors as drug lords, terrorists, and foreign insurgents—will not want to engage the U.S. military on its terms. They will choose instead political and military strategies designed to dissuade the United States from using force, or, if the United States does use force, to exhaust American will, circumvent or minimize U.S. strengths, and exploit perceived U.S. weaknesses. Asymmetric challenges can arise across the spectrum of conflict that will confront U.S. forces in a theater of operations or on U.S. soil.

*Terrorism.* Much of the terrorism noted earlier will be directed at the United States and its overseas interests. Most anti–U.S. terrorism will be based on perceived ethnic, religious, or cultural grievances. Terrorist groups will continue to find ways to attack U.S. military and diplomatic facilities abroad. Such attacks are likely to expand increasingly to include U.S. companies and American citizens. Middle East and Southwest Asian-based terrorists are the most likely to threaten the United States.

*Weapons of Mass Destruction.* WMD programs reflect the motivations and intentions of the governments that produce them and, therefore, can be altered by the change of a regime or by a regime's change of view. Linear projections of WMD are intended to assess what the picture will look like if changes in motivations and intentions do not occur.

Short- and medium-range ballistic missiles, particularly if armed with WMD, already pose a significant threat overseas to U.S. interests, military forces, and allies. By 2015, the United States, barring major political changes in these countries, will face ICBM threats from North Korea, probably from Iran, and possibly from Iraq, in addition to long-standing threats from Russia and China.

. . . Other means to deliver WMD against the United States will emerge, some cheaper and more reliable and accurate than early-generation ICBMs. The likelihood of an attack by these means is greater than that of a WMD attack with an ICBM. The goal of the adversary would be to move the weapon within striking distance by using short- and medium-range missiles deployed on surface ships or covert missions using military special operations forces or state intelligence services. Non-missile delivery means, however, do not provide the same prestige, deterrence, and coercive diplomacy associated with ICBMs.

. . . Chemical and biological threats to the United States will become more widespread; such capabilities are easier to develop, hide, and deploy than nuclear weapons. Some terrorists or insurgents will attempt to use such weapons against U.S. interests—against the United States itself, its forces or facilities overseas, or its allies. Moreover, the United States would be affected by the use of such weapons anywhere in the world because Washington would be called on to help contain the damage and to provide scientific expertise and economic assistance to deal with the effects. Such weapons could be delivered through a variety of means, including missiles, unmanned aerial vehicles, or covertly via land, air, and sea.

. . . Over the past decade, a slow but persistent transformation has occurred in the arms procurement strategies of states. Many states are attempting to diversify sources of arms for reasons that vary from fears of arms embargoes, to declining defense budgets, or to a desire to acquire limited numbers of cutting-edge technologies. Their efforts include developing a mix of indigenous production; codeveloping, coproducing, or licensing production; purchasing entire weapon systems; or leasing capabilities. At the same time, many arms-producing states, confronted with declining domestic arms needs but determined to maintain defense industries, are commercializing defense production and aggressively expanding arms exports.

Together, the above factors suggest:

Technology diffusion to those few states with a motivation to arm and the economic resources to do so will accelerate as weapons and militarily relevant technologies are moved rapidly and routinely across national borders in response to increasingly commercial rather than security calculations. For such militarily related technologies as the Global Positioning System, satellite imagery, and communications, technological superiority will be difficult to maintain for very long. In an environment of broad technological diffusion, nonmaterial elements of military power—strategy, doctrine, and training—will increase in importance over the next 15 years in deciding combat outcomes.

Export regimes and sanctions will be difficult to manage and less effective in controlling arms and weapons technology transfers. The resultant proliferation of WMD and long-range delivery systems would be destabilizing and increase the risk of miscalculation and conflict that produces high casualties.

Advantages will go to states that have a strong commercial technology sector and develop effective ways to link these capabilities to their national defense industrial base. States able to optimize private and public sector linkages could achieve significant advancements in weapons systems.

The twin developments outlined above—constrained defense spending worldwide combined with increasing military technological potential—preclude accurate forecasts of which technologies, in what quantity and form, will be incorporated in the military systems of future adversaries. In many cases, the question will not be which technologies provide the greatest military potential but which will receive the political backing and resources to reach the procurement and fielding stage. Moreover, civilian technology development already is driving military technology development in many countries.

The events of September 2001 have shown that the United States cannot afford to ignore this warning given by its top intelligence analysts. The events have also shown that conventional attacks and explosives remain a major threat at a time when it is still not possible to predict when and how attackers will emerge with the capability and willingness to use WMD in the U.S. homeland. It is a fact, however, that there are already a number of potential threats from foreign states and terrorists, and that such attacks will become increasingly easy to execute. There will also be a growing risk that such attacks can inflict levels of damage far beyond any previous act of terrorism or the kind of natural disasters with which federal, state, and local governments must normally deal.

Attacks involving large amounts of high explosives or chemical, biological, radiological, and nuclear (CBRN) attacks have long been technically feasible, and the "globalization" of chemical and biological technologies and production facilities is making some weapons easier to develop or acquire. Nuclear proliferation continues and the levels of control over weapons, fissile material, and radioactive material are uncertain. Attacks using such weapons can involve a wide range of different levels of casualties, but they can involve attacks that could kill well over ten thousand to one hundred thousand Americans with economic, physical, psychological, and political effects that are radically different from any covert, terrorist, or extremist attacks that have occurred to date.

## THE GROWING FOCUS ON TERRORISM

These risks help explain why the Clinton and Bush Administrations have seen these risks as a critical aspect of homeland defense. The United States has steadily refined its policy toward terrorism and the risk of such attacks since the Vice President's Task Force on Terrorism issued a report in 1985 that highlighted the need for improved, centralized, interagency coordination of the significant federal assets to respond to terrorist incidents. The U.S. response to potential threats from covert attacks by state actors, their proxies, or independent extremists and terrorists has changed even more since the mid-1990s.

The National Defense Authorization Act for FY1994, Public Law No. 103–160, Section 1703 (50 USC 1522) mandated the coordination and integration of all Department of Defense (DOD) chemical and biological defense programs. As part of this coordination and integration, the secretary of defense was directed to submit an assessment and a description of plans to improve readiness to survive, fight, and win in a nuclear, biological, and chemical (NBC) contaminated environment.

The bombing of the federal building in Oklahoma City led to the issuance of Presidential Decision Directive 39 (PDD-39) in June 1995. PDD-39 built on the previous directive and contained three key elements of a national strategy for combating terrorism: (1) reduce vulnerabilities to terrorist attacks and prevent and deter terrorist acts before they occur; (2) respond to terrorist acts that do occur—crisis management—and apprehend and punish terrorists; and (3) manage the consequences of terrorist acts, including providing emergency relief and restoring capabilities to protect public health and safety and essential government services. This directive also further elaborated on agencies' roles and responsibilities and some specific measures to be taken regarding each element of the strategy.[2]

These policies have since been further developed by two key PDDs—62 and 63—which were issued in 1998. PDD-62 reaffirmed the basic principles of PDD-39, but clarified and reinforced the specific missions of the U.S.

agencies charged with defeating and defending against terrorism, and created a new and more systematic federal approach to fighting the emerging threat posed by WMD, such as programs to deter terrorist incidents involving CBRN weapons and to manage the consequences if such incidents should occur. PDD-63 called for a national effort to ensure the security of critical infrastructure. It covered critical infrastructure protection (CIP) cyber crime and the security of government and private-sector infrastructure to ensure national security, national economic security, and public health and safety.

New legislation has also shaped U.S. policy. The Defense against Weapons of Mass Destruction Act, contained in the National Defense Authorization Act for FY1997 (title XIV of PL 104–201, September 23, 1996), established the Nunn-Lugar-Domenici Domestic Preparedness Program. This act made the DOD the lead federal agency for implementing the program, and is to work in cooperation with the Federal Bureau of Investigation (FBI), the Department of Energy (DOE), the Environmental Protection Agency (EPA), the Department of Health and Human Services (HHS), and the Federal Emergency Management Agency (FEMA).[3] Equally important, major new funds have been spent on federal programs to deal with these threats, and federal spending increased by at least 43 percent between FY1998 and FY2001.

## TERRORISM VERSUS ASYMMETRIC WARFARE

At the same time, there is no way for federal, state, and local governments to predict what risks attackers will actually take when launching attacks on the United States, or to predict the kind of event or crisis that could suddenly change their willingness to use any given means and level of attack. There also is no reason to limit the threat to "terrorism." States and proxy terrorist groups may conduct or sponsor sophisticated attacks on the U.S. homeland, and they have little incentive to declare war and many incentives to avoid attribution. There are no clear boundaries that separate one form of attack from another or that allow the U.S. government to predict where and how it will have to defend itself against an attack or to strike first to prevent one from happening.

While it is tempting for governments to plan for the kind of near simultaneous hijacking of four aircraft or any other cleanly defined single incident with which governments can best cope, there is no reason to assume that an attacker must follow such rules. Multiple attacks can greatly complicate defense and response. A single attack can use a variety of weapons ranging from a "conventional" weapon like an aircraft or a truck bomb to a mix of biological agents or a mix of chemical and information warfare. One attacker can piggyback on the attack of another, and attacks on the U.S. homeland can be linked to attacks on Americans overseas or our allies. The very threat of an attack can be used to try to deter the United States from attacking or exercising its diplomatic or military power, or it can be used to try to force a domestic political agenda on federal, state, or local governments.

The U.S. military, for example, is increasingly concerned that foreign states or well-organized terrorist groups may attack embarking U.S. troops at an air base, port, or assembly facility. Federal, state, and local civil authorities often focus on urban terrorist attacks that are totally decoupled from U.S. strategic and military interests, and see the U.S. military as a source of aid in an emergency. Some military analysts, however, feel the most probable reason any state or movement would take the risk of using a biological weapon would be to halt U.S. military deployments. If such an attack were successful, it could be that the U.S. military would have to turn to state and local authorities for emergency medical and other forms of assistance.

What is clear is that homeland defense must respond to a constantly changing threat, especially to the kind that may be impossible to predict, the emergence of new patterns of attack for years to come. At the same time, many of the actions necessary to defend the U.S. homeland will take years— sometimes well over a decade—to fully implement. In many cases, research and development is required, and the end result must then be transformed into deployed and effective capabilities at the federal, state, and local levels. Such action can only be cost effective if it has a reasonable life cycle or period of effectiveness.

As a result, the United States must make decisions now to shape programs that will affect its capabilities as much as a quarter of a century in the future. It must do so knowing that it cannot predict what new threats will or will not emerge, and that grave uncertainties exist regarding the emergence of new methods of attack and defense and the balance of technology between them. The world can evolve in radically different directions and is almost certain to do so. The level of foreign threats can vary sharply by region, and the level of domestic threats can change strikingly. George Santayana's warning that those who cannot remember the past are condemned to repeat it is as valid as ever, but those who ignore the uncertainty of future change may well face far more serious problems.

These uncertainties have polarized part of the debate over the threat posed by WMD and other means of attack which produce mass casualties. There are those who believe passionately that such attacks on the U.S. homeland are inevitable, while others believe the threat is unreal and an exaggeration that has grown out the search for new threats following the end of the Cold War. Many in both camps focus almost exclusively on the forms of "terrorism" that do not involve the potential threat from states engaging in asymmetric warfare, state sponsorship of terrorist or extremist groups, or the slow emergence of more sophisticated terrorist entities or networks.

There is often a conceptual gap in homeland defense among the threats posed by overt attacks using ballistic missiles, asymmetric warfare, and "terrorism." At the same time, there are debates over how the threat should be categorized and prioritized, what response measures are needed, if any, and what kinds of attack are most likely. So far, these debates have provided many insights as to what may happen, but no basis for resolving the many uncertainties involved.

## NOTES

1. U.S. General Accounting Office, GAO Report to Congressional Requesters, "Combating Terrorism, Federal Agencies' Efforts to Implement National Policy and Strategy," GAO/NSIAD-97-254, September 1997, 15.

2. U.S. General Accounting Office, GAO Report to Congressional Requesters, "Combating Terrorism, Federal Agencies' Efforts to Implement National Policy and Strategy," GAO/T-NSIAD-98-164, April 23, 1998, 3.

3. "Combating Terrorism," GAO/T-NSIAD-98-164, 4.

*Chapter 2*

# Risk Assessment: Planning for "Non-patterns" and Potential Risk

The United States must learn to defend against uncertainty. There is no way to predict the probable nature of the threat that can be firmly rooted in either an analysis of past patterns of attack, or a clearly identifiable threat from specific countries or foreign and domestic extremists. Furthermore, U.S. planning and analysis often tends to react to an emotive and generic approach to terrorism, and/or generalize from patterns and incidents that simply do not justify such generalizations. There has been only limited, sporadic efforts to develop national net assessments of the threat posed by foreign terrorism and no matching effort to create comprehensive net assessment of domestic threats. The net assessments that have addressed foreign terrorism have generally failed to address higher levels of asymmetric warfare and to provide any net technical assessment of how methods of attack may evolve in the future and what technology can do to improve defense.

## LOOKING BEYOND EMOTIONAL DEFINITIONS OF TERRORISM

Many elements of the U.S. government seem to find it difficult to accept the fact that asymmetric warfare is only illegal or illegitimate in the eyes of those who do not need to use such tactics, or find them to be the most effective form of attack, and the fact that the future threat posed by covert or proxy attacks by state actors may be at least as important, and far more lethal, than the threat posed by foreign and domestic terrorist-extremist groups and individuals.

With the exception of the DOD and the Central Intelligence Agency (CIA), the U.S. government tends to use a relatively narrow definition of the word "terrorism" based on the currently most probable threats rather than examine the full range of possible asymmetric threats and consider how they may evolve over time. This focus on a narrow definition of "terrorism" has three major negative side effects: First, the threat analysis and characterization is based on the idea that the threat to the U.S. homeland comes only from illegal or illegitimate actors, driven largely by extreme political or ideological motives. Second, it leads federal planners to downplay or ignore the risk that governments may launch covert CBRN attacks against the United States or use proxies to do so, giving "terrorists" an access to far more sophisticated weapons than would otherwise be the case. And finally, it leads many agencies to define threats in terms of attacks that would produce limited to moderate casualties, with ten thousand deaths or less.

The term "terrorism" has often been taken to imply attacks by small groups or independent organizations, rather than attacks by well-organized, nonstate actors or asymmetric warfare by states. This problem is compounded by the fact that federal agencies use different definitions of terrorism:

- The State Department uses a statutory definition of terrorism: "premeditated, politically motivated violence against noncombatant targets by subnational groups or clandestine agents, usually intended to influence an audience."[1]

- The FBI defines terrorism more broadly: "the unlawful use of violence, committed by a group of two or more individuals against persons or property to intimidate or coerce a government, the civilian population, or any segment thereof, in furtherance of political or social objectives." The FBI's definition of terrorism is broader than the State's definition, in that the terrorist act can be done by a group of two or more individuals for social as well as political objectives. Because of this broader definition, the FBI includes in its annual reports on terrorism in the United States acts such as bombings, arson, kidnapping, assaults, and hijackings committed by persons who may be suspected of associating with militia groups, animal rights groups, and others. Federal agencies also use different terms to describe their programs and activities for combating terrorism. For example, the FBI uses "counterterrorism" to refer to the full range of its activities directed against terrorism, including preventive and crisis management efforts. On the other hand, the DOD uses the term "counterterrorism" to refer to offensive measures to prevent, deter, and respond to terrorist attack and "antiterrorism" to cover defensive measures to reduce the vulnerability of individuals and property to terrorist acts.[2]

- FEMA defines terrorism as: "Terrorism is the use of force or violence against persons or property in violation of the criminal laws of the United States for purposes of intimidation, coercion, or ransom. Terrorists often use threats to create fear among the public, to try to convince citizens that their government is powerless to prevent terrorism, and to get immediate publicity for their causes."[3]

- The GAO uses the term "combat terrorism" to refer to the full range of federal programs and activities applied against terrorism, domestically and abroad, regardless of the source or motive.

- The Rand Corporation definition of terrorism is: "Terrorism is violence, or the threat of violence, through acts designed to coerce others into actions they otherwise would not undertake or into refraining from actions that they desired to take. All terrorist acts are crimes. Many would also be violations of the rules of war, if a state of war existed."[4]

A focus on "terrorism" as distinguished from "war" also leads government agencies to fail to come to grips with the issues that asymmetric warfare and terrorism involving truly massive attacks on the United States raise in terms of international law, the ability to use given levels of force to defend against such attacks, the changes taking place in the "rules of war," and the uncertain ability to even define whether a "state of war" actually exists. In many cases, it is assumed that peacetime norms will be adequate and that defense can consist of normal civil legal efforts in counterterrorism and response can be carried out largely at the state and local level. The cases where the president might have to declare a state of national emergency and where defense and response become tied to a conflict or to levels of attack beyond the capability of civil agencies receive only limited attention.

From a functional perspective, however, ignoring the risk of asymmetric warfare does not encourage objective planning and analysis. Neither does using definitions of "terrorism" that include virtually any act of violence other than one committed in the context of a declared war and involving the overt use of a properly identified military weapons system in full compliance with the most stringent interpretation of the Geneva convention. The proof lies in the fact that a number of federal agencies do not currently fit covert or proxy attacks by states into their rhetoric, while others exclude the unstable, insane, criminal, and religiously motivated. Homeland defense must respond to the full range of threats.

## RETHINKING THE MID- AND LONG-TERM RISK OF CBRN ATTACK

Much of the federal literature on the risks posed by terrorism—even when it involves the analysis of possible CBRN and WMD attacks—also understates the problem of uncertainty. At least in the open literature, this seems to have contributed to five problems in planning and analysis:

1. a lack of sophisticated pattern analysis and threat characterization;
2. a failure to look beyond past patterns of attack and examine the full range of possible futures;

3. a lack of explicit near- and mid-term net assessments of how the balance of means of attack can evolve relative to defensive and response options;
4. a failure to analyze the nature and impact of the many uncertainties in CBRN lethality and effects data; and
5. a reluctance to explicitly consider the full implications of large-scale and complex attack options for response and defense.

There is nothing new about potential threats to the United States from terrorism or even terrorism using WMD and there were many precedents before September 2001. There were at least fifty-two incidents of terrorist threats to use WMD between 1968–1994.[5] However, there is no agreement within the federal government as to how to count and categorize the past pattern of threats to the U.S. homeland. Furthermore, some departments and agencies count attempts in ways clearly designed to suit their programs without defining the attempts in terms of seriousness and capability. Some threat counts seem to define every person in the United States who writes or speaks the word "anthrax" as a terrorist threat.

Many analysts do firmly believe that the terrorist threat to the United States is increasing, as is the potential willingness to use WMD. A June 2000 report by the National Commission on Terrorism made a strong case that this threat was imminent more than a year before the attack on the World Trade Center and the Pentagon:

> If most of the world's countries are firmer in opposing terrorism, some still support terrorists or use terrorism as an element of state policy. Iran is the clearest case. The Revolutionary Guard Corps and the Ministry of Intelligence and Security carry out terrorist activities and give direction and support to other terrorists. The regimes of Syria, Sudan, and Afghanistan provide funding, refuge, training bases, and weapons to terrorists. Libya continues to provide support to some Palestinian terrorist groups and to harass expatriate dissidents, and North Korea may still provide weapons to terrorists. Cuba provides a safehaven to a number of terrorists. Other states allow terrorist groups to operate on their soil or provide support that, while failing short of state sponsorship, nonetheless gives terrorists important assistance.
>
> The terrorist threat is also changing in ways that make it more dangerous and difficult to counter.
>
> International terrorism once threatened Americans only when they were outside the country. Today international terrorists attack us on our own soil. Just before the millennium, an alert U.S. Customs Service official stopped Ahmad Ressam as he attempted to enter the United States from Canada— apparently to conduct a terrorist attack. This fortuitous arrest should not inspire complacency, however. On an average day, over one million people enter the United States legally and thousands more enter illegally. As the [1993] World Trade Center bombing demonstrated, we cannot rely solely on existing border controls and procedures to keep foreign terrorists out of the United States.

Terrorist attacks are becoming more lethal. Most terrorist organizations active in the 1970s and 1980s had clear political objectives. They tried to calibrate their attacks to produce just enough bloodshed to get attention for their cause, but not so much as to alienate public support. Groups like the Irish Republican Army and the Palestine Liberation Organization often sought specific political concessions.

Now, a growing percentage of terrorist attacks are designed to kill as many people as possible. In the 1990s a terrorist incident was almost 20 percent more likely to result in death or injury than an incident two decades ago. The World Trade Center bombing in New York killed six and wounded about 1,000, but the terrorists' goal was to topple the twin towers, killing tens of thousands of people. The thwarted attacks against New York City's infra-structure in 1993—which included plans to bomb the Lincoln and Holland tunnels—also were intended to cause mass casualties. In 1995, Philippine authorities uncovered a terrorist plot to bring down 11 U.S. airliners in Asia. The circumstances surrounding the millennium border arrests of foreign na-tionals suggest that the suspects planned to target a large group assembled for a New Year's celebration. Overseas attacks against the United States in recent years have followed the same trend. The bombs that destroyed the military barracks in Saudi Arabia and two U.S. Embassies in Africa inflicted 6,059 casualties. Those arrested in Jordan in late December had also planned attacks designed to kill large numbers.

The trend toward higher casualties reflects, in part, the changing motiva-tion of today's terrorists. Religiously motivated terrorist groups, such as Usama bin Ladin's group, al-Qaida, which is believed to have bombed the U.S. Embassies in Africa, represent a growing trend toward hatred of the United States. Other terrorist groups are driven by visions of a post-apocalyptic future or by ethnic hatred. Such groups may lack a concrete political goal other than to punish their enemies by killing as many of them as possible, seemingly without concern about alienating sympathizers. Increasingly, attacks are less likely to be followed by claims of responsibility or lists of political demands.

The shift in terrorist motives has contributed to a change in the way some international terrorist groups are structured. Because groups based on ideo-logical or religious motives may lack a specific political or nationalistic agenda, they have less need for a hierarchical structure. Instead, they can rely on loose affiliations with like-minded groups from a variety of countries to support their common cause against the United States.

Al-Qaida is the best-known transnational terrorist organization. In addi-tion to pursuing its own terrorist campaign, it calls on numerous militant groups that share some of its ideological beliefs to support its violent cam-paign against the United States. But neither al-Qaida's extremist politico-religious beliefs nor its leader, Usama bin Ladin, is unique. If al-Qaida and Usama bin Ladin were to disappear tomorrow, the United States would still face potential terrorist threats from a growing number of groups opposed to perceived American hegemony. Moreover, new terrorist threats can suddenly emerge from isolated conspiracies or obscure cults with no previous history of violence.[6]

## PATTERNS AND NON-PATTERNS IN THE NUMBER OF ATTACKS

The risks described in the National Commission on Terrorism's report are all too real. At the same time, the incidents it cited did not provide conclusive evidence that there was a trend toward an increased terrorist threat to the United States. Before September 2001, the United States had not yet been the target of extensive covert attacks by either foreign states or terrorists/extremists. In fact, U.S. territory had been surprisingly free of such attacks by state actors, extremists, or independent terrorists when one examines the patterns of attack against those in other regions.[7] According to the State Department's numbers, terrorist incidents in the United States declined sharply after the early 1980s, when they averaged thirty to fifty a year, and there was only one incident in the United States involving casualty levels approaching "superterrorism": the World Trade Center bombing in 1993.

Table 2.1 summarizes these patterns and serves as a warning about the dangers of oversimplified pattern analysis in terrorism. There are striking and sudden variations in the number of incidents by region, and in the overall frequency of terrorism. Perceptions also rarely track with reality. The Middle East, for example, is often seen as the center of global terrorism. In practice, however, this has not been true since the early 1990s and has recently been ranked as a region with a relatively low number of terrorist incidents.

It should be noted that there are severe definitional problems in the numbers shown in Table 2.1 that reflect long-standing problems in the way the State Department analyzes terrorism, which deprives the table's analysis of much of its potential value. The State Department only counts acts of terrorism with a political motive and does not count acts where the motive might be religious, quasi-criminal, or is simply irrational. There have been major attacks on U.S. embassies, airliners, barracks, and private-sector facilities *outside* the United States, and some have been sufficiently violent to indicate that if the attackers had WMD they might have used them. There also have been *serious* attempts that did not succeed and that are not counted. Furthermore, there is no clear correlation between the number of attacks and the seriousness of the consequences.

## CASUALTIES VERSUS INCIDENTS: THE LACK OF CORRELATION

The historical pattern in the total casualties from all attacks is shown in Table 2.1, along with the number of American casualties. There was a rise in the number of American casualties before the attacks on the World Trade Center and the Pentagon, but they remained a small proportion of the total, and most occur outside the United States. As such, these data did

Table 2.1
Attacks on the U.S. Homeland versus Attacks on Other Regions

| Total International Terrorist Attacks by Region | 1989 | 1990 | 1991 | 1992 | 1993 | 1994 | 1995 | 1996 | 1997 | 1998 | 1999 |
|---|---|---|---|---|---|---|---|---|---|---|---|
| Africa | - | - | - | - | 6 | 25 | 10 | 11 | 11 | 21 | 52 |
| Asia | - | - | - | - | 37 | 24 | 16 | 11 | 21 | 49 | 72 |
| Eurasia | - | - | - | - | 5 | 11 | 5 | 24 | 42 | 14 | 35 |
| Latin America | - | - | - | - | 97 | 58 | 92 | 84 | 128 | 110 | 116 |
| Middle East | - | - | - | - | 100 | 116 | 45 | 45 | 37 | 31 | 25 |
| Western Europe | - | - | - | - | 185 | 88 | 272 | 121 | 52 | 48 | 85 |
| North America | - | - | - | - | 1 | 0 | 0 | 0 | 13 | 0 | 2 |
| Worldwide Total | - | - | - | - | 431 | 322 | 440 | 296 | 304 | 273 | 387 |

*Source:* Adapted from U.S. State Department, *Patterns of Global Terrorism, 1998,* Department of State Publication 10610, Office of the Secretary of State, Office of the Coordinator for Counterterrorism, released April 1999, and U.S. Department of State, *Patterns of Global Terrorism, 1999,* Department of State Publication 10610, Office of the Secretary of State, Office of the Coordinator for Counterterrorism, released April 2000.

not support an estimate that the U.S. homeland was now the subject of an emerging pattern of attack and that Americans remain a small portion of the total casualties in any given year.

At the same time, it was all too clear that foreign states, extremists, and terrorists have been willing to attack Americans in the past and that the United States does not enjoy any special immunity. These data also do not cover attempts, as distinguished from successes.

It is also clear from Table 2.1, and from the additional data in Charts 2.1 to 2.4, that the patterns in the number of incidents and casualties varied sharply by year and did not provide a way to predict the size of the casualties in a given region. For example, the State Department reported that the number of international terrorist incidents fell from a peak of 666 in 1987 to 296 in 1996, a 25-year low. Of the 296 international incidents during 1996, only 73 were against U.S. persons and facilities overseas. However, the total casualties resulting from international terrorist incidents

**Chart 2.1**
**Terrorist Incidents Involving Americans versus Total Incidents**

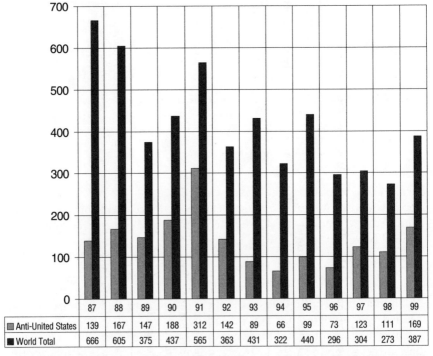

| | 87 | 88 | 89 | 90 | 91 | 92 | 93 | 94 | 95 | 96 | 97 | 98 | 99 |
|---|---|---|---|---|---|---|---|---|---|---|---|---|---|
| Anti-United States | 139 | 167 | 147 | 188 | 312 | 142 | 89 | 66 | 99 | 73 | 123 | 111 | 169 |
| World Total | 666 | 605 | 375 | 437 | 565 | 363 | 431 | 322 | 440 | 296 | 304 | 273 | 387 |

*Source*: Adapted by Anthony H. Cordesman from DCI Counterterrorist Center, "International Terrorism in 1997: A Statistic View." (March 1993), <http://www.odci.gov/cia/di/productions/terrorism>; 1998, and U.S. State Department, *Patterns of Global Terrorism, 1994 through the 1999 edition*, Department of State Publication 10610, Office of the Secretary of State, Office of the Coordinator for Counterterrorism.

Chart 2.2
Terrorist Incidents in the United States, 1980–2000

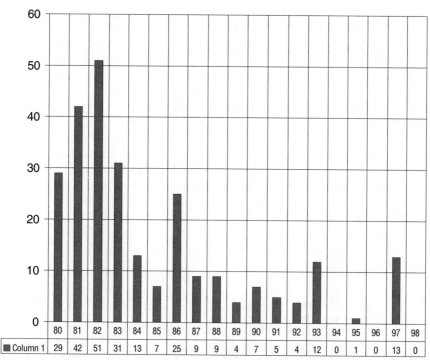

| | 80 | 81 | 82 | 83 | 84 | 85 | 86 | 87 | 88 | 89 | 90 | 91 | 92 | 93 | 94 | 95 | 96 | 97 | 98 |
|---|---|---|---|---|---|---|---|---|---|---|---|---|---|---|---|---|---|---|---|
| ■ Column 1 | 29 | 42 | 51 | 31 | 13 | 7 | 25 | 9 | 9 | 4 | 7 | 5 | 4 | 12 | 0 | 1 | 0 | 13 | 0 |

*Source*: Adapted by Anthony H. Cordesman from DCI Counterterrorist Center, "International
Terrorism in 1997: A Statistical View" (March 1998), <http://www.odci.gov/cia/di/produc-
tions/terrorism>, and U.S. General Accounting Office, GAO Report to Congressional Requesters, "Combating Terrorism, Federal Agencies' Efforts to Implement National Policy
and Strategy," GAO/NSIAD-97-254, September 1997, 14.

during 1996 were among the highest ever recorded—311 persons killed and
2,652 wounded. A total of 24 Americans were killed and another 250 were
wounded.[8] Moreover, by 1999, the number of terrorist incidents had
climbed back to a more normal number: 387.

The FBI recorded 23 acts of terrorism in the United States between 1989
and the end of 1993. It only recorded one domestic terrorist incident in the
United States in 1995, but this was the bombing of a federal building in
Oklahoma City. That incident was the most destructive ever on U.S. soil.
It killed 168 and wounded 500 persons.[9]

There were a total of 111 attacks on U.S. citizens in 1998. However,
these attacks only resulted in twenty-three U.S. casualties, in spite of the
fact many of the attacks used exceptionally violent means. A total of 96
out of 111 attacks used bombs, and an additional 5 were fire bombings.[10]
The number of attacks rose to 169 in 1999, including 111 bombings, 22
kidnappings, 12 fire bombings, 11 armed attacks, and 3 hijackings. This

**Chart 2.3**
**Terrorist Casualties Involving Americans, 1987–1999**

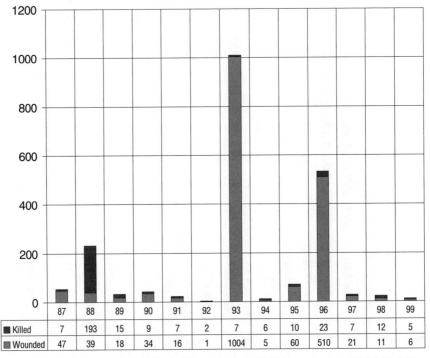

| | 87 | 88 | 89 | 90 | 91 | 92 | 93 | 94 | 95 | 96 | 97 | 98 | 99 |
|---|---|---|---|---|---|---|---|---|---|---|---|---|---|
| ■ Killed | 7 | 193 | 15 | 9 | 7 | 2 | 7 | 6 | 10 | 23 | 7 | 12 | 5 |
| ■ Wounded | 47 | 39 | 18 | 34 | 16 | 1 | 1004 | 5 | 60 | 510 | 21 | 11 | 6 |

*Sources*: Adapted by Anthony H. Cordesman from DCI Counterterrorist Center, "International Terrorism in 1997: A Statistic View" (March 1998), <http://www.odci.gov/cia/di/productions/terrorism>; and U.S. State Department, *Patterns of Global Terrorism, 1994 through the 1999 edition*, Department of State Publication 10610, Office of the Secretary of State, Office of the Coordinator for Counterterrorism.

pattern provided no warning that thousands would die in a single attack on September 11, 2001.

## U.S. AND AMERICAN CASUALTIES VERSUS INTERNATIONAL CASUALTIES

The most serious limitation in the data currently available on the patterns in terrorism is that there is no reliable estimate of the number of attempts to conduct large-scale attacks or to use CBRN weapons. As a result, some analysts conclude that these patterns do not reveal any serious risk, while others conclude that attacks like those by Aum Shinrikyo are evidence of a growing trend toward WMD attacks because they could have been far more deadly if the movement had used sarin more intelligently or succeeded in effectively weaponizing anthrax.

Chart 2.4
**Anti–U.S. Attacks by Region, 1994–1999**

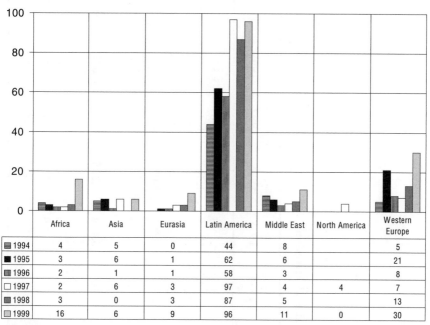

| | Africa | Asia | Eurasia | Latin America | Middle East | North America | Western Europe |
|---|---|---|---|---|---|---|---|
| 1994 | 4 | 5 | 0 | 44 | 8 | | 5 |
| 1995 | 3 | 6 | 1 | 62 | 6 | | 21 |
| 1996 | 2 | 1 | 1 | 58 | 3 | | 8 |
| 1997 | 2 | 6 | 3 | 97 | 4 | 4 | 7 |
| 1998 | 3 | 0 | 3 | 87 | 5 | | 13 |
| 1999 | 16 | 6 | 9 | 96 | 11 | 0 | 30 |

*Source*: Adapted by Anthony H. Cordesman from DCI Counterterrorist Center, "International Terrorism in 1997: A Statistic View" (March 1998), <http://www.odci.gov/cia/di/productions/terrorism>.

In spite of the lessons that will be learned from the events of September 11, 2001 there is no way to resolve this debate from pattern analysis per se. It seems likely that intended lethality of many attempted attacks was considerably more lethal than the end result, and the limited casualties shown in Table 2.2 are more a result of poor planning and/or lack of access to more lethal means than of any deliberate effort at restraint.

Table 2.2 also shows that the limited number of casualties that are U.S. citizens grossly understated the number of actual casualties from attacks on U.S. facilities and in attacks in which there are some U.S. casualties. For example, such attacks produced a total of 184 killed and wounded in 1999, of which 133 were businesspeople, 9 were diplomats, 9 were military, 7 were in government, and 26 were "other." The State Department reports that only eleven casualties were U.S. citizens, but it is clear that the number of U.S. casualties would rise sharply if more terrorist attacks had been executed within the U.S. homeland.

This is a clear warning to all of those who still argue that the risks that weapons of mass destruction will be used can be based on past patterns of behavior. The kind of data shown in Table 2.2 and Charts 2.1 through 2.4

Table 2.2
Patterns in Total International and U.S. Casualties from International Terrorism

| International Casualties from Terrorism by Region | 1991 | 1992 | 1993 | 1994 | 1995 | 1996 | 1997 | 1998 | 1999 |
|---|---|---|---|---|---|---|---|---|---|
| Africa | - | - | 7 | 55 | 8 | 80 | 28 | 5,379 | 185 |
| Asia | - | - | 135 | 17 | 5,639 | 1,507 | 344 | 635 | 690 |
| Eurasia | - | - | 1 | 151 | 29 | 20 | 27 | 12 | 3 |
| Latin America | - | - | 66 | 329 | 46 | 18 | 11 | 194 | 9 |
| Middle East | - | - | 178 | 256 | 445 | 1,097 | 480 | 68 | 31 |
| Western Europe | - | - | 117 | 126 | 287 | 503 | 17 | 405 | 16 |
| North America | - | - | 1,006 | 0 | 0 | 0 | 7 | 0 | 0 |
| **Worldwide Total (all nationalities)** | - | - | 1,510 | 934 | 6,454 | 3,225 | 886 | 6,693 | 934 |
| Total U.S. Citizen Casualties | | | | | | | | | |
| Killed | 7 | 2 | 7 | 6 | 10 | 23 | 7 | 12 | 5 |
| Wounded | 16 | 1 | 1,004 | 5 | 60 | 510 | 21 | 11 | 6 |
| Total | 23 | 3 | 1,011 | 11 | 70 | 533 | 28 | 23 | 11 |

| Patterns in Anti–U.S. Attacks | 1991 | 1992 | 1993 | 1994 | 1995 | 1996 | 1997 | 1998 | 1999 |
|---|---|---|---|---|---|---|---|---|---|
| *Anti–U.S. Attacks By Region* | | | | | | | | | |
| Africa | - | - | - | 4 | 3 | 2 | 2 | 3 | 16 |
| Asia | - | - | - | 5 | 6 | 1 | 6 | 0 | 6 |
| Eurasia | - | - | - | - | 1 | 1 | 3 | 3 | 9 |
| Middle East | - | - | - | 8 | 6 | 3 | 4 | 5 | 11 |
| Europe | - | - | - | 5 | 21 | 8 | 7 | 13 | 30 |
| Latin America | - | - | - | 44 | 62 | 58 | 97 | 87 | 96 |
| Total | - | - | - | 66 | 99 | 73 | 119 | 111 | 168 |
| *Anti–U.S. Attacks by Type of Event* | | | | | | | | | |
| Armed Attack | - | - | - | 9 | 8 | 3 | 5 | 5 | 11 |
| Vandalism | - | - | - | 1 | 9 | 0 | 0 | 0 | 0 |
| Barricade Hostage | - | - | - | 0 | 0 | 0 | 0 | 0 | 1 |
| Occupation | - | - | - | 0 | 0 | 0 | 0 | 0 | 2 |
| Hijacking | - | - | - | 0 | 0 | 0 | 0 | 0 | 3 |
| Arson | - | - | - | 0 | 6 | 7 | 2 | 1 | 6 |
| Assault | - | - | - | 1 | 0 | 1 | 0 | 0 | 0 |
| Kidnapping | - | - | - | 10 | 11 | 6 | 8 | 4 | 20 |
| Bombing | - | - | - | 43 | 65 | 55 | 108 | 96 | 111 |
| Fire Bombing | - | - | - | 2 | 0 | 1 | 0 | 5 | 12 |
| Total | - | - | - | 66 | 99 | 73 | 123 | 111 | 166 |

continued

Table 2.2 (continued)

| Patterns in Anti–U.S. Attacks | 1991 | 1992 | 1993 | 1994 | 1995 | 1996 | 1997 | 1998 | 1999 |
|---|---|---|---|---|---|---|---|---|---|
| *Total Worldwide Casualties from Attacks on U.S. Facilities and Attacks in Which U.S. Citizens Suffered Casualties* | | | | | | | | | |
| Other | - | - | - | 26 | 22 | 19 | 14 | 3 | 26 |
| Government | - | - | - | 1 | 2 | 1 | 4 | 0 | 7 |
| Military | - | - | - | 0 | 2 | 4 | 1 | 0 | 9 |
| Diplomat | - | - | - | 2 | 6 | 1 | 3 | 19 | 9 |
| Business | - | - | - | 38 | 70 | 50 | 104 | 1 | 133 |
| **Total** | - | - | - | 67 | 102 | 75 | 126 | 23 | 184 |

*Source:* Adapted from U.S. State Department, *Patterns of Global Terrorism, 1994 through the 1999 edition*, Department of State Publication 10610, Office of the Secretary of State, Office of the Coordinator for Counterterrorism.

do not support any kind of statistically valid pattern analysis that can lead to reliable estimates of the nature of future attacks on the U.S. homeland.

If anything, the variations in the data are so wide that they provided a statistical "proof," long before the strikes of the World Trade Center and the Pentagon, that there is no empirical basis for predicting future patterns that goes beyond pure speculation. Analysts of terrorism may assert anything they please, but there simply is no evidence to support such assertions that can be tied to the negligible number of terrorist attacks that have as yet occurred in the United States or the highly erratic patterns in attacks outside the United States. If anything, the patterns to date would indicate that there is little meaningful foreign threat to the U.S. homeland and that terrorism is something that happens outside it.

## CONSIDERING THE THREAT FROM STATE AND NON-STATE ACTORS

Even if pattern analysis of "terrorism" did provide clearer results, it is far from certain that it would provide a useful picture of the present and future threat to the U.S. homeland. This threat is not limited to terrorism per se, but rather the combination of threats posed by asymmetric warfare, covert attacks, proxy attacks, *and* what the United States now normally labels "terrorism." It also includes the threat posed by foreign *and domestic* extremist violence, regardless of whether attacks have a political motive. Accordingly, there are serious dangers in focusing attention on the historical threat posed by relatively limited attacks by small groups and individuals, rather than the much larger threats that can be posed by state-sponsored asymmetric warfare.

### States, "Terrorists," and Acts of War

The threat that states will play a role in launching or supporting large-scale attacks has long been recognized in U.S. strategy and military doctrine and DOD reports. However, the semantic loading that most civil departments and agencies gave to the term "terrorist" led some officials and analysts to ignore the potential seriousness of covert or proxy attacks driven by state actors. It also led some planners to ignore the fact that there are no true international norms that prevent such forms of asymmetric warfare—regardless of whether the United States and its allies would like to create them.

Former Secretary of Defense William Cohen's FY2001 report to the president and Congress clearly reflected this broader threat:

> The Department of Defense prevents conflicts and other threats by limiting the spread of dangerous military technologies, combating transnational

threats, and providing security reassurance. Limiting the Spread of Dangerous Military Technologies: DOD limits the spread of dangerous military technologies, through efforts to reduce or eliminate NBC capabilities and through activities to prevent NBC and missile technology proliferation. . . . DOD combats transnational threats through its activities to prevent terrorism, reduce U.S. vulnerability to terrorist acts, and decrease the production and flow to the United States of illegal drugs. Such activities include efforts to enhance intelligence collection capabilities, protect critical infrastructure (including combating cyber-terrorism), support joint interagency counterdrug task forces operating overseas and in international air and sea space contiguous to U.S. borders, and support to U.S. and host nation drug law enforcement agencies.[11]

The same kind of warning was contained in the DOD's January 2001 report on proliferation:

U.S. conventional military superiority paradoxically creates an incentive for adversary states to acquire NBC weapons. Because our potential adversaries know that they cannot win a conventional war against us, they are more likely to try asymmetric methods such as employing biological or chemical weapons or threatening the use of nuclear weapons. This strategy also applies to particular terrorist groups intent on inflicting a large number of casualties or causing panic, if such groups judge that conventional means are inadequate and they do not fear political or military retaliation.

The Quadrennial Defense Review (QDR), the Department of Defense's (DOD) most recent strategic-level defense review, published in May 1997, concluded that the threat or use of chemical or biological weapons is a likely condition of future warfare and could occur in the very early stages of war to disrupt U.S. military operations and deployments of men and supplies into theater.

Asymmetric warfare—that is, countering an adversary's strengths by focusing on its weaknesses—is not a new concept. Because of U.S. and allied conventional force superiority, some states may see asymmetric strategies, such as the employment of biological or chemical agents, as a means of avoiding direct engagements with dominant U.S. conventional forces and a way to "level the playing field." This strategy also applies to particular terrorist groups intent on inflicting a large number of casualties or causing panic, if such groups judge that conventional means are inadequate and they do not fear political or military retaliation.

The terrorist threat of today is far more complex than that of the past. Violent, religiously, and ethnically motivated terrorist organizations now share the stage with the more traditional, politically motivated movements. State sponsors, including Iran, Iraq, Libya, Syria, Sudan, North Korea, and Cuba, continue to provide vital support to a disparate mix of terrorist groups. As recent history shows, homegrown organizations and disaffected individuals have also demonstrated an increasing willingness to act on U.S. soil. Not only is the threat more diverse, but the increasing sophistication of organizations and their weaponry also make them far more dangerous. The Oklahoma City and 1993 World Trade Center bombings have already demonstrated the devastating effects of conventional explosives in the hands of terrorists.[12]

This situation did not change with the end of the Clinton Administration. President George W. Bush, Secretary of State Colin Powell, and Secretary of Defense Donald Rumsfeld all warned, months before the September 2001 strikes, of the risks of asymmetric warfare and of CBRN attacks on the United States. Yet, much of the U.S. analysis of response measures focused on attacks of relatively limited size and consequences. FEMA, DOD, the Department of Justice (DOJ), and the HHS (including the U.S. Centers for Disease Control [CDC]) did not have a working definition of mass casualties. The metropolitan medical response systems that HHS was establishing across the nation used a limit of one thousand casualties for planning local medical systems and equipping and supplying the response teams, even though the HHS stated that its planning considered three tiers of threats: one thousand casualties or less, one thousand to ten thousand casualties, and ten thousand casualties or more.[13]

Similarly, a number of the GAO analyses that dealt with "combating terrorism" concluded that the risk of covert attacks or terrorist incidents using WMD might be limited because small independent terrorist groups and extremists would be unable to acquire or build sophisticated and highly lethal weapons. This kind of reasoning could lead the United States to ignore the fact that it faces an equally serious threat of covert or indirect attacks by states that could use such weapons and produce casualties far in excess of ten thousand.[14]

The U.S. government officials in civil agencies that do warn of CBRN attacks tend to focus on relatively limited uses of such weapons by terrorist organizations. Louis Freeh, then director of the FBI, warned on a number of occasions that the United States must plan to deal with attacks involving WMD, and has quoted statistics on attempted acts of terrorism that are less reassuring than the data on successful acts of terrorism quoted earlier. At the same time, he has focused on criminal cases and terrorism:

The FBI views the proliferation of weapons of mass destruction (WMD) as a serious and growing threat to our national security. Pursuant to our terrorism mandate and statutory requirements, we are developing within the inter-agency setting broad-based, pro-active programs in support of our mission to detect, deter, or prevent the threat of nuclear, chemical, and biological weapons, their delivery systems, and WMD proliferation activities occurring in or directed at the United States.

Our programs cover the broad spectrum of Foreign Counterintelligence (FCI), criminal, and counterterrorism investigations, focusing on persons or organizations involved in WMD proliferation activities.

During 1997, the FBI initiated over 100 criminal cases pertaining to nuclear, biological, and chemical threats, incidents, or investigations (excluding proliferation cases). Many of these threats were determined to be non-credible; however, this represents a threefold increase over 1996. Credible cases have resulted in arrests and prosecutions by the FBI, and state and local authorities. In support of this growing problem, legislative changes by Congress over the past three years have strengthened the FBI's powers to investigate and bring to prosecution those individuals involved in WMD proliferation.

The FBI has also investigated and responded to a number of threats that involved biological agents and are attributed to various types of groups or individuals. For example, there have been apocalyptic-type threats that actually advocate destruction of the world through the use of WMD. We have also been made aware of interest in biological agents by individuals espousing white-supremacist beliefs to achieve social change; individuals engaging in criminal activity, frequently arising from jealousy or interpersonal conflict; individuals and small anti-tax groups, and some cult interest. In most cases, threats have been limited in scope and have targeted individuals rather than groups, facilities, or critical infrastructure. Threats have surfaced which advocate dissemination of a chemical agent through air ventilation systems. Most have made little mention of the type of device or delivery system to be employed, and for this reason have been deemed technically not feasible. Some threats have been validated. As an example, during 1997, a group with white supremacist views pled guilty to planning to explode tanks containing the deadly industrial chemical hydrogen sulfide as a diversionary act to their primary activity, an armored car robbery.

The FBI has experienced an increase in the number of cases involving terrorist or criminal use of WMD. These cases frequently have been small in scale and committed primarily by individuals or smaller splinter/extremist elements of right-wing groups that are unrelated to larger terrorist organizations.

For example: As most of you will remember, on April 24, 1997, B'nai B'rith headquarters in Washington, D.C., received a package containing a petri dish labeled "Anthracis Yersinia," a nonexistent substance and a threat letter. Although testing failed to substantiate the perceived threat, the significant response mobilized to mitigate the situation highlights the disruption, fears, and complexity associated with these types of cases.

On September 17, 1997, an individual was indicted in violation of Title 18, U.S.C. Section 175(A)/Biological Weapons Anti-Terrorism Act for knowingly possessing a toxin (ricin and nicotine sulfate) for use as a weapon and knowingly possessing a delivery system designed to deliver or disseminate a toxin. On October 28, 1997, he pled guilty to manufacturing a toxin (ricin) for use as a weapon. On January 7, 1998, he was sentenced to 12 years and 7 months in federal prison to be followed by 5 years of supervised release.

In what the FBI considers a significant prevention, the FBI arrested four members of a white supremacist organization in Dallas, Texas, who planned to bomb a natural gas refinery, which could have caused a release of a deadly cloud of hydrogen sulfide. This act was planned to divert law enforcement attention from the group's original objective of committing an armored car robbery. On video, the subjects discussed their complete disregard for the devastating consequences of their intended actions. The four were indicted on several charges including use of weapons of mass destruction. The group pled guilty to several criminal charges and are awaiting sentencing.[15]

Barbara Y. Martinez, deputy director of the FBI for National Domestic Preparedness Office, gave a similar warning in 1999:

Terrorist events such as the World Trade Center bombing, the bombing of the Alfred P. Murrah federal building in Oklahoma City, and the pipe bomb at the Olympic Games in Atlanta revealed the United States' increased susceptibility to terrorist assaults. These attacks, coupled with the March 1995 Tokyo subway attack, where the weapon was the chemical nerve agent sarin, exposed the threat of use of WMD within the United States. The threat of WMD use in the United States is real, however, we must not inflate nor understate the actual threat. The United States is experiencing an increased number of hoaxes involving the use of chemical or biological agents perpetrated by individuals wishing to instill fear and disrupt communities. Yesterday's bomb threat has been replaced with a more exotic biological or chemical threat. While the FBI continues to investigate these hoaxes, other ongoing investigations reveal that domestic extremists, as well as international terrorists with open anti–U.S. sentiments, are becoming more interested in the potential use of chemical and biological agents.

Examining the increased number of WMD criminal cases the FBI has opened over the past several years highlights the potential threat of use we face. WMD criminal cases are those cases primarily dealing with the use, threatened use, or procurement of chemical and biological materials with intent to harm within the United States. These criminal cases have shown a steady increase since 1995, rising from 37 in 1996 to 74 in 1997, 181 in 1998, and 114 to date for 1999, with three-quarters of these cases threatening a biological release. The biological agent most often cited in 1998 and 1999 was anthrax. Despite the increase in fabricated threats, the WMD threat remains. Since the early 1990s, the FBI has investigated a number of domestic extremist groups and associated individuals interested in procuring or ready to employ chemical or biological agents against innocent civilians. In February 1999, members of a right-wing splinter group were sentenced to 292 months (over 24 years) in prison for threatening to use a weapon of mass destruction against federal officials. These individuals intended to modify a cigarette lighter in order to shoot cactus quills tainted with HIV–blood or rabies.[16]

The same is true of the CIA. George Tenet, director of central intelligence, issued a warning in March 2000 that seems particularly prescient given the events of September 2001:

Although 1999 did not witness the dramatic terrorist attacks that punctuated 1998, our profile in the world and thus our attraction as a terrorist target will not diminish any time soon. We are learning more about the perpetrators every day . . . and I can tell you that they are a diverse lot motivated by many causes.

Usama bin Ladin is still foremost among these terrorists, because of the immediacy and seriousness of the threat he poses. The connections between Bin Ladin and the threats uncovered in Jordan, Canada, and the United States during the holidays are still being investigated, but everything we have learned recently confirms our conviction that he wants to strike further blows against America. Despite these and other well-publicized disruptions, we believe he could still strike without additional warning. Indeed, Usama bin Ladin's organization and other terrorist groups are placing increased emphasis on developing surrogates to carry out attacks in an effort to avoid detection. For example, the Egyptian Islamic Jihad (EIJ) is linked closely to bin Ladin's organization and has operatives located around the world—including in Europe, Yemen, Pakistan, Lebanon, and Afghanistan. And, there is now an intricate web of alliances among Sunni extremists worldwide, including North Africans, radical Palestinians, Pakistanis, and Central Asians.

I am also very concerned about the continued threat Islamic extremist groups pose to the Middle East Peace Process. The Palestinian rejectionist groups, HAMAS (Islamic Resistance Movement) and PIJ (Palestine Islamic Jihad), as well as Lebanese Hizbollah continue to plan attacks against Israel aimed at blocking progress in the negotiations. HAMAS and PIJ have been weakened by Israeli and Palestinian Authority crackdowns, but remain capable of conducting large scale attacks. Recent Israeli arrests of HAMAS terrorist operatives revealed that the group had plans underway for major operations inside Israel.

Some of these terrorist groups are actively sponsored by national governments that harbor great antipathy toward the United States. Although we have seen some dramatic public pressure for liberalization in Iran, which I will address later, and even some public criticism of the security apparatus, the fact remains we have yet to find evidence that the use of terrorism as a political tool by official Iranian organs has changed since President Khatami took office in August 1997.

Mr. Chairman, we remain concerned that terrorist groups worldwide continue to explore how rapidly evolving and spreading technologies might enhance the lethality of their operations. Although terrorists we've preempted still appear to be relying on conventional weapons, we know that a number of these groups are seeking chemical, biological, radiological, or nuclear (CBRN) agents. We are aware of several instances in which terrorists have contemplated using these materials.

- Among them is bin Ladin, who has shown a strong interest in chemical weapons. His operatives have trained to conduct attacks with toxic chemicals or biological toxins.

- HAMAS is also pursuing a capability to conduct attacks with toxic chemicals.

Terrorists also are embracing the opportunities offered by recent leaps in information technology. To a greater and greater degree, terrorist groups, including Hizbollah, HAMAS, the Abu Nidal organization, and bin Ladin's al-Qaida organization are using computerized files, e-mail, and encryption to support their operations.

. . . we have had our share of successes, but I must be frank in saying that this has only succeeded in buying time against an increasingly dangerous threat. The difficulty in destroying this threat lies in the fact that our efforts will not be enough to overcome the fundamental causes of the phenomenon—poverty, alienation, disaffection, and ethnic hatreds deeply rooted in history. In the meantime, constant vigilance and timely intelligence are our best weapons.[17]

Events have shown that there are good reasons for the priorities that are implicit in these statements. Conventional attacks on the U.S. homeland are ongoing threats, and are now more probable than the threat of weapons of mass destruction. Comparatively low-level WMD attacks are now more probable than high-level WMD attacks. At the same time, the September 2001 attacks showed that risk alone may not deter a determined attacker, and the tacit assumption that state actors will not attack in the future can lead to a seriously distorted American approach to homeland defense.

## Planning for Major Attacks and Asymmetric Warfare by State Actors

There is good reason to use the word "war" rather than "terrorism" since the attacks on the World Trade Center and the Pentagon. It may be valid to label state actors as "terrorists" when they or their proxies attack innocent civilians or economic targets without a declaration of war. However, such labeling has such a heavy emotional content that it may lead U.S. planners to pay insufficient attention to the fact that most hostile states have little choice other than to wage asymmetric warfare and may pursue rational and focused strategies that are only acts of "terrorism" when seen from an American perspective. The United States exists in a world where there are many current and potentially hostile states. It makes good sense to call such states "enemies," but labeling them as "terrorist" is as dysfunctional in some ways as calling them "freedom fighters."

Ironically, the now-dated U.S. use of the term "rogue state" never seemed to have led the U.S. government to take the possibility of such attacks as seriously as it did the risk of Soviet use of unconventional warfare during the Cold War. The United States has also downplayed the mid- and long-term risk of such attacks from states like China. These are states that have little near-term prospect of becoming peer threats, but which could develop extremely lethal forms of asymmetric threats to the U.S. homeland. It is not yet clear what talking about "states of concern" means, but the phrase does not seem to convey much urgency about dealing with asymmetric warfare (or anything else).

Such statements do, however, help illustrate how diverse the threat really is. They also help show why an effective homeland defense strategy and program must plan for attacks using WMD. Just as there is no way to predict whether attacks on the U.S. homeland will be made by states, proxies, independent nonstate actors, and/or terrorists/extremists, there is no way to predict what mix of different kinds of weapons will be used, whether WMD will be used, or whether equally costly attacks can be carried out using conventional explosives.

An effective homeland defense strategy must look beyond the threats posed by individuals and private groups, and take account of the fact that other states can launch direct asymmetric attacks on the U.S. homeland. These attacks may or may not be covert in the sense that an effort is made to conceal the state responsible, the nature of the attack, or that the attack has taken place at all. States may also use proxies like terrorists or extremists. In all of these cases, if the primary sponsor is a hostile state, such attacks become an act of war and must be treated as such.

## The Threat of "Proxies" and "Networks"

The United States must give equal priority to assessing the risks posed by the links between states and nonstate actors and by the secondary links between various nonstate groups. A significant amount of the present open literature on terrorism assumes that such networks and common interests already exist. It often does so on the basis of insufficient evidence or without regard to the limits of such ties. At the same time, little attention seems to be paid to the ways in which future transfers of technology, WMD, and money can take place between states and such groups in the future. The assumption often seems to be that potentially hostile states will not take the risk of aiding terrorist and extremist groups in CBRN attacks in peacetime. While this may well be true, risk perceptions can change radically in a crisis or war.

The United States politicizes links between states and terrorists/extremists in ways that can be severely misleading. For example, current State Department reporting sharply downplays Syria's role in supporting the Hizbollah in proxy attacks on Israel and exaggerates the role of Iran by default. Pakistan's role in support of bin Ladin and Afghan extremists, and the role of Saudi and other sources of terrorist financing, has also been downplayed for political reasons.

## Dealing with Nuance and Complex Motives

There is also a tendency to oversimplify the radically differing nature of terrorist and extremist groups that have no currently visible ties to states. Far too much of the public official U.S. literature on such groups lumps them together as if their motives, behavior, and capabilities were similar. Buzz words are developed to characterize terrorists as "right," "left," "religious," "lone," "fanatic," "leaderless," "rational," and "irrational."

As a result, there seems to be little independent assessment of which groups might act as proxies or in alliance with hostile states. Such an approach fails to develop a nuanced approach as to exactly what given groups and types of individuals believe in, and whether they do or do not pose a direct threat to the U.S. homeland. In the process, it ignores the long history of the sudden appearance of factions and splinter groups and the fact that they often are willing to take far more extreme risks than their parent group or the state(s) that fund it.

Accurate intelligence on the character and dynamics of every group—and its level of outside and state support—may not be possible, but every effort needs to be made to clearly distinguish between given groups and to determine what they may be able to do with or without state aid and on a continuing basis. Groups and individuals may emerge that are willing to attack the U.S. homeland with little regard to U.S. retaliation and with few goals other than causing the maximum amount of damage to American citizens and institutions. Their political agendas could include complex political and religious ideologies, pragmatic strategic and tactical objectives, or paranoid fantasies. Such attackers could also be American, rather than foreign. This is critical to warning, defense, and effective response if attacks do succeed.

Once again, the very lack of an extensive history of attacks on the U.S. homeland means the United States must consider future capabilities more than current intentions and look beyond the most probable set of threats. It is equally important to understand that serious new threats can emerge with little warning or public agenda, and that advances in biotechnology and information warfare will probably increase threat capabilities with time.

## CONSIDERATION OF THE FULL SPECTRUM OF POSSIBLE TYPES AND METHODS OF ATTACK: THE NEED TO CONSIDER "WORST CASES"

While the most probable forms of terrorist attack still range in lethality from low-lethality modes like conventional weapons and explosives to very limited uses of chemical and biological weapons, these limits do not apply to states or their proxies. States can already launch attacks using extremely lethal modes like nuclear and biological weapons. State and proxy attacks can be launched to support covert warfare, be conducted with or without warning and attribution, and/or use more than one method of attack at the same time. In some biological attacks, the United States may not even know it is under attack for days or weeks after the attack, or even be certain that it has been under attack at all.

If the United States only had to consider past attacks, it might be able to concentrate on attacks using conventional weapons and explosives or limited uses of chemical and biological weapons. However, the fact that the

United States may face threats from state actors, combined with the ongoing changes in the technology and availability of highly lethal WMD, means that the United States must also prepare to defend its homeland against an equally broad spectrum of possible levels and means of attack. U.S. plans and programs must consider much higher levels of attack than those posed by ordinary terrorists and the possible use of WMD to attack the U.S. government and/or institutions, to kill as many Americans as possible, or to broadly attack the U.S. economy and infrastructure.

The United States must consider a possible future in which the use of WMD becomes a common aspect of asymmetric warfare and in which complex and sophisticated attacks are conducted against the United States and its allies. While there are few current indications that such a future will occur, it is certainly becoming technically feasible for a steadily wider range of state actors and sophisticated terrorists. America's conventional military strength and the potential development of national missile defenses will tend to push hostile states toward such a form of asymmetric warfare. Furthermore, if theater conflicts evolve toward such forms of asymmetric warfare and the use of WMD becomes more common in theater conflicts or internal struggles outside the United States, the resulting willingness to use WMD could easily spill over into threats or attacks on the U.S. homeland.

Such "worst cases" may become a future reality over the next quarter of a century. As a result, the United States must not only consider scenarios involving complex and highly lethal biological attacks and multiple use of high-yield nuclear devices, but also the program implications. These include (1) the value of homeland defense as a deterrent against the evolution of such a future, (2) the need to shape research and development programs to deal with the scale and nature of such attacks, and (3) the need to consider the problems such attacks create for response planning.

## MAKING OFFENSE, DETERRENCE, DENIAL, DEFENSE, AND RETALIATION PART OF HOMELAND DEFENSE

The need to consider all the implications of the threat posed by state actors and proxies has other implications. When the federal government views that threat of CBRN attacks largely in terms of foreign and domestic terrorism, there is a natural tendency to focus on defense and response. When the threat is broadened to include state actors, the U.S. government must pay equal attention to the fact that the best homeland defense may often be a good offense.

PDDs 39 and 62, for example, view U.S. policy largely in terms of what can be done within the United States to prevent a terrorist act and then respond to it if defense fails. These data also seem to indicate that the threat is viewed as primarily directed at the United States, rather than by theater-driven motives that may see our friends and allies as targets of equal priority. There is no sign of an effort to create a postwar concept for using offensive capabilities as a deterrent, defense, and method of retaliation, and to redefine extended deterrence.

Defense and response is not an adequate way of dealing with the CBRN threat. If attackers are foreign, federal efforts to strengthen offensive, deterrent, and retaliatory capabilities may be at least as productive as efforts to strengthen denial, defense, and response measures. Effective deterrence requires that the United States be able to identify the full range of actors that threaten the United States and develop a convincing threat of immediate action to retaliate and deny attackers the ability to repeat or escalate their attacks. This, in turn, requires the United States to be able to distinguish whether states under crisis conditions are directly or indirectly involved in unconventional attacks, regardless of whether they use proxies or cover organizations.

This will not be easy in the case of well-planned attacks by states, or state-controlled or state-driven actors. Nevertheless, one key to successful defense will be the ability to clearly distinguish acts of war and who is behind them, to be able to react quickly and decisively, and to convince the world such action is justified. Grim as the prospect may be, the United States may have to create a convincing threat that it will respond to nuclear or biological attacks on its homeland with nuclear attacks on the population centers of any state that carries out such attacks, regardless of whether the method of attack is covert or uses proxies.

Similarly, deterrence, denial, and retaliation against attacks by independent nonstate actors requires the United States to be able to clearly distinguish whether states are or are not involved in such attacks, what level of action host-states can credibly be expected to take, and what level of damage the United States can inflict in retaliation.

These are not game-theoretic issues. The United States was not ready to take decisive action after the attack on the U.S. Marine Corps barracks in Lebanon. It was ready to take military action against Libya for one series of incidents but not for the bombing of Pan Am Flight 103. It could not identify the target in the case of the attack on Al Khobar. It struck against targets in Afghanistan and the Sudan after the embassy bombings in Kenya and Tanzania, but with only limited effectiveness. It has never found a clear target to attack in response to the attack on the USS *Cole*. The response to the attacks on the World Trade Center and the Pentagon may prove to be very different, but the lack of any warning of such attacks shows that intelligent attackers can be expected to make every effort to avoid identification and retaliation and to shelter behind international public opinion and civilian populations. The stakes will be infinitely higher when the issue is nuclear and/or biological attacks on targets in the United States.

The United States must also recognize the fact that most foreign threats to the United States that involve the use of WMD are likely to emerge as a result of theater-driven conflicts and confrontations rather than antagonism to the United States per se. The United States will be perceived as an enemy because of its support to regional friends and allies. As a result, the threat posed by state actors and terrorists will generally involve the United States and at least one major ally and must be countered in the theater involved as well as the U.S. homeland. At the same time, effective counterterrorist, deterrent, offensive, and retaliatory action—as well as effective denial, defense, and response action—will have to be part of a coalition effort. The United States will have to obtain help from its allies and have some obligation to protect them.

This, indeed, is one of the critical weaknesses of the present PDDs affecting counterterrorism and most of the federal literature on the subject. Such an approach ignores the true nature of American power and vulnerability, the assets our friends and allies can provide, and our need to develop coalition capabilities. It ignores the fact that nearly 40 percent of the total federal spending on counterterrorism in recent years has gone to protect U.S. forces, embassies, and other facilities overseas. Ironically, the United States has almost reversed the lessons of the Cold War, and has gone from a nearly exclusive focus on responding to the threat of WMD with deterrence through offensive retaliation to one focused largely on "civil defense."

## LINKING HOMELAND DEFENSE TO COUNTERPROLIFERATION

Just as an effective homeland defense policy must be based on the use of offense and defense, and must be linked to U.S. theater and coalition warfare planning, it cannot be separated from an effective counterproliferation policy:

- Like missile defense, counterproliferation deals with a national and international threat, and one that directly involves our allies and U.S. forces and citizens abroad.

- Although the current U.S. policy debate is obsessed with the word "terrorist," threat analysis indicates that the most lethal attacks will be covert or asymmetric attacks by states, state-sponsored groups, or large independent organizations capable of using WMD in asymmetric warfare.

- The U.S. response cannot merely be passive in terms of interception of threats in U.S. territory and response measures. It must be directly linked to intelligence gathering, retaliation, and deterrence, which again involve our allies and forces overseas.

- Nuclear and biological weapons represent the more important threats, even though they may not be as likely as attacks using chemical weapons or toxins. The United States can deal with attacks involving WMD where the level of casualties is so low that they cannot be distinguished from the effects of attacks using conventional weapons. Tragic as such attacks may be, state and local resources can cope. They cannot cope with attacks involving effective nuclear or biological weapons.

• There is no practical prospect of limiting conventional attacks through efforts to influence potential suppliers. Control regimes like Nunn-Lugar and the Chemical Weapons Convention (CWC) may well, however, be one of the most effective forms of homeland defense.

These issues highlight one of the most complex problems the United States faces in terms of national security policy and in allocating its scarce national resources. The United States must develop, fund, and implement a global counterproliferation policy of which both homeland defense and counterterrorism are essential parts. In the process, it must prepare to deal with an extremely wide range of threats with high-potential lethality, but any one of which has relatively low probability. It must develop internal defense measures against foreign and domestic threats and response measures. Any one set of steps involves high costs to deal with threats that individually have low probability.

This presents major problems for programming that go far beyond the narrow scope of the present PDDs dealing with terrorism. There are important synergies in intelligence, active and passive defense, deterrence and retaliation, and response measures. However, there are also homeland defense means that involve expensive and unique activities that may well require trade-offs with other military capabilities if they are ever to be funded.

## NOTES

1. See 22 U.S.C. Sec. 2656f(d). The term "noncombatant" includes military personnel who, at the time of the incident, are unarmed and/or not on duty. This legislation also requires the State Department to submit annual reports to Congress on international terrorism.

2. U.S. General Accounting Office, GAO Report to Congressional Requesters, "Combating Terrorism, Federal Agencies' Efforts to Implement National Policy and Strategy," GAO/NSIAD-97-254, September 1997, 16.

3. See <http://www.fema.gov/library/terror.htm>.

4. "Combating Terrorism," GAO/NSIAD-97-254, 16; First Annual Report of the Advisory Panel to Assess Domestic Response Capabilities for Terrorism Involving the Use of Weapons of Mass Destruction, *I. Assessing the Threat* (December 15, 1999), iii, <http://www.rand.org/organization/nsrd/terrpanel/html>.

5. Bruce Hoffman, *Responding to Terrorism across the Technological Spectrum* (Santa Monica, Calif.: Rand Corporation, 1993), 3.

6. National Commission on Terrorism, *Countering the Changing Threat of International Terrorism* (June 2000), <http://www.fas.org/irp/threat/commission.html>.

7. The State Department does not distinguish the type of terrorist responsible for attacks.

8. "Combating Terrorism," GAO/NSIAD-97-254.

9. "Combating Terrorism," GAO/NSIAD-97-254.

10. Adapted from U.S. State Department, *Patterns of Global Terrorism, 1998*, Department of State Publication 10610, Office of the Secretary of State, Office of the Coordinator for Counterterrorism (released April 1999), <http://www.state.gov/www/global/terrorism/1998Report/sponsor.html>.

11. Secretary William Cohen, *Annual Report to the President and the U.S. Congress, FY2001*, Internet ed. (Washington, D.C.: U.S. Department of Defense).

12. Office of the Secretary of Defense, *Proliferation—Threat and Response, January 2001*, Internet ed. (Washington, D.C.: U.S. Department of Defense, January 2001), section 2.

13. U.S. General Accounting Office, GAO Report to Congressional Requesters, "Combating Terrorism: Opportunities to Improve Domestic Preparedness, Program Focus and Efficiency," GAO/NSIAD-99-3, November 12, 1998; U.S. General Accounting Office, GAO Report to Congressional Requesters, "Combating Terrorism: Observations on the Nunn-Lugar-Domenici Domestic Preparedness Program," GAO-T-NSIAD-99-16, October 2, 1998; and U.S. General Accounting Office, GAO Report to Congressional Requesters, "Combating Terrorism: Need for Comprehensive Threat and Risk Assessment of Chemical and Biological Attacks," GAO-T-NSIAD-99-163, September 1999.

14. "Combating Terrorism," GAO/NSIAD-99-3; "Combating Terrorism," GAO-T-NSIAD-99-16; and "Combating Terrorism," GAO-T-NSIAD-99-163.

15. Statement for the Record of Louis J. Freeh, Director Federal Bureau of Investigation on "Threats to U. S. National Security," before the Senate Select Committee on Intelligence (January 28, 1998), <http://www.fbi.gov/pressrm/congress/congress98/threats.htm>.

16. Statement for the Record of Mrs. Barbara Y. Martinez, Deputy Director, National Domestic Preparedness Office Federal Bureau of Investigation on "Preparedness for Terrorism Response," before the United States House of Representatives Transportation and Infrastructure Committee, Subcommittee on Oversight, Investigations, and Emergency Management (June 9, 1999), <http://www.fbi.gov/pressrm/congress/congress99/comterr.htm>.

17. Statement by Director of Central Intelligence, George J. Tenet, before the Senate Foreign Relations Committee on "The Worldwide Threat in 2000: Global Realities of Our National Security," as prepared for delivery (March 21, 2000).

*Chapter 3*

# Threat Prioritization: Seeking to Identify Current and Future Threats

There are two further issues that the United States must deal with in defining the threat: the possible nature of the attackers and the possible means of attack. In broad terms, the United States has done a good job of identifying potential attackers and the means that they might use. It does, however, need to improve its threat and risk assessments in terms of the ways in which it analyzes attackers and determines if they might use WMD.

## POTENTIAL STATE ACTORS

The United States is inherently vulnerable to covert foreign attack. America is an extraordinarily open society dependent on massive volumes of foreign trade and immigration. It has nearly one hundred thousand miles of shoreline and six thousand miles of borders. Some 475 million people and 142 million trucks and vehicles cross the border every year. There are 21.4 million major container-sized cargo shipments a year, plus countless break bulk and individual shipments. The legal trade across the U.S. borders arrives daily at 3,700 terminals in 301 ports of entry.[1]

Customs searches a tiny percentage of legal shipments into the United States, and much of the processing is pro forma. Most air forwarding enters the United States without any inspection. Containers can enter the duty-free areas of U.S. ports and remain there for thirty days before a declaration is required. Roughly eight million containers enter the United States each year, and one container takes an average of five inspectors three hours to search. In practice, one container enters southern California every twenty seconds and almost none are searched. Seven thousand trucks went from Windsor, Canada, to Detroit in one day in February 2000, and one truck has to be cleared through Customs every twelve seconds in Detroit. The volume of illegal traffic is massive and includes an estimated 376 metric tons of cocaine a year. (It also, however, includes an equally massive amount of other goods, including some five to ten million pounds of chloroflourocarbons [CFCs].) Cargo threat amounts to $10 billion worth of goods a year, most of which involves shipments whose nature and character cannot be proven.[2]

As for immigration, even if one ignores legal immigrants and the constant movement of U.S. citizens across our borders, there are five million illegal immigrants in the United States, roughly 2.7 million of which are undocumented.[3]

State actors are one of the major potential sources of foreign attack, particularly of attacks using sophisticated CBRN weapons. U.S. officials have identified seven states that now pose a possible threat in using WMD in unconventional or covert attacks against the United States. These states include major powers like Russia and China, which do not seem pose an immediate threat to the United States, but which have such broad ranging capabilities to manufacture WMD that their capabilities cannot be ignored.

They also include five more hostile powers that have some potential capability to use WMD to attack the U.S. homeland. The U.S. secretary of state has designated seven states as sponsors of terrorism: Cuba, Iran, Iraq, Libya, North Korea, Sudan, and Syria. Six of these states—Iran, Iraq, Libya, North Korea, the Sudan, and Syria—have access to WMD. Only one—North Korea—now presents more than a marginal risk since it has nuclear weapons, but all of these powers will probably acquire the capability to produce a highly lethal biological weapon over the next five to ten years.

### A Department of State Assessment of State Threats

The State Department report on terrorism issued in April 2000 summarizes the threat from foreign states as follows:

> Iran, Iraq, Syria, Libya, North Korea, Cuba, and Sudan remain the seven governments that the U.S. Secretary of State has designated as state sponsors of international terrorism. Iran continued to support numerous terrorist groups—including the Lebanese Hizbollah, HAMAS, and the Palestinian Islamic Jihad (PIJ)—in their efforts to undermine the Middle East peace process through terrorism. Although there were signs of political change in Iran in 1999, the actions of certain state institutions in support of terrorist groups made Iran the most active state sponsor of terrorism. Iraq continued to provide safehaven and support to a variety of Palestinian rejectionist groups, as well as bases, weapons, and protection to the Mujahedin-e Khalq (MEK), an

Iranian terrorist group that opposes the current Iranian regime. Syria continued to provide safehaven and support to several terrorist groups, some of which oppose the Middle East peace process. Libya had yet to fully comply with the requirements of the relevant UN Security Council resolutions related to the trial of those accused of downing Pan Am Flight 103 over Lockerbie, Scotland. North Korea harbored several hijackers of a Japanese Airlines flight to North Korea in the 1970s and maintained links to Usama bin Ladin and his network. Cuba continued providing safehaven to several terrorists and U.S. fugitives and maintained ties to other state sponsors and Latin American insurgents. Finally, Sudan continued to serve as a meeting place, safehaven, and training hub for members of bin Ladin's al-Qaida, Lebanese Hizbollah, al-Jihad, al-Gama'at, PIJ, HAMAS, and the Abu Nidal Organization (ANO).

State sponsorship has decreased over the past several decades. As it decreases, it becomes increasingly important for all countries to adopt a "zero tolerance" for terrorist activity within their borders. Terrorists will seek safehaven in those areas where they are able to avoid the rule of law and to travel, prepare, raise funds, and operate. In 1999 the United States actively researched and gathered intelligence on other states that will be considered for designation as state sponsors.[4]

This State Department report describes the level of support for terrorism in each state as follows:

- Cuba: Cuba continued to provide safehaven to several terrorists and U.S. fugitives in 1999. A number of Basque ETA terrorists who gained sanctuary in Cuba some years ago continued to live on the island, as did several U.S. terrorist fugitives.

    Havana also maintained ties to other state sponsors of terrorism and Latin American insurgents. Colombia's two largest terrorist organizations, the Revolutionary Armed Forces of Colombia and the National Liberation Army (ELN), both maintained a permanent presence on the island. In late 1999, Cuba hosted a series of meetings between Colombian government officials and ELN leaders.

- Iran: Although there were signs of political change in Iran in 1999, the actions of certain state institutions in support of terrorist groups made Iran the most active state sponsor of terrorism. These state institutions, notably the Revolutionary Guard Corps and the Ministry of Intelligence and Security, continued to be involved in the planning and execution of terrorist acts and continued to support a variety of groups that use terrorism to pursue their goals.

    A variety of public reports indicate Iran's security forces conducted several bombings against Iranian dissidents abroad. Iranian agents, for example, were blamed for a truck bombing in early October of a Mujahedin-e Khalq (MEK) terrorist base near Basrah, Iraq, that killed several MEK members and non–MEK individuals.

    Iran continued encouraging Hizbollah and the Palestinian rejectionist groups—including HAMAS, the Palestinian Islamic Jihad, and Ahmad Jibril's

PFLP–GC—to use violence, especially terrorist attacks, in Israel to undermine the peace process. Iran supported these groups with varying amounts of money, training, and weapons. Despite statements by the Khatami administration that Iran was not working against the peace process, Tehran stepped up its encouragement of, and support for, these groups after the election of Israeli Prime Minister Barak and the resumption of Israel-Syria peace talks. In a gesture of public support, President Khatami met with Damascus-based Palestinian rejectionist leaders during his visit to Syria in May. In addition, Iranian Supreme Leader Khamenei reflected Iran's covert actions aimed at scuttling the peace process when he sponsored a major rally in Tehran on November 9 to demonstrate Iran's opposition to Israel and peace. Hizbollah and Palestinian rejectionist speakers at the rally reaffirmed their support for violent *jihad* against Israel. A Palestinian Islamic Jihad representative praised a bombing in Netanya that occurred days before and promised more such attacks.

Tehran still provided safehaven to elements of Turkey's separatist PKK that conducted numerous terrorist attacks in Turkey and against Turkish targets in Europe. One of the PKK's most senior at-large leaders, Osman Ocalan, brother of imprisoned PKK leader Abdullah Ocalan, resided at least part time in Iran. Iran also provided support to terrorist groups in North Africa and South and Central Asia, including financial assistance and training.

Tehran accurately claimed that it also was a victim of terrorism, as the opposition Mujahedin-e Khalq conducted several terrorist attacks in Iran. On April 10 the group assassinated Brigadier General Ali Sayyad Shirazi, the Iranian Armed Forces Deputy Chief of the Joint Staff.

- Iraq: Iraq continued to plan and sponsor international terrorism in 1999. Although Baghdad focused primarily on the antiregime opposition at home and abroad, it continued to provide safehaven and support to various terrorist groups.

Press reports stated that, according to a defecting Iraqi intelligence agent, the Iraqi intelligence service had planned to bomb the offices of Radio Free Europe in Prague. Radio Free Europe offices include Radio Liberty, which began broadcasting news and information to Iraq in October 1998. The plot was foiled when it became public in early 1999.

The Iraqi opposition publicly stated its fears that the Baghdad regime was planning to assassinate those opposed to Saddam Hussein. A spokesman for the Iraqi National Accord in November said that the movement's security organs had obtained information about a plan to assassinate its secretary general, Dr. Iyad 'Allawi, and a member of the movement's political bureau, as well as another Iraqi opposition leader.

Iraq continued to provide safehaven to a variety of Palestinian rejectionist groups, including the Abu Nidal Organization, the Arab Liberation Front (ALF), and the former head of the now-defunct May 15 Organization, Abu Ibrahim, who masterminded several bombings of U.S. aircraft.

Iraq provided bases, weapons, and protection to the MEK, an Iranian terrorist group that opposes the current Iranian regime. In 1999, MEK cadre based in Iraq assassinated or attempted to assassinate several high-ranking Iranian government officials, including Brigadier General Ali Sayyad Shirazi, Deputy Chief of Iran's Joint Staff, who was killed in Tehran on April 10.

- Libya: In April 1999, Libya took an important step by surrendering for trial the two Libyans accused of bombing Pan Am Flight 103 over Lockerbie, Scotland, in 1988. The move responded directly to the U.S.–UK initiative; concerted efforts by the Saudi, Egyptian, and South African governments; and the active engagement of the UN Security Council and the UN Secretary General. At year end, however, Libya still had not complied with the remaining UN Security Council requirements: payment of appropriate compensation; acceptance of responsibility for the actions of its officials; renunciation of, and an end to, support for terrorism; and cooperation with the prosecution and trial. Libyan leader Qadhafi repeatedly stated publicly during the year that his government had adopted an antiterrorism stance, but it remained unclear whether his claims of distancing Libya from its terrorist past signified a true change in policy.

  Libya also remained the primary suspect in several other past terrorist operations, including the La Belle discotheque bombing in Berlin in 1986 that killed two U.S. servicemen and one Turkish civilian and wounded more than 200 persons. The trial in Germany of five suspects in the bombing, which began in November 1997, continued in 1999.

  In 1999, Libya expelled the Abu Nidal Organization and distanced itself from the Palestinian rejectionists, announcing that the Palestinian Authority was the only legitimate address for Palestinian concerns. Libya still may have retained ties to some Palestinian groups that use violence to oppose the Middle East peace process, however, including the PIJ and the PFLP–GC.

- North Korea: The Democratic People's Republic of Korea (D.P.R.K.) continued to provide safehaven to the Japanese Communist League—Red Army Faction members who participated in the hijacking of a Japanese Airlines flight to North Korea in 1970. P'yongyang allowed members of the Japanese Diet to visit some of the hijackers during the year. In 1999 the D.P.R.K. also attempted to kidnap in Thailand a North Korean diplomat who had defected the day before. The attempt led the North Korean Embassy to hold the former diplomat's son hostage for two weeks. Some evidence also suggests the D.P.R.K., in 1999, may have sold weapons directly or indirectly to terrorist groups.

- Pakistan: In 1999, the United States increasingly was concerned about reports of Pakistani support for terrorist groups and elements active in Kashmir, as well as Pakistani relations with the Taliban, which continued to harbor terrorists such as Usama bin Ladin. In the Middle East, the United States was concerned that a variety of terrorist groups operated and trained inside Lebanon with relative impunity. Lebanon also was unresponsive to U.S. requests to bring to justice terrorists who attacked U.S. citizens and property in Lebanon in previous years.

- Sudan: Sudan in 1999 continued to serve as a central hub for several international terrorist groups, including Usama bin Ladin's al-Qaida organization. The Sudanese government also condoned Iran's assistance to terrorist and radical Islamist groups operating in and transiting through Sudan.

  Khartoum served as a meeting place, safehaven, and training hub for members of the Lebanese Hizbollah, Egyptian Gama'at al-Islamiyya, al-Jihad, the Palestinian Islamic Jihad, HAMAS, and Abu Nidal Organization. Sudan's support to these groups included the provision of travel documentation, safe passage, and refuge. Most of the groups maintained offices and other forms of representation in the capital, using Sudan primarily as a secure base for organizing terrorist operations and assisting compatriots elsewhere.

Sudan still had not complied with UN Security Council Resolutions 1044, 1054, and 1070 passed in 1996—which demand that Sudan end all support to terrorists—despite the regime's efforts to distance itself publicly from terrorism. They also require Khartoum to hand over three Egyptian Gama'at fugitives linked to the assassination attempt in 1995 against Egyptian President Hosni Mubarak in Ethiopia. Sudanese officials continued to deny that they were harboring the three suspects and that they had a role in the attack.

- Syria (1998 report): There is no evidence that Syrian officials have engaged directly in planning or executing international terrorist attacks since 1986. Syria, nonetheless, continues to provide safehaven and support to several terrorist groups, allowing some to maintain training camps or other facilities on Syrian territory. Ahmad Jibril's Popular Front for the Liberation of Palestine–General Command and the Palestine Islamic Jihad, for example, have their headquarters in Damascus. In addition, Syria grants a wide variety of terrorist groups—including HAMAS, the PFLP–GC, and the PIJ—basing privileges or refuge in areas of Lebanon's Bekaa Valley under Syrian control.

  Although Damascus claims to be committed to the Middle East peace process, it has not acted to stop anti-Israeli attacks by Hizbollah and Palestinian rejectionist groups in southern Lebanon. Syria allowed—but did not participate in—a meeting of Palestinian rejectionist groups in Damascus in December to reaffirm their public opposition to the peace process. Syria also assists the resupply of rejectionist groups operating in Lebanon via Damascus. Nonetheless, the Syrian government continues to restrain the international activities of some groups and to participate in a multinational monitoring group to prevent attacks against civilian targets in southern Lebanon and northern Israel.[5]

The June 2000 report of the National Commission on Terrorism added Afghanistan and Greece to the states that the State Department designates as terrorism sponsors or "not cooperating fully":

The U.S. government has not designated Afghanistan as a state sponsor of terrorism because it does not recognize the Taliban regime as the government of Afghanistan.

In 1996, the Taliban regime gained control of the capital of Afghanistan and began asserting its control over much of the country. Since then it has provided a safehaven to terrorist groups and terrorist fugitives wanted by U.S. law enforcement, including Usama bin Ladin—who is under indictment for his role in the bombings of U.S. Embassies in Kenya and Tanzania in 1998. The Taliban also supports the training camps of many of these terrorist groups.

. . . In 1996, Congress enacted a law that authorizes the President to designate as "not cooperating fully" states whose behavior is objectionable but not so egregious as to warrant designation as a "state sponsor of terrorism." This law has not been effectively used.

Some countries use the rhetoric of counterterrorist cooperation but are unwilling to shoulder their responsibilities in practice, such as restricting the travel of terrorists through their territory or ratifying United Nations conventions on terrorism. Other states have relations with terrorists that fall short of the extensive criteria for designation as a state sponsor, but their failure to act against terrorists perpetuates terrorist activities. Newer terrorist groups, many of which are transnational in composition and less influenced by state agendas, can take advantage of such states for safehaven.

To address these categories of countries, in 1996 Congress authorized the President to designate countries as "not cooperating fully with U.S. antiterrorism efforts" and to embargo defense sales to such states. To date, only Afghanistan has been so designated, and that designation arose from the legal difficulty of putting Afghanistan on the state sponsor list without appearing to recognize the Taliban as the legitimate government.

Two other countries that present difficulties for U.S. counterterrorism policy are Pakistan and Greece. Both are friendly nations and Greece is a NATO ally.

. . . Greece has been disturbingly passive in response to terrorist activities. It is identified by the U.S. government as "one of the weakest links in Europe's effort against terrorism" (Patterns of Global Terrorism, 1999. U.S. Department of State). Since 1975 there have been 146 terrorist attacks against Americans or American interests in Greece. Only one case has been solved and there is no indication of any meaningful investigation into the remaining cases. Among the unresolved cases are the attacks by the Revolutionary Organization 17 November, which has claimed responsibility for the deaths of 20 people, including four Americans, since 1975. Greek authorities have never arrested a member of 17 November, which is a designated FTO. The Turkish leftist group, the Revolutionary People's Liberation Party/Front (DHKP–C), also an FTO, has murdered four Americans since 1979 and maintains an office in Athens despite United States protests. Last year, senior Greek government officials gave assistance and refuge to the leader of the Kurdish terrorist group, the Kurdish Workers Party (PKK).[6]

## A Department of Defense Assessment of Threats from Foreign States

There is a rough correlation between the states the United States has identified as potential threats and the states capable of delivering WMD. A recent DOD report on chemical and biological weapons summarizes the developments in several key states as follows:

- China: China possesses an advanced biotechnology infrastructure as well as the requisite munitions production capabilities necessary to develop, produce, and weaponize biological agents. Although China has consistently claimed that it has never researched or produced biological weapons, it is nonetheless believed likely that it retains a biological warfare capability begun before acceding to the BWC.

China is believed to have an advanced chemical warfare program that includes research and development, and production and weaponization capabilities. Its current inventory is believed to include the full range of traditional chemical agents. It also has a wide variety of delivery systems for chemical agents to include artillery rockets, aerial bombs, sprayers, and short-range ballistic missiles. Chinese forces, like those of North Korea, have conducted defensive CW training and are prepared to operate in a contaminated environment. As China's program is further integrated into overall military operations, its doctrine, which is believed to be based in part on Soviet-era thinking, may reflect the incorporation of more advanced munitions for CW agent delivery. China has signed and ratified the CWC.

- Libya: Libya's biological warfare program is believed to remain in the early research and development phase. Progress has been slow due in part to an inadequate scientific and technical base. Though Libya may be able to produce small quantities of usable agent, it is unlikely to transition from laboratory work to production of militarily significant quantities until well after the year 2000. Libya acceded to the BWC in 1982.

  Libya has experienced major setbacks to its chemical warfare program, first as a result of intense public scrutiny focused on its Rabta facility in the late 1980s and more recently on its Tarhuna underground facility. Nevertheless, Libya retains a small inventory of chemical weapons as well as a CW agent production capability. Prior to closing its Rabta plant in 1990, Libya succeeded in producing up to 100 tons of blister and nerve agent at the site. Although the site was re-opened in 1995, ostensibly as a pharmaceutical plant, the facility is still believed capable of producing CW agents. CW–related activities at the Tarhuna site are believed to be suspended. Libya has not ratified the CWC and is not likely to do so in the near future.

- India: India has a well-developed biotechnology infrastructure that includes numerous pharmaceutical production facilities bio-containment laboratories (including BL-3) for working with lethal pathogens. It also has qualified scientists with expertise in infectious diseases. Some of India's facilities are being used to support research and development for BW defense purposes. These facilities constitute a substantial capability for offensive purposes as well. India is a signatory to the BWC of 1972.

  India also has an advanced commercial chemical industry, and produces the bulk of its own chemicals for domestic consumption. New Delhi ratified the CWC in 1996. In its required declarations, it acknowledged the existence of a chemical warfare program. New Delhi has pledged that all facilities related to its CW program would be open for inspection. Pakistan has a capable but less well-developed biotechnology infrastructure than India. Its facilities, while fewer in number, could nonetheless support work on lethal biological pathogens. Moreover, Pakistan is believed to have the resources and capabilities necessary to support a limited-offensive biological warfare research and development effort. Like India, Pakistan is a signatory to the BWC.

- Iran: Iran's biological warfare program, which began during the Iran-Iraq War, is now believed to generally be in the advanced research and development phase. Iran has qualified, highly trained scientists and considerable expertise with pharmaceuticals. It also possesses the commercial and military infrastructure needed to produce basic biological warfare agents and may have produced pilot quantities of usable agent. Iran is a signatory to the BWC of 1972.

Iran initiated a chemical weapons program in the early stages of the Iran-Iraq War after it was attacked with chemical weapons. The program has received heightened attention since the early 1990s with an expansion in the chemical production infrastructure as well as its munitions arsenal. Iran currently possesses munitions containing blister, blood, and choking agents and may have nerve agents as well. It has the capability to deliver CW agents using artillery shells and aerial bombs. Iran has ratified the CWC, declared agents and chemical agent production facilities, and is obligated to open suspected sites to international inspection and eliminate its CW program.

- Iraq: Prior to the Gulf War, Iraq developed the largest and most advanced biological warfare program in the Middle East. Though a variety of agents were studied, Iraq declared anthrax, botulinum toxin, and aflatoxin to have completed the weaponization cycle. During the Gulf War, coalition bombing destroyed or damaged many key facilities associated with BW activity. However, it is suspected that a key portion of Iraq's BW capability, in the form of agent-filled munitions, was hidden and may have subsequently escaped damage. Nonetheless, Iraq declared, after the war, that all BW agent stockpile and munitions were unilaterally destroyed. United Nations Special Commission (UNSCOM) activity has, however, revealed this assertion as well as many others related to BW activity, to be inaccurate and misleading. As with its chemical program, Iraq intends to re-establish its BW capabilities if afforded the opportunity by the relaxation or cessation of UNSCOM inspection activity.

Iraq had a mature chemical weapons program prior to the Gulf War that included a variety of nerve agents, such as tabun (GA), sarin (GB), and GF, as well as the blister agent mustard, available for offensive use. Iraq also undertook a program, begun in 1985 and continuing uninterrupted until December 1990, to produce the advanced nerve agent VX. Recent UNSCOM findings indicate that Iraq had weaponized VX in Al Hussein missile warheads. Although Iraq's chemical warfare program suffered extensive damage during the Gulf War and subsequently from UNSCOM activity, Iraq retains a limited capability to re-constitute key parts of its chemical warfare program. Moreover, UNSCOM, despite having destroyed over 700 metric tons of agent, is still unable to verify elements of Iraqi declarations such as the disposal of chemical precursors, as well as the destruction of all chemical munitions. The comprehensive nature of Iraq's previous chemical warfare activity and the consistent pattern of denial and deception employed by Iraqi authorities indicate a high-level intent to rebuild this capacity, should Iraq be given the opportunity.

- North Korea: North Korea has been pursuing research and development related to biological warfare since the 1960s. Pyongyang's resources presently include a rudimentary (by Western standards) biotechnology infrastructure that is sufficient to support the production of limited quantities of toxins, as well as viral and bacterial biological warfare agents. In the early 1990s, an open press release by a foreign government referred to applied military biotechnology work at numerous North Korean medical institutes and universities dealing with pathogens such as anthrax, cholera, and plague. North Korea possesses a sufficient munitions-production infrastructure to accomplish weaponization of BW agents. North Korea acceded to the Biological and Toxins Weapons Convention (BWC) in 1987.

By comparison, North Korea's chemical warfare program is believed to be mature and includes the capability, since 1989, to indigenously produce bulk quantities of nerve, blister, choking, and blood chemical agents as well as a variety of different filled munitions systems. North Korea is believed to possess a sizable stockpile of chemical weapons, which could be employed in offensive military operations against the South. North Korea has also devoted considerable scarce resources to defensive measures aimed at protecting its civilian population and military forces from the effects of chemical weapons. Such measures include extensive training in the use of protective masks, suits, detectors, and decontamination systems. Though these measures are ostensibly focused on a perceived threat from U.S. and South Korean forces, they could also support the offensive use of chemical weapons by the North during combat. North Korea has yet to sign the Chemical Weapons Convention (CWC) and is not expected to do so in the near-term, due to intrusive inspection and verification requirements mandated by the agreement.

- Pakistan: Pakistan has a less well-developed commercial chemical industry but is expected to eventually have the capability to produce all precursor chemicals needed to support a chemical weapons stockpile. Like India, Pakistan has numerous munitions systems which could be used to deliver CW agent, including artillery, aerial bombs, and missiles. Pakistan has ratified the CWC, but submitted a null declaration.

- The Former Soviet Union (FSU): The FSU's offensive biological warfare program was the world's largest and consisted of military facilities and nonmilitary research and development institutes. Nonmilitary activity was centrally coordinated and performed largely through a consortium of institutes known as Biopreparat. This network of facilities was created in 1973 as a cover for activity related to biological warfare. This huge organization at one time employed up to 25,000 people and involved nearly 20 research, development, and production facilities. The Russian government has committed to ending the former Soviet BW program, although serious questions about offensive BW capabilities remain. Key components of the former program remain largely intact and may support a possible future mobilization capability for the production of biological warfare agents and delivery systems. Moreover, work outside the scope of legitimate biological defense activity may be occurring at selected facilities within Russia. Such activity, if offensive in nature, would contradict statements by top Russian political leaders that offensive activity has ceased.

  While former Soviet biological warfare facilities existed in Ukraine, Kazakhstan, and Uzbekistan, none are currently active. Moreover, the governments in these new republics are not believed to have plans to establish any future BW capability. Also, Belarus has no program and no intention of establishing one. Ukraine, Belarus, and Uzbekistan have ratified the BWC, while Kazakhstan has not yet signed it.

Russia has acknowledged the world's largest stockpile of chemical agents, amounting to approximately 40,000 metric tons. This stockpile, consisting mostly of weaponized agent includes artillery, aerial bombs, rockets, and missile warheads. Actual agents include a variety of nerve and blister agents. Additionally, some Russian chemical weapons incorporate agent mixtures, while others have added thickening materials in order to increase agent persistence. Russian officials do not deny that CW research has continued but claim that it is for defensive purposes and therefore not proscribed by the CWC. Many of the components for new binary agents developed under the former-Soviet program have legitimate civilian applications and are not considered on the CWC's schedule of chemicals.

- Syria: Syria has a limited biotechnology infrastructure but could support a limited biological warfare effort. Though Syria is believed to be pursuing the development of biological weapons, it is not believed to have progressed much beyond the research and development phase and may have produced only pilot quantities of usable agent. Syria has signed, but not ratified, the BWC. Syria has a mature chemical weapons program, begun in the 1970s, incorporating nerve agents, such as sarin, which have completed the weaponization cycle. Future activity will likely focus on CW infrastructure enhancements for agent production and storage, as well as possible research and development of advanced nerve agents. Munitions available for CW agent delivery likely include aerial bombs as well as SCUD missile warheads. Syria has not signed the CWC and is unlikely to do so in the near future.[7]

## The Probable Lack of Well-Defined Strategic Warning of a Threat from State Actors and Unpredictable Behavior in a Crisis

None of the State Department and DOD descriptions of hostile and proliferating states imply that any of the previously listed states are now likely to take the risk of attacking the United States. They do, however, have dangerous capabilities, and U.S. policy cannot be based on current threats. A covert or proxy attack by Iran would have seemed much more likely during the tanker war of 1987–1988, and an Iran willing to build missiles with ranges capable of reaching the United States may well have contingency plans for other forms of attack. If the Persian Gulf War had not taken place, Iraq would pose a much greater threat, and if sanctions are lifted, it may develop such attack capabilities in an effort to either deter U.S. action in the Persian Gulf or punish it for any attack on the Iraqi leadership. North Korea remains unpredictable. The behavior of any regime can change suddenly in a crisis. For example, the United States never had to seriously evaluate Serbian chemical warfare capabilities before its intervention in Kosovo.

There also is no reason to assume the United States can now identify its future attackers. Attacks by state actors may well come from one of the roughly 170 states that are not a threat today. New proliferators continue to emerge and states can develop biological and chemical weapons with little or no warning. The transfer of fissile material from state to state could sharply reduce the lead times in nuclear proliferation, and today's "friend" or "neutral" could easily become tomorrow's enemy.

Table 3.1 shows that list of today's known proliferators is also considerably longer than the list of today's known threats. It is uncertain how much strategic warning the United States will have of the fact that a proliferating state might take hostile action. Under normal conditions, it seems likely that virtually any state actor would show great restraint in attacking the U.S. homeland because of the risks of retaliation. As a result, it seems more likely that a nonstate actor would take such risks than a state. "Normal," however, is an uncertain term.

There are several interactive reasons why the United States might not receive adequate strategic warning and/or "normal" behavior might not restrain a state:

- Crisis behavior is very different from normal behavior. For example, the ability to threaten or attack the United States might be exercised if a regime felt that it was fatally threatened by U.S. military action or a U.S.–supported coalition, or that an attack on the United States might force the United States or international community to take action that would aid it in a conflict. Iraq's horizontal escalation in using missiles against Israel is an example of such crisis behavior.

- The lead times and indicators that identify proliferating states are changing with time. The spread of chemical, biological, and associated delivery system technologies is proliferating throughout much of the developing world, as is the ability to use fissile material in a nuclear weapon. The United States can have steadily less confidence in the time it has in which to detect proliferation and in the material indications that proliferation is taking place.

- The United States has not established a clear doctrine of massive retaliation in reprisal for such attacks, and the threat the United States might reply with massive conventional attacks or by using nuclear weapons may become steadily less convincing with time.

- A hostile state actor might attempt to conceal an attack in several ways that would offer a reasonable chance that it would not be detected or that it could avoid massive retaliation:
  - It could build up or support an independent extremist or terrorist movement and use it as a proxy, as Syria and Iran have used the Hizbollah and Hamas. In many cases, such movements have several state supporters, and the particular state using a proxy to attack the U.S. might not be possible to identify. The ambiguities surrounding the attack on Pan Am Flight 103, the USAF compound at Al Khobar, and USS *Cole* are cases in point.
  - A hostile state might use a crisis or conflict involving another state hostile to the U.S. as a cover for its attack. In the case of Iran or Iraq, for example, attacking the U.S. homeland during a crisis with the other state might succeed in hiding the true nature of the attacker and causing the U.S. to retaliate against a regional enemy.

- Biological attacks with long lead times before their affects become apparent may be very difficult to characterize. Attacks on animals and agriculture could be extremely costly to the U.S., but would be difficult to characterize, and the U.S. has no apparent retaliatory doctrine for dealing with such attacks.

- A hostile state might piggyback on a more conventional form of covert attack by another state, or a separate attack by a hostile terrorist or extremist movement.

These uncertainties *do not* mean that state-driven, covert attacks on the U.S. homeland are likely, with or without the use of WMD. They do mean, however, that it is dangerous to attempt to assign a relative probability based on current, precrisis, or peacetime behavior.

## FOREIGN TERRORISTS AND EXTREMISTS

Analyzing the threat from foreign terrorists and extremists require a focus on current and future capabilities, rather than on current intentions. Tables 2.1 and 2.2 have already shown that terrorist and extremist violence comes in uncertain cycles. The most recent data on the actions of foreign terrorists and extremists confirms this pattern. The State Department reports that there were 304 international terrorist attacks during 1997, 273 attacks during 1998, and 387 during 1999. Taken at face value, 1998 seems a low year for terrorism. In fact, it had the fewest annual incidents since 1971 and only 70 percent of the incidents in 1999. The total number of persons killed or wounded in terrorist attacks, however, was the highest on record: 741 persons died and 5,952 persons suffered injuries. Twelve U.S. citizens died in terrorist attacks in 1998, all in the Nairobi bombing. Each was an embassy employee or dependent. Eleven other U.S. citizens were wounded in terrorist attacks in 1999, including six in Nairobi, Kenya, and one in Dar es Salaam, Tanzania. Three-fifths of the total attacks—166—were bombings. The foremost type of target was business related.[8]

There are no similar patterns to look at in terms of foreign terrorist and extremist attacks on the United States. The State Department did not report any successful foreign terrorist attacks in the U.S. homeland between the World Trade Center bombing in 1993 and the attacks on the World Trade Center and the Pentagon in 2001. However, the United States was the target of the devastating bombings of the U.S. embassies in Nairobi and Dar es Salaam in August 1998. In Nairobi, the U.S. embassy was located in a congested downtown area, and 213 persons were killed in the attack, and about 4,500 were wounded. In Dar es Salaam, ten persons were killed and seventy-seven wounded.

More broadly, about 40 percent of all the attacks the State Department reported in 1998—a total of 111—were directed against U.S. targets.

Table 3.1
Global Challenges: Who Has Weapons of Mass Destruction?

| Country | Type of Weapon of Mass Destruction | | | Long-Range Missiles | |
|---|---|---|---|---|---|
| | Chemical | Biological | Nuclear | Theater | Intercontinental |
| *East-West* | | | | | |
| Britain | Breakout | Breakout | Deployed | Deployed | SLBMs |
| Canada | - | Technology | Technology | - | - |
| France | Breakout | Breakout | Deployed | Deployed | SLBMs |
| Germany | Breakout | Breakout | Technology | Technology | - |
| Serbia | Deployed | - | - | Deployed | - |
| Sweden | - | - | Technology | - | - |
| Russia | Residual | Residual | Deployed | Technology | ICBMs/SLBMs |
| United States | Residual | Breakout | Deployed | Technology | ICBMsS/SLBMs |
| *Middle East* | | | | | |
| Egypt | Residual | Breakout | - | Deployed | - |
| Israel | Breakout | Breakout | Deployed | Deployed | Technology/Booster |
| Iran | Deployed? | Breakout | Technology | Deployed | Technology/Booster |
| Iraq | Deployed | Deployed | Technology | Technology | ? |
| Libya | Deployed | Research | - | Deployed | ? |
| Syria | Deployed | Technology? | - | Deployed | - |
| Yemen | Residual | - | - | - | - |

*Asia and South Asia*

| | | | | | ICBMs/SLBMs |
|---|---|---|---|---|---|
| China | Deployed? | Breakout? | Deployed | Deployed | Technology |
| India | Breakout? | Breakout? | Deployed | Deployed | - |
| Japan | Breakout | Breakout | Technology | Technology | Technology? |
| Pakistan | Breakout? | Breakout? | Deployed | Deployed | Technology/Booster |
| North Korea | Deployed | Deployed | Technology | Deployed | - |
| South Korea | Breakout? | Breakout | Technology | Technology? | - |
| Taiwan | Breakout? | Breakout | Technology | - | - |
| Thailand | Residual | - | - | - | |
| Vietnam | Residual | - | - | - | |

*Other*

| | | | | | |
|---|---|---|---|---|---|
| Argentina | - | - | Technology | Technology | - |
| Brazil | - | - | Technology | Technology | - |
| South Africa | - | - | Technology | Technology | - |

However, the majority of these attacks—a total of 77—were bombings of a single target: the multinational oil pipeline in Colombia, which terrorists regard as a U.S. target.

### Continuing Threats and Counterterrorist Action

Experts reportedly warned that the failure to attack the U.S. homeland, before September 2001, did not reflect a lack of potential threats. Louis Freeh, then director of the FBI, summarized the threat posed by foreign terrorists as follows in a testimony before the Senate Committee on Appropriations Subcommittee for the Departments of Commerce, Justice, and State, the Judiciary, and Related Agencies on February 4, 1999:

The current international terrorist threat can be divided into three general categories that represent a serious and distinct threat to the United States. These categories also reflect, to a large degree, how terrorists have adapted their tactics since the 1970s by learning from past successes and failures, from becoming familiar with law enforcement capabilities and tactics, and from exploiting technologies and weapons that are increasingly available to them in the post–Cold War era.

The first threat category, state sponsors of terrorism, violates every convention of international law. State sponsors of terrorism currently designated by the Department of State are: Iran, Iraq, Syria, Sudan, Libya, Cuba, and North Korea. Put simply, these nations view terrorism as a tool of foreign policy. In recent years, the terrorist activities of Cuba and North Korea appear to have declined as the economies of these countries have deteriorated. However, the terrorist activities of the other states I mentioned continue, and in some cases, have intensified during the past several years.

The second category of the international terrorist threat is represented by more formal terrorist organizations. These autonomous, generally transnational, organizations have their own infrastructures, personnel, financial arrangements, and training facilities. These organizations are able to plan and mount terrorist campaigns on an international basis and actively support terrorist activities in the United States.

Extremist groups such as Lebanese Hizbollah, the Egyptian al-Gama'at al- Islamiyya, and the Palestinian Hamas have supporters in the United States who could be used to support an act of terrorism here. Hizbollah ranks among the most menacing of these groups. It has staged many anti-American attacks in other countries, such as the 1983 truck bombings of the United States Embassy and the United States Marine Corps barracks in Beirut, the 1984 bombing of the United States Embassy Annex in Beirut, and the 1985 hijacking of TWA Flight 847 during which United States Navy diver Robert Stehem, a passenger on the flight, was murdered by the hijackers. Elements of Hizbollah were also responsible for the kidnapping and detention of United States hostages in Lebanon throughout the 1980s.

The activities of American cells of Hizbollah, Hamas, and al Gama'at al-Islamiyya generally revolve around fund-raising and low-level intelligence gathering. In addition, there are still significant numbers of Iranian students attending United States universities and technical institutions. A significant number of these students are hardcore members of the pro-Iranian student organization known as the Anjoman Islamie, which is comprised almost exclusively of fanatical, anti-American, Iranian Shiite Muslims. The Iranian government relies heavily on these students studying in the United States for low-level intelligence and technical expertise. However, the Anjoman Islamie also represents a significant resource base on which the government of Iran can draw to maintain the capability to mount operations against the United States, if it so decides.

The third category of international terrorist threat stems from loosely affiliated extremists, characterized by rogue terrorists such as Ramzi Ahmed Yousef and international terrorist financier Usama bin Ladin. These loosely affiliated extremists may pose the most urgent threat to the United States because these individuals bring together groups on an ad hoc, temporary basis. By not being encumbered with the demands associated with maintaining a rigid, organizational infrastructure, these individuals are more difficult for law enforcement to track and infiltrate. Individuals such as Ramzi Yousef and Usama bin Ladin have also demonstrated an ability to exploit mobility and technology to avoid detection and to conduct terrorist acts. Fortunately, in 1995, we were able to capture Yousef and return him to the United States to stand trial for the February 1993 bombing of the World Trade Center and the conspiracy to attack American aircraft overseas. Yousef was convicted in two trials and sentenced to life imprisonment.

The FBI believes that the threat posed by international terrorists in each of these categories will continue for the foreseeable future. As attention remains focused on Usama bin Ladin in the aftermath of the East African bombings, I believe it is important to remember that rogue terrorists such as bin Ladin represent just one type of threat that the United States faces. It is imperative that we maintain our capabilities to counter the broad range of international terrorist threats that confront the United States.

For many of us in this room, the threat of international terrorism was literally brought home by the World Trade Center bombing in February 1993. Although the plotters failed in their attempt to topple one of the twin towers into the other, an outcome that would have produced thousands of casualties, they succeeded in causing millions of dollars worth of damage in a blast that killed 6 persons and injured more than 1,000. After his capture in 1995, Ramzi Yousef, the convicted mastermind behind the New York City bombing and other terrorist acts, conceded to investigators that a lack of funding forced his group's hand in plotting the destruction of the World Trade Center. Running short of money, the plotters could not assemble a bomb as large as they had originally intended. The timing of the attack was also rushed by a lack of finances. Incredibly, the plotters' desire to recoup the deposit fee on the rental truck used to transport the bomb helped lead investigators to them. As horrible as that act was, it could very well have been much more devastating.

We are fortunate that in the nearly six years since the World Trade Center bombing, no significant act of foreign-directed terrorism has occurred on

American soil. At the same time, however, we have witnessed a pattern of terrorist attacks that are either directed at United States interests or initiated in response to U.S. government policies and actions. Among these acts are:

. . . As these examples illustrate, the threat of terrorism is real both at home and abroad. Usama bin Ladin readily acknowledges trying to obtain chemical and biological weapons for use in his jihad, or holy war, against the United States. We also know that domestic terrorist groups have also expressed interest in chemical and biological agents. The willingness of terrorists to carry out more large-scale incidents designed for maximum destruction places a larger proportion of our population at risk. Today, Americans engaged in activities as routine as working in an office building, commuting to and from work, or visiting museums and historical sites in foreign lands, can become random victims in a deadly game acted out by international terrorists. America's democratic tradition and global presence make United States citizens and interests targets for opportunists who are willing to shed the blood of innocents for their causes.[9]

The FBI did claim, however, that part of the reason for the low incidence of recent attacks on the United States was that the United States had steadily stepped up its counterterrorism efforts, and there were a number of cases in which the United States had shown it could take action against terrorists who attack Americans:

- On November 4, 1998, indictments were returned before the U.S. District Court for the Southern District of New York in connection with the two U.S. Embassy bombings in Africa. Charged in the indictment were: Usama bin Ladin, his military commander Muhammad Atef, and al-Qaida members Wadih El Hage, Fazul Abdullah Mohammed, Mohammed Sadeek Odeh, and Mohamed Rashed Daoud al-Owhali. Two of these suspects, Odeh and al-Owhali, were turned over to U.S. authorities in Kenya and brought to the United States to stand trial. Another suspect, Mamdouh Mahmud Salim, was arrested in Germany in September and extradited to the United States in December. On December 16, five others were indicted for their role in the Dar es Salaam Embassy bombing: Mustafa Mohammed Fadhil, Khalfan Khamis Mohamed, Ahmed Khalfan Ghailani, Fahid Mohommed Ally Msalam, and Sheikh Ahmed Salim Swedan.

- In June 1998, Mohammed Rashid was turned over to U.S. authorities overseas and brought to the United States to stand trial on charges of planting a bomb in 1982 on a Pan Am flight from Tokyo to Honolulu that detonated, killing one passenger and wounding fifteen others. Rashid had served part of a prison term in Greece in connection with the bombing until that country released him from prison early and expelled him in December 1996, in a move the United States called "incomprehensible." The nine-count U.S. indictment against Rashid charges him with murder, sabotage, bombing, and other crimes in connection with the Pan Am explosion.

- Three additional persons convicted in the bombing of the World Trade Center in 1993 were sentenced last year. Eyad Mahmoud Ismail Najim, who drove the explosive-laden van into the World Trade Center, was sentenced to 240 years in prison and ordered to pay $10 million in restitution and a $250,000 fine. Mohammad Abouhalima, who was convicted as an accessory for driving his brother to the Kennedy International Airport knowing he had participated in the bombing, was sentenced to eight years in prison. Ibrahim Ahmad Suleiman received a ten-month sentence on two counts of perjury for lying to the grand jury investigating the bombing.

- In May 1998, Abdul Hakim Murad was sentenced to life in prison without parole for his role in the failed conspiracy in January 1995 to blow up a dozen U.S. airliners over the Pacific Ocean. Murad received an additional sixty-year sentence for his role and was fined $250,000. Ramzi Ahmed Yousef, who was convicted previously in this conspiracy and for his role in the World Trade Center bombing in 1993, is serving a life prison term.[10]

This list of arrests and thwarted attempts was scarcely evidence that a threat did not exist; rather, it was evidence that a threat did exist and had not been successful.

## Major Foreign Terrorist Groups and Extremists

There is no comprehensive list of foreign terrorist organizations, and any attempt to make such a list would run up against a host of problems in distinguishing between "freedom fighters," nonviolent opposition movements, and terrorists. Many of the groups involved have major internal divisions and splinter groups and new groups keep emerging. The State Department has, however, designated a list of key movements that it feels can be described as terrorist:

- **Abu Nidal Organization** (ANO; aka Fatah Revolutionary Council, Arab Revolutionary Council, Arab Revolutionary Brigades, Black September, and Revolutionary Organization of Socialist Muslims International terrorist organization): Led by Sabri al-Banna. Split from PLO in 1974. Made up of various functional committees, including political, military, and financial. Has carried out terrorist attacks in 20 countries, killing or injuring almost 900 persons. Targets include the United States, the United Kingdom, France, Israel, moderate Palestinians, the PLO, and various Arab countries. Major attacks included the Rome and Vienna airports in December 1985, the Neve Shalom synagogue in Istanbul and the Pan Am Flight 73 hijacking in Karachi in September 1986, and the City of Poros day-excursion ship attack in July 1988 in Greece. Suspected of assassinating PLO deputy chief Abu Iyad and PLO security chief Abu Hul in Tunis in January 1991. ANO assassinated a Jordanian diplomat in Lebanon in January 1994 and has been linked to the killing of the PLO representative there. Has not attacked Western targets since the late 1980s. *Has received considerable support, including safehaven, training, logistic assistance, and financial aid from Iraq, Libya, and Syria (until 1987), in addition to close support for selected operations.*

- **Abu Sayyaf Group** (ASG): Smallest and most radical of the Islamic separatist groups operating in the southern Philippines. Split from the Moro National Liberation Front in 1991 under the leadership of Abdurajik Abubakar Janjalani, who was killed in a clash with Philippine police on December 18, 1998. Some members have studied or worked in the Middle East and developed ties to Arab *mujahidin* while fighting and training in Afghanistan. Uses bombs, assassinations, kidnappings, and extortion payments to promote an independent Islamic state in western Mindanao and the Sulu Archipelago, areas in the southern Philippines heavily populated by Muslims. Raided the town of Ipil in Mindanao in April 1995, the group's first large-scale action. Suspected of several small-scale bombings and kidnappings in 1998. *Probably receives support from Islamic extremists in the Middle East and South Asia.*

- **Alex Boncayao Brigade** (ABB): The ABB, the urban hit squad of the Communist Party of the Philippines, was formed in the mid-1980s. Responsible for more than 100 murders and believed to have been involved in the 1989 murder of U.S. Army Col. James Rowe in the Philippines. Although reportedly decimated by a series of arrests in late 1995, the murder in June 1996 of a former high-ranking Philippine official, claimed by the group, demonstrates that it still maintains terrorist capabilities. In March 1997 the group announced that it had formed an alliance with another armed group, the Revolutionary Proletarian Army.

- **Armed Islamic Group*** (GIA): An Islamic extremist group, the GIA aims to overthrow the secular Algerian regime and replace it with an Islamic state. The GIA began its violent activities in early 1992 after Algiers voided the victory of the Islamic Salvation Front (FIS)—the largest Islamic party—in the first round of legislative elections in December 1991. Frequent attacks against civilians, journalists, and foreign residents. In the last several years the GIA has conducted a terrorist campaign of civilian massacres, sometimes wiping out entire villages in its area of operations and frequently killing hundreds of civilians. Since announcing its terrorist campaign against foreigners living in Algeria in September 1993, the GIA has killed more than 100 expatriate men and women—mostly Europeans—in the country. Uses assassinations and bombings, including car bombs, and it is known to favor kidnapping victims and slitting their throats. The GIA hijacked an Air France flight to Algiers in December 1994, and suspicions centered on the group for a series of bombings in France in 1995. *Algerian expatriates and GIA members abroad, many of whom reside in Western Europe, provide some financial and logistic support. In addition, the Algerian government has accused Iran and Sudan of supporting Algerian extremists and severed diplomatic relations with Iran in March 1993.*

- **Aum Supreme Truth*** (Aum; aka Aum Shinrikyo): A cult established in 1987 by Shoko Asahara, Aum aims to take over Japan and then the world. Its organizational structure mimics that of a nation-state, with "finance," "construction," and "science and technology" ministries. Approved as a religious entity in 1989 under Japanese law, the group ran candidates in a Japanese parliamentary election in 1990. Over time, the cult began to emphasize the imminence of the end of the world and stated that the United States would initiate

"Armageddon" by starting World War III with Japan. The Japanese government revoked its recognition of Aum as a religious organization in October 1995, but in 1997 a government panel decided not to invoke the Anti-Subversive Law against the group, which would have outlawed the cult. On March 20, 1995 Aum members simultaneously released sarin nerve gas on several Tokyo subway trains, killing 12 persons and injuring up to 6,000. The group was responsible for other mysterious chemical incidents in Japan in 1994. Its efforts to conduct attacks using biological agents have been unsuccessful. Japanese police arrested Asahara in May 1995, and he remained on trial facing seventeen counts of murder at the end of 1998. In 1997 and 1998 the cult resumed its recruiting activities in Japan and opened several commercial businesses. Maintains an Internet homepage that indicates Armageddon and anti-U.S. sentiment remain a part of the cult's world view. *At the time of the Tokyo subway attack, the group claimed to have 9,000 members in Japan and up to 40,000 worldwide. Its current strength is unknown. Operates in Japan, but previously had a presence in Australia, Russia, Ukraine, Germany, Taiwan, Sri Lanka, the former Yugoslavia, and the United States.*

- **Basque Fatherland and Liberty\*** (ETA; aka Euzkadi Ta Askatasuna): Founded in 1959 with the aim of establishing an independent homeland based on Marxist principles in Spain's Basque region and the southwestern French provinces of Labourd, Basse-Navarra, and Soule. Primarily bombings and assassinations of Spanish government officials, especially security and military forces, politicians, and judicial figures. In response to French operations against the group, ETA also has targeted French interests. Finances its activities through kidnappings, robberies, and extortion. The group has killed more than 800 persons since it began lethal attacks in the early 1960s. ETA was responsible for murdering six persons in 1998 but did not carry out any known killings in 1999. In late November 1999, the ETA broke the "unilateral and indefinite" cease-fire it had held since September 16, 1998. *Operates primarily in the Basque autonomous regions of northern Spain and southwestern France, but also has bombed Spanish and French interests elsewhere. Has received training at various times in the past in Libya, Lebanon, and Nicaragua. Some ETA members allegedly have received sanctuary in Cuba. Also appears to have ties to the Irish Republican Army through the two groups' legal political wings.*

- **bin Ladin, Usama:** The bombings of the U.S. Embassies in Nairobi, Kenya, and Dar es Salaam, Tanzania, on 7 August 1998 underscored the global reach of Usama bin Ladin—a long-time sponsor and financier of Sunni Islamic extremist causes—and his network. A series of public threats to drive the United States and its allies out of Muslim countries foreshadowed the attacks. The foremost threat was presented as a Muslim religious decree and published on 23 February 1998 by bin Ladin and allied groups under the name "World Islamic Front for Jihad against the Jews and Crusaders." The statement asserted that it was a religious duty for all Muslims to wage war on U.S. citizens, military and civilian, anywhere in the world. *Bin Ladin leads a broad-based, versatile organization. Suspects named in the wake of the Embassy bombings— four Egyptians, one Comoran, one Jordanian, three Saudis, one U.S. citizen,* one or possibly two Kenyan citizens, and one Tanzanian—reflect the range of al-Qaida operatives. The diverse groups under his umbrella afford bin Ladin resources beyond those of the people directly loyal to him. With his own inherited wealth, business interests, contributions from sympathizers in various countries, and support from close allies like the Egyptian and South Asian groups that signed his so-called fatwa, he funds, trains, and offers logistic help to extremists not directly affiliated with his organization.

Bin Ladin seeks to aid those who support his primary goal—driving U.S. forces from the Arabian Peninsula, removing the Saudi ruling family from power, and "liberating Palestine"—or his secondary goals of removing Western military forces and overthrowing what he calls corrupt, Western-oriented governments in predominantly Muslim countries. To these ends, his organization has sent trainers throughout Afghanistan as well as to Tajikistan, Bosnia, Herzegovina, Chechnya, Somalia, Sudan, and Yemen, and has trained fighters from numerous other countries, including the Philippines, Egypt, Libya, Pakistan, and Eritrea. Using the ties al-Qaida has developed, bin Ladin believes he can call on individuals and groups virtually worldwide to conduct terrorist attacks. His Egyptian and South Asian allies, for example, publicly threatened U.S. interests in the latter half of 1998. Bin Ladin's own public remarks underscore his expanding interests, including a desire to obtain a capability to deploy weapons of mass destruction.

On November 4, 1997 indictments were returned in the U.S. District Court for the Southern District of New York in connection with the two U.S. Embassy bombings in Africa. Charged in the indictment were: Usama bin Ladin, his military commander Muhammad Atef, and Wadih El Hage, Fazul Abdullah Mohammed, Mohammed Sadeek Odeh, and Mohamed Rashed Daoud al-Owhali, all members of al-Qaida. Two of these suspects, Odeh and al-Owhali, were turned over to U.S. authorities in Kenya and brought to the United States to stand trial. Another suspect, Mamdouh Mahmud Salim, was arrested in Germany and extradited to the United States in December. On December 16, five others were indicted for their role in the Dar es Salaam Embassy bombing: Mustafa Mohammed Fadhil, Khalfan Khamis Mohamed, Ahmed Khalfan Ghailani, Fahid Mohommed Ally Msalam, and Sheikh Ahmed Salim Swedan.

- **Continuity Irish Republican Army** (CIRA; aka Continuity Army Council): Radical terrorist group formed in 1994 as the clandestine armed wing of Republican Sinn Fein, a political organization dedicated to the reunification of Ireland. Established to carry on the republican armed struggle after the Irish Republican Army announced a cease-fire in September 1994. Bombings, assassinations, kidnappings, extortion, and robberies. Targets include British military and Northern Irish security targets and Northern Irish Loyalist paramilitary groups. Also has launched bomb attacks against predominantly Protestant towns in Northern Ireland. Does not have an established presence or capability to launch attacks on the UK mainland. Fewer than 50 activists. *The group probably receives limited support from IRA hard-liners that are dissatisfied with the IRA cease-fire, and other republican sympathizers. Suspected of receiving funds and arms from sympathizers in the United States.*

- **Democratic Front for the Liberation of Palestine\*** (DFLP): Marxist-Leninist organization founded in 1969 when it split from the Popular Front for the Liberation of Palestine (PFLP). Believes Palestinian national goals can be achieved only through revolution of the masses. In early 1980s occupied political stance midway between Arafat and the rejectionists. Split into two factions in 1991; Nayif Hawatmah leads the majority and more hard-line faction, which continues to dominate the group. Joined with other rejectionist groups to form the Alliance of Palestinian Forces (APF) to oppose the Declaration of Principals signed in 1993. Broke from the APF—along with the Popular Front for the Liberation of Palestine (PFLP)—over ideological differences. Has made limited moves toward merging with the PFLP since the mid-1990s. In the 1970s conducted numerous small bombings and minor assaults and some more spectacular operations in Israel and the occupied territories, concentrating on Israeli targets. *Involved only in border raids since 1988, but continues to oppose the Israel–PLO peace agreement. Conducts occasional guerrilla operations in southern Lebanon. Receives limited financial and military aid from Syria.*

- **al-Gama'at al-Islamiyya** (Islamic Group, IG): The group issued a cease-fire in March 1999 and has not conducted an attack inside Egypt since August 1998. Signed Usama bin Ladin's *fatwa* in February 1998 calling for attacks against U.S. civilians but publicly has denied that it supports bin Ladin. Shaykh Umar Abd al-Rahman is al-Gama'at's preeminent spiritual leader, and the group publicly has threatened to retaliate against U.S. interests for his incarceration. Primary goal is to overthrow the Egyptian government and replace it with an Islamic state. Armed attacks against Egyptian security and other government officials, Coptic Christians, and Egyptian opponents of Islamic extremism. Al-Gama'at has launched attacks on tourists in Egypt since 1992, most notably the attack in November 1997 at Luxor that killed 58 foreign tourists. Also claimed responsibility for the attempt in June 1995 to assassinate Egyptian President Hosni Mubarak in Addis Ababa, Ethiopia. *The Gama'at has never specifically attacked a U.S. citizen or facility but has threatened U.S. interests.*

- **HAMAS** (Islamic Resistance Movement): Formed in late 1987 as an outgrowth of the Palestinian branch of the Muslim Brotherhood. Various HAMAS elements have used both political and violent means, including terrorism, to pursue the goal of establishing an Islamic Palestinian state in place of Israel. Loosely structured, with some elements working clandestinely and others working openly through mosques and social service institutions to recruit members, raise money, organize activities, and distribute propaganda. HAMAS's strength is concentrated in the Gaza Strip and a few areas of the West Bank. Also has engaged in peaceful political activity, such as running candidates in West Bank Chamber of Commerce elections. In August 1999, Jordanian authorities closed the group's Political Bureau offices in Amman, arrested its leaders, and prohibited the group from operating on Jordanian territory. *Receives funding from Palestinian expatriates, Iran, and private benefactors in Saudi Arabia and other moderate Arab states. Some fund-raising and propaganda activity take place in Western Europe and North America.*

- **Harakat ul-Mujahidin** (HUM): Formerly the Harakat ul-Ansar, which was designated a foreign terrorist organization in October 1997. HUM is an Islamic militant group based in Pakistan that operates primarily in Kashmir. Leader Fazlur Rehman Khalil has been linked to bin Ladin and signed his *fatwa* in February 1998 calling for attacks on U.S. and Western interests. Operates terrorist training camps in eastern Afghanistan and suffered casualties in the U.S. missile strikes on bin Ladin-associated training camps in Khowst in August 1998. Fazlur Rehman Khalil subsequently said that HUM would take revenge on the United States. Has conducted a number of operations against Indian troops and civilian targets in Kashmir. Linked to the Kashmiri militant group al-Faran that kidnapped five Western tourists in Kashmir in July 1995; one was killed in August 1995, and the other four reportedly were killed in December of the same year. Has several thousand armed supporters located in Azad Kashmir, Pakistan, and India's southern Kashmir and Doda regions. Supporters are mostly Pakistanis and Kashmiris, and also include Afghans and Arab veterans of the Afghan war. Uses light and heavy machine guns, assault rifles, mortars, explosives, and rockets. Based in Muzaffarabad, Pakistan, but members conduct insurgent and terrorist activities primarily in Kashmir. The HUM trains its militants in Afghanistan and Pakistan. *Collects donations from Saudi Arabia and other Gulf and Islamic states and from Pakistanis and Kashmiris. The source and amount of HUA's military funding are unknown.*

- **Hizbollah\*** (Party of God; aka Islamic Jihad, Revolutionary Justice Organization, Organization of the Oppressed on Earth, and Islamic Jihad for the Liberation of Palestine Radical Shia): Group formed in Lebanon; dedicated to creation of Iranian-style Islamic republic in Lebanon and removal of all non-Islamic influences from the area. Strongly anti-West and anti-Israel. Closely allied with, and often directed by, Iran but may have conducted operations that were not approved by Tehran. *Known or suspected to have been involved in numerous anti-U.S. terrorist attacks, including the suicide truck bombing of the U.S. Embassy and U.S. Marine barracks in Beirut in October 1983 and the U.S. Embassy annex in Beirut in September 1984. Elements of the group were responsible for the kidnapping and detention of U.S. and other Western hostages in Lebanon. The group also attacked the Israeli Embassy in Argentina in 1992. Operates in the Bekaa Valley, the southern suburbs of Beirut, and southern Lebanon. Has established cells in Europe, Africa, South America, North America, and elsewhere. Receives substantial amounts of financial; training; weapons; explosives; and political, diplomatic, and organizational aid from Iran and Syria.*

- **Irish Republican Army** (IRA; aka Provisional Irish, Republican Army [PIRA]): The Provos Radical terrorist group formed in 1969 as clandestine armed wing of Sinn Fein, a legal political movement dedicated to removing British forces from Northern Ireland and unifying Ireland. Has a Marxist orientation. Organized into small, tightly knit cells under the leadership of the Army Council. Bombings, assassinations, kidnappings, extortion, and robberies. Before its cease-fire in 1994, targets included senior British government officials, British military and Royal Ulster Constabulary targets in Northern Ireland, and a

British military facility on the European Continent. The IRA has been observing a cease-fire since July 1997; the group's previous cease-fire was from September 1, 1994 to February 1996. *Has received aid from a variety of groups and countries and considerable training and arms from Libya and, at one time, the PLO. Is suspected of receiving funds and arms from sympathizers in the United States. Similarities in operations suggest links to the ETA.*

- **Islamic Movement of Uzbekistan** (IMU): Coalition of Islamic militants from Uzbekistan and other Central Asian states opposed to Uzbekistani President Islom Karimov's secular regime. Goal is establishment of Islamic state in Uzbekistan. Recent propaganda also includes anti-Western and anti-Israeli rhetoric. Believed to be responsible for five car bombs in Tashkent. Instigated two hostage crises in Kyrgyzstan in the fall, including a two-and-one-half-month crisis in which IMU militants kidnapped four Japanese and eight Kyrgyzstanis. Militants probably number in the thousands. Most militants believed to be in Afghanistan in the winter (1999–2000), though some may have remained in Tajikistan. Area of operations includes Uzbekistan, Tajikistan, Kyrgyzstan, Afghanistan, and Iran. *Support from other Islamic extremist groups in Central Asia. IMU leadership broadcasts statements over Iranian radio.*

- **Jamaat ul-Fuqra**: Islamic sect that seeks to purify Islam through violence. Led by Pakistani cleric Shaykh Mubarik Ali Gilani, who established the organization in the early 1980s. Gilani now resides in Pakistan, but most cells are located in North America and the Caribbean. Members have purchased isolated rural compounds in North America to live communally, practice their faith, and insulate themselves from Western culture. Fuqra members have attacked a variety of targets that they view as enemies of Islam, including Muslims they regard as heretics and Hindus. *Attacks during the 1980s included assassinations and firebombings across the United States. Fuqra members in the United States have been convicted of criminal violations, including murder and fraud. Operates in North America and Pakis*tan.

- **Japanese Red Army\*** (JRA; aka Anti-Imperialist International Brigade [AIIB]): An international terrorist group formed around 1970 after breaking away from Japanese Communist League-Red Army Faction. Led by Fusako Shigenobu, believed to be in Syrian-garrisoned area of Lebanon's Bekaa Valley. Stated goals are to overthrow Japanese government and monarchy and help foment world revolution. Organization unclear but may control or at least have ties to Anti-Imperialist International Brigade (AIIB). Also may have links to Antiwar Democratic Front, an overt leftist political organization in Japan. Details released following arrest in November 1987 of leader Osamu Maruoka indicate that JRA may be organizing cells in Asian cities, such as Manila and Singapore. *Has had close and long-standing relations with Palestinian terrorist groups—based and operating outside Japan—since its inception.* During the 1970s JRA conducted a series of attacks around the world, including the massacre in 1972 at Lod Airport in Israel, two Japanese airliner hijackings, and an attempted takeover of the U.S. Embassy in Kuala Lumpur. In April 1988, JRA operative Yu Kikumura was arrested with explosives on the New Jersey Turnpike, apparently planning an attack to coincide with the bombing of a USO club in Naples and a suspected JRA operation that killed five, including a U.S. servicewoman. Kikumura was convicted of these charges and is serving a lengthy prison sentence in the United States. In March 1995, Ekita Yukiko, a longtime JRA activist, was arrested in Romania and subsequently deported to Japan. Eight others have been arrested since 1996, but leader Shigenobu remains at large. *Location unknown, but possibly based in Syrian-controlled areas of Lebanon.*

- al-Jihad* (aka Jihad Group, Islamic Jihad, Vanguards of Conquest, and Talaa' al-Fateh): Egyptian Islamic extremist group active since the late 1970s. Appears to be divided into two factions: one led by Ayman al-Zawahiri—who currently is in Afghanistan and is a key leader in terrorist financier Usama bin Ladin's new World Islamic Front—and the Vanguards of Conquest (Talaa' al-Fateh) led by Ahmad Husayn Agiza. Abbud al-Zumar, leader of the original Jihad, is imprisoned in Egypt and recently joined the group's jailed spiritual leader, Shaykh Umar Abd al-Rahman, in a call for a "peaceful front." Primary goal is to overthrow the Egyptian government and replace it with an Islamic state. Increasingly willing to target U.S. interests in Egypt. Specializes in armed attacks against high-level Egyptian government officials. The original Jihad was responsible for the assassination in 1981 of Egyptian President Anwar Sadat. Appears to concentrate on high-level, high-profile Egyptian government officials, including cabinet ministers. Claimed responsibility for the attempted assassinations of Interior Minister Hassan al-Alfi in August 1993 and Prime Minister Atef Sedky in November 1993. *Has not conducted an attack inside Egypt since 1993 and never has targeted foreign tourists there. Has threatened to retaliate against the United States, however, for its incarceration of Shaykh Umar Abd al-Rahman and, more recently, for the arrests of its members in Albania, Azerbaijan, and the United Kingdom. The Egyptian government claims that Iran, Sudan, and militant Islamic groups in Afghanistan—including Usama bin Ladin—support the Jihad factions. Also may obtain some funding through various Islamic nongovernmental organizations.*

- Kach and Kahane Chai*: Stated goal is to restore the biblical state of Israel. Kach (founded by radical Israeli-American rabbi Meir Kahane) and its offshoot Kahane Chai, which means "Kahane Lives" (founded by Meir Kahane's son Binyamin following his father's assassination in the United States), were declared to be terrorist organizations in March 1994 by the Israeli Cabinet under the 1948 Terrorism Law. This followed the groups' statements in support of Dr. Baruch Goldstein's attack in February 1994 on the al-Ibrahimi Mosque—Goldstein was affiliated with Kach—and their verbal attacks on the Israeli government. *Have threatened to attack Arabs, Palestinians, and Israeli government officials. Claimed responsibility for several shootings of West Bank Palestinians that killed four persons and wounded two in 1993. Receives support from sympathizers in the United States and Europe.*

- Kurdistan Workers' Party* (PKK): Established in 1974 as a Marxist-Leninist insurgent group primarily composed of Turkish Kurds. In recent years has moved beyond rural-based insurgent activities to include urban terrorism. Seeks to establish an independent Kurdish state in southeastern Turkey, where the population is predominantly Kurdish. Primary targets are Turkish government security forces in Turkey but the PKK has bombed tourist sites and hotels and kidnapped foreign tourists. *Operates in Turkey, Europe, the Middle East, and Asia. Has received safehaven and modest aid from Syria, Iraq, and Iran. The Syrian government claims to have expelled the PKK from its territory in October 1998.*

- **Liberation Tigers of Tamil Eelam\*** (LTTE): Known front organizations: World Tamil Association (WTA), World Tamil Movement (WTM), the Federation of Associations of Canadian Tamils (FACT), the Ellalan Force, and the Sangillan Force. The most powerful Tamil group is in Sri Lanka, founded in 1976. Uses overt and illegal methods to raise funds, acquire weapons, and publicize its cause of establishing an independent Tamil state. Began its armed conflict with the Sri Lankan government in 1983 and relies on a guerrilla strategy that includes the use of terrorist activities. Controls most of the northern and eastern coastal areas of Sri Lanka and has conducted operations throughout the island. Headquartered in the Jaffna peninsula, LTTE leader Velupillai Prabhakaran has established an extensive network of checkpoints and informants to keep track of any outsiders who enter the group's area of control. *The LTTE's overt organizations support Tamil separatism by lobbying foreign governments and the United Nations. Also uses its international contacts to procure weapons, communications, and bombmaking equipment. Exploits large Tamil communities in North America, Europe, and Asia to obtain funds and supplies for its fighters in Sri Lanka. Some Tamil communities in Europe also are involved in narcotics smuggling.*

- **Loyalist Volunteer Force** (LVF): Extremist terrorist group formed in 1996 as a splinter of the mainstream loyalist Ulster Volunteer Force (UVF). Seeks to subvert a political settlement with Irish nationalists in Northern Ireland by attacking Catholic politicians, civilians, and Protestant politicians who endorse the Northern Ireland peace process. Composed of hard-liners formerly associated with the UVF. Mark "Swinger" Fulton now leads the LVF following the assassination in December 1997 of LVF founder Billy "King Rat" Wright. Announced a unilateral cease-fire on May 15, 1998 and, in a move unprecedented among Ulster terrorist groups, decommissioned a small but significant amount of weapons on December 18, 1998. While the LVF decommissioned a small but significant amount of weapons in December 1998, it did not repeat this gesture in 1999. LVF bombs often have contained Powergel commercial explosives, typical of many loyalist groups. LVF attacks have been particularly vicious: LVF terrorists killed an 18-year-old Catholic girl in July 1997 because she had a Protestant boyfriend. Murdered numerous Catholic civilians with no political or terrorist affiliations following Billy Wright's assassination. Also has conducted successful attacks against Irish targets in Irish border towns.

- **Manuel Rodriguez Patriotic Front** (FPMR): Founded in 1983 as the armed wing of the Chilean Communist Party and named for the hero of Chile's war of independence against Spain. Splintered into two factions in the late 1980s, and one faction became a political party in 1991. The dissident wing FPMR/D is Chile's only remaining active terrorist group. FPMR/D attacks civilians and international targets, including U.S. businesses and Mormon churches. In 1993, FPMR/D bombed two McDonald's restaurants and attempted to bomb a Kentucky Fried Chicken restaurant.

- **Mujahedin-e Khalq Organization** (MEK or MKO; aka National Liberation Army of Iran [NLA, the militant wing of the MEK], the People's Mujahidin of Iran [PMOI], National Council of Resistance [NCR], Muslim Iranian Student's Society [front organization used to garner financial support]): Formed in the 1960s by the college-educated children of Iranian merchants, the MEK sought to counter what it perceived as excessive Western influence in the Shah's regime. Following a philosophy that mixes Marxism and Islam, it has developed into the largest and most active armed Iranian dissident group. Its history is studded with anti-Western activity, and, most recently, attacks on the interests of the clerical regime in Iran and abroad. Worldwide campaign against the Iranian government stresses propaganda and occasionally uses terrorist violence. *During the 1970s, the MEK staged terrorist attacks inside Iran and killed several U.S. military personnel and civilians working on defense projects in Tehran. Supported the takeover in 1979 of the U.S. Embassy in Tehran. In April 1992, conducted attacks on Iranian embassies in 13 different countries, demonstrating the group's ability to mount large-scale operations overseas. Recent attacks in Iran include three explosions in Tehran in June 1998 that killed three persons and the assassination of Asadollah Lajevardi, the former director of the Evin Prison. In April 1999, Brigadier General Ali Sayyad Shirazi, the deputy joint chief of staff of Iran's armed forces, was killed in Tehran by a MEK operative. In the 1980s, the MEK's leaders were forced by Iranian security forces to flee to France. Most resettled in Iraq by 1987. In the mid-1980s, it did not mount terrorist operations in Iran at a level similar to its activities in the 1970s. In recent years, it has claimed credit for a number of operations in Iran. Beyond support from Iraq, the MEK uses front organizations to solicit contributions from expatriate Iranian communities.*

- **National Liberation Army** (ELN)—Colombia: Pro-Cuban, anti–U.S. guerrilla group formed in January 1965. Primarily rural based, although it has several urban fronts, particularly in the Magdalena Medio region. Entered peace talks with Colombian Civil Society in mid-1998 and was preparing to participate in a national convention in early 1999. Conducted weekly assaults on oil infrastructure (typically pipeline bombings) and has inflicted massive oil spills. Extortion and bombings against U.S. and other foreign businesses, especially the petroleum industry. Annually conducts several hundred kidnappings for profit, including foreign employees of large corporations. Forces coca and opium poppy cultivators to pay protection money and attacks government efforts to eradicate these crops.

- **New People's Army** (NPA): The guerrilla arm of the Communist Party of the Philippines (CPP), NPA is an avowedly Maoist group formed in December 1969 with the aim of overthrowing the government through protracted guerrilla warfare. Although primarily a rural-based guerrilla group, the NPA has an active urban infrastructure to conduct terrorism and uses city-based assassination squads called sparrow units. Derives most of its funding from contributions of supporters and so-called revolutionary taxes extorted from local businesses. The NPA primarily targets Philippine security forces, corrupt politicians, and drug traffickers. Opposes any U.S. military presence in the Philippines and attacked U.S. military interests before the U.S. base closures in 1992. *Estimated between 6,000 to 8,000 members.*

- **Orange Volunteers** (OV): Extremist Protestant terrorist group comprised largely of disgruntled Loyalist hard-liners who split from groups observing the cease-fire. OV seeks to prevent a political settlement with Irish nationalists by attacking Catholic civilian interests in Northern Ireland. Bombings, arson, beatings, possibly robberies. *Possibly around 20 hardcore members, many of whom are experienced in terrorist tactics and bombmaking.*

- **The Palestine Islamic Jihad\*** (PIJ): Originated among militant Palestinians in the Gaza Strip during the 1970s; a series of loosely affiliated factions rather than a cohesive group. Committed to the creation of an Islamic Palestinian state and the destruction of Israel through holy war. Because of its strong support for Israel, the United States has been identified as an enemy of the PIJ. Also opposes moderate Arab governments that it believes have been tainted by Western secularism. Has threatened to retaliate against Israel and the United States for the murder of PIJ leader Fathi Shaqaqi in Malta in October 1995. *Conducted suicide bombings against Israeli targets in the West Bank, Gaza Strip, and Israel. Has threatened to attack U.S. interests in Jordan. Receives financial assistance from Iran and limited assistance from Syria.*

- **Palestine Liberation Front\*** (PLF): Broke away from the PFLP–GC in mid-1970s. Later split again into pro–PLO, pro-Syrian, and pro-Libyan factions. Pro–PLO faction led by Muhammad Abbas (Abu Abbas), who became a member of PLO Executive Committee in 1984 but left it in 1991. *The Abu Abbas–led faction has conducted attacks against Israel. Abbas's group also was responsible for the attack in 1985 on the cruise ship* Achille Lauro *and the murder of U.S. citizen Leon Klinghoffer. A warrant for Abu Abbas's arrest is outstanding in Italy. Receives support mainly from Iraq. Has received support from Libya in the past.*

- **The Party of Democratic Kampuchea** (Khmer Rouge): Communist insurgency trying to overthrow the Cambodian government. Under Pol Pot's leadership, conducted a campaign of genocide, killing more than 1 million persons during its four years in power in the late 1970s. Defections starting in 1996 and accelerating in spring 1998 appear to have shattered the Khmer Rouge as a military force, but hard-line remnants still may pose a threat in remote areas. Virtually has disintegrated as a viable insurgent organization because of defections, but hard-line remnants continue low-level attacks against government troops in isolated areas. Some small groups may have turned to banditry. Also targets Cambodian and ethnic Vietnamese villagers and occasionally has kidnapped and killed foreigners traveling in remote rural areas.

- **Popular Front for the Liberation of Palestine** (PFLP): Marxist-Leninist group founded in 1967 by George Habash as a member of the PLO. Joined the Alliance of Palestinian Forces (APF) to oppose the Declaration of Principles signed in 1993 and has suspended participation in the PLO. Broke away from the APF, along with the DFLP, in 1996 over ideological differences. Has made limited moves toward merging with the DFLP since the mid-1990s. *Committed numerous international terrorist attacks during the 1970s. Since 1978 has conducted numerous attacks against Israeli or moderate Arab targets, including killing a settler and her son in December 1996. Receives most of its financial and military assistance from Syria and Libya.*

- **Popular Front for the Liberation of Palestine–General Command** (PFLP–GC): Split from the PFLP in 1968, claiming it wanted to focus more on fighting and less on politics. Violently opposed to Arafat's PLO. Led by Ahmad Jabril, a former captain in the Syrian Army. *Closely tied to Syria and Iran. Has conducted numerous cross-border terrorist attacks into Israel using unusual means, such as hot-air balloons and motorized hang gliders. Headquartered in Damascus with bases in Lebanon and cells in Europe. Receives logistic and military support from Syria and financial support from Iran.*

- **al-Qaida:** Established by Usama bin Ladin about 1990 to bring together Arabs who fought in Afghanistan against the Soviet invasion. Helped finance, recruit, transport, and train Sunni Islamic extremists for the Afghan resistance. Current goal is to "reestablish the Muslim State" throughout the world. Works with allied Islamic extremist groups to overthrow regimes it deems "non-Islamic" and remove Westerners from Muslim countries. Issued statement under banner of "The World Islamic Front for Jihad against the Jews and Crusaders" in February 1998, saying it was the duty of all Muslims to kill U.S. citizens, civilian or military, and their allies everywhere. *Conducted the bombings of the U.S. Embassies in Nairobi; Kenya; and Dar es Salaam, Tanzania on August 7 that killed at least 301 persons and injured more than 5,000 others. Claims to have shot down U.S. helicopters and killed U.S. servicemen in Somalia in 1993 and to have conducted three bombings targeted against the U.S. troop presence in Aden, Yemen in December 1992. Linked to plans for attempted terrorist operations, including the assassination of the Pope during his visit to Manila in late 1994; simultaneous bombings of the U.S. and Israeli Embassies in Manila and other Asian capitals in late 1994; the midair bombing of a dozen U.S. trans-Pacific flights in 1995; and a plan to kill President Clinton during a visit to the Philippines in early 1995. Continues to train, finance, and provide logistic support to terrorist groups that support these goals. May have from several hundred to several thousand members. Also serves as the core of a loose umbrella organization that includes many Sunni Islamic extremist groups, including factions of the Egyptian Islamic Jihad, the Gama'at al-Islamiyya, and the Harakat ul-Mujahidin. The Embassy bombings in Nairobi and Dar es Salaam underscore al-Qaida's global reach. Bin Ladin and his key lieutenants reside in Afghanistan, and the group maintains terrorist training camps there. Bin Ladin, son of a billionaire Saudi family, is said to have inherited around $300 million that he uses to finance the group. Al-Qaida also maintains money-making businesses, collects donations from like-minded supporters, and illicitly siphons funds from donations to Muslim charitable organizations.*

- **Qibla and People Against Gangsterism and Drugs** (PAGAD): Qibla is a small radical Islamic group led by Achmad Cassiem, who was inspired by Iran's Ayatollah Khomeini. Cassiem founded Qibla in the 1980s, seeking to establish an Islamic state in South Africa. PAGAD began in 1996 as a community anticrime group fighting drug lords in Cape Town's Cape Flats section. PAGAD now shares Qibla's anti-Western stance as well as some members and leadership. Though distinct, the media often treat the two groups as one. *Qibla routinely protests U.S. policies toward the Muslim world and uses radio station 786 to promote its message and mobilize Muslims.* PAGAD is suspected of conducting 170 bombings and 18 other violent actions in 1998 alone. Qibla and PAGAD may have masterminded the bombing on 15 August of the Cape Town Planet Hollywood. Often use the front names Muslims Against Global Oppression (MAGO) and Muslims Against Illegitimate Leaders (MAIL) when anti-Western campaigns are launched. *Qibla is estimated at 250 members. Police estimate there are at least 50 gunmen in PAGAD, and the size of PAGAD-organized demonstrations suggests it has considerably more adherents than Qibla. Operate mainly in the Cape Town area, South Africa's foremost tourist venue. Probably have ties to Islamic extremists in the Middle East.*

- **Real IRA** (RIRA; aka True IRA): Formed in February–March 1998 as clandestine armed wing of the 32-County Sovereignty Movement, a "political pressure group" dedicated to removing British forces from Northern Ireland and unifying Ireland. The 32-County Sovereignty Movement opposed Sinn Fein's adoption in September 1997 of the Mitchell principles of democracy and nonviolence and opposed the amendment in May 1998 of Articles 2 and 3 of the Irish Constitution, which lay claim to Northern Ireland. Former IRA "quartermaster general" Mickey McKevitt leads the group; Bernadette Sands-McKevitt, his common-law wife, is the vice-chair of the 32-County Sovereignty Movement. Most Real IRA activists are former IRA members; the group has inherited a wealth of experience in terrorist tactics and bombmaking. Targets include British military and police in Northern Ireland and Northern Irish Protestant communities. Claimed responsibility for the car bomb attack in Omagh, Northern Ireland on August 15, which killed 29 and injured 220 persons. Announced a cease-fire after that bombing. Has attempted several unsuccessful bomb attacks on the UK mainland. *About 70 members, plus limited support from IRA hard-liners dissatisfied with the current IRA cease-fire and other republican sympathizers. Suspected of receiving funds from sympathizers in the United States. Press reports claim Real IRA leaders also have sought support from Libya.*

- **Red Hand Defenders** (RHD): Extremist terrorist group composed largely of Protestant hard-liners from loyalist groups observing a cease-fire. RHD seeks to prevent a political settlement with Irish nationalists by attacking Catholic civilian interests in Northern Ireland. RHD has carried out numerous pipe bombing and arson attacks against "soft" civilian targets such as homes, churches, and private businesses to cause outrage in the republican community and to provoke IRA retaliation. RHD claimed responsibility for the car bombing murder on 15 March of Rosemary Nelson, a prominent Catholic nationalist lawyer and human rights campaigner in Northern Ireland. *Approximately 20 hardcore members, many of whom have considerable experience in terrorist tactics and bombmaking.*

- **Revolutionary Armed Forces of Colombia** (FARC): The largest, best-trained, and best-equipped insurgent organization in Colombia. Established in 1964 as a rural-based, pro-Soviet guerrilla army. Organized along military lines and includes several urban fronts. Has been anti–United States since its inception. The FARC agreed in 1998 to enter into preliminary peace talks with the Colombian government. The Pastrana administration demilitarized five large rural municipalities to meet FARC conditions for peace talks. (President Pastrana traveled to this area on 7 January 1999 to inaugurate peace talks with guerrilla leaders, although the FARC's senior-most leader failed to attend.) Still conducts bombings, murders, kidnappings, extortion, hijackings, as well as armed insurgent attacks against Colombian political, military, and economic targets. In March 1999 the FARC brutally murdered three U.S. Indian rights activists on Venezuelan territory whom they had kidnapped in Colombia. Foreign citizens often are targets of FARC kidnappings for ransom. Has well-documented ties to narcotics traffickers, principally through the provision of armed protection. *During 1999 continued its bombing campaign against oil pipelines. Armed attacks against Colombian political, economic, military, and police targets. Many members pursue criminal activities, carrying out hundreds of kidnappings for profit annually. Foreign citizens often are targets of FARC kidnappings. Group has well-documented ties to narcotics traffickers, principally through the provision of armed protection for coca and poppy cultivation and narcotics production facilities, as well as through attacks on government narcotics eradication efforts. Approximately 8,000–12,000 armed combatants and an unknown number of supporters, mostly in rural areas.*

- **Revolutionary Organization 17 November** (17 November): Radical leftist group established in 1975 and named for the student uprising in Greece in November 1973 that protested the military regime. *Anti-Greek establishment, anti–U.S., anti-Turkey, anti–NATO, and committed to the ouster of U.S. bases, removal of Turkish military presence from Cyprus, and severing of Greece's ties to NATO and the European Union (EU). Possibly affiliated with other Greek terrorist groups. Initial attacks were assassinations of senior U.S. officials and Greek public figures. Added bombings in 1980s. Since 1990 has expanded targets to include EU facilities and foreign firms investing in Greece and has added improvised rocket attacks to its methods.*

- **Revolutionary People's Liberation Party/Front*** (DHKP/C; aka Devrimci Sol [Revolutionary Left] and Dev Sol): Originally formed in 1978 as Devrimci Sol, or Dev Sol, a splinter faction of the Turkish People's Liberation Party/Front. *Renamed in 1994 after factional infighting, it espouses a Marxist ideology and is virulently anti–U.S. and anti–NATO. Finances its activities chiefly through armed robberies and extortion. Has concentrated attacks against current and retired Turkish security and military officials. Began a new campaign against foreign interests in 1990. Assassinated two U.S. military contractors and wounded a U.S. Air Force officer to protest the Gulf War. Launched rockets at U.S. Consulate in Istanbul in 1992. Assassinated prominent Turkish businessman in early 1996, its first significant terrorist act as DHKP/C. Turkish authorities thwarted DHKP/C attempt in June 1999 to fire light antitank weapon at U.S. Consulate in Istanbul. Conducts attacks in Turkey—primarily in Istanbul—Ankara, Izmir, and Adana. Raises funds in Western Europe.*

- **Revolutionary People's Struggle** (ELA): Extreme leftist group that developed from opposition to the military junta that ruled Greece from 1967 to 1974. Formed in 1971, ELA is a self-described revolutionary, anti-capitalist, and anti-imperialist group that has declared its opposition to "imperialist domination, exploitation, and oppression." *Strongly anti–U.S. and seeks the removal of U.S. military forces from Greece. In 1986, stepped up attacks on Greek government and commercial interests. Raid on a safehouse in 1990 revealed a weapons cache and direct contacts with other Greek terrorist groups, including 1 May and Revolutionary Solidarity. In 1991, ELA and 1 May claimed joint responsibility for over 20 bombings. Greek police believe they have established a link between the ELA and the Revolutionary Organization 17 November. Has not claimed responsibility for a terrorist attack since January 1995.*

- **Sendero Luminoso** (SL; Shining Path): Larger of Peru's two insurgencies, SL is among the world's most ruthless guerrilla organizations. Formed in the late 1960s by then university professor Abimael Guzman. Stated goal is to destroy existing Peruvian institutions and replace them with peasant revolutionary regime. Guzman's capture in September 1992 was a major blow, as were arrests of other SL leaders in 1995, defections, and Peruvian President Fujimori's amnesty program for repentant terrorists. Has engaged in particularly brutal forms of terrorism, including the indiscriminate use of bombs and selective assassinations. Conducted fewer attacks in 1998, generally limited to rural areas. Almost every institution in Peru has been a target of SL violence. It also opposes any influence by foreign governments, as well as by other Latin American guerrilla groups, especially the MRTA. Detonated explosives at diplomatic missions of several countries in Peru in 1990, including an attempt to car bomb the U.S. Embassy in December. Has bombed diplomatic missions of several countries in Peru, including the U.S. Embassy. Conducts bombing campaigns. Has attacked U.S. businesses since its inception. Approximately 30,000 persons have died since Shining Path took up arms in 1980 in its aim to turn Peru into a Communist state. Although SL continued to clash with Peruvian authorities and military units, armed operations declined in 1999 because recent arrests have decimated the group's leadership. *Membership is unknown but estimated to be a few hundred armed militants. SL's strength has been vastly diminished by arrests and desertions. Approximately 1,500 to 2,500 armed militants; larger number of supporters, mostly in rural areas.*

- **Sikh Terrorism:** Sikh Terrorism is sponsored by expatriate and Indian Sikh groups who want to carve out an independent Sikh state called Khalistan (Land of the Pure) from Indian territory. Active groups include Babbar Khalsa, International Sikh Youth Federation, Dal Khalsa, and Bhinderanwala Tiger Force. A previously unknown group, the Saheed Khalsa Force, claimed credit for the marketplace bombings in New Delhi in 1997. Militant cells are active internationally and extremists gather funds from overseas Sikh communities. *Sikh expatriates have formed a variety of international organizations that lobby for the Sikh cause overseas. Most prominent are the World Sikh Organization and the International Sikh Youth Federation.*

- **Tupac Amaru Revolutionary Movement** (MRTA): Traditional Marxist-Leninist revolutionary movement formed in 1983. Aims to rid Peru of imperialism and establish Marxist regime. Has suffered from defections and government counterterrorist successes in addition to infighting and loss of leftist support. Previously responsible for large number of anti–U.S. attacks; recent activity has dropped off dramatically. Most members have been jailed. Nonetheless, in December 1996, 14 MRTA members overtook the Japanese Ambassador's residence in Lima during a diplomatic reception, capturing hundreds. Government forces stormed the residence in April 1997 rescuing all but one of the remaining hostages. Has not conducted a significant terrorist operation since then. *Believed to have fewer than 100 remaining members.*

- **Al Ummah:** Radical Indian Muslim group founded in 1992 by S. A. Basha. Believed responsible for the Coimbatore bombings in Southern India in February 1998. Basha and 30 of his followers were arrested and await trial for those bombings.

- **Zviadists:** Extremist supporters of deceased former Georgian President Zviad Gamsakhurdia. Following Gamsakhurdia's ouster in 1991, his supporters launched a revolt against his successor, Eduard Shevardnadze. Suppressed in late 1993, and Gamsakhurdia committed suicide in January 1994. Some Gamsakhurdia sympathizers have formed a weak legal opposition in Georgia, but others remain violently opposed to Shevardnadze's rule and seek to overthrow him. Some Gamsakhurdia government officials fled to Russia following Gamsakhurdia's ouster and now use Russia as a base of operations to bankroll anti-Shevardnadze activities. Attempted two assassinations against Shevardnadze in August 1995 and February 1998. *Took UN personnel hostage following the February 1998 attempt, but released the hostages unharmed. May have received support and training in Chechen terrorist training camps. Chechen mercenaries participated in the assassination attempt against Shevardnadze in February 1998. Zviadists conducted no violent activity in 1999.*[11]

While no group on this list has been associated with a serious effort to acquire WMD except for Aum Shinrikyo, some have conducted large-scale conventional attacks on Americans. Moreover, September 2001 events show that foreign terrorism (1) poses a continuing risk to the U.S. homeland and (2) is linked to state actors in ways that could lead to the transfer of WMD and make it difficult to assign the blame for attacks.

According to CIA Director George Tenet, "terrorist groups are actively searching the Internet to acquire information and capabilities for chemical, biological, radiological, and even nuclear attacks. Many of the 29 officially designated terrorist organizations have an interest in unconventional weapons, and, in 1998, Usama bin Ladin declared their acquisition a 'religious duty.'" Reporting by the DOD has also made it clear that at least one major terrorist group hostile to the United States has sought advanced chemical weapons, and U.S. intelligence experts indicate that it is also interested in biological weapons like anthrax:

The Usama bin Ladin network's reported interest in NBC materials is a key concern in terms of possible future threats to U.S. interests. The network's interest in NBC materials has been noted since the early 1990s and, in 1999, Usama bin Ladin made public statements defending the right of the Muslim community to pursue NBC capabilities. The bombings of the U.S. Embassies in Nairobi, Kenya, and in Dar es Salaam, Tanzania, on August 7, 1998 underscored the global reach of Usama bin Ladin—a longtime sponsor and financier of extremist causes—and brought to full public awareness his transition from sponsor to terrorist. A series of public threats to drive the United States and its allies out of Muslim countries foreshadowed the attacks, including what was presented as a *fatwa* (Muslim legal opinion) published on February 23, 1998 by bin Ladin and allied groups under the name "World Islamic Front for Jihad Against the Jews and Crusaders." The statement asserted it was a religious duty for all Muslims to wage war on U.S. citizens, military and civilian, anywhere in the world.

. . . Bin Ladin has stated publicly that terrorism is a tool to achieve the group's goal of bringing Islamic rule to Muslim lands and "cleanse" them of Western influence and corruption. To this end, bin Ladin, in 1999, led a broad-based, versatile organization. Suspects named in the wake of the Embassy bombings—Egyptians, one Comoran, one Palestinian, one Saudi, and U.S. citizens—reflect the range of al-Qaida operatives.

The diverse groups under his umbrella afford bin Ladin resources beyond those of the people directly loyal to him. With his own inherited wealth, business interests, contributions from sympathizers in various countries, and support from close allies like the Egyptian and South Asian groups that signed his *fatwa*, he funds, trains, and offers logistic help to extremists not directly affiliated with his organization. He seeks to aid those who support his primary goals—driving U.S. forces from the Arabian Peninsula, removing the Saudi ruling family from power, and "liberating Palestine"—or his secondary goals of removing Western military forces and overthrowing what he calls corrupt, Western-oriented governments in predominantly Muslim countries.

His organization has sent trainers throughout Afghanistan as well as to Tajikistan, Bosnia, Chechnya, Somalia, Sudan, and Yemen and has trained fighters from numerous other countries, including the Philippines, Egypt, Libya, Pakistan, and Eritrea. Using the ties al-Qaida has developed, bin Ladin believes he can call on individuals and groups virtually worldwide to conduct terrorist attacks.

. . . In 1998, acting on convincing information from a variety of reliable sources that the network of radical groups affiliated with Usama bin Ladin had planned, financed, and carried out the bombings of our embassies in Nairobi and Dar es Salaam and planned future attacks against Americans, the United States carried out strikes on one of the most active terrorist bases in the world. Located in Afghanistan, it contained key elements of the bin Ladin network's infrastructure and has served as a training camp for literally thousands of terrorists from around the globe. The U.S. military also struck a plant in Khartoum, Sudan, that was linked by intelligence information to chemical weapons and to the bin Ladin terror network. The strikes were deemed a necessary and proportionate response to the imminent threat of further terrorist attacks against U.S. personnel and facilities and demonstrated that the U.S. government will seek out terrorists around the world, no matter where they try to seek refuge.

. . . In December 1998, bin Ladin gave a series of interviews in which he denied involvement in the East Africa bombings but said he "instigated" them and called for attacks on U.S. citizens worldwide in retaliation for the strikes against Iraq. Bin Ladin's public statements then ceased under increased pressure from his Taliban hosts. Nonetheless, in 1999, bin Ladin continued to influence like-minded extremists to his cause, and his organization continued to engage in terrorist planning. His Egyptian and South Asian allies, for example, continued publicly to threaten U.S. interests.

The Usama bin Ladin network's reported interest in NBC materials is a key concern in terms of possible future threats to U.S. interests. The network's interest in NBC materials has been noted since the early 1990s and, in 1999, Usama bin Ladin made public statements defending the right of the Muslim community to pursue NBC capabilities being stolen from industrial and research facilities. In the short run, reports of nuclear theft, whether real or scams, will continue.[12]

Moreover, there are no rules that say only major terrorist groups—or only the groups the United States can now identify—will pose the most critical future threats. The State Department list is only part of the roughly 130 groups that are normally labeled as terrorist, a list that excludes many foreign and domestic extremist groups and individuals, or "loners," by definition. At the same time, it is so long, so diverse, and so unstable that it is tempting to ignore the real-world cases involved and talk in terms of generalities. It is only by looking at specific cases, that the diversity in the threat—and the cumulative risk to U.S. interests, U.S. allies, and the U.S. homeland—becomes clear.

There are many additional groups that are opposed to friendly governments and might target Americans in retaliation for any U.S. aid to the allied governments involved. The portion of the text describing each group that is shown in italics also shows that many groups have ties to hostile state actors, and that in many cases, states have provided them with explosives and weapons like antitank-guided missiles and light antiaircraft missiles. Furthermore, such movements can splinter with little or no warning into more extreme and violent factions and subfactions. Coupled to the sometimes sudden emergence of major new anti-American groups like those led by bin Ladin, it is clear that threats can suddenly arise that would take extreme risks and that could seek vengeance or simply kill as many Americans as possible.

### Threats from Foreign Students and Immigrants

The foreign terrorist threat includes the potential threat from foreign students and immigrants—*although it should be stressed that native-born*

*Americans have so far posed a much more serious threat than any posed by foreign visitors or residents that are not directly involved with terrorist groups.* The National Commission on Terrorism identified foreign students studying in the United States as potential threats in its June 2000 report:

> Of the large number of foreign students who come to this country to study, there is a risk that a small minority may exploit their student status to support terrorist activity. The United States lacks the nationwide ability to monitor the immigration status of these students.
>
> In spite of elaborate immigration laws and the efforts of the Immigration and Naturalization Service, the United States is, de facto, a country of open borders. The commission found that the massive flows of people across U.S. borders make exclusion of all foreign terrorists impossible. There are more than 300 million legal crossings each year at the U.S./Mexican land border alone. Millions more stream through our airports.
>
> Beyond the millions who legally come and go, over four million persons reside illegally in the United States. About half of them entered the country without inspection, meaning they crossed U.S. borders between inspection stations or entered by small boat or aircraft. Roughly another two million people entered the United States with a valid visitor's visa, but overstayed their visa and remained here to live. That said, of the millions who come here to live or visit only a minuscule portion of all foreigners in the United States attempt to harm the country in any way.
>
> While the problems of controlling America's borders are far broader than just keeping out terrorists, the Commission found this an area of special concern. For example, thousands of people from countries officially designated as state sponsors of terrorism currently study in the United States. This is not objectionable in itself as the vast majority of these students contribute to America's diversity while here and return home with no adverse impact on U.S. national security. However, experience has shown the importance of monitoring the status of foreign students. Seven years ago, investigators discovered that one of the terrorists involved in bombing the World Trade Center had entered the United States on a student visa, dropped out, and remained illegally. Today, there is still no mechanism for ensuring the same thing won't happen again.
>
> One program holds promise as a means of addressing the issue. The Coordinated Interagency Partnership Regulating International Students (CIPRIS), a regional pilot program mandated by the 1996 Illegal Immigration Reform and Immigrant Responsibility Act (IIR/IRA) collects and makes readily available useful and current information about foreign student visa holders in the United States. For example, CIPRIS would record a foreign student's change in major from English literature to nuclear physics. The CIPRIS pilot program was implemented in 20 southern universities and is being considered for nationwide implementation after an opportunity for notice and comment. The Commission believes that CIPRIS could become a model for a nationwide program monitoring the status of foreign students.[13]

One needs to be careful about such a generic approach to counterterrorism. The commission raises a potentially valid issue, but it is not clear that there is as yet any clear history of foreign students in the United States actually going back to their original country to participate in the development of threats to the U.S. homeland. At the same time, there are a massive number of illegal persons in the United States that are not students or that never entered under student visas, while many American citizens have ties to foreign countries. It is difficult to argue with the idea that the United States has a right to track the activities of foreign students in broad terms and to ensure that they comply with the law. At the same time, there is a thin margin between tracking and creating ethnic or national stereotypes and "threats" for which there is no real justification. Furthermore, it is worth pointing out that many foreign students with advanced technical training stay in the United States and play a critical role in contributing to the American economy.

## DOMESTIC TERRORISTS AND EXTREMISTS

It is equally difficult to profile American terrorists and extremists, particularly because many are not associated with well-established ideologies and individuals and ad hoc factions can be as dangerous as organized groups. Louis Freeh summarized this threat as follows in his testimony before the Senate Committee on Appropriations Subcommittee for the Departments of Commerce, Justice, and State, the Judiciary, and Related Agencies on February 4, 1999:

> Domestic terrorist groups are those which are based and which operate entirely within the United States, or its territories, and whose activities are directed at elements of the U.S. government or its civilian population. Domestic terrorist groups represent interests that span the full political spectrum, as well as social issues and concerns. FBI investigations of domestic terrorist groups or individuals are not predicated on social or political beliefs; rather, they are based on planned or actual criminal activity. The current domestic terrorist threat primarily comes from right-wing extremist groups, Puerto Rican extremist groups, and special interest extremists.
>
> Right-wing Extremist Groups: The threat from right-wing extremist groups includes militias, white-separatist groups, and anti-government groups. All right-wing extremist groups tend to encourage massing weapons, ammunition, and supplies in preparation for a confrontation with federal law enforcement, as well as local law enforcement who are often perceived as agents for the state/federal government.
>
> The goal of the militia movement is to defend and protect the United States Constitution from those who want to take away the rights of Americans. The militia movement believes that the United States Constitution gives Americans the right to live their lives without government interference. The FBI is not concerned with every single aspect of the militia movement since many militia members are law-abiding citizens who do not pose a threat of violence. The FBI focuses on radical elements of the militia movement capable

and willing to commit violence against government, law enforcement, civilian, military, and international targets (UN, visiting foreign military personnel). Not every state in the union has a militia problem. Militia activity varies from states with almost no militia activity (Hawaii, Connecticut) to states with thousands of active militia members (Michigan, Texas).

The American militia movement has grown over the last decade. Factors contributing to growth include:

- GUNS—The right to bear arms is an issue that almost all militia members agree on. Most militia members believe a conspiracy exists to take away their guns. The national system of instant background checks for all gun buyers, mandated by the 1993 Brady Act and which actually was implemented on November 30, 1998, has further angered many militia groups. These militia members see this new law as another example of how the government is conspiring to take away their guns. The banning of semiautomatic assault weapons has also angered many militia members.

- STATE LAWS—Militias resent state laws forbidding them to gather together to fire weapons. Sixteen states have laws that prohibit all militia groups and 17 states have laws that prohibit all paramilitary training.

- MISTRUST OF FEDERAL LAW ENFORCEMENT—is frequently mentioned in militia literature and overall militia mythology. FBI and Bureau of Alcohol, Tobacco and Firearms (ATF) actions, such as Ruby Ridge, the Branch Davidians, and the Freeman standoff, are cited, and thus are hated and distrusted by many militia members.

- TAXES—Militia members believe that they pay too many taxes and that those tax dollars are wasted by a huge, uncaring, and inefficient bureaucracy in Washington, D.C. Since the Internal Revenue Service collects federal taxes, it is widely hated by militia members.

- THE UNITED NATIONS—is perceived as an organization bent on taking over the world and destroying American democracy and establishing "the New World Order." The New World Order theory holds that, one day, the United Nations will lead a military coup against the nations of the world to form a one-world government. United Nations troops, consisting of foreign armies, will commence a military takeover of America. The United Nations will mainly use foreign troops on American soil because foreigners will have fewer reservations about killing American citizens. Captured United States military bases will be used to help conquer the rest of the world.

Most of the militia movement has no racial overtones and does not espouse bigotry; there are some black and Jewish militia members. However, the pseudo-religion of Christian Identity, as well as other hate philosophies, have begun to creep into the militia movement. This scenario is currently being played out in the Michigan Militia, arguably the largest militia group in America. Lynn Van Huizen, leader of the Michigan Militia Corps, is currently trying to oust Christian Identity factions from his group. Christian

Identity is a belief system that provides both a religious base for racism and anti-Semitism, and an ideological rationale for violence against minorities. This pattern of racist elements seeping into the militia movement is a disturbing trend, as it will only strengthen the radical elements of the militias.

Many white supremacist groups adhere to the Christian Identity belief system, which holds that the world is on the verge of a final apocalyptic struggle between God/Christ and Satan (The Battle of Armageddon) in which Aryans (European Caucasians) must fight Satan's heirs: Jews, nonwhites, and their establishment allies (i.e., the federal government). The Christian Identity belief system (also known as Kingdom Identity) provides a religious base for racism and anti-Semitism, and an ideological rationale for violence against minorities and their white allies. Christian Identity teaches that the white race is the chosen race of God, whites are the "true Israelites," and Jews are the Children of Satan. Adherents believe that Jews have increasingly gained control of the U.S. federal government and are attempting to enslave the white population by enacting laws subjugating the white people, such as affirmative action, pro-choice, and anti-gun statutes.

To prepare for Armageddon, many Identity adherents engage in survivalist and paramilitary training, storing foodstuffs and supplies, and caching weapons and ammunition.

. . . Due to Christian Identity adherents' widespread propaganda efforts and Identity's racist/anti-Semitic/anti-government appeal, there are a number of churches and diverse organizations throughout the United States that embrace the doctrines of Identity. Identity beliefs are also increasingly found in the rhetoric of all types of right-wing extremist groups, including, but not limited to, militias, survivalist communes, the Ku Klux Klan, neo-Nazis, skinheads, tax protesters, and common law courts. Thus, with the approaching millennium, there is a greater potential for members from such Identity influenced groups to engage in violent activities as well.

Other Anti-Government Groups: The other right-wing anti-government groups include Freemen, "sovereign" citizens, and common law courts. The Freemen and sovereign citizens believe they have the right to renounce their citizenship, after which they do not have to comply with any laws or rules and the federal government would have no influence over them. In addition, some, like the Freemen, believe they have the right to issue their own money that is called "certified comptroller warrants."

Some members of the right wing have formed their own system of laws to enforce and follow (called common law courts) to replace the existing court system. The common law courts have no basis in jurisprudence, but participants claim legitimacy based on the laws of the Old Testament, English common law, the Magna Carta, and commercial law. Some common law courts have issued arrest warrants, but as of yet, there are no reports that any of these arrests have been accomplished.

Puerto Rican Extremist Groups: A resurgence in Puerto Rican extremism has occurred in the past six months. A nearly decade-long hiatus in terrorist activity ended on March 31, 1998, with the detonation of an incendiary device at the "Superaquaduct" construction project in Arecibo, Puerto Rico. On June 9, 1998, a bomb exploded outside a branch of Banco Popular in

Rio Piedras, Puerto Rico. The EPB–Macheteros publicly claimed responsibility for the attacks, citing environmental concerns and opposition to the privatization of the Puerto Rico Telephone Company.

Puerto Rican extremism remains a concern to the FBI. Traditionally, the Puerto Rican Terrorists have targeted United States establishments and interests in an effort to gain Puerto Rican independence. On December 13, 1998, Puerto Ricans voted in a non-binding referendum concerning Puerto Rico's political status. Voters were given the opportunity to vote for independence, continued commonwealth status, statehood, free association, or none of the above. Independence garnered precious little support in the referendum, receiving a mere 2.5% of the vote, according to media reports. Despite the lack of popular support for independence, militant independence activists continue to pursue independence through illegal means. Recently, July 25, 1998 marked the 100-year anniversary of the United States invasion of Puerto Rico during the Spanish-American War. In addition, several convicted Puerto Rican terrorists remain incarcerated within the federal prison system, and militant pro-independence activists continue to lobby for their release. The militant independentistas may engage in violence as a response to the prisoners' continued incarceration, or as a symbolic commemoration of over 100 years of American control over the island.

Special Interest Extremists: Special interest or single-issue extremists advocate violence and/or criminal activity with the goal of effecting change in policy vis à vis one specific aspect of society. The most recognizable single-issue terrorists at the present time are those involved in the violent animal rights, anti-abortion, and environmental protection movements. Each of these issues evoke strong emotions within society at large, and violent aberrants continue to tarnish the legitimate public debate on each issue.

The FBI continues to vigorously investigate various bombings of abortion clinics and incidents of violence targeting abortion providers across the country. The January 1998 bombing of an abortion clinic in Birmingham, Alabama, has resulted in a significant allocation of FBI manpower and resources to the investigation of the bombing. The recent assassination of Dr. Barnett Slepian in Buffalo, New York, serves as an acute reminder of the very real threat posed by anti-abortion extremists.

Animal rights extremists continue to pose significant challenges for law enforcement as well. Various arsons and other incidents of property destruction have been claimed by the Animal Liberation Front (ALF) and the Earth Liberation Front (ELF). For example, on October 19, 1998, the Vail Ski Resort suffered a series of arson attacks that damaged or destroyed eight separate structures and resulted in approximately $12 million in property damage. In a communiqué issued to various news agencies in Colorado, ELF claimed responsibility for the arsons in retaliation for the resort's plans to expand its ski areas. The group claimed that the proposed expansion would destroy the last remaining habitat in Colorado for the lynx.

Although the frequency of terrorist incidents within the United States has decreased in number, the potential for destruction has increased as terrorists have turned toward large improvised explosive devices to inflict maximum damage. The ease with which people can obtain the recipes for manufacturing explosives and developing chemical and biological weapons facilitates the potential of a major incident. As technology and materials become more accessible, the possibility of misuse and subsequent fatalities increases. One has only to look at the bombing of the Murrah Federal Building, in Oklahoma City, to see the devastating potential for a terrorist act. Prior to April 19, 1995, no one would have believed that Americans would commit such a tragic act against other Americans. But they did, and the potential for another such incident continues.[14]

The Oklahoma City bombing showed that "loners" and leaders of ill-informed extremist groups can pose a major threat. At the same time, the United States has a long history of disturbed individuals who have attempted mass killings. Virtually all of the killings to date have been carried out by using automatic weapons and bombs, but there is no clear reason that this should be true in the future. "Loner" mass killings in the United States are generally carried out by well-educated white males, most of which are fully functional and capable of working at complex tasks.[15] Nothing precludes them from using simple chemical devices and biological weapons in the future.

### The Implications of Past Terrorist Attacks

The U.S. government lacks any standard way of defining and reporting the patterns in actual acts of terrorism in the U.S. homeland. The FBI reporting of such acts since 1990 is, however, summarized in Table 3.2. The largest number of terrorist strikes have occurred in the western states and Puerto Rico. Attacks in Puerto Rico accounted for about 60 percent of all terrorist incidents between 1983 and 1991 that occurred on U.S. territory.[16]

It is important to note that only two incidents in these FBI statistics—the World Trade Center bombing in 1993 and the Oklahoma City bombing in 1995—have approached the level of violence that indicates that some response is required that goes beyond normal law enforcement and the existing counterterrorism capabilities of the Department of Justice.

Press reports produce the appearance of a more threatening environment than law enforcement reports, but this appearance does not seem to reflect the reality. Work by the Center for Non-Proliferation Studies at the Monterey Institute of International Studies highlights the fact that many of the apparent increases in CBRN terrorism are the result of hoaxes and different methods of report. The Center's effort to use media to find such instances found 175 reports of chemical, biological, and nuclear terrorism in 1999, of which 104 occurred in the United States. This was a major apparent rise since the Center's database contained a total of 687 incidents since 1900 as of February 23, 2000. Taken at face value, 25 percent of all recorded incidents occurred in 1999 alone. A total of 35 percent of the 494 biological incidents that occurred during 1900 to 1999 occurred in 1999. Most of these incidents, however, were part of a flood of false reports of anthrax threats that began in October 1998. A total of 81 out of the 104 incidents reported in the United States were anthrax threats, and 85 of the 104 incidents were hoaxes or pranks. Aside from hoaxes, here was one token possession of ricin in the United States, one token possession of sarin, and two personal attacks using cyanide. Interestingly enough, 55 out of the 104 incidents in the United States had a criminal motive, and only 49 could be assigned any kind of political or ideological motive. While the United States was the focus of false reports of biological attacks, a total of 99 of the 175 incidents worldwide were hoaxes or pranks. Most of the actual use of agents consisted of tear gas. There was one report of a radiological incident and two involving nuclear facilities, neither of which were confirmed.[17]

At the same time, no one can dismiss the fact that even one incident that involved a WMD could have catastrophic effects, and that extremists have attempted to use such weapons against the U.S. homeland. More lethal attacks have been attempted in the past. Covert terrorist and extremist efforts to use WMD against targets in the United States date back to the extensive efforts made by German agents to use biological warfare to attack U.S. agriculture during World War I. Domestic terrorists from an organization called RISE actively attempted to use typhoid and a number of other diseases as biological weapons against U.S. targets as early as 1972.[18] Muharem Kurbegovic, the psychologically disturbed "alphabet bomber," attempted to use chemical weapons in 1973–1974.[19] The Rajneeshees, a cult in Oregon, successfully used bioterrorism in the form of food poisoning using Salmonella in an effort to influence local politics during August–September 1984.[20] Other organizations, like the Arm of the Lord, were detected attempting to poison water supplies in the mid-1980s, and right-wing groups like the Minnesota Patriots Council were detected trying to obtain biological agents in the early 1990s.[21]

The bombing of the U.S. embassy in Dar es Salaam and the bomb that detonated near the U.S. embassy in Nairobi on August 7, 1998, provided grim warnings of how lethal new attacks in the United States could be even if they do not involve CBRN weapons, long before the attacks on the World Trade Center and the Pentagon. The toll in both bombings, in terms of lives lost, persons injured, and damage to buildings, was substantial. In Dar es Salaam, eleven persons were killed, seven of whom were foreign service nationals employed by the United States at the embassy. Another seventy-four persons were injured, including two American citizens and five foreign-service nationals. In Nairobi, where the U.S. embassy was located in a congested downtown area, 213 persons were killed, including 12 American citizens and 32 foreign-service nationals employed at the embassy.

Table 3.2
Chronological Summary of Terrorist Incidents in the United States: 1990–1997*

| Date | Location | Incident Type | Group |
|---|---|---|---|
| 1-12-90 | Santurce, P.R. | Pipe bombing | Brigada Internacionalista Eugenio Maria de Hostos de las Fuerzas Revolucionarias Pedro Albizu Campos (Eugenio Maria de Hostos International Brigade of the Pedro Albizu Campos Revolutionary Forces) |
| 1-12-90 | Carolina, P.R. | Pipe bombing | Brigada Internacionalista Eugenio Maria de Hostos de las Fuerzas Revolucionarias Pedro Albizu Campos (Eugenio Maria de Hostos International Brigade of the Pedro Albizu Campos Revolutionary Forces) |
| 2-22-90 | Los Angeles, Calif. | Bombing | Up the IRS, Inc. |
| 4-22-90 | Santa Cruz County | Malicious destruction | Earth Night Action Group Calif. of Property |
| 5-27-90 | Mayaguez, P.R. | Arson | Unknown Puerto Rican group |
| 9-17-90 | Arecibo, P.R. | Bombing | Pedro Albizu Group Revolutionary Forces |
| 9-17-90 | Vega Baja, P.R. | Bombing | Pedro Albizu Group Revolutionary Forces |
| 2-3-91 | Mayaguez, P.R. | Arson | Popular Liberation Army |
| 2-18-91 | Sabana Grande, P.R. | Arson | Popular Liberation Army |
| 3-17-91 | Carolina, P.R. | Arson | Unknown Puerto Rican group |

| Date | Location | Incident | Group |
|------|----------|----------|-------|
| 4-1-91 | Fresno, Calif. | Bombing | Popular Liberation Army |
| 7-6-91 | Punta Borinquen P.R. | Bombing | Popular Liberation Army |
| 4-5-92 | New York, N.Y. | Hostile takeover | Mujahedin-e-Khalq |
| 11-19-92 | Urbana, Ill. | Attempted Fire bombing | Mexican Revolutionary Movement |
| 12-10-92 | Chicago, Ill. | Car fire and attempted Fire bombing (two incidents) | Boricua Revolutionary Front |
| 2-26-93 | New York, N.Y. | Car bombing | International radical terrorists. |
| 7-20-93 | Tacoma, Wash. | Pipe bombing | American Front Skinheads |
| 7-22-93 | Tacoma, Wash. | Bombing | American Front Skinheads |
| 11-27/28-93 | Chicago, Ill. | Fire bombing (nine incidents) | Animal Liberation Front |
| 4-19-95 | Oklahoma City, Okla. | Truck bombing | Pending investigation |
| 4-1-96 | Spokane, Wash. | Pipe bomb/bank | Robbery Phineas Priesthood |
| 7-12-96 | Spokane, Wash. | Pipe bomb/bank | Robbery Phineas Priesthood |
| 7-27-96 | Atlanta, Ga. | Pipe bomb | Pending investigation |
| 1-2-97 | Washington, D.C. | Letter-bomb | Pending investigation |
| 1-2-97 | Leavenworth, Kans. | Letter-bomb | Pending investigation |

*There were no incidents of terrorism in 1994.

Source: Federal Bureau of Investigation, Terrorism in the United States (Washington, D.C.: Counterterrorism Threat Assessment and Warning Unit, National Security Division, 1997).

Approximately forty-five hundred persons were treated for injuries, including thirteen Americans and sixteen foreign-service nationals.

Other warnings emerge when one looks beyond statistics and at FBI and State Department descriptions of the incidents involved. Attacks and plots involving Americans or American interests include:

- The 1993 murders of two CIA employees and the wounding of several others by Mir Amal Kasi in Langley, Virginia.
- The March 1995 attack against three employees of the U.S. consulate in Karachi, Pakistan, which resulted in the deaths of two Americans.
- The July 1995 hostage taking of four Western tourists, including an American, by terrorists in Kashmiri, India.
- The plot by Shayk Omar Abdel Rahman and his followers to bomb several New York City landmarks, including the United Nations building, the Holland and Lincoln tunnels, and several federal buildings.
- The November 1995 bombing of a Saudi Arabian National Guard building in Riyadh, Saudi Arabia, which resulted in the deaths of five U.S. citizens assigned to the U.S. military training mission to Saudi Arabia.
- The June 1996 bombing at the Al-Khobar Towers, Dhahran, Saudi Arabia, which resulted in the deaths of 19 U.S. servicemen and the injury of 240 other military personnel and dependents.
- A plot led by Ramzi Yousef to destroy numerous U.S. air carriers in a simultaneous operation.
- A plot, also led by Ramzi Yousef, to kidnap and kill U.S. diplomats and foreign officials in Pakistan.
- The November 1997 ambush and massacre of foreign tourists in Luxor, Egypt, which appears to have been undertaken to pressure the U.S. government to release Shayk Rahman from federal prison.
- The November 1997 murder of four U.S. businessmen and their driver in Karachi, Pakistan, believed to be in retaliation against the FBI's capture and rendition of Mir Amal Kasi.
- The kidnapping of seven Americans during 1998 in Colombia by terrorist groups, bringing the total number of U.S. citizens reported kidnapped in that country between 1980 and 1998 to ninety-two, of which twelve Americans have died in captivity.
- The arrest in February 1998 of Larry Wayne Harris for packaging a vaccine strain of anthrax and claiming to attack Las Vegas.
- The December 1998 kidnapping of a group of Western tourists, including two Americans, by terrorists in Yemen, during which four hostages were killed and one American hostage wounded when Yemeni security forces attempted a rescue operation.
- In mid-December 1999, U.S. authorities arrested Ahmed Ressam, an Algerian national, as he entered the United States from Canada at Port Angeles, Washington. The vehicle he was driving was carrying explosives and detonating

devices. The Canadian government cooperated closely in the follow-up investigation into Ressam's activities and associates in Canada. Some Algerians arrested in connection with this case apparently are "Afghan alumni," who trained with the *mujahidin* in Afghanistan and are linked to Usama bin Ladin. Canada has a long-standing cooperative relationship with the United States on counterterrorist matters, and the two countries meet regularly to discuss ways to enhance this cooperation and improve border security. While a potentially serious incident was avoided with Ressam's arrest, at year end Canada and the United States remained concerned about the possibility of a heightened threat of terrorism in North America, and the two countries were exploring new mechanisms for exchanging information on individuals with links to terrorism.

- In 2000, the USS *Cole*, while refueling in Aden, was attacked with a terrorist bomb.

While this list only includes foreign attackers, some domestic paramilitary groups or "militias" have attempted to use WMD and that they are organized to attack American civil society. There is no precise count of such groups, but various recent estimates indicate that there are some 435 to 800 "patriot" groups, and that 171 to 441 are identifiable militia groups—a number that does not include so-called phantom cell groups like the one that Timothy McVeigh, the Oklahoma City bomber, believed in. The lower range of this estimate of patriot groups excludes 457 active "hate" groups, and this separation of patriot and hate groups seems the more valid approach. According to some law enforcement estimates, three hundred thousand people may belong to the patriot and hate groups, although the overwhelming majority of these people have no tendency toward violence and pose no threat to anyone.[22]

## PROBABILITY VERSUS PROBABILITY THEORY

There is a large range of literature that attempts to identify the most probable sources of attacks on the U.S. homeland and the most probable forms of terrorist attack. While such literature is sometime useful, it can also be highly misleading. Searching for the most probable form of one or several of the virtually countless variations of low-probability attacks is simply terrible mathematics. It is a fundamental principle of probability theory that under these conditions, the cumulative probability of a truly low-probability event occurring will always be higher than the cumulative probability of a small set of the slightly higher-probability events. Put more simply, history shows that contingency and scenario analysis is at best diagnostic, not predictive, and that it is the wild card that is most likely to actually be played.

Ironically these realities do not support either those who argue that CBRN attacks are unlikely or those who argue that they are inevitable.

Those who try to argue that today's identifiable threats from state actors, terrorists, and extremists present a clear and decisive rationale for extensive homeland defense programs dealing with CBRN attacks are stretching the evidence beyond its limits. At the same time, those who argue such programs are not necessary on the grounds that such threats cannot be clearly and decisively identified ignore very real risks. It would be much easier to shape U.S. programs if this were not the case. But there are times when the United States must learn to live with complexity and uncertainty and the reality that it will have to continuously modify its programs and policies to deal with such threats as they do, or do not, evolve.

## NOTES

1. Stephen E. Flynn, draft version of "Border Control Blues," *Foreign Affairs* 79, no. 6 (November–December 2000).

2. Flynn, "Border Control Blues."

3. Flynn, "Border Control Blues."

4. Adapted from the U.S. State Department, *Patterns of Global Terrorism, 1999*, Department of State Publication 10610, Office of the Secretary of State, Office of the Coordinator for Counterterrorism (released April 2000), <http://www.state.gov/www/global/terrorism/1999Report/sponsor.html>.

5. Adapted from the U.S. State Department, *Patterns of Global Terrorism, 1999*.

6. National Commission on Terrorism, *Countering the Changing Threat of International Terrorism* (June 2000), <http://www.fas.org/irp/threat/commission.html>.

7. U.S. Department of Defense, *Chemical and Biological Defense Program, Annual Report to the Congress* (Washington, D.C.: U.S. Department of Defense, March 2000), 6–10.

8. Adapted from the U.S. State Department, *Patterns of Global Terrorism, 1998*, Department of State Publication 10610, Office of the Secretary of State, Office of the Coordinator for Counterterrorism (released April 1999), <http://www.state.gov/www/global/terrorism/1998Report/sponsor.html; and also adapted from the U.S. State Department, *Patterns of Global Terrorism, 1999*.

9. See <http://www.fbi.gov/pressrm/congress/congress99/freehct2.htm>.

10. Adapted from the U.S. State Department, *Patterns of Global Terrorism, 1998*; and also adapted from the U.S. State Department, *Patterns of Global Terrorism, 1999*.

11. The State Department list includes groups that were designated foreign terrorist organizations on October 8, 1997, pursuant to the Antiterrorism and Effective Death Penalty Act of 1996 (denoted by an asterisk), but also includes other major groups that were active in 1998. Terrorist groups whose activities were limited in scope in 1998 are not included.

12. Office of the Secretary of Defense, *Proliferation—Threat and Response, January 2001*, Internet ed. (Washington, D.C.: U.S. Department of Defense, January 2001), "Transnational Threats."

13. National Commission on Terrorism, *Countering the Changing Threat of International Terrorism* (June 2000), <http://www.fas.org/irp/threat/commission.html>.

14. See <http://www.fbi.gov/pressrm/congress/congress99/freehct2.htm>.

15. See the series in the *New York Times*, 8–12 April 2000.

16. See <http://www.fema.gov/library/terror.htm>.

17. Gavin Cameron, Jaspon Pate, Diana McCauley, and Libsay DeFazio, "1999 WMD Terrorism Chronology: Incidents Involving Sub-National Actors and Chemical, Biological, Radiological, and Nuclear Materials," *The Non-Proliferation Review* (Summer 2000): 157–174.

18. See the work by Seth Carus in Jonathan B. Tucker, ed., *Toxic Terror, Assessing Terrorist Use of Chemical and Biological Weapons* (Cambridge, Mass.: Belfer Center for Scientific and International Affairs, 2000), 55–70.

19. See the work by Jeffrey D. Simon in Tucker, *Toxic Terror*, 71–94.

20. See the work of Carus in Tucker, *Toxic Terror*, 116–137.

21. See the work of Jessica Eve Stern in Tucker, *Toxic Terror*, 139–157; and the work of Jonathan B. Tucker and Jason Pate in Tucker, *Toxic Terror*; also see Morris Dees, *Gathering Storm: America's Militia Threat* (New York: HarperCollins, 1996).

22. Estimates of membership as high as twelve million have been made but seem absurd. For a partial list, see the Militia Watchdog Links Page, <http://www.militia.watchdog.org/ml.htm>.

## Chapter 4

# Types of Attack: Determining Future Methods of Attack and the Needed Response

From a public policy viewpoint, these uncertainties mean the United States must prepare for a wide variety of low-probability attacks on the United States, rather than to emphasize any given form of attack or group of attackers. The United States must plan its homeland defense policies and programs for a future in which there is no way to predict the weapon that will be used or the method chosen in which that weapon will be delivered. That delivery can range from a small suicide attack by an American citizen, to the covert delivery of a nuclear weapon by a foreign state. There is no reason the United States should assume that some convenient Gaussian curve or standard deviation will make small- or medium-level attacks a higher priority over time than more lethal forms.

The U.S. government is still deciding how to come to grips with these problems and how to assess possible methods of attack. A GAO report that summarized CIA and FBI views on these issues reached the following conclusions, although it must be stressed that the analysis focused on the normal historical pattern of actions by terrorists/extremists, and largely excluded attacks by state actors, proxy attacks, or covert attacks:

> The possibility that terrorists may use chemical or biological materials may increase over the next decade, according to intelligence agencies. According to the Central Intelligence Agency (CIA), interest among non-state actors, including terrorists, in biological and chemical materials is real and growing and the number of potential perpetrators is increasing. The CIA also noted that many such groups have international networks and do not need to be

tied to state sponsors for financial and technical support. Nonetheless, the CIA continues to believe that terrorists are less likely to use chemical and biological weapons than conventional explosives. We previously reported that, according to intelligence agencies, terrorists are less likely to use chemical and biological weapons than conventional explosives, at least partly because chemical and biological agents are difficult to weaponize and the results are unpredictable.

. . . The CIA classified the specific agents identified in intelligence assessments that would more likely be used by foreign-origin terrorists. The CIA also classified the intelligence judgments about the chances that state actors with successful chemical and/or biological warfare programs would share their weapons and materials with terrorists or terrorist groups. Unlike the foreign-origin threat, the FBI's analysts' judgments concerning the more likely chemical and biological agents that may be used by domestic-origin terrorists have not been captured in a formal assessment. However, FBI officials shared their analyses of the more likely biological and chemical threat agents on the basis of substances used or threatened in actual cases.

In analyzing domestic-origin threats, FBI officials grouped chemical and biological agents and did not specify individual agents as threats. Although the FBI has not addressed the specific types of chemical or biological weapons that may be used by domestic terrorists in the next 2 to 5 years, FBI officials believe that domestic terrorists would be more likely to use or threaten to use biological agents than chemical agents.

The FBI's observation is based on an increase in reported investigations involving the use of biological materials. In 1997, of the 74 criminal investigations related to weapons of mass destruction, 30 percent (22) were related to the use of biological materials. In 1998, there were 181 criminal investigations related to weapons of mass destruction, and 62 percent (112) were related to the use of biological materials. Most of these investigations involved threats or hoaxes. The FBI estimated that in 1997 and 1998, approximately 60 percent of biological investigations were related to anthrax hoaxes.

The FBI ranks groups of chemical and biological agents on its threat spectrum according to the likelihood that they would be used.

- Biological toxins: any toxic substance of natural origin produced by an animal or plant. An example of a toxin is ricin, a poisonous protein extracted from the castor bean.

- Toxic industrial chemicals: chemicals developed or manufactured for use in industrial operations such as manufacturing solvents, pesticides, and dyes. These chemicals are not primarily manufactured for the purpose of producing human casualties. Chlorine, phosgene, and hydrogen cyanide are industrial chemicals that have also been used as chemical warfare agents.

- Biological pathogens: any organism (usually living) such as a bacteria or virus capable of causing serious disease or death. Anthrax is an example of a bacterial pathogen.

- Chemical agents: a chemical substance that is intended for use in military operations to kill, seriously injure, or incapacitate people. The FBI excludes from consideration riot control agents and smoke and flame materials. Two examples of chemical agents are sarin (nerve agent) and mustard gas (blister agent).[1]

The First Annual Report of the Advisory Panel to Assess Domestic Response Capabilities for Terrorism Involving the Use of Weapons of Mass Destruction, also known as the Gilmore Commission, took a somewhat different path. It downplayed the CBRN threat largely because of the current technical problems nonstate actors confront in using WMD:

Many government officials and concerned citizens believe that it is not a question of if, but when, an incident will occur that involves the use by a terrorist of a chemical, biological, radiological, and nuclear (CBRN) weapon—a so-called "weapon of mass destruction" (WMD)—that is designed, intended, or has the capability to cause "mass destruction" or "mass casualties." In recent years, some have depicted terrorist incidents as causing catastrophic loss of life and extensive structural and environmental damage as not only possible but probable. Such depictions do not accurately portray the full range of terrorist threats. . . . While such a devastating event is within the realm of possibility . . .

In our opinion, some fundamental questions should be answered before the federal government builds and expands programs, plans, and strategies to deal with the threat of WMD terrorism: How easy or difficult is it for terrorists (rather than state actors) to successfully use chemical or biological WMDs in an attack causing mass casualties? And if it is easy to produce and disperse chemical and biological agents, why have there been no WMD terrorist attacks before or since the Tokyo subway incident? What chemical and biological agents does the government really need to be concerned about? We have not yet seen a thorough assessment or analysis of these questions. It seems to us that, without such an assessment or analysis and consensus in the policy-making community, it would be very difficult—maybe impossible—to properly shape programs and focus resources.

Statements in testimony before the Congress and in the open press by intelligence and scientific community officials on the issue of making and delivering a terrorist WMD sometimes contrast sharply. On the one hand, some statements suggest that developing a WMD can be relatively easy. For example, in 1996, the Central Intelligence Agency Director testified that chemical and biological weapons can be produced with relative ease in simple laboratories, and in 1997, the Central Intelligence Agency Director said that "delivery and dispersal techniques also are effective and relatively easy to develop." One article by former senior intelligence and defense officials noted that chemical and biological agents can be produced by graduate students or laboratory technicians and that general recipes are readily available on the Internet.

On the other hand, some statements suggest that there are considerable difficulties associated with successfully developing and delivering a WMD. For example, the Deputy Commander of the Army's Medical Research and Materiel Command testified in 1998 about the difficulties of using WMDs, noting that "an effective, mass-casualty producing attack on our citizens would require either a fairly large, very technically competent, well-funded terrorist program or state sponsorship." Moreover, in 1996, the Director of the Defense Intelligence Agency testified that the agency had no conclusive information that any of the terrorist organizations it monitors were developing chemical, biological, or radiological weapons and that there was no conclusive information that any state sponsor had the intention to provide these weapons to terrorists. In 1997, the Central Intelligence Agency Director testified that while advanced and exotic weapons are increasingly available, their employment is likely to remain minimal, as terrorist groups concentrate on peripheral technologies such as sophisticated conventional weapons.[2]

## ILLUSTRATIVE ATTACK SCENARIOS

Federal, state, and local governments are almost certainly correct in assuming that the *current* threat of conventional attack is notably higher than the risk of CBRN attack, and that the use of relatively low levels of CBRN attack is currently higher than the risk of high levels of CBRN attack.

The attacks on the World Trade Center and the Pentagon are evidence of this fact. The analysis of the nature and lethality of the threat changes considerably, however, if states conduct covert CBRN attacks, or give them to proxies or independent movements. It also changes that, over time, as technology makes the use of biological weapons more available and as the time horizon for estimating the risk of some form of high-level CBRN attack is extended to the quarter of the country, U.S. planners must consider shaping long-term programs and research, development, test, and evaluation (RDT&E) activities.

Under these conditions, there are many scenarios where different types of CBRN weapons could have lethalities and costs up to several orders of magnitude higher than those that occurred as a result of the first World Trade Center, Oklahoma City, and Aum Shinrikyo attacks. Consider the following scenarios:

- A radiological powder is introduced into the air conditioning systems of several high-rise office buildings, hotels, and so on, possibly in several cities over a matter of weeks. Symptoms are only detected over days or weeks and public warning is given several weeks later. The authorities now detect the presence of such a powder, but cannot estimate its long-term lethality and have no precedents for decontamination. Local tourism collapses, no one will enter the building area, and the buildings eventually have to be torn down and rebuilt.

- A Country X or a Country X-backed terrorist group smuggles in parts for a crude gun-type nuclear device. The device is built in a medium-sized commercial truck. The group uses a U.S. Department of Defense weapons effects manual, maps a U.S. city to maximize fallout effects in an area filled with buildings with heavy metals, and waits for a wind maximizing the fallout impact. The group also searches the U.S. literature response measures to pick wind patterns that complicate the response effort and affect a maximum number of first responders. The bomb explodes with a yield of only a few kilotons, but with high levels of radiation. Immediate casualties are serious and the long-term death rate mounts steadily with time.

- Several workers move drums labeled as cleaning agents into a large shopping mall, large public facility, subway, train station, or airport. They dress as cleaners and are wearing what appear to be commercial dust filters or have taken the antidote for the agent they will use. They mix the feed stocks for a persistent chemical agent at the site during a peak traffic period.

- Immunized terrorists carry anthrax powder into a building or urban area in containers designed to make them look like shopping bags, brief cases, suitcases, and so on. They pick sites where their study of federal, state, and local governments indicate that detection is unlikely and local response capabilities are limited. They slowly scatter the powder as they walk through the areas. The United States does not detect the attacks until days or weeks after they occur. It then finds it has no experience with decontaminating a number of large buildings or areas where anthrax has entered the air system and is scattered throughout closed areas. After long debates over methods and safety levels, the facilities and areas are temporarily abandoned. (A variation on this scenario is the use of a form of inhaled anthrax modified to prevent effective immunization and use of normal medical treatment).

- A Country X or a Country X-backed terrorist group seeking to "cleanse" the United States introduces a modified type culture of Ebola or a similar virus into urban areas. It scatters infectious cultures for which there is no effective immunization and only limited treatment, capitalizing on years of strategic warning regarding what vaccines the United States is developing and stockpiling and on the open literature on the limits to U.S. detection and response capabilities. By the time the attack(s) are detected, they have reached epidemic proportions, causing the collapse of medical facilities and emergency response capabilities. Other nations and regions have no alternative other than to isolate the part of the United States under attack, letting the disease take its course.

- A Country X or a Country X-backed terrorist group modifies the valves on a Japanese remote-controlled crop spraying helicopter that has been imported legally for agricultural purposes. It uses this system at night or near dawn to spray a chemical or biological agent at altitudes below radar coverage in a line-source configuration. Alternatively, it uses a large home-built remotely polited vehicle with simple GPS guidance. The device eventually crashes undetected into the sea or in the desert. Delivery of a chemical agent achieves far higher casualties than a conventional military warhead. A biological agent would be equally effective and the first symptoms might appear days after the actual attack—by which time the cause would be impossible to determine and treatment could be difficult or impossible.

- A truck filled with what appears to be light gravel is driven through the streets of a city during rush hour or another heavy traffic period. A visible powder does come out through the tarpaulin covering the truck, but the spread of the powder is so light that no attention is paid to it. The driver and his assistant are immunized against the modified form of anthrax carried in the truck, which is being released from behind the gravel or sand in the truck. The truck slowly quarters key areas of the city. Unsuspected passersby and commuters not only are infected, but also carry dry spores home and into other areas. By the time the first major symptoms of the attack occur some three to five days later, anthrax pneumonia is an epidemic and some septicemic anthrax has appeared. Some 40 percent to 65 percent of the exposed population dies and medical facilities collapse, causing serious, lingering secondary effects.

- A Country X or a Country X-backed terrorist group scatters high concentrations of a radiological, chemical, or biological agent in various areas in a city, and trace elements into the processing intakes to the local water supply. When the symptoms appear, the terrorist group makes its attack known, but claims that it has contaminated the local water supply. The authorities are forced to confirm that water is contaminated and mass panic ensues.

- Immunized terrorists carry small amounts of anthrax or a similar biological agent onto a passenger aircraft like a B-747, quietly scatter the powder, and deplane at a regular scheduled stop. No airport detection system or search detects the agent on the plane. Some 70 percent to 80 percent of those who fly on the aircraft die as a result of symptoms that only appear days later. It takes weeks to detect the fact that the aircraft remains contaminated.

- Several identical nuclear devices are smuggled out of the former Soviet Union. One of the devices is disassembled to determine the precise technology and coding system used in the weapon's permissive action link. This allows users to activate the remaining weapons. The weapon is then disassembled to minimize detection with the fissile core shipped covered in lead. The weapon is successfully smuggled into the periphery of an urban area outside any formal security perimeter. A ten-plus-kiloton ground burst destroys a critical area and blankets the region in fallout.

- The same device is shipped to a U.S. port area in a modified standard shipping container, equipped with considerable shielding and detection and triggering devices, which set it off either when the container is opened or by using information from a GPS that sets it off automatically when it reaches the proper coordinates. The direct explosive effect is significant, and even if it detonates at Customs, the damage and "rain out" contaminate a massive local area.

- A Country X or a Country X-backed terrorist group develops a radiation fallout model using local weather data that it confirms by sending out scouts with simple commercial wind measurement equipment and cellular phones. It waits for the ideal wind pattern and detonates a nuclear device for maximum contamination of a city or critical economic areas. Alternatively, the same group uses a similar weather model, waits for the proper wind pattern, and allows the wind to carry a biological agent over a city.

- Simultaneous release takes place of anthrax spores at ten to twenty scattered subway platforms during rush hour, and at commuter rail stations as well. No notice is given of the attack. Incubation takes one to seven days, and the attack is only detected when massive numbers of cases in the acute phase exhibit flu-like symptoms and then enter the breathing difficulty and shock phase (one to two days after incubation). Several million commuters are potentially exposed, but the locations of the attack are unknown, and effective triage is now impossible. Prompt treatment is no longer possible. Local and regional medical facilities collapse.

- An illegal smallpox culture is used or stolen. The agent is planted in the air duct of aircraft flying to an airport in the target country. The first cases occur two weeks after the flight(s). Widespread infection presents major problems because of a lack of the ability to trace passengers and secondary infections. Mass panic affects national medical facilities and some 10 to 30 percent of those infected die.

- A freighter carrying fertilizer enters a port and docks. In fact, the freighter has mixed the fertilizer with a catalyst to create a massive explosion that also disseminates a large amount of a radiological and/or biological agent. Response focuses on the damage done by the resulting explosion. The scattering of a radiological or biological weapon over the area is only detected days later.

- A large terrorist device goes off in a populated and critical economic or military assembly area—scattering mustard or nerve gas. Emergency teams react quickly and deal with the chemical threat and the residents are evacuated. Only later it becomes clear that the device also included a biological agent and that the response to this "cocktail" killed most emergency response personnel and the evacuation rushed the biological agent to a much wider area.

- Country X or a proxy group attacks U.S. agriculture with a foreign pest or disease that could be transmitted by normal commerce and that is genetically enhanced. The United States suffers major economic damage and never knows it is under attack. Alternatively, it uses a mix of normal plant diseases plus an add-on weaponized agent. The United States fails to react to the added agent until it discovered the true scale of the problem weeks later, it then finds it has only limited near- to mid-term countermeasures. It never conclusively identifies its attacker.

- Country X or a terrorist or proxy group attacks the United States with a biological agent in very small amounts in many areas in the United States. The United States is forced to mount a massive nation-wide preemptive effort at vast expense, even though it is only under limited attack. The attack is tailored to counter the highly detailed open literature on U.S. federal, state, and local detection and response capabilities.

- A local terrorist group produces ricin from castor beans and either distributes the toxin through the air intake of a government building or sprays it from a truck moving down a street. The first symptoms do not appear until three hours later and there is no known treatment. Significant deaths occur within thirty-six to seventy-two hours.

This list of possible attack scenarios illustrates the fact that a wide range of highly lethal CBRN attacks are practical, although most would *now* require an attacker to at least have access to the level of technology available only to governments. Second, it shows how dangerous it is to assume that attacks have to follow any rules or be carried out in a predictable way. Third, it shows that many attacks can defeat "first response" as well as avoid early U.S. efforts at detection or containment and/or can be tailored to bypass or counter many of the measures the United States is currently exploring for homeland defense. Fourth, it illustrates the fact that attackers can use more than one means of attack at the same time. Finally, it illustrates the dangers of leaving any gap in homeland defense between responding to overt warfare like missile attacks and to relatively limited attacks by terrorists.

### "CONVENTIONAL" MEANS OF ATTACK

Homeland defense clearly should not emphasize CBRN attacks, at the cost of defending against more conventional means of attack. The previous scenarios do not mean that attacks using conventional explosives are not lethal or more probable than CBRN attacks. Most terrorist/extremist attacks to date on Americans inside and outside the United States have used conventional explosives, and the World Trade Center and Oklahoma City bombings show that such attacks can be very costly. There are also good reasons why some federal agencies see the large-scale use of conventional explosives as a "weapon of mass destruction."

The DOD has carried out many vulnerability analyses over the years that have highlighted critical targets for conventional attack ranging from communications grids to political leadership. Some of these studies focused on the risk of using high-explosive attacks by Soviet Spetznaz during the Cold War, and exposed the vulnerability of key plants and military facilities in the United States. U.S. utility companies have carried out vulnerability studies and have found other important "weak links" in the U.S. infrastructure. They have found that conventional attacks could be far more lethal if the attacker had the expertise to target vulnerabilities and place explosives more precisely than terrorists have done in the past.

There is also no reason that attackers cannot combine conventional explosives with the use of WMD. Sophisticated attackers might well find that a mix of different forms of attacks would do most to increase damage or political effect. One such scenario might be mixing a conventional bomb with a chemical or biological weapon, with the idea that the rush of response teams into the bombed area would greatly increase the number of casualties.

As a result, it is clear that the United States needs to continue improving many of its capabilities to detect conventional forms of attack, improve its regular counterterrorism and law enforcement activity, improve its defenses, and consider finding ways of reducing conventional vulnerability, as well as deal with CBRN attacks.

## WEAPONS OF MASS DESTRUCTION

The previous scenarios do indicate, however, that the United States must fully recognize the risk posed by CBRN weapons and how they differ sharply in character and in their effects. Each form of weapon can be used in ways that present radically different problems for defense and response. The key differences in the character and use of each type of weapon are summarized in Table 4.1, and it is clear that each can have very different impacts, regardless of whether it is used against military or civilian targets.

The broad differences in the lethality of each type of weapon are equally important, and are shown in Table 4.2. It should be noted, however, that much depends on the size of the weapon and the way in which it is employed. The actual design of a given weapon or device is almost totally unpredictable but will be critical in determining its actual lethality. Once again, there also are no clear precedents or paradigms that can be used for planning homeland defense.

These problems are compounded by the fact that theoretical lethality models are filled with gross uncertainties, and there is little chance that any current database, model, or simulation can be used to accurately predict the actual consequences of the use of such weapons. The data in Tables 2.5 and 2.6 are typical of such models and they are derived from models whose primary purpose was to examine what state actors could do when using bombs and missiles in warfare. They were not intended to reflect the character and lethality of the CBRN weapons in the kind of smaller attacks that might take place under covert conditions, or by proxies, terrorists, and extremists. There is also good historical reason to question whether chemical weapons are normally as lethal as Tables 4.1 and 4.2 imply. They fail to distinguish between methods of delivery of biological weapons and tacitly assume the optimal use of dry micropowders when actual attacks may use much cruder "wet" weapons with limited or no lethality.

There is also no reason to assume that effects of WMD should be measured in terms of mass casualties or mass destruction. With the exception of nuclear weapons, they can be used in virtually any size, and attackers can exploit their different effects to attack small targets and highly localized areas as well as cities and large populated areas. Even nuclear weapons are available in fractions of a kiloton and chemical, biological, and radiological weapons can be used for the purposes of assassination or attacking individual buildings.

Attackers will generally have a political or ideological motive. The psychological and political aspects of using WMD cannot be quantified in

Table 4.1
Key Characteristics of Weapons of Mass Destruction

Chemical Weapons

*Destructive Effects*:    Poisoning skin, lungs, nervous system, or blood. Contaminating areas, equipment, and protective gear for periods of hours to days. Forcing military units to don highly restrictive protection gear or use incapacitating antidotes. False alarms and panic. Misidentification of the agent, or confusion of chemical with biological agents (which may be mixed) leading to failure of defense measures. Military and popular panic and terror effects. Major medical burdens that may lead to mistreatment. Pressure to deploy high cost air and missile defenses. Paralysis or disruption of civil life and economic activity in threatened or attacked areas.

*Typical Targets*:    Infantry concentrations, air bases, ships, ports, staging areas, command centers, munitions depots, cities, key oil and electrical facilities, desalinization plants.

*Typical Missions*:    Killing military and civilian populations. Intimidation. Attack of civilian population or targets. Disruption of military operations by requiring protective measures or decontamination. Area or facility denial. Psychological warfare, production of panic, and terror.

*Limitations*:    Large amounts of agents are required to achieve high lethality, and military and economic effects are not sufficiently greater than careful target conventional strikes to offer major war fighting advantages. Most agents degrade quickly, and their effect is highly dependent on temperature and weather conditions, height of dissemination, terrain, and the character of built-up areas. Warning devices far more accurate and sensitive than for biological agents. Protective gear and equipment can greatly reduce effects, and sufficiently high numbers of rounds, sorties, and missiles are needed to ease the task of defense. Leave buildings and equipment reusable by the enemy, although persistent agents may require decontamination. Persistent agents may contaminate the ground the attacker wants to cross or occupy and force use of protective measures or decontamination.

Biological Weapons

*Destructive Effects*:    Infectious disease or biochemical poisoning. Contaminating areas, equipment, and protective gear for periods of hours to weeks. Delayed effects and tailoring to produce incapacitation or killing, treatable or non-treatable agents,

Table 4.1 (continued)

and be infectious on contact only or transmittable. Forcing military units to don highly restrictive protection gear or use incapacitating vaccine antidotes. False alarms and panic. High risk of at least initial misidentification of the agent, or confusion of chemical with biological agents (which may be mixed) leading to failure of defense measures. Military and popular panic and terror effects. Major medical burdens that may lead to mistreatment. Pressure to deploy high cost air and missile defenses. Paralysis or disruption of civil life and economic activity in threatened or attacked areas.

*Typical Targets*: Infantry concentrations, air bases, ships, ports, staging areas, command centers, munitions depots, cities, key oil and electrical facilities, desalinization plants. Potentially far more effective against military and civil area targets than chemical weapons.

*Typical Missions*: Killing and incapacitation of military and civilian populations. Intimidation. Attack of civilian population or targets. Disruption of military operations by requiring protective measures or decontamination. Area or facility denial. Psychological warfare, production of panic, and terror.

*Limitations*: Most wet agents degrade quickly, although spores, dry encapsulated agents, and some toxins are persistent. Effects usually take some time to develop (although not in the case of some toxins). Effects are unpredictable, and are even more dependent than chemical weapons on temperature and weather conditions, height of dissemination, terrain, and the character of built-up areas. Major risk of contaminating the wrong area. Warning devices uncertain and may misidentify the agent. Protective gear and equipment can reduce effects. Leave buildings and equipment reusable by the enemy, although persistent agents may require decontamination. Persistent agents may contaminate the ground the attacker wants to cross or occupy and force use of protective measures or decontamination. More likely than chemical agents to cross the threshold where nuclear retaliation seems justified.

**Nuclear Weapons**

*Destructive Effects*: Blast, fire, and radiation. Destruction of large areas and production of fallout and contamination—depending on character of weapon and height of burst. Contaminating

continued

**Table 4.1 (continued)**

---

|  |  |
|---|---|
|  | areas, equipment, and protective gear for periods of hours to days. Forcing military units to don highly restrictive protection gear and use massive amounts of decontamination gear. Military and popular panic and terror effects. Massive medical burdens. Pressure to deploy high cost air and missile defenses. Paralysis or disruption of civil life and economic activity in threatened or attacked areas. High long term death rates from radiation. Forced dispersal of military forces and evacuation of civilians. Destruction of military and economic centers, and national political leadership and command authority, potentially altering character of attacked nation and creating major recovery problems. |
| *Typical Targets:* | Hardened targets, enemy facilities and weapons of mass destruction, enemy economic, political leadership, and national command authority. Infantry and armored concentrations, air bases, ships, ports, staging areas, command centers, munitions depots, cities, key oil and electrical facilities, desalinization plants. |
| *Typical Missions:* | Forced dispersal of military forces and evacuation of civilians. Destruction of military and economic centers, and national political leadership and command authority, potentially altering character of attacked nation and creating major recovery problems. |
| *Limitations:* | High cost. Difficulty of acquiring more than a few weapons. Risk of accidents or failures that hit friendly territory. Crosses threshold to level where nuclear retaliation is likely. Destruction or contamination of territory and facilities attacker wants to cross or occupy. High risk of massive collateral damage to civilians if this is important to attacker. |

---

*Source*: Adapted by Anthony H. Cordesman from Office of Technology Assessment, *Proliferation of Weapons of Mass Destruction: Assessing the Risks*, U.S. Congress OTA-ISC-559, Washington, D.C. (August 1993), 56–57.

any one form. They can be exploited in ways where the number of casualties and the amount of physical damage may be far less important than the impact on public opinion, crowd behavior, and the political perceptions of foreign states. The very threat of such attacks can cause panic, and the risk of contamination can deny the use of a facility even if contamination is minimal or no longer exists. At the same time, a successful biological or nuclear attack on U.S. territory might radically change world perceptions of American strength and vulnerability, even if the target was poorly chosen and casualties were limited.

This latter point is ignored in some studies. The fact that an attacker would be perceived in radically different terms if he or she successfully used a WMD against the United States is viewed only as a deterrent to using such weapons. In fact, it is a double-edged sword. There is no other way many attackers could change perceptions of their importance so quickly. Aum Shinrikyo is not memorable for the casualties it caused, but rather because it used chemical weapons and prepared biological weapons. Missiles were Iraq's only memorable response during the Persian Gulf War.

## CHEMICAL WEAPONS AS MEANS OF ATTACK

Chemical weapons have not been used effectively in attacks on the U.S. homeland. Reports that the bombers of the World Trade Center considered trying to add a chemical weapon like sodium cyanide to their explosives seem to be untrue. These reports led to an unsubstantiated assertion by the trial judge.[3] There have, however, been a number of attempts to use chemical weapons by domestic extremists and individuals. For example, in 1997, members of the Ku Klux Klan plotted to place an improvised explosive device on a hydrogen sulfide tank at a refinery near Dallas, Texas.[4] There is a well-established, low-level risk that such weapons will be used in the future, although there is no way to predict the frequency of such attacks, their scale, potential success, or lethality.

There is a wide range of countries involved in the development of chemical weapons. Table 4.3 provides a recent unclassified overview of chemical weapons activities by nation. It is, however, only a partial list. The U.S. intelligence community is tracking a total of approximately twenty-five nations that are believed to be carrying out some form of state-sponsored chemical and/or biological weapons development. At least two foreign terrorist groups are believed to have active chemical and biological weapons efforts.

Effective planning for homeland defense must consider the fact that the United States currently has limited ability to properly characterize the impact of chemical weapons in any form of attack. Many terrorist uses of chemical weapons will not be inherently more lethal or more painful than the use of explosives. At the same time, it must consider the risk that chemical attacks can produce much larger levels of damage and virtually any use of such weapons will have a far different psychological impact. Chemical weapons are weapons of terror and intimidation as well as a means of producing casualties and physical destruction.

Table 4.2
The Comparative Effects of Biological, Chemical, and Nuclear Weapons Delivered against a Typical Urban Target

*Using missile warheads*: Assumes one Scud-sized warhead with a maximum payload of 1,000 kilograms. The study assumes that the biological agent would not make maximum use of this payload capability because this is inefficient. It is unclear this is realistic.

| | Area Covered in Square Kilometers | Deaths Assuming 3,000–10,000 people Per Square Kilometer |
|---|---|---|
| *Chemical*: 300 kilograms of sarin nerve gas with a density of 70 milligrams per cubic meter | 0.22 | 60–200 |
| *Biological*: 30 kilograms of anthrax spores with a density of 0.1 milligram per cubic meter | 10.00 | 30,000–100,000 |
| *Nuclear*: One 12.5-kiloton nuclear device achieving 5 pounds per cubic inch of overpressure | 7.80 | 23,000–80,000 |
| One 1-megaton hydrogen bomb | 190.00 | 570,000–1,900,000 |

*Using one aircraft delivering 1,000 kilograms of sarin nerve gas or 100 kilograms of anthrax spores:* Assumes the aircraft flies in a straight line over the target at optimal altitude and dispensing the agent as an aerosol. The study assumes that the biological agent would not make maximum use of this payload capability because this is inefficient. It is unclear whether this is realistic.

| | Area Covered in Square Kilometers | Deaths Assuming 3,000–10,000 people Per Square Kilometer |
|---|---|---|
| *Clear sunny day, light breeze:* | | |
| Sarin nerve gas | 0.74 | 300–700 |
| Anthrax spores | 46.00 | 130,000–460,000 |
| *Overcast day or night, moderate wind:* | | |
| Sarin nerve gas | 0.80 | 400–800 |
| Anthrax spores | 140.00 | 420,000–1,400,000 |
| *Clear calm night:* | | |
| Sarin nerve gas | 7.80 | 3,000–8,000 |
| Anthrax spores | 300.00 | 1,000,000–3,000,000 |

*Source:* Adapted by Anthony H. Cordesman from Office of Technology Assessment, *Proliferation of Weapons of Mass Destruction: Assessing the Risks*, US Congress OTA-ISC-559, Washington, D.C. (August 1993), 53–54.

Table 4.3
U.S. Department of Defense Estimate of Potential National Threats Involving Chemical Weapons

China

Beijing is believed to have an advanced chemical warfare program including research and development, production, and weaponization capabilities. China's chemical industry has the capability to produce many chemicals, some of which have been sought by states trying to develop a chemical warfare capability. Foreign sales of such chemicals have been a source of foreign exchange for China. The Chinese government has imposed restrictions on the sale of some chemical precursors and its enforcement activities generally have yielded mixed results. While China claims it possesses no chemical agent inventory, it is believed to possess a moderate inventory of traditional agents. It has a wide variety of potential delivery systems for chemical agents, including cannon artillery, multiple rocket launchers, mortars, land mines, aerial bombs, SRBMs, and MRBMs.

Chinese military forces most likely have a good understanding of chemical warfare doctrine, and its forces routinely conduct defensive chemical warfare training. Even though China has ratified the CWC, made its declaration, and subjected its declared chemical weapons facilities to inspections, we believe that Beijing has not acknowledged the full extent of its chemical weapons program.

India

India is an original signatory to the CWC. In June 1997, it acknowledged that it had a dedicated chemical warfare production program. This was the first time India had publicly admitted that it had a chemical warfare effort. India also stated that all related facilities would be open for inspection, as called for in the CWC, and subsequently, it has hosted all required CWC inspections. While India has made a commitment to destroy its chemical weapons, its extensive and well-developed chemical industry will continue to be capable of producing a wide variety of chemical agent precursors should the government change its policy. In the past, Indian firms have exported a wide array of chemical products, including Australia Group–controlled items, to several countries of proliferation concern in the Middle East. (Australia Group–controlled items include specific chemical agent precursors, microorganisms with biological warfare applications, and dual-use equipment that can be used in chemical or biological warfare programs.) Indian companies could continue to be a source of dual-use chemicals to countries of proliferation concern.

Iran

Iran has acceded to the Chemical Weapons Convention (CWC) and in a May 1998 session of the CWC Conference of the States Parties, Tehran, for the first time, acknowledged the existence of a past chemical weapons program. Iran admitted developing a chemical warfare program during the latter stages of the Iran-Iraq war as a "deterrent" against Iraq's use of chemical agents against Iran. Moreover, Tehran claimed that after the 1988 cease-fire, it "terminated" its program. However, Iran has yet to acknowledge that it, too, used chemical weapons during the Iran-Iraq War.

Table 4.3 (continued)

---

Nevertheless, Iran has continued its efforts to seek production technology, expertise, and precursor chemicals from entities in Russia and China that could be used to create a more advanced and self-sufficient chemical warfare infrastructure. As Iran's program moves closer to self-sufficiency, the potential will increase for Iran to export dual-use chemicals and related equipment and technologies to other countries of proliferation concern. In the past, Tehran has manufactured and stockpiled blister, blood, and choking chemical agents, and weaponized some of these agents into artillery shells, mortars, rockets, and aerial bombs. It also is believed to be conducting research on nerve agents. Iran could employ these agents during a future conflict in the region. Lastly, Iran's training, especially for its naval and ground forces, indicates that it is planning to operate in a contaminated environment.

### Iraq

Since the Gulf War, Baghdad has rebuilt key portions of its industrial and chemical production infrastructure; it has not become a state party to the CWC. Some of Iraq's facilities could be converted fairly quickly to production of chemical warfare agents. Following Operation Desert Fox, Baghdad again instituted a rapid reconstruction effort on those facilities to include former dual-use chemical warfare-associated production facilities, destroyed by U.S. bombing. In 1999, Iraq may have begun installing or repairing dual-use equipment at these and other chemical warfare-related facilities. Previously, Iraq was known to have produced and stockpiled mustard, tabun, sarin, and VX, some of which likely remain hidden. It is likely that an additional quantity of various precursor chemicals also remains hidden.

In late 1998, UNSCOM reported to the UN Security Council that Iraq continued to withhold information related to its chemical program. UNSCOM cited an example where Baghdad seized from inspectors a document discovered by UNSCOM inspectors, which indicated that Iraq had not consumed as many chemical munitions during the Iran-Iraq War as had been declared previously by Baghdad. This document suggests that Iraq may have an additional 6,000 chemical munitions hidden. Similarly, UNSCOM discovery in 1998 of evidence of VX in Iraqi missile warheads showed that Iraq had lied to the international community for seven years when it repeatedly said that it had never weaponized VX.

Iraq retains the expertise, once a decision is made, to resume chemical agent production within a few weeks or months, depending on the type of agent. However, foreign assistance, whether commercial procurement of dual-use technology, key infrastructure, or other aid, will be necessary to completely restore Iraq's chemical agent production capabilities to pre–Desert Storm levels. Iraqi doctrine for the use of chemical weapons evolved during the Iran-Iraq War, and was fully incorporated into Iraqi offensive operations by the end of the war in 1988. During different stages of that war, Iraq used aerial bombs, artillery, rocket launchers, tactical rockets, and sprayers mounted in helicopters to deliver agents against Iranian forces. It also used chemical agents against Kurdish elements of its own civilian population in 1988.

continued

Table 4.3 (continued)

---

## Libya

Libya has made progress with its chemical warfare effort. However, it remains heavily dependent on foreign suppliers for precursor chemicals, mechanical and technical expertise, and chemical warfare-related equipment. From 1992 to 1999, UN sanctions continued to limit the type and amount of support Tripoli receives from abroad. However, following the suspension of UN sanctions in April 1999, Libya wasted no time in reestablishing contacts with foreign sources of expertise, parts, and precursor chemicals for its program. Clearly, Tripoli has not given up its goal of reestablishing its offensive chemical warfare ability and continues to pursue an indigenous chemical warfare production capability.

Prior to 1990, Libya produced about 100 tons of chemical agents—mustard and some nerve agent—at a chemical facility at Rabta. However, it ceased production there in 1990 due to intense international media attention and the possibility of military intervention, and fabricated a fire to make the Rabta facility appear to have been seriously damaged. Libya maintains that the facility is a pharmaceutical production plant and announced in September 1995 that it was reopening the Rabta pharmaceutical facility. Although production of chemical agents has been halted, the Rabta facility remains part of the Libyan chemical weapons program, and future agent production cannot be ruled out. After 1990, the Libyans shifted their efforts to trying to build a large underground chemical production facility at Tarhunah. However, the pace of activity there has slowed, probably due to increased international attention. The Libyans claim that the Tarhunah tunnel site is a part of the Great Man-made River Project, a nationwide irrigation effort. Libya has not become a state party to the CWC.

## North Korea

Like its biological warfare effort, we believe North Korea has had a long-standing chemical warfare program. North Korea's chemical warfare capabilities include the ability to produce bulk quantities of nerve, blister, choking, and blood agents, using its sizeable, although aging, chemical industry. We believe it possesses a sizeable stockpile of these agents and weapons, which it could employ should there be renewed fighting on the Korean peninsula.

North Korea is believed to be capable of weaponizing such stocks for a variety of delivery means. These would include not only ballistic missiles, but also artillery and aircraft, and possibly unconventional means. In fact, the United States believes that North Korea has some long-range artillery deployed along the demilitarized zone (DMZ) and ballistic missiles, some of which could deliver chemical warfare agents against forward-based U.S. and allied forces, as well as against rear-area targets. North Korean forces are prepared to operate in a contaminated environment; they train regularly in chemical defense operations and are taught that South Korean and U.S. forces will employ chemical munitions. North Korea has not signed CWC, nor it is expected to do so in the near future.

Table 4.3 (continued)

---

### Pakistan

Pakistan ratified the CWC in October 1997 and did not declare any chemical agent production or development. Pakistan has imported a number of dual-use chemicals that can be used to make chemical agents. These chemicals also have commercial uses and Pakistan is working towards establishing a viable commercial chemical industry capable of producing a variety of chemicals, some of which could be used to make chemical agents. Chemical agent delivery methods available to Pakistan include missiles, artillery, and aerial bombs.

### Russia

Moscow has acknowledged the world's largest stockpile of chemical agents of 40,000 metric tons of agent. The Russian chemical warfare agent inventory consists of a comprehensive array of blister, choking, and nerve agents in weapons and stored in bulk. These agents can be employed by tube and rocket artillery, bombs, spray tanks, and SRBM warheads. In addition, since 1992, Russian scientists familiar with Moscow's chemical warfare development program have been publicizing information on a new generation of agents, sometimes referred to as "Novichoks." These scientists report that these compounds, some of which are binaries, were designed to circumvent the CWC and to defeat Western detection and protection measures. Furthermore, it is claimed that their production can be hidden within commercial chemical plants. There is concern that the technology to produce these compounds might be acquired by other countries.

As a state party to the CWC, Russia is obligated to declare and destroy its chemical weapons stockpile and to forego the development, production, and possession of chemical weapons. However, we believe that the Russians probably have not divulged the full extent of their chemical agent and weapon inventory. Destruction facilities are being planned at Shchuch'ye and Gornyy, two of the seven declared storage locations for the Russian chemical warfare stockpile; these efforts are being funded in large part by foreign assistance programs.

Nevertheless, Russia admitted it could not meet its first obligation to destroy one percent of its stockpile by April 2000. Subsequently, the Organization for the Prohibition of Chemical Weapons (OPCW) granted Russia an extension until April 2002, but with the stipulation that it must also meet 20 percent destruction deadline by the same date, as called for under the CWC. However, international experts agree that it will be extremely difficult for Russia to destroy its huge chemical arsenal by 2007 as mandated by the CWC. Even if Russia were to be granted a five-year extension by the OPCW, it is unlikely that Russia's declared stockpile will be completely destroyed because of serious technical, ecological, financial, and political problems.

### Syria

Syria is not a state party to the CWC and has had a chemical warfare program for many years, although it has never used chemical agents in a conflict. Damascus already has a stockpile of the nerve agent sarin that can be delivered by aircraft or

continued

**Table 4.3** (continued)

---

ballistic missiles. Additionally, Syria is trying to develop the more toxic and persistent nerve agent VX. In the future, Syria can be expected to continue to improve its chemical agent production and storage infrastructure. Damascus remains dependent on foreign sources for key elements of its chemical warfare program, including pre-cursor chemicals and key production equipment. For example, during 1999, Syria sought chemical warfare-related precursors and expertise from foreign sources.

**Sudan**
Sudan has been interested in acquiring a chemical warfare capability since the 1980s and has sought assistance from a number of countries with chemical warfare programs. We believe that Iraq, in particular, has provided technical expertise to Khartoum. In addition, the finding of a known VX precursor chemical near a pharmaceutical facility in Khartoum suggests that Sudan may be pursuing a more advanced chemical warfare capability. Sudan acceded to the CWC in 1999, although allegations of Sudanese chemical warfare use against rebels in southern Sudan have persisted. These, and prior allegations of chemical warfare use, have not been confirmed. Further, Khartoum's desire to present a more moderate image and alleviate its international isolation will cause Sudan to proceed with its chemical warfare program with caution.

---

*Source*: Adapted by Anthony H. Cordesman from Office of the Secretary of Defense, *Proliferation and Response* (Washington, D.C.: U.S. Department of Defense, January 2001).

### The Impact and Variety of Possible Chemical Weapons

Experts like the U.S. Centers for Disease Control (CDC) have found that the United States may face a wide range of threats from different types of chemical weapons and toxic agents, many of which are not normally considered to be weapons. A CDC study in April 2000 noted that the chemical agents that might be used by terrorists range from sophisticated military agents to toxic chemicals commonly used in industry. The criteria it suggested for determining priority chemical agents include:

- chemical agents already known to be used as weaponry;
- availability of chemical agents to potential terrorists;
- chemical agents likely to cause major morbidity or mortality;
- potential of agents for causing public panic and social disruption; and
- agents that require special action for public health preparedness.[5]

The CDC study listed several categories of chemical agents as presenting enough of a threat to require active public health planning. These included nerve agents, such as tabun (ethyl N, N-dimethylphosphoramido-cyanidate), sarin (isopropyl methylphosphanofluoridate), soman (pinacolyl methyl phosphonofluoridate), GF (cyclohexylmethylphosphonofluoridate), and VX (o-ethyl-[S]-[2-diisopropylaminoethyl]-methylphosphonothiolate). They included blood agents such as hydrogen cyanide and cyanogen chloride; and blister agents such as lewisite (an aliphatic arsenic compound, 2-chlorovinyldichloroarsine), nitrogen and sulfur mustards, and phosgene oxime. They also included pulmonary agents like phosgene, chlorine, and vinyl chloride; and incapacitating agents like BZ (3-quinuclidinyl benzilate).

Other agents were more commercial in character. They included heavy metals like arsenic, lead, and mercury, and volatile toxins like benzene, chloroform, and trihalomethanes. Other types of agents included explosive nitro compounds and oxidizers, such as ammonium nitrate combined with fuel oil. They included pulmonary agents like phosgene, chlorine, and vinyl chloride; persistent and nonpersistent pesticides; and dioxins, furans, and polychlorinated biphenyls. They included flammable industrial gases and liquids like gasoline and propane; and poison industrial gases, liquids, and solids, like the cyanides and nitriles. Finally, they included corrosive industrial acids and bases like nitric and sulfuric acid.

Many of the items on this list are widely available on the U.S. market and include commercial organo-phospates and parathion. The military list of possible agents is much longer and includes additional toxic smokes, herbicides, flame materials, and toxic industrial compounds.[6] As a result, it is hardly surprising that the CDC study also noted that there was no way to predict precisely what chemicals might be used, particularly in low-level attacks. This created major problems for response planning:

> Because of the hundreds of new chemicals introduced internationally each month, treating exposed persons by clinical syndrome rather than by specific agent is more useful for public health planning and emergency medical response purposes. Public health agencies and first responders must render the most aggressive, timely, and clinically relevant treatment possible by using treatment modalities based on syndromic categories (e.g., burns and trauma, cardiorespiratory failure, neurologic damage, and shock). These activities must be linked with authorities responsible for environmental sampling and decontamination.

### The Probable Lethality and Effectiveness of Chemical Attacks

Just as it is easy to underestimate the importance of conventional explosives, it is easy to exaggerate the lethality of most chemical weapons. Many forms of lower-level attacks using chemical weapons might do no more damage than conventional weapons. For example, the World Trade Center bombing killed six and injured over one thousand, and could easily have killed hundreds if the bomb had been better placed.[7] Large high-explosive weapons can easily be equal to chemical and radiological weapons as "weapons of mass destruction."

It is also an illusion that the effects of chemical weapons are always radically worse or more repellent than the damage done conventional weapons. No one who has actually visited a battlefield and seen anyone with a fragmentation wound in the stomach and then seen a prisoner affected by a moderate dose of mustard gas is going to accept for a second that one casualty is somehow worse than another.[8]

The characteristics of a representative range of chemical weapons are summarized in Parts 1 to 3 of Chart 4.1, along with a rough comparison of their lethality to the lethality of a thousand-pound bomb. It should again be noted that the relatively high lethality estimates in Part 1 are derived from extremely questionable military literature, and that there has been little historical correlation between such theoretical lethality models and real-world casualties.[9]

While there are good models, as well as bad, much of the military effects data on chemical weapons in the unclassified literature is based on theoretical models whose inherent validity is suspect and do not track with either the historical data on the use of chemical weapons in World War I or Iraq's use of chemical weapons in the Iran-Iraq War. There are also extremely sharp variations in such estimates. Some estimates give nerve gas near nuclear lethalities, while others indicate that the effects could be highly localized and produce random concentrations with much more limited numbers of deaths.[10]

In many cases, the results of limited primate testing is generalized on extraordinarily tenuous grounds, and then scaled-up using models of how weaponized chemical vapors are deposited that ignore temperature, wind, and heat conditions and assume optimal scattering of the vapor evenly over large areas. These same problems affect the lethality modeling of biological and nuclear weapons as well as chemical weapons, but the higher estimates of lethality in such chemical weapons effects modeling seems uniquely exaggerated. This is particularly true when the input data are drawn from unclassified estimates that are ultimately drawn from Soviet literature on missile warhead behavior, some of which seems to be little more than analytic nonsense.

The December 15, 1999 report of the Gilmore Commission provides what seems to be a more accurate picture of the probable lethality of chemical attacks on the U.S. homeland:

> Developing a means to disseminate sarin effectively is likely to prove a far greater challenge to terrorists than is producing the agent itself. Although sarin's high volatility greatly simplifies weaponization, terrorists who may seek to cause mass casualties will need a fairly sophisticated means of spreading the agent in sufficiently large quantities over their intended target area.

Chart 4.1—Part 1
The Relative Killing Effect of Chemical Weapons under Different Conditions
of Aerosol Delivery (Numbers of dead from delivery of 1,000 kilograms)

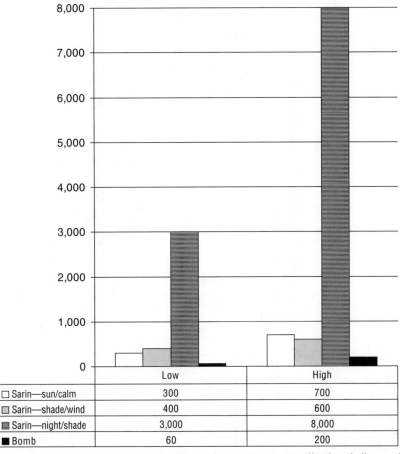

|  | Low | High |
|---|---|---|
| ☐ Sarin—sun/calm | 300 | 700 |
| ▨ Sarin—shade/wind | 400 | 600 |
| ▥ Sarin—night/shade | 3,000 | 8,000 |
| ■ Bomb | 60 | 200 |

*Sources:* Adapted by Anthony H. Cordesman from Victor A. Utgoff, *The Challenge of
Chemical Weapons* (New York: St. Martin's, 1991), 238–242; and Office of Technology
Assessment, *Proliferation of Weapons of Mass Destruction: Assessing the Risks*, U.S. Con-
gress OTA-ISC-559, Washington, D.C., August 1993, 56–57.

For wide coverage in an open area, such as a city, an airplane equipped with
a suitable industrial or crop sprayer could be a satisfactory mechanism for
dissemination. Alternatively, terrorists could equip a truck and drive through
the target area, taking care, of course, to ensure that its passengers are properly sealed off from the chemical agent. Temperature, wind speed, inversion
conditions, and other meteorological factors, however, would likely determine

**Chart 4.1—Part 2**
**The Relative Casualty Effect of Chemical Weapons under Military Conditions**
(Percent of Casualties)

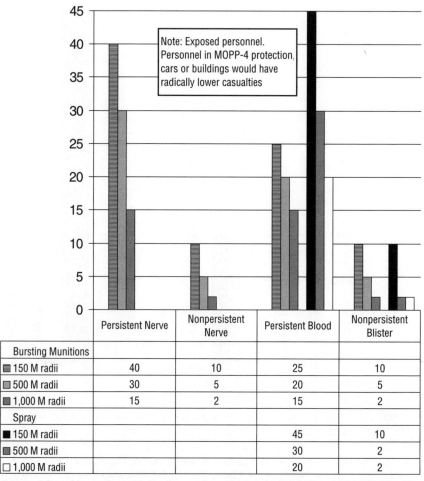

Note: Exposed personnel. Personnel in MOPP-4 protection, cars or buildings would have radically lower casualties

| | Persistent Nerve | Nonpersistent Nerve | Persistent Blood | Nonpersistent Blister |
|---|---|---|---|---|
| Bursting Munitions | | | | |
| 150 M radii | 40 | 10 | 25 | 10 |
| 500 M radii | 30 | 5 | 20 | 5 |
| 1,000 M radii | 15 | 2 | 15 | 2 |
| Spray | | | | |
| 150 M radii | | | 45 | 10 |
| 500 M radii | | | 30 | 2 |
| 1,000 M radii | | | 20 | 2 |

*Source*: Adapted by Anthony H. Cordesman from Table 1-3 of FM-37 and USACHPPM, *The Medical NBC Battlebook*, USACHPPM Technical Guide 244, 5–7.

the effectiveness of any attack. For example, as sarin and other chemical agents are exposed to the environment, they tend to be dispersed by the wind, which necessitates the use of large amounts of material to ensure that a given target receives a sufficiently high dose. In fact, the need to produce and disperse sufficiently large amounts of sarin or other chemical agents to achieve the mass-casualty levels that may be sought by terrorists arguably drawn to chemical weapons in the first place ironically may be the biggest disincentive for their use.

**Chart 4.1—Part 3**
**Exclusion Areas for Release from Bulk Tank of Hazardous Chemicals (quantity in tons/ exclusion area in kilometers)**

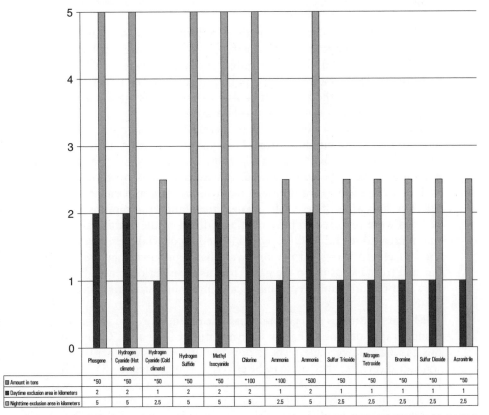

| | Phosgene | Hydrogen Cyanide (Hot climate) | Hydrogen Cyanide (Cold climate) | Hydrogen Sulfide | Methyl Isocyanide | Chlorine | Ammonia | Ammonia | Sulfur Trioxide | Nitrogen Tetroxide | Bromine | Sulfur Dioxide | Acronitrle |
|---|---|---|---|---|---|---|---|---|---|---|---|---|---|
| Amount in tons | *50 | *50 | *50 | *50 | *50 | *100 | *100 | *500 | *50 | *50 | *50 | *50 | *50 |
| Daytime exclusion area in kilometers | 2 | 2 | 1 | 2 | 2 | 2 | 1 | 2 | 1 | 1 | 1 | 1 | 1 |
| Nighttime exclusion area in kilometers | 5 | 5 | 2.5 | 5 | 5 | 5 | 2.5 | 5 | 2.5 | 2.5 | 2.5 | 2.5 | 2.5 |

*Source*: Adapted by Anthony H. Cordesman from JP 3-11 (Draft); and USACHPPM, *The Medical NBC Battlebook*, USACHPPM Technical Guide 244, 5–7.

A U.S. Defense Department model illustrates the problem. Releasing ten kilograms (22 pounds) of sarin into the open air under favorable weather conditions covers about one-hundredth of a square kilometer with lethal effects. Since population densities in U.S. urban areas are typically around 5,000 people per square kilometer, such an attack would kill about 50 people.

Releasing 100 kilograms (220 pounds) of sarin into the open air affects about ten times as much area and therefore would kill approximately 500 people. Releasing 1,000 kilograms (2,200 pounds) into the open air would cover several square kilometers, killing about 10,000 people. Thus, only in an open-air attack using amounts approaching 1,000 kilograms of sarin would the effects become distinctly greater than that attainable by such traditional terrorist means as conventional explosives. One way for terrorists to overcome these problems would be to carry out an attack in an enclosed space, such as a domed stadium, office building, or subway system.[11]

The effectiveness data used by the U.S. Army are also relatively conservative and are summarized in Table 4.4. It is clear, however, that such data are highly nominal and provide only a tenuous basis for predicting casualty effects. The same is true of a potential sabotage or terrorist release of toxic chemicals of the kind that is also shown in this table. Only nominal area of evacuation—not lethality—data are available.

Such estimates do not mean that chemical attacks could not be highly lethal under some circumstances. For example, in 1984 an incident took place in Bhopal, India, where a disgruntled employee at a pesticide plant precipitated an explosion in one of the storage tanks by adding water to it. This led to the massive release of methylisocyanate and the noxious fumes affected thousands of people living near the plant. Four months later, 1,430 persons were reported to have died as a direct result of the leak—a figure that increased to the 3,800 reported by Indian officials seven years later. A total of eleven thousand persons were listed as having been disabled or harmed from exposure to the gas. This case was serious enough to lead to laws that require public reporting on all similar industrial risks in the United States.

Military estimates also generally assume prompt medical action and some assume rapid decontamination or evacuation of the area. Chemical weapons can have lingering effects as poisons, and act as contact or food poisons for days after they cease to be effective as mass agents. BVX, HD, HN, L, and HL are all persistent agents that can remain lethal for weeks.[12] Effective and timely decontamination could well be impossible. Casualty recognition can be difficult with some weapons where there is either a psychomimetic agent or a quiescent period in terms of symptoms. In some cases, the use of antidotes like Atropine could create medical problems of their own. In others, severe exposure can require up to a week of intensive treatment for nerve gas and months to years for inhaled blistering agents.[13]

Historically, however, the preattack estimates of chemical weapon lethality have borne no relation to either actual lethality in combat or the area actually covered. After more than five years of using chemical weapons, for example, the Iraqis still found that even nerve gas was often more useful in area denial, forcing rapid withdrawals, or in creating panic than as a killing mechanism per se.[14] The tendency to estimate lethality in terms of neat wind-borne ellipses or "plumes" has also confused the lethality issue. Under most real-world conditions, it is likely that small chemical weapons would have limited areas of lethality, and that wide-area coverage would require far larger amounts of the agent than are likely to be feasible in state covert, proxy, terrorist, or extremist attacks on the U.S. homeland.

Table 4.4
Key Chemical Weapons

---

NERVE AGENTS: Agents that quickly disrupt the nervous system by binding to enzymes critical to nerve functions, causing convulsions and/or paralysis. Must be ingested, inhaled, and absorbed through the skin. Very low doses cause a running nose, contraction of the pupil of the eye, and difficulty in visual coordination. Moderate doses constrict the bronchi and cause a feeling of pressure in the chest, and weaken the skeletal muscles and cause filibration. Large doses cause death by respiratory or heart failure. Can be absorbed through inhalation or skin contact. Reaction normally occurs in 1–2 minutes. Death from lethal doses occurs within minutes, but artificial respiration can help and atropine and the oximes act as antidotes. The most toxic nerve agents kill with a dosage of only 10 milligrams per minute per cubic meter, versus 400 for less lethal gases. Recovery is normally quick, if it occurs at all, but permanent brain damage can occur:

Tabun (GA)
Sarin (GB)—nearly as volatile as water and delivered by air. A dose of 5 mg/min/m$^3$ produces casualties, a respiratory dose of 100 mg/min/m$^3$ is lethal. Lethality lasts 1–2 days.
Soman (GD)
GF
VR-55 (improved soman)—a thick, oily substance which persists for some time.
VK/VX—a persistent agent roughly as heavy as fuel oil. A dose of 0.5 mg/min/m$^3$ produces casualties, a respiratory dose of 10 mg/min/m$^3$ is lethal. Lethality lasts 1–16 weeks.

BLISTER AGENTS: Cell poisons that destroy skin and tissue, cause blindness upon contact with the eyes, and which can result in fatal respiratory damage. Can be colorless or black oily droplets. Can be absorbed through inhalation or skin contact. Serious internal damage if inhaled. Penetrates ordinary clothing. Some have delayed and some have immediate action. Actual blistering normally takes hours to days, but effects on the eyes are much more rapid. Mustard gas is a typical blister agent and exposure of concentrations of a few milligrams per meter over several hours generally at least causes blisters and swollen eyes. When the liquid falls onto the skin or eyes it has the effect of second or third degree burns. It can blind and cause damage to the lungs leading to pneumonia. Severe exposure causes general intoxication similar to radiation sickness. HD and HN persist up to 12 hours. L, HL, and CX persist for 1–2 hours. Short of prevention of exposure, the only treatment is to wash the eyes, decontaminate the skin, and treat the resulting damage like burns:

Sulfur Mustard (H or HD)—adose of 100 mg/min/m$^3$ produces casualties, a dose of 1,500 mg/min/m$^3$ is lethal. Residual lethality lasts 2–8 weeks.
Distilled Mustard (DM)
Nitrogen Mustard (HN)
Lewisite (L)
Phosgene Oxime (CX)
Mustard Lewisite (HL)

continued

Table 4.4 (continued)

CHOKING AGENTS: Agents that cause the blood vessels in the lungs to hemorrhage, and fluid to build up, until the victim chokes or drowns in his or her own fluids (pulmonary edema). Provide quick warning though smell or lung irritation. Can be absorbed through inhalation. Immediate to delayed action. The only treatment is inhalation of oxygen and rest. Symptoms emerge in periods after exposure of seconds up to 3 hours:

> Phosgene (CG)
> Diphosgene (DP)
> PS Chloropicrin
> Chlorine Gas

BLOOD AGENTS: Kill through inhalation. Provide little warning except for headache, nausea, and vertigo. Interferes with use of oxygen at the cellular level. CK also irritates the lungs and eyes. Rapid action and exposure either kills by inhibiting cell respiration or it does not—casualties will either die within seconds to minutes of exposure or recover in fresh air. Most gas masks have severe problems in providing effective protection against blood agents:

> Hydrogen Cyanide (AC)—a dose of 2,000 mg/min/m$^3$ produces casualties, a respiratory dose of 5,000 mg/min/m$^3$ is lethal. Lethality lasts 1–4 hours.
> Cyanogen Chloride (CK)—a dose of 7,000 mg/min/m$^3$ produces casualties, a respiratory dose of 11,000 mg/min/m$^3$ is lethal. Lethality lasts 15 minutes to 1 hour.

TOXINS: Biological poisons causing neuromuscular paralysis after exposure of hours or days. Formed in food or cultures by the bacterium clostridium Botulinum. Produces highly fatal poisoning characterized by general weakness, headache, dizziness, double vision and dilation of the pupils, paralysis of muscles, and problems in speech. Death is usually by respiratory failure. Antitoxin therapy has limited value, but treatment is mainly supportive:

> Botulin toxin (A)—six distinct types, of which four are known to be fatal to man. An oral dose of 0.001 mg is lethal. A respiratory dose of 0.02 mg/min/m$^3$ is also lethal.

DEVELOPMENTAL WEAPONS: A new generation of chemical weapons is under development. The only publicized agent is perfluoroisobutene (PFIB), which is an extremely toxic, odorless, and invisible substance produced when PFIB (Teflon) is subjected to extreme heat under special conditions. It causes pulmonary edema or dry-land drowning when the lungs fill with fluid. Short exposure disables and small concentrations cause delayed death. Activated charcoal and most existing protection equipment offer no defense. Some sources refer to "third" and "fourth" generation nerve gasses, but no technical literature seems to be available.

CONTROL AGENTS: Agents which produce temporary irritating or disabling effects when in contact with the eyes or inhaled. They cause flow of tears and irritation of upper respiratory tract and skin. They can cause nausea and vomiting:

**Table 4.4 (continued)**

---

can cause serious illness or death when used in confined spaces. CS is the least toxic gas, followed by CN and DM. Symptoms can be treated by washing of the eyes and/or removal from the area. Exposure to CS, CN, and DM produces immediate symptoms. Staphylococcus produces symptoms in 30 minutes to 4 hours, and recovery takes 24–48 hours. Treatment of Staphylococcus is largely supportive:

> Tear
> Chlororacetophenone (CN)
> O-Chlorobenzyl-malononitrile (CS)
> Adamsite (DM)
> Staphylococcus

INCAPACITATING AGENTS: Agents which normally cause short term illness, psychoactive effects (delirium and hallucinations). Can be absorbed through inhalation or skin contact. The psychoactive gases and drugs produce unpredictable effects, particularly in the sick, small children, elderly, and individuals who already are mentally ill. In rare cases they kill. In others, they produce a permanent psychotic condition. Many produce dry skin, irregular heart beat, urinary retention, constipation, drowsiness, and a rise in body temperature, plus occasional maniacal behavior. A single dose of 0.1 to 0.2 milligrams of LSD-25 will produce profound mental disturbance within a half hour that lasts 10 hours. The lethal dose is 100 to 200 milligrams:

> BZ
> LSD
> LSD Based BZ
> Mescaline
> Psilocybin
> Benzilates

---

One "wild card" that might change this situation is the potential existence of the so-called fourth-generation chemical weapons. According to some reports, Russia developed far more lethal chemical weapons during the Cold War and brought them to production readiness. At least some experts believe that it is possible that far more lethal chemical weapons exist than are listed in unclassified studies. Like many reports of advanced biological weapons, however, it is unclear that such agents really exist and there is no way to assess what states or terrorist/extremist movements might acquire them.

### Methods of Delivery

Most chemical weapons are not easy to handle or deliver and even nerve gas would have to be used in large amounts to achieve high levels of coverage and lethality. Obtaining suitable delivery systems can be a real problem, although covert attacks can be conducted from fixed locations in an urban area. Suitable dual-use delivery systems are readily available in the form of crop duster aircraft and simple spray generators that can be readily adapted for the delivery of a variety of agents.

At the same time, the quantities of chemical agent required to conduct low-level attacks are relatively small when compared to industrial production of similar commercial chemicals, which pose problems for detection. Terrorists could employ chemical weapons agents in a variety of means utilizing simple containers such as glass bottles. The lethality of any given chemical weapon would also increase strikingly if it was used in a closed environment like an office building with a forced air system, or disseminated under ideal conditions in an urban environment.

Lethality may also be only one consideration in choosing the means of delivery for a covert or chemical terrorist attack. Much would depend on the perceptions of the attacker of the full range of postattack impacts of using a chemical weapon. It is far from clear, for example, that civilians would ever accept a building as safe where persistent chemical agents had been used, regardless of the success of contamination efforts. The Persian Gulf War syndrome and Agent Orange are one thing in the context of U.S. military serving over seas; chemical attacks are quite another in the context of civilians living in America.

As is the case of virtually all forms of attack on the U.S. homeland, the psychological and political impact of a given strike would also be as important as the resulting physical damage or body count. An attack on the U.S. Capitol with minor casualties would have far more symbolic and political impact than a high-casualty attack on a hotel. Attacks on targets with high-media profiles and live new coverage can be important almost regardless of their effectiveness. The visible physical symptoms of chemical weapons, their horrifying reputation, and their alien nature will be a critical "effect," although many forms of fragmentation wounds cause at least as much suffering in practice.

### Detection and Interception

Chemical weapons can impose serious problems in terms of detection. The flow of people and goods across the Canadian, Mexican, Alaskan, and Hawaiian borders and between the East and West Coast is so intense, it is unclear that any detection system would find the amounts used in covert, proxy, and extremist/terrorist attacks—even assuming that truly cost-effective and reliable detection devices become readily available and could cover binary or trinary ingredients. Even if reliable, and low-cost detectors and systems become readily available—as some experts assume—this does not mean that they will be able to cover enough area to cope with the volume of commercial shipping into the United States and provide a reliable method of detection and defense. Any gaps in coverage are likely to be openly documented, and the details of U.S. detection systems are likely to become part of the open literature—giving foreign attackers much of the information they need.

The domestic production of weapons will probably only be detectable by receiving a warning through human intelligence or by tracing the flow of key equipment and ingredients, which may be legally and physically impossible. Once a weapon is actually used, detection may also be too late. This would certainly be true in the case of an attack exploiting a closed-air system, and might well be true of a modified drone or crop sprayer. Even if an antidote or safe area is available, it is unclear that anyone would have the time and capacity to react to a first use or that defense would be affordable.

The problems in developing effective interception, defense, and response measures can be compounded by using more than one group of attackers and by mixing agents that require different kinds of protection and decontamination. They can be compounded by the use of persistent agents, near simultaneous attacks in a number of areas, and sequential attacks designed to target those who respond to initial attacks. Furthermore, it is far from clear whether the detection and sensor systems necessary to cover entire urban areas and provide detection and characterization of an attack will be cost-effective.

### Acquiring Chemical Weapons

Many experts believe that most attackers will find it difficult to obtain the necessary chemical weapons, in the necessary amounts, and to develop an effective delivery system or device.[15] Acquiring chemical agents would not be a problem for most governments, but the ease with which most domestic or foreign terrorists can obtain or manufacture such weapons has sometimes been exaggerated. The December 1999 report by the Gilmore Commission makes the following points:

> It has sometimes been claimed that producing sarin and other nerve agents is a relatively easy process, to the extent, according to one authority, that "ball-point pen ink is only one chemical step removed."[16] While sarin may be less complicated to synthesize than other nerve agents, the expertise required to produce it should not, however, be underestimated. The safety challenges involved would, at a minimum, require skill, training, and special equipment to overcome. For this reason, the level of competency required for producing sophisticated chemical nerve agents, including sarin, will likely be on the order of a graduate degree in organic chemistry and/or actual experience as an organic chemist—not simply a knowledge of college-level chemistry, as is sometimes alleged.[17]

A GAO analysis of the issue found that,

Experts from the scientific, intelligence, and law enforcement communities we spoke with agreed that toxic industrial chemicals can cause mass casualties and require little, if any, expertise or sophisticated methods. Generally, toxic industrial chemicals can be bought on the commercial market or stolen, thus avoiding the need to manufacture them. Chlorine, phosgene, and hydrogen cyanide are examples of toxic industrial chemicals. DOD classified further details concerning the use of toxic industrial chemicals.

Experts believe that unlike toxic industrial chemicals, for various reasons, most G and V chemical nerve agents are technically challenging for terrorists to acquire, manufacture, and produce. Examples of the G-series nerve agents are tabun (GA), sarin (GB), and soman (GD). VX is an example of a V-series nerve agent. According to chemical experts, developing nerve agents requires synthesis of multiple precursor chemicals. On the basis of our review of a technical report, we concluded that some 11 steps in the production process are difficult and hazardous. Although tabun production is relatively easy, containment of a highly toxic gas (hydrogen cyanide) is a technical challenge. Production of sarin, soman, and VX requires the use of high temperatures and generates corrosive and dangerous by-products. Moreover, careful temperature control, cooling of the vessel, heating to complete chemical reactions, and distillation could be technically unfeasible for terrorists without a sophisticated laboratory infrastructure. Blister chemical agents such as sulfur mustard, nitrogen mustard, and lewisite can be manufactured with ease or with only moderate difficulty. However, experts told us that buying large quantities of the precursor chemicals for these agents is difficult due to the Chemical Weapons Convention.

. . . Chemical experts believe that chemical agents need to be in vapor or aerosol form (a cloud of suspended microscopic droplets) to cause optimal inhalation exposure and to cause an effect. Vapors and aerosols remain suspended in the air and are readily inhaled deep into the lungs. Another method is to spray large droplets or liquid for skin penetration. A chemical agent could be disseminated by explosive or mechanical delivery. Further, chemical agents can be disseminated in vapor, aerosol, or bulk droplet form from delivery devices.

According to the experts, terrorists could disseminate chemical agents using simple containers such as glass bottles with commercial sprayers attached to them or fire extinguishers. However, the chemical agent would need to withstand the heat developed if disseminated by explosives. Moreover, according to chemical experts, the successful use of chemical agents to cause mass casualties requires high toxicity, volatility (tendency of a chemical to vaporize or give off fumes), and stability during storage and dissemination. Rapid exposure to a highly concentrated agent in an ideal environment would increase the number of casualties. These experts agree that disseminating a chemical agent in a closed environment would be the best way to produce mass casualties. Weather affects exterior dissemination, particularly sunlight, moisture, and wind. Some chemical agents can be easily evaporated by sunlight or diluted by water. The experts stated that it is also difficult to target an agent with any precision or certainty to kill a specific percentage of individuals outdoors. For example, wind could transport a chemical agent away from the designated target area.

. . . The 1995 attack by Aum Shinrikyo, an apocalyptic religious sect, in the Tokyo subway using the chemical nerve agent sarin elevated concerns about chemical and biological terrorism. Twelve people were killed and many more were injured as a result of that incident. Some experts have noted that despite substantial financial assets, well-equipped laboratories, and educated scientists working in the laboratories, Aum Shinrikyo did not cause more deaths because of the poor quality of the chemical agent and the dissemination technique used.[18]

It should be noted, however, that these views again reflect the tendency to see the threat of "terrorism" as being separate from the more sophisticated threats that could be posed by proxy attacks and state actors. The risks could change radically if states became involved and used or provided the chemical weapon. There has been at least one successful terrorist use of chemical weapons without state aid. The Tamil Tigers used commercially obtained chlorine gas on a besieged Sri Lankan special forces group at East Kiran in June 1990. The attack worked, although all the Tigers did was take drums of the chemical from a nearby paper plant, wait for the right prevailing wind, and open the drums.[19] It is also dangerous to rule out industrial sabotage. Sabotage by one man at a plant at Bophal in 1984 did, after all, kill far more people than the attacks of Aum Shinrikyo.

At the same time, the GAO analysis ignores the availability of a wide range of commercial poisons that can be used to produce limited numbers of casualties and are described in detail in the unclassified military literature issued by the U.S. Army.

It should also be noted that the Advisory Panel drew most of its database from models tailored to the use of chemical weapons in largely open-air conditions. It is not clear that such models are valid in built-up or urban areas. Tanker trucks could be used to deliver the chemicals needed to deliver an agent in office buildings. Some lethal gases or chemicals rise, but all current chemical weapons are actually vapors that are heavier than air. An attacker could exploit these characteristics in those buildings with large open spaces or forced-air systems, or by the use of elevator shafts and other vertical corridors.

The dissemination and persistence of chemical weapons in attacks launched from outside a closed-air system like a large office building would be a function of heat, wind patterns, and terrain obstruction. Even under military conditions, real-world dissemination never follows the neat, predictable elliptical patterns used in military models. Concentrations vary sharply over the dissemination area and "skip effects" can blow lethal concentrations substantial distances down wind.

An attack on an urban area using a delivery system like a commercial aircraft or aircraft modified as a drone that is either crashed into an urban area or used as a line source sprayer would deposit chemical weapons over the complex surface of urban "canyons." Depending on the time of year, temperature, and so on, such an agent might either be remarkably persistent near the ground or be deposited over large vertical areas with little lethality. At present, the open literature simply does not provide a useful basis for drawing any conclusions, and this presents major problems in assessing risk and the value of given detection, characterization, and response measures.

### The Impact of Technological Change

Finally, it is not clear from open sources how changes in chemical technology and production over the coming twenty-five years will affect the ways in which state actors, proxies, and terrorist/extremist groups can attack against the United States. Key issues include:

- Advances in the way chemical weapons can be manufactured and used—including changes in related technologies like remote-controlled crop sprayers, and so on
- The possible existence of fourth-generation weapons that are far more lethal than existing nerve gases
- Whether control regimes and regulatory/safety controls will outpace any advances in the ability to make chemical weapons and use new commercially available ingredients
- The level of security the United States can develop to prevent the transit of chemical weapons or precursors into the United States
- The capability and cost of new detection and characterization systems, and the ability to cost-effectively deploy them
- Advances in protection and treatment

It should be noted in this regard that the GAO has repeatedly cited the lack of comprehensive risk assessments as a problem in federal programs.[20] The unclassified literature the federal government issues on the risk posed by chemical weapons tends to ignore the need to forecast changes in risk, just as it tends to use generic lethality data of uncertain provenance and value.

### The Aum Shinrikyo Case Study

It is also somewhat misleading for GAO to state that Aum Shinrikyo did not cause more deaths "despite substantial financial assets, well-equipped laboratories, and educated scientists working in the laboratories . . . because of the poor quality of the chemical agent and the dissemination technique used."[21] Aum experimented with a wide range of chemical weapons, including nerve agents like sarin, tabun, soman, and VX, and considered hydrogen cyanide, and possibly phosgene and mustard. Aum selected sarin precisely because it was relatively easy to manufacture and any problems with the result are more a reflection on Aum's peculiar internal structure and lack of effective organization than the technical problems in manufacturing chemical weapons per se.[22]

Aum does seem to have been successful in buying the formula for sarin from a Russian agent and in getting all of the necessary equipment to successfully make it. It is also important to note that Iraq produced its first mustard gas in small lots at a university-affiliated facility in less than six months. Iraq initially rejected rushing forward with the manufacture of sarin because it was not persistent and was unstable under heat and daylight conditions, not because of the difficulty in making small amounts.

Aum attempted several different chemical attacks. It evidently staged its first attack on a rival religious leader in 1993. Its first successful attack was on the judges in a civil suit against Aum in Matsumoto in June 1994, where a heating element, fan, and sprayer on a refrigeration truck were used to kill 7 people and injure 144. The Tokyo subway attack that took place in March 1995 killed only twelve people but injured more than a thousand. The delivery mechanism consisted of plastic bags of sarin punctured in subway cars, where puddles of diluted sarin were allowed to evaporate. This was an extremely crude delivery method, and even so the Japanese authorities reported some effects for as many as 5,000 people, while the prosecutors claimed 3,398 were injured.

Better tactics in using the same dissemination technique could easily have produced far more lethal results and there are a number of other simple and more effective dissemination techniques.[23] For example, Aum could have achieved high-lethality results by introducing the same agent into the closed-air systems in many high-rise office buildings or simply by releasing pools of sarin over wide areas in the floor of the Kasumigaseki subway station, rather than leaving it in bags in subway cars. Aum planned similar attacks for May 5 and July 4, 1995, and it is still unclear why they failed.

There are different descriptions of what Aum did, and some illustrate how the risk could have been much greater. Reporting by Chris Bullock describes the Aum attacks as follows:

> Now the event stands out historically for several reasons: first of all, this was the first use of nerve agent in a terrorist setting; it was a use not by a state but by a private group of individuals against civilians.
>     . . . The Tokyo subway attack, the objective of the attack, was not to kill hundreds or thousands of random strangers in the Tokyo subway. It had a

very specific purpose: the cult had learned that the police in Tokyo had been trained the week before in chemical protective gear and tactics by the military, in anticipation of raids against cult facilities that were set to begin on Monday, March 20, 1995. The reason the cult decided to attack the Tokyo subway on Monday, March 20, was to kill as many policemen on their way to work as possible. You see, all of those trains converged at Kasumigaseki station, which serves the headquarters of the Japanese police agency.

You see, Aum's actions, I would argue, were perfectly logical. We've heard them characterized as an insane cult, an end-of-the-world cult, a group of mad scientists in Buddhist monk clothing. Well, actually, I would argue that Aum's actions were perfectly logical. They had established their own value system. They essentially set themselves up as a society in conflict with larger society. A self-legitimized group that rejected and ultimately was going to have to confront that society at some level. Given that they didn't have enough men, enough guns, [or] enough bullets to fight society and fight the police, let alone the military, they had to go with an asymmetric option, they had to find a trump card, and to this end it made perfect sense to think about weapons of mass destruction.[24]

### Political and Psychological Effects

These latter points tend to argue that any attacker striking at targets in the U.S. homeland would have major problems in getting the amounts of agent needed to achieve high casualties and then in delivering it. They also imply that biological weapons would be vastly preferred in terms of handling and delivering the mass of agent required for highly lethal attacks.

However, none of the points in the Gilmore Commission or the Rand study would be of critical importance in attacks where the main consequence was intended to be psychological and/or political. It should also be noted that a number of multiple, near simultaneous, small attacks could have a major impact in causing public fear and panic, forcing the United States into a massive defensive response and dominating media coverage.

For example, out of the 5,010 Japanese that reported to hospitals after the Aum attack on the Tokyo subway during the first twenty-four hours, 74 percent showed no symptoms of nerve agent exposures and were diagnosed as "worried well." By this standard, there were three to four times more psychological victims of the attack than there were physiological victims. Israel exhibited a similar pattern in response to Iraq's Scud attacks during the Persian Gulf War, as did Iran during Iraq's Scud attacks on its cities during the Iran-Iraq War.[25]

Once again, there is no reason to tie perceptions of the seriousness of the use of WMD to actual mass destruction or mass casualties. If anything, attackers might feel they could make more political or psychological gains by demonstrating the ability to attack without creating the political backlash that would come from large numbers of deaths.

### The Problem of Response

In spite of these problems, chemical weapons are the WMD that most first responders and law enforcement agencies feel with which they are most prepared to deal. They feel that most chemical attacks present many of the same problems and uncertainties as dealing with the shipment of similar hazardous materials (HAZMAT) or large-scale industrial accidents. They already have to prepare for such HAZMAT incidents, and the estimated total casualties from most chemical attacks are unlikely to put an impossible burden on medical services. The law enforcement aspects and forensics of dealing with chemical attacks present challenges, but law enforcement experts believe most incidents will have a clear location and chains of evidence.

The United States has made advances in chemical weapons attack detection, at least at the military level. The Army and Marine Corps have fielded the M21 Remote Sensing Chemical Agent Alarm (RSCAAL) to provide standoff detection of nerve and blister agents. The hand-held Improved Chemical Agent Monitor (ICAM) provides all deployable units with a rapid, chemical agent monitoring and identification capability for nerve and blister agent vapors. There is a broad consensus, however, that there are still major problems in rapid detection and characterization and in training and equipping suitable emergency medical personnel and facilities. These problems would be least significant if a chemical weapon was used in a single closed area. They could be more serious if a chemical weapon was combined with an explosive device in attacking a building or facility and responders had to characterize and deal with two sets of destructive effects at the same time.

These problems would be most serious, however, if a chemical attack could be conducted in enough volume to cover a large area. A truly successful attack against a crowded subway could, for example, saturate response services and present major problems in determining the area covered by the agent, how many people were actually exposed, and with what effect. The number of false reports and people seeking cautionary or panic medical treatment would rise sharply. The fear of sequential or follow-on attacks would grow, and so would the problems in decontamination.

The most serious problems would occur if very large amounts of agent could be broadly disseminated or industrial sabotage—such as the Bophal incident—had the same effect. No currently deployed detection system can accurately measure the plume or area coverage of such an attack, and most detection systems would present problems in reliably characterizing the exact weapon used and/or the amount of the weapon present in given areas. In many cases, little is also known about what constitutes a lethal dose, symptomology, treatment, and long-term effects.

While sophisticated individual detection and characterization devices are available and much more reliable and advanced systems are completing development, there are as of yet no rapidly deployable arrays that can be used in urban environments and most responders have no funds to acquire them. There are no current plans to broadly disseminate gas masks or the antidote to nerve gas before a crisis—even if warning occurs—and there are severe limits on the ability to treat large numbers of gas victims even in urban areas.

While most urban responders have plans for handling the public relations aspects of chemical accidents, it is far from clear that these plans would work in dealing with major chemical or sequential attacks. It is also clear that national and local media have, at best, token preparations to report on such attacks and to perform a civil defense role. The psychological dimension also presents problems because it is not clear that the normal decontamination of areas, facilities, and buildings will not leave trace problems or that the public can be convincingly reassured of what is and is not safe. More broadly, the long-term medical effects of a large-scale attack are very difficult to characterize, and the Persian Gulf War has shown how the resulting uncertainties can create major medical, psychological, and political problems.

Fortunately, under most conditions these problems may prove moot. Although some models indicate that limited amounts of sophisticated chemical weapons can produce thousands of casualties, it is more likely that a serious chemical attack or incident would produce a thousand casualties or less. It would take a highly sophisticated group to launch multiple attacks and produce large amounts of a highly lethal agent. As a result, it seems unlikely that either defenders or responders will have to deal with the kind of chemical attack(s) that could cripple a significant part of the economy, paralyze a city, vastly oversaturate available response and medical facilities, cause lasting panic and a loss of faith in political institutions, or threaten the fabric of American society. In this sense, chemical weapons differ fundamentally from biological and nuclear weapons.

Nevertheless, the threat posed by chemical weapons illustrates the need to be able to measure the existing capabilities of federal, state, and local defenders and responders, to determine what can be done to improve their capabilities with minimal or no additional resources, and then to expressly address what level of additional capability the nation is and is not willing to fund. At present, federal efforts are just beginning to develop a detailed picture of existing national capabilities, and much of the governmental effort at every step is concerned with basic endeavors to understand the problem, coordinate, and train. There is no question that this is producing real progress, but it does not create a system or architecture for homeland defense, and no one has seriously addressed the question of "how much is enough?"

One key problem is that defense and response against "small" chemical, biological, and radiological attacks must generally begin at the local level, and state and federal aid will come hours or days after the event. Local law enforcement, emergency services, and medical services must bear the brunt of trying to stop or contain an incident if there is warning and ameliorate the consequences if it succeeds. In the case of most chemical attacks, like most high-explosive attacks, local and regional capabilities will be decisive in determining the outcome. Regional and federal resources cannot be brought to bear in time without extensive and precise warning.

This, however, raises the question of what local resources are needed, and what federal role, if any, is needed to provide them. So far, this question has tended to be answered more in terms of counterterrorism than response, and emergency response capabilities are better trained and organized than medical services. There are serious variations in response capability, however, and it is not clear what standards need to be set for each urban area or to deal with attacks on critical facilities in areas that lack the resources approaching those of major cities.

It is also obvious from the testimony and briefings of both responders and medical professionals that public health has been steadily downsized in ways that limit the ability to handle the patient loads from chemical attacks more so than the higher patient loads from biological and nuclear attacks. These problems seem likely to grow as more public resources are shifted to dealing with the aging and are compounded by a search for cost-effectiveness among medical professionals that is reducing emergency medical facilities and placing sharp limits on intensive care units and respirators.

This again illustrates the fact that effective homeland defense cannot be separated from national health policy and the overall problems in balancing out treatment cost, the need to provide continuing peacetime services, and changing priorities to meet an aging population and deal with welfare reform. At present, cost and capacity constraints are so severe that medical facilities often cannot participate effectively in exercises and training for homeland defense.

The briefings of responders and law enforcement officials raise two other problems that affect chemical attacks as well as other large-scale attacks. One is the need to provide some kind of cost-effective detection and characterization system that can be rapidly deployed before or after an attack and that can provide an accurate picture of how much of what agent is present in what area. Models lack the accuracy to substitute for measurement. At present, more effort seems to be going into improving individual detectors than into creating deployable and affordable systems that can be available for local use—a problem compounded by the need to provide biological and nuclear detection and characterization as well as chemical. This kind of real-time information is critical not only to first responders, but also to the efficient use and allocation of regional, state, and federal aid.

Another problem that arises with large-scale chemical incidents is the potential conflict between the law enforcement priorities necessary to obtain evidence and convictions, the need to take every possible measure to prevent follow-on attacks, the need to provide immediate emergency services, and long-standing problems in using U.S. intelligence assets to support defense and response inside U.S. territory when it may involve U.S. citizens. Considerable progress has been made in improving such coordination at the federal, state, and local level but much of this progress seems tailored to dealing with low-level attacks where (normally) criminal procedures and civil rights can be given priority. There does not as yet seem to be a clear doctrine for dealing with escalating levels of crisis where the need to take immediate and urgent action may have higher priority.

## BIOLOGICAL WEAPONS AS A MEANS OF ATTACK

One way of describing the risks posed by biological weapons is to describe the world that existed when natural outbreaks of disease were a recurrent fact of life. A recent WHO study provides a good overview of the impact of disease on history:

It is arguable whether war or the devastation wrought by infectious disease has had a greater historic influence on political boundaries. Up until the Second World War, it was pestilence—and not warfare—that claimed the lives of Europe's soldiers. Napoleon Bonaparte can lay blame for his ignominious retreat from Moscow—not on the Russians, nor even the Russian winter. By far, his deadliest opponent was typhus; a louse-borne infection that reduced a healthy Grande Armee of 655,000 to a pitiful and demoralized 93,000— who wound up straggling home and surviving just long enough to pass the rickettsia on to neighbours and loved ones. The subsequent epidemic killed another two million, carrying off 250,000 civilians in Germany alone.

In the New World, it was not superior Spanish firepower, nor their reliance on horses that resulted in the conquest and enslavement of the Amerindians. By far the greatest allies of the self-proclaimed, "liberators of the heathens" were smallpox, influenza, and measles. Formerly unknown in the Americas, the first recorded smallpox epidemic hit the fledgling colony of Santo Domingo in 1495, destroying 80% of the local indigenous population. That same outbreak was also responsible for the deaths of hundreds of Spanish soldiers after the battle of Vega Real in 1495.

In 1515, another flare-up in Puerto Rico spared the Spanish but extirpated the locals. By the time Hernando Cortes and his rogue's army of mercenaries and missionaries set foot on Mexico's shores, smallpox, measles and influenza had already insinuated themselves as a kind of microbial fifth column among the local population. How a ragtag army of 300 men (albeit armed with muskets, riding horses, and unbridled greed) could defeat the highly organized and warlike Aztecs can never be satisfactorily explained except by factoring in the inroads European diseases made into a people entirely devoid of immunity. Conquistador and expedition scribe Bernal Diaz described the resultant carnage from infectious disease thus: "We could not walk without treading on the bodies and heads of dead Indians. The dry land was piled with corpses." In the space of 10 years, historians estimate that Mexico's population plummeted from some 25 million to 6.5 million owing to epidemics of infectious disease—a drop of 74%. In North America, later events echoed those in Mexico but with one not-so-subtle difference. By the 1600s, colonizers knew enough about epidemiology to maliciously inflict deadly diseases on locals by providing "gifts" of blankets and clothing infested with smallpox and typhus-bearing lice—the first recorded acts of biological warfare.[26]

Biological weapons have never been used successfully in large-scale combat or in covert and terrorist attacks. Japan was the only nation in World War II that made confirmed use of biological weapons, and it used relatively crude means. While Japan used biological weapons against twelve Chinese cites, the total number of deaths does not seem to have exceeded ten thousand—many of which were caused under controlled conditions by experiments using human beings as live subjects.[27] Other nations confined their efforts to experimentation or to developing such weapons for retaliatory purposes. For example, Britain produced over five million seed cakes of animal anthrax to be dropped by bombers during World War II.

The past, however, is unlikely to be a representative prologue of the future. As Table 4.5 shows, a wide range of powers developed far more effective biological weapons after World War II, and the development of biological weapons in the form of dry, storable micropowders dates back to the 1950s. Furthermore, Table 4.6 shows that the United States lists a number of countries where biological weapons efforts are continuing, and U.S. intelligence experts indicate that a classified list would be over twice as long.

As has been touched on earlier, the technology necessary to produce biological weapons is proliferating as part of the broad transfer of biotechnology throughout the world. Many, if not most of the key technologies involved, are now commercialized for food processing and pharmaceutical purposes. Modern biological weapons have become far more lethal and easy to deliver since World War II and have been stockpiled. For example, the United States had stockpiles of seven weapons in 1969, and was testing advanced biological warheads for the Polaris and Shark cruise missile, at the same time it renounced the use of biological weapons.[28] Russia, France, Britain, China, and North Korea also had extensive stocks of such weapons in 1972, when the Biological Weapons Convention (BWC) was opened for signature. In spite of the fact that 140 nations have now signed or ratified the BWC, U.S. intelligence exports estimate that at least 15 countries still stockpile such weapons.

Table 4.5
Biological Weapons: Known Development of Agents by the Major Powers before the BWC

| Agent | Canada | France | Germany | Japan | UK | USA | Russia |
|---|---|---|---|---|---|---|---|
| *Bacteria* | | | | | | | |
| Anthrax | + | + | + | + | + | + | + |
| Brucella | | + | | | | + | + |
| Chlamydia psittaci | | | | | + | | |
| Dysenteria | | + | | + | + | + | + |
| Gas gangrene | | + | + | + | | | |
| Leprosy | | | | + | | | |
| Tuberculosis | | | | | | | + |
| Pseudomonas mallei | | + | + | + | | + | + |
| Pseudomonas Pseudomallei | | + | | + | | + | |
| Tetanus | | + | | + | + | | + |
| Typhoid | | + | | + | + | | + |
| Typhus | | + | | + | + | | |
| Vibro Cholera | | | + | + | + | + | + |
| Yersinia Pestis | | | + | + | + | + | + |
| *Viruses* | | | | | | | |
| Ebola | | + | | | + | + | + |
| Encephalitis | | + | | | | + | + |
| FMD | | | + | | | | + |
| Fowl plague | | + | | | | + | |

| Agent | | | | | | | |
|---|---|---|---|---|---|---|---|
| Influenza | | | | + | | + | + |
| Newcastle disease | | + | | | | | + |
| Rinderpest | + | + | + | | | + | |
| Korean haemorrhagic fever | | | | + | | | |
| *Toxins* | | | | | | | |
| Botulin | + | + | | + | + | + | + |
| Ricin | | + | | + | + | + | + |
| Saxitoxin | | | | | | + | + |
| Staphylococcus | | | | | | + | + |
| Enterotoxin B | | | | | | | |
| Snake Toxins | | | | + | | | |
| Tetrodotoxin (fish poison) | | | | + | + | | |
| *Arthropods* | | | | | | | |
| Potato beetles | | + | + | | | | |
| *Fungi* | | | | | | | |
| Coccidioides immitis | | | | + | | + | |
| *Other* | | | | | | | |
| Malaria | | | | + | | | |
| Weeds | | | + | | | | |
| Phytopathogens | | | | | | + | + |
| Fish pathogens | | | | | | | + |

*Source*: SIPRI and IDA.

**Table 4.6**
**U.S. Department of Defense Estimate of Potential National Threats Involving Biological Weapons**

---

### China
China continues to maintain some elements of an offensive biological warfare program it is believed to have started in the 1950s. China possesses a sufficiently advanced biotechnology infrastructure to allow it to develop and produce biological agents. Its munitions industry is sufficient to allow it to weaponize any such agents, and it has a variety of delivery means that could be used for biological agent delivery. China is believed to possess an offensive biological warfare capability based on technology developed prior to its accession to the BWC in 1984. China actively participates in international efforts to negotiate a BWC compliance protocol.

Since 1984, China consistently has claimed that it never researched, produced, or possessed any biological weapons and never would do so. Nevertheless, China's declarations under the voluntary BWC declarations for confidence building purposes are believed to be inaccurate and incomplete, and there are some reports that China may retain elements of its biological warfare program.

### India
India has many well-qualified scientists, numerous biological and pharmaceutical production facilities, and biocontainment facilities suitable for research and development of dangerous pathogens. At least some of these facilities are being used to support research and development for biological warfare defense work. India has ratified the BWC.

### Iran
Iran has a growing biotechnology industry, significant pharmaceutical experience, and the overall infrastructure to support its biological warfare program. Tehran has expanded its efforts to seek considerable dual-use biotechnical materials and expertise from entities in Russia and elsewhere, ostensibly for civilian reasons. Outside assistance is important for Iran, and it is also difficult to prevent because of the dual-use nature of the materials and equipment being sought by Iran and the many legitimate end uses for these items.

Iran's biological warfare program began during the Iran-Iraq War. Iran is believed to be pursuing offensive biological warfare capabilities and its efforts may have evolved beyond agent research and development to the capability to produce small quantities of agent. Iran has ratified the BWC.

### Iraq
Iraq's continued refusal to disclose fully the extent of its biological program suggests that Baghdad retains a biological warfare capability, despite its membership in the BWC. After four and one-half years of claiming that it had conducted only "defensive research" on biological weapons Iraq declared reluctantly, in 1995, that it had produced approximately 30,000 liters of bulk biological agents and/or filled munitions. Iraq admitted that it produced anthrax, botulinum toxins and aflatoxins, and that it prepared biological agent-filled munitions, including missile warheads and aerial bombs. However, UNSCOM believed that Iraq had produced substantially greater amounts than it has admitted—three to four times greater.

Table 4.6 (continued)

Iraq also admitted that, during the Persian Gulf War, it had deployed biological agent-filled munitions to airfields and that these weapons were intended for use against Israel and coalition forces in Saudi Arabia. Iraq stated that it destroyed all of these agents and munitions in 1991, but it has provided insufficient credible evidence to support this claim.

The UN believes that Baghdad has the ability to reconstitute its biological warfare capabilities within a few weeks or months, and, in the absence of UNSCOM inspections and monitoring during 1999 and 2000, we are concerned that Baghdad again may have produced some biological warfare agents.

### Libya
Libya has ratified the BWC, but has continued a biological warfare program. This program has not advanced beyond the research and development stage, although it may be capable of producing small quantities of biological agent. Libya's program has been hindered by the country's poor scientific and technological base, equipment shortages, and a lack of skilled personnel, as well as by UN sanctions in place from 1992 to 1999. Without foreign assistance and technical expertise to help Libya use available dual-use materials, the Libyan biological warfare program is not likely to make significant progress beyond its current stage. On the other hand, with the suspension of UN sanctions, Libya's ability to acquire biological-related equipment and expertise will increase.

### North Korea
North Korea has acceded to the Biological and Toxin Weapons Convention (BWC), but nonetheless has pursued biological warfare capabilities since the 1960s. Pyongyang's resources include a rudimentary (by Western standards) biotechnical infrastructure that could support the production of infectious biological warfare agents and toxins such as anthrax, cholera, and plague. North Korea is believed to possess a munitions-production infrastructure that would allow it to weaponize biological warfare agents and may have biological weapons available for use.

### Pakistan
Pakistan is believed to have the resources and capabilities to support a limited biological warfare research and development effort. Pakistan may continue to seek foreign equipment and technology to expand its bio-technical infrastructure. Pakistan has ratified the BWC and actively participates in compliance protocol negotiations for the treaty.

### Russia
The FSU offensive biological program was the world's largest and consisted of both military facilities and civilian research and development institutes. According to Ken Alibek, the former Deputy Director of BIO-PREPARAT, the principal Soviet government agency for biological weapons research and development, by the early 1970s, the Soviet Union had developed a biological warfare employment doctrine, where biological weapons were categorized as strategic or operational. Alibek stated that they were not to be employed as tactical weapons. Strategic biological agents,

continued

Table 4.6 (continued)

those to be used on "deep targets," such as the continental United States, were the lethal variety and included smallpox, anthrax, and plague. Operational agents, those intended for use on medium-range targets, but well behind the battlefront, were the incapacitating variety and included tularemia, glanders, and Venezuelan equine encephalitis.

For both strategic and operational employment, the Soviet goal was to create large numbers of casualties and extensive disruption of vital civilian and military activities. The former Soviet Biological Warfare Program was a massive program involving tens of thousands of personnel. Thousands of tons of agent were reportedly produced annually, including anthrax, smallpox, plague, tularemia, glanders, and Venezuelan equine encephalitis. Perceived for strategic use against targets in the United States. Dual-use nature of virtually all materials involved in production process makes it difficult to determine conclusively the exact size and scope of the former Soviet program, or any remaining effort.

The former Deputy Director further stated that although the Soviet Union became a signatory to the 1972 BWC, it continued a massive program to develop and manufacture biological weapons. Alibek claims that in the late-1980s and early-1990s, over 60,000 people were involved in the research, development, and production of biological weapons in the Soviet Union. The annual production capacity of all of the facilities involved was several thousand tons of various agents.

The Russian government has publicly committed to ending the former Soviet biological weapons program and claims to have ended the program in 1992. Nevertheless, serious concerns remain about Russia's offensive biological warfare capabilities and the status of some elements of the offensive biological warfare capability inherited from the FSU. Since the breakup of the Soviet Union, more extensive downsizing and restructuring of the program have taken place. Many of the key research and production facilities have taken severe cuts in funding and personnel. However, some key components of the former Soviet program may remain largely intact and may support a possible future mobilization capability for the production of biological agents and delivery systems. Despite Russian ratification of the BWC, work outside the scope of legitimate biological defense activity may be occurring now at selected facilities within Russia, and the United States continues to receive unconfirmed reports of some ongoing offensive biological warfare activities.

### Syria
Syria has signed but not ratified the BWC but nonetheless is pursuing the development of biological weapons. Syria's biotechnical infrastructure is capable of supporting limited agent development. However, the Syrians are not believed to have begun any major effort to put biological agents into weapons. Without significant foreign assistance, it is unlikely that Syria could manufacture significant amounts of biological weapons for several years.

*Source*: Adapted by Anthony H. Cordesman from Office of the Secretary of Defense, *Proliferation and Response* (Washington, D.C.: U.S. Department of Defense, January 2001).

### Categorizing the Biological Threat

Modern biological weapons offer many potential advantages. They employ living agents or toxins produced by natural or synthetic agents to kill or injure humans, domestic animals, and crops. As Table 4.7 shows, there are a wide range of agents with many different effects and they offer a wide range of ways to attack American citizens, crops, and livestock. They also are nearly ideal terror weapons with massive psychological as well as physiological consequences.

Such weapons fall into five main medical categories: bacterial agents (anthrax, plague, brucellosis, and typhoid fever); rickettsial agents (typhus, Rocky Mountain spotted fever, and Q fever); viral agents (smallpox, influenza, yellow fever, encephalitis, dengue fever, chikungunga, and Rift Valley fever, and hemorrhagic fevers like Ebola, Marburg and Lassa); toxins (botulinum, staphylococcus enterotoxin, shigella toxin, and aflatoxin); and fungal (coccidiodomyocosis). There are other antiplant and antianimal weapons that are not used against humans.

This helps explain why the CDC has concluded that the U.S. public health system and primary health care providers must be prepared to address varied biological agents, including pathogens that are rarely seen in the United States. It has stated that,

> High-priority agents include organisms that pose a risk to national security because they
>
> - can be easily disseminated or transmitted person-to-person;
> - cause high mortality, with potential for major public health impact;
> - might cause public panic and social disruption; and
> - require special action for public health preparedness.[29]

There are many different ways to categorize biological weapons according to lethality. The CDC divides them into three main categories: Category A, Category B, and Category C. The Category A weapons are high-priority agents that include organisms that pose a risk to national security because they can be easily disseminated or transmitted person-to-person; cause high mortality, with potential for major public health impact; might cause public panic and social disruption; and require special action for public health preparedness. They include:

- variola major (smallpox)
- *Bacillus anthracis* (anthrax)
- *Yersinia pestis* (plague)
- *Clostridium botulinum* toxin (botulism)

Table 4.7
Key Biological Weapons

| Disease | Infectivity | Transmissibility | Incubation Period | Mortality | Therapy |
|---|---|---|---|---|---|
| *Viral* | | | | | |
| Chikungunya fever | high? | none | 2–6 days | very low (–1%) | none |
| Dengue fever | high | none | 5–2 days | very low (–1%) | none |
| Eastern equine encephalitis | high | none | 5–10 days | high (+60%) | developmental |
| Tick borne encephalitis | high | none | 1–2 weeks | up to 30% | developmental |
| Venezuelan equine encephalitis | high | none | 2–5 days | low (–1%) | developmental |
| Hepatitis A | - | - | 15–40 days | - | - |
| Hepatitis B | - | - | 40–150 days | - | - |
| Influenza | high | none | 1–3 days | usually low | available |
| Yellow fever | high | none | 3–6 days | up to 40% | available |
| Smallpox (Variola) | high | high | 7–16 days | up to 30% | available |
| *Rickettsial* | | | | | |
| Coxiella Burneti (Q fever) | high | negligible | 10–21 day | low (–1%) | antibiotic |
| Mooseri | - | - | 6–14 days | - | - |
| Prowazeki | - | - | 6–15 days | - | - |
| Psittacosis | high | mod-high | 4–15 days | mod-high | antibiotic |
| Rickettsi (Rocky Mountain spotted fever) | high | none | 3–10 days | up to 80% | antibiotic |
| Tsutsugamushi | - | - | - | - | - |
| Epidemic typhus | high | none | 6–15 days | up to 70% | antibiotic/vaccine |

| Bacterial | | | | | |
|---|---|---|---|---|---|
| Anthrax (pulmonary) | mod-high | negligible | 1–5 days | usually fatal | antibiotic/vaccine |
| Brucellosis | high | none | 1–3 days | ~25% | antibiotic |
| Cholera | low | high | 1–5 days | up to 80% | antibiotic/vaccine |
| Glanders | high | none | 2–1 days | usually fatal | poor antibiotic |
| Meloidosis | high | none | 1–5 days | usually fatal | moderate antibiotic |
| Plague (pneumonic) | high | high | 2–5 days | usually fatal | antibiotic/vaccine |
| Tularemia | high | negligible | 1–10 days | low to 60% | antibiotic/vaccine |
| Typhoid fever | mod-high | mod-high | 7–21 days | up to 10% | antibiotic/vaccine |
| Dysentery | high | high | 1–4 days | low to high | antibiotic/vaccine |
| **Fungal** | | | | | |
| Coccidioidomycosis | high | none | 1–3 days | low | none |
| Coccidiodes Immitis | high | none | 10–21 days | low | none |
| Histoplasma | | | | | |
| Capsulatum | - | - | 15–18 days | - | - |
| Norcardia Asteroides | - | - | - | - | - |
| **Toxins[a]** | | | | | |
| Botulinum toxin | high | none | 12–72 hours | high neromusclar paralysis | vaccine |
| Mycotoxin | high | none | hours or days | low to high | ? |
| Staphylococcus | moderate | none | 24–48 hours | incapacitating | ? |

[a]Many sources classify as chemical weapons because toxins are chemical poisons.

*Sources:* Adapted by Anthony H. Cordesman from Report of the Secretary General, Department of Political and Security Affairs, *Chemical and Bacteriological (Biological) Weapons and the Effects of Their Possible Use* (New York: United Nations, 1969), 26, 29, 37–52, 116–117; *Jane's NBC Protection Equipment, 1991–1992*; James Smith, "Biological Warfare Developments," *Jane's Intelligence Review* (November 1991), 483–487; and USACHPPM, *The Medical NBC Battlebook*, USACHPPM Technical Guide 244, 4-22-4-26.

- *Francisella tularensis* (tularaemia)
- filoviruses
  - Ebola hemorrhagic fever
  - Marburg hemorrhagic fever
- arenaviruses
  - Lassa (Lassa fever)
  - Junin (Argentine hemorrhagic fever) and related viruses

Category B agents include biological weapons that are moderately easy to disseminate, cause moderate morbidity and low mortality, and require specific enhancements of CDC's diagnostic capacity and enhanced disease surveillance. They include:

- *Coxiella burnetti* (Q fever)
- *Brucella* species (brucellosis)
- *Burkholderia mallei* (glanders)
- alphaviruses
  - Venezuelan encephalomyelitis
  - eastern and western equine encephalomyelitis
- ricin toxin from *Ricinus communis* (castor beans)
- epsilon toxin of *Clostridium perfringens*
- *Staphylococcus* enterotoxin B

There is a subset of Category B agents that includes pathogens that are food- or water-borne. These pathogens include but are not limited to:

- *Salmonella* species
- *Shigella dysenteriae*
- *Escherichia coli* O157:H7
- *Vibrio cholerae*
- *Cryptosporidium parvum*

Category C agents include emerging pathogens that could be engineered for mass dissemination in the future because of their availability, ease of production and dissemination, and potential for high morbidity and mortality and major health impact. The preparedness for Category C agents requires ongoing research to improve disease detection, diagnosis, treatment, and prevention. They include:

- Nipah virus
- hanta viruses
- tick borne hemorrhagic fever viruses

- tick borne encephalitis viruses
- yellow fever
- multi-drug-resistant tuberculosis

Many of these weapons offer a means of attack that is potentially cheap, lethal, and hard to detect. At the same time, much depends on how well they are weaponized, in terms of the agent and the way in which it is delivered. For example, the same disease is generally far more lethal in the form of a dry micro-powder that can be disseminated and inhaled over a wide area than as a wet agent. Explosive warheads may waste much of the agent, while spraying it upwind in a line source delivery may be highly effective. Wind patterns, temperature, and the presence of ultraviolet light can affect lethality and the life of the agent. As a result, the same amount of the same agent can be several orders of magnitude more lethal under optimal weaponization and delivery conditions and potentially highly lethal agents can have minimal effectiveness under the wrong weaponization and delivery conditions.

This helps explain why the lethality models involved in estimating the impact of biological weapons are far more uncertain than those associated with conventional explosives, chemical weapons, and the immediate effects of nuclear weapons.[30] There is also little historical experience on which to build. Up until 1945, the development of biological weapons had only limited success. In fact, a recent history of biological weapons has found that every major power in World War II failed to develop highly effective weapons while its scientists either lied about their success or exaggerated their potential success, and their intelligence experts grossly exaggerated the potential threat from other states.[31]

The CDC also warns that there is no way to know in advance which newly emergent pathogens might be employed by terrorists and that it is imperative to link "bioterrorism preparedness efforts with ongoing disease surveillance and outbreak response activities as defined in CDC's emerging infectious disease strategy."[32]

Other estimates of the biological weapons that might be used by states or terrorists illustrate this point. The NATO handbook dealing with biological warfare lists thirty-one agents. A Russian panel assessing microbiological agents identified eleven that were "very likely to be used." The top four were smallpox, plague, anthrax, and botulism. These four were chosen because they can all be delivered as aerosols and have theoretical lethality rates of 30 percent to 80 percent, and smallpox and anthrax are particularly attractive because they are easy for states to produce in large quantities, and the organism is resistant to destruction. The other items on the list included tularemia, glanders, typhus, Q fever, Venezuelan equine encephalitis, Marburg, and the influenza viruses.[33]

It should be noted that none of these lists include biological weapons directed at livestock or food groups, or the use of "eco-weapons" such as introducing new strains of agricultural disease or new plants, animals, and insects that could exploit vulnerabilities in the ecological balance of the United States. There is ample recent experience to show, however, that such attacks occur regularly in the course of nature and as part of global transit and trade. They could, potentially, be highly effective.

The sheer diversity of biological weapons—and the difficulties in predicting how they will be weaponized and how strains of the disease will have been altered during militarization—presents major problems in detecting, characterizing, and responding to such threats, particularly because they may be used in covert attacks. As the CDC notes:

> They present different challenges and require an additional dimension of emergency planning that involves the public health infrastructure. Covert dissemination of a biological agent in a public place will not have an immediate impact because of the delay between exposure and onset of illness (i.e., the incubation period). Consequently, the first casualties of a covert attack probably will be identified by physicians or other primary health care providers. For example, in the event of a covert release of the contagious variola virus, patients will appear in doctors' offices, clinics, and emergency rooms during the first or second week, complaining of fever, back pain, headache, nausea, and other symptoms of what initially might appear to be an ordinary viral infection. As the disease progresses, these persons will develop the papular rash characteristic of early-stage smallpox, a rash that physicians might not recognize immediately. By the time the rash becomes pustular and patients begin to die, the terrorists would be far away and the disease disseminated through the population by person-to-person contact. Only a short window of opportunity will exist between the time the first cases are identified and a second wave of the population becomes ill. During that brief period, public health officials will need to determine that an attack has occurred, identify the organism, and prevent more casualties through prevention strategies (e.g., mass vaccination or prophylactic treatment). As person-to-person contact continues, successive waves of transmission could carry infection to other worldwide localities. These issues might also be relevant for other person-to-person transmissible etiologic agents (e.g., plague or certain viral hemorrhagic fevers).
>
> Certain chemical agents can also be delivered covertly through contaminated food or water. In 1999, the vulnerability of the food supply was illustrated in Belgium, when chickens were unintentionally exposed to dioxin-contaminated fat used to make animal feed. Because the contamination was not discovered for months, the dioxin, a cancer-causing chemical that does not cause immediate symptoms in humans, was probably present in chicken meat and eggs sold in Europe during early 1999. This incident underscores the need for prompt diagnoses of unusual or suspicious health problems in animals as well as humans, a lesson that was also demonstrated by the recent outbreak of mosquito-borne West Nile virus in birds and humans in New

York City in 1999. The dioxin episode also demonstrates how a covert act of food-borne biological or chemical terrorism could affect commerce and human or animal health.

... Early detection of and response to biological or chemical terrorism is crucial. Without special preparation at the local and state levels, a large-scale attack with variola virus, aerosolized anthrax spores, a nerve gas, or a food-borne biological or chemical agent could overwhelm the local and perhaps national public health infrastructure. Large numbers of patients, including infected persons and the "worried well," would seek medical attention, with a corresponding need for medical supplies, diagnostic tests, and hospital beds. Emergency responders, health-care workers, and public health officials could be at special risk, and everyday life would be disrupted as a result of widespread fear of contagion.

Preparedness for terrorist-caused outbreaks and injuries is an essential component of the U.S. public health surveillance and response system, which is designed to protect the population against any unusual public health event (e.g., influenza pandemics, contaminated municipal water supplies, or intentional dissemination of *Yersinia pestis,* the causative agent of plague). The epidemiologic skills, surveillance methods, diagnostic techniques, and physical resources required to detect and investigate unusual or unknown diseases, as well as syndromes or injuries caused by chemical accidents, are similar to those needed to identify and respond to an attack with a biological or chemical agent. However, public health agencies must prepare also for the special features a terrorist attack probably would have (e.g., mass casualties or the use of rare agents). Terrorists might use combinations of these agents, attack in more than one location simultaneously, use new agents, or use organisms that are not on the critical list (e.g., common, drug-resistant, or genetically engineered pathogens). Lists of critical biological and chemical agents will need to be modified as new information becomes available. In addition, each state and locality will need to adapt the lists to local conditions and preparedness needs by using the criteria provided in CDC's strategic plan.

Potential biological and chemical agents are numerous, and the public health infrastructure must be equipped to quickly resolve crises that would arise from a biological or chemical attack. However, to best protect the public, the preparedness efforts must be focused on agents that might have the greatest impact on U.S. health and security, especially agents that are highly contagious or that can be engineered for widespread dissemination via small-particle aerosols. Preparing the nation to address these dangers is a major challenge to U.S. public health systems and health-care providers. Early detection requires increased biological and chemical terrorism awareness among front-line health care providers because they are in the best position to report suspicious illnesses and injuries. Also, early detection will require improved communication systems between those providers and public health officials. In addition, state and local health-care agencies must have enhanced capacity to investigate unusual events and unexplained illnesses, and diagnostic laboratories must be equipped to identify biological and chemical agents that rarely are seen in the United States. Fundamental to these efforts is comprehensive, integrated training designed to ensure core competency in public health preparedness and the highest levels of scientific expertise among local, state, and federal partners.[34]

### Case Studies: Iraq and Russia

There are two nations whose activities in biological warfare have become relatively well known. Table 4.8 shows that Iraq was found to have weaponized a wide range of agents after the Persian Gulf War. The former Soviet Union successfully weaponized some thirty-seven agents before the end of the Cold War, including infectious agents designed to follow up a strategic nuclear attack on the United States with contagious diseases designed to decimate the population.[35] According to some sources, it involved sixty thousand to seventy thousand people.[36] The agents Russia developed included germ agents such as anthrax, smallpox, Ebola, and Venezuelan encephalitis and genetically engineered bugs for which there is no vaccine or prophylactic treatment.[37] An accidental release of an anthrax agent in Sverdlovsk, Russia, in 1979, affected an area some three miles downwind from the factory and infected eighty to two hundred Russians. It killed animals in villages as far as thirty miles downwind.[38]

Ken Alibek, a senior Russian official in the Soviet Union's Bioweapons Directorate program summarizes the effort as follows:

> When I came to the United States we had a lot of discussions on how, for example, one or another country would be developing biological weapons. And do you know what was interesting to me, it's a widely accepted idea in this country that biological weapons could be developed just in one case; if there is protection or treatment or prophylaxis against another agent. In the United States, until this country terminated its program, there was a requirement; if there was no treatment or prophylaxis you cannot use a given agent for developing and manufacturing biological weapons. People were trying just to apply exactly the same mentality to other countries involved in developing biological weapons. For example, for the Soviet Union, the best biological weapons were biological weapons without any possible treatment and prophylaxis. Ebola was considered one of the best possible agents for biological weapons; Marburg, smallpox and huge number of attempts to genetically alter diseases like plague, anthrax, tularemia. In the late '80s the country was able to start developing new prototypes of bacterial biological weapons based on multi-resistant strains, meaning that all existing treatments available in the West wouldn't be possible to apply because these agents would overcome antibiotic treatments. We cannot ignore this situation. I'm 100% sure that some biological weapons and their killing capability are more effective than some forms of nuclear weapons.[39]

While Russia no longer seems to pose a direct threat to the United States, it is important to note that this program may lead to the transfer of critical weapons technologies to state actors or terrorists. An April report by the GAO found that such a threat is all too real:

The former Soviet Union's biological weapons institutes continue to threaten U.S. national security because they have key assets that are dangerous and vulnerable to misuse, according to State and Defense Department officials. These assets include as many as 15,000 underpaid scientists and researchers, specialized facilities and equipment (albeit often in a deteriorated condition), and large collections of dangerous biological pathogens. These assets could harm the United States if hostile countries or groups were to hire the institutes or biological weapons scientists to conduct weapons-related work. Also of concern is the potential sale of dangerous pathogens to terrorist groups or countries of proliferation concern. State and Defense officials told us that since 1997, Iran and other countries have intensified their efforts to acquire biological weapons expertise and materials from former Soviet biological weapons institutes. In addition, deteriorated physical safety and security conditions could leave dangerous pathogens vulnerable to theft or distribution into the local environment. Finally, much of the former Soviet biological weapons program's infrastructure, such as buildings and equipment, still exists primarily in Russia. While most of these components have legitimate biotechnological applications, they also harbor the potential for renewed production of offensive biological agents.

... About 50 former Soviet biological weapons institutes continue to exist today—most of which are in Russia. Defense Department officials told us that the Russian Ministry of Defense still manages at least four former Soviet military biological weapons institutes to which Russia has consistently refused to grant the United States access. A senior Science Center official noted that the Russian government has not restricted the Center's access to former Soviet nonmilitary biological weapons institutes that receive U.S. assistance. While the Science Center has funded projects and gained access to more than 30 such institutes, the official noted that at least 15 other nonmilitary institutes have not received Center funding.

The Science Center official also estimated that there may be as many as 5,000 senior former Soviet biological weapons scientists who could pose significant proliferation risks and another 10,000 personnel who have weapons-relevant skills. At the six institutes that we visited in December 1999, institute officials said their institutes had lost as much as one-half of their former workforce but noted that they had released administrative and technical support staff in efforts to retain their senior scientists. The senior Science Center official also said these highly trained senior scientists, many with doctorates or other advanced degrees, represent the intellectual core of the world's largest and most sophisticated biological weapons program.

During our visit to the six institutes, we observed that many of these institutes have retained physical assets that could be applied to biological weapons research. Officials at two of the Russian institutes—the State Research Center for Virology and Biotechnology (Vector) and the State Research Center for Applied Microbiology (Obolensk)—said they continue to conduct research

Table 4.8
The Effects of Iraq's Biological Weapons

| Disease | Weapon | Main Symptoms | Incubation Period | Untreated Fatality Rate | Contagious? |
|---------|--------|---------------|-------------------|-------------------------|-------------|
| Anthrax (Pulmonary) *Bacillus Anthrax* | Bacterial spore in vapor or dry micro-powder | High fever, difficult breathing, rapid pulse, chest pains, shock, and toxic blood poisoning. | 1–5 days | 90% as a military agent. Antibiotics only effective after short period. | No |
| Botulism *Clostridium Botulinum* bacterium | Botulinum toxin in vapor or dry micro-powder | Fatigue, nausea, headache, constipation, thirst, fever, cramps, dizziness, blurred vision, problems in swallowing, followed by respiratory paralysis and death. | 2–36 hours | 65% | No |
| Gas Gangrene *Clostridium perfingens* | Vapor or mist | Enters open wounds. Toxins kill muscle cells and cause bloating, shock, jaundice, and sometimes death. | 2–36 hours | 25% | No |

| Aflatoxin | Powered mold or vapor | High concentrations can confuse and incapacitate, and later cause jaundice, internal bleeding, and liver cancer. | Hours to years | ? | No |
|---|---|---|---|---|---|
| Ricin | Castor bean derivative in powder or vapor form. Can ingest or inject. | Can be an insecticide or weapon. Kills cells and impedes breathing and circulation, causes nausea, vomiting, bloody diarrhea, stupor, convulsions, shock, liver damage, and death. | 10 hours. Lethal amounts kill in 2 days. | ? | No |
| Plague, pneumonic *Yersina pestis* bacterium | Vapor, possibly dry powder | Infection of lungs, and causes fever, headache, pneumonia. hemorrhages, and heart failure. | 2–5 days | 95% | Yes, extremely. |
| Smallpox *Variola* virus | Vapor, possibly dry power | Headache, chills, fever, and lesions of skin and mucous membranes. | 12 days | 25–40% | Yes, extremely |

*Sources:* Adapted by Anthony H. Cordesman from work by the Monterey Institute; CIA report of February 19, 1998; and *Washington Post*, 22 February 1998, A-28.

on [dangerous] live pathogens for legitimate [or illicit] purposes. . . . Several former Soviet biological weapons institutes continue to maintain vast collections of dangerous pathogens that could be used for legitimate public health research or for an offensive biological weapons program.

. . . These threat assets could be misused if third parties obtained access either to the scientists, the institutes, or the pathogens themselves. The assets could also be subject to unauthorized access or used to sustain or renew an offensive biological weapons program. . . . State, Defense, and Energy Department officials said the dire financial conditions at former Soviet biological weapons institutes could encourage the proliferation of weapons expertise to countries or groups of concern. This proliferation could occur either if former Soviet biological weapons scientists emigrate to countries of proliferation concern in search of higher pay or if such countries or terrorist groups engage impoverished institutes in research that would augment their biological weapons programs. State and Defense officials told us that since 1997 Iran and other countries of proliferation concern have intensified their efforts to acquire biological weapons expertise and materials from at least 15 former Soviet biological weapons institutes.

An unclassified Central Intelligence Agency report notes that these countries and terrorist groups could make dramatic leaps forward in their biological weapons programs by importing talent from Russia.[40] Another unclassified Central Intelligence Agency report notes that Russia is a significant source of biotechnology expertise for Iran and that Russia's world-leading biological weapons program makes it an attractive target for Iranians seeking technical information and training on biological weapons production processes.[41]

Five of the six institute directors told us of significant reductions of funding since the breakup of the former Soviet Union. Officials at Russia's State Research Center for Applied Microbiology told us that their operating budget dropped from about $25 million in 1991 to about $2.5 million in 1999. Institute officials said the actual purchasing power of the scientists' salaries had decreased by more than 75 percent during this time. Numerous senior scientists told us their current salaries ranged from $40 to $80 a month.

Institute officials at the six institutes we visited said most of the scientific staff that had left their institutes had gone to the United States or Europe. Although none of the institute officials reported knowledge of scientists moving to countries of proliferation concern, the former Deputy Chief of Biopreparat and various media reports identify instances in which scientists have moved to such countries. Officials at three institutes we visited reported that, in the past, representatives of countries of proliferation concern had approached them seeking to initiate questionable dual-use research. Officials at the three institutes told us they had refused these offers because of a pledge made to U.S. executive branch officials as a condition of receiving U.S. assistance. The pledge includes avoiding cooperation with countries of proliferation concern or with terrorists.

. . . Officials from the Departments of State and Defense said they are concerned that dangerous pathogen stocks could be stolen and used for illicit purposes or that an industrial accident could occur. These officials cited a recent nongovernmental report that identified several instances of theft or diversion of dangerous pathogens, including smallpox, plague, and anthrax, from institutes in Russia, Georgia, and Kazakhstan. The Defense Department notes that providing physical security is difficult because of the small size of pathogen vials. Also, pathogens cannot be detected using X-ray machines. For example, a seed culture of dried anthrax spores could be carried in a sealed plastic vial the size of a thumbnail, making detection almost impossible. Also of concern is the potential sale of dangerous pathogens to terrorist groups or countries of proliferation concern.

Although some institutes had impressive equipment and modern facilities, we also observed [they] are often unused. Deteriorated conditions may be compounded by potential human error such as the case of the 1979 accidental release of anthrax from a Soviet military facility in Sverdlovsk, Russia (now Yekaterinburg), which resulted in the deaths of at least 66 people.

. . . Russia could potentially sustain or renew an offensive biological weapons program by using the former Soviet program's existing human and physical assets, according to State and Defense Department officials. Such assets include the institutes, which supported a covert national offensive biological weapons program that continued in spite of the Biological and Toxin Weapons Convention. The Department of Defense has reported 16 that the United States remains concerned about Russia's biological weapons capabilities and its compliance with the Convention. State and Defense officials told us in March 2000 that they remain concerned that offensive research may continue to take place at the Russian Ministry of Defense facilities to which the United States has no access. Another issue of concern is that the leadership of the former Soviet biological weapons program remains largely in place. In a January 2000 report, the Defense Department stated that the same generals who directed the Soviet biological weapons program continue to lead the greatly reduced Russian military defensive biological weapons program, while the same Soviet ex-general continues to direct Biopreparat.[42]

## State Actor, Proxy, and Terrorist/Extremist Incidents to Date

While some sources claim that there has been almost no use of biological weapons in covert and terrorist attacks to date, this does not seem to be the case. Work by W. Seth Carus indicates that there are fifty-one cases of reported biological terrorism, of which twenty-four involved significant activity and five involved confirmed use. In addition, there are seventy-seven cases of criminal use of biological agents and poisons, forty-nine of which can be confirmed, and ninety-three more cases where the perpetrators cannot be characterized clearly as either terrorist or criminals. There are nineteen cases involving allegations of covert state activity, of which eleven can be documented.[43]

This does not mean that there have not been more cases where false reports have been made. Carus found a total of 234 reported cases, of which 150 involved significant activity. A total of 109 cases out of the 150 involved threats or hoaxes, but 10 involved a serious interest in biological agents, 10 more involved actual efforts to acquire biological agents, and 21 more involved actual acquisition and use. It is interesting to note that sixteen of the latter twenty-one cases of actual use involved criminal activity and only five involved terrorism.[44]

The tempo of such activity also seems to be increasing. A total of thirty-three out of forty-nine confirmed criminal cases occurred in the 1990s, and sixteen out of the twenty-four confirmed criminal uses. If one includes all possibilities including threats and hoaxes, 123 out of 150 cases occurred in the 1990s, versus 9 during 1980–1989, 8 during 1970–1979, 1 during 1960–1969, 1 during 1950–1959, 1 during 1940–1949, 3 during 1930–1939, 0 during 1920–1929, 3 during 1910–1919, and 1 during 1900–1909.[45] The actual level of casualties, however, has remained limited. Carus estimates that there were 881 casualties as a result of bio-crimes and bioterrorism, of which 130 resulted from bio-crimes and 751 from one successful incident of bioterrorism. These casualties produced only ten deaths, only one of which has occurred since 1945.[46]

There have been several serious terrorist and extremist efforts to use biological weapons. Germany's Red Army Faction, Italy's Red Brigades, and some Palestinian groups have, at least, discussed the manufacture and use of chemical and biological weapons. Chemical poisons have been used in ways that skate the definition of biological weapons. Palestinian terrorists once poisoned a shipment of Jaffa oranges from Israel, and a shipment of Chilean grapes shipped to the United States was dusted with cyanide. In 1984, a member of the Baghwan Shree Rajneesh cult used salmonella gastroenteritis to poison the salad bars in a town in Oregon and 751 people became ill.[47] In 1989, a cell of the German Baader-Meinhof gang was discovered with a culture of *Clostridium botulinum*.

Aum Shinrikyo is the one known case in which a terrorist/extremist group had vast financial resources and actively attempted to use biological weapons. It is not clear, however, that it represents anything other than a fluke. Few religious extremist movements turn to radical terrorism of the kind that involves the potential use of WMD. Aum's vast financial resources, ability to buy modern equipment, and access to some scientists also does not mean that a cult based on a narrow view of the world sets the standard for effective planning and work efforts.

There are also different views of Aum's success. According to some sources, Aum attempted to acquire the Ebola virus in Zaire, and success-fully manufactured and tried to use anthrax and botulinum in attacks in Japan in 1995.[48] One report even talks about spraying anthrax from the top of Aum's building in Tokyo for four days. It does seem that Aum attempted eleven different uses of biological weapons. According to one source, four involved the use of botulinum toxin between April 1990 and March 1995, and against targets such as civilians in Tokyo, U.S. bases in

Yokohama, and the airport at Narita. Four involved attacks using anthrax during the period from late June through July 1993, and all intended to kill large numbers of civilians in Tokyo.[49]

Experts debate whether this failure was the result of any inherent problems in manufacturing the agent or limitations in the method of attack, and some feel Aum failed because it used a vaccine strain of anthrax and a form of botulism that was very slow to reproduce.[50] Still another source summarizes Aum's efforts as follows:

> The first experiment with this was in April 1990, while most of the cult members were at a retreat on an island near Okinawa. One team was left behind expressly for the purposes of experimentally releasing Botulin toxin from a car around the Japanese Parliament building, around the Diet. There were no reports of any casualties, any injuries associated with that release.
>
> Three years later, having worked toward trying to perfect their technology, working out of a new laboratory now, the cult attempted once again to release Botulin toxin. They had modified a truck or a car rather, as a spray vehicle, and this time they were intending to release their Botulin toxin to coincide with the wedding of the Crown Prince. And to that end they drove around the Imperial Palace grounds as well as government buildings in Tokyo. At that time they also visited the U.S. Naval base outside of Tokyo and attempted to release Botulin toxin in that area as well. However, once again there were no health effects associated with that release, at least none that were reported.
>
> In late June of '93, that same month, disappointed perhaps over the inability of their Botulin toxin to effect any lasting effects, the cult attempted to release anthrax spores, or did release anthrax spores, from their office building laboratory in Tokyo itself. Now at the time there were reports of foul smells, brown steam spots on cars and the sidewalk, some pet deaths, plant deaths and what-have-you, but again, no reports of any human casualties associated with that release.[51]

Another source directly contradicts these assertions. It denies that Aum actively sought Ebola or Q fever, produced botulinum toxin with any success, or made an effective attempt to use anthrax. In fact, it claims that Aum attempted to modify an animal vaccine culture.[52] It denies that Aum had any success in genetic engineering and reports that Aum successfully used molecular engineering or reengineered E. coli to place a botulinum toxin inside it.

The most interesting aspect of this view is that it indicates that Aum failed to be successful because it never made many of the reported attempts and because it was so extreme it could not carry out complex efforts efficiently. It is interesting to note that a U.S. Army simulation in the 1960s of the use of anthrax in the New York subway produced an estimated ten thousand deaths, and one expert estimated that as many as three million might have died if tularemia had been used instead.[53]

## The Yugoslav Smallpox Incident

It is interesting to contrast the various views of the Aum experience with a natural outbreak of disease in a developed country, which could just as easily have been the result of a biological attack:

> the only guidance we have on what to expect from a smallpox release comes from the experience of two natural outbreaks, one in Germany in 1970, which led to a total of 20 people being infected, and a far worse outbreak in Yugoslavia in 1972. . . . When a pilgrim returned to the famous Kosovo province, he was seen by a number of different friends on return. These friends came from a number of different areas and about two weeks later, a group of cases occurred, eleven cases.
>
> Yugoslavia had seen no smallpox since 1927, so this was 1972, 45 years since they'd had any smallpox. Yugoslavia, like most of Europe, was regularly vaccinating the population, so it was a moderately well vaccinated population. The physicians however, had had no experience in diagnosing smallpox and all of the eleven cases in the first generation were missed. One of the cases was a haemorrhagic case. Haemorrhagic smallpox is very uniformly fatal, within usually five to seven days. The individual normally puts out a great deal of virus, but the diagnosis is often missed. In this case it was a 30-year-old schoolteacher who came down with this disease, was given penicillin; his condition deteriorated, he was moved subsequently to another hospital, a district hospital, finally to the capital city, his blood pressure began to fall, he was evacuated to an intensive care unit, and at the intensive care unit he died. Only two days after his death was it recognized that smallpox was present in Yugoslavia.
>
> That person, that one schoolteacher, infected some 35 others in the hospital throughout his stay, including a number of physicians and nurses. And then by the time it was discovered, there were some 150 cases already present in Yugoslavia. The problem that the Yugoslav government was then faced with, as this was reported to other countries, they closed their borders, literally closed their borders—this would be Austria, Italy, Greece—and simply stopped all transport across the border, be it boat or train or plane, Yugoslavia was isolated.
>
> They saw no option but to go ahead and vaccinate the entire country, which they did over a period of some 10 to 12 days, they vaccinated some 19 million people. They were faced with a number of contacts of cases; they wanted to isolate them, so that if they did come down with smallpox they would already be isolated and would not continue to spread the disease. And so they took over whole hotels, apartment blocks, and cordoned them off with barbed wire and police, and admitted the people in to this area for a two-week stay, and no one left those once they were quarantined. And they did this for some 10,000 people.[54]

### Cases in the United States

There have been a number of domestic extremist attempts to use such weapons in the United States although many were little more than threats and none have been particularly successful. Some food poisoning efforts have succeeded in causing illness, but a few sick and dead scarcely compare with an average of nine thousand deaths from food poisoning a year in the United States from natural causes. The FBI reports that:

- Thirty-seven cases involving chemical and biological weapons were opened in 1996.
- There were seventy-four cases opened in 1997, twenty-two of which were related to biological agents.
- There were 181 cases opened in 1998, 112 of which were biological.
- As of late May 1999, 123 cases had been opened in 1999, 100 of which were biological.
- In 1998 and 1999 combined, over three-quarters of the cases opened threatened the release of biological weapons; the most common threat was anthrax.[55]

Most of these cases can be dismissed as mere threats and extortion attempts, often by deeply disturbed "loners." FBI sources do indicate, however, that some involved relatively well-equipped home labs and that there were some successful efforts to produce ricin, botulinum, and anthrax.

### The Lethality and Effectiveness of Current Biological Weapons

Chart 4.2 shows that biological weapons can be far more lethal than chemical weapons. The lethal dose for botulinum toxin, for example, is 0.001 micrograms per kilogram of body weight, while the lethal dose for VX—the most lethal form of nerve gas—is 15 micrograms per kilogram of body weight. In theory, one milligram of anthrax spores contains one million infective doses.

Chart 4.3 and Tables 4.7 and 4.8 show that efficient modern biological weapons can be extremely lethal or merely incapacitating. They can be infectious or transmitted only by contact with a wet or dry delivery medium. They can be quick or slow to react, and can be chosen from weapons for which there are well-known and proven cures or from weapons for which there is no present vaccine or effective treatment. It should be noted, however, that most of the estimates of the impact of attacks used in this study are drawn from military models where the threat was assumed to be weaponized.

As in the case with chemical weapons any such lethality estimates are extremely uncertain although, the CDC and Defense Threat Reduction Agency (DTRA) are working on more sophisticated classified models. There is no operational experience to back up theoretical estimates, and the limited test data supporting such estimates is often highly dated and has little to do with modern, highly weaponized agents. In many cases, the assumption is made that delivery will occur under near optimal conditions and that

**Chart 4.2**
**The Relative Killing Effect in Numbers of Dead for Biological versus Chemical Weapons with an Optimal Aerosol Delivery**

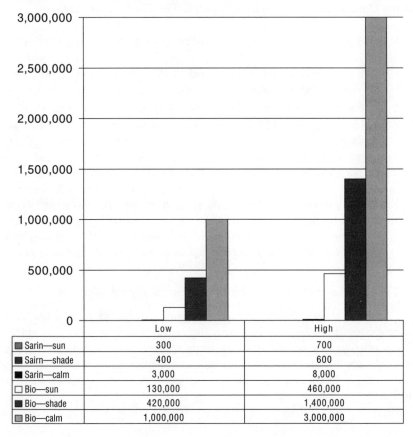

| | Low | High |
|---|---|---|
| Sarin—sun | 300 | 700 |
| Sairn—shade | 400 | 600 |
| Sarin—calm | 3,000 | 8,000 |
| Bio—sun | 130,000 | 460,000 |
| Bio—shade | 420,000 | 1,400,000 |
| Bio—calm | 1,000,000 | 3,000,000 |

the agent will behave in a manner that is somewhat similar to a natural epidemic. In the case of biological weapons, however, these uncertainties affect a far wider range of potential casualties.

### Anthrax As a Case Example

Johns Hopkins has attempted to create a consensus estimate of the threat posed by key biological weapons, including anthrax. It was forced to turn to a World Health Organization (WHO) estimate dating back to 1970 that estimated that the release of 50 kilograms of anthrax over a developed urban area of 5 million could infect as many as 250,000 people, of whom 100,000 could be expected to die. This same WHO study, however, estimated that in other sections fifty kilograms of anthrax could kill "only" about thirty-six thousand and incapacitate another forty-five thousand.[56]

A 1993 report by the Office of Technology Assessment (OTA) of the U.S. Congress estimated that between 130,000 and 3 million would die following the release of 100 kilograms of aerosolized anthrax over the greater Washington area with economic costs of $26.2 billion per 100,000 persons exposed. A chart in the same study estimated that 100 kilograms of a 1- to 5-micron aerosol of anthrax could kill 3 million people in the Washington area, versus 750,000 to 1.9 million for a one-megaton bomb.[57] Other U.S. government studies indicate that it could take in excess of 2,000 kilograms of agent to produce the same range of casualties in the OTA study.[58]

These figures illustrate a range of uncertainty in lethality approaching two orders of magnitude—a range some U.S. Army experts indicate is not atypical of classified studies. The risks of basing deterrence, detection, warning, and response on such estimates are also illustrated by the fact that the Soviet release of anthrax at Sverdlovsk killed only sixty-eight out of only seventy-nine people who became ill, although a cloud of the agent might theoretically have killed one hundred thousand or more. The Soviet government also made only a minimal effort to decontaminate the area and vaccinated only forty-seven thousand of the city's one million inhabitants.

These basic uncertainties regarding lethality are matched by equal uncertainties as to how to measure the area over which an agent has a given degree of effectiveness. Most models assume a symmetrical and relatively even deposit of given amounts of agent over a given area in spite of the fact that all operational tests indicate that wind patterns and other factors lead to irregular patterns of concentration. They also do little more than speculate difficulty of estimating exposure in urban areas where much of the population may stay indoors and where the life and effectiveness of the agent may vary according to the presence of sunlight and heat.[59]

Although anthrax is the best studied biological weapon, it seems fair to say that the effectiveness of any given weaponization of the agent will only be determined when it is actually used, and that its real-world lethality could range from negligible to catastrophic. Furthermore, the weaponized version of anthrax is inhaled while virtually all cases that occur in nature are cutaneous.

While Iraq produced over eight thousand liters of concentrated anthrax solution before the Persian Gulf War, there is little practical experience with anthrax as a human disease. Only eighteen cases of inhalation have been recorded in the United States between 1900 and 1978, two of which were the result of laboratory experiments. In contrast, 2,000 cases of cutaneous anthrax are reported each year, a total of 224 cases were reported in the United States during 1944–1994, and 10,000 people died during an epidemic in Zimbabwe between 1979 and 1985. This helps explain why

**Chart 4.3—Part 1**
**The Nominal Lethality of Different Biological Weapons (numbers of dead from delivery of 1,000 kilograms)**

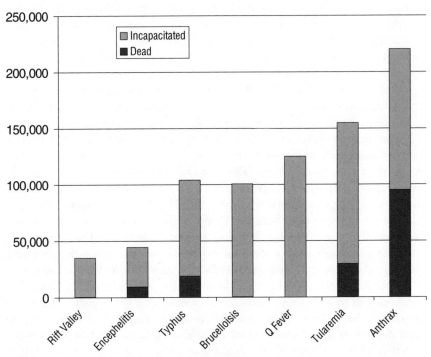

| Agent | Downwind Reach (kilometers) | Casualties | |
|---|---|---|---|
| | | Dead | Incapacitated |
| Rift Valley fever | 1 | 400 | 35,000 |
| Tick-borne encephalitis | 1 | 9,500 | 35,000 |
| Typhus | 5 | 19,000 | 85,000 |
| Brucellosis | 10 | 500 | 100,000 |
| Q fever | 20+ | 150 | 125,000 |
| Tularemia | 20+ | 30,000 | 125,000 |
| Anthrax | 20++ | 95,000 | 125,000 |

*Source*: World Health Organization, *Health Aspects of Chemical and Biological Weapons* (Geneva: World Health Organization, 1970).

estimates of the lethality of weaponized inhalational anthrax have to be based on primate data, and why the range of uncertainty for a lethal dose of a 1- to 5-micron dry agent ranges from 2,500 to 55,500 spores.[60] The DOD *Medical NBC Battlebook* does not give lethality data per se, but it

**Chart 4.3—Part 2**
**The Nominal Lethality of Different Biological Weapons (numbers of dead from delivery of 1,000 kilograms)**

| 20–90% Deaths in 1–10 Days | 20–100% Deaths in 5–20 Days | 50–100% Incapacity for 2 Weeks |
|---|---|---|
| Anthrax[bc] | Brucellosis[c] | Brill-Zinsser disease |
| Bolivian hemor. fever | Blastomycosis | Dengue fever |
| Ebola infection | Congo Crim. hem. fever[d] | Eastern equine encephalitis |
| Glanders[d] | Monkey herpes B | Epidemic typhus[d] |
| Lassa infection[d] | Korean hemor. fever[d] | Legionellosis |
| Marburg infection | Japanese encephalitis | Murine typhus |
| Plague[bd] | Monkeypox infection | Q fever[c] |
| Smallpox[abd] | Omsk hemor. fever[d] | Rift Valley fever |
| Yellow fever[b] | Russian S/S encephalitis | Salmonellosis |
| Melioidosis | Tularemia[bc] | Scrub typhus[d] |
| | Argentine hemor. fever[d] | |
| | Bolivian hemor. fever[d] | |
| | Influenze[d] | |

[a]Untreated; days are numbers of days after symptoms appear
[b]Vaccine available—if not genetically altered
[c]Known to be weaponized
[d]Probably weaponized

*Sources*: Kenneth Alibeck, "Biological Weapons Protection," Hadron, Inc., June 1, 2000; and USACHPPM, *The Medical NBC Battlebook*, USACHPPM Technical Guide 244, 4-20-4-21.

does show a range of eight thousand to fifty thousand spores for an infective dose.[61]

This leads to equally large uncertainties over detection and treatment, particularly since the Soviet experience in Sverldovsk showed that cases occurred over a period two to forty-three days after exposure, and primate data indicates that weaponized spores can cause lethal effects fifty-eight to ninety-eight days after exposure. The diagnostics and post mortems at Sverdlovk produced a wide range of symptoms and effects that made diagnosis difficult. If an attack is covert, it is also unlikely that the disease would be recognized quickly. The limited Soviet and Russian experience with the disease indicates that first-stage symptoms are close to those of the flu—a problem that could make initial diagnosis difficult. Even if a deliberate early effort is made to use diagnostic testing for anthrax, it would take six to twenty-four hours to confirm the disease. With the course of the disease normally lasting only three days before death, that presents serious problems in organizing the proper response. A delay of even hours in administering antibiotics can be fatal.[62]

Treatment presents further problems because there are no clinical studies of inhalational anthrax in human beings, a weaponized agent can be tailored to increase its lethality and resistance to treatment, and rapid vaccination would not be practical even if the vaccine was known to be effective against the strain used in the weapon. The U.S. vaccine, which may or may not be effective, is normally given in a six-dose series and the United States does not regard the human-live attenuated vaccine developed by the former Soviet Union as safe.

The communicability of a weaponized version of the disease is unclear, and containment and quarantine might be necessary. Serious problems could also arise in dealing with dead bodies since cremation seems to be the only safe form of corpse disposal.[63]

### Botulism As a Case Example

These uncertainties become progressively more serious with less-familiar weaponized agents. For example, some U.S. Army experts believe that it takes at least thirty-five times more botulinum to create a lethal dose than the U.S. estimates in much of its published lethality data.[64] This uncertainty is of some interest because Iraq produced tons of botulism toxin. (The *Medical NBC Battlebook* does not give a lethal dose, but states that the infective dose is 0.001 *ug*/kilogram [type A].[65])

There is virtually no empirical data in normal medicine with aerosolized botulinum toxin, but it is expected to produce symptoms normal to the food borne version. Symptoms could begin anywhere from twenty-four hours to several days after exposure. The initial symptoms would be those of the flu or cold until more characteristic motor symptoms appeared. The U.S. Army is still investigating a vaccine that counters five of the seven neurotoxins in the disease, and seems to leave significant antibodies for more than a year, while the CDC has a vaccine that deals with three out of the seven neurotoxins. A higher-risk heptavalent antitoxin for neurotoxins A-G is available from the U.S. Army Medical Research Institute of Infectious Disease, but it requires a protocol with informed consent.[66]

### Plague As a Case Example

Plague is a known natural killer and is estimated to have killed over one-third of the population in the Middle East and Europe in major outbreaks in 541 A.D. and 1346, and another 12 million people in China and India in 1855. Japan, however, is the only nation known to have tried to use botulinum in recent combat. Unit 731 dropped plague-infected fleas over China on several occasions and caused some cases of plague, although the true scale of the resulting illnesses and deaths is unknown.[67]

Once again, the little reliable data on lethality and estimates differ sharply. The WHO estimated in 1970 that the release of an aerosol of 50 kilograms of Y Pestis over a city of 5 million would infect 150,000 people and kill 36,000—creating a zone of infection 10 kilometers long and lasting an hour.[68] The former Soviet Union also conducted a massive weaponization effort during the Cold War that involved ten institutes and thousands of scientists.

U.S. Army experts working on the weapon, however, never succeeded in developing a highly effective agent before they terminated research in 1970. Once again, there are serious questions as to what dose would be lethal and how much agent would be required. The DOD *Medical NBC Battlebook* does not give lethality data per se, but it does show a range of one hundred to five hundred organisms for an infective dose.[69]

A military agent would not behave as a normal disease. Most natural cases are caused by infection from fleas or direct contact with the infected, and only 2 percent of the 390 cases in the United States between 1947 and 1996 were the kind of pneumonic plague that would be used in weapons. The most recent cases involving large outbreaks of pneumonic plague date back to outbreaks in Manchuria in 1910–1911 and in India in and 1920–1921, with one small case in Madagascar in 1997. These cases produced nearly 100 percent lethality among those infected, but they do not set a clear precedent for understanding the behavior of an aerosol weapon.

What is clear is that warning, detection, and treatment would present major response problems. The signs of plague only develop one to six days after infection, with a mean time of two to four days, and can initially be confused with a cold or flu. The more severe symptoms are similar to viral pneumonia and might not be seen as plague. There are no widely available rapid diagnostic tests, and it could take many states days to perform a conclusive set of tests. The only vaccine for plague was discontinued in 1999 and was never effective in dealing with pneumonic as distinguished from bubonic plague.

The use of streptomycin and other drugs can be highly effective, but it requires treatment to begin within twenty-four hours of exposure to avoid high lethality rates. There are also strains of Y Pestis that are highly immune to normal treatment and that might be weaponized.[70] The live-attenuated vaccines used in some countries have serious side effects and do not seem effective against aerosol agents, and the formaline-inactivated vaccine produced in the United States does not reliably protect animals against aerosols.[71]

Once again, there is no empirical evidence for judging the infectivity of a weaponized agent, how a cloud of agent would behave, or the real-world lethality of the agent. The disease is so dangerous, however, that immediate decisions would have to be taken as to who to contain and/or quarantine.

### Smallpox As a Case Example

Smallpox has not been a disease threat in the United States for more that a quarter of a century, but it is highly lethal, with a fatality rate approaching 30 percent among the nonvaccinated. In theory, it was eradicated in 1977, and only two tightly controlled samples are supposed to exist in the United States and Russia. However, the former Soviet Union evidently was still involved in the large-scale weaponization of the agent in 1980, while a number of developing states began their biological warfare programs in the 1960s and may have retained cultures. U.S. intelligence suspects Iran, Libya, North Korea, and Syria may have retained cultures for military purposes.[72]

At this point in time, there are over 114 million unvaccinated Americans and the value of vaccination over thirty years ago is uncertain. The CDC does have a stockpile of fifteen million doses of the vaccine in the United States, but only a maximum of six to seven million doses still seem to be effective.[73] The U.S. Army has, however, contracted with BioReliance to make three hundred thousand more doses for military use. BioReliance is developing an improved vaccine and indicates it has a longer-term capability to make and store ten to fifteen million doses.[74]

The natural aerosolized version of variola major is vulnerable to heat and humidity, but again there is no way to translate the normal behavior of the disease into the effectiveness of a military agent or to predict its transmissibility between human beings, although each generation of infection can easily expand the number of cases by ten to twenty times. It is known that only a few virons are needed to infect a human being and they are only two hundred nanometers in diameter. Once again, there are serious questions as to what dose would be lethal and how much agent would be required. The DOD *Medical NBC Battlebook* does not give lethality data per se, but it does show an *assumed* range of ten to one hundred organisms for an infective dose.[75]

Smallpox has an incubation period of seven to seventeen days, with the normal period beginning around twelve days. It then takes one to three days for clear symptoms to appear in the form of typical skin eruptions, followed by a seven- to ten-day progression of the disease requiring constant isolation and intensive medical treatment.[76] As a result, warning and detection would be difficult, and death usually occurs five or six days after the appearance of the characteristic rash, leaving limited time for treatment. Vaccination is only effective through a maximum of two to four days after exposure, although the first symptoms do not appear for roughly two weeks, supportive therapy has only moderate effectiveness, and cases require isolation to prevent further transmission of the disease. In one case, a single patient infected people on three floors of a hospital because of transmission through the air vents. Decontamination is difficult and must be very thorough.[77]

The problem of deciding who to contain and/or quarantine would again force largely speculative decisions.

### Detect, Defend, and Respond to What?

The sheer range of uncertainty in such estimates creates massive problems in judging the priority the United States should give to defense against biological weapons, deterring and retaliating against their use, and developing suitable response measures. Even if such weapons are not developed in ways that deliberately defeat current vaccines and medical treatment, many forms of biological attacks, and some chemical attacks as well, would present major problems in terms of effective medical treatment.

A recent GAO study concludes that this would be true even if the biological agent was a relatively well-known weapon like anthrax:

> Medical preventive measures and treatments are available for some but not all chemical and biological agents. Early treatment following exposure to chemical agents is critical. The availability of effective medical defenses from or treatments for a chemical or biological agent could be a risk factor and influence terrorists' choice of weapon. The lack of an effective vaccine or antibiotic antiviral treatment for biological agents or of an antidote for chemical agents would pose a potential public health challenge but also pose a significant risk for terrorists as well. In the absence of medical defenses, a chemical or biological agent if effectively acquired, processed, and disseminated could become a more desirable choice because it might result in greater casualties. However, processing, testing, and disseminating the agent could equally endanger terrorists because they, too, would have no effective protection against the agent.
>
> Medical and biological warfare experts agree that anthrax when inhaled is an agent of concern due in large part to the difficulty of diagnosis and treatment once symptoms appear and its very high lethality. We recently testified on DOD's anthrax vaccination program, pointing out that:
>
> - the anthrax vaccine is effective for preventing anthrax infections through the skin such as those sometimes contracted by unprotected workers who handle wool and hides and
> - the vaccine appears to be effective against inhalation anthrax in animal species for some, but not all, strains.
>
> However, due to the absence of known correlates of immunity, the results of the animal studies cannot be extrapolated with certainty to humans. DOD is in the process of vaccinating military personnel against anthrax. The efficacy of the vaccine for inhalation anthrax in humans has not been proven. According to CDC, supplies of the plague vaccine do not exist in the United States; however, small supplies of killed plague vaccine may exist in Australia and the United Kingdom. CDC does not consider a vaccine useful to control an outbreak nor protect a population against a terrorist incident.
>
> Further, there are no vaccines for other potential biological agents such as Ebola and other hemorrhagic fevers, brucellosis, glanders, or staphylo-

coccal enterotoxin B. Post-exposure treatment for inhalation anthrax consists of using the vaccine and the antibiotic ciproflaxin, but treatment must begin immediately after exposure and before the influenza-like symptoms appear. . . . Because the symptoms mimic common influenza, proper diagnosis may come too late for effective treatment. . . . DOD believes it is prudent to vaccinate U. S. military forces against anthrax exposure, even though efficacy for inhalation anthrax has been based on animal testing.

Similarly, there are no specific antidotes for a number of chemical agents such as the toxic industrial chemicals chlorine and phosgene. Treatment for exposure to these chemical agents consists largely of decontamination, first aid, and respiratory support. An antidote kit comprised of amyl or sodium nitrite exists for hydrogen cyanide. Appendixes I and II contain information on medical treatments for chemical and biological agents, respectively.

Prevention and treatments are available for a number of other agents. For example, there is an effective vaccine for known strains of smallpox, and there are new investigative vaccines for several other possible biological agents, including botulinum, Q fever, Venezuelan equine encephalitis, and tularemia. Antidotes such as atropine, pralidoxime chloride, and diazepam can be used to counteract the effects of a number of chemical nerve agents. The treatment for some chemical and biological agents includes respiratory support with a ventilator. The types and quantities of vaccines, pharmaceuticals, and other items that should be available in the event of a chemical or biological attack can be determined through a methodologically sound threat and risk assessment.[78]

### Means of Delivery

Some of these issues become clearer after a review of different means of delivery. Unlike chemical weapons and most nuclear weapons, biological agents generally are compact and low in weight. They can be disseminated in a wide number of ways—such as insects, the contamination of water and food supplies, contact, spreading powders or liquids, and by aerosol. The DOD reports that dissemination of infectious agents through aerosols, either as droplets from liquid suspensions or by small particles from dry powders, is by far the most efficient method.[79] Tests conducted during the 1950s and 1960s showed that an aerosol cloud of fine (two to five microns) particles behaves more like a gas than a suspension and penetrates interior as well as exterior spaces. The United States found that release from ships, aircraft, and tall buildings could achieve some lethality over distances of fifty to one hundred miles, although without anything approaching uniform density.[80]

The military means for delivering biological weapons include artillery, missiles, and aerial sprayers. There are two basic types of actual munitions: point-source bomblets and line-source tanks. Within each category there can be multiple shapes and configurations. Biological weapons munitions and delivery systems are very interdependent; frequently, the munition dictates the delivery system. With the evolution of sophisticated line-source hardware, the agent, munition, and delivery system must be carefully integrated. Like chemical weapons, the effectiveness of biological weapons munitions is dependent on meteorological conditions and many are also sensitive to exposure to daylight.

Covert attacks against the U.S. homeland could involve a wide range of different methods of delivery. They could include disseminating agents through contact, using the wind, or spreading them from high buildings, crop sprayers, commercial aircraft, and helicopters. Arthropod vectors and the contamination of food and water supplies could be significant modes of dissemination for biological weapons agents. Since only relatively small quantities of relatively impure agent are required for terrorist use, the range of possible agents and methods of delivery are almost unlimited.

The DOD estimates indicate that the quantity of an agent could be small (a single gram, possibly less). Production and purification methods and dissemination means could range from simple to complex. All of the elements of such a program might go undetected until use occurred. Broad areas or individual buildings are potential targets. In the case of buildings, off-the-shelf aerosol generators could be used to disperse a biological agent into the air inlet ducts of the target structure. This is especially true in the case of toxins, in that a much less toxic agent could be employed and/or that quantities of agent required would be much less than for other targets.

Attacks could involve a *mix* of different biological weapons that require radically different treatments. Because some weapons take a long time before their effects are clear, attacks using multiple agents of "cocktails" could be carried out over days or weeks before their nature and impact became clear. Attacks on agriculture or humans could be masked as the natural outbreak of disease. Accidental "attacks" on American agriculture have been common, and have often had a major impact. Such "attacks" have consisted of importing the wrong pet, diseases brought in the form of a few infected animals or plants, and insects and parasites that have arrived on birds, aircraft, cars, and ships. These have all had a major impact on given crops and have affected the ecology of whole states, particularly in the southern and western United States and Hawaii. The potential lethality of such attacks is further illustrated by the costs of "mad cow" disease (variant Cruzfeldt Jakob disease or VCJD) in Europe, and the fact that one infected pig could destroy an entire swine industry in Taiwan. The introduction of foot-and-mouth disease into Great Britian has demonstrated a similar level of vulnerabillity. Such a form of delivery offers many advantages: it could be virtually undetectable, it could be unattributable, it might never been seen as a deliberate attack, and its effects could be lasting and nationwide.

## Manufacturing Biological Weapons

The manufacture of highly effective biological weapons to use against humans does, however, present significant problems. Producing such weapons is not a problem for most governments, but the ease with which most domestic or foreign terrorists/extremists can obtain or manufacture such weapons has sometimes been exaggerated.

A recent GAO analysis of the issue found that:

> According to experts in the many fields associated with the technical Biological Agents aspects of dealing with biological agents, including those formerly with state-sponsored offensive biological weapon programs, terrorists working outside a state-run laboratory infrastructure would have to overcome extraordinary technical and operational challenges to effectively and successfully weaponize and deliver a biological agent to cause mass casualties. Terrorists would require specialized knowledge from a wide range of scientific disciplines to successfully conduct biological terrorism and cause mass casualties. For example, biological agents have varying characteristics.
>
> Information and technical data from these experts, intelligence, and authoritative documented sources indicate that some biological agents such as smallpox are difficult to obtain. In the case of other biological agents such as anthrax and tularemia (both of which are bacteria), it is difficult to obtain a virulent strain (one that causes disease and injury to humans). Other agents such as plague are difficult to produce. Biological toxins such as ricin require large quantities to cause mass casualties, thereby increasing the risk of arousing suspicion or detection prior to dissemination. Furthermore, some agents such as Q fever incapacitate rather than cause death. Finally, many agents are relatively easy to grow, but are difficult to process into a form for a weapon.
>
> . . . According to experts from former biological warfare programs, to survive and be effective, a virulent biological agent must be grown, handled, and stored properly. This stage requires time and effort for research and development. After cultivation, the agent is wet. Terrorists would need the means to sterilize the growth medium and dispose of hazardous biological wastes. Processing the biological agent into a weaponized form requires even more specialized knowledge.
>
> According to a wide range of experts in science, health, intelligence, and biological warfare and the technical report we reviewed, the most effective way to disseminate a biological agent is by aerosol. This method allows the simultaneous respiratory infection of a large number of people. Microscopic particles that are dispersed must remain airborne for long periods and may be transported by the wind over long distances. The particles are small enough to reach the tiny air sacs of the lungs (alveoli) and bypass the body's natural filtering and defense mechanisms.
>
> According to experts, if larger particles are dispersed, they may fall to the ground, causing no injury, or become trapped in the upper respiratory tract, possibly causing infections but not necessarily death. From an engineering standpoint, it is easier to produce and disseminate the larger particles than the microscopic particles. Other critical technical hurdles include obtaining the proper size equipment to generate proper size aerosols, calculating the correct output rate (speed at which the equipment operates), and having the correct liquid composition.

According to key experts with experience in biological warfare, biological agents can be processed into liquid or dry forms for dissemination. Anthrax is the disease caused by the biological agent Bacillus anthracis. Throughout the report we use the related disease term when referring to biological agents. We found that the disease term is used synonymously with the biological agent in discussions with the many experts we interviewed and documentation we reviewed.

They pose difficult technical challenges for terrorists to effectively cause mass casualties. These experts told us that liquid agents are easy to produce. However, it is difficult to effectively disseminate aerosolized liquid agents with the right particle size without reducing the strength of the mixture. Further, the liquid agent requires larger quantities and dissemination vehicles that can increase the possibility of raising suspicion and detection. In addition, experts told us that in contrast, dry biological agents are more difficult to produce than liquid agents, but dry agents are easier to disseminate.

Dry biological agents could be easily destroyed when processed, rendering the agent ineffective for causing mass casualties. A leading expert told us that the whole process entails risks. For example, powders easily adhere to rubber gloves and pose a handling problem. Effectively disseminating both forms of agent can pose technical challenges in that the proper equipment and energy sources are needed. A less sophisticated product and dissemination method can produce some illness and/ or deaths. DOD classified further details on technical challenges of effectively processing and disseminating biological agents.

According to the experts we spoke with, exterior dissemination of biological agents can be disrupted by environmental (e.g., pollution) and meteorological (e.g., sun, rain, mist, and wind) conditions. Once released, an aerosol cloud gradually decays and dies as a result of exposure to oxygen, pollutants, and ultraviolet rays. If wind is too erratic or strong, the agent might be dissipated too rapidly or fail to reach the desired area. Interior dissemination of a biological agent through a heating and air conditioning ventilation system could cause casualties. But this method also has risks. Security countermeasures could intercept the perpetrators or apprehend them after the attack. Successful interior dissemination also requires knowledge of aerodynamics. For example, the air exchange rate in a building could affect the dissemination of a biological agent. Regardless of whether a liquid or dry agent is used in interior or exterior environments, experts believe that testing should be done to determine if the agent is virulent and disseminates properly. The numerous steps in the process of developing a biological weapon increase the chances of a terrorist being detected by authorities.[81]

The Gilmore Commission drew somewhat similar conclusions:

the situation now facing a terrorist, who may seek to use a CBRN weapon to achieve mass effects, could change dramatically because of new discoveries, further advances in technology, or other material factors. This is particularly true with respect to potential improvements in aerosolization techniques and processes; advances in the isolation, purification, stability, and quality of certain biological strains; or enhancements to delivery devices, such as nozzles or other sprayers. Future progress in any two or more areas would be especially troubling.

. . . There are at least four primary acquisition routes that terrorists could conceivably pursue in acquiring a biological warfare capability. They are purchasing a biological agent from one of the world's 1,500 germ banks, as Larry Wayne Harris did; theft from a research laboratory, hospital, or public health service laboratory, where agents are cultivated for diagnostic purposes; isolation and culturing of a desired agent from natural sources; or obtaining biological agents from a rogue state, a disgruntled government scientist, or a state sponsor.

The principal obstacle is less the development of a biological agent than the development of a genuinely lethal strain of the agent in sufficient quantities to cause mass casualties—precisely as Aum's experience indicates. Acquiring the "most infectious and virulent culture for the seed stock is the greatest hurdle," a former senior official in the U.S. military's biological warfare program maintains.

As Aum clearly demonstrated, this is not an easily surmountable obstacle. The most obvious route would be by attempting to acquire the strain from nature, e.g., obtaining potentially lethal anthrax spores from soil and then culturing sufficient quantities to produce mass casualties. While theoretically conceivable, this is nonetheless difficult in practice and doubtless well beyond the capabilities of most terrorist groups.

Acquiring a biological agent of sufficient virulence is only one of the prerequisites for conducting biological terrorism on a mass scale. As Ken Alibek, one of the former Soviet Union's leading biological weapons scientists has argued, the "most virulent culture in a test tube is useless as an offensive weapon until it has been put through a process that gives it stability and predictability. The manufacturing technique is, in a sense, the real weapon, and it is harder to develop than individual agents."

. . . Airborne viral agents, in particular, are extraordinarily difficult to work with, since the mass production, packaging, and storage of viruses are by themselves difficult and complicated tasks, demanding advanced biotechnical skills, in addition to the attendant risks to personnel involved in the process. In the specific case of botulinum toxins, there are difficulties in purifying these agents, which then will likely become unstable once they are purified. According to one biological warfare authority, "maintaining the high toxicity in the culture and the properties of the toxin as you purify it are what you have to have a lot of years [of experience] to know how to do."

The same problem of maintaining toxicity during the purification process hampered U.S. government researchers during the Cold War. They discovered that attempting to achieve 95 percent purity of a biological agent—the level needed to render it effective as a weapon—in turn reduced the bulk amount of the toxin by 70–80 percent.

Producing other types of bioterrorism agents similarly requires training, advanced techniques, and specialized equipment. In the case of B. anthracis, for example, transforming the bacterium into spore form suitable for use in a wide-scale terrorist attack necessitates a combination of skill and extreme care during a production technique that involves the application of heat or chemical shock. During all stages of the process, B. anthracis, like all other biological agents, must also be continuously tested to ensure its purity and lethality and thus its utility for weapons purposes. Although small-scale laboratory testing might be concealed, any larger-scale tests will likely invite the attention of law enforcement or intelligence agencies.

Indeed, any group aiming at developing a weapon capable of inflicting mass casualties would almost certainly require sophisticated, though not exotic, laboratory equipment. According to the Central Intelligence Agency, this would include "fermenters, large-scale lyophilizers or freeze dryers, class II or III safety hoods, High-Efficiency Particulate Air (HEPA) filters, and centrifuges."

Estimates for the cost of equipping a facility for the production of biological agents for mass-casualty terrorist operations vary widely but would likely seem to fall anywhere in the $200,000 to $2 million range—certainly not trivial sums. Although there remains a widespread public perception that it is easy to acquire and use highly lethal biological agents, there is no clear consensus among analysts about how much scientific and technological expertise and prior training are needed. Some authorities maintain that having an "experimental microbiologist and a pathologist, or someone who combines these capabilities, would be crucial [s]upplemented with a little help and advice from an aerosol physicist and a meteorologist."

Other experts are even more conservative in their assessments. In their view, the creation of a mass-casualty biological weapon would entail scientific teams composed of persons highly trained in "microbiology, pathology, aerosol physics, aerobiology, and even meteorology."

The acquisition of dedicated staff with the appropriate scientific and engineering knowledge and credentials may, therefore, be the greatest hurdle to developing an effective biological terrorism capability. Finding trained and skilled personnel, who could also overcome obstacles of perhaps working in less-than-ideal environments and who are willing to participate in mass murder, is a profound organizational roadblock, inherent to terrorist development of biological weapons, that is perhaps too readily discounted.

In addition, the paranoid, stressful, and fantasy-prone atmosphere almost certain to be present in a terrorist organization most likely to seek to acquire biological weapons would make it difficult for personnel to perform efficiently the careful and demanding work required for a successful program. In the case of Aum, the atmosphere within the cult, characterized by extreme paranoia, intense stress, and widespread delusion, likely contributed to its failure to develop an effective biological weapons capability. That atmosphere could exist in any number of potential terrorist organizations with similar intentions or motivations.

Finally, terrorists intent on inflicting hundreds of thousands of casualties with biological agents would have to create an aerosol cloud to disseminate the toxin. Aerosol clouds can be created from biological agents in either a mud-like liquid ("slurry") form or in a dried, talcum powder-like form. The latter is far more difficult. In the case of B. anthracis, turning the spores into a powder requires the use of large and expensive centrifuges and drying apparatus. Powder, moreover, clings to surfaces, making it difficult to handle and more probable that those handling it will accidentally infect themselves.

In addition, the drying process needed to create a pathogenic powder tends to kill inordinate amounts of the organisms. The use of slurry, on the other hand, while less technically challenging, still presents significant problems. For example, the slurry must be continuously refrigerated until it is used, and unless it is extremely pure, material is likely to settle at the bottom of a container and clog the sprayer or aerosol dissemination device. As is detailed below, this is precisely what happened when Aum Shinrikyo members sprayed what they believed to be a lethal strain of B. anthracis from the roof of a Tokyo building in 1993. A slurry concoction is also tricky to disseminate as an aerosol of particles of an optimal size—in other words, that will readily be inhaled into the victims' lungs. Disseminating particles of the proper size (1-5 microns) is critical to the success of any large-scale attack. Building a disseminator capable of dispersing 1- to 5-micron particles in dry form would, however, be a major technical hurdle for any prospective biological terrorist.

That being said, the dissemination itself could conceivably be physically accomplished in any number of different ways: from low-flying airplanes, crop dusters, trucks equipped with sprayers, or with an aerosol canister situated in one place and activated by a remote timing device.

Even if a terrorist group succeeded in producing a virulent biological agent, even if it conducted rigorous tests to ensure that virulence was maintained, and even if it prepared the agent properly for aerosolization and acquired the proper equipment with which to disseminate it, at least one major hurdle would remain. As bioagents are aerosolized and become airborne, they decay rapidly. It is estimated, for example, that 90 percent of the microorganisms in a slurry are likely to die during the process of aerosolization.

. . . In sum, while the technical challenges in producing an effective biological weapon are not insurmountable, they are neither as straightforward nor as simple as has often been claimed and presented publicly. The latter view, based on the limited information previously available, has heretofore primarily served as the basis for the public and for many decision makers to draw conclusions about the direction of related public policy. The level of difficulty was in fact what Aum discovered for itself and why it elected to pursue, in tandem with its continuing biological weapons R&D program, a concerted and even more expensive effort to produce chemical weapons.

Moreover, as previously mentioned, the requirements to amass personnel, money, facilities, equipment; to conduct testing; and to execute related logistics tasks, will materially increase the risk of exposure to detection by intelligence and law enforcement agencies.[82]

### Changes in Technology and the Difficulty of Manufacture

These cautions are useful, but it must be stressed that these comments on the difficulties in manufacturing biological weapons apply largely to attacks on human beings by either individuals or terrorist and extremist groups working without the aid of a state.

They also reflect to the current state of the art in biotechnology. The steady dissemination of the required technology and equipment is reducing the problems in making biological weapons. For example, a recent survey of fourteen hundred U.S. academic institutions found that 16 percent possessed human, animal, or plant pathogens that appear on the draft BWC's list of biological agents. Another 11 percent have high-level containment facilities, 7 percent conduct research on vaccines, 5 percent perform research for the military or DOD to develop defenses against biological weapons, and 3 percent have high-volume bioreactors.[83]

In the twenty-five years that have followed the development of recombinant DNA technologies, over two thousand firms have been founded in the United States alone. More generally, there are roughly 1,308 U.S. companies now actively commercializing biotechnology. They employ 108,000 to 116,000 people, and the market for such products is estimated to grow from $7.6 billion in 1996 to $24 billion in 2006. These figures do not include the growth of agriculture biotechnology, which may be as much of a source of threat as the technology tailored to deal with humans and which is expected to grow from $295 million in 1996 to $1.74 billion in 2006. Unlike most companies, such firms also train a large number of individuals in research and development. Biotech firms spent $69,000 per employee on research and development in 1995, versus a U.S. corporate average of $7,651.[84] While there are no precise figures, much of this activity involves foreign scientists and technical personnel.

Other regions are not yet as advanced. For example, Japan is estimated to lag roughly ten years behind the United States in biotechnology (a factor to be considered in assessing Aum Shinrikyo), but the volume is growing. Japan's pharmaceutical market is now worth about $37 billion. Europe is also experiencing significant growth. The number of biotechnology firms grew from 486 in 1994 to 584 in 1995, and the number of employees grew from 16,100 to 17,200. What is more significant is that spending on research and development increased by 21 percent in one year, to $795 million.[85]

Technology transfer from the former Soviet Union, however, is a very serious potential problem. The Cold War effort involved sixty thousand to seventy thousand people.[86] There is no meaningful current accounting of their whereabouts. It is clear, however, that at least seventy-five thousand Russian scientific workers emigrated between 1989–1992, and many have left since. There are also repeated unconfirmed reports that some of these scientists are working in Iran and North Korea.

The DOD has warned that even the production and development of biological weapons by foreign states might not be detected, much less by terrorist or extremist groups:

> A state might elect to build large-scale facilities unique to this function, as was done in the United States prior to 1969. Such facilities would be, in principle, more susceptible to detection. However, there is no requirement to do this. The lower cost (by a considerable margin) and less readily observable

approach would be to employ an in-place civilian facility as the site for agent production.

Production equipment will vary, depending on the quantity of material desired, the methods selected for production, and the agent selected. Unlike CW agents, where production is measured in the tons, BW agent production is measured in the kilograms to tens of kilograms. Assessments of BW verification sometimes assume that the problem is to detect production of as little as 10 kilograms of BW agent.

There is nothing unique about the types of equipment (or technology) that might be employed in a BW program. For example, biological safety cabinets have been adopted universally for biomedical research as well as commercial production of infectious disease products, reagents, and so forth. Fermenters, centrifuges, purification, and other laboratory equipment are used not only by the biomedical community, but have other academic and commercial applications as well, such as wineries, milk plants, pharmaceutical houses, and agricultural products. Production of beer, antibodies, enzymes, and other therapeutic products, such as insulin and growth hormone, involves the use of fermenters ranging in size from 10,000 to 1 million liters; such fermenters could produce significant quantities of BW agent. Key technologies have an intrinsic dual-use character.[87]

The problems in detection would be compounded by the fact that neither states nor independent groups have to adopt the safety procedures used by the United States. The DOD report also notes that while the United States developed elaborate containment facilities for conducting infectious disease research at facilities like the Fort Detrick Biological Warfare Research and Development Laboratories during the Cold War, "Other countries do not necessarily share these safety concerns."[88] Iraq did not follow such procedures and did not provide all of its dispersed biological weapons with guards or special security storage arrangements during the Persian Gulf War.

### The Growing Lethality of Biological Weapons and Growing Ease of Manufacture

Biological weapons also represent an area where the rapid pace of technical change creates the ability to make far more effective weapons. Biotechnology can offer many benefits.[89] At the same time, genetic engineering and other new technologies can now be employed to overcome product deficiencies in the classic agents and toxins normally addressed in such discussions. Moreover, toxins that exist in nature in small amounts were once considered not to be potential threat agents because of their limited availability. Today, the DOD estimates that a number of natural toxins could be produced through genetic engineering techniques in sufficient quantities for an adversary to consider producing them as an offensive weapon. There are many microorganisms or their metabolic byproducts (toxins) that can now meet all of the criteria for effective biological weapons agents.[90]

Studies like those of the Jason project indicate that this situation will become much worse in the future. Genetically engineered pathogens can be designed to have any or all of the following attributes:

- *Safer handling and deployment*, including the elimination of risks from accidents or misuse—the "boomerang effect."

- *Easier propagation and/or distribution*, thereby eliminating the need for a normally hydrated bioagent or any use of aerosols. Microorganisms with enhanced aerosol and environmental stability.

- *Improved ability to target the host*, including the possible targeting of specific races or ethnic groups with given genetic characteristics.

- *Greater transmissivity and infectivity*: Engineering a disease like Ebola to be as communicable as measles. Microorganisms resistant to antibiotics, standard vaccines, and therapeutics.

- *New weapons*: Benign microorganisms, genetically altered to produce a toxin, venom, or bioregulator.

- *Increased problems in detection*: Immunologically altered microorganisms able to defeat standard identification, detection, and diagnostic methods. Problems in diagnosis, false diagnosis, and lack of detection by existing detectors, long latency, and binary initiation.

- *Greater toxicity, more difficult to treat*: Very high morbidity or mortality, resistant to known antibacterial or antiviral agents; defeats existing vaccines; and produces symptoms designed to saturate available specialized medical treatment facilities.

- *Combinations of some or all of the above.*[91]

### New Types of Biological Weapons

While any such analysis is speculative, scientists postulate that the following new types of biological weapons are now deployable or can be manufactured during the coming decade:

- *Binary biological weapons* that use two safe-to-handle elements that can be assembled before use. This could be a virus and helper virus like Hepatitis D or a bacterial virulence plasmid like E. coli, plague, anthrax, and dysentery.

- *Designer genes and life forms*, which could include synthetic genes and gene networks, synthetic viruses, and synthetic organisms. These weapons include DNA shuffling, synthetic forms of the flu—which killed more people in 1918 than those who died in all of World War I and which still kills about thirty thousand Americans a year—and synthetic microorganisms.

- *"Gene therapy" weapons* that use transforming viruses or similar DNA vectors carrying Trojan horse genes (retrovirus, adenovirus, poxvirus, HSV-1). Such weapons can produce single individual (somatic cell) or inheritable (germline) changes. It can also remove immunities and wound-healing capabilities.

- *Stealth viruses* can be transforming or conditionally inducible. They exploit the fact that humans normally carry a substantial viral load, and examples are the herpes virus, cytomegalovirus, Epstein-Barr, and SV40 contamination that are normally dormant or limited in infect but can be transformed into far more lethal diseases. They can be introduced over years and then used to blackmail a population.

- *Host-swapping diseases*: Viral parasites normally have narrow host ranges and develop an evolutionary equilibrium with their hosts. Disruption of this equilibrium normally produces no results, but it can be extremely lethal. Natural examples include AIDS, hanta virus, Marburg, and Ebola. Tailoring the disruption for attack purposes can produce weapons that are extremely lethal and for which there is no treatment. A tailored disease like AIDS could combine serious initial lethality with crippling long-term effects lasting decades.

- *Designer diseases* involve using molecular biology to create the disease first and then constructing a pathogen to produce it. It could eliminate immunity, target normally dormant genes, or instruct cells to commit suicide. Apoptosis is programmed cell death, and specific apoptosis can be used to kill any mix of cells.[92]

### Changes in Disease: Piggybacking on the Threat from Nature

Alternatively, an attacker might take advantage of the fact that the world—and Americans—are under constant natural attack from evolution. A recent national intelligence estimate found that at least twenty well-known diseases had emerged in resistant form during the last twenty years, including tuberculosis, malaria, and cholera.[93] The strains of streptococcus pnemoniae, staphylococcus aureus, and mycobacterium tuberculosis in the United States are now 10 percent to 35 percent immune to treatment.

At least thirty previously unknown diseases have emerged since 1973, including HIV, Ebola, Hepatitis C, and Nipah virus for which there are no known cures. As a result, the annual deaths from infectious diseases in the United States have doubled to 170,000 a year from their historic low in 1980. Many have been caused by new immigrants such as the West Nile virus. Europe continues to suffer from new zoonotic diseases like Creutzfeldt-Jakob or "mad cow disease," which have had massive economic consequences even with minor human losses. (A total of seventy deaths have occurred over a period of six years, with some seven additional cases still alive.)[94]

To put these trends in perspective, 890,000 Americans are now infected with HIV/AIDS, 4 million are chronic carriers of Hepatitis C, 27,000 a year now catch tuberculosis—which is 32 percent to 52 percent resistant to established drugs—and 14,000 a year die of streptococcus pnemoniae and staphylococcus aureus. The flu now kills about thirty thousand Americans a year—twice the number as in 1972–1984. CDC experts predict a new epidemic—similar to the one that killed 500,000 Americans in 1918—could kill 197,000 to 227,000 in spite of improvements in medical treatment.[95]

More massive outbreaks of resistant diseases are taking place outside the United States, and tuberculosis, malaria, hepatitis, and HIV/AIDS continue to surge. For example, roughly 700,000 died from AIDS in 1993, and 2.3 million in 1998. There are an estimated 5.8 million infections and many in developed countries: the HIV population in Russia could reach 1 million by 2000, and double by 2002. There were 33.4 million people infected with AIDS in 1998, and there were more than 40 million by the end of 2000.

The inability to predict the impact of even a well-established disease is illustrated by the fact that the WHO predicted that deaths from HIV/AIDS would peak in 2006 with 1.7 million deaths, and the death rate was already 2.3 million in 1998. The cumulative global economic cost of AIDS is already estimated to have reached $500 billion.[96]

The WHO has warned that "globalism" means that developed countries like the United States are becoming progressively more vulnerable to the new variants of disease emerging in the developing world:

... wealthy countries which have exclusively focused efforts on fighting disease within their own borders, while failing to help eliminate them globally. Proliferating elsewhere, many bacteria, viruses, and parasites mutate, become drug resistant, and venture back to wealthy countries via modern transportation.

Resistance is also seen where health workers have exclusively focused on providing drugs for their patients while inadvertently failing to take time to ensure proper diagnosis, prescription, and adherence to treatment.

Antimicrobial resistance is a natural biological phenomenon. But it becomes a significant public health problem where it is amplified many-fold owing to human misuse and neglect. Drug resistance is the most telling sign that we have failed to take the threat of infectious diseases seriously. It suggests that we have mishandled our precious arsenal of disease-fighting drugs, by overusing them in developed nations and, paradoxically, misusing and underusing them in developing nations. In all cases, half-hearted use of powerful antibiotics now will eventually result in less effective drugs later.

This report describes the growing threat of antimicrobial resistance. It documents how once life-saving medicines are increasingly having as little effect as a sugar pill. Microbial resistance to treatment could bring the world back to a pre-antibiotic age.

Before long, we may have forever missed our opportunity to control and eventually eliminate the most dangerous infectious diseases. Indeed, if we fail to make rapid progress during this decade, it may become very difficult and expensive—if not impossible—to do so later. We need to make effective use of the tools we have now.

The eradication of smallpox in 1980, for example, happened not a moment too soon. Just a few years' delay and the unforeseen emergence of HIV would have undermined safe smallpox vaccination in populations severely affected by HIV.

While many exciting research efforts are currently underway, there is no guarantee that they will yield new drugs or vaccines in the near future. Since 1970, no new classes of antibacterials have been developed to combat infectious diseases. On average, research and development of anti-infective drugs takes 10 to 20 years. Currently, there are no new drugs or vaccines ready to emerge from the research and development pipeline.

Moreover, for the major infectious killers, research and development funding continues to be woefully inadequate. A very small percentage of all global health research and development funding is currently devoted to finding new drugs or vaccines to stop AIDS, acute respiratory infections (ARI), diarrhoeal diseases, malaria, and TB. The pharmaceutical industry reports that it costs them a minimum of U.S. $500 million just to bring one drug to market. Combined funding for research and development into ARI, diarrhoeal diseases, malaria, and TB last year was under that amount.

Although prevention through vaccination continues to be the ultimate weapon against infection and drug resistance, no vaccines are available to prevent five of the six major infectious killers. Yet it is a needless tragedy that 11 million people perish each year awaiting the advent of newer miracle drugs and vaccines. Prevention and treatment strategies using tools available now can be provided to populations throughout the world to help eliminate high-burden diseases of poverty.

We need not stand by helplessly watching antimicrobial resistance increase and drug effectiveness decrease. As this report shows, resistance can be contained. When an infection is addressed in a comprehensive and timely manner, resistance rarely becomes a public health problem. The most effective strategy against antimicrobial resistance is to get the job done right the first time—to unequivocally destroy microbes—thereby defeating resistance before it starts.

Today—despite advances in science and technology—infectious disease poses a more deadly threat to human life than war. This year—at the onset of a new millennium—the international community is beginning to show its intent to turn back these microbial invaders through massive efforts against diseases of poverty—diseases which must be defeated now, before they become resistant. When diseases are fought wisely and widely, drug resistance can be controlled and lives saved.

. . . As early as half a century ago—just a few years after penicillin was put on the market—scientists began noticing the emergence of a penicillin-resistant strain of Staphylococcus aureus, a common bacterium that claims membership among the human body's normal bacterial flora. Resistant strains of gonorrhoea, dysentery-causing shigella (a major cause of premature death in developing countries) and salmonella rapidly followed in the wake of staphylococcus 20 to 25 years later.

From that first case of resistant staphylococcus, the problem of anti-microbial resistance has snowballed into a serious public health concern with economic, social, and political implications that are global in scope and cross all environmental and ethnic boundaries. Multi drug-resistant tuberculosis (MDR-TB) is no longer confined to any one country or to those co-infected with HIV, but has appeared in locations as diverse as eastern Europe, Africa, and Asia among health care workers and in the general population. Penicillin-resistant pneumococci are likewise spreading rapidly, while resistant malaria is on the rise, disabling and killing millions of children and adults each year. In 1990, almost all cholera isolates gathered around New Delhi (India) were sensitive to cheap, first-line drugs furazolidone, ampicillin, co-trimoxazole and nalidixic acid. Now, 10 years later, formerly effective drugs are largely useless in the battle to contain cholera epidemics.

In some areas of the world—most notably Southeast Asia—98% of all gonorrhoea cases are multi drug-resistant which in turn contributes to the sexual transmission of HIV. In India, 60% of all cases of visceral leishmaniasis—a sandfly-borne parasitic infection—no longer respond to an increasingly limited cache of first-line drugs; while in the industrialized world, as many as 60% of hospital-acquired infections are caused by drug-resistant microbes. These infections—the most recent of which are vancomycin-resistant Enterococcus (VRE) and methicillin-resistant Staphylococcus aureus (MRSA), are now no longer confined to wards but have crept into the community at large.

Although most drugs are still active, the lengthening shadow of resistance means that many of them may not be for long. In the case of tuberculosis, the emergence of multi drug-resistant bacteria means that medications that once cost as little as U.S. $20 must now be replaced with drugs a hundred times more expensive. Other diseases are likewise becoming increasingly impervious.[97]

This illustrates the fact that homeland defense cannot be separated from public health policy. The effectiveness of treatment for most of these diseases is now forecast to decline over the near- to mid-term, and humanitarian crises are projected to create a further problem. There were twenty-four major humanitarian crises in 1999, involving at least thirty-five million refugees and displaced people. Furthermore, immigration had reached the point where 180 million people lived outside the country of their birth. Roughly 88 percent of the population growth in Europe in the 1990s came from immigration.[98]

Future attackers could piggyback on the natural evolution of disease to use new or resistant weapons, or genetically engineer diseases that might not be distinguished from a natural outbreak—at least not quickly and in a form where the attacker could not be identified. They could also use stealth attacks and proxies to deliver new or resistant diseases, and the previous data show that some attacks on the United States might take years to mature—which makes detection and retaliation extremely difficult.

## Agricultural and Ecological Attacks

As has been discussed earlier, the uncertainties surrounding biological attacks on human beings are compounded by the risk of biological attacks on crops and livestock, which could be combined with attacks on human beings. Agriculture accounts for 13 percent of the U.S. gross national product and 17 percent of total employment (860,000 jobs), although less than 2 percent of the U.S. workforce is on farms.[99] The United States exports well over $140 billion worth of agricultural goods annually. It also has special regional and local vulnerabilities. Some 84 percent of its cattle are in the southwest, 60 percent of swine are in the northeast, and 78 percent of chickens are in the southeast Atlantic region. Some feedlots hold 150,000 to 300,000 cattle and 78 percent of all cattle pass through only 2 percent of the feedlots. Some pig farms hold ten thousand hogs and chicken farms pen over one hundred thousand birds.[100]

A DOD study issued in January 2001 notes that:

> The potential threats to U.S. agriculture and livestock can come from a variety of pathogens and causative agents. With one in eight jobs and 13 percent of the gross national product dependent on U.S. agricultural productivity, economic stability of the country depends on a bountiful and safe food supply system. Similar to the human population, the high health status of crop and livestock assets in the United States creates a great vulnerability to attack with biological agents. Attacks against U.S. agricultural assets might be tempting, due to the perceived relative ease of attack, the plausible deniability toward accusations, and the limited number of plant seed varieties in use. Indeed, the Soviet Union apparently planned to target U.S. agriculture and livestock as one element of a larger disruptive process and developed a range of biological agents that would be effective in this capacity.
>
> Consequences of compromising the productivity and safety of the U.S. food supply are primarily economic in nature. Disrupting the supply lines for food stocks or threatening the safety of those items supplied also may erode military readiness.
>
> Highly infectious naturally occurring plant and animal pathogens exist outside the U.S. borders and some agents are readily transported, inadvertently or intentionally, with little risk of detection. The Animal and Plant Health Inspection Service (APHIS) is the regulatory, first-response agency responsible for the diagnosis and management of all suspicious agricultural disease outbreaks. As a result of binding international agreements, select plant and animal disease outbreak confirmation, regardless of magnitude, can immediately have an impact on export trade. Depending on the agent, APHIS authority includes property seizure and total eradication of all plant or animal hosts within concentric zones of quarantine. Public trust in government and political stability can be threatened depending on the extent of disease transmission, the success of regulatory response procedures, and the duration of time to restore normalcy. Additional impacts include:

U.S. livestock markets would be vulnerable to the causative agents of diseases including anthrax, Q fever, brucellosis, FMD, Venezuelan equine encephalitis, hog cholera, African swine fever, avian influenza, Newcastle disease, Rift Valley fever, and rinderpest.

Soybean rust, which can easily be introduced and spreads quickly, could cause U.S. soybean producers, processors, livestock producers, and consumers to lose up to $8 billion annually, according to USDA estimates. An outbreak of FMD, which is also easily introduced, highly contagious, and persistent, in the U.S. livestock industry could cost as much as $20 billion over 15 years in increased consumer costs, reduced livestock productivity, and restricted trade, according to the USDA.[101]

The first major use of biological weapons in the twentieth century was Germany's attempt to infect Argentine, French, Mesopotamian, Romanian, and U.S. livestock during World War I (anthrax and glanders). France, Germany, and Japan are known to have developed more advanced agricultural weapons during World War II (anthrax, glanders, fungi, nematodes, riderpest virus, hoof and mouth disease, potato beetles, turnip weevils, turnip bugs, antler moths, potato stalk rot, and potato tuber decay), and some experts feel the Soviet Union may have attempted similar attacks on German horses on the eastern front in World War II.

During the Cold War, the United States weaponized and stockpiled wheat-stem rust and weaponized rice blast fungus, rinderpest, and foot and mouth disease (FMD). It carried out thirty anticrop attack tests between 1951 and 1969, and stockpiled at least five thousand kilograms of wheat and rice rust. The former Soviet Union weaponized and stockpiled FMD, rinderpest, African swine fever, vesicular stomatitis virus, contagious bovine pleuropneumonia, mutated avian influenza, contagious sheep ecthyma to attack animals, and wheat and barley mosaic streak viruses, potato virus, tobacco mosaic virus, brown grass virus, wheat fungal, and brown leaf rust to damage crops. It also used radar to track the use of insect clouds. Iraq seriously examined ways to attack the Iranian grain crop and livestock (wheat rust and camelpox) during the Iran-Iraq War. Neither Germany nor Iraq carried out effective attacks, although in Iraq's case this may have been because it was not ready to attack until the Iran-Iraq War was over.[102]

Nature has already shown how easy it might be for a sophisticated, technically informed state, group, or individual to attack crops and livestock by introducing a new parasite, predator, or disease. There is no clear record of how many times such problems have occurred naturally in the United States since World War II, but instances like the introduction of the Mediterranean Fruit Fly (which involved a group called the Breeders protesting the use of insecticides in California), cross-breeding of "killer bees," poisoning of Chilean grapes, importation of mosquitoes infected with the West Nile fever, and mere rumors that U.S. apples might be covered in carcinogens are examples of cases involving millions of dollars. There are a host of "rusts" and "smuts" that can attack grain crops. Wheat rust, for example, can affect most of the western and Great Plains wheat crop and some 12 percent of the California wheat crop was lost to this rust in one recent year. The following pathogens already threaten U.S. crops as a result of natural causes: soybean rust (soybean plant), ear rot (corn), karnal bunt (wheat), ergot (sorghum), bacterial blight (rice), ring rot (potatoes) and wirrega blotch (barley).

There is an even longer list of threats to U.S. livestock. They include animal disease, plant disease, FMD, vesicular stomatitis, rinderpest gibberella, African swine fever, highly pathogenic avian influenza, Rift Valley fever, lumpy skin disease, blue tongue, sheep and goat pox, swine vesicular disease, contagious bovine pleuropneumonia, Newcastle disease, African horse sickness, and classical swine fever.

Anthrax, FMD, rinderpest, and swine fever are well-researched ways to attack livestock.[103] In the case of "mad cow disease," less than two hundred cases of sickness over more than ten years cost billions of dollars. In contrast, FMD is extremely contagious and has seven variants, seventy subvariants, and airborne infections that have been spread up to 150 kilometers by winds. Even single cases of FMD have halted all exports of meat products from cloven-hoofed animals from some countries. The March 1997 outbreak of FMD in Taiwan forced the immediate destruction of 900,000 animals and an eventual total of up to 1.6 million, affecting exports that made up 41 percent of Japan's pork supply. The cost to the Taiwanese economy was $1 billion a year. Alternatively, African swine fever is nonvirulent against its natural hosts in Africa (ticks and warthogs), but is lethal enough against U.S. pigs to act as the equivalent of a swine Ebola.[104] The outbreak of foot-and-mouth disease in Great Britian in 2000–2001 cost billions of dollars and demonstrated that even one of the most advanced countries can be totally unprepared to deal with one of the best-known agricultural diseases.

The DOD has examined the possible impact of an attack using FMD— an agent that might be very difficult to distinguish from a natural outbreak and which could be manufactured and used by terrorist groups as well as by state actors—and has drawn the following conclusions:

> The foot and mouth disease (FMD) virus is a member of the Picornovirus family, and the disease is endemic in many areas of the world. However, the United States has not dealt with the FMD virus since the 1920s. Therefore, few veterinary practitioners currently have the ability to recognize early stages of FMD infection. This agent is somewhat unique, as the animal becomes infective shortly after exposure and prior to the onset of clinical symptoms.
>
> To disseminate the agent, the mere transport of sloughed nasal vesicular tissue and modest preservation in transport could easily start an epidemic.

For example, a single infected cow, or particularly a pig, can generate enough viral particles to infect vast geographical areas in a short period of time. FMD is characterized by a sudden rise in temperature, followed by an eruption of blisters in the mouth, nostrils, other areas of tender skin, and on the feet. The blisters grow larger and then break, exposing raw, eroded surfaces. Eating becomes difficult and painful, and because the soft tissues under the hoof are inflamed, the animal invariably becomes lame. Livestock raised for meat lose much weight, and dairy cattle and goats give far less milk.

FMD usually kills very young animals and causes pregnant females to abort. The Animal and Plant Health Inspection Service (APHIS) of the U.S. Department of Agriculture (USDA) does not permit imports of FMD seropositive animals. Considerable progress has been made toward developing an effective vaccine against FMD, but the cost (approximately $1 billion annually) of vaccinating all susceptible animals would be prohibitive. Moreover, the vaccine would not eradicate the disease. Consequently, the slaughter and incineration of all exposed animals is the only presently effective countermeasure to FMD. During an outbreak in the United Kingdom in 1967 and 1968, ore example, more than 430,000 animals were destroyed.[105]

While agricultural and ecological attacks do not offer quick results or the kind of shock impact that can decide the outcome of short wars or achieve high immediate visibility, they may also be extremely difficult to trace to any deliberate cause, have long-term effects that are very difficult to deal with, and offer a potential means of revenge and punishment even to weak movements and states.

This risk explains why the Department of Agriculture has the mission of detecting and defending against such attacks. As is the case with human biological weapons, however, it is far from clear how genetic engineering will change the balance between defense and attack. Virtually all of the advances in biotechnology that can affect human diseases can be applied to the agents to attack crops and livestock and with far fewer risks in handling the materials and in weapons development.

### The Problem of Response

Like chemical weapons, biological weapons can be a WMD with which most first responders and law enforcement agencies are able to deal. Attacks with limited medical effects can be dealt with as outbreaks of disease and be contained and treated accordingly. Attacks on critical or sensitive facilities present more serious individual risks, but so do chemical attacks and bombs used against the same target. Similarly, false threats only need to be taken seriously to the point of ensuring that they do not produce mass panic.

Most responders feel—probably correctly—that they already have to prepare for such incidents and that the estimated total casualties from most limited or crude biological attacks of the kind are unlikely to put an impossible burden on local and regional medical services. The law enforcement and forensics aspects of dealing with such biological attacks present challenges, but law enforcement experts believe most incidents will have a clear location and chains of evidence. This is more questionable in the case of attacks on livestock, crops, food, and the environment, but small, crude attacks of this kind also seem likely to be limited in effect and containable.

At the same time, there is the same broad consensus that there are still major problems in the rapid detection and characterization of even a limited and relatively crude biological attack, and in training and equipping suitable emergency medical personnel and facilities. These problems could be much more serious if a small and/or crude biological weapon were combined with an explosive or chemical device in attacking a building or facility and/or if responders had to characterize and deal with two sets of different biological weapons at the same time.

### Funding Half-Measures and False Solutions?

The problems in responding to biological attacks radically change character, however, if they involve an attack with enough agent to affect a large area, are conducted in a stealth or delayed mode, and/or use highly lethal militarized agents. Such attacks could rapidly exhaust the response capabilities of any urban area or region. They could also involve weapons with very different methods of transmission, effects, and treatment requirements than a normal outbreak or epidemic.

Early response is critical in dealing with most attacks. It is unclear, however, that the U.S. intelligence community is prepared to give warning of any kind against biological attacks. CIA director George Tenet testified to the Senate Foreign Relations Committee on March 20, 2000, that biological warfare programs, "are becoming self-sufficient, challenging our detection and deterrence efforts, and limiting our interdiction capabilities. . . . Biological and chemical weapons pose arguably the most daunting challenge for intelligence collectors and analysis." Tenet was referring largely to the threat posed by states, although he mentioned that a number of terrorist groups—such as Usama bin Laden—were seeking to develop or acquire biological and chemical weapons.[106] Given the risk that U.S. intelligence may not even detect the weaponization of biological agents, it seems almost certain that there is a much greater risk that any intelligence warning of a potential attack will not be able to name the agent(s) involved and indicate the degree to which genetic engineering, the use of militarized strains, cocktails of mixes of different agents, and/or weaponization affect dissemination, lethality, and the effectiveness of the agent.

Detection might well lag behind the deadlines for effective response and such attacks could infect or kill many local responders. Characterizing the risk of exposure and actual levels of exposure could prove to be a nightmare, as could separating real exposures from feared exposures. It is unclear that anyone is prepared to determine the area covered by the agent (assuming it is noninfectious) and how many people are actually exposed and with what effect. The number of false reports and people seeking cautionary or panic medical treatment would rise massively. The potential problem of halting movement and establishing quarantines could overload law enforcement as well as create major lethal and ethical issues. The fear of sequential or follow-on attacks would grow, as would the problems in decontamination.

Advances have been made in detection and characterization at the military level. In October 1996, the U.S. Army fielded its first biological defense unit equipped with state-of-the-art biological detection capabilities, the Biological Integrated Detection System (BIDS). In 1999, a second unit was fielded with the BIDS Phase II Pre-Planned Program Improvement (P3I). This phase provided technology insertion from concurrent development efforts to upgrade the Phase I (4-agent detection capability), core configuration to 8-agent detection capability, automated detectors, and computerized integration of detection equipment outputs. In addition, the Army fielded the Long Range Biological Standoff Detection System (LR-BSDS), used for remote detection of aerosols and particulates. Also, the Interim Biological Agent Detector (IBAD) has been installed on selected Navy ships to provide a mobile biological, point-detection capability.

The DOD is cautious about discussing the limits of current detection and characterization systems and technology and constraints in the conduct of research efforts to overcome these problems. These limitations are severe even when the threat is confined to military operations in a relatively limited military target against fully alert forces in the field:[107]

Because of the dual-use nature of BW [biological warfare] technology, it is extremely difficult to prevent BW proliferation. No matter how good individual protective equipment and collective protective structures become, their utility is limited unless there is adequate warning to mask and seek cover. This fact places a premium on developing effective battlefield BW detection systems. Currently available equipment can be broadly divided between point detection/identification systems and standoff systems.

Point detection and identification of biological agents in the field is done with vehicles and shelters containing manually operated, commercial off-the-shelf technology that use re-agent processes, fluidics, and spectrometry. Standoff systems, which can either be stationary or mounted on platforms like helicopters, rely on Light Detection and Ranging (LIDAR) technology to spot clouds of suspect particulate matter in the atmosphere from a distance. Both types of systems are capable of providing early warning, though point-detection systems must be remotely deployed in an ensemble well upwind of friendly forces to be most effective.

The lack of sensitivity to low concentrations of biological aerosols and slow processing speed are the most critical shortcomings of our currently fielded point sensors. Since contamination can only be avoided with early warning, a sensor that reacts quickly to the earliest manifestation of a biological agent is the *sine qua non* of survival on the battlefield. Although an indication of the presence of agent can be provided very quickly by the Aerosol Particle Sizer (APS) component of the system, there is no way to tell whether the particles activating the trigger are harmful until the collection and identification functions are completed. This process takes from 15 to 45 minutes for high concentrations of agent. Low concentrations of agent require even longer detection cycles for the sensor systems. The extraordinary potency of these pathogens at even minute counts of agent-containing particles per liter of air suggests that troops are very likely to be exposed to disease-causing concentrations of them for some time before current point detection systems provide the warning to mask. But, as the impracticality of detecting to warn makes detecting to treat look like a more probable outcome of responding to a biological attack, medical technology assumes ever more importance in the attempt to counter BW.

The difficulty of relying only on established technologies or BW detection can be illustrated with an example. One recently proposed system involved distributing throughout the area of operations large numbers of point particle sensors linked to a sensor network command post—essentially a computer with algorithms to sort out the implications of alarms at different locations. An analysis of this system estimated that one false alarm per week per brigade with the allotted 24 sensors would result in the average divisional soldier being masked for 15 hours a week. To achieve this low a rate, already very disruptive to operational tempo, the system could allow no more than 0.006 false alarms per sensor per day—a standard not approached by contemporary capabilities. These concerns resulted in the elimination of the particle sensing units from the system.

While the rate of improvement in sensor performance against biological materials does not, at present, appear particularly promising, there are some grounds for encouragement due to the rapid and steady increase in the speed of information processing. It should, in theory, be possible to increase the efficiency of detection technology by linking networks of sensors. Digitized information networks, for a start, are faster than the analog networks they are replacing, and sensors incorporating some computing ability may eventually be able to pick out critically relevant returns rather than transmitting volumes of unprocessed data. The use of programmed algorithms to process returns in sensor network command posts has been pursued as a promising application of information-processing technology to the detection and warning problem. This was the approach taken in the system discussed earlier that sought to link large numbers of particle sensors to a central unit. The hope was that this technology would permit the prediction of directional trends and speeds of agent clouds. But the potential for such systems is stunted by the stubborn limitations of the sensors themselves, and the likelihood that marginal improvements in them will be more than matched by substantial changes and improvements in the agents they are attempting to detect. Though the continual drama of advances in information technology seems to have given life to a generalized optimism about the prospects for across-the-board improvements in military technology, this case suggests that there are some defense problems not susceptible to the solutions offered by the information revolution.

The difficulties posed by the proliferation of biological weapons may demonstrate that, contrary to popular expectations, technical challenges do not of necessity generate increasingly ingenious technical responses in an unceasing reciprocal process. The likelihood that the detection problem will experience only gradual improvement means that some areas of technology, like information technology, may be limited in the contributions they can make to it, while others are made more important. The possibility that proliferating states may develop new agents, such as modified viruses, makes it desirable that the limited set of classical agents available for presumptive identification with the current antibody-based identification technology be expanded. There are also gene-based systems in the inventory that use well-established polymerase chain reaction techniques to provide highly sensitive and specific identification of putative agents. These systems are two to three times slower than small, cheap hand-held assays, and their size, weight, and power requirements have, until recently, been thought to render them impractical for the field. They have now been operationally deployed with encouraging results in Theater Army Medical Laboratories (TAML), where they can be operated and maintained by experienced technicians. Their identification technology is able to identify most classical agents within their incubation periods, except for the fast-acting toxins. These latter agents are, in any case, more appropriately analyzed by more rapid immunoassay technologies such as the enzyme-linked immunosorbent assay (ELISA) or the even faster, more sensitive electro-chemiluminescence (ECL), both of which can be deployed with the TAML.

. . . The need to have diagnostic tests directed at both endemic organisms and BW agents has become more apparent, since nonspecific symptoms of naturally occurring diseases (e.g., fever, fatigue, or respiratory complaints) may be identical to initial symptoms of biological agent infection. Technological advances have allowed for the development of rapid diagnostic tests for specific biological warfare agents, to include naturally occurring and bioengineered microbial organisms. Detectors that sample environmental organisms may not be sensitive or specific enough to identify "new" or emerging agents that have epidemic potential in a military or public health setting. In addition, with the advent of genetically manipulated variants, the need to have rapid and accurate means to determine antibiotic sensitivities, genomic sequences, and virulence factors, especially in bioengineered organisms, may become more important. Confirmatory evaluation at established reference laboratories within the United States requires a highly responsive system involving well-defined procedures in the collection, preparation, handling, and shipment of diagnostic specimens. The TAML is a group of professionals who deploy before or with military units to survey and sample the environment and determine the conditions. Samples are either evaluated by the deployed team in the field or packaged and shipped to reference laboratories for additional testing. DOD continues to identify appropriate technologies to bring the best tools to the war fighter through such institutions as the U.S. Army Medical Research Institute for Infectious Diseases (USAMRIID). Prototype systems are being developed and fielded at the installation and unit levels. The biological defense program aggressively pursues technology advances in standoff detection, remote early-warning detection, sensor miniaturization, and improved agent identification sensitivity. . . .

The DOD reports that there are similar problems in trying to provide adequate treatment and medical services, although a number of research efforts are promising and stockpiling some vaccines may be of value. Once again it is critically important to understand that the department is addressing a prescribed, bounded combat environment and not the much larger potential target base in the U.S. homeland.[108]

There are serious but not insurmountable organizational and medical obstacles to the success of post-exposure treatment. The number of known bioagents to which U.S. personnel in either Southwest Asia (SWA) and Northeast Asia (NEA) are considered most likely to be exposed is at least as high as ten. The daunting logistical prospect of procuring vaccines, prophylaxes, and other treatments for all these agents suggests, at first glance, that the availability of appropriate medical countermeasures is the first and principal limiting factor on the post-exposure strategy; and, of course, the medicines must be supplied in the right place and at the right moment to all personnel who might have been exposed. But the applicability of certain treatments to multiple diseases (doxycycline, for instance, can be used against plague, tularemia, anthrax, brucellosis, and Q-fever) would lighten the logistical burden.

The research being done to develop polyvalent or multidisease resistant vaccines could eventually make a valuable contribution to our medical countermeasures, particularly in meeting the unpredictable threat of modified viruses. But this would only be the case if scientists succeed in creating vaccines that could actually short circuit the pathogenic mechanisms common to all agents. A limited number of conventional, single-disease vaccines (anthrax, smallpox, plague, and botulinum) should be adequate to protect U.S. forces against most biological weapons currently suitable for large-scale operational use. Though this would establish a major element of force protection, the engineering of novel viruses for military use could be a matter for increasing concern in the future.

. . . Medical prophylaxes, pretreatments, and therapies are necessary to protect personnel from the toxic or lethal effects of exposure to all validated threat agents, as well as other potential threats. DOD has fielded a number of medical countermeasures that greatly improve individual protection, treatment, and diagnoses. Vaccines are the most effective and least costly protection from biological agents. There has been significant progress within the area of biological defense vaccine policy and development. The department has established policy, responsibilities, and procedures for stockpiling biological agent vaccines and determined which personnel should be immunized and when the vaccine should be administered. DOD also has identified biological agents that constitute critical threats and determined the amount of vaccine that should be stocked for each threat. Other preventive and therapeutic measures, such as broad-spectrum antibiotics, may be used for treatment following a biological attack with bacterial agent.

. . . Anthrax is a biological warfare agent that has been produced and weaponized by adversaries of the United States. A small amount of anthrax spores, distributed under proper conditions, can generate a large number of fatalities among individuals who are not properly protected. While protective clothing and gas masks provide excellent front-line defense against anthrax and other biological agents, their effective use requires rapid and early detection of the agent. Current detection devices may not provide enough time for personnel to don protective equipment before exposure. Ideally, the United States should be able to deter the use of anthrax. As Secretary of Defense William Cohen warned in 1998, if any state "even contemplates using WMD against our forces, we will deliver a response that's overwhelming and devastating." In the event deterrence fails, however, an added level of protection must be provided to our forces. For protection against anthrax, there is a safe and effective vaccine licensed by the Food and Drug Administration (FDA).

. . . Medical countermeasures for biological threat agents are limited but improving. A Joint Medical Biological Defense Research Program is developing countermeasures to protect U.S. forces and thereby deter, constrain, and defeat the use of biological agents. A primary objective is the development of vaccines, drug therapies, diagnostic tools, and other medical products that are effective against biological agents. Efforts are focused on maintaining the technological capability to meet present requirements and counter future threats, providing individual-level prevention and protection and providing training in medical management of biological casualties. A research program directed at the development of safe and effective antiviral drugs is also in progress. Current medical biological defense program research involves pre- and post-exposure BW countermeasures as well as diagnostics, including the following:

- Characterize the biochemistry, molecular biology, physiology, and physical structure of BW threat agents.
- Investigate the disease mechanisms and natural body defenses against BW agents.
- Determine the mechanism of action of these threat agents in animal model systems.
- Develop and compare potential vaccine candidates and characterize their effects in animal models.
- Establish safety and efficacy data for candidate.
- Vaccines. Develop medical diagnostics to include field confirmatory and reference laboratory techniques. Develop effective casualty treatment

protocols using antitoxins, antibiotics, antivirals, and other pharmaceuticals to prevent death and maximize return to duty.

... Research, Development, Test, and Evaluation (RDT&E) efforts are underway to develop vaccines against all validated threat agents, including plague, smallpox, and tularemia, although it will take a number of years to successfully complete all of these vaccines....There are a number of medical biological defense products transitioning to advanced development and in varying stages of review for licensure by the FDA. These include vaccines for botulinum and Venezuelan Equine Encephalitis (VEE), plague, brucella, Marburg (filovirus), and a common diagnostic system for rapid biological agent identification and agent prophylaxis.

The current weapons effects literature simply cannot prepare defenders and responders for what would really happen if large amounts of given agents were broadly disseminated or highly infectious military agents were used. No currently deployed detection system can accurately measure the area coverage of such an attack, and most projected detection systems—including most biochips—would present problems in reliably characterizing the exact weapon used and/or the amount of the weapon present in given areas or the degree to which it does or does not mimic the patterns of a normal disease. While more sophisticated individual detection and characterization devices are becoming available and much more reliable and advanced systems are completing development, there are as yet no rapidly deployable arrays that can be used in urban environments and most responders have no funds to acquire them. In fact, the National Security Council (NSC) was just beginning to examine the kinds of "systems" that might be required in August 2000.

The resulting response problems will be greatly complicated by the steady decline in public health funding and in the number of hospitals and emergency facilities per patient that has affected the United States and virtually every nation in the West. The United States saw over one thousand hospitals close in the 1990s, medical services shift to minimize stocks and any kind of surplus capacity, and many emergency wards close. In the late 1990s, nearly 30 percent of America's remaining hospitals were losing money. The U.S. Public Health Service and state and local public health departments have been badly underfunded, and the overall system can barely cope with its normal caseload.[109]

No hospital in the country can deal with more than fifty to one hundred patients requiring isolation. It can also take a critical twenty-four to forty-eight hours to move federal and state resources to a local facility once (and if) an attack is detected, and hospitals are not funded to do anything to bridge the gap. Furthermore, it is far from clear that detection of some kind of bio-attack is any guarantee that such an attack can be characterized in a sufficiently precise way to allow hospitals/caregivers and local, state, and federal authorities to know what kind of services and treatment to provide and what kind of aid to ask for.[110]

The end result could easily be to funnel patients into a public health system and hospital network with almost no surplus capability, which has neither the facilities nor the stockpiles to treat the result of a biological attack and which would be incapable of rapidly diagnosing the exact nature of an attack. While similar problems would occur in responding to any major CBRN attack, biological attacks ultimately place a critical response burden on hospitals and advanced medical facilities. The creation of federal groups like the Office of Emergency Preparedness in HHS and the Bioterrorism Preparedness and Response Office of the CDC and the training of state and local health departments and of military and National Guard personnel are all useful measures. So is the creation of the seven thousand volunteer force in thirty-person Disaster Medical Assistance Teams, although few members of the teams are doctors. No system can work, however, if it cannot treat the patient load, and the burden of treatment-isolation-quarantine would be far greater in the case of an infectious attack, particularly one that was only detected after it had spread.

Current plans to stockpile vaccines and given types of treatment aids seem to assume that attacks will be limited and will not involve militarized or highly effective agents or mixes of agents that cannot be detected and/or treated as regular diseases. This may well be valid, but it is unclear that the classified work done by the military services, DTRA, and CDC in looking at the full range of biological agents have yet been translated into anything approaching reliable effects models, and that planning which is not familiar with the full range of militarized agents and military risks is always valid for more than limited and unsophisticated attacks. They also tacitly assume that attacks can be detected and characterized in time to react and that vaccines can be moved to effective public health authorities who can discriminate who should be vaccinated and carry out the actual vaccination in time to be effective.

Biotechnology may well give the "defense" as many advantages, or more, than the "offense." However, anyone can promise the biological equivalent of the philosopher's stone and universal solvent and some programs seem to be very poorly justified and grossly oversold. Many of the stockpiling, vaccine, and research and development programs underway do not seem to have been supported by any kind of net technical assessment of the cost to defeat them, the advances taking place in possible attack technologies, and what the cost of national deployment would really be. Many RDT&E programs are being oversold and overhyped in what seem to be dangerously oversimplistic terms. In many cases, no effort is made to describe their probable deployment and life-cycle costs or even what actual deployment would entail.

### The Need for Constantly Updated Net Technical Assessments

These problems are compounded by what seems to be the lack of any clear net assessment of the probable trends in the offensive and defensive capabilities of biotechnology. Some programs hype the problem and some hype the solution. Many assume that a solution that works with current biotechnology will be valid five, ten, or more years in the future, and that sophisticated attackers will not choose new means of attack even though they have years of public warning of the measures the United States plans to take to reduce its vulnerability. These problems are made worse by a flood of policy and strategic studies literature with no supporting references to technology.

The unclassified literature is filled with unsubstantiated and poorly referenced assertions and efforts to sell given programs. The gap between "science" based on normal patterns of disease and the different risks posed by militarized agents is brutally and almost constantly apparent. It is true that no one net technical assessment can hope to accurately predict the future, but the need for well-funded assessments that have classified and unclassified versions is painfully clear.

These problems are compounded by a failure to integrate suggested response and RDT&E efforts for biological attacks into a realistic overall set of procedures that take account of day-to-day public heath needs, real-word pressures to reduce the cost and level of medical services, and the impact of dealing with the aging of the American population. Biological warfare planners and responders sometimes seem to assume that they have an axiomatic priority for resources. They plainly do not.

### Reconsidering the Practical Problems in Defense and Response

The threat posed by biological weapons illustrates the need to be able to measure the existing capabilities of federal, state, and local defenders and responders, to determine what can be done to improve their capabilities with minimal or no additional resources, and then to expressly address what level of additional capability the nation is and is not willing to fund. At present, federal efforts are just beginning to develop a detailed picture of existing national capabilities, and much of the governmental effort at every effort is concerned with basic efforts to understand the problem, coordinate, and train. There is no question that this effort is producing progress, but it does not create a system or architecture for homeland defense, and no one has seriously addressed the question of "how much is enough?"

Biological weapons offer an extraordinarily wide spectrum of means of attack with highly unpredictable effects and lethality. They can vary from limited use of toxins by individuals up to extremely lethal attacks by state actors. It also seems prudent to assume that biological weapons present a serious potential threat in spite of the lack of any past history of effective use and the problems in manufacturing, handling, and delivering them.

Homeland defense requires the United States to consider the following factors:

- The psychological and political impact of using such weapons can be varied according to the means of attack. Weapons can be designed to kill or incapacitate, or to attack livestock, plants, and specific foods.

- The amount of biological weapons needed to achieve a given effect are usually far smaller than for conventional or chemical weapons. Some are easy to smuggle and safe to handle by personnel who have had suitable medical treatment.

- Some biological weapons are so lethal, they potentially approach the lethality of nuclear weapons.

- While the technical skills involved in making such agents are high, biological weapons can be relatively easy to manufacture if such skills are present and the required equipment available, both of which are becoming increasingly common.

- Biological weapons are hard to detect and characterize, particularly if more than one type of weapon is used or if the nation is not on the alert.

- Defense is difficult at best. Effective vaccines and treatment are often not available or must be administered very quickly. Casualties often require intensive and long-term care and therapy, possibly saturating available care.

- The impact of an attack can be timed in ways that favor the attacker. The time before the effects of an attack varies. It may be hours, days, or weeks before an attack is apparent, and this could severely restrict warning, detection, and the value of treatment.

- The United States would find it extremely difficult to estimate the seriousness of the attack and react accordingly. It is difficult to characterize the scale of the threat and its impact until symptoms appear and the casualties can be judged by the number of sick or poisoned.

- Unprotected medical and emergency personnel are highly vulnerable if they enter areas they do not know have been attacked or attempt treatment when no cure is available.[111]

It is not clear that anyone can assign valid probabilities to the kinds of biological attacks that will be made on the U.S. homeland. It is clear that the frequency of given types of attacks is not a meaningful criterion. There already is a flood of false anthrax threats and attacks, and the frequent efforts by extremists and disturbed individuals to use chemical and biological weapons on a small scale are almost certain to continue. Some attacks will almost certainly eventually succeed. In fact, some attacks on food and agricultural products have already succeeded.

### The Problem of Large-Scale or Highly Efficient Attacks

The key risk is the kind of highly lethal attack that would involve more sophisticated weapons. The United States cannot afford to ignore the fact that a single, well-executed, covert attack by a state actor or proxy could produce casualties on the order of tens of thousands—easily resulting in more cumulative casualties than hundreds of small attacks. It could also involve far more stable agents that would survive exposure to heat and light, and involve strains or genetic manipulation to reduce or eliminate the effect of conventional medical treatment. There are no rules preventing multiple attacks and/or the use of multiple biological weapons at the same time, and attacks that hit medical and response capabilities as well as civilians.

The lead times involved in developing an effective deterrent and defense present another critical issue. Advances in biotechnology and food processing, and the proliferation of these technologies and related delivery and weaponization technology, are steadily increasing the ease with which nations and terrorist/extremist groups can acquire the means to make biological weapons. The use of "dry" storage biological weapons is likely to become widespread over the next five to ten years and the necessary skills may become available. Genetic engineering is introducing a whole new set of risks to the equation.

The lack of clear lethality and effects data also has major implications for homeland defense:

- It may not be possible to detect and characterize a biological attack (or attacks) until it is too late to provide effective treatment, to determine what levels of medical resources are required, or to know how many response and treatment capabilities have been attacked and what level of patient flow will result. Much of the current response planning tacitly assumes that either incidents will be small and familiar enough to allow existing response capabilities to work or that attacks will be detected and characterized in ways that allow effective response planning for reasons that are not clearly explained.

- Much of the response planning assumes that it is possible to predict the required medical treatment based on limited experience with civil incidents and epidemics. It is not clear that the "scaling" involved in estimating the effect of terrorist, extremist, or covert use of more sophisticated weapons is more than speculative, and many studies do not cite the special evidence and method used to scale up civil cases into estimates of how biological weapons would behave.

- The uncertainty created by the ability to modify or engineer new weapons or forms of existing weapons greatly compounds these problems. There do not seem to be net assessments of the balance between changes in offensive and defensive biotechnology that allow the United States to predict future lethalities or the effectiveness of many proposed response measures.

- Most of the measures the United States takes to provide homeland defense against biological weapons immediately become part of the open literature, and many take years of lead-time to become effective. While this can act as a deterrent, it can also act as a road map for states and sophisticated extremists in finding the weaknesses in U.S. defenses. The ability to select or tailor biological weapons that remain lethal in spite of U.S. efforts at defense has had only limited analysis.

- There are a number of detailed problems in detection, characteristics, and effects analysis. For example, reliable models of biological weapons effects do not seem to exist that cover attacks in major urban areas involving massive complexes of high-rise steel and glass buildings. The containment and transmission effects of modern cities are extremely difficult to model.

- Most effects estimates only apply to the use of one biological weapon, but attacks using "cocktails" of several biological weapons were found to be the most effective method of mass attack during the Cold War.

- There is often a gap between generic data on the treatment needed for a given biological weapon and the assumed level of treatment required. There is the tacit or explicit assumption that a weapon can be treated as a conventional disease and that enough will be known about effects and exposure for treatment to be applied.

- Much of the federal, state, and local response literature effectively dodges around the issue of triage and the problem of choosing who will receive limited medical treatment and how these victims will be selected. It does not describe what is done with the assumed dying and untreatable or to contain those who may transmit diseases. It also does not address the issue of how hospitals and caregivers can determine what level of resources are needed for those who can be treated—a critical issue given the limited specialized medical facilities in most areas in the United States.

- Corpse disposal may be a major problem, as may disposal of dead animals and birds. This aspect of response seems to be largely ignored.

- Even military medical handbooks fail to address the psychological impacts of prompt and longer-term effects.

### Other Problems in the Present Response Effort

The briefings of responders and law enforcement officials raise other problems that affect biological attacks and other large-scale CBRN attacks in ways that may seriously limit the adequacy of present federal, state, and local efforts to deal with the problem:

- Large-scale biological attacks highlight the conflict between the normal civil rights considerations affecting interference with civil liberties, the law enforcement priorities necessary to obtain evidence and convictions, and the need to take every possible measure to prevent follow-on attacks, the need to provide immediate emergency services, and long-standing problems in using U.S. intelligence assets to support defense and response inside U.S. territory when it may involve U.S. citizens.

- Intelligence warning of the exact nature of a probable biological attack can be absolutely critical to an effective response—although it may be difficult or impossible. The ability to identify the specific disease that may be used in attacks would greatly simplify detection and treatment. So would warning of the potential difference between relatively unsophisticated attacks using familiar diseases and toxins and more sophisticated attacks using dry micro-powders, unfamiliar agents, strains bred to resist treatment or decay, or genetically engineered disease. In many cases, effective response may be impossible without such warning.

- There is a need to provide some kind of cost-effective detection and characterization system that can be rapidly deployed before or after an attack and that will provide an accurate picture of how much of what agent is present in what area. Models lack the accuracy to substitute for measurement. At present, more effort seems to be going into improving individual detectors than into creating deployable and affordable systems that can be available for local use—a problem compounded by the need to provide biological and nuclear detection and characterization as well as chemical. This kind of real-time information is critical not only to first responders, but to the efficient use and allocation of law enforcement and intelligence resources in defense and regional, state, and federal aid in response.

- No one really seems to want to confront the issue of triage and of deciding who gets treatment, who is left at risk, and who dies. This simply is not a realistic approach. Triage cannot be improvised by practitioners without a major risk of wasting inadequate resources on moving the dead and leaving the curable untreated. Creating systems to decide what level of risk is involved in urging people to stay put or evacuate, how to control the media, and what level of detail to provide should not be left up to responders in a crisis. Such planning can only be done at a federal level, but it is uncertain that the leadership and moral courage is present to do it.

Dealing with the psychological and political impacts of biological weapons present additional problems. While most urban responders have at least token plans for handling the public relations aspects of biological accidents, it is far from clear that these plans would work in dealing with major attacks or sequential attacks. It is clear that national and local media are not prepared to report on such attacks and to perform a civil defense role. The psychological dimension also presents problems because it is not clear that the normal decontamination of areas, facilities, and buildings will not leave trace problems or that the public can be convincingly reassured of what is and is not safe. More broadly, the long-term medical effects of a large-scale attack are very difficult to characterize, and the Persian Gulf War has shown how the resulting uncertainties can create major medical, psychological, and political problems.

### Cost-Effectiveness of Real-World Options

There are options for improving U.S. defense and response capabilities to biological attacks, some of which the government is already aggressively exploring and many of which apply to all forms of major CBRN attacks. The existing federal effort is discussed in depth in the following chapters of this analysis, which discuss the present size and nature of the federal effort by department and agency. At the same time, it is clear that the following options and issues need continuing examination—particularly in the light of the cumulative long-term risk of major biological (and nuclear) attacks:

- The role of intelligence in defense and response needs to be addressed to determine the probable ability to detect the development of biological weapons, the specific agents under development, the strain, and the nature of the delivery systems. The need to communicate warning to responders and treatment facilities as well as defenders also needs to be addressed.

- Zero-based investigation is needed of the probable effects and lethality of biological weapons that examines the use of normal diseases and militarized strains. This should, specifically, include the issue of weaponization and the effect of different levels of efficiency in weaponization.

- Specialized intelligence and defense capabilities must be developed for warning, detection, characterization, and defense. This is not only a task for the national intelligence, security, and law enforcement community, but also for federal, state, and local law enforcement and state National Guard units. The problem of finding cost-effective mixes of specialized CBRN expertise and linking these efforts to response activities will present a constant challenge in terms of law, resources, organization, and training.

- As part of the development of intelligence, defense, and response capabilities, explicit analysis is needed of the trade-offs between the risk posed by mass attack and the separation of foreign intelligence from law enforcement, and the priority given to prosecution versus defense. The scale of treatment and the needed response times call for almost total integration of the intelligence, defense, and response effort, but this now presents major legal and organizational problems.

- The ability to convincingly identify attackers needs to be determined, as well as the possible timelines, as part of an effort to create a credible threat of retaliation and punishment at the military and law enforcement levels.

- A major research and development effort is already underway to improve detectors. The role that new technical aids—such as strain analysis, VNTR analysis, localization, phylogentics, DNA tags, and pathogen isotopes—needs to be addressed as part of an effort to determine what can be done to improve warning, detection, characterization, response, and treatment.

- The CDC and DTRA evidently are already examining models that are capable of providing a more realistic picture of the effects of biological weapons in urbanized environments and how they might behave in real-world attacks. These seem to include the use of modern militarized agents. Virtually the same need exists to improve the modeling of all forms of CBRN attack.

- As part of this effort, the need to be able to model and predict the effect of the atmospheric boundary level and to estimate the combined impact of air movements, temperature, and day-night conditions in an urbanized environment is critical to predicting effects and the capability for detection. The need for models capable of reflecting local wind and weather conditions and water flows is equally important. Nominal models of plumes and weather effects are now so uncertain that they may do more harm than good in providing guidance for detection and response.

- Zero-based investigation is needed of how to link the detection and characterization of biological agents to a system capable of measuring the scale and lethality of attacks. Efforts to develop advanced real-time detectors need to be tied to a clear plan for deployment as a system—including fixed versus mobile sensor arrays and the possible use of municipal vehicles as sensor platforms. This should include the ability to provide the data needed to identify the need for containment, isolation, treatment, disposal, and decontamination. This examination must address fundamental cost-effectiveness issues as to whether systems can or should be deployed without strategic and tactical warning, and can be rapidly deployed and should consider the real-world problems of developing such systems to deal with infectious diseases and their epidemiology.

- The problem of providing integrated detection and characterization of all forms of CBRN attack must be addressed at the same time, along with their cost-effectiveness. The limits of such systems, their level of accuracy and error, and their ability to reliably address the scale and area of coverage of attacks must be addressed.

- The potential role of any such detection and characterization system must be examined in a broader context. Methods of transmitting data to defenders, responders, and caregivers—including hospitals and public health facilities—need to be identified. As part of such systems, a clear linkage needs to be established between local detection and characterization and communication of the results to state, regional, and federal authorities. Methods need to be developed to use the results to immediately alert caregivers and local, state, and federal authorities to assemble the necessary containment and treatment resources. Contingency plans need to be developed to use the media to alert those in and near the affected area as to what to do in the presence of a given agent(s).

- Current efforts to develop detectors need to be recalibrated to consider the problems of telemetry and triage—including presymptomatic triage.

- The cost-effectiveness of vaccine stockpiling needs careful examination. Focusing on anthrax and smallpox may be a valid option. It may also drive attackers to choose other diseases or develop strains/genetically engineered variants that are immune. The option of "silver bullet" antibiotics and vaccines capable of dealing with a wide range of existing diseases, militarized strains, and genetically modified diseases needs full net technical assessment.

- The cost-effectiveness of enhancing local public health capability needs examination as does the overall cost-effectiveness of developing suitable local government response systems. It is easy to call for federal support and HHS/FEMA training and aid efforts. The tangible benefits per dollar in terms of lasting capabilities to deal with attacks are far from clear.

- Adding courses on biodefense to current medical and postgraduate training may be cost-effective.

- The hospital seems to be the current weak link in most serious bioattacks. The cost-effectiveness of federal programs, regulations, and tax credits in creating hospitals with improved CBRN and biodefense treatment capabilities needs serious examination. At present, far too much of the defense/response effort would simply end in overloading existing medical treatment facilities.

- Efforts are already underway to create specialized National Guard and reserve CBRN defense units. The capability to contain, isolate, perform triage, and treat the wounded seems to be the critical current weak link in such efforts, and is compounded by the lack of well-funded public health programs capable of organizing and training reserves of local caregivers.

- Civil defense options need to be reexamined in terms of building design and modification, personal defense equipment, and possible home protection and care options. These need to be examined in terms of their real-world cost-effectiveness and of their value in dealing with the full spectrum of CBRN attacks.

- A comprehensive plan is needed for dealing with local, state, and national media. This must involve education efforts, voluntary agreement to provide coverage that will inform without creating panic or misinformation, and some effort to provide clearly official coverage that viewers and listeners will trust. Consideration is needed of bringing back some form of authorized civil defense network in the effect of large-scale nuclear and biological attacks.

- Much of the current planning effort sees one major attack with one agent used in a form that federal, state, and local authorities clearly detect and characterize as the "worst case." Defense and response needs to examine cases involving multiple attacks, deception and false alarms, false characterization, and late detection. The problem of dealing with contagious disease outbreaks that are only detected after they have reached at least scatter regional or national levels is particularly important.

- The nation needs to be prepared for the "morning after." A clear plan is needed for presidential response and national leadership in the event of a successful attack and to prepare the American people for follow-on attacks and the need for a U.S. response.

- The issue of retaliation and counteroffensive options in the event of foreign attacks must be transformed into credible options that can be communicated in ways that reassure our allies, that can create a clear context for American counterattacks that the world will understand, and that will deter attackers.

The problem with this list is obvious, particularly when considered in the light of the need for federal response to existing public health care and entitlements needs, the existence of the full spectrum of CBRN attacks, the additional risks posed by missile and critical infrastructure attacks, and existing national security requirements. The checklist of necessary options is *very* long, the short-term risks are low, the effectiveness of most options is uncertain, and the cumulative cost is high. Furthermore, it is not possible to prioritize defense and response at this point in time, and the effectiveness of any program may be determined by its weakest and/or most expensive link. Anyone can call for action. Developing an affordable and well-justified program is an entirely different matter.

## RADIOLOGICAL WEAPONS AS MEANS OF ATTACK

Another method of attack would be a radiological weapon that employed conventional explosives or other means to scatter radioactive material. Radiological weapons are generally felt to be suitable largely for terror, political, and area denial purposes, rather than mass killings. Unlike nuclear weapons, they spread radioactive material contaminating personnel, equipment, facilities, and terrain. The radioactive material acts as a toxic chemical to which exposure eventually proves harmful or fatal.

There are two types of radiological weapons. A *radiological dispersal device* (RDD) includes any explosive device utilized to spread radioactive material upon detonation. Any improvised explosive devise could be used by placing it in close proximity to radioactive material. A *simple RDD* spreads radiological material without the use of an explosive. Any nuclear material (including medical isotopes or waste) can be used in this manner.

The main potential sources of such weapons—barring covert transfer from outside the United States—are hospital radiation therapy (iodine-125, cobalt-60, and cesium-137), radio-pharmaceuticals (iodine-131, iodine-123, technetium-99, thalium-201, and xenon-133), nuclear power plant fuel rods (uranium-235), and universities, laboratories, radiography, and gauging (cobalt-60, cesium-137, iridium-192, and radium-226). Such materials can be delivered by a wide variety of means, including human agents, the destruction of a facility or vessel containing radioactive material, shipments or remote control devices that explode and disseminate the agent, placement in facilities or water supplies, or using aircraft, missiles, and rockets. Radiological dispersal weapons (RDWs) can also be used to contaminate livestock, fish, and food crops.

The effectiveness of such weapons is controversial and the impact can vary sharply because of the time required to accumulate a disabling or significant dose of radiation through ingestion, inhalation, or exposure. According to U.S. military reporting on their effects, "There are no official casualty predictions for radiological dispersal weapons (RDWs). Because of the nature of the weapon, verification of the use of the weapon may prove difficult."[112] Other findings of the DOD provide important insights into the potential effectiveness of RDWs:

> Such a weapon would not produce a nuclear yield; but would spread contamination. While such weapons would produce far less immediate damage

than devices that result in nuclear detonations, radiological weapons have enormous potential for intimidation. Targeting a nuclear reactor in an antagonist's territory to produce an accident releasing nuclear material would be another option.

There are hundreds of nuclear reactors and many more nuclear sources throughout the world, such as radiological materials used in hospitals. Both international and national measures control these items and associated materials and thereby contribute to proliferation prevention. However, post-war investigations in occupied Iraq showed that at least some of these control regimes could be circumvented, even by a state that was a nominal adherent to the Nuclear Non-Proliferation Treaty. Near-term concerns include the accumulation of large quantities of plutonium from reactors that is intended for reprocessing and/or storage, and the status of nuclear materials in the New Independent States that previously comprised the Soviet Union.[113]

## The Practical Chances of Using Radiological Weapons

A December 1999 report by the Gilmore Commission drew the following conclusions about the ability of terrorist groups to use radiological weapons:

In the view of some authorities, theft of a nuclear device or building a weapon "in house" are the least-probable courses of action for a prospective nuclear terrorist. Far more likely—for all the reasons cited above—is the dispersal of radiological material in an effort to contaminate a target population or distinct geographical area.

The material could be spread by radiological dispersal devices (or RDDs)— i.e., "dirty bombs" designed to spread radioactive material through passive (aerosol) or active (explosive) means. Alternatively, the material could be used to contaminate food or water. This latter option is, however, considerably less likely given the huge quantities of radioactive material that would be required. The fact that most radioactive material is not soluble in water means that its use by a terrorist would be unlikely and impractical, if the purpose is to contaminate reservoirs or other municipal water supplies, because the radioactive material will settle out or be trapped in filters. Those factors, coupled with the fact that any radioactive material will present safety risks to the terrorists themselves, collectively indicate the serious difficulties for any adversary attempting to store, handle, and disseminate it effectively.

Radiological weapons kill or injure by exposing people to radioactive materials, such as cesium-137, iridium-192, or cobalt-60. Victims are irradiated when they get close to or touch the material, inhale it, or ingest it. With high enough levels of exposure, the radiation can sicken and kill. Radiation (particularly gamma rays) damages cells in living tissue through ionization, destroying or altering some of the cell constituents essential to normal cell functions.

The effects of a given device will depend on whether the exposure is "acute" (i.e., brief, one time) or "chronic" (i.e., extended). There are a number of possible sources of material that could be used to fashion such a device, including nuclear waste stored at a power plant (even though such waste is not highly radioactive), or radiological medical isotopes found in many hospitals or research laboratories. Although spent fuel rods are sometimes mentioned as potential sources of radiological material, they are very hot, heavy, and difficult to handle, thus making them a poor choice for terrorists. Other sources, such as medical devices, might be much easier to steal and handle. These materials, however, have a lower specific activity than the materials in reactor fuel rods (although large unshielded sources are quite dangerous). Presumably, terrorists could steal a device (either in transit or at the service facility or user location) and remove the radioactive materials.

Radioactive materials are often sintered in ceramic or metallic pellets. Terrorists could then crush the pellets into a powder and put the powder into an RDD. The RDD could then be placed in or near a target facility and detonated, spreading the radiological material through the force of the explosion and in the smoke of any resulting fires. Of course, the larger the radioactive material dispersal area, the smaller the resulting dose rate. Although incapable of causing tens of thousands of casualties, a radiological device, in addition to possibly killing or injuring any people who came into contact with it "could be used to render symbolic targets or significant areas and infrastructure uninhabitable and unusable without protective clothing."

A combination fertilizer truck bomb, if used together with radioactive material, for example, could not only have destroyed one of the New York World Trade Center's towers but might have rendered a considerable chunk of prime real estate in one of the world's financial nerve centers indefinitely unusable because of radioactive contamination. The disruption to commerce that could be caused, the attendant publicity, and the enhanced coercive power of terrorists armed with such "dirty" bombs (which, for the reasons cited above, are arguably more likely threats than terrorist use of an actual fissile nuclear device), is disquieting.[114]

At the same time, a DOD study notes that, "Iraqi and Russian separatists Chechnya have already demonstrated practical knowledge of RDWs. The availability of material to make RDWs will inevitably increase in the future as more countries pursue nuclear power (and weapons) programs and radioactive material becomes more available."[115]

### The Practical Risks and Effects of Using Radiological Weapons

There is no question that small amounts of radioactive materials can be used to attack, threaten, and contaminate, and that the risk of radiation poses a serious psychological problem. Covert attacks might produce slow radiation poisoning, and agents might be deliberately designed to make cost-effective decontamination difficult, time-consuming, or impossible.

The limited use of small amounts of radiological weapons present the problem that there are no reliable criteria for determining what dose is dangerous or lethal, particularly if effects like long-term increases in the cancer rate are included. Responders also differ sharply in terms of their use of sophisticated radiation detectors and most are far more concerned with evacuation than the difficult problems of dealing with medical and decontamination aftermaths. In broad terms, however, these effects are somewhat similar to those of using a chemical weapon. They are not catastrophic and even the contamination of most critical facilities could be dealt with—at the cost of interruptions in service and efficiency.

The large-scale weaponization of radiological materials presents a different issue. The previous comments make some relatively casual assumptions about how easy or difficult it is to obtain and convert radioactive materials into a form that can be broadly disseminated over a wide area. These comments may be valid, but they also may not. There are significant disputes over how easy it is to grind up radioactive materials and spread them over an area larger than a single facility, and the unclassified literature seems to be based on generalizations rather than detailed technical analysis. This does not mean that such attacks are not possible, but it does mean that considerably more evidence is needed as to what can and cannot be done.

One possible option is a systematic attack on a nuclear power plant. This would require considerable expertise, access to the basic design of the plant and ideally to a full set of plans, and either an exceptionally efficient saboteur or a trained team. In most cases, it would require considerable time and effort to bypass safeguards and controls. The possible venting or overload of a reactor could then act as a radiological weapon, however, and cover hundreds of square kilometers as well as have a major potential affect on regional power supplies and some aspects of the U.S. military nuclear program.[116]

Alternatively, an attacker might seize significant amounts of radioactive material from spent fuel storage, during the nuclear fuel cycle—which involves milling, conversion, enrichment, fuel fabrication, and disposal of waste—as well as reactor operations. A seizure of spent fuel would be particularly dangerous during the first 150 days after the downloading of the reactor because iodine-131 and iodine-123 are present, extremely volatile, and affect the thyroid.[117]

Work by the DOD indicates that the following problems exist in trying to detect and estimate the impact of radiological weapons:

- The impact of prompt radiation is extremely difficult to estimate, and lethal and serious doses can vary sharply according to exposure even in the same areas. Even personnel equipped with dosimeters present major problems in triage because dosimeter readings cannot be used to judge whole body radiation, and a mix of physical symptoms have to be used to judged the seriousness of exposure. The impact of radiation poisoning also changes sharply if the body has experienced burns or physical trauma.[118] In the case of treatable patients, significant medical treatment may be required for more than two months after exposure.

- Prompt detection and decontamination can have a major effect, and about 95 percent of external agents can be removed by simply removing outer clothing and shoes.[119]

- The spread of airborne radioactive particulates can vary sharply according to the size and nature of a weapon and its placement and in the size and lethality of particles and water vapor. While most will settle within twenty-four hours, this will vary according to wind pattern and movement through the affected area. The drop in actual radiation of the affected material is generally much slower, but logarithmic. Radiation at the first hour after the explosion is down about 90 percent, and radiation is only about 1 percent of the original level after two days. Radiation only drops to trace levels, however, after three hundred hours.[120]

- The test data on the longer-term (after twenty-four hours) effects of radiation are highly uncertain and the longer-term impacts of radiation are so speculative as to be impossible to estimate. As a result, virtually all estimates of the impact of RDWs ignore the long-term casualties (ninety-six hours to seventy years or more) caused by radiation, such as cancer, and the impact of a weapon on the environment in terms of the poisoning of water and food supplies. The data on treatment of exposures from zero to 530 cGy of exposure do not even seem to call for recording the probable level of exposure.[121]

- The problem is further complicated by trying to estimate the specific mix of radioisotopes and radionuclides that will be produced and then become induced in the soil. The hazard prediction models used by the DOD are under review, and it is not clear when new models will be available.[122]

- There is often a gap between generic data on radiation and the assumed level of treatment required. Much of the federal, state, and local response literature effectively dodges around the issue of triage and the problem of choosing who will receive limited medical treatment and how these victims will be selected in the case of large scale exposures. It does not describe what is done with the assumed dying and untreatable, and some literature seems to assume that doses from zero to 70 cGy can be largely ignored, while other literature is more concerned with long-term effects. The broader issue of what indicators will be used for triage and deciding treatment and what treatment should actually be employed is generally not addressed because so many different RDWs and types of attack are possible.

- The characterization of RDWs presents a significantly greater problem than does detection, and estimating the type and effects of a specific RDW is difficult. This is particularly true of contamination with RDWs or if detection only occurs after significant exposure. Because of the limitations of dosimeters and other detection equipment, bioassay is generally needed to determine the level and type of effects. This is critical with inhalation and ingestion.[123]

- Postattack radiological surveys can be very difficult for the same reasons.[124]

- Corpse disposal may be a major problem as may disposal of dead animals and birds. This aspect of response seems to be largely ignored.

- Even military medical handbooks fail to address the psychological impacts of prompt and longer-term effects.
- Food and water contamination can be a problem and add to the response burden in any major attack.[125]

Experts agree that considerably more study is needed of the different kinds of agents that might be used, of their different effects and risks, of the problem of characterizing the weapon versus detecting radiation, and of how triage, monitoring, and treatment need to be applied. The same is true of decontamination. As is the case with chemical and biological weapons, there is also a need for far more analysis of what kind of detection grids or systems are needed, of what level of shielding or masking would be effective, and of how to predict dissemination and effects.

More broadly, responders correctly assume that destruction and lethality are key criteria, but the main purpose of such an attack might be political or psychological. As is the case with chemical and biological weapons, public and world perceptions of the impact of such attacks would initially be based on the fact they occurred at all. It is also far from clear how the public would react to even the most successful decontamination effort and how well the United States could guarantee the effectiveness of such a decontamination effort. Past incidents of nuclear smuggling and black market sales have also demonstrated that it is far easier to obtain some form of radioactive material than fissile material.

## NUCLEAR WEAPONS AS MEANS OF ATTACK

No one questions the dangers posed by a covert or terrorist attack using nuclear weapons. Table 4.9 shows a list of known nuclear powers that are not allies of the United States, and several of which may become hostile in the future. A number of other countries are conducting nuclear weapons research efforts, have carried out enough nuclear research to deploy weapons relatively quickly, or could build a nuclear weapon if they could find a source of fissile material.

The real question is whether any state actor would take the risk of conducting a covert or proxy attack or of aiding an extremist/terrorist group, and whether any extremist/terrorist group could acquire or make a weapon on its own. At present, these factors seem to limit the probability of a nuclear attack on the United States. However, effective homeland defense must deal with the risk of such attacks over at least a twenty-five-year period, and the process of proliferation described earlier does not create high confidence that the United States can count on future restraint. International peacetime restraint is also not a valid basis for estimating risk. Much of the risk stems from how actors would behave in a contingency involving an extreme crisis in which past patterns of behavior could change quickly and with little warning.

Table 4.9
U.S. Department of Defense Estimate of Potential National Threats Involving
Nuclear Weapons

---

## China

China currently has over 100 nuclear warheads and is increasing the size, accuracy, and survivability of its nuclear missile force. It is likely that the number of deployed Chinese theater and strategic systems will increase in the next several years. However, as its strategic requirements evolve, it may change the pace of its modernization effort for its nuclear missile force (particularly if the United States deploys NMD); any warhead improvements will complement China's missile modernization effort. China currently is not believed to be producing fissile material for nuclear weapons, but has a stockpile of fissile material sufficient to improve or increase its weapons inventory. China has ratified the NPT and signed the CTBT, and has declared it will never use its nuclear forces against a non-nuclear weapons state. China maintains a no-first use pledge in its strategic nuclear doctrine and regards its strategic nuclear force as a deterrent against intimidation or actual attack. Thus, China's stated doctrine reportedly calls for a survivable long-range missile force that can hold a significant portion of the U.S. population at risk in a retaliatory strike. As China's strategic forces and doctrine further evolve, Beijing will continue to develop and deploy more modern ICBMs and SLBMs

## India

On 11 and 13 May 1998, India conducted what it claimed were five nuclear explosive tests. According to Indian officials, the 11 May tests included a fission device with a yield of about 12 kilotons, a thermonuclear device with a yield of about 43 kilotons, and a third test with a yield of about 0.2 kilotons. An Indian spokesman stated that the first set of tests was intended "to establish that India has a proven capability for a weaponized nuclear program."

India claimed that its 13 May tests had yields of about 0.5 and 0.2 kilotons, which were carried out to generate additional data for computer simulations. According to the Chairman of India's Atomic Energy Commission, the tests enabled India to build "an adequate scientific database for designing the types of devices that [India] needs for a credible nuclear deterrent." The tests triggered international condemnation and the United States imposed wide-ranging sanctions against India.

The tests were India's first since 1974, and reversed the previously ambiguous nuclear posture where Indian officials denied possession of nuclear weapons. Indian officials cited a perceived deterioration of India's security environment, including increasing Pakistani nuclear and missile capabilities and perceived threats from China, to justify the tests. India has a capable cadre of scientific personnel and a nuclear infrastructure, consisting of numerous research and development centers, 11 nuclear power reactors, uranium mines and processing plants, and facilities to extract plutonium from spent fuel. With this large nuclear infrastructure, India is capable of manufacturing complete sets of components for plutonium-based nuclear weapons, although the acquisition of foreign nuclear-related equipment could benefit New Delhi in its weapons development efforts to develop and produce more sophisticated nuclear weapons. India probably has a small stockpile of nuclear

**Table 4.9 (continued)**

weapon components and could assemble and deploy a few nuclear weapons within a few days to a week. The most likely delivery platforms are fighter-bomber aircraft. New Delhi also is developing ballistic missiles that will be capable of delivering a nuclear payload in the future.

India is in the beginning stages of developing a nuclear doctrine. In August 1999, the Indian government released a proposed nuclear doctrine prepared by a private advisory group appointed by the government. It stated that India will pursue a doctrine of credible minimum deterrence. The document states that the role of nuclear weapons is to deter the use or the threat of use of nuclear weapons against India, and asserts that India will pursue a policy of "retaliation only." The draft doctrine maintains that India "will not be the first to initiate a nuclear strike, but will respond with punitive retaliation should deterrence fail." The doctrine also reaffirms India's pledge not to use or threaten to use nuclear weapons against states that do not possess nuclear weapons. It further states that India's nuclear posture will be based on a triad of aircraft, mobile land-based systems, and sea-based platforms to provide a redundant, widely dispersed, and flexible nuclear force. Decisions to authorize the use of nuclear weapons would be made by the Prime Minister or his "designated successor(s)." The draft doctrine has no official standing in India, and the United States has urged Indian officials to distance themselves from the draft, which is not consistent with India's stated goal of a minimum nuclear deterrent. India expressed interest in signing the CTBT, but has not done so. It has pledged not to conduct further nuclear tests pending entry into force of the CTBT. Indian officials have tied signature and ratification of the CTBT to developing a domestic consensus on the issue. Similarly, India strongly opposed the NPT as discriminatory but it is a member of the IAEA. Only four of India's 13 operational nuclear reactors currently are subject to IAEA safeguards. In June 1998, New Delhi signed a deal with Russia to purchase two light-water reactors to be built in southern India; the reactors will be under facility-specific IAEA safeguards. However, the United States has raised concerns that Russia is circumventing the 1992 NSG guidelines by providing NSG trigger list technology to India, which does not allow safeguards on all of its nuclear facilities. India has taken no steps to restrain its nuclear or missile programs. In addition, while India has agreed to enter into negotiations to complete a fissile material cutoff treaty, it has not agreed to refrain from producing fissile material before such a treaty would enter into force.

**Iran**
Although a signatory to NPT and the CTBT, Iran also is seeking fissile material and technology for weapons development through an elaborate system of military and civilian organizations. We believe Iran also has an organized structure dedicated to developing nuclear weapons by trying to establish the capability to produce both plutonium and highly enriched uranium. Iran claims to desire the establishment of a complete nuclear fuel cycle for its civilian energy program. In that guise, it seeks to obtain whole facilities that could be used in numerous ways in support of efforts to produce fissile material for a nuclear weapon. The potential availability of black

continued

Table 4.9 (continued)

market fissile material also might provide Iran a way to acquire the fissile material necessary for a nuclear weapon.

Iran's success in achieving a nuclear capability will depend, to a large degree, on the supply policies of Russia and China or on Iran's successful illicit acquisition of adequate quantities of weapons-usable fissile material. Russia is continuing work on a 1,000-megawatt power reactor at Bushehr. Although Russian officials have provided assurances that Russian cooperation with Iran will be limited to the Bushehr reactor project during the period of its construction, the United States Government is aware that a number of Russian entities are engaged in cooperation with Iran that goes beyond this project. One of Iran's primary goals is the acquisition of a heavy water-moderated, natural uranium-fueled nuclear reactor and associated facilities suitable for the production of weapons-grade plutonium. Although Bushehr will fall under IAEA safeguards, Iran is using this project to seek access to more sensitive nuclear technologies from Russia and to develop expertise in related nuclear technologies. Any such projects will help Iran augment its nuclear technology infrastructure, which in turn would be useful in supporting nuclear weapons research and development.

In the past, Chinese companies have been major suppliers of nuclear-related facilities and technology albeit under IAEA safeguards. China pledged in 1997 that it would not undertake any new nuclear cooperation with Iran and that it would close out its two existing projects—a small research reactor and a zirconium production facility, which will produce cladding for nuclear fuel—as soon as possible. (Neither of these two projects poses a significant proliferation concern.) China also agreed to terminate cooperation on a uranium conversion project. This project would have allowed Iran to produce uranium hexafluoride or uranium dioxide, which are the feedstock materials for the manufacture of weapons-grade plutonium. In addition, China announced new export controls in June 1998 that cover the sale of dual-use nuclear equipment. China appears to be living up to its 1997 commitments.

### Iraq

Iraq has ratified the NPT. Nevertheless, before the Gulf War, Iraq had a comprehensive nuclear weapons development program that was focused on building an implosion-type device. The program was linked to a ballistic missile project that was the intended delivery system. From April 1991 to December 1998, Iraqi nuclear aspirations were held in check by IAEA/UNSCOM inspections and monitoring. All known weapons-grade fissile material was removed from the country. Although Iraq claims that it destroyed all of the specific equipment and facilities useful for developing nuclear weapons, it still retains sufficient skilled and experienced scientists and engineers as well as weapons design information that could allow it to restart a weapons program.

Iraq would need five or more years and key foreign assistance to rebuild the infrastructure to enrich enough material for a nuclear weapon. This period would be substantially shortened should Baghdad successfully acquire fissile material from a foreign source.

Table 4.9 (continued)

**Libya**

Libya has ratified the NPT, but has not signed the CTBT and has long intended to develop or acquire nuclear weapons. Libya has made little progress, however, as its nuclear program lacks well-developed plans, expertise, consistent financial support, and adequate foreign suppliers. In the face of these difficulties, nonetheless, Libya likely will continue to try to develop a supporting infrastructure. Libya has a Soviet-supplied research reactor at Tajura that is under IAEA safeguards. The Russians may become actively involved in the modernization of the Tajura nuclear research center and, in 1999, Tripoli and Moscow resumed discussions on cooperation involving the Tajura reactor as well as a potential power reactor deal. Should this civil sector work come to fruition, Libya could gain opportunities to conduct nuclear weapons-related research and development. Libya reportedly also is trying to recruit foreign scientists and technicians to aid its program.

**North Korea**

The 1994 Agreed Framework between the United States and North Korea froze nuclear weapons material production at the Yongbyon and Taechon facilities. However, the United States believes North Korea produced and diverted sufficient plutonium for at least one nuclear weapon prior to the agreement. (In any event, North Korea will have to satisfy the International Atomic Energy Agency (IAEA) as to its exact plutonium holdings before key nuclear components can be delivered for the two light-water reactors that are to be provided under the Agreed Framework.) North Korea removed spent fuel from the Yongbyon reactor in 1994. Had Pyongyang reprocessed the spent fuel from the Yongbyon reactor, it could have produced enough plutonium for several nuclear weapons. As part of the Agreed Framework, the IAEA has maintained a continuous presence at Yongbyon, and IAEA personnel have monitored canning of the spent fuel from the reactor. The canning of all accessible spent fuel rods and rod fragments, which was carried out by a team from the United States, under the auspices of the Department of Energy (DOE), was completed in April 2000. The U.S. team maintains a presence at the site to continue maintenance activities. In 1998, the United States became concerned about an underground construction project at Kumchang-ni, in northern North Korea. The site was believed to be large enough to house a plutonium production facility and possibly a reprocessing plant. Through successful negotiations, U.S. officials were permitted to visit the facility at Kumchang-ni in May 1999. Based on the 1999 team's findings, it was concluded that the facility as then concurrently configured, was not suited to house graphite-moderated reactors or reprocessing operations. A second visit to Kumchang-ni was conducted in May 2000, during which the team found no evidence to contradict the 1999 conclusions. In the summer of 1999, the United States dispatched former Secretary of Defense William Perry to consult with North Korea on key U.S. security concerns such as its nuclear and missile programs. In the North Korea Policy Review, Dr. Perry concluded that the nuclear freeze instituted at Yongbyon's facilities remained in effect, although the U.S. remains concerned about possible continuing North Korean interest in a

continued

Table 4.9 (continued)

nuclear weapons program. Moreover, there is some evidence that North Korea has tried to procure technology that could have applications in its nuclear program. North Korea has ratified the NPT. It has not signed the Comprehensive Test Ban Treaty (CTBT). Dr. Perry recommended that the U.S. should seek the complete and verifiable cessation of testing, production, and deployment of missiles exceeding the parameters of the MTCR, and the complete cessation of export sales of such missiles and the equipment and technology associated with them.

## Pakistan

As a response to India's tests, Pakistan conducted its own series of nuclear tests in May 1998. Pakistan claimed to have tested six devices, five on 28 May and one on 30 May. Dr. A. Q. Khan, a key figure in Pakistan's nuclear program, claimed the five devices tested on 28 May were boosted fission devices: a "big bomb" and four tactical weapons of low yield that could be used on small missiles. He also claimed that Pakistan could conduct a fusion or thermonuclear blast if it so desired. The United States imposed additional sanctions against Pakistan as a result of these tests. Pakistan has a well-developed nuclear infrastructure, including facilities for uranium conversion and enrichment and the infrastructure to produce nuclear weapons. Unlike the Indian nuclear program, which uses plutonium for its weapons, Pakistan's program currently is based on highly-enriched uranium. However, Pakistan is also developing the capability to produce plutonium for potential weapons use. An unsafeguarded heavy-water research reactor built at Khushab will produce plutonium that could be reprocessed for weapons use at facilities under construction. In the past, China supplied Pakistan with nuclear materials and expertise and has provided critical assistance in the production of Pakistan's nuclear facilities. Pakistan also acquired a significant amount of nuclear-related and dual-use equipment and materials from various sources principally in the FSU and Western Europe. Acquisition of nuclear-related goods from foreign sources will remain important if Pakistan chooses to continue to develop and produce more advanced nuclear weapons, although we expect that, with the passage of time, Pakistan will become increasingly self-sufficient. Islamabad likely will increase its nuclear and ballistic missile stockpiles over the next five years.

Islamabad's nuclear weapons are probably stored in component form. Pakistan could probably assemble the weapons fairly quickly and has aircraft and possibly ballistic missiles available for delivery. Pakistan's nuclear weapons program has long been dominated by the military, a dominance that likely has continued under the new military government and under Pakistan's new National Command Authority (NCA), announced in February 2000. While Pakistan has yet to divulge publicly its nuclear doctrine, the new NCA is believed to be responsible for such doctrine, as well as nuclear research and development and wartime command and control. The NCA also includes two committees that advise Pakistan's Chief Executive, General Musharraf, about the development and employment of nuclear weapons.

Pakistan remains steadfast in its refusal to sign the NPT, stating that it would do so only after India joined the Treaty. Consequently, not all of Pakistan's nuclear facilities are under IAEA safeguards. Pakistani officials have stated that signature

Table 4.9 (continued)

---

of the CTBT is in Pakistan's best interest, but that Pakistan will do so only after developing a domestic consensus on the issue, and have disavowed any connection with India's decision. Like India, Pakistan expressed its intention to sign the CTBT, but, so far, has failed to do so. While Pakistan has provided assurances that it will not assemble or deploy its nuclear warheads, nor will it resume testing unless India does so first; it has taken no additional steps. Pakistan has agreed to enter into negotiations to complete a fissile material cutoff agreement, but has not agreed to refrain from producing fissile material before a cutoff treaty would enter into force.

### Russia

Moscow increasingly has stated it will rely more heavily on its nuclear forces for deterrent purposes, especially given the serious deterioration of their conventional forces' capability. Russia conditionally ratified (START II) in May 2000, which, once it enters into force, will limit the number of operational launchers and deployed warheads to 3,000–3,500. In June 1999, former President Yeltsin proposed discussions with the United States for further force reductions in the context of a START III Treaty, with proposed force levels of 1,500–2,000.

The Russian nuclear warhead stockpile is being reduced as a result of tactical nuclear warhead reduction initiatives, while the START I Treaty (which entered into force in December 1994) and system aging have resulted in the reduction of deployed strategic warheads. In December 2000, the stockpile was estimated to be well under 25,000 warheads, a reduction of over 11,000 warheads since eliminations began in 1992. By the end of 2010, the overall stockpile will likely be further reduced, depending on the economic situation in Russia, Moscow's willingness and ability to abide by tactical nuclear warhead reduction pledges, and future arms control agreements. Moscow has consolidated many of its strategic and tactical warheads at central storage locations, and numerous warhead storage sites for holding warheads have been deactivated since the early 1990s. While this consolidation has improved security, current resource shortages have subjected the nuclear storage system to stresses and risks for which it was not designed. Indeed, warhead reductions have had the collateral effect of increasing near- to mid-term fissile material storage requirements, pending the long-term elimination of relevant weapons-usable fissile materials.

While Russia's strategic nuclear forces will retain considerable capability over the next ten years and will serve as its primary means of deterrence, the overall force is expected to continue to decrease because of arms control, economic constraints, and aging equipment. Within ten years, the number of operational strategic warheads will continue to decline. At the same time, however, production of warheads will continue into the 21st century as new strategic missile systems are deployed and obsolete warheads replaced.

For strategic delivery, Russia retains a significant strategic ballistic missile force of some 1,130 operational ICBMs and SLBMs. There no longer are any operationally deployed ICBMs in Ukraine, Kazakhstan, and Belarus. More than 1,250 FSU ICBMs and SLBMs have been removed from the overall force since 1991.

continued

Table 4.9 (continued)

This force is likely to decline further as a result of systems aging, chronic funding problems, and arms control agreements. On the other hand, Russia has begun deployment of a new ICBM, the SS-27 (TOPOL-M), and has other missiles planned for deployment in the 21st century. Russia has ratified the NPT and the CTBT.

Because of economic and other difficulties facing Russia and its armed forces, tactical nuclear weapons will remain a viable component of its general purpose forces for at least the next decade. Russia likely believes that maintaining tactical nuclear forces is a less expensive way to compensate for its current problems in maintaining conventional force capabilities. In late 1991 and early 1992, Russia agreed in the Presidential Nuclear Initiatives to a dramatic reduction in its tactical nuclear forces, including the elimination of its ground-launched tactical weapons. Russia still has significant numbers and types of delivery systems capable of performing the tactical nuclear mission. For example, Russia continues to have large inventories of tactical SRBMs (SS-21s), deactivated SCUDs, and a variety of artillery capable of delivering NBC weapons. In fact, Russia employed its tactical SRBMs (with conventional warheads) against the Chechens in the fall of 1999. Air systems include fighter aircraft and bombers. Naval tactical nuclear systems include torpedoes, anti-shipping and anti-submarine warfare missiles, and air-launched munitions carried on naval aircraft. Further, Russia's industrial base can support production of the full range of solid- and liquid-propellant ballistic missiles, space launch vehicles, and all associated technologies.

In November 1993, the Russian Ministry of Defense formally dropped its wholly declaratory "no first use" of nuclear weapons policy. In its place, the Ministry of Defense published its Basic Provisions of the Military Doctrine of the Russian Federation, in which it articulated its current nuclear policy: "The Russian Federation will not employ its nuclear weapons against any state party to the treaty on the nonproliferation of nuclear weapons, dated 1 July 1968, which does not possess nuclear weapons except in the cases of (a) an armed attack against the Russian Federation, its territory, armed forces, other troops, or its allies by any state that is connected by an alliance agreement with a state that does not possess nuclear weapons or; (b) joint actions by such a state with a state possessing nuclear weapons in the carrying out or in support of any invasion or armed attack upon the Russian Federation, its territory, armed forces, other troops, or its allies."

The current Russian doctrine and strategy involving the use of nuclear weapons, reiterated in October 1999, states that "the possibility of the use of nuclear weapons has not been excluded if the situation deteriorates during the course of conventional war." A revised version of this document was approved by then-Acting President Putin in January 2000, which further lowers the threshold for nuclear use in order to protect Russia's national interests and territorial integrity; it states: "The application of all forces and means, including nuclear weapons, if necessary to repel armed aggression, if all other measures for resolving the crisis situation have been exhausted or proven ineffective." In April 2000, the Russians elaborated on this threshold, stating that "the Russian Federation retains the right to use nuclear weapons in response to the use of nuclear weapons, or other types of weapons of mass destruction against itself or its allies, and also in response to large scale

**Table 4.9** (continued)

---

aggression with the use of conventional weapons in situations critical to the national security of the Russian Federation."

**Syria**
Syria is not pursuing the development of nuclear weapons. However, it retains an interest in nuclear technology and has a small Chinese-supplied research reactor, which is under IAEA safeguards. In addition, in May 1999, Syria signed a broad nuclear cooperation agreement with Russia, which includes the construction of a small light-water research reactor, which will be subject to IAEA safeguards. Syria currently lacks the infrastructure and trained personnel to establish a nuclear weapons program. Syria has ratified the NPT, but has not signed the CTBT.

---

*Source*: Adapted by Anthony H. Cordesman from Office of the Secretary of Defense, *Proliferation and Response* (Washington, D.C.: U.S. Department of Defense, January 2001).

### Lethality and Effectiveness

There are many uncertainties associated with the employment of nuclear weapons in covert, proxy, or terrorist/extremist attacks on the United States.[126] There is no way to predict the yield or how successful given proliferants will be in implementing fusing, yield enhancement, delivery system accuracy, and other technologies. Many studies simply assume a baseline case of a weapon using 1950s vintage U.S. technology—a simple fission weapon with a tens of kilotons yield that could be delivered by aircraft or tactical missiles. However, it is at least conceivable that a state might smuggle a thermonuclear weapon into the United States or explode one off its coasts, and fission weapons can range in yield from less than a kiloton to one hundred kilotons or even megatons.

A nuclear detonation releases vast amounts of energy that is manifested as blast effects. In the case of a small (ten kiloton) fission weapon, the blast is roughly 50 percent of the total energy, while the remainder is heat (35 percent) and nuclear radiation (15 percent). About 4 percent of this radiation is prompt ionizing radiation and 10 percent is fallout. The electromagnetic pulse (EMP)—a powerful radio wave—accounts for the remaining one percent.[127] Thermal energy becomes the dominant method of destruction in high yield weapons, however, such as thermonuclear or fusion weapons. The height-of-burst also has a critical impact on its effects. If the fireball does not touch the ground, there may not be militarily significant fallout. At higher altitudes, however, the EMP from a nuclear weapon can damage electronic equipment at considerable distances.

These factors are of critical importance in estimating the lethality of a covert or terrorist nuclear attack because the explosion is likely to take place at ground-level or a relatively low altitude, which produces maximum fall-out at the cost of diminished blast, thermal, and radiation effects. Most attacks are also likely to take place in cities, which would contain the radiation, blast, and thermal effects beyond the fireball, but ensure that a high population density was affected by fallout. It is important to note that most nuclear effects research for war fighting purposes assumes that a weapon will be used at much higher altitudes to avoid fallout and not interfere with military operations and that the weapon will affect a relatively open space.[128]

To put such yields into historical perspective, the weapon used at Hiroshima on August 6, 1945, had a nominal yield of twelve kilotons; the weapon used at Nagasaki on August 9, 1945, had a yield of twenty-three kilotons. The thermonuclear weapon the United States tested at the Bikini Atoll in the spring of 1954 had a yield of fifteen megatons, while the former Soviet Union tested a fifty-megaton weapon in 1961. This latter test had a yield over four thousand times larger than the yield of the weapon at Hiroshima.

Even a one-kiloton device, however, could have a massive impact, particularly because such devices are likely to be set off near ground level and be inefficient enough to increase the amount of direct fallout. An OTA study estimated that a one-kiloton terrorist device would still produce 5 psi overpressure out to 442 meters, and 600 rems of radiation out to 808 meters. (This compares with 4.4 miles for 5 psi for a one-megaton weapon and 600 rems to 2.7 kilometers.) It should be noted, however, that buildings normally cut these distances by about 25 percent in the case of blast and 75 percent in the case of direct radiation.[129]

Table 4.10 and Chart 4.4 show that yield can have a major impact on lethality, and that it is dangerous to assume that any response team will be able to characterize the impact of an explosion until it actually occurs. At the same time, Chart 4.5 warns that even a relatively lethal nuclear weapon would not necessarily be more lethal than even a relatively simple biological weapon.

Once again, the data on the lethality and the damage posed by such threats also suffers from major problems that could be of great importance in homeland defense:

- There are no reliable models of nuclear weapons effects in major urban areas involving massive complexes of high-rise steel and glass buildings. The containment effects of modern cities are extremely difficult to model. Military studies indicate, for example, that modern buildings can reduce the effect of blast, thermal, and radiation by 40 percent to 60 percent, but they do not specifically address modern heating and air conditioning systems, and the

**Chart 4.4**
The Nominal Lethality of Different Nuclear Weapons (seriousness of effect in
kilometers as a function of yield)

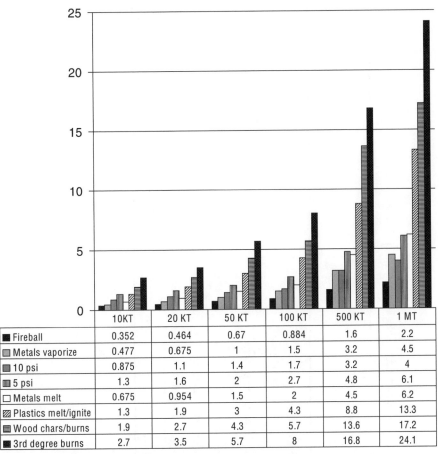

| | 10KT | 20 KT | 50 KT | 100 KT | 500 KT | 1 MT |
|---|---|---|---|---|---|---|
| ■ Fireball | 0.352 | 0.464 | 0.67 | 0.884 | 1.6 | 2.2 |
| ▨ Metals vaporize | 0.477 | 0.675 | 1 | 1.5 | 3.2 | 4.5 |
| ▥ 10 psi | 0.875 | 1.1 | 1.4 | 1.7 | 3.2 | 4 |
| ▥ 5 psi | 1.3 | 1.6 | 2 | 2.7 | 4.8 | 6.1 |
| ▢ Metals melt | 0.675 | 0.954 | 1.5 | 2 | 4.5 | 6.2 |
| ▨ Plastics melt/ignite | 1.3 | 1.9 | 3 | 4.3 | 8.8 | 13.3 |
| ▤ Wood chars/burns | 1.9 | 2.7 | 4.3 | 5.7 | 13.6 | 17.2 |
| ■ 3rd degree burns | 2.7 | 3.5 | 5.7 | 8 | 16.8 | 24.1 |

*Source*: Adapted by Anthony H. Cordesman from the Royal United Services Institute, *Nuclear Attack: Civil Defense* (London: RUSI/Brassey's, 1982), 30–36.

sheltering effects are not designed to take glass into account and the internal impact on the building.[130]

- Nuclear explosions create a wide range of different effects that can interact on the human body. The recent literature on military models for predicting casualties indicates that such models are not reliable, and states that, "The US Army Office of the Surgeon General is developing a system of casualty estimation that will provide rapid and reasonably accurate estimates of the number of types of casualties produced by a given enemy nuclear attack." This system, however, is not yet available.[131] The military handbook on the subject

Table 4.10—Part 1
**The Thermal and Blast Effects of Nuclear Weapons: The U.S. Department of Defense Estimates**

*Radii of Effects in Kilometers versus Weapons Yield*

| Effect | 1 KT | 20 KT | 100 KT | 1 MT | 10 MT |
|---|---|---|---|---|---|
| Nuclear Radiation (1,000 cGy or lethal dose in open) | 0.71 | 1.30 | 1.60 | 2.30 | 3.7 |
| Blast (50% incidence of translation with subsequent impact on a nonyielding surface) | 0.28 | 1.00 | 1.40 | 3.80 | 11.7 |
| Thermal (50% incidence of 2nd degree burns to bare skin | | | | | |
| Kilometer visibility) | 0.77 | 1.80 | 3.20 | 4.80 | 14.5 |
| Duration of Thermal Pulse in Seconds | 0.12 | 0.32 | 0.90 | 2.40 | 6.40 |

*Ranges in Kilometers for Probabilities of Flying Debris*

| | Probability of Serious Injury | | |
|---|---|---|---|
| **Yield in KT** | 1% | 50% | 99% |
| 1 | 0.28 | 0.22 | 0.17 |
| 10 | 0.73 | 0.57 | 0.44 |
| 20 | 0.98 | 0.76 | 0.58 |
| 50 | 1.40 | 1.10 | 0.84 |
| 100 | 1.90 | 1.50 | 1.10 |
| 200 | 2.50 | 1.90 | 1.50 |
| 500 | 3.60 | 2.70 | 2.10 |
| 1,000 | 4.80 | 3.60 | 2.70 |

*Ranges in Kilometers for Translational (Blast) Injuries*

| Yield in KT | Range for Probability Blunt Injuries and Fractures | | | | Range for Probable Fatal Injuries | |
|---|---|---|---|---|---|---|
| | -1% | 50% | 99% | | -1% | 50% |
| 1 | 0.38 | 0.27 | 0.19 | | 0.27 | 0.19 |
| 10 | 1.00 | 0.75 | 0.53 | | 0.75 | 0.53 |
| 20 | 1.30 | 0.99 | 0.71 | | 0.99 | 0.71 |
| 50 | 1.90 | 1.40 | 1.00 | | 1.40 | 1.00 |
| 100 | 2.50 | 1.90 | 1.40 | | 1.90 | 1.40 |
| 200 | 3.20 | 2.50 | 1.90 | | 2.50 | 1.90 |
| 500 | 4.60 | 3.60 | 2.70 | | 3.60 | 2.70 |
| 1,000 | 5.90 | 4.80 | 3.60 | | 4.80 | 3.60 |

*Source:* Adapted from Table 2-1 and Table 2-7 of FM 8-10-7; Table 4 of FM-8-9, Part 1; and USACHPPM, *The Medical NBC Battlebook*, USACHPPM Technical Guide 244, 2-2, 2-3.

continued

Table 4.10—Part 2
The Thermal and Blast Effects of Nuclear Weapons - Part Two: The British RUSI Estimates

*Radius of Effect in Kilometers*

| Yield in Kilotons | Metals Vaporize | Metals Melt | 3rd Wood Burns | 5 psi Degree Burns | 3 psi 160 mph Winds | 116 mph Winds |
|---|---|---|---|---|---|---|
| 10 | 0.337 | 0.675 | 1.3 | 1.9 | 1.3 | 1.6 |
| 20 | 0.477 | 0.954 | 1.9 | 2.7 | 1.6 | 2.0 |
| 50 | 0.754 | 1.500 | 3.0 | 4.3 | 2.0 | 2.7 |
| 100 | 1.000 | 2.000 | 4.3 | 5.7 | 2.7 | 3.5 |
| 200 | 1.500 | 2.800 | 5.7 | 8.0 | 3.5 | 4.5 |

*Impact of Killing Effects by Yield*

| | | Radius in Nautical Miles | | |
| | | 40 KT | 170 KT | 1MT |
| --- | --- | --- | --- | --- |
| Cause | Effect | | | |
| Overpressure (crushing) | Lethality threshold | 0.10 | 0.15 | 0.25 |
| | Severe lung damage | 0.70 | 1.10 | 2.10 |
| | Broken eardrums | 0.30 | 0.50 | 0.80 |
| Translation | Personnel in open (1%) | 0.90 | 1.60 | 3.30 |
| | Personnel near structures (1%) | 1.00 | 1.90 | 3.80 |
| | Personnel near structures (50%) | 0.60 | 1.00 | 2.10 |
| Thermal | 3rd degree burn (100%) | 1.50 | 2.60 | 5.20 |
| | No burns (100%) | 2.80 | 4.80 | 8.70 |
| | Retinal burn—daytime safe distance | 20.00 | 23.00 | 25.00 |
| Radiation | Lethal does (1,000 rads) | 0.70 | 0.80 | 0.90 |
| | No immediate harm (100 rads or less) | 1.00 | 1.10 | 1.20 |

*Source:* Adapted by Anthony H. Cordesman from Royal United Services Institute, *Nuclear Attack: Civil Defense* (London: RUSI/Brassey's, 1982), 30–36; and Office of Technology Assessment, *The Effects of Nuclear War*, U.S. Congress, OTA-NS-89; Washington, D.C. (May 1979), 43–46.

Chart 4.5
**The Relative Killing Effect of Chemical versus Biological versus Nuclear Weapons**

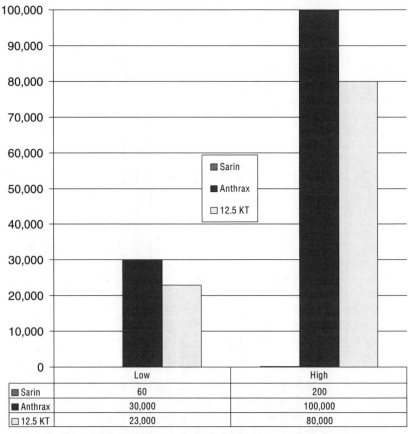

| | Low | High |
|---|---|---|
| ■ Sarin | 60 | 200 |
| ■ Anthrax | 30,000 | 100,000 |
| □ 12.5 KT | 23,000 | 80,000 |

*Sources*: Adapted by Anthony H. Cordesman from Victor A. Utgoff, *The Challenge of Chemical Weapons* (New York: St. Martin's, 1991), 238–242; and Office of Technology Assessment, *Proliferation of Weapons of Mass Destruction: Assessing the Risks*, U.S. Congress OTA-ISC-559, Washington, D.C., August, 1993, 56–57.

acknowledges that medical facilities will probably be saturated or collapse in the event of a major attack, but effectively dodges the problem of diagnosis and triage, and assumes that adequate medical professionals and facilities are available to allow extended triage and preventive medical treatment.[132] The DTRA is working on more sophisticated models tailored to attacks on the United States but it again is unclear when any unclassified results will be available.

- The impact of prompt radiation is extremely difficult to estimate, and lethal and serious doses can vary sharply according to exposure even in the same areas. Even personnel equipped with dosimeters present major problems in triage because dosimeter readings cannot be used to judge whole body radiation, and a mix of physical symptoms have to be used to judged the seriousness of exposure. The impact of radiation poisoning also changes sharply if the body has experienced burns or physical trauma.[133] In the case of treatable patients, significant medical treatment may be required for more than two months after exposure.

- Fallout can vary sharply according to the size and nature of a weapon and its placement, and in the size and lethality of particles and water vapor. While most fallout settles within twenty-four hours, this varies according to wind pattern and movement through the affected area. The drop in actual radiation of the affected material is much slower, but logarithmic. Radiation at the first hour after the explosion is down about 90 percent, and radiation is only about 1 percent of the original level after two days. Radiation only drops to trace levels, however, after three hundred hours.[134]

- The test data on the longer-term (after twenty-four hours) effects of radiation are highly uncertain and the longer term impacts of radiation are so speculative as to be impossible to estimate. As a result, virtually all estimates of the impact of nuclear weapons ignore the long-term casualties (ninety-six hours to seventy years or more) caused by radiation, such as cancer, and the impact of a weapon on the environment in terms of the poisoning of water and food supplies. The data on treatment of exposures from zero to 530 cGy of exposure do not even seem to call for recording the probable level of exposure.[135]

- There is little data on the steadily growing seriousness of EMP on urban areas filled with computers and solid-state communications and control devices.[136]

- Most models of fallout assume relatively neat patterns of distribution or plumes that give state and local responders a relatively clear picture of probable lethality and casualty effects. It is uncertain how realistic these models really are. Weather patterns could produce far more erratic patterns of distribution, and some estimates indicate that the "worst case" area covered by the overall plume could easily be twice the area used as the reference case. There is little detailed or parametric modeling of these uncertainties and of the burden they place on response teams. These uncertainties are also much greater for the much larger areas covered by low levels of radiation over time.

- The problem is further complicated by trying to estimate the specific mix of radioisotopes and radionuclides that will be produced and then become induced in the soil. The hazard prediction models used by the DOD are under review, and it is not clear when new models will be available.[137]

- There is often a gap between generic data on radiation, burn, and physical effects and the assumed level of treatment required. Much of the federal, state, and local response literature effectively dodges around the issue of triage and the problem of choosing who will receive limited medical treatment and how these victims will be selected. It does not describe what is done with the assumed dying and untreatable. The broader issue, however, is what indicators will be used for triage and deciding treatment and what treatment should actually be employed.

- Food and water contamination can be a serious problem and add to the response burden in any major attack.[138] Fallout presents special problems since sheltered civilians may not have access to safe water and urban water systems may be affected.

- Corpse disposal may be a major problem as may disposal of dead animals and birds. This aspect of response seems to be largely ignored.

- Even military medical handbooks fail to address the psychological impacts of prompt and longer-term effects.

### Is There a Threat from State Actors, Proxies, Terrorists, and Extremists? The Problem of Getting the Weapon

Two other key questions shaping the nuclear threat are whether state actors can obtain such weapons and will take the risk of using them covertly or giving them to a proxy, and whether terrorists can obtain such weapons or obtain the fissile material they need to make such weapons. The answers to these questions are heavily dependent on whether nuclear weapons become available from an existing nuclear weapons state or a state or independent group can obtain fissile material.[139]

The basic design features and technology needed for nuclear weapons are well understood. Iran and North Korea are estimated to have nuclear weapons or to be able to acquire them in five years. The International Atomic Energy Agency (IAEA) found in 1992 that Iraq had two fully functional implosion weapon designs and the skills needed to make the timing devices, neutron initiators, and high-explosive lenses for these weapons.

There are two primary ways of making a nuclear device. The first route is a gun-assembly weapon—like the one used at Hiroshima that propels a subcritical mass of uranium-235 (U-235) into a second, also subcritical, mass of U-235, in order to produce the critical mass needed for a nuclear explosion. The second route is to make an implosion weapon like the one used at Nagasaki. In such a device, an outer shell of chemical high explosives surrounds a subcritical sphere of fissionable nuclear material, for example, plutonium-239 (Pu-239). Precise detonation of the "entire" sphere results in an implosion that produces a critical mass and the resulting nuclear explosion.

Unlike most means of attack, the two basic materials needed for any such weapon—U-235 and Pu-239—are difficult to obtain. This is particularly true of the optimal weapons-grade nuclear materials for a weapon, although mixed isotope plutonium (reactor-grade material) can be used in nuclear weapons. The DOD reports that such a device would be less efficient and might have a less predictable yield. However, a weapon using nonweapons-grade plutonium was successfully detonated in a 1960s' test.[140]

Production of fissile material is probably impossible for most terrorist and extremist movements. At present, Russia seems to be the only state that might lose control over weapons-grade U-235 or P-239, although the DOD feels this risk is diminishing:

> Security of weapons-usable nuclear materials in Russia is another serious concern. While the Russian government is committed to nuclear security, continuing turmoil in society, corruption, and resource shortages complicate this commitment. The combination of lax security for nuclear materials at some facilities, poor economic conditions, and the growing power of organized crime in Russia mean that the potential for the theft and subsequent smuggling of these materials will continue to cause concern.

> At the same time, the Russians have taken seriously the threat from a potential Chechen insurgent attack on a nuclear power facility and have made security upgrades. In the past, there have been incidents of weapons-usable materials being diverted from Russian nuclear facilities. The largest seizures of such materials outside of the FSU occurred in 1994, where 2.7 kilograms of Highly Enriched Uranium (HEU) were found in the Czech Republic and about 360 grams of plutonium was seized in Germany. However, confirmed incidents of smuggling of weapons-usable nuclear materials, primarily plutonium and HEU, have declined but continued at a low rate. This decrease may be due to several factors: decreased smuggling through Western Europe, where detection is more likely; shifting of smuggling pathways through the southern tier of former Soviet states, where detection is highly unlikely; or improved security at Russian nuclear facilities. Nevertheless, reports of theft of nuclear materials continue to emanate from the former Soviet block countries.

> For example, in September 1999 one kilogram of reportedly uranium-235 (enrichment unconfirmed) was seized in the Republic of Georgia. In another recent case, 10 grams of weapons-grade HEU was confiscated in Bulgaria. In addition to reports of actual nuclear materials being offered for sale, there have been numerous accounts of radioactive isotopes such as californium-252, strontium-90, and cesium-137.

> However, in the longer term, the implementation of the U.S.–sponsored Material Protection, Control, and Accountability Program at Russian nuclear facilities likely will lead to a reduction of the number of incidents of diversion of weapons-usable materials. HEU and plutonium are also being recovered from Russia's ongoing warhead elimination effort, although a considerable degree of uncertainty remains about the overall security of Russia's large inventory of nuclear material. Several programs are under way to alleviate the security problems for this material.

> First, the U.S. DOE is assisting former Soviet states with physical security improvements at nuclear facilities in an effort to institute accurate accounting procedures for nuclear materials.

> Second, pursuant to a Cooperative Threat Reduction (CTR) implementing agreement with the Russian Ministry of Atomic Energy, DOD is helping to build a state-of-the-art storage facility for long-term secure storage of HEU and plutonium from disassembled nuclear weapons. This facility is located

at Mayak, about 1,400 kilometers east of Moscow near the Ural mountains. Third, the United States is purchasing 500 metric tons of HEU derived from disassembled Russian warheads. This material is being blended down in Russia into low-enriched uranium suitable for use in nuclear power reactors. Shipments to the United States began in 1993 and will continue over the next 20 years; as of mid-2000, about 100 tons of HEU had been transferred from Russia to the United States.

Finally, Russia has agreed to shut down its remaining plutonium-producing reactors. DOD is assisting the Russian Ministry of Atomic Energy pursuant to a CTR implementing agreement in the conversion of reactor cores so they will not produce weapons-grade plutonium. The weapons-grade plutonium produced since January 1997 will be placed under bilateral safeguards. Concern about security is not confined to nuclear items, but extends also to facilities in the FSU that house chemical or biological warfare-related materials. In addition, numerous scientists and technicians previously involved in key programs face severe salary reduction, complete loss of pay, [and] unemployment. States, such as Iran, that are seeking to establish their own weapon capabilities may try to exploit the situation by attempting to recruit such individuals. However, Western programs, such as the International Science and Technology Center (ISTC), the U.S. Civilian Research and Development Foundation (CRDF), the Nuclear Cities Initiative (NCI), and the Initiatives for Proliferation Prevention (IPP) are expressly designed to address this "brain drain" problem.[141]

These problems in obtaining fissile material led the Gilmore Commission to draw somewhat optimistic conclusions about the ability of terrorist groups to use nuclear weapons:

> Perhaps the only certain way for terrorists to achieve bona fide mass destruction would be to use a nuclear weapon. In this area, however, the challenges are arguably the most formidable. Although the collapse of the Soviet Union heightened Western fears about security at Russian military facilities, it appears that Russian strategic and tactical weapons are perhaps more secure than had been initially feared. Where there may be particular concern, however, is during their transportation for maintenance or dismantling, when the Russian weapons apparently are not subject to the same strict security measures.
>
> But even if terrorists were able to steal or acquire through black market purchase a stolen nuclear weapon, they would still face a number of significant obstacles in using or detonating it. Strategic nuclear warheads are immense and would be extremely difficult to move either easily or clandestinely.
>
> Tactical nuclear weapons, such as artillery projectiles, admittedly, are far lighter and easier to conceal, making them potentially much more attractive items for terrorist theft or illicit acquisition. Moreover, many tactical nuclear weapons, and most strategic nuclear devices, are equipped with permissive action links (PALs) or other protective mechanisms designed to prevent accidental or unauthorized detonation.

In addition, some nuclear devices have tamper-proof seals that will disable the weapon if unauthorized personnel attempt to disassemble it. It would be extremely difficult, therefore, for terrorists to circumvent or overcome these built-in protective measures; some of the smaller tactical weapons (including the KGB's alleged nuclear bombs concealed in small suitcases) admittedly may have had little or no protective devices or locks installed and, thus, the safety measures designed to thwart unauthorized detonation would be more easily overcome.

In the absence of assurance about the status and control of all Russian nuclear weapons, we must remain vigilant. Terrorists who were either unable or unwilling to steal a nuclear device or were unsuccessful in obtaining one on the putative black market that has surfaced in the countries of the former Soviet Union and Warsaw Pact, might attempt to build one.

Their first hurdle, however, would be in acquiring sensitive nuclear material (SNM), that is, either highly enriched uranium (HEU) or plutonium (Pu) suitable for fashioning a nuclear device. Mining and processing uranium or building a reactor to create plutonium would of course be impractical (although, it should be noted, Aum's most grandiose aims embraced this possibility); terrorists would, therefore, have to steal SNM or conceivably purchase it on the black market. A number of authorities in recent years repeatedly have expressed concern about illicit access to nuclear materials and technology, particularly in the former Soviet Union. Minatom, the Russian entity with responsibility for nuclear weapons, has itself complained about a lack of qualified personnel and adequate control systems, and the security at HEU storage facilities has also been reported to be grossly inadequate.

Given this apparent lack of security, and the fact that 250 tons of HEU and 50 tons of weapons-grade plutonium has been stockpiled in Russia, the risk of illicit acquisition from SNM storage facilities should be considered a serious threat. Potentially less worrying, however, is the supposed "black market" for these substances. Between 1992 and 1996, more than 1,000 claims were made involving the illicit sale and smuggling of nuclear material; however, only six instances were substantiated, and none of those involved the quantities needed to construct an effective "homemade" device that could cause mass casualties—thereby suggesting that the black market, if it exists at all, is limited in size and grossly exaggerated in impact.

. . . To be sure, small amounts of SNM have been diverted illegally, apparently from Russian facilities. It is worth noting, however, that all of the SNM stolen to date is not sufficient to make a single nuclear device and that reported thefts of weapons-grade material have dropped in recent years. Ongoing improvements in Russian nuclear security procedures should further reduce the incidents of theft.[142]

Building a nuclear device capable of producing mass destruction presents Herculean challenges for terrorists and indeed even for states with well-funded and sophisticated programs. According to one analysis, minimum requirements include "personnel, skills, information, money, facilities, equipment, supplies, security, special nuclear materials . . . and, usually, other specialized and hard-to-obtain material."

According to another assessment, a successful program hinges on obtaining enough fissile material to form a super-critical mass for each of its nuclear weapons (thus permitting a chain reaction); arriving at weapon design that will bring that mass together in a tiny fraction of a second, before the heat from early fission blows the material apart; and designing a working device small and light enough to be carried by a given delivery vehicle. It is important to emphasize that the above represents the minimum requirements. If each one is not met, concludes the assessment, "one ends up not with a less powerful weapon, but with a device that cannot produce any significant nuclear yield at all or cannot be delivered to a given target."

That being said, it is clear that certain types of nuclear devices are easier to create than others. Two types of weapons systems, for example, can create nuclear fission: the implosion device and the "gun" type. In the former, explosives compress a sphere of HEU or plutonium into a small ball, thus achieving supercriticality and a nuclear chain reaction. Even the simplest implosion weapon, however, requires the fabrication of complex components, such as high-explosive lenses, high-performance detonation systems, and fusing and firing circuitry.

The gun-type device, on the other hand, employs HEU exclusively. Using a high explosive, the system fires a subcritical HEU projectile into a subcritical cylinder of HEU to form a solid mass of critical material. Although it uses relatively scarce HEU, the gun-type device is considered technically easier to fabricate; and many analysts accordingly argue that terrorists attempting to make a bomb "in house" will build a gun-type device.

There is disagreement, however, about what level of expertise and other resources are required to construct such a weapon. According to one authority, "most states and some exceptionally capable non-state actors" could build a highly destructive 10-kiloton weapon in several months at a cost of a few hundred thousand dollars—assuming they had access to sufficient quantities of fissile material.

Other experts, however, are far more skeptical in their estimates of the capabilities required. Although much of the information about nuclear weapons design and production has become public knowledge during the past 50 years, it is still extraordinary for non-state entities to attempt to embark on a nuclear weapons R&D program.

Indeed, even technical requisite knowledge and hands-on experience are not enough to build an effective nuclear weapon. As an Office of Technology Assessment report explains, "[k]nowledge must be supplemented by industrial infrastructure and the resources to carry a nuclear weapon program to completion. The technologies for building cars and propeller-driven airplanes date back to early in this century, but many countries still cannot build them indigenously."

Moreover, the fact that a number of states—despite aid from other nuclear powers, their own intense motivations, the provision of considerable resources, alongside concerted espionage activities designed to support their R&D programs—still struggle to build a nuclear weapon capability, suggests that the technical challenges remain immense.

In the case of South Africa, for example, it took scientists and engineers—who were endowed with a large and sophisticated infrastructure—four years to build their first gun-type system. Nevertheless, any nuclear weapons program will inevitably involve a number of people, and significant resources, equipment, and facilities. As noted earlier, all of that activity inevitably will materially increase the risk of exposure of the terrorist group to detection by intelligence and law enforcement agencies.[143]

Such comments, however, again assume that a state does not use a nuclear weapon in an asymmetric attack, provide a nuclear device to a terrorist movement, or offer a sanctuary and fissile material. These risks led the National Commission to draw different conclusions about the risks a state might provide independent groups with nuclear material:

> Terrorists could acquire more deadly CBRN capabilities from a state. Five of the seven nations the United States identifies as state sponsors of terrorism have programs to develop weapons of mass destruction. A state that knowingly provides agents of mass destruction or technology to a terrorist group should worry about losing control of the terrorists' activities and, if the weapons could be traced back to that state, the near certainty of massive retaliation. However, it is always difficult and sometimes dangerous to attempt to predict the actions of a state. Moreover, a state in chaos, or elements within such a state, might run these risks, especially if the United States were engaged in military conflict with that state or if the United States were distracted by a major conflict in another area of the world.
>
> The Commission was particularly concerned about the persistent lack of adequate security and safeguards for the nuclear material in the former Soviet Union (FSU). A Center for Strategic International Studies panel chaired by former Senator Sam Nunn concluded that, despite a decade of effort, the risk of "loose nukes" is greater than ever. Another ominous warning was given in 1995 when Chechen rebels, many of whom fight side-by-side with Islamic terrorists from bin Ladin's camps sympathetic to the Chechen cause, placed radioactive material in a Moscow park.[144]

U.S. intelligence experts have become increasingly concerned that Pakistan may develop surplus fissile material production capacity over the next few years. At least some analysts have also raised the issue of whether a China that became hostile might sell fissile material in the future. A number of experts on proliferation also question why any state that does contemplate a nuclear attack on the United States would risk the use of an easily attributable ballistic missile attack, rather than use of a far less attributable covert or proxy attack. The perceived risk of fissile transfers or nuclear weapons use may also change over time. If nuclear weapons and highly lethal biological weapons are used against targets elsewhere in the world, the end result might well be to make the nuclear threat to the United States far more "thinkable."

### The Problem of Delivery

Most nuclear weapons are large and potentially detectable. This is particularly true of large boosted or thermonuclear weapons that states might use to launch a catastrophic attack on the United States and of the kind of relatively crude or implosion device that an extremist or foreign terrorist might be able to build. Most primitive gun devices would, for example, be at least two meters long and weigh well over one thousand pounds.

A crude implosion device might be more compact, but would still be very heavy. At the same time, the former Soviet Union seems to have built small nuclear weapons weighing less than two hundred pounds, somewhat similar to the atomic demolition munitions the United States withdrew from service years ago. The advanced thermonuclear devices it uses on its MIRV missiles are relatively compact and weigh well under one thousand pounds. As is the case with yield, there are no rules regarding the size and weight of a nuclear device, particularly if one can be acquired or stolen from a nuclear power. It is also possible that the fissile core of a weapon could be delivered in separate component form and then matched with the rest of the weapon. This would sharply reduce the size and detectability of even a crude basic weapon.

Radiation would present a detectability problem, as it would for radiological weapons. Nuclear devices can, however, be shielded and the core of a weapon might be smuggled into the United States in many different ways. Thousands of large containers enter U.S. ports every day, and less than 3 percent are searched or inspected. The northern and southern borders are porous enough so that some drug smugglers do not even bother to carefully conceal the drugs they are smuggling, and a device might be routed through a relatively open border for small craft like Alaska or Hawaii.

Several attack models also involve rigging weapons to go off if the storage device is opened, is scanned in certain ways, or even if a GPS unit indicates it is in a U.S. port and approaching customs. Unless excellent human intelligence is available to the United States, unmanned delivery would offer a relatively high assurance of success and a self-destruct device would reduce the risk of attribution—particularly in a broad crisis. Detonation on detection, scan, or entry into a port area before customs is now sufficiently low tech so that it can be used by a wide range of potential attackers.

### Dealing with the Risk and Impact of Nuclear Attacks

There is no present way to predict whether a state actor, proxy, or terrorist/extremist will be willing to take the risk of launching a nuclear attack on the United States over the coming decades or be able to acquire a weapon or device. Like the more lethal forms of biological weapons, the use of nuclear weapons would almost certainly lead to massive U.S. retaliation if the United States could identify the attacker, and would pose a high level of risk.

At the same time, this judgment assumes that the attacker is deterrable. This is not necessarily true of a regime under extremists that acts because it feels it has no other choice or is certain it will fall in any case. It is not true of a proxy, terrorist, or extremist that is willing to accept destruction or martyrdom to achieve a goal. It is not true of a state or terrorist that assumes—rightly or wrongly—that an attack cannot be attributed or will be ambiguous enough so that it can escape dramatic punishment. It is also at least possible that such an attack could occur as the result of escalation to the use of WMD in another theater in which the United States is deeply involved—such as Korea, the Taiwan Straits, Israel, and so on.

The problem with such risk assessments—and with similar risk assessments affecting chemical and biological weapons—is that history is often shaped by extreme events that occur without warning and that are only explainable long after the event. History is also filled with examples in which escalation was not gradual or "rational" and in which the weaker side acted in unpredictable ways. No one looking at the history of the twentieth century has any reason to assume that sudden catastrophic events will not occur in the twenty-first century. At the same time, no one can assume that because such events can occur, they will occur. There simply is no clear nexus of probabilities on which to act.

### Problems in Responding to a Nuclear Attack

There are also problems in the way defenders and responders currently deal with nuclear weapons:

- Far too much current response planning seems to treat nuclear weapons the way that it treats attacks using highly sophisticated biological weapons. It treats them as sufficiently improbable so that it tacitly assumes that legal procedures and civil rights issues can be treated in the same way as much more moderate and limited attacks using explosives, chemical weapons, and unsophisticated biological weapons. There is no true sense of emergency. It is tacitly assumed that a state of true emergency would follow the use of a nuclear weapon, rather than from convincing evidence that an attack is planned or underway.

- The focus on terrorist weapons leads to a lack of concern over efforts to determine the type and size of a weapon in the attacker's hands and providing defenders and responders with as clear a set of warning signals as possible. If a state is involved, the prospect of a boosted or thermonuclear weapon being available may grow steadily over time, and there is no guarantee that the loss or sale of a former Soviet Union weapon would involve a small or limited yield. Just as all WMD are not the same, all nuclear weapons are not the same and intelligence and defense must give early characterization high priority.

- Responders are well aware that even a relatively small nuclear event would saturate, if not destroy, their capabilities. As a result, most local and state responders concentrate on planning for events they can manage and making limited preparations to deal with nuclear effects on an ad hoc basis. This seems perfectly realistic given current resources. There is, however, a basic policy issue that needs to be addressed: What—if anything—can be done cost-effectively to provide serious response capability to a nuclear attack beyond regional improvisation and limited federal aid?

- Many models and simulations, including those publicly briefed by DTRA, assume relatively simplistic blast, thermal, immediate radiation, and plume/fallout models. Work is underway to model urban effects more realistically and to develop workable real-time monitoring and detection grids that can characterize and predict fallout and plume effects. It is not clear, however, what systems are practical, and serious problems seem to exist in determining the threshold of radiation to be used for warning and response and the level of accuracy needed when radiation is deposited in very different levels over a given region. The present models seem to present a serious risk of misleading responders and to have uncertainties in affected area coverage with factors of at least two to three. There is a possible need for zero-based parametric modeling.

- Like mass biological incidents, no one really seems to want to confront the issue of triage, and of deciding who gets treatment, who is left at risk, and who dies. This simply is not a realistic approach. Triage cannot be improvised by practitioners without a major risk of wasting inadequate resources on moving the dead and leaving the curable untreated. Creating systems to decide what level of risk is involved in urging people to stay put or evacuate, how to control the media, and what level of detail to provide should not be left up to responders in a crisis. Such planning can only be done at a federal level, but it is uncertain that the leadership and moral courage is present to do it.

- Responders correctly focus on immediate effects. Serious questions do arise, however, as to dealing with lower levels of radiation that affect the mid- to long-term death rate, but which may or may not merit immediate response and treatment. This issue was ignored in civil defense planning during the Cold War because there was no way to deal with it in a mass attack on the United States. It cannot be ignored in a limited attack. As Hiroshima and Nagasaki showed, the physical and psychological impacts can last more than half a century, and there is a serious risk of "syndromes" where the exposed and nonexposed alike become major problems.

- Decontamination and recovery planning and options seem to be far too ad hoc. It is unclear what level of pre-event capability is cost-effective, but this should not be left up to chance.

Once again, it is also important to note that the psychological and political impact of any nuclear explosion would be vast, regardless of the damage it inflicted. As a result, even an explosion at sea or in the air outside U.S. territory would, under some scenarios, be a victory for an attacker.

Any strike on U.S. territory would be even more of a victory, and in many U.S. ports, an explosion at sea-level would deposit immense amounts of slightly radioactive water or "rain out" over a wide area, plus do major direct damage to an American city. Like some biological weapons, nuclear weapons are also "stand-off" weapons. They do not need to be near the target to do major damage. In fact, offsetting a weapon upwind from a city or facility and setting it off at ground level would produce massive fallout problems over a wide area. This, however, greatly increases the detection and intercept area and the potential problems in carrying out and coordinating detection and defense activities.

### Rethinking the Unthinkable about Nuclear Attacks on the U.S. Homeland

It is far harder to make specific recommendations about courses of action as to how to better respond to such. A great deal of detailed program planning, cost analysis, and net technical assessment is needed which have not yet been performed. However, possible priorities include:

- Improved modeling of real-world urban effects. Modeling of fallout and "rain out" plumes in ways tailored to improve response planning.

- Near real-time fallout corridor modeling and data mining. Modeling for needed level of state, regional, and federal response.

- Detection and diagnostic systems—either distributed or rapidly deployable (e.g., the public transportation sensor grid).

- Monitoring of actual distribution of fallout and weapons effects to give local responders a more precise picture of short- and long-term response requirements. Real-time transmission to responders and state, regional, and federal actors (there is often a twelve- to forty-eight-hour time window for critical response actions).

- Systems for instant detection and diagnostics, and guidance for response and triage. Dosimeters are useless for this purpose. Need clearly defined stay-or-flee guidance.

- Cheap portable systems for real-time triage analysis.

- Improved detection and characterization of residual threats, decontamination technologies, and decontamination effectiveness measuring systems.

- Hospital technology solutions and rapidly deployable care technology.

- Cheap, simple, civil defense options, such as masks, advice at no cost to those who need advice and want to acquire safety technology, and media warning and advice alert systems.

### NOTES

1. U.S. General Accounting Office, GAO Report to Congressional Requesters, "Combating Terrorism: Need for Comprehensive Threat and Risk Assessment of

Chemical and Biological Attacks," GAO-T-NSIAD-99-163, September 1999, 18–17.

2. First Annual Report of the Advisory Panel to Assess Domestic Response Capabilities for Terrorism Involving the Use of Weapons of Mass Destruction, *I. Assessing the Threat* (December 15, 1999), <http://www.rand.org/organization/nsrd/terrpanel/html>.

3. See John V. Parachini, "The World Trade Center Bombers (1993)," in Jonathan B. Tucker, ed., *Toxic Terror, Assessing Terrorist Use of Chemical and Biological Weapons* (Cambridge, Mass.: Belfer Center for Scientific and International Affairs, 2000), 185–207.

4. Robert M. Burnham, Chief, Domestic Terrorism Section, FBI, before the United States Senate Subcommittee on Clean Air, Wetlands, Private Property, and Nuclear Safety, March 16, 1999.

5. Ali S. Khan, MD, Alexandra M. Levitt, MA, Ph.D., Michael J. Sage, M.P.H., et al., U.S. Centers for Disease Control, *Biological and Chemical Terrorism: Strategic Plan for Preparedness and Response Recommendations of the CDC Strategic Planning Workgroup*, April 21, 2000 / 49 (RR04), 1–14, <http://www.cdc.gov/epo/mmwr/preview/mmwrhtml/rr4904a1.html>.

6. See USACHPPM, *The Medical NBC Battlebook*, USACHPPM Technical Guide 244, 5-43-5-54.

7. Parachini, "The World Trade Center Bombers (1993)," 185–207.

8. The DOD defines the technical risk posed by chemical weapons as:

Chemical weapons (CW) are compounds used in military operations or as terrorist weapons to kill, incapacitate, or seriously injure personnel through their chemical properties. Most CW agents useful as military weapons are not gases, although poison gas is a term commonly used. While chlorine gas was used in World War I, most agents are liquids, which facilitate munitions loading and contribute to stability in storage and transportation. When employed, these liquids are dispersed as droplets. These droplets can either penetrate the skin or vaporize and become a respiration hazard.

Chemical agents are either persistent or nonpersistent. Persistent agents may last from hours to days. Nonpersistent agents last minutes to hours. Agents can be lethal or non-lethal. The effects induced can include blistering, choking, blocking the ability of body tissue to absorb oxygen, convulsions, and paralysis. Reports indicate that the 1995 Japanese subway incident involved sarin, an agent that attacks the nervous system.

The precursor chemicals and intermediate stages in the production process for two classical CW agents, nerve and blister agents, have agricultural and industrial uses. For example, Thiodiglycol, which has been used to produce ballpoint pen ink, can be converted to mustard agent by a simple (single) chlorination step. The technology and most of the production equipment, moreover, even the military hardware necessary for delivery and dissemination, are dual-use. Detection and discrimination between legitimate and illegal production are difficult. Facilities producing pesticides, insecticides, and fire retardant chemicals could be converted to CW production. There are strong external similarities between civilian and military facilities, although the latter may have observable security measures such as restricted access areas and fences, and possibly storage areas used for chemical munitions. Knowledgeable personnel are readily available; a relatively small number of chemical engineers and technicians are needed for production of chemical weapons.

## CW THREATS DURING THE GULF WAR

While the defensive capabilities of U.S. and other Coalition forces improved rapidly, CW/BW defensive readiness at the outset of the crisis was quite low. Coalition forces embarked on extraordinary measures to correct these weaknesses, largely by building up the preparedness of individuals to protect themselves in the event of CW/BW attack. On balance, these gains did lead to a significant potential for U.S. forces to operate on a contaminated battlefield. While the outcome would have been unaffected, the tempo of the Operation Desert Storm campaign could have been hindered had U.S. troops been forced to remain fully protected by masks and suits. Temperatures during Operation Desert Storm were comparatively cool; data indicate that risks of heat exhaustion would have been sharply higher in the summer, making protracted use of personal protective gear impractical. Studies have also shown that protective equipment dramatically impedes crew performance. The masks hinder communications, and the suits impair the ability to operate equipment. High-speed combat requiring close coordination between crews manning complex systems becomes quite difficult.

## THE IRAQI THREAT

Iraq had developed a substantial CW capability including research and development facilities; stockpiles of CW munitions; a variety of delivery systems; and the doctrine and training to employ integrated CW and conventional fire effectively on the battlefield. Iraq was the first nation to use nerve agents on the battlefield—attacking unprepared Iranian troops in 1984. By 1990, Iraq had the largest CW agent production capability in the Third World, annually producing thousands of tons of blister and nerve agents.

Source: *Conduct of the Persian Gulf War*, p. 640.

CW–suitable dual-use delivery systems are readily available ranging from SCUD missiles and unmanned aerial vehicles to sophisticated cruise and ballistic missiles. If need be, crop duster aircraft and simple spray generators can be readily adapted for delivery of a variety of agents. The quantities of chemical agent required are relatively small when compared to industrial production of similar commercial chemicals, which poses significant problems for detection. The low technology required lends itself to proliferation and even potential terrorist use. Terrorists could employ CW agents in a variety of means utilizing simple containers such as glass bottles, commercial compressed gas bottles, or propane tanks.

### Military Significance

Chemical weapons are the only NBC munitions that have been used in post–World War II large-scale conflicts, most recently during the Iran-Iraq war. Consequently, there is cause for concern that proliferators may perceive that international responses (ranging from sanctions to military action) are less likely, given the use of CW.

CW impacts military operations in a number of ways. Large numbers of people (combatants and civilians) can be killed if suitable protective equipment or shelters are not available and properly utilized. There may be large numbers of non-fatal casualties. This was the characteristic experience when CW was employed during World War I. The volume of injured personnel can overwhelm the military medical evacuation and treatment system, impacting operations.

If CW employment is anticipated, forces are required to operate in protective ensembles that degrade operational performance, especially under adverse climatic conditions. Even though forces using appropriate protective equipment may be immune to CW effects, their ability to accomplish tasks is greatly reduced. Furthermore, equipment, facilities, and territory are contaminated. This impacts the ability of forces to maneuver. It also can have a major effect on ports, airfields, and other essential facilities that support operations.

Once CW use occurs, decontamination operations are required. These operations can be time consuming. They may require forces to be diverted from other missions. In some instances, current technology decontamination equipment damages equipment. Perhaps most significantly, psychological effects impacting the ability of personnel to perform their missions can occur.

CW employment involves a number of factors, including agent type; the dissemination method (and its dispersion efficiency); droplet size; and meteorological conditions, including temperature, wind speed and direction, and inversion conditions. Agent dispersion can be very dependent on environmental factors, such as wind direction and speed.

Chemical agents can be used as limited area effects (battlefield) or large area effects weapons, to include areas with civilian populations. Unlike nuclear or biological weapons (BW), effective chemical agent attacks sometimes require significant numbers of munitions to achieve large area coverage. This can be an advantage in some situations since it means that the consequences of CW use are more predictable and hence more readily integrated into war plans. (<http://www.defenselink.mil/pubs/prolif/access_tech.html>)

9. See Center for Counterproliferation Research, "The Effects of Chemical and Biological Weapons on Operations, What We Know and Don't Know," National Defense University, February 1997; P2NBC2 Report No. 90–1, Physiological and Psychological Effects of NBC Environment and Sustained Operations on Systems in Combat, *P2NBC2 Test Reports*, "Program Overview," U.S. Army Chemical School, Ft. McClellan, Alabama, January 4, 1990, CB–013725.0; P2NBC2 Report No. 90-2, Physiological and Psychological Effects of NBC Environment and Sustained Operations on Systems in Combat, *P2NBC2 Test Reports*, "Program Overview," U.S. Army Chemical School, F. McClellan, Alabama, January 4, 1990, CB–013726; P2NBC2, Physiological and Psychological Effects of NBC Environment and Sustained Operations on Systems in Combat, *P2NBC2 Test Reports*, "Program Wrap-Up, Annotated List of Findings," U.S. Army Chemical School, Ft. McClellan, Alabama, January 1995, EAI Report 69–2/95/002F; John A. Mojecki, "Combined Arms in a Nuclear/Chemical Environment (CANEn), Phase IIA; and Summary Evaluation, "ORI, Inc. for Commandant," U.S. Army Chemical School, Ft. McClellan, Alabama, May 31, 1987.

10. USACHPPM, *Medical NBC Battlebook*, 5-7–5-12, is very cautious about estimating lethality, and confines its estimates to limited data on exposed troops and civilian hazard prediction methods. See also Field Manual 3–7 and JP 3–11(Draft).

11. See pages 27–28 of the report; see also Wayman C. Mullins, "An Overview and Analysis of Nuclear, Biological, and Chemical Terrorism: The Weapons, Strategies and Solutions to a Growing Problem," *American Journal of Criminal Justice* 16, No. 2 (1992): 108–109. The model used for these calculations is known as VLSTRACK 3.0 and was developed by the Dahlgren Division, Naval Surface Warfare Center, Dahlgren, Virginia.

12. USACHPPM, *Medical NBC Battlebook*, 5–21.

13. USACHPPM, *Medical NBC Battlebook*, 5-8–5-25.

14. The data on World War I are limited and can be interpreted in many ways, particularly since well-planned delivery generally only occurred after the force be-

ing attacked was equipped with gas masks and changes had taken place in field medical treatment. I have talked extensively to Iraqi field commanders during the Iran-Iraq War, visited some battlefields where chemical weapons were used, and discussed these issues with Western intelligence analysts who attempted to characterize the results of such attacks using limited data. In general, the operational lethality was limited, although the use of chemical weapons seems to have had a major impact on Iranian tactical behavior after early 1997.

15. For a good technical summary of the issues involved in making such weapons, see Office of Technology Assessment, *Background Paper: Technologies Underlying Weapons of Mass Destruction*, U.S. Congress, OTA-BP-ISC-115, Washington, D.C. (December 1993).

16. Mullins, "An Overview and Analysis," 108–109.

17. First Annual Report of the Advisory Panel, *Assessing the Threat*, 91–94.

18. "Combating Terrorism," GAO/NSIAD-99-163, 12.

19. "Combating Terrorism," GAO/NSIAD-99-163, 12.

20. "Combating Terrorism," GAO/NSIAD-99-163; and U.S. General Accounting Office, GAO Report to Congressional Requesters, "Combating Terrorism: Observations on the Threat of Chemical and Biological Terrorism," GAO/NSIAD-00-50, October 20, 1999.

21. Aum Shinrikyo carried out an expensive research and development effort, which the Rand Corporation indicates has cost estimates as high as $30 million. The program had an eighty-man program in state-of-the-art facilities, and was led by a Ph.D.–level scientist. Nevertheless, it took at least a year between the time of conception and the initial production of sarin. The Tokyo subway attack, and an earlier sarin attack in Matsumoto, succeeded in killing only a dozen people, although several thousand were affected.

22. David E. Kaplan, "Aum Shinrikyo," in Jonathan B. Tucker, ed., *Toxic Terror, Assessing Terrorist Use of Chemical and Biological Weapons* (Cambridge, Mass.: Belfer Center for Scientific and International Affairs, 2000), 207–226.

23. See Kaplan, "Aum Shinrikyo," 207–226; National Police Agency, "White Paper on Police 1996," Tokyo Police Association, 1997; and "Briefing Paper on Aum, 1995," as quoted by David E. Kaplan.

24. Chris Bullock, "Biological Terrorism" (transcript of a program on biological warfare chaired by Professor D. A. Henderson, director of the Johns Hopkins Center for Biodefense Studies, August 29, 1999, <http://www.infowar.com/wmd/99/wmad 091699aj.shtml>, September 16, 1999).

25. W. Seth Carus, "Working Paper, Bioterrorism and Biocrimes, the Illicit Use of Biological Agents in the 20th Century" (Washington, D.C., Center for Counterproliferation Research, National Defense University, August 1998), 3.

26. World Health Organization, *Overcoming Antimicrobial Resistance: World Health Report on Infectious Diseases 2000*, Internet ed. (June 2000), <http://www.who.org>.

27. Thomas V. Inglesby, "The Germs of War," *Washington Post*, 9 December 1998.

28. Bullock, "Biological Terrorism." If the naval trials had gone forward, the U.S. naval biological weapons trials flotilla would have been the equivalent of the fifth largest navy in the world.

29. Khan, Levitt, Sage et al., *Biological and Chemical Terrorism*, 1–14.

30. See Center for Counterproliferation Research, "Effects of Chemical and Biological Weapons on Operations"; P2NBC2 Report No. 90–1, Physiological and Psychological Effects of NBC Environment and Sustained Operations on Systems in Combat, *P2NBC2 Test Reports*, "Technical Papers and Bibliographies," U.S. Army Chemical School, Ft. McClellan, Alabama, January 4, 1990, CB-013725.0; P2NBC2 Report No. 90–2, Physiological and Psychological Effects of NBC Environment and Sustained Operations on Systems in Combat, *P2NBC2 Test Reports*, "Program Overview"; P2NBC2, Physiological and Psychological Effects of NBC Environment and Sustained Operations on Systems in Combat, *P2NBC2 Test Reports*, "Program Wrap-Up"; and Mojecki, "Combined Arms in a Nuclear/Chemical Environment."

31. Erhard Geissler and John Ellis van Courtland Moon, eds., *Biological and Toxin Weapons: Research, Development, and Use from the Middle Ages to 1945*, SIPRI Chemical and Biological Weapons Studies (Oxford: Oxford University Press, 1999).

32. U.S. Centers for Disease Control, *Preventing Emerging Infectious Diseases: A Strategy for the 21st Century* (Atlanta, Ga.: U.S. Department of Health and Human Services, 1998).

33. Donald A. Henderson, "The Looming Threat of Bioterrorism," *Science* 283 (February 26, 1999): 1279–1282.

34. Khan, Levitt, Sage et al., *Biological and Chemical Terrorism*, 1–14.

35. See Ken Alibek, *Biohazard* (New York: Random House, 1999). At that time, the Soviet Union had two programs, a long-standing military program and a new program started in 1975 that used Soviet biotechnology industry as a front. This was a major effort that included a significant percentage of Soviet life and biomedical scientists. It was called "Biopreparat," and was extremely secret. The Soviet Union developed the capability to produce large amounts of agent and some estimates indicate capacities—before it collapsed—of the order of hundreds, even thousands of tons in facilities distributed throughout the former Soviet Union. It also had mobilization plans to take all this production from zero to weapons in a relatively short period of time. The current status of this program and the location of its scientists, equipment, agents, and stockpiles is unknown.

36. Brad Roberts, ed., *Hype or Reality? The New Terrorism and Mass Casualty Attacks* (Alexandria, Va.: Chemical and Biological Arms Control Institute, 2000), 87.

37. For a brief summary, see Al J. Venter, "Spectre of Biowar Remains," *Jane's Defense Weekly*, 28 April 1999, 22–23.

38. Bullock, "Biological Terrorism."

39. Bullock, "Biological Terrorism."

40. Statement of Special Assistant to the Director of Central Intelligence for Nonproliferation, John A. Lauder on the Worldwide Biological Warfare Threat to the House Permanent Select Committee on Intelligence As Prepared for Delivery on March 3, 1999 (Langley, Va.: Central Intelligence Agency).

41. Unclassified Report to Congress on the Acquisition of Technology Relating to Weapons of Mass Destruction and Advanced Conventional Munitions, January 1 to June 30, 1999 (Langley, Va.: Central Intelligence Agency, February 2, 2000); U.S. General Accounting Office, "Nuclear Nonproliferation: Concerns With DOE's

Efforts to Reduce the Risks Posed by Russia's Unemployed Weapons Scientists," GAO/RCED-99-54, February 19, 1999.

42. U.S. General Accounting Office, "Biological Weapons: Effort to Reduce Former Soviet Threat Proposes Benefits, Offers New Risks," GAO/NSIAD-00-138, April 2000.

43. See Carus, "Bioterrorism and Biocrimes," 7–8; see also Jeffery D. Simon, *Terrorists and the Potential Use of Biological Weapons: A Discussion of Possibilities*, Rand Report R-3771-AFMIC, December 1989; Brad Roberts, ed., *Terrorism with Chemical and Biological Weapons* (Alexandria, Va.: Chemical and Biological Arms Control Institute, 1997; Ronh Purver, *Chemical and Biological Terrorism: The Threat According to the Open Literature*, Canadian Security Intelligence Service, June 1995; and George W. Christopher et. al., "Biological Warfare, A Historical Perspective," *JAMA* 278, No. 5 (August 6, 1997).

44. Carus, "Bioterrorism and Biocrimes," 7–8.

45. Carus, "Bioterrorism and Biocrimes," 11–12.

46. Carus, "Bioterrorism and Biocrimes," 21–25.

47. Roberts, *Hype or Reality?*, 214–216.

48. Margaret Hamburg, U.S. Department of Health and Human Services, Associated Press, February 5, 2000.

49. See Kaplan, "Aum Shinrikyo," 207–226; National Police Agency, "White Paper on Police 1996"; and "Briefing Paper on Aum, 1995," as quoted by David E. Kaplan.

50. David Kaplan and Andrew Marshall, *The Cult at the End of the World* (New York: Crown, 1996), 94–97; and Carus, "Bioterrorism and Biocrimes," 25.

51. Bullock, "Biological Terrorism."

52. See Milton Leiternberg, "The Experience of the Japanese Aum Shinrikyo Group and Biological Agents," in *Hype or Reality? The New Terrorism and Mass Casualty Attacks*, ed. Brad Roberts (Alexandria, Va.: Chemical and Biological Arms Control Institute, 2000), 159–169.

53. Carus, "Bioterrorism and Biocrimes," 27.

54. The WHO decided to eradicate smallpox in 1959 and began an active campaign in 1966. The outbreak in Yugoslavia was the last major outbreak, although a last case was reported in Somalia in 1977. The WHO announced the disease was eradicated in 1980. Ken Alibeck charges in *Biohazard*, however, that the former Soviet Union had twenty tons of the agent stockpiled for delivery in missile warheads, and U.S. experts feel Russia may be continuing weapons research at facilities like Sergiyev Posad near Moscow. Iraq and North Korea are believed to retain small stocks of the disease culture. The CDC retains 15.4 million doses of vaccine, but there are 270 million citizens in the United States. See "Controversy Surrounds Smallpox Decisions," *The CBW Chronicle*, Issue 6 (August 1999).

55. Robert M. Burnham, Chief, Domestic Terrorism Section, FBI, before the House of Representatives Subcommittee on Oversight and Investigations, May 20, 1999.

56. World Health Organization, *Health Aspects of Biological Weapons* (Geneva: World Health Organization, 1970), 98–99.

57. Office of Technology Assessment, *Proliferation of Weapons of Mass Destruction: Assessing the Risks*, U.S. Congress, OTA-ISC-559, Washington, D.C. (August 1993), 53–53.

58. Thomas V. Inglesby et al., "Anthrax As a Biological Weapon: Medical and Public Health Management," *JAMA* 281, No. 18 (May 12, 1999): 1735–1745; World Health Organization, *Health Aspects of Chemical and Biological Weapons* (Geneva: World Health Organization, 1970); Office of Technology Assessment, *Proliferation of Weapons of Mass Destruction*; A. F. Kaufman, M. I. Meltzer, and G. P. Schmid, "The Economic Impact of a Bioterrorist Attack," *Emerging Infectious Diseases* 3 (1997): 83–94.

59. I reviewed such models and test results extensively while acting as the NBC program manager at the Defense Advanced Research Projects Agency. Also see M. Meselson, J. Guillemin, M. Hugh-Jones et al., "The Sverdlovsk Anthrax Outbreak of 1979," *Science* (1994): 1202–1208; and W. A. Perkins, "Public Health Implications of Airborne Infection," *Bacterial Review* (1961): 347–355.

60. Inglesby et al., "Anthrax As a Biological Weapon," 1735–1745, 1736–1737; and USACHPPM, *Medical NBC Battlebook*, 4–31.

61. USACHPPM, *Medical NBC Battlebook*, 4–31.

62. Inglesby et al., "Anthrax As a Biological Weapon," 1735–1745, 1736–1737.

63. Inglesby et al., "Anthrax As a Biological Weapon," 1735–1745, 1736–1737; USACHPPM, *Medical NBC Battlebook*, 4–31.

64. Carus, "Bioterrorism and Biocrimes," 14–15.

65. USACHPPM, *Medical NBC Battlebook*, 4–30.

66. USACHPPM, *Medical NBC Battlebook*, 4-31–4-32.

67. Thomas V. Inglesby et al., "Plague As a Biological Weapon: Medical and Public Health Management," *JAMA* 283, No. 18 (May 3, 2000): 1735–1745, 2281–2289.

68. World Health Organization, *Health Aspects of Chemical and Biological Weapons*.

69. USACHPPM, *Medical NBC Battlebook*, 4–31.

70. Inglesby et al., "Plague As a Biological Weapon," 1735–1745, 2281–2289.

71. USACHPPM, *Medical NBC Battlebook*, 4-34–4-35.

72. *Washington Post*, 24 August 2000, E-1.

73. Donald A Henderson, Thomas V. Inglesby et al., "Smallpox As a Biological Weapon: Medical and Public Health Management," *JAMA* 281, No. 18 (June 9, 1999): 2127–2137.

74. *Washington Post*, 24 August 2000, E-1.

75. USACHPPM, *Medical NBC Battlebook*, 4-31.

76. Henderson, Inglesby et al., "Smallpox As a Biological Weapon," 2127–2137.

77. Henderson, Inglesby et al., "Smallpox As a Biological Weapon," 2127–2137; and USACHPPM, *Medical NBC Battlebook*, 4–37.

78. "Combating Terrorism," GAO/NSIAD-99-163, 12.

79. See <http://www.defenselink.mil/pubs/prolif/access tech.html>.

80. Bullock, "Biological Terrorism."

81. "Combating Terrorism," GAO/NSIAD-99-163, 12.

82. First Annual Report of the Advisory Panel, *Assessing the Threat*, 73–88.

83. Ronald M. Atlas and Richard E. Weller, "Academe and the Threat of Biological Terrorism," *The Chronicle of Higher Education*, 13 August 1999.

84. Office of Technology, *Meeting the Challenge U.S. Industry Faces the 21st Century: The US Biotechnology Industry* (Washington, D.C.: U.S. Department of Commerce, 2000), 9–10.

85. Office of Technology, *Meeting the Challenge*, 9–10.

86. Roberts, *Hype or Reality?*, 87.

87. See <http://www.defenselink.mil/pubs/prolif/access tech.html>.

88. See <http://www.defenselink.mil/pubs/prolif/access tech.html>.

89. See the forecast in National Intelligence Council, "Global Trends 2015: A Dialogue about the Future with Nongovernment Experts," Washington, D.C., Central Intelligence Agency (December 2000), <http://www.odci.gov/cia/publications/globaltrends2015/index.html>.

90. For a good technical summary of the issues involved in making such weapons, see Office of Technology Assessment, *Technologies Underlying Weapons of Mass Destruction*.

91. Briefing on the Jason 1997 summer study, Malcolm R. Dando, "The Impact of Biotechnology," in *Hype or Reality? The New Terrorism and Mass Casualty Attacks*, ed. Brad Roberts (Alexandria, Va.: Chemical and Biological Arms Control Institute, 2000), 193–206.

92. Briefing on the Jason 1997 summer study, Malcolm R. Dando, "The Impact of Biotechnology," in *Hype or Reality? The New Terrorism and Mass Casualty Attacks*, ed. Brad Roberts (Alexandria, Va.: Chemical and Biological Arms Control Institute, 2000), 193–206.

93. National Intelligence Council, "The Global Infectious Disease Threat and Its Implications for the United States," CIA NIE-99-17D (January2000), <http://www.cia.gov/cia/publications/nie/report/nie99-17d.htm>.

94. *The Economist*, 22 July 2000, 54–55.

95. National Intelligence Council, "Global Infectious Disease Threat."

96. National Intelligence Council, "Global Infectious Disease Threat."

97. World Health Organization, *Overcoming Antimicrobial Resistance*.

98. National Intelligence Council, "Global Infectious Disease Threat."

99. S. Koonin, Study Leader, "Civilian Biodefense," Jason 1999, JSR-99-105 (July 1999).

100. See Jonathan Ban, "Agricultural Biological Warfare: An Overview," *The Arena* (Alexandria), CBACI, no. 9 (June 2000).

101. Office of the Secretary of Defense, *Proliferation and Response* (Washington, D.C.: U.S. Department of Defense, January 2001), "Transnational Threats."

102. See Ban, "Agricultural Biological Warfare."

103. Koonin, "Civilian Biodefense."

104. Koonin, "Civilian Biodefense."

105. Office of the Secretary of Defense, *Proliferation and Response*.

106. *Reuters*, 21 March 2000, 20, 22.

107. Office of the Secretary of Defense, *Proliferation and Response* (Washington, Department of Defense, January 2001), Section II, "The Challenge of Developing Biological Weapons Detection Systems."

108. Office of the Secretary of Defense, *Proliferation and Response*.

109. Briefing by Tara Otoole, "Biological Weapons: National Security Threat, Public Health Emergency," Johns Hopkins Central for Civilian Biodefense Studies, Baltimore, Md., August 2000.

110. Tara Otoole, "Testimony to the Hearing on Terrorism Preparedness, Medical First Response," Subcommittee on National Security, Veterans Affairs, and International Relations, Committee on Government Reform, House of Represen-

tatives, Johns Hopkins Center for Civilian Biodefense Studies, Baltimore, Md., September 22, 1999.

111. Briefing on the Jason 1997 summer study, Malcolm R. Dando, "The Impact of Biotechnology," in *Hype or Reality? The New Terrorism and Mass Casualty Attacks*, ed. Brad Roberts (Alexandria, Va.: Chemical and Biological Arms Control Institute, 2000), 193–206.

112. USACHPPM TG-238; and USACHPPM, *Medical NBC Battlebook*, 3-4–3-6.

113. See <http://www.defenselink.mil/nubs/i2rolif/access tech.html>.

114. First Annual Report of the Advisory Panel, *Assessing the Threat*, 114–117.

115. USACHPPM, *Medical NBC Battlebook*, 3–4.

116. Joint Publication 3–11(Draft), Table E-2-6; USACHPPM TG-238; and USACHPPM, *Medical NBC Battlebook*, 3-16–3-17.

117. USACHPPM, *Medical NBC Battlebook*, 3-4–3-6; International Atomic Energy Agency, "Summary Report on the Post Accident Review Meeting on the Post Accident Review Meeting on the Chernobyl Accident," International Nuclear Safety Center, <http://www.insc.anl.gov>; Uranium Information Center, <http://www.uic.com.au>; and <http://www.ulondon.org/netpower.html>);

118. USACHPPM, *Medical NBC Battlebook*, 2-5–2-23.

119. USACHPPM, *Medical NBC Battlebook*, 3–30.

120. USACHPPM, *Medical NBC Battlebook*, 2–15.

121. See AFRRI, AmedP-6©; and USACHPPM, *Medical NBC Battlebook*, 2–15

122. USACHPPM, *Medical NBC Battlebook*, 3-16–3-17; Joint Publication 3–11 (Draft), FM 8–9 and FM 8–10–7; AMEED Center and School's, *Effects of Nuclear Weapons and Directed Energy on Military Operations*; and U.S. Department of Defense, 5100.52-M, *Nuclear Accident Response Procedures Manual–NARP*.

123. USACHPPM, *Medical NBC Battlebook*, 3-35–3-39.

124. See USACHPPM, *Medical NBC Battlebook*, 3-32–3-34.

125. See AMEED Center and School, *Effects of Nuclear Weapons and Directed Energy on Military Operations*, especially 1–34; and USACHPPM, *Medical NBC Battlebook*, 3-15–3-16.

126. See Center for Counterproliferation Research, "Effects of Chemical and Biological Weapons on Operations"; P2NBC2 Report No. 90–1, Physiological and Psychological Effects of NBC Environment and Sustained Operations on Systems in Combat, *P2NBC2 Test Reports*, "Technical Papers and Bibliographies"; P2NBC2 Report No. 90–2, Physiological and Psychological Effects of NBC Environment and Sustained Operations on Systems in Combat, *P2NBC2 Test Reports*, "Program Overview"; P2NBC2, Physiological and Psychological Effects of NBC Environment and Sustained Operations on Systems in Combat, *P2NBC2Test Reports*, "Program Wrap-Up"; and Mojecki, "Combined Arms in a Nuclear/Chemical Environment."

127. FM 8–10–7, Figure 2–1.

128. See Table 2–1 and Table 2–7 of FM 8–10–7 and Table 4 of FM 8–9, Part 1; and USACHPPM, *Medical NBC Battlebook*, 2-2–2-3.

129. Office of Technology Assessment, *The Effects of Nuclear War*, U.S. Congress, OTA-NS-89, Washington, D.C. (May 1979), 43–46.

130. See USACHPPM, *Medical NBC Battlebook*, section 2; Field Manual (FM) 1.1-31-2; FM 3–7; and FM 8–10–7.

131. USACHPPM, *Medical NBC Battlebook*, 2–6.

132. USACHPPM, *Medical NBC Battlebook*, 2-6–2-23, 2-28–2-29; FM 8–9, Table 6–2; and FM 8–10–7, Table 4–2.

133. USACHPPM, *Medical NBC Battlebook*, 2-5–2-23.

134. USACHPPM, *Medical NBC Battlebook*, 2–15.

135. See AFRRI, AmedP-6©; and USACHPPM, *Medical NBC Battlebook*, 2–15

136. These issues are poorly dealt with in most weapons effect manuals, but are discussed in summary form in Office of Technology Assessment, *Effects of Nuclear War*.

137. USACHPPM, *Medical NBC Battlebook*, 3-16–3-17; Joint Publication 3–11 (Draft), FM 8–9 and FM 8–10–7; AMEED Center and School's, *Effects of Nuclear Weapons and Directed Energy on Military Operations*; and U.S. Department of Defense, 5100.52-M *Nuclear Accident Response Procedures Manual—NARP*.

138. See AMEED Center and School, *Effects of Nuclear Weapons and Directed Energy on Military Operations*, especially 1–34; and USACHPPM, *Medical NBC Battlebook*, 3-15–3-16.

139. For a good technical summary of the issues involved in making such weapons, see Office of Technology Assessment, *Technologies Underlying Weapons of Mass Destruction*; and Office of Technology Assessment, *Effects of Nuclear War*.

140. See <http://www .defenselink.mil/pubs/prolif/access tech.html>.

141. Office of the Secretary of Defense, *Proliferation and Response*.

142. Office of the Secretary of Defense, *Proliferation: Threat and Response* (Washington, D.C.: U.S. Government Printing Office, 1997), <http://www.defenselink.mil/pubs/prolif97/trans.htrnl#terrorism>.

143. First Annual Report of the Advisory Panel, *Assessing the Threat*, 94–115.

144. National Commission on Terrorism, *Countering the Changing Threat of International Terrorism* (June 2000), <http://www.fas.org/irp/threat commission.html>.

*Chapter 5*

# Threat Assessment and Prioritization: Identifying Threats

It would be nice to be able to predict the future, although the success of Cassandra's curse may be a warning that accurate prediction alone is never enough. At this point in time, however, the situation is so volatile and unpredictable that it is not possible to predict a future in which the threat of covert attacks by state actors, their proxies, or independent extremists and terrorists requires a major homeland defense effort. The United States and its citizens are almost certain to come under attack in some form, but it is not yet clear that such attacks will involve methods of attack that produce mass casualties or mass destruction. A trend analysis and an assessment of current threats indicate that such a future is *possible*, but it does not firmly indicate that it is *probable*.

At the same time, the analysis of possible methods of attack and the evolving technologies involved indicate that the United States cannot prudently ignore the risk that CBRN weapons will be used against the U.S. homeland in the future and that there are no technical barriers to such use in the near term. Leaving a power vacuum in terms of credible deterrence and retaliation, active detection and defense within U.S. territory, and effective response measures will create an open invitation to strike at the U.S. homeland in an era where asymmetric warfare is the only counter that most of America's enemies have to its conventional military power. It also risks making the U.S. homeland a hostage to the threat of such attacks when enemies attack U.S. friends and allies.

## DR. PANGLOSS VERSUS CHICKEN LITTLE
## AND THE BOY WHO CRIED WOLF

That said, there is no effective way to prioritize which method of attack will be used, if any. Choosing a given mix of threats and methods of attack at this point in time is simply guesswork. In fact, it is difficult to assign any clear priority to attacks on U.S. citizens versus attacks on U.S. facilities or agriculture. It is certainly true that the United States is more likely to experience limited than mass attacks, but mass attacks by definition are far more lethal. There are many tactical and technical reasons that biological attacks could become a method of choice, but there is no evidence as yet that they will be. There seems to be a high level of deterrence of nuclear attacks by states, but the United States is embarked on a massive missile defense effort because such deterrence may fail and covert or proxy attacks with nuclear or highly lethal biological weapons offer a number of advantages over missile attacks.

The sheer scale of the uncertainties involved may explain why some policymakers and experts have decided to choose the Dr. Pangloss school, which minimizes the risk that such attacks will become frequent and common enough to justify large-scale homeland defense activity. Others favor the Chicken Little and the Boy Who Cried Wolf school, which sees successful large-scale attacks as almost inevitable. It explains why there is sometimes more rhetoric and passion than detailed analysis. It also helps explain the search to categorize or compartmentalize potential threats in ways that make them easier to understand, and to explain the sometimes desperate search within the U.S. government to narrow down the range of cases to a level where it is possible to assign priorities for action, regardless of whether there are valid reasons for doing so.

As has been pointed out earlier, the evidence simply does not yet exist to make such choices. Furthermore, selecting the slightly more probable cases out of a large set of unlikely cases may be a natural human tendency, but it is terrible probability theory. Given the current set of variables, it is the much larger set of even less probable cases that is more likely to occur.

This point is critical in determining the priority for any integrated approach to CBRN defense and response measures. It warns that taking action for action's sake, or proposing measures with artificial deadlines or rigid parameters of effectiveness, is likely to be functionally pointless—if "politically correct." The same is true of measures that assume the level and type of attack is predictable or that do not treat CBRN attacks in an integrated form where all forms of attack are considered. Measures that can be countered at low cost or by turning to other forms of attack are particularly likely to be ineffective in a democracy where more measures, which lack flexibility and adaptability, are likely to be highly publicized and where attackers may have ample warning of precisely what the limits and gaps of those measures are.

As a result, it is essential that the U.S. government does not tolerate programs and activities that are not justified in explicit terms by an analysis of the methods and costs of countering them and an honest statement of their risks and limitations. It must also be said in this light that bureaucracy and congressional politics can be some of the strongest allies an attacker can have. Compartmentation, false claims of effectiveness, and a failure to analyze program weaknesses and the cost of defeating them are tendencies that are all too common in given programs and departments. Similarly, a congressional tendency to mandate action for action's sake, while politicizing given threats and countermeasures, will scarcely serve the public interest. It may be argued that such approaches have a deterrent effect. This may be true in the case of lazy or incompetent potential attackers, but it is unlikely to be the case when the United States faces serious ones.

## THE PROBLEM OF DETECTION, WARNING, AND RESPONSE

The threat posed by CBRN weapons is extremely diverse and extremely uncertain. The uncertainties affecting each category of weapon are compounded by the fact that sophisticated attackers can use mixes or "cocktails" of different weapons or sequence of attacks to expose responders to sequential attacks. As a result, any analysis of methods of attack confirms the fact that there are no real rules to the game. Attacks can range from empty threats or ineffective weapons to attacks that can achieve high lethality over major urban areas or destroy much of a significant sector of the American economy.

This raises basic issues as to how to integrate the need to defend and respond to all types of CBRN events. At present, the emphasis seems to be on response to chemical and biological events involving moderate (no more than one thousand to ten thousand) casualties. The idea that defense must escalate in intensity—at a growing potential cost to civil rights and normal legal procedures—seems to have had only limited consideration. Detection and characterization often are tacitly approached by weapons type, rather than as part of an integrated and affordable CBRN system. The same is true of medical response and treatment. There seems to be little study of the degree to which different types of CBRN attacks require unique detection and response efforts and of the degree to which some kind of synergy is possible.

## LIVING WITH COMPLEXITY AND UNCERTAINTY: A FLEXIBLE AND EVOLUTIONARY APPROACH

The United States needs to plan flexibly for a wide spectrum of threats over time, rather than for some limited set in a climate of artificial crisis.

It needs to adapt and evolve its approach to the threat of covert attacks by state actors, their proxies, or independent extremists and terrorists, and develop contingency capabilities. It needs to avoid committing large resources to a limited set of cases that may never happen and exaggerating any aspect of the threat—either in terms of actors or methods—simply because it cannot afford any unnecessary distraction or waste. At the same time, it must plan now for the future that may occur, and not simply wait until the threats outlined in this book become tangible.

The GAO has made this point well in repeated reports on federal efforts and has made repeated calls for improved threat assessment. A report issued in April 2000 stated that:[1]

> A well-organized and efficient national counterterrorism program starts with a rigorous assessment of the terrorist threat the United States faces. Included in the analysis should be a clear examination on the qualifications to that threat. Adjusted threat scenarios would feed a risk analysis for use in developing a strategy. A strategy should have a desired outcome to attempt to achieve and to measure progress against. Resource decisions should be based on both a threat and risk assessment, and a strategy with a clear desired outcome.
>
> Intelligence agencies continuously assess the foreign and domestic terrorist threats to the United States. The U.S. foreign intelligence community, which includes the Central Intelligence Agency and others, monitors the foreign-origin terrorist threat to the United States. In addition, the FBI gathers intelligence and assesses the threat posed by domestic sources of terrorism. According to the U.S. intelligence community, conventional explosives and firearms continue to be the weapons of choice for terrorists. The FBI reports an increasing number of domestic cases involving U.S. persons attempting or threatening to use such materials. The intelligence community also reports an increased possibility that terrorists may use CBRN agents in the next decade.
>
> What is important about intelligence agency threat assessments is the very critical distinction between what is conceivable or possible and what is likely in terms of the threat of a terrorist attack. Some of the public statements made by intelligence community officials about the terrorist CBRN threat do not include important qualifications to the information they present. Based on our reading of the classified threat documents, such as national intelligence estimates, such qualifications include the fidelity and amount of credible intelligence, the terrorists' intentions versus their capabilities, whether the target is military or civilian, whether the target is international or domestic, and whether the enemy is a government or terrorists without foreign government sponsorship.
>
> . . . In a prior report, we have recommended that the federal government conduct sound threat and risk assessments to define and prioritize requirements and properly focus programs and investments in combating terrorism. The critical first step in a sound threat and risk assessment process is the threat analysis. The analysis should identify and evaluate each threat in terms of

capability and intent to attack an asset, the likelihood of a successful attack, and its consequences. The result of this analysis should be a list of potential terrorist attack scenarios. Next the risk assessment should be a deliberate, analytical effort that results in a prioritized list of risks (i.e., threat-asset-vulnerability combinations) that can be used to select countermeasures to create a certain level of protection or preparedness. Without the benefits that a threat and risk assessment provides, many agencies have been relying on worst case scenarios to generate countermeasures or establish their programs. Worst case scenarios are extreme situations and, as such, may be out of balance with the threat. In our view, by using worst case scenarios, the federal government is focusing on vulnerabilities (which are unlimited) rather than credible threats (which are limited). By targeting investments based on worst case scenarios, the government may be over funding some initiatives and programs and under funding the more likely threats the country will face.

As an example, we have testified that the Department of Health and Human Services is establishing a national pharmaceutical and vaccine stockpile that does not match intelligence agencies' judgments of the more likely chemical and biological agents that terrorists might use. In some of our current work at other federal agencies, we are continuing to find that worst case scenarios are being used in planning efforts to develop programs and capabilities.[2]

. . . we have recommended that the threat and risk assessments be conducted at the local level as a tool to target federal assistance programs. In addition, since we last testified before this Subcommittee, we also recommended that the FBI perform a national-level threat and risk assessment. The FBI has agreed in principle with our recommendations and FBI officials recently updated us on their progress. Regarding local threat and risk assessments, the FBI and the Department of Justices' Office of Justice Programs are about to send out threat and risk assessment information for local governments to use. The local jurisdictions will then send their assessments to their respective state governments to compile and analyze. The state governments will use the findings to develop a statewide domestic preparedness strategy. The FBI has agreed to lead a national-level threat and risk assessment, but has noted certain limitations. For example, because of the restrictions it faces on the use of law enforcement intelligence information, its efforts will first concentrate on the threats posed by various CBRN agents, as opposed to threats posed by specific terrorist groups. The FBI would then combine this with threat information in a classified assessment. The FBI officials did not have an estimate as to when they would formally begin their national assessment, but they estimated it would take about 6 months.

The events of September 11, 2001 indicated that the GAO understated the seriousness of this need for analysis. It does not consider the need to examine how the technology of offense and defense can affect threat assessments over time and the need for forecasts that look ten to twenty years into the future. It also tends to downplay the risk of covert attacks from state actors, or the use of proxy attacks, and it fails to assess the grave uncertainties in estimating the short- and long-term effects of using CBRN weapons—uncertainties so great that they could alter the damage and casualty estimates in many scenarios.

It is also far from clear that threat and risk assessments can be used to create a set of scenarios that focus the defense effort or that prioritize it around a select and well-defined group of scenarios. Once again, the problem is to determine the range of low-probability events the United States may have to react to and what this means for deterrence, offense, defense, and response. While it is most likely that the United States will have to react to a series of relatively low-level events in the near term, the cumulative probability that the United States may have to react to much more serious events over the mid to long term may be equally high. As a result, threat and risk assessments must consider nuclear and highly lethal biological attacks.

Having said this, it is clear that such an approach to assessing and prioritizing risk goes against the American character. Complexity and uncertainty are not conditions that Americans easily tolerate. Patience is not a great American virtue, and turning away from the specter of an urgent artificial crisis to evolving a response that has long organizational and technical lead-times is a response that is normally forced on the United States, rather than one it accepts. The United States did not win the Cold War with a careful and systematic process of deterrence and containment because it wanted to. It did so because the conditions of the Cold War evolved in ways that gave it no other choice.

## THE "MORNING AFTER," MULTIPLE ATTACKS; THE "MORNING AFTER" AND THE "LEARNING CURVE EFFECT"

There is a final set of points that must be made about all of the forms of attack analyzed in this study. The fact the United States cannot currently assess and prioritize the risk and form of attacks that will take place on the U.S. homeland may well mean that it cannot prevent multiple or sequential attacks from taking place. At the same time, the psychological and political impact of using weapons that produce mass destruction or mass casualties will change with each use.

Multiple attacks can suddenly make the "unthinkable" and "unacceptable" cease to be unthinkable or unacceptable. Attackers will learn whether such attacks are feasible and whether their political, financial, and military results can be tailored to achieve their objectives. Americans will learn they can and must live with occasional attacks and that they must do whatever is necessary to deter, retaliate, defend, and respond. As horrible as such a world may now seem, the events of September 2001 have shown it is one that the United States may have to learn to live in, and this may mean redefining the levels of casualties that are acceptable. Americans have, after all, learned to live with a high casualty and death rate from many other causes including crime, accidents, disease, and drugs. One key reality of homeland defense is that one lives with what one must.

There has generally been a subconscious or implicit denial of these realities in much of the literature on homeland defense. Much of our planning and analysis has been based on the assumption that the United States can anticipate the nature of future attacks and react effectively. There has been a similar failure to realize that the United States may have to deal with multiple attacks, follow-on attackers, and evolving and changing sources and methods of attack in which the attackers will attempt to adapt to every U.S. countermeasure. For example, few present scenarios examine mixes of chemical and biological weapons, "cocktails" of different biological weapons, and/or the simultaneous use of information warfare. There are no guarantees that attacks on the U.S. homeland will reach this level of intensity or become a paradigm of international and domestic politics over the next twenty-five years. At the same time, there are no guarantees they will not.

Similar problems affect much of the thinking about response measures. The search to create an effective response to every attack is a noble goal. However, there is no indication that such an effort will be feasible or remotely cost effective. At the same time, there is equally little guarantee that any given response will be effective until a clear threat emerges and some pattern of attack allows the United States to evolve an effective response. Even then, the previous analysis has shown that many forms of biological attack may have no effective defensive response for years to come, if ever.

If there is any good news about such bad news, it is that the strikes on the World Trade Center and the Pentagon have shown that actual attacks produce a "learning curve effect" that aids defense. The U.S. government, media, industry, and public learn how to deal with each new type of attack and attacker. There is no grimmer and more tragic way to learn, but adapting to reality is often more practical than guessing at what the future will bring. It is unlikely that the United States will face a full spectrum of complex threats at the same time, as such, its detection, defense, and response capabilities can be tailored to deal with tangible and predictable problems. So can dealing with issues like federal, state, and local jurisdiction and many of the painful issues involved in maintaining the rule of law and human rights.

It should be noted in this regard that much of the success of homeland defense will be determined by how the United States reacts and adapts over time after successful attacks. Creating a leakproof defense is a noble goal, but it is also probably a fantasy in any world where covert, proxy, and terrorist/extremist attacks on the United States, its allies, or indeed any other group of states become common. Accordingly, one key aspect of assessing and prioritizing such threats is to understand how much the world can change after the first attack and how much broader the U.S. response may have to be when responding to a single attack or set of attacks. The risk that the United States or its allies may come under covert, proxy, or terrorist/extremist attack using WMD may be an enduring one based on a new paradigm of world conflict.

Furthermore, it should be noted that every aspect of U.S. defense planning—deterrence, offense, defense, and response—must also adapt. In many cases, it may take weeks, months, or years to firmly identify an attacker. Technology may cut these times in many cases, but not all. Once a pattern of actual attacks begins, the United States may have to fundamentally rethink its criteria for using its offensive capabilities to deter and retaliate. This could easily involve retaliation based on far more limited evidence, involving massive amounts of civilian casualties and collateral damage, and drastic reprioritization of the priority given to national self-defense in the U.S. view of international law. At the same time, it could involve major shifts in collective antiterrorism and effective defense with U.S. friends and allies and new forms of arms control efforts.

## NOTES

1. GAO, "Combating Terrorism: Issues in Managing Counterterrorist Programs," Statement of Norman J. Rabkin, Testimony Before the Subcommittee on Oversight, Investigations, and Emergency Management, Committee on Transportation and Infrastructure, House of Representatives," GAO/T-NSIAD-00-145, April 6, 2000.

2. GAO, "Combating Terrorism: Observations on Biological Terrorism and Public Health Initiatives," GAO/T-NSIAD-99-112, March 16,1999, and "Combating Terrorism: Need for Comprehensive Threat and Risk Assessments of Chemical and Biological Attack," GAO/NSIAD-99-163, September 7, 1999.

*Chapter 6*

# U.S. Government Efforts to Create a Homeland Defense Capability

The United States does not yet have a clearly defined strategy or cohesive program for dealing with asymmetric warfare; even though this was a priority with the Clinton Administration and remains a high priority of the George W. Bush Administration. The federal government never made a proper survey of its programs in this area before the strikes of September 2001 changed its priorities and led Congress to add tens of billions of dollars to such programs. It failed to develop a cohesive program and budget for counterterrorism, critical infrastructure protection (CIP), and counterproliferation activities.

Even the DOD, which is the only part of the government with a detailed program budget and future year plan, only made a crude effort to analyze its homeland defense activities in ways that looked beyond the next budget year. The rest of the U.S. government suboptimized around the more familiar threat of terrorism and forms of counterterrorist and response activity, without fully examining the impact of higher levels of asymmetric warfare.

The U.S. government has, however, followed the same basic principles in dealing with terrorism since the 1970s: Make no concessions to terrorists, pressure state sponsors of terrorism, and apply the rule of law to terrorists as criminals.

The May 1972 Lod Airport massacre and the Munich Olympics the following September resulted in the Nixon Administration's creation of the Cabinet Committee to Combat Terrorism in 1972. Chaired by the Secretary of State, the committee included the secretaries of defense, treasury, and transportation; the attorney general; directors of the CIA and FBI, and the UN ambassador. The committee's attempt to obtain a new draft UN convention to suppress terrorism marked the beginning of a long series of U.S. government initiatives to formulate and strengthen international conventions and treaties covering every aspect of the control of international terrorism, from aircraft hijacking to the prevention of hostage-taking, for example, the 1973 hijack pact with Cuba. A U.S. working group was also set up, consisting of senior members of the Cabinet committee.

In 1976, the State Department established the Office for Combating Terrorism to provide expert assistance and an operational focus for crisis management when dealing with international incidents. During the Carter Administration, the Nixon Cabinet committee was abolished and replaced by the Special Coordination Committee (SCC) of the National Security Council. With the 1979 kidnapping of the entire U.S. mission in Tehran, terrorism became identified as a national security issue not only by the government but also by the American public.

In the face of the Tehran hostage crisis the Reagan Administration put international terrorism high on its list of national security priorities. According to Paul Wilkinson, the urgency with which the Reagan Administration pursued this aim was based on the belief that the Soviet Union was behind a vast conspiracy to use terrorism to destabilize the free world and that U.S. security was being threatened by exported subversion and terrorism from revolutionary regimes in Cuba and Nicaragua.[1] This urgency coincided with Claire Sterling's publication of *The Terror Network* and U.S. State Department dossiers of alleged evidence of Cuban and Nicaraguan aid to Marxist guerrillas in El Salvador. With the October 1983 massacre of U.S. Marines and French troops by Shi'ites using truck bombs, U.S. counterterrorism policy increasingly centered on employing military options and on how to retaliate against state sponsors of such attacks. The United States not only lost more lives in Lebanon in 1983 than in the previous fifteen years of terrorism, according to Wilkinson, but was also forced to alter and limit its policy options in the Middle East. Not surprisingly, shortly thereafter, on April 3, 1984, President Reagan signed a new National Security Decision Directive ordering the U.S. government to develop military options to deal with international terrorism. On the same day, Secretary of State George Schultz spoke of the necessity to use force to combat state-sponsored international terrorism, starting a debate on the utility and nature of the use of force that continues unabated.

Meanwhile during the early 1970s through the early 1990s, the United States had experienced little terrorism of the type seen overseas during the same period. Hijackings abated, as did like violence. Early disputes over who was in charge in the event of such terrorist incidents were generally concluded with an understanding that the FBI was in charge. The only exceptions to this were (1) an early victory by the U.S. Federal Aviation

Administration in assuming the lead during hijackings once the aircraft door was shut or (2) the almost successful attempt in the early months of the first Reagan Administration by the newly appointed FEMA director—a California confidante of President Reagan—to take over the domestic response. The attempted takeover was unsuccessful, and FEMA was left with only responsibility for the consequences of the incident—responsibility to which, as it turned out, FEMA only halfheartedly paid lip service to. It was not until the mid-1990s, and the bombings in New York City and Oklahoma City, that the U.S. government focused seriously on domestic response, relying primarily on the FBI. The joining of the possibility of domestic attacks with concerns about weapons of mass destruction, arising in the aftermath of the Tokyo subway attack, presented a challenge hitherto not faced by the U.S. government.

This U.S. policy on terrorism was formalized in 1986, when the Reagan Administration issued National Security Decision Directive 207 (NSDD 207). This shift to a more formal policy came as the result of the findings of the 1985 Vice President's Task Force on Terrorism, which highlighted the need for improved, centralized interagency coordination of the significant assets the federal government had to respond to terrorist incidents. NSDD 207 reaffirmed the lead agency responsibilities for implementing this policy. The State Department was made responsible for international terrorism policy, procedures, and programs, and the FBI was made responsible for dealing with domestic terrorist acts while acting through the Department of Justice.

The U.S. response to the potential threats from covert attacks by state actors, their proxies, or independent extremists and terrorists have, however, evolved significantly since the mid-1990s. The first major shift in policy came in the National Defense Authorization Act for Fiscal Year 1994, Public Law No.103-160, Section 1703 (50 USC 1522). This law mandated the coordination and integration of all Department of Defense chemical and biological (CB) defense programs. As part of this coordination and integration, the Secretary of Defense was directed to submit an assessment and a description of plans to improve readiness to survive, fight, and win in a nuclear, biological, and chemical (NBC) contaminated environment. Since that time, 50 USC 1522 has provided the essential authority to ensure the elimination of unnecessarily redundant programs, focusing funds on DOD and program priorities, and enhancing readiness.

## KEY PRESIDENTIAL DECISION DIRECTIVES AND
## LEGISLATION AFFECTING THE FEDERAL RESPONSE

The bombing of the federal building in Oklahoma City led to the issuance of Presidential Decision Directive 39 (PDD-39) in June 1995. PDD-39 built on the previous directive and contained three key elements of a national strategy for combating terrorism: (1) reduce vulnerabilities to terrorist attacks and prevent and deter terrorist acts before they occur; (2) respond to terrorist acts that do occur—crisis management—and apprehend and punish terrorists; and (3) manage the consequences of terrorist acts, including providing emergency relief and restoring capabilities to protect public health and safety and essential government services. This directive further elaborates on agencies' roles and responsibilities and some specific measures to be taken regarding each element of the strategy.[2]

These policies were further developed by two key Presidential Decision Directives, PDD-62 and PDD-63 issued in May 1998.

- PDD-62 reaffirmed the basic principles of PDD-39, but clarified and reinforced the specific missions of the U.S. agencies charged with defeating, and defending against, terrorism, and created a new and more systematic federal approach to fighting the emerging threat posed by weapons of mass destruction (WMD). This includes programs to deter terrorist incidents involving chemical, biological, radiological, and nuclear weapons, and to manage the consequences if such incidents should occur.
- PDD-63 called for a national effort to assure the security of critical infrastructure. It covers both critical infrastructure protection and cyber-crime, and the security of both government and private sector infrastructure to ensure national security, national economic security, and public health and safety.

As a result of PDD-39 and PDD-62, the federal response to domestic incidents is now formally divided into crisis management, led by the FBI, and consequence management led by FEMA. According to the GAO

Two Presidential Decisions Directives—Number 39 issued in June 1995 and Number 62 issued in May 1998—define U.S. policy to combat terrorism. These presidential directives and implementing guidance divide the federal response to terrorist attacks into two categories—crisis management and consequence management. Crisis management includes efforts to stop a terrorist attack, arrest terrorists, and gather evidence for criminal prosecution. Consequence management includes efforts to provide medical treatment and emergency services, evacuate people from dangerous areas, and restore government services. The presidential directives also organize federal efforts to combat terrorism along a lead agency concept. The Department of Justice, through the Federal Bureau of Investigation (FBI), is the lead federal agency for crisis management of domestic terrorist incidents. For managing the consequences of domestic terrorist incidents, state and local authorities are primarily responsible. The Federal Emergency Management Agency (FEMA) is the lead federal agency for consequence management if state or local authorities request federal assistance.[3]

New legislation has also shaped U.S. policy. "The Defense Against Weapons of Mass Destruction Act," contained in the National Defense

Authorization Act for Fiscal Year 1997 (Title XIV of P.L. 104-201, September 23, 1996), established the Nunn-Lugar-Domenici Domestic Preparedness Program. This act made the Department of Defense the lead federal agency for implementing the program, in cooperation with the FBI, the Department of Energy, the Environmental Protection Agency, the Department of Health and Human Services, and the Federal Emergency Management Agency.[4]

The United States gave significantly higher priority to the full range of threats posed by WMD. On June 8, 1998, President Clinton forwarded to Congress a FY1999 budget amendment that included a proposal to: (1) build a civilian stockpile of antidotes and vaccines to respond to a large-scale biological or chemical attack; (2) improve the public health surveillance system to detect biological or chemical agents rapidly and to analyze resulting disease outbreaks; (3) provide specialized equipment and training to states and localities for responding to a biological or chemical incident; and (4) expand the National Institutes of Health's research into vaccines and therapies.

The Omnibus Consolidated and Emergency Supplemental Appropriations Act (PL 105–277) included $51 million for the CDC to begin developing a pharmaceutical and vaccine stockpile for civilian populations. The act also required that HHS submit an operating plan to the House and Senate Committees on Appropriations before obligating the funds. The FY2000 request for HHS's bio-terrorism initiative was $230 million, including $52 million for the CDC to continue procurement of a national stockpile.

## ONGOING CHANGES IN THE STRUCTURE OF THE FEDERAL EFFORT

The number of federal players involved in combating the threats posed by state actors, their proxies, or independent extremists and terrorists increased substantially after PDD-39 was issued in June 1995, and has laid the groundwork for steps the nation must now take. The GAO has reported that the number of players now involves more than forty federal agencies, bureaus, and offices in combating terrorism.

For example, Department of Agriculture (USDA) representatives now attend counterterrorism crisis response exercise planning functions. The U.S. Army's director of military support has created a new office to implement the Nunn-Lugar-Domenici Domestic Preparedness Program, which has a new mission of training U.S. cities' emergency response personnel to deal with terrorist incidents using chemical and biological WMD. It plans to create another office to integrate another new player—the National Guard and reserves—into the terrorism consequence management area.

Similarly, the National Guard and reserves have established ten WMD Civil Support Teams (CSTs), formerly known as Rapid Assessment and Initial Detection (RAID) teams, throughout the country and now have a total of twenty-seven teams in early 2001.[5] Five more WMD CSTs were appropriated for FY2001, but there have been difficulties in finding funds for these. The U.S. Marine Corps has established the Chemical Biological Incident Response Force. Further, the DOE has redesigned its long-standing Nuclear Emergency Search Team into various Joint Technical Operations Teams and other teams. At least one DOE laboratory is offering consequence management services for chemical and biological, as well as nuclear, incidents. The Public Health Service is in the process of establishing 120 Metropolitan Medical Strike Teams throughout the country in addition to three deployable "national asset" National Medical Response Teams and existing Disaster Medical Assistance Teams. There are many more examples of new players in the terrorism arena.

## THE GROWTH OF THE FEDERAL EFFORT

These rapid changes in the way the federal government deals with terrorism have been accompanied by an even more rapid growth in federal spending. This has created major problems in tracking and assessing the federal effort in dealing with terrorism, before Congress began to pour massive new funds into homeland defense in September 2001. Strategy and planning are meaningless unless they are properly implemented, and the only way to assess implementation is to follow the money and assess individual programs in terms of their objectives, effectiveness, and cost.

Unfortunately, reporting on the key programs contributing to homeland defense has been a definitional and statistical nightmare. At this writing, it is still unclear whether the Bush Administration will be any more successful than the Clinton Administration in bringing order to the process. While the federal effort reflects steadily improving coordination, there are still major bureaucratic rivalries, duplicative programs, and differing priorities. Furthermore, current reporting focuses far too heavily on the construction costs for the physical protection of foreign and domestic federal facilities, and far too little on the broader national response effort needed to protect the American people and economy. The current level of program analysis also ignores related activity in asymmetric warfare, deterrent and offensive activities, arms control, and many forms of counterproliferation. The terrorism-counterterrorism bias discussed earlier means that most federal studies of homeland defense are so narrowly defined that they exclude key activities and options. The Bush Administration is also caught up in a series of broader budget debates and transition problems, which means it will be FY2003, at the earliest, before this administration can hope to shape a cohesive program and budget of its own.

What is clear is that major increases have taken place in those portions of the federal budget that the GAO, OMB, and DOD do include in homeland defense. The GAO reported in 1997 that seven key federal agencies spent more than an estimated $6.5 billion on federal efforts to combat terrorism, excluding classified programs and activities in FY1997. Some key agencies' spending on terrorism-related programs had increased dramatically. For example, FBI terrorism-related funding and staff-level authorizations tripled between FY1995 and FY1997, and Federal Aviation Administration (FAA) spending to combat terrorism also tripled.[6]

The Office of Management and Budget (OMB) reporting to Congress on enacted and requested terrorism-related funding for FY1998 and FY1999, stated that more than seventeen agencies had classified and unclassified programs. These agencies were authorized a total of $6.5 billion for FY1998, and $6.7 billion for FY1999. OMB's figures are lower than the GAO's for FY1997, but different definitions and interpretations of how to attribute terrorism-related spending in broader accounts can cause a difference of billions of dollars.[7] For example, the OMB later reported that actual spending in 1998 totaled $7.658 billion consisting of $5.871 billion for combating terrorism, $645 million for combating WMD, and $1.142 billion for CIP.[8]

### The FY2000 Program

President Clinton's administration did issue a detailed "guesstimate" as to the amount of federal spending on homeland defense when it submitted its FY2000 budget request:

In his FY2000 budget request, President Clinton will propose $10 billion to address "terrorism and terrorist-emerging tools" including nearly $1.4 billion in defense against chemical and biological terrorism. A further $1.46 billion will be requested for CIP, $231 million for nonproliferation and transnational antiterrorism efforts, and $230 million for bio-terrorism programs at the Department of Health and Human Services.[9]

The Clinton Administration provided the following breakdown of how the FY2000 program was allocated to different activities:

*Funding for Domestic Preparedness and Critical Infrastructure Protection:* The President's FY2000 budget includes requests for $2.849 billion for critical infrastructure protection, computer security, and domestic preparedness against a weapons of mass destruction attack. The budget request also proposed $7.162 billion for conventional counterterrorism security programs.

*Domestic Preparedness against Weapons of Mass Destruction:* In May 1999 the President proposed adding $300 million for a new weapons of mass destruction domestic preparedness program. As a result, the 1999 enacted level was $1.281 billion. The President's FY2000 funding request for countering the threat of terrorist use of weapons of mass destruction continues and expands the program to $1.385 billion. The FY2000 request included increases of $30 million above the previous level for research into new vaccines and medicines, an additional $15 million to fund Public Health Surveillance to detect an attack, and an additional $13 million to create new metropolitan medical response teams. Highlights of the FY2000 budget included:

$52 million to continue procurement of a national stockpile of specialized medicines to protect the civilian population.

$611 million for training and equipping emergency personnel in U.S. cities, planning and exercising for weapons of mass destruction contingencies, and strengthening public health infrastructure.

$206 million to protect U.S. government facilities.

$381 million for research and development, including pathogen genome sequencing, vaccines, new therapies, detection and diagnosis, decontamination, and disposition of nuclear material.

*Critical Infrastructure Protection and Computer Security*: The President's FY2000 request included $1.464 billion for protection of critical infrastructure and computer security. This represented a 40 percent increase in the two budget years since the President created the Critical Infrastructure Protection Commission. The highlights of this program included:

Critical Infrastructure Applied Research Initiative ($500 million).

Intrusion and Detection Systems: In addition to ongoing Department of Defense funding, $2 million will be spent to design and evaluate a similar system for other Federal agencies.

Information Sharing and Analysis Centers (ISACs): As part of the public-private partnership, we will provide $8 million to support the initial establishment of ISACs.

*Cyber Corps*: This program addresses the shortage of highly skilled computer science expertise in the government and enable agencies to recruit a cadre of experts to respond to attacks on computer networks. It will use existing personnel flexibilities, scholarship, and financial assistance programs and $3 million to examine new scholarship programs to retrain, retain, and recruit computer science students.

*Counterterrorism Security*: In addition to the programs above, the President's FY2000 budget request for all antiterrorism and counterterrorism programs was $8.547 billion, a 12 percent increase over the FY1999 enacted level and an 18 percent increase over FY1998.

The President also requested a supplemental appropriation in FY1999 of $2.064 billion after the Africa bombings. This included $1.4 billion to provide additional security measures to diplomatic and consular facilities and [to] rebuild the two embassies destroyed in Dar es Salaam and Nairobi.[10]

## The FY2001 Program

An OMB estimate of FY2001 federal spending on combating terrorism indicated that spending would total $9.3 billion for FY2001, a 43 percent increase. Within these amounts, WMD preparedness spending has increased from $645 million in FY1998 to $1.55 billion in FY2001, a 141 percent increase.[11]

According to the GAO, however, the requested FY2001 budget for counterterrorism, including CIP, as of April 6, 2000, was $11.117 billion.

> In addition to reporting on the increase in the number of programs, we have testified twice on the rapid increase in federal funding to combat terrorism. The Office of Management and Budget (OMB) reported 1998 actual spending at $7.658 billion consisting of $5.871 billion for combating terrorism, $.645 billion for combating weapons of mass destruction and $1.142 billion for critical infrastructure protection. The President's budget request for FY2001 totals $11.117 billion consisting of $7.538 billion for combating terrorism, $1.552 billion for combating weapons of mass destruction and $2.027 billion for critical infrastructure protection. As proposed in the President's budget request, total funding would increase about 45 percent from 1998 to 2001, with component increases of about 28 percent for combating terrorism, about 140 percent for combating weapons of mass destruction, and about 77 percent for critical infrastructure protection. As noted in our earlier work, funding has increased dramatically at the Departments of Health and Human Services, Justice, and at the FBI.[12]

Part of the problem in estimating federal expenditures is that they are subject to constant change. For example, the president requested an additional $300 million for new counterterrorism initiatives on May 17, 2000:

> President Clinton announced a plan today to invest an additional $300 million in critical programs to strengthen the Nation's counterterrorism efforts.
>
> The funding would enhance the federal government's work to deter and detect terrorist activity, applying lessons learned from the counterterrorism effort undertaken during Millennium celebration events. The request proposes $89 million for the Department of Justice and $87 million for the Department of the Treasury to fund extra personnel, new equipment, and additional joint operations and infrastructure improvements. An additional $159 million is proposed for other agencies to support these efforts.
>
> Highlights of the initiative include:
>
> - Increasing the number of Joint Terrorism Task Forces located throughout the United States. The Task Forces were established to integrate the resources and expertise of the law enforcement authorities of the Federal Bureau of Investigation (FBI), the Immigration and Naturalization Service (INS), the U.S. Customs Service, ATF, Secret Service and state and local law enforcement.

- Improving monitoring on the northern border with secure communications equipment and advanced monitoring equipment, including high resolution day and night camera technology.

- Expanding INS forensic capabilities at the government's federal crime lab dedicated to the forensic examination of potentially fraudulent travel documents.

- Supporting the establishment of a new interagency National Terrorist Asset Tracking Center to analyze the financing of terrorist organizations and expand the Office of Foreign Asset Control at the Department of the Treasury.

- Increasing the number of Department of Justice prosecutors and legal staff to support the prosecution of terrorists.

- Increasing the Department of the Treasury's Counterterrorism Fund that was established to cover costs associated with efforts to counter, investigate, or prosecute domestic or international terrorism.

Today's request builds on activities already being undertaken. In FY2000, reprogramming funds the majority of the package. A fully offset FY2001 budget amendment will be submitted to Congress.[13]

## THE DETAILS OF THE FEDERAL EFFORT

The most accurate detailed estimate of the federal efforts, before massive changes began to take place as a result of the attacks on the World Trade Center and the Pentagon, was the work done by OMB in response to a requirement in Section 1051 of the FY1998 National Defense Authorization Act (PL 105–85). This legislation requires the administration to provide information on executive branch funding efforts to combat terrorism. Subsequent legislation (Section 1403 of PL 105–261) requires an annex to this report that shows spending on domestic preparedness.

Table 6.1 and Charts 6.1 to 6.3 show the past patterns in total federal spending on defense and response against terrorism, although it must again be stressed that they are so narrowly defined that they exclude most DOD activity relating to deterrence or offensive of foreign state and terrorist threats and to counterproliferation and asymmetric warfare. They also exclude State Department, DOD, and DOE activity in relevant areas of counterproliferation and arms control

According to the data in Table 6.1, the total funding for all forms of federal action dealing with terrorism rose from $7.658 billion in FY1998 to $11.338 billion in FY2001. This is a rise of 48 percent. The total funding designed specifically to deal with the threat from WMD rose from $645 million in FY1998 to $1.554 billion in FY2001, a rise of 141 percent. The rise in CIP was from $1.142 billion to $2.027 billion, a rise of 78 percent. These figures reveal an extremely rapid rate of growth in new program areas, and this was before Congress added billions more in September 2001.

Chart 6.1
Federal Spending on Terrorism, WMD, and CIP by Category, FY1998–FY2001
(current $US millions)

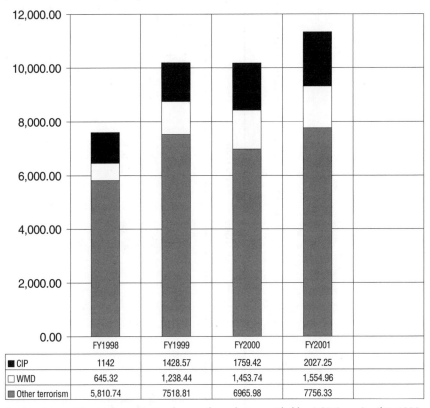

| | FY1998 | FY1999 | FY2000 | FY2001 | |
|---|---|---|---|---|---|
| ■ CIP | 1142 | 1428.57 | 1759.42 | 2027.25 | |
| □ WMD | 645.32 | 1,238.44 | 1,453.74 | 1,554.96 | |
| ■ Other terrorism | 5,810.74 | 7518.81 | 6965.98 | 7756.33 | |

*Source*: Adapted by Anthony H. Cordesman from data provided by ACDA on April 1, 1999.
Belarus and Kazakhstan report zero in every category.

## The Changing Patterns in Federal Spending

A review of Table 6.1 and Charts 6.1 to 6.3 reveals the following more detailed patterns in federal spending during FY1998–FY2001:

- The federal effort is broadly distributed among twenty-three major federal departments and agencies. The largest efforts are carried out in the national security area, which includes the DOD and intelligence agencies and which received slightly over 51 percent of the total funding programmed for FY2001. The second largest recipient has been the State Department, largely because of the high cost of improving physical security at U.S. embassies.

Table 6.1
OMB Estimate of Total Federal Spending on Terrorism (as of June 2000) (government spending for combating terrorism, WMD and CIP in current $US billions)

| | FY1998 | FY1999 | FY2000 | FY2001 |
|---|---|---|---|---|
| Federal Government | 7,658.08 | 10,185.82 | 10,179.14 | 11,338.54 |
| *Combat Terrorism* | 6,516.08 | 8,757.26 | 8,419.71 | 9,311.30 |
| Law enforcement and investigative activities | 2,654.72 | 2,686.77 | 2,820.04 | 3,025.51 |
| Physical security of government facilities and employees | 2,893.72 | 4,356.44 | 3,637.49 | 4,259.24 |
| Physical security of national populace | 146.66 | 256.83 | 249.86 | 266.76 |
| Preparing for and responding to terrorist acts | 417.84 | 930.21 | 984.41 | 947.00 |
| Research and development | 403.14 | 527.01 | 727.91 | 812.79 |
| *WMD Preparedness* | 645.31 | 1,238.44 | 1,453.74 | 1,554.96 |
| Law enforcement and investigative activities | 71.82 | 102.30 | 93.77 | 142.53 |
| Physical security of government | 175.09 | 199.35 | 200.58 | 185.41 |
| Physical security of national populace | 3.39 | 3.83 | 3.61 | 3.62 |
| Preparing for and responding to WMD terrorism | 155.26 | 564.20 | 618.74 | 633.48 |
| Research and development | 239.75 | 368.76 | 537.04 | 589.92 |

| Critical Infrastructure Protection | | | | |
|---|---|---|---|---|
| Federal infrastructure protection | 1,142.02 | 1,428.55 | 1,759.43 | 2,027.18 |
| Education and training | 1,038.81 | 1,278.92 | 1,584.26 | 1,699.03 |
| Intrusion monitoring and response | 37.54 | 48.50 | 79.45 | 105.00 |
| Legislative initiatives and legal issues | 127.63 | 186.27 | 213.37 | 249.27 |
| Multiple program areas | 0.12 | 0.20 | 0.20 | 0.23 |
| Reconstitution | 242.45 | 282.72 | 397.21 | 369.05 |
| System protection | 26.19 | 30.18 | 16.29 | 5.64 |
| Threat/vulnerability/risk assessments | 533.32 | 631.13 | 710.23 | 740.69 |
| CIP assistance/outreach to private sector | 71.56 | 99.92 | 167.51 | 229.15 |
| Education and training | 103.21 | 149.66 | 175.17 | 328.15 |
| Intrusion monitoring and response | 1.14 | 1.60 | 1.60 | 2.50 |
| Legislative initiatives and legal issues | 3.75 | 5.20 | 4.70 | 6.62 |
| Multiple program areas | 1.58 | 2.60 | 2.60 | 3.60 |
| Public awareness/outreach | 37.99 | 70.78 | 61.14 | 133.92 |
| Reconstitution | 0.00 | 0.00 | 2.30 | 3.10 |
| System protection | 0.00 | 0.00 | 0.00 | 2.13 |
| Threat/vulnerability/risk assessments | 37.31 | 43.15 | 57.05 | 72.14 |
| | 21.44 | 26.33 | 45.78 | 104.14 |

*Source:* Adapted by Steve Chu and Preston Golson from Executive Office of the President, Office Management and Budget, "Annual Report to Congress on Combating Terrorism," May 2000.

**Chart 6.2**
**Distribution of Federal Spending on Terrorism, WMD, and CIP by Category, FY2001 (current $US millions)**

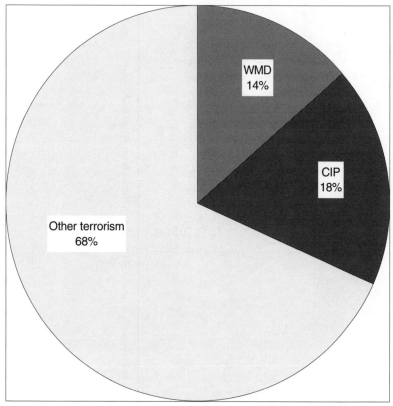

WMD
14%

CIP
18%

Other terrorism
68%

*Source*: Adapted by Anthony H. Cordesman from the Executive Office of the President, Office Management and Budget, "Annual Report to Congress on Combating Terrorism," May 2000.

- The "civil" effort reflects a similar rise in spending on physical protection, which is a key reason for the rise in spending by agencies like the DOE, General Services Administration (GSA), and Transportation and Energy. There has, however, been an important increase in funding for law enforcement, and the funding for the DOJ rose by nearly 50 percent during FY1998–FY2000.

- Most federal spending on terrorism is not directly related to either the threat posed by WMD (14 percent) or to CIP (18 percent). Spending on other activities totaled 68 percent in the FY2001 budget request.

- The main increases in the overall federal effort to combat terrorism took place in funding to improve physical protection for government facilities and employees (from $2.9 billion to $4.3 billion), in preparing for and responding

**Chart 6.3—Part 1**
**Federal Spending on Terrorism, WMD, and CIP by Agency, FY1998–FY2001**
**(current $US millions)**

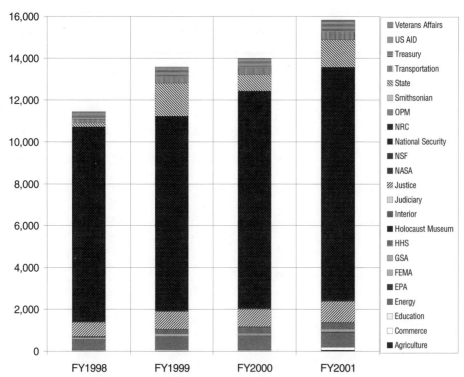

*Source*: Adapted by Anthony H. Cordesman from the Executive Office of the President, Office Management and Budget, "Annual Report to Congress on Combating Terrorism," May 2000.

to terrorist acts (from $418 million to $947 million), and in research and development (from $403 million to $813 million.)

- In contrast, law enforcement—the traditional focus of the federal effort—rose from $2.7 million to $3.0 billion. This latter rise was still quite significant, but law enforcement spending dropped from 41 percent of all spending in FY1998 to 32 percent in FY2001.

- The rise in spending to directly counter the threat of the use of WMD, in contrast, did not involve major increases in spending on physical protection for either government or the national populace. It did lead to a near doubling of law enforcement spending and massive increases in preparing for and responding to WMD terrorism (from $155 million to $633 million) and on research and development (from $240 million to $590 million).

- The growth in the CIP effort was more broadly distributed by category, although the outreach to the private sector tripled (from $103 million to $328 million), as did the federal efforts in education and intrusion monitoring and response.

Chart 6.3—Part 2
Federal Spending on Terrorism, WMD, and CIP by Agency, FY1998–FY2001
(current $US millions)

|  | FY1998 | FY1999 | FY2000 | FY2001 |
|---|---|---|---|---|
| Agriculture | 10.90 | 12.92 | 14.84 | 59.17 |
| Commerce | 38.89 | 53.66 | 40.15 | 125.70 |
| Education | 3.59 | 4.45 | 5.23 | 2.51 |
| Energy | 500.48 | 614.65 | 669.59 | 708.83 |
| EPA | 2.12 | 2.24 | 2.08 | 5.50 |
| FEMA | 5.92 | 17.61 | 31.57 | 35.99 |
| GSA | 89.60 | 136.50 | 92.80 | 132.36 |
| HHS | 37.75 | 187.51 | 299.67 | 292.97 |
| Holocaust Museum | 0.00 | 2.00 | 0.00 | 0.00 |
| Interior | 12.21 | 15.61 | 12.31 | 11.49 |
| Judiciary | 7.00 | 8.00 | 10.60 | 11.20 |
| Justice | 672.70 | 848.08 | 826.04 | 994.76 |
| NASA | 41.00 | 43.00 | 66.00 | 61.00 |
| NSF | 19.15 | 21.42 | 26.65 | 43.85 |
| National Security | 5470.68 | 5867.73 | 6520.11 | 6582.97 |
| NRC | 3.48 | 3.41 | 3.21 | 3.49 |
| OPM | 0.00 | 0.00 | 2.00 | 7.00 |
| Smithsonian | 0.00 | 0.00 | 0.00 | 0.05 |
| State | 186.00 | 1579.00 | 791.00 | 1312.00 |
| Transportation | 189.63 | 295.66 | 327.89 | 397.49 |
| Treasury | 364.27 | 416.90 | 424.21 | 527.24 |
| US AID | 5.68 | 54.89 | 5.83 | 5.01 |
| Veterans Affairs | 0.01 | 0.04 | 17.33 | 17.39 |

*Source*: Adapted by Anthony H. Cordesman from the Executive Office of the President, Office Management and Budget, "Annual Report to Congress on Combating Terrorism," May 2000.

It is important to note that these totals include all federal spending and not simply efforts to react to the threat posed to the U.S. homeland. As a result, they give a somewhat misleading view of how the United States is attempting to defend against the threat posed by state actors, their proxies, or independent extremists and terrorists even according to the relatively narrow definition of homeland defense activity used in the OMB analysis. For example, CIP is often excluded from the analysis of U.S. counter-terrorism efforts and includes different threats such as information warfare.

At the same time, any effort to break out federal spending into neat categories presents major problems in categorization, which is compounded by constant changes in the structure of federal effort. Furthermore, the spending formally included in reports on efforts to deal directly with the threat of state actors, their proxies, or independent extremists and terrorists using WMD is only a relatively small portion of total federal spending, much of the spending in other areas improves the quality of law enforcement and offers some protection against the use of such weapons. There are also broad categories of federal spending, like spending on national health care, the offensive and deterrent capabilities of the DOD, and the civil emergency capabilities of agencies like FEMA, all of which have a major impact in countering terrorism and in consequence management.

### Planning and Programming the Overall Federal Effort

This latter point is particularly important because it reflects the serious real-world limits on how efficiently the federal government can hope to be in allocating resources. The initial increases in funding produced a near feeding frenzy as departments and agencies competed for major new sources of funding. As noted in a 1998 GAO report:

> More money is being spent to combat terrorism without any assurance of whether it is focused on the right programs or in the right amounts . . . [and] key interagency management functions were not clearly required or performed. For example, neither the National Security Council nor the Office of Management and Budget (OMB) was required to regularly collect, aggregate, and review funding and spending data relative to combating terrorism on a crosscutting, government-wide basis. Further, neither agency had established funding priorities for terrorism-related programs within or across agencies' individual budgets or ensured that individual agencies' stated requirements had been validated against threat and risk criteria before budget requests were submitted to the Congress. Because government-wide priorities have not been established and funding requirements have not necessarily been validated based on an analytically sound assessment of the threat and risk of terrorist attack, there is no basis to have a reasonable assurance that funds are being spent on the right programs in the right amounts and that unnecessary program and funding duplication, overlap, misallocation, fragmentation, and gaps have not occurred.[14]

The federal government has since made major efforts to improve its coordination, planning, programming, budgeting, and coordination efforts. The National Defense Authorization Act for FY1998 (PL 105–85, November 18, 1997) required OMB to establish a reporting system for executive agencies on the budgeting and expenditure of funds for programs and activities to combat terrorism. OMB is also to collect the information, and the president is to report the results to the Congress annually, including information on the programs and activities, priorities, and duplication of efforts in implementing the programs.[15] OMB made its first report in 1998, and the reports that have followed reflect a steadily improving coordination effort within and between federal agencies.

The Clinton Administration also made efforts to develop an integrated federal approach to dealing with the threat posed by state actors, their proxies, or independent extremists and terrorists. As part of this effort, the administration developed more specific guidance for federal agencies in two documents: A "Five-Year Interagency Counter-Terrorism Plan," and a "National Plan for Infrastructure Systems Protection."

The Clinton Administration tasked the NSC with leading the interagency working groups involved with terrorism, the threat from WMD, and critical infrastructure protection, and with ensuring that the policies are properly prioritized and executed in agency programs and budget. An annual review by the NSC is intended to ensure that agencies structure their activities efficiently and effectively and to develop a comprehensive and cross-cutting national program.

The Bush Administration has begun similar efforts, but there are obvious limits to what these efforts can accomplish, particularly when they must be conducted in the turmoil of the aftermath of the strikes on the World Trade Center and the Pentagon and are not linked to any clear future year plans for the activities and expenditures of each relevant department and agency. While it is easy to talk about creating a coordinated federal plan and efficiently programming resources accordingly, the sheer scale of the current federal effort, its rapid recent growth, and agency efforts to compete for new resources make such efforts largely impossible.

These problems become even more clear in the detailed analyses of agency and departmental efforts in the next chapter, and are further complicated by the fact that there is no way to relate the character and size of various federal efforts to those of state and local governments and of the private and civil sectors. For example, response capabilities for given types of attack differ so much by urban area that it becomes extremely difficult for agencies to develop a common approach that can react to these differences.

The Gilmore Commission and GAO both found that serious problems still existed in the conceptual approach to such coordination effort and that the federal government still had a long way to go in developing a well-coordinated and effective program. The GAO testified in June 2000 that:

> One of the major deficiencies in federal efforts to combat terrorism is the lack of linkage between the terrorist threat, a national strategy, and agency resources. Much of the federal efforts to combat terrorism have been based on vulnerabilities rather than an analysis of credible threats. For example, agencies have used and are still using improbable "worst case scenarios" to plan and develop programs. While there has been a major effort to develop a national strategy, to date the strategy does not include a clear desired

outcome to be achieved. Resources to combat terrorism have increased in terms of budgets and programs. These increased resources have not been clearly linked to a threat analysis and we have found cases where some agency initiatives appear at odds with the judgments of the intelligence community.

This situation also creates the potential for agencies to develop their own programs without adequate coordination, leaving the potential for gaps and/or duplication. Efforts to track and coordinate federal spending across agencies have started, but they have only begun to tackle the important task of prioritizing programs.

We have recommended, and the executive branch has agreed to, conducting threat and risk assessments to improve federal efforts to combat terrorism. Specifically, such assessments could be an important step to develop a national strategy and to target resources. The federal government cannot prepare for CBRN incidents on its own. Several improvements are also warranted in intergovernmental relations between federal, state and local governments. For example, we found that federal agencies developed some of their assistance programs without coordinating them with existing state and local emergency management structures.

In addition, the multitude of federal assistance programs has led to confusion on the part of state and local officials. One step to improve coordination and reduce confusion has been the creation of the National Domestic Preparedness Office within the Department of Justice to provide "one stop shopping" to state and local officials in need of assistance. This office has recently prepared a draft plan on how it will provide assistance.

Another intergovernmental issue requiring resolution is the matter of command and control at the site of a terrorist incident. Roles of the federal government versus the state and local governments need to be further clarified to prevent confusion. The federal government is making some progress in addressing these command and control issues through exercises. Federal exercises, in contrast to earlier years, are now practicing crisis and consequence management simultaneously and including state and local participation.

Finally, the Gilmore Panel report found many of the same problems that we have been reporting on, such as the need for (1) more rigorous analyses of the threat, (2) better management of federal programs, (3) improvements in coordination with state and local officials, and (4) a national strategy to combat terrorism. In addition, the report raises some interesting points for Congress to consider in the future as it oversees federal programs to combat terrorism.[16]

There are no prefect answers to these problems and there may not even be good ones by the standards of more conventional efforts dealing with more predictable problems. As has already been discussed in depth, the range of threats simply are not predictable enough for given agencies to attempt more than a constantly evolving and uncertain process of suboptimization. Put differently, departments and agencies must often do what they can to improve their capabilities at the margin, rather than seek to create building blocks in some kind of coherent homeland defense.

Uncoordinated and episodic individual federal efforts are almost certain to fail in giving the United States the capability it needs to defend against nuclear and highly lethal biological attacks. They may give the impression of defense and response capability, but the end result may not be able to cope with high levels of attack, which may well force all levels of government to improvise radically with little warning and under intense pressure. Marginal improvements in resources may fail to deal with response requirements or be impossible to allocate efficiently within the time windows required. This is particularly true because there currently seems to be little practical understanding of what a "worst case" or high-level attack would really do and how uncertain its effects now are.

Finally, the past coordination effort only focused on those federal programs identified as being directly designed to defend or respond to the threat state actors, their proxies, or independent extremists and terrorists pose to the U.S. homeland. This is almost certainly *not* the right way to create the most effective overall program to actually improve homeland defense. Such a program must explicitly consider the offensive, deterrent, and retaliatory capabilities of U.S. military and intelligence agencies and the role their activities overseas can play in creating an effective deterrent to foreign attacks on the United States.

### Antiterrorism, Counterterrorism, and Core Spending

OMB reports that there has been an ongoing debate on how to prioritize each group of activities, but the distinctions between such federal activities are often artificial and it is obvious from the budget presentations of different departments and agencies that the United States is still seeking to find a balance. Much of the spending in both categories, however, does not go to homeland defense per se.

Chart 6.4 shows the patterns in federal expenditures, less expenditures on CIP. OMB reports that these expenditures are broadly divided into antiterrorism spending, which includes protection against terrorism and management of the consequences of an attack, and methods to counter terrorism, which include efforts to preempt and prosecute terrorism.

### Antiterrorism

In the case of antiterrorism, the United States has spent massive sums on force protection in recent years, and this includes embassy security and the protection of U.S. troops overseas. According to an OMB estimate, spending in this area grew by 47 percent from FY1998–FY2001, largely because of the need to improve the protection of embassies. The Clinton administration requested $4.259 million for such activities in FY2001, or roughly 55 percent of all of the money dedicated to antiterrorism spending. The U.S. National Security community accounts for 51 percent of the federal funding in antiterrorism, largely because of force protection efforts.

**Chart 6.4**
**Federal Spending on Terrorism and WMD by Category, FY1998–FY2001**
**(current $US millions)**

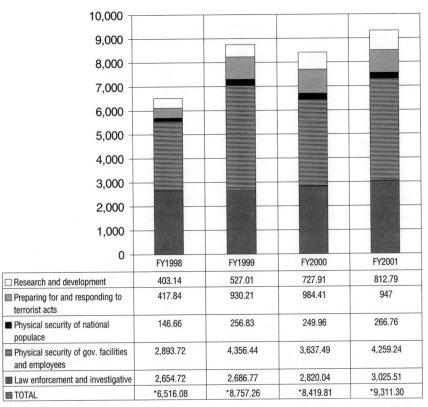

| | FY1998 | FY1999 | FY2000 | FY2001 |
|---|---|---|---|---|
| ☐ Research and development | 403.14 | 527.01 | 727.91 | 812.79 |
| ▧ Preparing for and responding to terrorist acts | 417.84 | 930.21 | 984.41 | 947 |
| ■ Physical security of national populace | 146.66 | 256.83 | 249.96 | 266.76 |
| ▤ Physical security of gov. facilities and employees | 2,893.72 | 4,356.44 | 3,637.49 | 4,259.24 |
| ■ Law enforcement and investigative | 2,654.72 | 2,686.77 | 2,820.04 | 3,025.51 |
| ▨ TOTAL | *6,516.08 | *8,757.26 | *8,419.81 | *9,311.30 |

*Source*: Adapted by Anthony H. Cordesman from the Executive Office of the President, Office Management and Budget, "Annual Report to Congress on Combating Terrorism," May 2000.

Federal antiterrorism efforts, however, have involved very little broadly based spending on the protection of the national populace and infrastructure. Funds to improve the physical security of the national populace and infrastructure facilities in the United States increased by 80 percent since FY1998, but accounted for only 3 percent of the FY2001 request for antiterrorism funding. Most of this spending went to defend largely against conventional attacks, and does not enhance protection against the use of WMD in ways that would attack from beyond a relatively limited security perimeter of selected federal facilities. According to OMB, most of this money went to one narrow area, aviation security, in the form of increased inspections and training assistance to security companies.

Law enforcement and investigation activities directed at antiterrorism include criminal investigations and intelligence assessments by a wide range of agencies. The Bureau of Alcohol, Tobacco, and Firearms funds activities related to trafficking in illegal firearms, the recovery of explosives, and tracing projects. GSA investigates building security. Justice and Treasury concentrate on terrorism-related criminal investigations, and the Federal Aviation Administration, GSA, Coast Guard, intelligence community, and Nuclear Regulatory Commission conduct defensive intelligence assessments in their areas of responsibility. The Clinton administration has proposed a $112 million rise in spending in FY2001 in this category, a 6 percent rise over FY2000. The Bush Administration's approach is not yet clear.

### Counterterrorism

Federal spending on counterterrorism has been dominated by law enforcement and investigative activities, which use over 70 percent of total spending. The effort to preempt and prosecute terrorists seeks to meet the goals set forth in PDD-62 relating to the apprehension and prosecution of terrorists. The Clinton Administration sought to increase this aspect of the FY2001 budget request by $235 million, of which $148 million would go to the Justice and Treasury Departments to detect and deter terrorist activity. An additional $87 million was to go to the national security agencies.

The effort to prepare and respond to terrorist acts have been dominated by spending by the FBI and national security agencies, which were allocated nearly 80 percent of the FY2001 request. The FBI effort included investigations and operations and training, forensics, and criminal justice activities. A substantial amount of this founding, however, went to aid foreign countries or deal with terrorist attacks on Americans overseas. For example, the administration sought to fund a crisis response or Foreign Emergency Support Team (FEST) aircraft to transport teams to terrorist incidents to assist host nations in managing or resolving a crisis. This area of federal funding also included Treasury Department activities in planning and securing protective activities.

Research and development funding for counterterrorism accounted for 80 percent of all research and development funding, and is conducted by the national security agencies, FBI, and DOE. Much of this funding went to research to prevent or respond to the use of WMD, and most recent increases in this category have been dominated by funding for such research.

### "Core Spending" on Terrorism

Much of the activity in antiterrorism and counterterrorism has focused on worldwide federal activities and has gone only to protect federal buildings and facilities. Accordingly, Charts 6.5 and 6.6 provide a different breakout of the patterns in total federal spending on counter–WMD terrorism. They eliminate spending on activities like CIP and show only the

**Chart 6.5**
**Core Federal Spending on Counterterrorism and Counter–WMD by Activity, FY1998–FY2001 (current $US millions)**

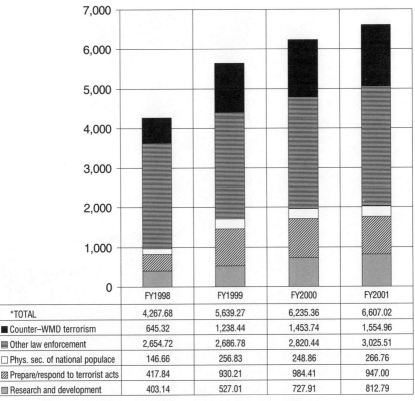

| | FY1998 | FY1999 | FY2000 | FY2001 |
|---|---|---|---|---|
| *TOTAL | 4,267.68 | 5,639.27 | 6,235.36 | 6,607.02 |
| ■ Counter–WMD terrorism | 645.32 | 1,238.44 | 1,453.74 | 1,554.96 |
| ▤ Other law enforcement | 2,654.72 | 2,686.78 | 2,820.44 | 3,025.51 |
| ☐ Phys. sec. of national populace | 146.66 | 256.83 | 248.86 | 266.76 |
| ▨ Prepare/respond to terrorist acts | 417.84 | 930.21 | 984.41 | 947.00 |
| ▦ Research and development | 403.14 | 527.01 | 727.91 | 812.79 |

*Source*: Adapted by Anthony H. Cordesman from the Executive Office of the President, Office Management and Budget, "Annual Report to Congress on Combating Terrorism," May 2000.

core federal spending on threats by state actors, their proxies, or independent extremists and terrorists. It must be stressed that such a categorization is highly artificial, but it seems to provide a somewhat more accurate picture of the trends in federal spending designed to directly deter, defend, and/or respond to direct attacks on the U.S. homeland.

The total expenditures in these charts are much lower than those shown in the previous tables and charts, and total less than half the figures shown earlier. The total expenditures for FY2001 are only 46 percent of the total for CIP, WMD, and other terrorism, and 56 percent of the total for WMD, and other terrorism. At the same time, they are still considerable. "Core spending" increased from $3,797.46 million in FY1998 to $5,237.47

**Chart 6.6**
**Distribution of Core Federal Spending on Terrorism and WMD by Activity: FY2001**
**(current $US millions)**

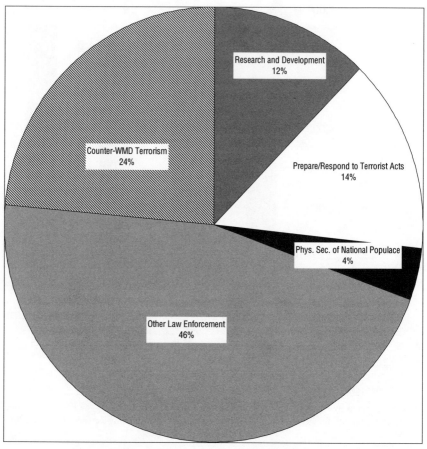

*Source*: Adapted by Anthony H. Cordesman from Executive Office of the President, Office Management and Budget, "Annual Report to Congress on Combating Terrorism," May 2000.

million in FY2001, or by 38 percent. This involved a 141 percent increase in spending to deal with WMD, and a more than 36 percent increase in related research and development activity. This also involved a 12 percent increase in other law enforcement and investigation activities, a 19 percent increase in preparations and response to terrorist acts—almost all of which has gone to protection against attacks using weapons of mass destruction—and a more than 80 percent increase in efforts to improve the physical security of the populace.

**Chart 6.7**
**Federal Spending on WMD Preparedness by Activity, FY1998–FY2001**
**(current $US millions)**

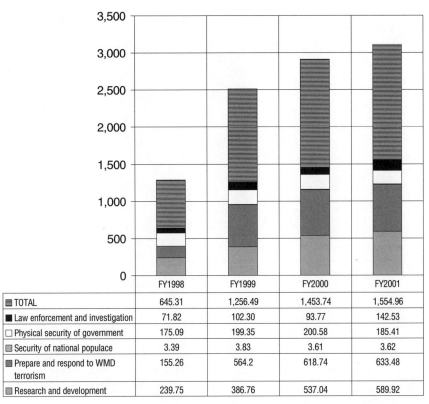

| | FY1998 | FY1999 | FY2000 | FY2001 |
|---|---|---|---|---|
| ▤ TOTAL | 645.31 | 1,256.49 | 1,453.74 | 1,554.96 |
| ■ Law enforcement and investigation | 71.82 | 102.30 | 93.77 | 142.53 |
| ☐ Physical security of government | 175.09 | 199.35 | 200.58 | 185.41 |
| ▨ Security of national populace | 3.39 | 3.83 | 3.61 | 3.62 |
| ■ Prepare and respond to WMD terrorism | 155.26 | 564.2 | 618.74 | 633.48 |
| ▨ Research and development | 239.75 | 386.76 | 537.04 | 589.92 |

*Source*: Adapted by Anthony H. Cordesman from the Executive Office of the President, Office Management and Budget, "Annual Report to Congress on Combating Terrorism," May 2000.

### Spending on Preparedness for Attacks Using Weapons of Mass Destruction

Only a relatively small number of federal programs have been dedicated specifically to dealing with the threat that state actors, their proxies, or independent extremists and terrorists pose to the U.S. homeland, and these programs often apply at least indirectly to the protection of U.S. forces overseas and U.S. friends and allies. The size and nature of these programs are shown in Charts 6.7 and 6.8. Total federal expenditures grew from $645.31 million in FY1998 to a request for $1,554.96 in FY2001, or by a factor of 2.4. In the process, they grew from 8 percent of total federal combating terrorism and CIP spending in FY1998 to 14 percent in FY2001.

**Chart 6.8**
**Federal Spending on WMD by Agency, FY1998–FY2001 (current $US millions)**

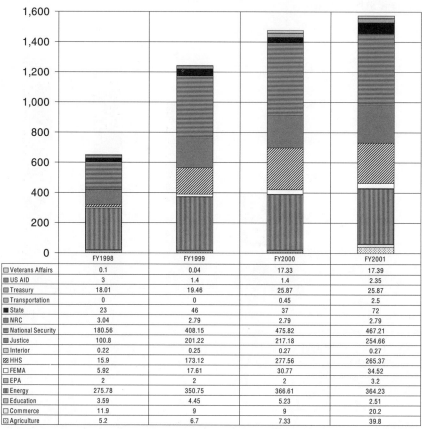

| | FY1998 | FY1999 | FY2000 | FY2001 |
|---|---|---|---|---|
| Veterans Affairs | 0.1 | 0.04 | 17.33 | 17.39 |
| US AID | 3 | 1.4 | 1.4 | 2.35 |
| Treasury | 18.01 | 19.46 | 25.87 | 25.87 |
| Transportation | 0 | 0 | 0.45 | 2.5 |
| State | 23 | 46 | 37 | 72 |
| NRC | 3.04 | 2.79 | 2.79 | 2.79 |
| National Security | 180.56 | 408.15 | 475.82 | 467.21 |
| Justice | 100.8 | 201.22 | 217.18 | 254.66 |
| Interior | 0.22 | 0.25 | 0.27 | 0.27 |
| HHS | 15.9 | 173.12 | 277.56 | 265.37 |
| FEMA | 5.92 | 17.61 | 30.77 | 34.52 |
| EPA | 2 | 2 | 2 | 3.2 |
| Energy | 275.78 | 350.75 | 366.61 | 364.23 |
| Education | 3.59 | 4.45 | 5.23 | 2.51 |
| Commerce | 11.9 | 9 | 9 | 20.2 |
| Agriculture | 5.2 | 6.7 | 7.33 | 39.8 |

*Source*: Adapted by Anthony H. Cordesman from the Executive Office of the President, Office Management and Budget, "Annual Report to Congress on Combating Terrorism," May 2000.

As Chart 6.8 shows, most of the money has been allocated to the DOD and intelligence community (National Security) and DOE—both of which have special expertise in these areas. Their combined budgets rose from a total of $456 million in FY1998 to $831 million in FY2001. HHS had a massive increase in such funding—$16 million in FY1998 to $265 million in FY2001—because of the threat of biological warfare. The same was true for the USDA, which has gone from $5 million to $40 million. The State Department saw its budget increase from $23 million to $72 million.

The budget of the DOJ has more than doubled from $100 million in FY1998 to $254 million in FY2001. Treasury increased from $18 million to $26 million, FEMA from $6 million to $35 million, and the Department of Commerce (DOC) from $12 to $20 million.

WMD programs seek to deter incidents involving the use of massive conventional bombs and CBRN weapons and manage the consequences if they are used. Most of this spending goes to antiterrorism efforts, and roughly 90 percent has been devoted to defensive efforts. This spending responds to PPD-62 and the need to enhance domestic preparedness. The FBI is the lead agency for crisis management where there is a credible threat of a WMD incident. FEMA is the lead agency for consequence management, when the incident or threat has subsided and the key priority is to restore order and deliver emergency assistance. Other agencies contribute according to their mission. DOE deals with radiological issues, HHS with medical impacts, and so on. The DOD provides support and has established a joint task force for support to civil authorities and to coordinate federal, state, and local authorities as part of its new Joint Forces Command.

These expenditures also have had to cover foreign incidents. The State Department has responsibility for consequence management and for initial U.S. coordination of such action through FEST. The DOD plays a major role in domestic- and foreign-related activities because of its long experience with WMD.

### WMD Antiterrorism Activities

The main activity in WMD antiterrorism is preparing for and responding to WMD terrorism. Spending increased from $89 million in FY1998 to $566 million in FY2000, after PDD-62 created a new requirement for a concerted effort to improve domestic preparedness. It also assigned DOJ, FEMA, HHS, and DOD responsibility as lead agencies for WMD crisis management, consequence management, medical response, and training for state and local authorities, and established a new interagency working group to deal with these issues. Four major initiatives are underway as part of this effort:

- Federal assistance to state and local authorities: The federal government provides training, equipment, and planning and technical expertise. Funding is planned to increase by 15 percent in FY2001 and shift emphasis from training to equipment grants as the first groups of the 120 largest cities in the United States complete training and begin to procure specialized equipment.

- Medical defense: Activity includes public health surveillance of people and the nation's food supply, development of a stockpile of vaccines and therapeutics, and other planning for the medical aspects of a WMD incident. An 8 percent increase in funding is planned for public health infrastructure for FY2001, and includes a more active program for epidemiological capacity to improve detection and the reporting of outbreaks and for food supply protection. The role of the USDA is enhanced to strengthen its ability to identify and protect against terrorist attacks aimed at crops or livestock.

- Federal special response: A large-scale WMD incident would overwhelm the response capabilities of state and local authorities. Federal response units will be needed from a variety of agencies, each with a specific expertise and mission. The DOE provides nuclear response teams. The EPA provides HAZMAT management teams. HHS provides medical response teams. The FBI provides forensic response teams. And the DOD provides explosive ordnance disposal teams. Funding doubled between FY1998 and FY1999, but then dropped slightly in FY2000 after the start-up cost of the DOD WMD CSTs were paid for.

- Federal contingency planning and exercises: These prepare federal agencies and departments to respond to terrorist incidents. There has only been modest program growth since FY1999.

The United States also had three smaller mission areas: physical security of government, physical security of the national populace, and law enforcement and investigation. The FY2001 request for all three programs was $259 million. Much of this spending goes to protecting government facilities with WMD-related materials.

### WMD Counterterrorism

The majority of WMD counterterrorism resources fall into two main categories within the national security community. The first is law enforcement and investigation. It totaled $73 million in FY2001, and spending increased by 40 percent since FY1998. The second is preparing for and responding to terrorist acts, which totaled $67 million in FY2001. Some of this activity is classified, but it also includes DOC implementation activities for the CWC, which accounts for most of the increase over FY2001. The other funding in this area is for participation in joint task forces and planning WMD counterterrorism activities.

### Research and Development for Defense against WMD

At this point in time, most federal spending on WMD concentrates on research and development. The Clinton administration determined that this was the highest priority area for spending. It made a 50 percent increase ($129 million) in FY1999, and a 30 percent increase ($111 million) in FY2001. This spending has had strong congressional support, and have been focused on dealing with three main scientific and technological challenges:

- Preventing or forestalling the release of a WMD payload
- Detecting and responding to a threatened or actual release
- Managing the health, environmental, and law enforcement consequences of such an incident

What is clear from this analysis is that progress has been made, but the U.S. effort up until September 2001 fell far short of a major national commitment. Effective efforts also require an exceptional degree of interagency coordination, which has been the responsibility of the White House Office of Science and Technology Policy. This agency chairs an interagency working group to determine vulnerabilities and shortfalls in the U.S. effort to mitigate or respond to WMD, determine research and development objectives, coordinate agency research and development activities, and identify new requirements. The Clinton administration has sought to enhance the links between researchers and customers for their research and development products, such as the agencies responsible for meeting first responder and technical needs. How the Bush Administration will change this situation is unclear, but it is clear it must do so if it is to be effective.

## NOTES

1. Paul Wilkinson in "Trends in International Terrorism and the American Response," *Terrorism and International Order*, The Royal Institute of International Affairs, 1986, pp. 49–50.

2. U.S. General Accounting Office, GAO Report to Congressional Requesters, "Combating Terrorism, Federal Agencies' Efforts to Implement National Policy and Strategy," GAO/T-NSIAD-98-164, April 23, 1998, 3.

3. U.S. General Accounting Office, "Combating Terrorism: Issues in Managing Counterterrorist Programs," GAO/T-NSIAD-00-145," April 6, 2000, <http://www.gao.gov/new.items/ns00145t.pdf>.

4. "Combating Terrorism," GAO/T-NSIAD-98-164, April 23, 1998, 4.

5. Cragin, Charles, "Defense Leaders Commentary: The Facts on WMD Civil Support Teams," March 31, 2000, <http://www.defenselink.mil/news/Mar2000/n0331200_20003311.html>.

6. U.S. General Accounting Office, GAO Report to Congressional Requesters, "Combating Terrorism, Federal Agencies' Efforts to Implement National Policy and Strategy," GAO/NSIAD-97-254, September 1997.

7. "Combating Terrorism" GAO/NSIAD-97-254, 6.

8. "Combating Terrorism," GAO/T-NSIAD-00-145, 5.

9. Center for Nonproliferation Studies, Monterey Institute of International Studies, "Agency Structures for Terrorism Response," <http://www.cns.miis.edu/research/cbw/response.htm>.

10. White House, Office of the Press Secretary for Immediate Release, "Funding for Domestic Preparedness and Critical Infrastructure Protection," Fact Sheet, January 22, 1999.

11. Executive Office of the President, Office of Budget and Management, "Annual Report to Congress on Combating Terrorism," May 2000.

12. "Combating Terrorism," GAO/T-NSIAD-00-145.

13. White House, Office of the Press Secretary, "Announcement on Counterterrorism Funding Request," May 17, 2000, http://www.state.gov/www/global/terrorism/000517_pres_funding.html.

14. "Combating Terrorism," GAO/T-NSIAD-98-164, 1998.

15. See U.S. General Accounting Office, "Combating Terrorism: Spending on Government-wide Programs Requires Better Management and Coordination," GAO/NSIAD-98-39, December 1, 1997; and U.S. General Accounting Office, "Combating Terrorism: Threat and Risk Assessments Can Help Prioritize and Target Program Investments," GAO/NSIAD-98-74, April 9, 1998.

16. See Report of the Advisory Panel to Assess Domestic Response Capabilities for Terrorism Involving Weapons of Mass Destruction (known as the Gilmore Panel, as its chairman is James S. Gilmore III); and Statement of Norman J. Rabkin, Director National Security Preparedness Issues, National Security and International Affairs Division, before the Subcommittee on Oversight, Investigations, and Emergency Management, Committee on Transportation and Infrastructure, House of Representatives, U.S. General Accounting Office, "Combating Terrorism: Issues in Managing Counterterrorist Programs," GAO/T-NSIAD-00-145," April 6, 2000.

*Chapter 7*

# Federal Efforts by Department and Agency

Any outside effort to characterize federal efforts by department and agency faces formidable problems, particularly at a time when the Bush Administration is reexamining every aspect of the Clinton Administration and is making changes of its own in reaction to the events of September 2001. Federal departments and agencies generally do a poor job in providing unclassified reporting on any aspect of their counterterrorism programs. Many fail to provide the details of their activities. Of those who do report, many discuss the threat but only provide a vague description of their actual programs and no detailed description of the money being spent. No agency provides a meaningful description of its future program, future costs, milestones, or measures of effectiveness. The level of cooperation with state and local agencies is rarely described, and when it is, the discussion tends to be discussed in anecdotal terms on terms of meaningless measures of effort, like numbers of undefined exercises, training sessions, and so on.

Research and development programs receive little detailed description. The description that is provided often concentrates on the threat being dealt with, and agencies provide little program detail. There is no evidence that any department or agency has provided a technology net assessment to examine whether its programs will provide defensive capabilities that outpace advances in offensive capability. There is virtually no discussion of the risk posed by countermeasures or the cost to defeat current and planned programs. There is no discussion of the outyear costs of research and development activity or of estimated deployment schedules, measures of effectiveness, and life cycle costs. Almost without exception, there is no way to be certain to what degree which given programs in given departments or agencies are actually focused on CBRN and other counterterrorism activities, or have simply recast ongoing or desired programs to compete for such funds.

The OMB reports in response to the National Defense Authorization Act do, however, provide an overview of department and agency activity directly relating to the defense and response against terrorism and some insight into spending by department and agency. They do not cut across individual agency efforts where, for example, it is possible to determine whether there is anything approaching a coherent program to deal with biological warfare. Yet, they do provide considerable detail on key activities within each agency.

The OMB data on spending by department and agency are shown in Table 7.1. It is important to note four things about these data: First, they do not include expenditures on CIP, although some of these expenditures deal with the protection of physical infrastructure, rather than information systems, and would help homeland defense in the event of a CBRN attack. Second, there is no way to determine how much spending deals with domestic threats per se versus threats to U.S. interests abroad. Third, the data on "WMD Preparedness" programs is included in the totals for the programs to combat terrorism and is not additive to the figures shown for "Combating Terrorism." Fourth, they exclude programs relating to deterrence and offensive capabilities against foreign threats and relevant arms control activities, a significant amount of DOD activity dealing with asymmetric warfare, and a significant amount of data on DOD, State Department, and DOE counterproliferation activity that has a major impact on homeland defense. As has been discussed in Chapter 6, it is often difficult or impossible to really follow the money.

## DEPARTMENT OF AGRICULTURE

Even though accurate figures and program descriptions are not available, it is clear that a wide range of different federal departments and agencies are working on this aspect of homeland defense. For example, the USDA plays a critical role in preparing for biological attacks on U.S. agriculture, and in dealing with the impact of fallout and secondary effects from a nuclear attack. It is requested $10 million for FY2001 for new research and development into techniques to rapidly identify pathogens and toxins and to discover the geographic origin of the pathogens.[1]

## NATIONAL ANIMAL HEALTH EMERGENCY PROGRAM

Table 7.1 shows that the USDA's FY2001 request also included $5.9 million for Animal Plant Health Inspection Service's (APHIS) National

Animal Health Emergency Program. The program is designed for APHIS to train personnel to respond to animal disease outbreaks that threaten the agriculture economy. APHIS develops training for WMD terrorism, including decontamination of chemical and biological agents. Funding has also gone toward an awareness campaign to recognize foreign animal diseases, to develop an animal pathogen genetic library, to develop veterinary investigative tools, to update bioterrorism response plans, and to the National Emergency Management Operations Center. The National Emergency Management Operations Center provides leadership for national plant and animal health emergencies.[2]

The FY2000 OMB counterterrorism funding report on USDA counterterrorism spending shows a large increase in the funds requested for FY2001 compared to previous appropriations. The $41.28 million requested was 235 percent above FY2000 levels and 96 percent of the requested funds went to WMD preparedness.[3] However, Department of Agriculture officials privately state that these funding levels remain hopelessly inadequate.

## CENTRAL INTELLIGENCE AGENCY

Intelligence plays a critical role in asymmetric warfare and counterterrorism. As Brent Scowcroft, a former national security adviser under Presidents Gerald R. Ford and George Bush, has said,

> Prevention, not defense, should be at the heart of any terrorism strategy, and its primary instrument is intelligence operations. If we can penetrate terrorist operations and anticipate their moves, we can at least keep them off balance and frequently prevent terrorist acts. In the end, an offensive strategy designed to prevent and disrupt terrorist activities by funding our intelligence agencies rather than construction contractors is the surest way to provide security for all American citizens abroad—and in the United States as well.[4]

Experts have warned for years that the CIA and other elements of the Intelligence community lack the priorities and resources needed for this mission. They have warned that agencies do not have adequate "humint" or human intelligence collection resources and that law and regulation have severely limited the ability to recruit sources that are not "politically correct." They have warned that analytic capabilities are underfunded and do not have money for area travel, and that language training and expertise is inadequate. They have warned that "operations" capabilities to operate covertly and strike at hostile targets is grossly inadequate and sometimes nearly paralyzed by law, executive orders, and regulation.

It is uncertain whether any level of funding activity, and better mission priorities, could have prevented the events in September 2001. Any "intelligence failure" does, however, begin with a major resource failure, which took place in spite of all the warnings listed previously. Unfortunately,

**Table 7.1**
**OMB Estimate of Federal Spending on Terrorism by Agency (as of June 2000) (Government spending for combating terrorism, WMD, and CIP in current $U.S. billions)**

| | | | | |
|---|---|---|---|---|
| **Department of Agriculture** | | | | |
| *Combating Terrorism* | 10.20 | 11.70 | 12.33 | 41.28 |
| Physical security of government facilities and employees | 5.00 | 5.00 | 5.00 | 1.48 |
| Preparing for and responding to terrorist acts | 0.00 | 0.00 | 0.63 | 10.60 |
| Research and development | 5.20 | 6.70 | 6.70 | 29.20 |
| *WMD Preparedness* | 5.20 | 6.70 | 7.33 | 39.80 |
| Preparing for and responding to WMD terrorism | 0.00 | 0.00 | 0.63 | 10.60 |
| Federal planning and exercises | 0.00 | 0.00 | 0.00 | 0.26 |
| Other planning and assistance to state/local | 0.00 | 0.00 | 0.00 | 4.48 |
| Public health infrastructure/surveillance | 0.00 | 0.00 | 0.63 | 5.87 |
| Research and development | 5.20 | 6.70 | 6.70 | 29.20 |
| Basic research, including gene sequencing | 0.00 | 0.00 | 0.00 | 10.00 |
| Other | 5.20 | 6.70 | 6.70 | 19.20 |
| *OMB highlighted programs WMD/CIP | | | | |
| Research and development | - | - | - | 10.00 |
| Laboratory infrastructure improvements | - | - | - | 19.00 |
| National Animal Health Emergency Program | - | - | - | 5.90 |
| **Department of Commerce** | | | | |
| *Combating Terrorism* | 29.54 | 31.85 | 22.40 | 33.60 |
| Law enforcement and investigative activities | 5.80 | 3.90 | 3.90 | 15.10 |
| Physical security of government facilities and employees | 11.64 | 17.45 | 8.00 | 8.00 |
| Research and development | 12.10 | 10.50 | 10.50 | 10.50 |

| | | | | |
|---|---|---|---|---|
| *WMD Preparedness* | 20.20 | 9.00 | 9.00 | 11.90 |
| Law enforcement and investigative activities | 11.20 | 0.00 | 0.00 | 1.90 |
| Research and development | 9.00 | 9.00 | 9.00 | 10.00 |
| Basic research, including gene sequencing | 9.00 | 9.00 | 9.00 | 10.00 |
| *OMB highlighted programs | | | | |
| WMD programs | | | | |
| Bureau of Export Administration | 11.20 | - | - | - |
| **Department of Energy** | | | | |
| *Combating Terrorism* | 663.53 | 647.61 | 611.05 | 498.98 |
| Law enforcement and investigative activities | 0.94 | 0.94 | 0.94 | 0.94 |
| Physical security of government facilities and employees | 471.05 | 468.22 | 449.85 | 389.00 |
| Preparing for and responding to terrorist acts | 97.74 | 94.35 | 84.80 | 84.38 |
| Research and development | 93.80 | 84.10 | 75.46 | 24.66 |
| *WMD Preparedness* | 364.23 | 366.31 | 350.75 | 275.78 |
| Physical security of government | 174.45 | 189.62 | 192.25 | 186.50 |
| Preparing for and responding to WMD terrorism | 97.74 | 94.35 | 84.80 | 84.38 |
| Equipment for first responders | 9.55 | 8.00 | 1.40 | 2.10 |
| Federal planning/exercises | 3.40 | 3.05 | 3.05 | 2.58 |
| First responder training and exercises | 4.08 | 3.85 | 0.20 | 0.20 |
| Other | 1.45 | 1.45 | 1.16 | 0.50 |
| Special Response Units | 79.31 | 78.00 | 79.00 | 79.00 |
| Research and development | 92.04 | 82.34 | 73.70 | 22.90 |
| Basic Research, including gene sequencing | 14.00 | 11.00 | 4.80 | 3.00 |
| Detection/diagnostics | 22.50 | 21.00 | 16.50 | 14.50 |
| Modeling, simulation, and systems analyses | 6.74 | 6.74 | 2.00 | 3.60 |
| Other | 45.60 | 40.40 | 47.60 | 0.00 |
| Personal/environment decontamination | 3.20 | 3.20 | 2.80 | 1.80 |

continued

Table 7.1 (continued)

|  |  |  |  |  |
|---|---|---|---|---|
| *OMB Highlighted Programs |  |  |  |  |
| WMD programs |  |  |  |  |
| Nuclear Emergency Search Team | 44.00 | - | - | - |
| Technology development and applications | 25.00 | - | - | - |
| Radiological Assistance Program | 4.00 | - | - | - |
| Research and eevelopment | 92.00 | - | - | - |
| Nuclear safeguards, security, and emergency operations | N/A | 25.00 | - | - |
| **Environmental Protection Agency** |  |  |  |  |
| *Combating Terrorism* | 3.20 | 2.00 | 2.00 | 2.00 |
| Preparing for and responding to terrorist acts | 3.20 | 2.00 | 2.00 | 2.00 |
| *WMD Preparedness* | 3.20 | 2.00 | 2.00 | 2.00 |
| Preparing for and responding to WMD terrorism | 3.20 | 2.00 | 2.00 | 2.00 |
| Special response units | 3.20 | 2.00 | 2.00 | 2.00 |
| *OMB highlighted programs |  |  |  |  |
| WMD programs |  |  |  |  |
| WMD Coordinator, Equipment and Training | 3.20 | - | - | - |
| **Federal Emergency Management Agency** |  |  |  |  |
| *Combating Terrorism* | 34.52 | 30.77 | 17.61 | 5.92 |
| Physical security of government facilities and employees | 2.13 | 2.13 | 1.96 | 1.46 |
| Preparing for and responding to terrorist acts | 32.39 | 28.64 | 15.64 | 4.45 |
| *WMD Preparedness* | 34.52 | 30.77 | 17.61 | 5.92 |
| Physical security of government | 2.13 | 2.13 | 1.96 | 1.46 |
| Preparing for and responding to WMD terrorism | 32.39 | 28.64 | 15.64 | 4.45 |
| Federal planning/exercises | 4.95 | 4.50 | 3.02 | 0.92 |
| First responder training and exercises | 13.96 | 14.56 | 8.31 | 2.76 |
| Other | 0.08 | 0.08 | 0.00 | 0.00 |

| | | | | |
|---|---|---|---|---|
| Other planning and assistance to state/locals | 9.50 | 9.50 | 4.31 | 0.76 |
| Special response units | 3.90 | 0.00 | 0.00 | 0.00 |
| *OMB highlighted programs | | | | |
| WMD programs | | | | |
| Assistance to state and local authorities | 24.00 | - | - | - |
| Urban Search and Rescue Teams | 4.00 | - | - | - |
| **General Services Administration** | | | | |
| *Combating Terrorism* | 116.96 | 92.80 | 133.50 | 89.60 |
| Law enforcement and investigative activities | 15.39 | 15.10 | 15.30 | 13.90 |
| Physical security of government facilities and employees | 99.41 | 74.90 | 115.30 | 72.90 |
| Preparing for and responding to terrorist acts | 2.16 | 2.80 | 2.90 | 2.80 |
| **Department of Health and Human Services** | | | | |
| *Combating Terrorism* | 265.37 | 277.56 | 173.12 | 15.90 |
| Preparing for and responding to terrorist acts | 173.63 | 165.60 | 138.25 | 0.00 |
| Research and development | 91.74 | 111.96 | 34.87 | 15.90 |
| *WMD Preparedness* | 265.37 | 277.56 | 173.12 | 15.90 |
| Preparing for and responding to WMD terrorism | 173.63 | 165.60 | 138.25 | 0.00 |
| Medical responder training exercises | 2.00 | 1.00 | 3.00 | 0.00 |
| Other | 10.60 | 3.10 | 2.00 | 0.00 |
| Other planning and assistance to state/locals | 17.43 | 16.50 | 16.25 | 0.00 |
| Public health infrastructure/surveillance | 85.50 | 88.00 | 62.00 | 0.00 |
| Special response units | 6.10 | 5.00 | 4.00 | 0.00 |
| Stockpile of vaccines and therapeutics | 52.00 | 52.00 | 51.00 | 0.00 |
| Research and developments | 91.74 | 111.96 | 34.87 | 15.90 |
| Basic research, including gene sequencing | 21.76 | 21.76 | 17.23 | 13.00 |
| Detection/diagnostics | 8.28 | 5.68 | 5.68 | 0.00 |
| Other | 0.00 | 31.72 | 1.85 | 0.00 |

continued

**Table 7.1 (continued)**

| | | | | |
|---|---|---|---|---|
| Personal/collective protection | 0.00 | 0.00 | 0.00 | 1.20 |
| Therapeutics/treatments | 0.00 | 3.98 | 4.35 | 4.35 |
| Vaccines | 2.90 | 6.13 | 48.45 | 56.15 |
| *OMB highlighted programs | | | | |
| WMD programs | | | | |
| Strengthening the public health surveillance system for WMD | – | – | – | 87.00 |
| National Pharmaceutical Stockpile Program | – | – | – | 52.00 |
| Metropolitan Medical Response Systems and WMD preparedness | – | – | – | 30.00 |
| Research and development | – | – | – | 92.00 |
| **Holocaust Memorial Museum** | | | | |
| *Combating Terrorism* | 0.00 | 2.00 | 0.00 | 0.00 |
| Physical security of government facilities and employees | 0.00 | 2.00 | 0.00 | 0.00 |
| **Department of the Interior** | | | | |
| *Combating Terrorism* | 12.43 | 15.86 | 12.58 | 11.76 |
| Law enforcement and investigative activities | 10.92 | 14.01 | 9.66 | 9.66 |
| Physical security of government facilities and employees | 0.17 | 0.20 | 0.22 | 0.22 |
| Preparing for and responding to terrorist acts | 10.71 | 13.77 | 9.40 | 9.40 |
| WMD Preparedness | 0.05 | 0.05 | 0.05 | 0.05 |
| Law enforcement and investigative activities | 0.22 | 0.25 | 0.27 | 0.27 |
| Physical security of government facilities and employees | 0.17 | 0.20 | 0.22 | 0.22 |
| Preparing for and responding to WMD terrorism | 0.05 | 0.05 | 0.05 | 0.05 |
| Other | 0.05 | 0.05 | 0.05 | 0.05 |
| **Judiciary** | | | | |
| *Combating Terrorism* | 7.00 | 8.00 | 10.60 | 11.20 |
| Physical security of government facilities and employees | 7.00 | 8.00 | 10.60 | 11.20 |

**Department of Justice**

| | | | | |
|---|---|---|---|---|
| *Combating Terrorism* | 647.09 | 793.99 | 782.02 | 949.25 |
| Law enforcement and investigative activities | 346.90 | 328.91 | 346.24 | 409.53 |
| Physical security of government facilities and employees | 84.29 | 105.08 | 117.12 | 171.22 |
| Physical security of national populace | 29.00 | 41.76 | 31.67 | 30.79 |
| Preparing for and responding to terrorist acts | 159.90 | 301.37 | 250.12 | 307.26 |
| Research and development | 27.00 | 16.87 | 36.88 | 30.45 |
| *WMD Preparedness* | 100.80 | 201.22 | 217.18 | 254.66 |
| Law enforcement and investigative activities | 43.00 | 39.74 | 39.74 | 43.24 |
| Physical security of national populace | 1.00 | 1.44 | 1.22 | 1.23 |
| Preparing for and responding to WMD terrorism | 41.80 | 147.35 | 143.54 | 189.25 |
| Equipment for first responders | 12.00 | 95.00 | 85.00 | 88.00 |
| First responder training and exercises | 10.00 | 26.47 | 38.45 | 73.45 |
| Other | 1.80 | 2.00 | 2.20 | 2.80 |
| Other planning and assistance to state/locals | 18.00 | 23.88 | 17.89 | 25.00 |
| Research and development | 15.00 | 12.69 | 32.69 | 20.94 |
| Detection/diagnostics | 3.00 | 2.69 | 2.69 | 3.94 |
| Personal/collective protection | 12.00 | 10.00 | 30.00 | 17.00 |
| *OMB highlighted programs | | | | |
| WMD programs | | | | |
| Equipment grants for first responders | – | – | – | 78.00 |
| Domestic preparedness training | – | – | – | 31.00 |
| Hazardous Devices School | – | – | – | 4.60 |
| Center for Domestic Preparedness at Fort McClellan | – | – | – | 15.00 |
| Technology and standards development | – | – | – | 17.00 |

**National Security**

| | | | | |
|---|---|---|---|---|
| *Combating Terrorism* | 4,496.12 | 4,682.51 | 5,117.17 | 5,124.06 |
| Law enforcement and investigative activities | 2,042.33 | 2,067.79 | 2,213.24 | 2,213.52 |
| Physical security of government facilities and employees | 2,075.47 | 2,036.47 | 2,122.75 | 2,173.85 |

continued

283

Table 7.1 (continued)

| | | | | |
|---|---|---|---|---|
| Physical security of national populace | 0.15 | 0.04 | 0.15 | 0.15 |
| Preparing for and responding to terrorist acts | 104.20 | 256.18 | 358.58 | 233.84 |
| Research and development | 270.98 | 322.03 | 422.45 | 502.71 |
| *WMD Preparedness* | 180.56 | 408.15 | 475.81 | 467.21 |
| Law enforcement and investigative activities | 7.10 | 20.96 | 20.41 | 19.47 |
| Preparing for and responding to WMD terrorism | 2.71 | 156.39 | 161.50 | 100.74 |
| First responder training and exercises | 0.05 | 49.90 | 32.10 | 10.20 |
| Other planning and assistance to state/locals | 0.00 | 15.60 | 8.50 | 10.30 |
| Special response units | 2.66 | 90.89 | 120.90 | 80.24 |
| Research and development | 170.75 | 230.80 | 293.90 | 347.00 |
| Basic research, including gene sequencing | 44.50 | 0.00 | 6.25 | 37.50 |
| Detection/diagnostics | 0.25 | 34.10 | 48.45 | 62.30 |
| Modeling, simulation, and systems analyses | 0.00 | 8.60 | 10.00 | 10.00 |
| Other | 126.00 | 140.00 | 161.50 | 141.00 |
| Personal/collective protection | 0.00 | 0.00 | 0.00 | 10.00 |
| Personal/environmental decontamination | 0.00 | 6.50 | 17.10 | 21.00 |
| Therapeutics/treatments | 0.00 | 12.00 | 16.50 | 22.20 |
| Vaccines | 0.00 | 29.60 | 34.10 | 43.00 |
| *OMB highlighted programs | | | | |
| WMD programs | | | | |
| Terrorism Consequence Management Response Units | - | - | - | 80.00 |
| Coordination of civil support | - | - | - | 5.00 |
| Research and development | - | - | - | 340.00 |
| Airlift for Counterterrorism Response | - | - | 73.00 | N/A |

## Nuclear Regulatory Commission

| | | | | |
|---|---|---|---|---|
| *Combating Terrorism* | 3.48 | 3.21 | 3.21 | 3.24 |
| Law enforcement and investigative activities | 0.65 | 0.40 | 0.40 | 0.40 |
| Physical security of government facilities and employees | 0.42 | 0.40 | 0.40 | 0.40 |
| Physical security of national populace | 2.39 | 2.39 | 2.39 | 2.39 |
| Preparing for and responding to terrorist acts | 0.02 | 0.02 | 0.02 | 0.05 |
| *WMD Preparedness* | 3.04 | 2.79 | 2.79 | 2.79 |
| Law enforcement and investigative activities | 0.65 | 0.40 | 0.40 | 0.40 |
| Physical security of national populace | 2.39 | 2.39 | 2.39 | 2.39 |

## Smithsonian

| | | | | |
|---|---|---|---|---|
| *Combating Terrorism* | 0.00 | 0.00 | 0.00 | 0.05 |
| Physical security of government facilities and employees | 0.00 | 0.00 | 0.00 | 0.05 |

## Department of State

| | | | | |
|---|---|---|---|---|
| *Combating Terrorism* | 186.00 | 1,579.00 | 791.00 | 1,312.00 |
| Law enforcement and investigative activities | 27.00 | 53.00 | 46.00 | 80.00 |
| Physical security of government facilities and employees | 151.00 | 1,512.00 | 727.00 | 1,224.00 |
| Preparing for and responding to terrorist acts | 6.00 | 6.00 | 6.00 | 6.00 |
| Research and development | 2.00 | 8.00 | 2.00 | 2.00 |
| *WMD Preparedness* | 23.00 | 46.00 | 37.00 | 72.00 |
| Law enforcement and investigative activities | 19.00 | 41.00 | 33.00 | 68.00 |
| Preparing for and responding to WMD terrorism | 4.00 | 4.00 | 4.00 | 4.00 |
| Special response units | 4.00 | 4.00 | 4.00 | 4.00 |
| Research and development | 0.00 | 1.00 | 0.00 | 0.00 |
| Other | 0.00 | 1.00 | 0.00 | 0.00 |
| *OMB highlighted programs | | | | |
| WMD programs | | | | |
| Embassy security | - | - | - | 1,200.00 |
| Anti-Terrorism Assistance Program | - | - | - | 64.00 |
| Terrorism Interdiction Program | - | - | - | 4.00 |

continued

Table 7.1 (continued)

| | | | | |
|---|---|---|---|---|
| **Department of Transportation** | | | | |
| *Combating Terrorism* | 169.30 | 270.78 | 277.21 | 298.15 |
| Law enforcement and investigative activities | 3.90 | 4.21 | 4.48 | 4.68 |
| Physical security of government facilities and employees | 17.86 | 18.16 | 19.54 | 20.94 |
| Physical security of national populace | 99.78 | 193.58 | 199.08 | 216.50 |
| Preparing for and responding to terrorist acts | 3.16 | 3.04 | 3.52 | 6.03 |
| Research and development | 44.60 | 51.79 | 50.60 | 49.65 |
| *WMD Preparedness* | 0.00 | 0.00 | 0.45 | 2.50 |
| Preparing for and responding to WMD terrorism | 0.00 | 0.00 | 0.00 | 2.50 |
| Equipment for first responders | 0.00 | 0.00 | 0.00 | 2.50 |
| Research and development | 0.00 | 0.00 | 0.45 | 0.00 |
| Detection/diagnostics | 0.00 | 0.00 | 0.45 | 0.00 |
| *OMB highlighted programs WMD/CIP | | | | |
| National airspace system modernization | – | – | – | 49.90 |
| Aviation security | – | – | – | 312.00 |
| Protection of critical Coast Guard systems | – | – | – | 3.30 |
| Transportation Infrastructure Assurance Research and Development | – | – | – | 3.40 |
| Information sharing and threat dissemination | – | – | – | 1.00 |
| Global Positioning System protection | – | – | – | 0.15 |
| **Department of Treasury** | | | | |
| *Combating Terrorism* | 341.36 | 368.01 | 348.00 | 440.21 |
| Law enforcement and investigative activities | 213.13 | 212.13 | 189.53 | 285.73 |
| Physical security of government facilities and employees | 64.30 | 67.51 | 68.46 | 63.46 |
| Physical security of national populace | 15.34 | 19.06 | 16.58 | 16.58 |
| Preparing for and responding to terrorist acts | 47.89 | 68.52 | 70.70 | 71.70 |
| Research and development | 0.70 | 0.79 | 2.73 | 2.74 |

| | | | | |
|---|---|---|---|---|
| *WMD Preparedness* | 18.01 | 19.46 | 25.87 | 25.87 |
| Physical security of government facilities and employees | 5.14 | 5.14 | 8.84 | 8.84 |
| Preparing for and responding to WMD terrorism | 12.88 | 14.32 | 17.03 | 17.03 |
| Equipment for first responders | 0.99 | 2.02 | 2.23 | 2.23 |
| Other | 0.35 | 0.73 | 0.20 | 0.20 |
| Special response units | 11.53 | 11.57 | 14.60 | 14.60 |
| *OMB highlighted programs | | | | |
| WMD programs | | | | |
| Air Security Protective Operations | - | - | - | 16.00 |
| CIP Programs | | | | |
| Research and development | - | - | - | 4.00 |
| Public key infrastructure | - | - | - | 7.00 |
| **US AID** | | | | |
| *Combat Terrorism* | 5.68 | 54.89 | 5.83 | 5.01 |
| Physical security of government facilities and employees | 2.68 | 3.49 | 3.98 | 2.66 |
| Preparing for and responding to terrorist acts | 3.00 | 51.40 | 1.40 | 2.35 |
| *WMD preparedness* | 3.00 | 1.40 | 1.40 | 2.35 |
| Preparing for and responding to WMD terrorism | 3.00 | 1.40 | 1.40 | 2.35 |
| First Responder training and exercises | 0.30 | 1.40 | 1.40 | 2.35 |
| Other | 2.70 | 0.00 | 0.00 | 0.00 |
| **Department of Veterans Affairs** | | | | |
| *Combating Terrorism* | 0.01 | 0.04 | 0.00 | 0.00 |
| Preparing for and responding to terrorist acts | 0.01 | 0.00 | 0.00 | 0.00 |
| *OMB highlighted programs | | | | |
| WMD programs | | | | |
| Stockpiling pharmaceuticals | - | - | - | N/A |
| Training medical personnel | - | - | - | N/A |

*Denotes programs highlighted in the OMB report. Figures are part of the FY2001 budget.

Source: Adapted by Steve Chu and Preston Golson from the Executive Office of the President, Office Management and Budget, "Annual Report to Congress on Combating Terrorism," May 2000.

classification of the intelligence budget has done more to hide the inadequacy of resources and capabilities than it has done to protect the nation's secrets.

OMB does not report on such CIA activity except as part of the broader category of "National Security." The Center for Nonproliferation at the Monterey Institute of International Studies has, however, described the counterterrorism efforts of the CIA as follows:

> The Directorate of Central Intelligence's mission is to gather timely intelligence on terrorist groups abroad in order to prevent and prepare for terrorist attacks.
>
> **Interagency Intelligence Committee on Terrorism**
>
> More than 40 federal agencies, bureaus, and offices are members of this committee. The Committee shares information between agencies on activities of terrorist groups and countries sponsoring terrorism in order to assess terrorist threats. Another element of this project is the detailing of staff between organizations, including representatives of many intelligence agencies to the Counterterrorist Center.
>
> **Counterterrorist Center**
>
> The counterterrorist center is a hub for interagency intelligence sharing to further efforts to combat terrorism. The center has representatives from all major facets of the intelligence community, as listed below. According to a speech by President Clinton in 1995, "an FBI official serves as the deputy director of the Counterterrorist Center."
>
> The agencies contributing to the Counterterrorist Center are as follows: Federal Bureau of Investigation, National Security Agency, Defense Intelligence Agency, Bureau of Intelligence and Research of the State Department, and the Central Intelligence Agency.[5]

The National Commission on Terrorism, also known as the Bremer Commission, recommended that the CIA take a more aggressive role in recruiting informants and collecting information. The Bremer Commission criticized 1995 guidelines that set up a complicated approval process to recruit informants who may have committed human rights violations. The Commission recommended that the CIA stop using the 1995 guidelines and revert to the preexisting process when recruiting terrorist informants.

The Commission also noted that the Counterterrorist Center (CTC) was underfunded. As a result, the CTC has had to cut back planned operations. The Commission recommended that the CIA work with Congress to ensure that the CTC has adequate resources. The Commission also believed that the CIA, through its Foreign Language Executive Committee, needs the authority to expand the pool of linguists available to the U.S. government to create a surge capability. The Commission did have praise for the

CIA by saying the FBI should have reports officers like the CIA. Reports officers' primary mission is to determine what information should be shared with other agencies.[6]

One key problem for the CIA, as well as other national intelligence organizations, is that it cannot legally gather intelligence on American citizens and is not organized to provide data directly to state and local law enforcement agencies. There are good reasons to protect the civil rights of individual American citizens. At the same time, the attacks on the World Trade Center and the Pentagon raise serious questions as to whether the rules should be changed or modified if the threat involves mass terrorism and/or the potential use of nuclear and biological weapons. This aspect of asymmetric warfare and homeland defense has been raised in a number of different forms, but largely in the context of far less threatening forms of terrorist attack. The need for change may now be all too real.

## DEPARTMENT OF COMMERCE

The DOC plays a major role in export and import control and in enforcing some aspects of arms control. The DOC's Bureau of Export Administration requested $11.2 million for FY2001 to strengthen import and export controls on WMD materials and to implement CWC inspections. FY2001 requested funding for WMD preparedness includes an increase of $11.2 million.[7]

## DEPARTMENT OF DEFENSE

The current role of the DOD in defending and responding to counterterrorism highlights the gap between classic national defense roles like missile defense and the current approach to counterterrorism. DOD is responsible for the development of a national missile defense system. At present, however, there is no clearly defined mission for the DOD in dealing with response to a catastrophic event like a successful missile penetration and strike on a U.S. target.

The DOD is responsible for planning for asymmetric attacks by states using nuclear or highly lethal biological weapons, but its role in defending against similar attacks by state proxies or major foreign terrorist groups is far less clear. It plays a major role in counterproliferation and some aspects of arms control, and is responsible for creating offensive and defensive deterrent and strike options to deal with foreign-based threats, but this aspect of its efforts are rarely included in studies of homeland defense.

There are also gray areas where military operations can become directly linked to attacks on the U.S. homeland. One key contingency studied in a number of DOD analyses is a foreign state or terrorist attack on the facilities, ports, and airports used by U.S. forces embarking for deployment overseas. In such a case, any use of chemical, biological, or nuclear weapons would almost certainly involve significant damage to civilians—including military dependents—as well as U.S. military forces.

The DOD does control many of the assets the federal government could provide for defense and response against any attack on a purely civil target that required massive federal assistance. At the same time, it has sought to avoid playing the lead role in such a response effort and having its forces fully integrated into the federal defense and response effort for such high-level attacks. There are four good reasons for such reluctance: (1) past charges that it was attempting to usurp civil authority; (2) concern that it would be forced to fund the mission with existing resources; (3) concern it would see its primary missions diluted into a morass of conflicting state and local priorities; and (4) concern that it would be dragged into a political morass in dealing with the interagency process and Congress.

As a result, the DOD has been charged with supporting the FBI or FEMA in a terrorism crisis and had no lead designation, before the events of September 2001. This role may be appropriate when states or their proxies are not involved in an attack and when it is an isolated incident that does not require a state of national emergency. It is a potential recipe for disaster, however, at higher levels of attack. It highlights the de facto gap between the current focus civil agencies have on relatively low levels of terrorist attack and the very different threat that could occur from overt or covert state or state sponsored attacks.

It is also unclear that the present arrangements are really adequate even for dealing with terrorist attacks. The Bremer Commission recommended that the DOD be the lead agency if a catastrophic terrorist event overwhelms the capabilities of other federal agencies. The Commission advised the creation of contingency plans in case a devastating terrorist event forced the DOD to take the lead and advised the Secretary of Defense to create a unified command structure to prepare the DOD for the lead role. The Commission said:

> The Department of Defense's ability to command and control vast resources for dangerous, unstructured situations is unmatched by any other department or agency. According to current plans, DOD involvement is limited to supporting the agencies that are currently designated as having the lead in a terrorism crisis, the FBI and the Federal Emergency Management Agency (FEMA). But, in extraordinary circumstances, when a catastrophe is beyond the capabilities of local, state, and other federal agencies, or is directly related to an armed conflict overseas, the president may want to designate DOD as a lead federal agency. This may become a critical operational consideration in planning for future conflicts. Current plans and exercises do not consider this possibility.
>
> An expanded role for the DOD in a catastrophic terrorist attack will have policy and legal implications. Other federal agencies, the states, and local

communities will have major concerns. In preparing for such a contingency, there will also be internal DOD issues on resources and possible conflicts with traditional military contingency plans. These issues should be addressed beforehand.

Effective preparation also requires effective organization. The DOD is not optimally organized to respond to the wide range of missions that would likely arise from the threat of a catastrophic terrorist attack. For example, within DOD several offices, departments, Unified Commands, the Army, and the National Guard have overlapping responsibilities to plan and execute operations in case of a catastrophic terrorist attack. These operations will require an unprecedented degree of interagency coordination and communication in order to be successful.

There are neither plans for the DOD to assume a lead agency role nor exercises rehearsing this capability. Hence, these demanding tasks would have to be accomplished on an ad hoc basis by the military.[8]

The Bremer Commission further recommended increased funding for the NSA to allow it to close technology gaps and to ensure that it has the capability to collect terrorist information.[9] This recommendation not only seems sound, it is crucial if the United States is to prepare effectively for the future spectrum of attacks on the U.S. homeland, close the present gap between WMD and counterterrorism, and prepare for complex forms of asymmetric attack that could combine covert attacks with WMD and new forms of attack-like cyberwarfare. It is also essential if homeland defense is to be treated as a serious part of war fighting, rather than a largely passive and defense activity. The failure to plan for events like multiple, near simultaneous biological attacks using multiple agents is one case in point. So is the tendency to limit the examination of cyberwarfare and CIP attacks to limited acts of terrorism rather than fully examine vulnerability and response in the case of large-scale state-sponsored attacks or actual war.

### Analyzing the Role of the DOD

These problems make it extraordinarily difficult to in analyze the past role of the DOD, and the national security community as a whole, in homeland defense against CBRN attacks. Most budget and program reporting on this aspect of DOD activity has been designed to cover a highly compartmentalized definition of counterterrorism activity that excludes three basic elements of the problem. It has not included most counterproliferation activities, an analysis of asymmetric warfare capabilities, and large-scale cyber and information warfare. There is also no way to know what resources the DOD has been given that could be used for responding to a large-scale attack or in a national emergency.

This means, in turn, that there is no way to analyze the size and cost of DOD's efforts to defend the United States against attacks by foreign states and its overall role in intelligence, counterterrorism, and responding to CBRN attacks. It is also clear that the counterproliferation activities of the DOD have had a major additional impact on homeland defense. The secretary of defense announced a major defense counterproliferation initiative in 1993 to combat the CBRN threat. This initiative called for developing capabilities that will allow the United States to defeat an enemy using CBRN weapons, and the secretary has described the CBRN threat as the single greatest and most complex challenge currently facing the DOD.

The GAO reported on the progress DOD had made in implementing the initiative in May 2000:

> The U.S. National Military Strategy states that the continued proliferation of weapons of mass destruction, particularly chemical and biological weapons, has made their use by an adversary increasingly likely in a major theater war and smaller scale contingencies. These weapons are capable of causing mass casualties, and their threat or use can disrupt the planning and conduct of military operations. DOD believes effective deterrence against the use of these weapons depends on a range of nuclear and conventional response capabilities, as well as active and passive defenses and supporting command, control, communications, and intelligence. DOD estimates that for fiscal year 2001 it will invest over $7.3 billion on the research, development, and acquisition of such conventional response capabilities, with about $5.3 billion of that investment on missile defense. Although an unclassified estimate is unavailable, additional funding is spent to provide intelligence support for counterproliferation.
>
> To help ensure that DOD's counterproliferation policy objectives are met and that implementation of the Counterproliferation Initiative is integrated and focused, the Secretary of Defense, in 1996, established the Counterproliferation Council composed of senior DOD civilian and military officials. The Council is to monitor departmental progress on developing the strategy, doctrine, and force planning necessary to effectively execute its counterproliferation objectives. In 1997, DOD's Quadrennial Defense Review report stated that a key challenge the Department must meet to ensure it is prepared for the NBC threat is to institutionalize—integrate or make permanent—counterproliferation as an organizing principle in every facet of military activity.
>
> To review activities and programs related to countering proliferation threats within the Departments of Defense and Energy and the U.S. intelligence community, in 1993 the Congress established the Counterproliferation Program Review Committee. The Committee's charter includes addressing shortfalls in existing and programmed capabilities to counter the proliferation of NBC weapons of mass destruction and their delivery systems; identifying and eliminating undesirable redundancies or uncoordinated efforts; and establishing priorities for programs and funding. Since 1995, the Committee has submitted an annual report to the Congress detailing its findings and recommendations.
>
> DOD is taking steps to make the nuclear, biological, and chemical threat a matter of routine consideration within its activities and functions, such as

training and field exercises and the acquisition of weapon systems and equipment. Since the 1993 Defense Counterproliferation Initiative was announced, DOD has given greater emphasis to this threat in policy and planning documents, and the Joint Staff has made considerable effort to determine and prioritize the counterproliferation requirements of the unified commands. The services, particularly the Air Force, have increased the importance placed on counterproliferation requirements in their acquisition programs, training, and doctrine. Regional unified commands have incorporated counterproliferation concepts, equipment, and tasks into their planning and military exercises.

. . . While DOD has taken positive steps, it can do more to integrate and focus its response to the growing threat posed by the proliferation of nuclear, biological, and chemical weapons. DOD does not have an overarching joint counterproliferation doctrine document to provide a centralized picture of how DOD should respond in a nuclear, biological, and chemical environment across the spectrum of military operations. Such a document, which was recently approved for development, will help ensure that counterproliferation is being satisfactorily integrated in the entire body of joint doctrine. DOD also has not taken sufficient action to provide reasonable assurance that its weapon systems and equipment can survive and operate in a biological and chemical environment. Additionally, studies by DOD and a congressionally mandated commission indicate that DOD's organization structure may be too diffused to effectively manage and integrate the Department's counterproliferation mission.

DOD has not developed key strategy documents and management plans to aid in directing and managing its counterproliferation initiatives. Internal DOD reviews have identified the need for a comprehensive strategy for countering the proliferation of weapons of mass destruction and a military strategy for integrating offensive and defensive capabilities. There is also no management plan to guide, oversee, and integrate department-wide initiatives, which would include a reporting and evaluation process with performance measures to allow for a continual assessment of the Department's progress in achieving goals and objectives.

DOD primarily coordinates its counterproliferation activities with the Department of Energy and the intelligence community through the Counterproliferation Program Review Committee. DOD, Energy, and intelligence agency officials generally expressed satisfaction with the exchange of information that the Committee had provided about ongoing programs among the agencies. However, the Committee has taken little action to identify and eliminate undesirable redundancies among research and development programs, one of the primary reasons the Congress established it. The Committee does not have a process to facilitate such determinations and provide a basis to make decisions on eliminating undesired redundancies.

This report includes recommendations that the Secretary of Defense (1) develop strategies, a management plan, and performance measures to help guide and manage the implementation of DOD's counterproliferation actions; (2) include in the next Quadrennial Defense Review an examination of the Department's organization for counterproliferation; (3) take steps to help ensure that the nuclear, biological, and chemical threat is being given sufficient attention in military doctrine and in the design and development of weapon systems and equipment; and (4) devise and implement a mechanism to help identify and eliminate undesirable redundancies among counter-proliferation programs.[10]

These recommendations did not go far enough. There needs to be clear recognition within DOD and the entire federal government that homeland defense is not simply WMD, counterterrorism, or information security. Homeland defense involves a much broader matrix of national security efforts. Effective planning and analysis requires a full understanding of the overall nature of the DOD and other national security efforts in this area, and regardless of past PDDs and the work of the NSC. The federal government at present lacks even a raw conceptual picture of its current plans, capabilities, and spending.

Ironically, the DOD virtually says this in its January 2001 report on its counterproliferation activities:

> DOD is undertaking a variety of programs and activities, in coordination with other Federal departments and agencies, to deter the use of NBC weapons against U.S. and allied forces, as well as against the territories of the United States and its friends and allies. The effectiveness of these efforts will depend on close inter-agency coordination, close cooperation with our allies, sound program management of resources, and integration and institutionalization of the counterproliferation mission and capabilities within DOD.
>
> Through these efforts, we attempt to influence the perceptions and assess-ments of potential aggressors who possess NBC weapons regarding the re-solve and capabilities of the United States to deal with such threats. Indeed, the knowledge that the United States has a powerful and ready nuclear ca-pability, as well as global-reach, stand-off, precision-guided, conventional munitions; a highly trained, equipped, and motivated special operations force; and global intelligence and law enforcement, are significant deterrents to the use of these weapons. Effective deterrence will depend on a range of nuclear and conventional response capabilities, as well as active and passive defenses, counterforce and consequence management capabilities, and supporting com-mand, control, communications, and intelligence.
>
> In particular, military preparations for operations in an NBC environment will make clear that the threat or use of NBC weapons will not deter the United States from applying military power in defense of its national inter-ests. The United States is substantially improving its ability to fight and win under conditions where an adversary may use asymmetric means, thereby decreasing the coercive value of NBC weapons against us and deterring ad-versaries from threatening or using such weapons.
>
> DOD plays a vital role in supporting all facets of national counterpro-liferation policy. This section outlines steps the Department is taking to respond to the challenges of proliferation and to deal with the military threats posed by NBC weapons. The DOD response to proliferation takes three forms: prevention/deterrence; protection of U.S. civilians and military forces if faced with the threat or use of NBC weapons, including missile defenses; and possessing the ability to respond in emergency situations where WMD are implemented.

None of these efforts alone will halt the spread and use of WMD. Together, they form a framework that allows the United States and its allies to mitigate this central, post–Cold War threat.[11]

## The Size of the Current DOD Effort

Although the DOD pioneered program budgeting and the development of future year plans, its public program is even more opaque and lacking in any public evidence of long-term planning than that of any civil agency— although these problems may partly be for security reasons. The data in the OMB report to Congress on the federal budget summarized in Table 7.1 does not provide specific budget figures or program descriptions for the DOD. Instead, it is included as part of the OMB totals for "National Security." For a more detailed look into how the DOD spends on combating terrorism and counter–CBRN defense, see Chart 7.1.

Chart 7.1
Department of Defense Spending on Combating Terrorism and Counter–CBRN Defense (current $U.S. millions)

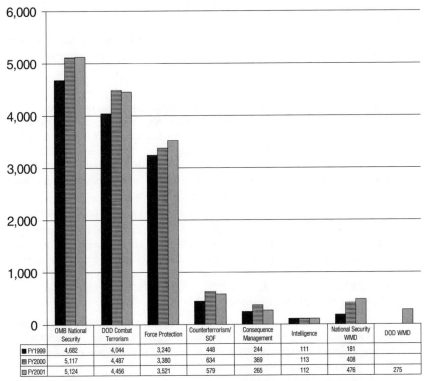

| | OMB National Security | DOD Combat Terrorism | Force Protection | Counterterrorism/ SOF | Consequence Management | Intelligence | National Security WMD | DOD WMD |
|---|---|---|---|---|---|---|---|---|
| FY1999 | 4,682 | 4,044 | 3,240 | 448 | 244 | 111 | 181 | |
| FY2000 | 5,117 | 4,487 | 3,380 | 634 | 369 | 113 | 408 | |
| FY2001 | 5,124 | 4,456 | 3,521 | 579 | 265 | 112 | 476 | 275 |

*Source*: Adapted by Anthony H. Cordesman from the Executive Office of the President, Office Management and Budget, "Annual Report to Congress on Combating Terrorism," May 2000.

One major recommendation for better coordination of homeland defense is that OMB be tasked with providing future reporting by federal agency, and that any sensitive figures on black programs either be rolled into other DOD programs or put into some general intelligence or "other agency" heading that could include NSA and CIA. There is no reason to grossly overclassify broad categories of data in the national security area. This made little real sense during the Cold War and it makes no sense in a context where enough data have to be declassified to allow effective government-wide planning. The present system of OMB reporting almost seems to be designed to avoid effective review by the NSC and Congress, much less by outside experts. It is also grossly inadaquate to deal with the major program and funding changes that must take place as a result of the new level of violence and vulnerability which emerged in September 2001.

As Table 7.2 shows, the DOD data track in broad terms with the OMB report in terms of total spending. This does not mean, however, that the differences between the two totals are measures of the money going to the intelligence community—although the DOD report makes no mention of any intelligence money going to the CIA, the NSA, or the Defense Intelligence Agency. There is no way to correlate the line-item data in the OMB and DOD reports and there seem to be a number of differences in the way each agency counts.

Several trends are apparent in the DOD data, however, that are not clear in the OMB data. Trends that warn that major changes be required in the level of homeland defense activity:

- The vast bulk of spending goes to force and facility protection activities under the heading of "antiterrorism." This has also been the area of the most rapid growth in recent years—rising from $3.2 billion in FY1999 to $3.5 billion in FY2001. In broad terms, protecting U.S. military forces and facilities overseas accounts for roughly 79 percent of all DOD spending on counterterrorism. There is no way to know, however, what percentage affects DOD activities in foreign countries and in the United States.

- Another major element is more a matter of accounting than reality. The entire Special Operations Command is stated to be a dedicated counterterrorism activity because the DOD includes resources that are dedicated and available to a given activity and personnel who dedicate 51 percent or more of their time to such efforts. As a result, counterterrorism spending is largely an artificial accounting construct. In FY2001, this included $557.9 million, or about 12 percent of total DOD spending.

- Terrorism consequence management is not a growth area and shrank from $369 million in FY2000 to $265 million in FY2001, as part of the DOD effort to reduce its responsibilities in this area. It was 5.9 percent of the total DOD effort in FY2001.

- Between FY1999 and FY2001, the DOD effort in domestic preparedness programs shrunk from $48.9 million to $10.2 million, or by nearly 80 percent. It was far less than 1 percent of the total DOD effort in FY2001.

- The consequence management response effort lost more than 50 percent of its funding between FY2000 and FY2001. It was 2 percent of the total DOD effort in FY2001.

- In contrast, RDT&E efforts in terrorism consequence management nearly doubled between FY1999 and FY2001, and rose from $89.0 million to $164.7 million. It was 3.7 percent of the total DOD effort in FY2001.

- Intelligence spending was nearly static between FY1999 and FY2001, at around $112 million, or 2.5 percent of the total effort. It is obvious that no new programs are underway and no new capabilities are being funded or developed. The funds shown in this heading do not, however, include any activity by the NSA or DIA, and virtually all go to the military services. Only about 4 percent are devoted to the Office of the Secretary of Defense.

- The DOD excludes all counterproliferation activity from its analysis of spending to combat terrorism. It also excludes most capabilities relating to asymmetric warfare.

- The DOD figures are meaningless in terms of measuring overall response capability and costs because these are contingency dependent. For example, any major emergency deployment of the National Guard, reserves, or active forces in reaction to a nuclear or large-scale biological attack could easily spend multiples of the total funding now shown for counterterrorism.

One key insight is that the DOD's total consequence management effort in FY2001 was only $265 million and is less than 6 percent of its total effort. Intelligence, which is not really defined, was static and funded at only $112 million. Reports that imply that there has been a massive homeland defense effort in the DOD relating to mass terrorism and CBRN attacks are flatly wrong, while the data that the DOD does provide make it impossible to understand what is really happening and to link counterproliferation and asymmetric warfare capability to homeland defense. This is a recipe for failure and further tragedies.

### Dedicated FY2001 DOD Expenditures for CBRN/WMD Homeland Defense

Another way to look at DOD activities is to count only those activities to combat terrorism that can be clearly and openly identified as directed toward CBRN attacks and WMD and that might have direct relevance to homeland defense. Any such estimate using the DOD report on combating terrorism must be tenuous at best.

**Table 7.2**
**Summary of the Budget Data in the Department of Defense Report on Combating Terrorism (current $U.S. millions)**

| Activities | FY1999 | FY2000 | FY2001 |
|---|---|---|---|
| *Antiterrorism* | | | |
| Physical security equipment | 192.4 | 185.9 | 205.2 |
| Physical security site improvements | 56.4 | 89.2 | 57.3 |
| Physical security management and planning | 58.3 | 55.6 | 58.1 |
| Security forces and technicians | 1,594.2 | 1,678.4 | 1,755.1 |
| Law enforcement | 861.9 | 884.3 | 906.8 |
| Security and investigative means | 428.6 | 427.3 | 473.0 |
| Research, development, rest and evaluation | 48.2 | 59.6 | 65.6 |
| Subtotal | 3,240.0 | 3,380.3 | 3,521.1 |
| *Counterterrorism* | | | |
| Special Operations Command | 446.5 | 620.8 | 554.9 |
| Research, development, test and evaluation | 1.9 | 3.4 | 3.0 |
| Subtotal | 448.4 | 624.2 | 557.9 |

| Terrorism Consequence Management | | | |
|---|---|---|---|
| Domestic preparedness programs | 48.9 | 32.1 | 10.2 |
| Consequence management response | 106.4 | 202.2 | 90.6 |
| Research, development, test and evaluation | 89.0 | 134.7 | 164.7 |
| Subtotal | 244.3 | 369.0 | 265.5 |
| *Intelligence* | | | |
| Counterintelligence | 107.1 | 106.8 | 106.0 |
| Research, development, rest and evaluation | 4.1 | 6.4 | 5.7 |
| Subtotal | 111.2 | 113.2 | 111.7 |
| **TOTAL** | **4,043.9** | **4,486.7** | **4,456.2** |
| *OMB National Security Total* | *(4,682.5)* | *(5,117.2)* | *(5,124.1)* |
| *Difference* | *638.6* | *630.5* | *667.9* |

*Source:* Adapted by Anthony H. Cordesman from the Department of Defense, Office of Combating Terrorism Policy and Support, *Combating Terrorism Activities, FY2001*, Washington, D.C., January 14, 2000.

Table 7.3 provides only a rough indication of just how small the dedicated effort may really be. While the total for combating terrorism is well in excess of $4 billion; the figure for core DOD activities that broadly affect the defense and response against CBRN attacks on the U.S. homeland is less than $300 million. This total accounts for a major part of the $467 million that OMB estimates is spent by all National Security agencies on such programs.

At the same time, there are, again, critical limits to any form of budget analysis based on either the OMB or DOD estimates. It is currently impossible to produce a valid analysis of the subset of DOD activities affecting the defense against the use of CBRN weapons by states, proxies, or terrorists and extremists, or to tie these aspects of homeland defense to other aspects of homeland defense. The figures in excess of $10 billion sometimes associated with such efforts are clearly statistical rubbish, as are any efforts to associate total DOD spending to combat terrorism with CBRN defense of the U.S. homeland. Only a minor amount of "combating terrorism" money goes to such efforts, and even some of that money actually supports many other functions.

### Key DOD Activities

The DOD has a number of specific responsibilities for homeland defense. According to a DOD report issued in 2001, the DOD plans to provide its resources for consequence management in accordance with several key principles.

- First, DOD will ensure an unequivocal chain of responsibility, authority, and accountability for its actions to ensure the American people that the military will follow all relevant laws when an emergency occurs. To this end, the assistant to the secretary of defense for civil support (ATSD–CS) will provide full-time civilian oversight for the domestic use of DOD CBRN consequence management assets in support of other federal agencies.

- Second, during a CBRN event, the DOD will always play a supporting role to the Lead Federal Agency (LFA) in accordance with the Federal Response Plan and will ensure complete compliance with the Constitution, the Posse Comitatus Act, and other applicable laws. The it routinely provides support and assistance to civilian authorities and has considerable experience balancing the requirement to protect civil liberties on one hand with the need to ensure national security on the other.

- Third, DOD chemical weapons equipment and assets are largely resident in its war fighting capabilities. However, many of these capabilities can be dual-use. Military units specializing in decontamination, medical support, logistics, transportation, and communications, for example, could assist in the domestic arena as well. The DOD will also emphasize its natural role, skills, and structure in support of the LFA, such as the ability to rapidly mobilize and provide mass logistical support.

**Table 7.3**
Core Department of Defense Efforts in Combating Terrorism that Broadly Affect
CBRN–Related Homeland Defense against State, Proxy, Terrorist, and Extremist
Attacks on Targets Other than DOD Facilities and Forces (current $U.S. millions)

| | |
|---|---:|
| *WMD preparedness* | |
| Preparing for and responding to WMD terrorism | |
| DLA | .066 |
| DTRA | 11.422 |
| Subtotal | 11.488 |
| First responder training | 10.2 |
| Air Force First Responder | 2.700 |
| Subtotal | 12.9 |
| Other planning and assistance to state/locals | |
| Navy—support to civil authorities/TCM | 5.574 |
| Special response units | |
| Terrorism Consequence Management Program | 76.4 |
| CBIRF | 4.369 |
| Subtotal | 80.769 |
| *TOTAL* | *110.731* |
| | |
| *Research and Development* | |
| Basic Research, including gene sequencing | |
| DARPA—Genetic sequencing of biological warfare agents | 12.5 |
| Detection/diagnostics | |
| CTTS | |
| DARPA—advanced diagnostics | 19.350 |
| DARPA—sensors | 24.056 |
| Subtotal | 46.454 |
| Modeling, simulation, and system analysis | |
| DARPA—consequence management | 10.0 |
| Personal/Collective Protection | |
| DARPA—Bio/chem defensive systems | 10.0 |
| Personal/environmental decontamination | |
| DARPA—external protection | 21.0 |
| Therapeutics/treatments | |
| DARPA—multipurpose | 22.2 |
| Vaccines | |
| DARPA—antivirals/immunizations | 21.3 |
| DARPA—Antibacterials/Antitoxins | 21.658 |
| Subtotal | 42.958 |
| *TOTAL* | *165.112* |
| **Grand Total** | **275.843** |

*Research and development calculated is the total of research and development from anti-
terrorism, counterterrorism, terrorism consequence management, and intelligence categories.
*Source*: Department of Defense, Office of Combating Terrorism Policy and Support, *Combating Terrorism Activities, FY2001*, Washington, D.C., January 14, 2000.

- Fourth, whereas active duty forces are the U.S. forward-deployed assets overseas, the DOD will employ the U.S. Army Reserve and National Guard as the forward-deployed units for consequence management in the domestic arena. In the event of a domestic CBRN event, certain units would be able to respond rapidly due to their geographic dispersion and proximity to major American cities. Moreover, many of the applicable capabilities such as decontamination, medical support, transportation, and communications are already contained in U.S. Army Reserve and National Guard units.

- Fifth, the DOD will deconflict LFA requests for support against ongoing war fighting requirements. Before providing support, the DOD will consider whether requested military capabilities are available domestically and whether it has the sufficient legal and budgetary authorities to provide the support to civil authorities.[12]

In order to respond to a domestic CBRN event, the DOD established a standing Joint Task Force for Civil Support (JTF–CS), subordinate to U.S. Joint Forces Command, to provide command and control of DOD support to the LFA for CBRN chemical weapons events in the continental United States (CONUS). The JTF–CS is involved in consequence management doctrine development, training and exercise management, planning development and review, and requirements identification. The U.S. Pacific Command and the U.S. Southern Command have parallel responsibilities for providing military assistance to civil authorities for states, territories, and possessions outside CONUS. The U.S. Joint Forces Command, in turn, provides technical advice and assistance to geographic commanders in chief conducting consequence management operations in response to CBRN incidents outside CONUS.[13]

The Office of the Secretary of Defense also directs the following efforts:

- Special Operations/Low-Intensity Conflict (SO/LIC): Has overall policy and resource oversight for domestic preparedness, and maintains the Counterterrorist Technical Support Program (CTTS), which is a fast-track research and development program for multiagency and international aspects of terrorism.

- Defense Threat Reduction Agency: Manages and coordinates the extensive technical expertise on chemical and biological defense within the DOD, and is also involved in counterproliferation, cooperative threat reduction activities, and special weapons technology.

- Director of Military Support: Located under the secretary of the army, within the office of the assistant secretary for installations, logistics, and environment, this office serves as the central point for the coordination of military support to civilian authorities.

- Reserve Component Consequence Management Program Integration Office: This office has been established under the command of the director of military support in order to integrate reserve and National Guard components into the national domestic preparedness strategy. This office will coordinate identification, training, equipping, and exercise of reservists and National Guard components.

## Antiterrorism and Force Protection

Antiterrorism and force protection efforts received most of the funding that DOD reports as part of its efforts to combat terrorism, but most such programs have little to do with mass terrorism or CBRN attacks of any kind. They are designed basically to deal with high explosives and direct assaults, with limited capability to deal with a direct intrusion of chemical, biological, or nuclear weapons.

In fact, one of the more interesting aspects of a detailed review of the service programs in this area is that there is considerable expense on intrusion and explosive detection and blast mitigation, but little on either CBRN or cyberattack detection. It is also unclear that the massive number of vulnerability assessments reflected in the FY1999–FY2001 budgets examined these aspects of the problem or any aspect of the possible impact on defense health facilities. It is unclear that current service regulations and technical manuals require such analysis, although protection against CBRN attacks is in the charter of each service force protection effort. (The only service to specifically mention this in its budget justification is the U.S. Navy.) Somewhat ironically, DOD law enforcement activities paid far more attention to CBRN attacks than any of the programs related to force and facility protection improvement and design.[14] Even the DTRA portion of the ongoing force protection effort does not explicitly touch on any CBRN–related effort in the DOD budget justification document.[15]

The Joint Chiefs of Staff (JCS) did, however, develop a WMD Planning Template Annex in FY1999, and directed a program to educate CINCs and their services in FY2000 and FY2001.[16] The DOD has also taken a number of actions to improve its antiterrorism/force protection (AT/FP) program since the 1995 Riyadh car bomb and the 1996 Khobar Towers bombing. The secretary of defense chose the chairman of the JCS to be the principal AT/FP adviser in September 1996, and the chairman announced DOD's goal of becoming the worldwide AT/FP leader. A July 2000 GAO report described the DOD AT/FP program as follows:

> The Assistant Secretary of Defense for Special Operations and Low-Intensity Conflict is the principal staff assistant and advisor to the Secretary of Defense for antiterrorism/force protection (AT/FP) policy. While this office focuses on policy, the Chairman of the Joint Chiefs of Staff and the Combating Terrorism directorate within the Joint Staff focus on implementing DOD's AT/FP program. The Joint Staff's responsibilities include reviewing the services' AT/FP budgets, developing standards, managing the Joint Staff Integrated Vulnerability Assessment program, and representing the geographic combatant commanders on AT/FP matters.

DOD policy makes commanders responsible for protecting their forces from terrorist attacks. For forces overseas, the responsibility rests with the geographic combatant commander and the installation commander, with the support of the service headquarters. The geographic combatant commanders are responsible for developing antiterrorism policies that apply at the installations in their areas of responsibility and that take precedence over service or other DOD component AT/FP policies. They are also responsible for determining the threat levels for each country in their area of responsibility, identifying the money and manpower needed to achieve sufficient AT/FP, and working with the services to provide the resources necessary. Finally, because all risks cannot be eliminated, the geographic combatant commanders are responsible for determining the types of risks their forces will face as they undertake their missions.

Installation commanders are responsible for protecting the people, assets, and facilities under their command from terrorist attacks. The installation commander, working with the installation AT/FP manager, is responsible for ensuring that AT/FP standards established by DOD, the geographic combatant commanders, the services, and the service headquarters are implemented. Additionally, because DOD recognizes that not all vulnerabilities can be addressed, installation commanders practice risk management—to decide what risks can be accepted and what risks are too great to be accepted. When the risk is unacceptable, the commander is responsible for taking action to mitigate the risk.

Although geographic combatant commanders have overall responsibility to protect forces assigned to them, individual services are responsible for funding an installation's AT/FP needs and for providing the required number of trained personnel. The majority of funds used for AT/FP activities (excluding the cost of military personnel) are located in the services' Operation and Maintenance appropriations. Operation and Maintenance appropriations are generally used to fund readiness activities, equipment maintenance, recruiting, pay for civilian employees (including contract security guards), and the everyday costs of running an installation. A number of subactivities within this appropriation fund specific expenses. Examples of the subactivities include real property maintenance, depot maintenance, and base operating support. The base operating support subactivity pays for expenses such as utilities, communications, security, building repair, and maintenance. Traditionally, the services have included funds for AT/FP in the base operating support subactivity, and AT/FP activities must compete against other activities for the same limited funding.

Shortly after the Khobar Towers bombing, the Secretary of Defense established the Chairman of the Joint Chiefs of Staff's Combating Terrorism Readiness Initiative Fund. The Fund, which is managed by the Joint Staff, was not intended to relieve the services of their responsibility to fund AT/FP projects; rather, it was intended to provide funding for emergency or other unforeseen high-priority, combating terrorism needs. In fiscal year 2000, the Fund totaled $15 million—$10 million of Operation and Maintenance funds and $5 million of procurement funds. This level of funding is scheduled to continue through fiscal year 2002. In fiscal years 2003 through 2007, the Fund will be reduced to a total of $10 million a year, according to DOD.[17]

The GAO has criticized the DOD for underfunding these AT/FP programs, for inadequately training AT/FP managers, and for incompletely
assessing vulnerabilities. The GAO said:

> Overall, military forces stationed overseas are better protected today than they
> were 3 years ago. The Joint Staff has developed DOD–wide construction stan-
> dards to ensure that antiterrorism/force protection measures are included in
> new construction. In addition, DOD has signed agreements with the Depart-
> ment of State and U.S. ambassadors or chiefs of mission to protect DOD
> personnel not under the jurisdiction of commanders. Geographic combatant
> commands have created permanent antiterrorism/force protection offices,
> hired permanent antiterrorism/force protection staff, and developed systems
> to monitor progress to correct vulnerabilities. Installation commanders are
> more aware of their responsibility to protect their forces from terrorist at-
> tack and, despite funding constraints, have addressed many security vulner-
> abilities. However, significant security and procedural antiterrorism/force
> protection problems continue at many installations. For example, some in-
> stallations have not developed plans to deal with terrorist attacks, others have
> no effective means of stopping unauthorized vehicles from entering the in-
> stallation, and some lack secure access to important intelligence information.
>
> Commanders are better able to determine their vulnerability to terrorist
> attacks than when we last reported. Vulnerability assessments are now be-
> ing conducted more routinely and are based on a defined set of criteria.
> However, vulnerability assessment reports do not provide specific actions to
> rectify problems mentioned in the reports. Additionally, there is no compre-
> hensive method in place to share solutions to common problems among dif-
> ferent installations.
>
> Limited antiterrorism funding and trained staff have affected the ability
> of commanders to correct known vulnerabilities. Funding for antiterrorism
> protection has been, and will likely continue to be, significantly less than what
> installation and geographic combatant commanders have determined they
> require, despite the fact that senior DOD leaders have designated anti-
> terrorism/force protection as a high priority item. For example, some over-
> seas service commands have repeatedly received less than 50 percent of the
> money the commands believe they require to correct or mitigate vulnerabili-
> ties. According to antiterrorism/force protection managers, this level of fund-
> ing has limited their ability to address vulnerabilities. Congress requires DOD
> to provide information on proposed antiterrorism/force protection funding
> and projects as part of its consolidated combating terrorism budget submis-
> sion; however, it does not require DOD to provide information on the num-
> ber of projects that remain to be funded. Without information on the types
> of projects that need funding, Congress does not have an accurate picture of
> the extent of the risk that U.S. forces face from terrorism. In addition, in-
> stallations we visited did not have adequately trained personnel dedicated to
> managing and implementing antiterrorism solutions.[18]

The GAO never explicitly addressed CBRN vulnerabilities as part of its
criticisms. It did report, however, that all services would face a shortage of

AT/FP funding in FY2001. It estimated that the services required $274.5 million and that the proposed budget was only $141.3 million, or 51 percent of the need. The JCS also estimated that AT/FP programs needed an extra $700 million over current FY2002–FY2005 spending plans. The GAO made the following recommendations to improve AT/FP:

> To improve the effectiveness and increase the impact of the vulnerability assessments and the vulnerability assessment reports, we recommend that the Secretary of Defense direct the Chairman of the Joint Chiefs of Staff to improve the vulnerability assessment reports provided to installations. Although the Joint Staff is planning to take some action to improve the value of these reports, we believe the vulnerability assessment reports should recommend specific actions to overcome identified vulnerabilities. In addition, the Joint Staff should develop an antiterrorism/force protection best practices or lessons learned program that would share recommendations for physical and process-oriented improvements. The program would assist installations in finding answers to common problems—particularly those installations that do not receive Joint Staff Integrated Vulnerability Assessment reports or others who have found vulnerabilities through their own vulnerability assessments.
>
> To provide Congress with the most complete information on the risks that U.S. forces overseas are facing from terrorism, we recommend that the Secretary of Defense direct the services to include in their next consolidated combating terrorism budget submission information on the number and types of antiterrorism/force protection projects that have not been addressed by the budget request and the estimated cost to complete these projects. Information on the backlog of projects should be presented by geographic combatant command.
>
> To ensure that antiterrorism/force protection managers have the knowledge and skills needed to develop and implement effective antiterrorism/force protection programs, we recommend that the Secretary of Defense direct the Assistant Secretary of Defense for Special Operations and Low-Intensity Conflict to expeditiously implement the Joint Staff's draft antiterrorism/force protection manager training standard and formulate a timetable for the services to develop and implement a new course that meets the revised standards. Additionally, the Assistant Secretary of Defense for Special Operations and Low-Intensity Conflict should review the course content to ensure that the course has consistency of emphasis across the services.[19]

As is the case with the OMB data, there is no way to tie the GAO estimates to the DOD reporting on such activity. The DOD reported that the AT/FP budget for FY2001 is $3.5 billion. There is a large discrepancy between the GAO and DOD estimates, and the only thing clear is that this level of funding must now be reassessed.

### Counterterrorism

As is noted earlier, the DOD budget category for counterterrorism, which is included in reports on homeland defense, explains nothing and is essentially the DOD's budget for the U.S. Special Forces Command. It includes the U.S. Army Special Forces Command, Naval Special Warfare Command and SEALS, U.S. Air Force Special Operations Command, and Joint Special Operations Command (JSOC). This effort does have a heavy RDT&E element ($87 million in FY2001), but most of the spending is on operating and procurement spending. The budget increased from $446 million in FY1999 to $621 million in FY2000, but dropped to $555 million in FY2001. Virtually all of the shift was procurement related.[20] Much of this program is black, but there are no indications of CBRN–dedicated programs in the DOD reporting and too little information to indicate how much spending really goes to combat terrorism as distinguished from all types of special forces missions

The CTTS Program, which was renamed the Combating Terrorism Technology Support Program in 2001, has the mission of developing technology and prototype equipment to combat terrorism and to include terrorist use of nuclear, biological, and chemical weapons. The CTTS integrates DOD advanced development efforts with government-wide and international efforts. The assistant secretary of defense for special operations and low-intensity conflict executes the CTTS Program, which addresses requirements identified by the Technical Support Working Group (TSWG), an interagency forum for combating terrorism. The CTTS helps fund the research and development for the TSWG under the Interagency Working Group on Counterterrorism.

The TSWG was established as a working group of the NSC's Interagency Working Group on Counterterrorism and acts as its technology development component. The CTTS and TSWG focus on the rapid development of equipment to address critical multiagency and future threat (counter- and antiterrorism) requirements. A significant portion of the CTTS funding and development efforts and TSWG technology requirements are directly related to countering nuclear, biological, and chemical weapons.

The Office of the Assistant Secretary of Defense (OASD) (SO/LIC) also coordinates WMD terrorist consequence management. "Activities funded consist of interagency user requirements related to the personal protection, detection, identification, containment, mitigation, and disposal of terrorist-employed chemical, biological, radiological, and nuclear materials."[21] The goal is to develop protective equipment and early warning devices for WMD incidents. The funding for the CTTS has decreased slightly for FY2001 because of the completion of various projects.

### Terrorism Consequence Management

Virtually all the activity that DOD reports that is directly related to CBRN threats to the U.S. homeland is funded as part of the Terrorism Consequence Management Program. As has been discussed earlier, this is not a growth area. Total funding shrank from $369 million in FY2000 to

$265 million in FY2001, largely because of a DOD effort to reduce its responsibilities in this area. The spending in this category was divided into three major program activities:

- Domestic preparedness programs, which shrunk from $48.9 million to $10.2 million between FY1999 and FY2001, or by nearly 80 percent. These programs train emergency responders, support Rapid Response Teams, and a Chemical-Biological Emergency Response Team. It funds an interagency FBI, FEMA, DOE, EPA, U.S. Public Health Service (USPHS), and DOD coordination group.

- Consequence management response programs that rose from $106 million in FY1999 to $202 million in FY2000, and than dropped to $91 million in FY2001. These efforts lost more than 50 percent of their funding between FY2000 and FY2001.

- RDT&E efforts in terrorism consequence management, which nearly doubled between FY1999 and FY2001, and rose from $89.0 million to $164.7 million.

Those efforts reflect a successful turf fight and a failed sense of mission. DOD can pass the buck, but not the task. This is an area where its efforts need comprehensive reassessment, in view of the attacks on the World Trade Center and the Pentagon.

### Domestic Preparedness Program

The Nunn-Lugar-Domenici Act tasked the secretary of defense with leading the Emergency Response Assistance Program to train first responders. To carry out the program, the secretary of defense was directed to consult with the director of FEMA, the secretary of energy, and the heads of other federal, state, and local agencies with expertise and responsibilities in the area of emergency response. The DOD is shifting most of the first responder training effort out of the department, but it has expanded its efforts in several other areas.

The Defense against Weapons of Mass Destruction Act of 1996, also known as the Nunn-Lugar-Domenici Act, designated the DOD as the lead agency for domestic preparedness for responding to and managing the consequences of a WMD attack and with leading the Emergency Response Assistance Program to train first responders.

The DOD established the Domestic Preparedness Program to train local and state first responders for a CBRN attack in response. The program was supposed to cover the 120 largest cities in the United States based on 1990 census data, and each city could request $300,000 in equipment that is loaned from the DOD for five years. Training was to be completed in the 120 largest cities by mid-2001. This effort is continuing, but the department is shifting much of the first responder training effort out of the department.

The U.S. Army's Soldier and Biological Chemical Command was made the organization within the DOD that administered the Domestic Preparedness Program.[22] The OMB reports that the total funding for the program during FY1997–FY1999 was $66.9 million. Funding for FY2000 was $12.6 million, and the funding request for FY2001 is $31 million.[23] The DOD report states that funding for the same heading was $48.9 million in FY1999, $32.1 million in FY2000, and $10.2 million in FY2001.[24] The difference between the OMB and DOD costing seems to be largely the result of the fact that the OMB report did not take account of plans to transfer much of the DOD activity to the DOJ.

In FY2000, the Clinton administration proposed to transfer the Domestic Preparedness Program to the DOJ beginning on October 1, 2000. As a result, DOJ will complete DOD's commitments to the 120 cities.[25] The current DOD budget plan will complete this transfer management of the Domestic Preparedness Program to the DOJ in FY2001. The DOD will retain management of some programs that utilize DOD resources. The DOD will still fund the Chem-Bio Database development component of the Rapid Response Information System and also the equipment-testing program.

A March 2000 GAO report summarized progress in the Domestic Preparedness Program as follows:

Defense developed the Domestic Preparedness Program to build on the existing knowledge and capabilities of those who would first deal with a WMD incident locally: fire, law enforcement, hazardous materials, and medical personnel. Defense planned to provide personnel in the 120 largest U.S. cities (based on city population) with training and expert advice regarding emergency responses to the use or threatened use of weapons of mass destruction or related materials. Defense targeted cities for the training because it wanted to deal with a single government entity that could choose the most appropriate personnel to be trained and to receive training equipment. Defense trains city personnel, who then provide similar instruction to their emergency responder communities.

The training is generally a week long and comprises six separate courses— emergency responder awareness, emergency responder operations, technician-hazardous materials, technician-emergency medical services, technician-hospital provider, and incident command. The awareness and operations courses, each 4-hour segments, generally train responders in how to recognize a WMD incident and how to protect themselves and their communities during such incidents. The technician courses vary in length from 8 to 16 hours and are primarily for individuals in those specialties. The incident command course, 8 hours in length, focuses on the management of an incident and includes an exercise during which participants role-play their responses.

As of September 30, 1999, Defense had completed training in 67 cities and trained approximately 19,000 individuals. This includes only those individuals directly trained by Defense instructors.[26]

Table 7.4
First Responders Trained through Domestic Preparedness
Program, FY1997–FY1999

| Responder community | Number trained |
| --- | --- |
| Firefighter | 5,100 |
| Law enforcement | 4,300 |
| Emergency medical services | 1,600 |
| Hospital provider | 2,800 |
| Military | 850 |
| Other | 4,350 |
| Total | 19,000 |

The GAO also provided the data in Table 7.4 on the overall output of these training efforts.

There have been problems in the program. The lack of interagency coordination in the Domestic Preparedness Program has been an example that critics like the GAO have cited in arguing for better federal integration of terrorism programs. DOJ administers the Metropolitan Firefighters Program and FEMA administers WMD courses at its National Fire Academy and Emergency Management Institute in Maryland. The problem is the potential for an actual overlap in first responders' training among the DOD, DOJ, and FEMA programs. Furthermore, another complaint is that it is inefficient for responders in each city to attend three programs from three departments when an integrated program would save time and resources.

The GAO made the following comments:

Federal training programs on weapons of mass destruction are not well coordinated, resulting in inefficiencies in the federal effort and concerns in the first responder communities. The Departments of Defense and Justice and the Federal Emergency Management Agency are providing similar awareness courses as part of their train-the-trainer programs. Defense and Justice plan to deliver their programs to individuals in the same 120 cities, and Justice also plans to train individuals in 135 additional jurisdictions. Through September 1999, Defense had trained individuals in 67 cities, and through mid-November 1999 Justice had trained individuals in 95 cities and metropolitan areas. Training from both agencies' programs was provided to individuals in 16 common cities. State and local officials and representatives of various responder organizations expressed concerns about duplication and overlap among the two federal training programs, courses offered by the Consortium, and other courses such as hazardous materials and other specialized training that first responders are required to complete. Some officials said that the number of federal organizations involved in weapons of mass destruction training creates confusion about which federal organization is in charge of that training. Officials were concerned that the Defense and Justice programs offered to cities and counties had bypassed the states' emergency management and training structures. As a result, some responders, such as state police, had been missed. And some officials were concerned that the Defense and Justice programs will not train responders in smaller communities. They pointed out the potential to reach responders in smaller communities through the use of state and local training organizations and the use of training tools such as video transmission of instructional materials to existing facilities at firehouses and National Guard armories. The responders' concerns are consistent with the conclusions reached by a forum of over 200 state and local responders in August 1998 and a June 1999 Justice report. Common themes included the need for concise information on federal programs, a centrally coordinated and standardized national training program (to ensure an effective and integrated response and to minimize redundancy), and the need to incorporate training related to terrorist incidents involving weapons of mass destruction into existing delivery mechanisms for emergency responder communities.

Efforts are under way to improve the federal government's role in weapons of mass destruction training, but more actions are needed to eliminate duplicative training and improve the efficiency of the Defense and Justice programs. Although Defense plans to transfer its Domestic Preparedness Program to Justice on October 1, 2000, and Justice was to provide Congress with a comprehensive plan for the transfer no later than December 15, 1999, that plan had not been issued as of March 1, 2000. According to Justice officials, Justice will complete Domestic Preparedness training in the 120 cities to honor Defense's commitments to those cities. It also still plans to deliver its Metropolitan Firefighters program to individuals in 255 cities and counties. Thus, in the near term, some cities will receive similar awareness courses under both programs. Justice officials said that in the longer term, they will assess the need to continue the Domestic Preparedness Program beyond the 120 cities based on a number of factors, including comprehensive needs assessments to be completed by the states and inputs from the first responder communities. In response to requests from the first responder community, Justice has established the interagency National Domestic Preparedness Office. The Office, recently funded under the Consolidated Appropriation Act for Fiscal Year 2000, is just getting organized. According to its draft action plan, it will provide an interagency forum for coordinating federal weapons of mass destruction assistance to state and local emergency responders. The Office has identified an ambitious list of tasks directed at many of the training concerns expressed by first responders.

To improve the efficiency of federal programs, we are recommending that the Secretary of Defense and the Attorney General eliminate duplicative training in the same metropolitan areas. We are also recommending that if the Department of Justice provides Domestic Preparedness Program training in more than the currently planned 120 cities, it should integrate the program with the Metropolitan Firefighters Program to capitalize on the strengths of each program and eliminate duplication and overlap.[27]

Serious questions arise as to whether the present training and equipment activity in this area are really suited to deal with large nuclear and biological attacks or incidents and realistically examine DOD, civil, federal, state, local, and private-sector needs and capabilities for more than low- to mid-level terrorism. There seems to be a great deal more emphasis on counting training activity in most reporting on this aspect of the DOD program than assessing whether the training is realistic and adequate.

The transfer of training responsibility to the DOJ also seems to have had a very uncertain rationale. The DOD may not like the responsibility, but transfer to a civil agency only seems suitable if the program focuses on incidents that can be dealt with by normal civil defense and response agencies and if DOD and civil agencies are not called on to deal with a major nuclear or biological incident or a series of asymmetric attacks by a foreign power, proxy, or highly sophisticated terrorist agency. Even then, it is not clear why the DOJ would be chosen instead of FEMA.

### Consequence Management Response Program

The Consequence Management Response Program is the largest operational component of the overall Terrorism Consequence Management Program, and had a total budget of $90.6 million in FY2001. This effort attempts to integrate the reserves into the response effort, and functions include detection, decontamination, supporting the civil authorities, ordnance disposal, and chemical and biological field sampling and characterization. It includes activities like the Civil Support (formerly Rapid Assessment Initial Detection) Teams. It also includes the efforts of the U.S. Army response task forces and support from specialized U.S. military institutes and facilities like the U.S. Army Research Institute of Chemical Defense (USAMRICD), the U.S. Army Medical Research Institute of Infectious Disease (USAMRIID), the U.S. Army Edgewood Chemical and Biological Forensic Analytic Center Modular On-Site Laboratory, the U.S. Army Radiological Control (RADCON) Team and U.S. Navy Radiological Control (RADCON) Team, and the U.S. Army Radiological Advisory Medical Team (RAMT).

The secretary of defense has appointed the assistant to the ATSD–CS to serve as the primary coordinator of these WMD consequence management programs. The ATSD–CS coordinates by chairing the DOD's WMD Preparedness Group, which ensures the DOD's consequence management capabilities and resources are efficiently used.

The WMD Preparedness Group consists of (1) the assistant secretaries for Health Affairs; Reserve Affairs; SO/LIC; Command, Control, Communications, and Intelligence; and Legislative Affairs; the General Counsel;

(2) the deputy undersecretaries for Comptroller and for Acquisition, Technology, and Logistics; and (3) senior representatives from the JCS, the Department of the Army, and the Defense Threat Reduction Agency. The ATSD–CS also represents the DOD in the interagency task force chaired by the President's National Coordinator for Security, Infrastructure Protection, and Counterterrorism.[28] Unfortunately the level of management and control is much more impressive than the level of activity and funding.

### Defense Threat Reduction Agency

The DTRA is a Combat Support Agency directed by the chairman and the JCS, and consists of military and DOD civilians to provide vulnerability assessment to better protect military and civilian personnel. DTRA also manages the Chemical/Biological Defense Program. This funding level is not adaquate to fund anything beyond a minimal planning, analysis, and exercise effort.

DTRA was established in October 1998 through the merger of the Defense Technology Security Administration, the Defense Special Weapons Agency, the On-Site Inspection Agency, and elements of the Office of the Secretary of Defense. Its mission is to provide a coherent, focused organization that will create the intellectual infrastructure for a new approach to deal with the weapons of mass destruction challenge by bringing into one organization the principal Department of Defense organizations with weapons of mass destruction expertise. Its expertise encompasses technology security activities; cooperative threat reduction programs; arms control treaty monitoring and on-site inspection; force protection; nuclear, biological, and chemical weapons defense; and counterproliferation.

### The Chemical/Biological Defense Program

The Chemical/Biological Defense Program is oriented primarily toward the support of war fighters but has a homeland defense component. Protection against chemical and biological weapons became a high priority after the Persian Gulf War. The National Defense Authorization Act for FY1994 directed the secretary of defense to improve the DOD's chemical and biological defense programs. The DOD integrated all programs into what is now the Chemical/Biological Defense Program managed by the DTRA with oversight from the deputy assistant to the secretary of defense for chemical and biological defense, who is responsible for planning, programming, budgeting, coordinating medical and nonmedical defenses, and overseeing management. The deputy assistance secretary is also the executive secretary of the Steering Committee, which consists of directors of the Defense Threat Reduction Agency, Defense Research and Engineering, representatives of the joint JCS, the assistant secretary of defense for strategy and threat reduction, the assistant secretary for health affairs, and top officials responsible for chemical and biological defense.[29]

The Chemical/Biological Defense Program is divided into three nonmedical defensive capabilities: contamination avoidance, protection, and decontamination. Contamination avoidance means detecting and avoiding contaminated areas, and decontamination means the restoration of fighting ability after a chemical and biological attack. The creation of the program has led to a steady increase in expenditures unrelated to homeland defense. For example, funding for chemical agents and munitions destruction, which are part of the DOD category of defense-wide Procurement Appropriations Account increased $24 million from $979 million for FY2000 to $1,004 million for the FY2001.[30]

The FY1999–FY2000 program was designed to fund the highest priority counterproliferation initiatives. The DOD reviewed its capabilities to protect against the asymmetric threats from chemical and biological weapons during 2000. As a result of the review, funding was identified to enhance and accelerate high-payoff technologies and advanced military chemical and biological defense systems. Accordingly, the FY2000–FY2001 budget submission includes $380 million in increased research and development funding for biological warfare defense and vaccines over FY2000–FY2005. It also provided additional FY1999 emergency supplemental funding to procure chemical and biological defense equipment for the National Guard and reserves to support the consequence management mission.

The DOD has acted on a May 1997 report of the Quadrennial Defense Review (QDR) and its recommendation to increase planned spending on counterproliferation by $1 billion over the FY1999–FY2003 program period. As a result, it continued to procure new chemical and biological defense equipment, and $732 million was allocated for chemical and biological defense efforts. The Chemical/Biological Defense Program also invested in technologies to provide improved capabilities that have minimal adverse impact on war fighting potential. At the same time, the program has cut funding for antiterrorism and force protection. It dropped from $2.841 billion in FY1999. The program's appropriation for FY2000 was $791 million, $410 million for research and development and $381 million for procurement.[31] Spending declined to $458 million in FY2001.

Most of Chemical/Biological Defense Program's counterterrorism activity has been oriented toward conventional explosives and chemical weapons as distinguished from biological warfare. In contrast, defense-wide RDT&E in more conventional counterterrorism activity increased from $25.0 million in FY1999 to $35.1 million in FY2001.[32] An additional $30 million in RDT&E was programmed in FY2001 for SO/LIC RDT&E, all of which is described as related to attacks using conventional explosives. The part of the Chemical/Biological Defense Program that relates directly to terrorism consequence management is also being cut. The DOD budget document indicates that funding dropped from $14.9 million in FY1999, to $9.2 million in FY2000, to $1.2 million in FY2001.[33]

The research agencies of the Chemical/Biological Defense Program include the Soldier and Biological Chemical Command, the Joint Program Office for Biological Defense, and the Defense Advanced Research Projects Agency. GAO testimony provides a brief description of these research agencies:

- The Soldier and Biological Chemical Command is organized around two integrated business areas, one of which is research, development, and acquisition. Nearly half of its research, development, and acquisition funding supports the Chemical and Biological Defense Program. The Command is engaged in the full range of research and development encompassing biological and chemical systems. Its business areas include chemical detection, biological detection, decontamination, protection, and supporting science and technology.

- The Joint Program Office for Biological Defense manages the Biological Warfare Agent Detection Program. The office monitors emerging technologies for advanced development, demonstration, and upgrades of fielded biological detection systems.

- The Defense Advanced Research Projects Agency's Biological Warfare Defense Program is an applied research program established under the authority of the National Defense Authorization Act for FY1997 (PL 104–201, as amended) to fund revolutionary new approaches to biological warfare defense. The Biological Warfare Defense Program pursues high-risk, high-potential technologies from the demonstration of technical feasibility through the development of prototype systems. The goal of the program is to "develop and demonstrate technologies to thwart the use of biological warfare agents (including bacterial, viral, and bioengineered organisms and toxins) by military and terrorist opponents. DARPA's primary strategy for accomplishing this goal is to create technologies applicable to broad classes of pathogens and toxins." DARPA focuses on detection, defense, and response of biological weapons. The DOD reports that funding for DARPA has increased every year from $84 million in FY1999 to $162 million for FY2001. The largest area of funding has been Sensors, which deal with the development of technology able to discern the type of bio agents used.[34]

This effort is relatively impressive, but it is focused on military operations overseas, and its practical value in homeland defense is often uncertain. There are also management, planning, and programming problems. The GAO has repeatedly criticized the Chemical/Biological Defense Program for not following the 1993 Government Performance and Results Act, which directs agencies to focus on program outcomes and performance rather than on program resources and activities.[35] The GAO criticized the Chemical/Biological Defense Program in August 1999 and again in May 2000:

Congressional reports and administrative guidance indicate that DOD programs such as the Chemical and Biological Defense Program should follow the Results Act's outcome-oriented principles, including the establishment of general goals; quantifiable, measurable, outcome-oriented performance goals; and related measures. Moreover, research organizations such as the Research Roundtable, the National Academy of Sciences, the National Academy of Engineering, and the Institute of Medicine have concluded that both applied and basic research programs supported by the federal government could be evaluated meaningfully in accordance with the Results Act framework.

DOD's Chemical and Biological Defense Program and its R&D activities have not incorporated key Results Act principles. Program goals are vague and unmeasurable and the performance measures emphasize activities rather than impacts. In the absence of explicit and measurable goals, it is difficult to assess the impact of the Program on war fighters' ability to survive, fight, and win in a chemical and biological environment.

Chemical and Biological Defense Program research and development organizations have incorporated Results Act principles inconsistently. Only one of three DOD organizations that engage in R&D activities in support of the Chemical and Biological Defense Program has adopted the Results Act planning and evaluation tools. The remaining two cited either the utilization of equivalent planning tools or the unique challenges of evaluating research and development activities as reasons for not adopting the Results Act processes.

Our August 1999 report recommended that the Secretary of Defense direct that actions be taken to develop a performance plan for the Chemical and Biological Defense Program based on the outcome-oriented management principles embodied in the Results Act. DOD concurred with the recommendation and agreed to develop a full, detailed, and coordinated plan for inclusion in its next DOD Chemical and Biological Defense Program Annual Report to Congress. Nevertheless, the next Report to Congress in March 2000 did not contain a plan containing the elements outlined in our recommendation. In the March 2000 Report to Congress, DOD established a new set of program goals and stated specific technology and systems goals will be included in a performance plan to be completed during calendar year 2000 and included in the next annual report to Congress.[36]

The GAO also recommended in March 2000 that the Chemical/ Biological Defense Program be coordinated with the other nonmedical chemical and biological research programs:

Each of the federally funded programs conducting non-medical research and development on threats from chemical and biological agents has its own mission objective. However, we found many similarities among these programs in terms of the research and development activities they engage in, the threats they intend to address, the types of capabilities they seek to develop, the technologies they pursue in developing those capabilities, and the organizations they use to conduct the work. For example, these programs conduct a similar range of research and development activities, such as evaluating the feasibility or showing the practical utility of a technology. With regard to threat, two of the programs (those in the Department of Defense and Defense Advanced Research Projects Agency) focus on threats to the military, and the other two (those in the Department of Energy and the Technical Support Working Group) focus on threats to civilians. However, the military and civilian user communities are concerned about many of the same chemical and biological substances (such as nerve agents) and possible perpetrators (such as foreign terrorists). In addition, we found that these programs are seeking to develop many of the same capabilities, such as detection and identification of biological agents. Furthermore, the types of technologies (such as mass spectroscopy) they pursue to achieve those capabilities may overlap. Finally, these programs may contract with the same groups of laboratories to perform research and development work.

Although the four programs we examined currently use formal and informal mechanisms for coordination, we found several problems that may hamper their coordination efforts. First, participation in formal and informal coordination mechanisms is inconsistent. For instance, several of these mechanisms do not include representatives of the civilian user community. Second, program officials cited a lack of comprehensive information on which chemical and biological threats to the civilian population are the most important and on what capabilities for addressing these threats are most needed. Third, several programs do not formally incorporate existing information on chemical and biological threats or needed capabilities in deciding what research and development projects to fund. Having and using detailed information on civilian chemical and biological threats and the capabilities needed to respond to those threats would enable coordination mechanisms to better assess whether inefficient duplication or critical research gaps exist, and if so, what changes should be made in federal research and development programs.[37]

### WMD Civil Support Teams

One of the original purposes of the Chemical/Biological Defense Program was to provide WMD CSTs with equipment adequate in a response to a chemical and biological incident under the National Guard and Reserve Component Equipment Program. These WMD CSTs were formerly known as National Guard Rapid Assessment and Initial Detection Teams. Their mission is to help local and state responders assess the situation, provide technical and medical advice, define requirements, and expedite state and federal support. A team consists of seven cells: command and control, reconnaissance, medical support, security, logistics, air liaison, and communications.[38]

The program was supposed to provide fifteen WMD CSTs with equipment, with ten equipped in FY1999 and five in FY2000. Ten teams have already been established and are stationed in the ten FEMA regions around the country.[39] The DOD is now establishing seventeen new WMD CSTs. However, funding for the Terrorism Consequence Management Program dropped from $107.2 million in FY2000 to $76.4 million in FY2001, and most funds are now be spent on the sustainment of the teams instead of initial fielding of new teams. There are no plans to field new WMD CSTs in FY2001. As a result, there will only be twenty-seven WMD CSTs by the end of 2001, rather than the forty-four that were originally planned. According to the DOD, it plans to retain one WMD Rapid Response Team in addition to seventeen CSTs.

The twenty-seven WMD CSTs the department has established are composed of twenty-two full-time National Guard personnel, and the governors of the states they are deployed in have command and control of the team.[40] The WMD CSTs are the first military responders. Their mission is to deploy rapidly, assist local first responders in determining the precise nature of an incident, provide expert medical and technical advice, and help pave the way for the identification and arrival of follow-on military support. They have a goal of reaching a WMD scene within four hours. Unless federalized, the CSTs will remain state National Guard assets that can be quickly accessed by proximate governors.

### Joint Task Force for Civil Support

The DOD established the JTF-CS to coordinate the department's WMD consequence management support to local and state officials. The task force is based in Norfolk, Virginia, and is led by a National Guard brigadier general. The task force has no standing forces but can mobilize quickly at FEMA's request of assistance. The task force also has operational command and control of WMD CSTs if the teams are federalized.[41] Five million dollars has been requested for FY2001 for the JTF-CS.

### Defense Logistics Agency

One of the Defense Logistics Agency's (DLA) responsibilities is the procurement of protective equipment and training for DLA agents to plan and react during a chemical and biological incident. Of the $2.2 million appropriated to the DLA in FY2001, however, only $66,000 went toward chemical and biological incident protection for the procurement of protective suits and masks and crisis management training.

### Specialized DOD Teams and Units for Defense and Response

The DOD has a number of specially trained and equipped units capable of performing detection and decontamination, providing command and control, exercising mortuary duties, transporting contaminated personnel, performing medical functions, and operating in a CBRN environment. Several DOD elements have a twenty-four-hour, on-call emergency response capability with personnel trained in biological, chemical, and explosive ordnance disposal operations. These personnel perform render-safe procedures; provide damage limitation, reconnaissance, recovery, sampling, mitigation, decontamination, and transportation; and provide or recommend final disposition of weaponized and nonweaponized nuclear, chemical, and biological materials. The units include:

- Joint Staff Integrated Vulnerability Assessments Teams (JSIVA): The operational teams that assess "facility vulnerability to terrorist operations and the means of reducing mass casualties. These assessments include: (1) Terrorist Options; (2) Physical Security; (3) Structural Engineering and Response; (4) Infrastructure Engineering; and (5) Operations."[42] The budget of the DTRA for FY2001 is $7.6 million, which will be spent on the salaries and expenses of the JSIVA teams.

- Consequence Management Advisory Team (CMAT): The CMAT is the team that satisfies the DTRA's responsibility for aiding other DOD organizations with WMD and radiological incidents. It "provides technical, consequence management planning, weapons effects modeling, general counsel, public affairs, and health physics expertise to augment CIMC staffs."[43] The funding for the CMAT in FY2001 is $300,000.

- U.S. Army 52nd Ordnance Group (EOD): "Provides military explosive ordnance disposal (EOD)/bomb squad units to defeat or mitigate the hazards from conventional, nuclear, or chemical military munitions and weapons of mass destruction (WMD) throughout CONUS as requested by local, state, and federal law enforcement or military authorities."[44]

- U.S. Army Soldier Biological and Chemical Command (SBCCOM): Develops technological countermeasures and equipment that provide rapid warning and facilitate quick response in the event of a chemical or biological incident. Under SBCCOM, the Edgewood Research and Development Center maintains a rapidly deployable mobile environmental monitoring and technical assessment system, the Mobile Analytical Response System. This system provides analytical assessment of chemical or biological hazards at an incident site. On order, SBCCOM deploys the Chemical/Biological Rapid Response Team (C/B-RRT). The mission of the C/B-RRT is to coordinate and manage all DOD technical capabilities tasked to support a crisis response or consequence management operation. The U.S. Army Technical Escort Unit is also under SBCCOM. It is a specialized unit with missions of escorting the movement of chemical or biological material and finding and destroying chemical or biological munitions. This unit maintains a twenty-four-hour, on-call alert team that will be tailored specifically to a current situation for crisis and consequence management responses.

- U.S. Army Response Task Forces (RTF): RTF aids the lead agency in consequence management operations by creating a command and control that coordinates all other DOD elements.

- U.S. Army Medical Research Institute of Chemical Defense (USAMRICD), Medical Chemical Biological Advisory Team (MCBAT): Is the lead source for medical information for chemical agents.

- U.S. Army Medical Research Institute of Infectious Diseases (USAMRIID): USAMRIID is the lead medical research laboratory for the U.S. Biological Defense Research Program. Its role is to protect against bioterrorism and biowarfare with the ideal prevention of immunization. It conducts research to develop technologies, procedures, and training programs for medical defense against biological warfare threats and naturally occurring infectious diseases. It is a tech-based research facility that creates countermeasures for biological agents. USAMRIID's facilities include the capability to contain and care for at biosaftey level three and four. It also has an Aeromedical Isolation Team that can respond anywhere in the world and transport back to the center. USAMRIID also provides counterterrorism support with threat evaluation, rapid bio agent identification, and as a general reference to biological agents. USAMRIID is the only biological containment laboratory in the DOD capable of studying infectious diseases. USAMRIID has many existing capabilities that can be employed for evaluating terrorist incidents from initial communication of the threat or incident to its resolution. These capabilities include assisting in the evaluation of threat capability in relation to a specific agent or agents, assisting in the evaluation of delivery methods and their impacts, identifying biological agents (infectious and toxic) in samples from an incident, providing special vaccines for limited numbers of personnel who respond to or are the target of such incidents, and handling specialized transport of a limited numbers of biological casualties under containment conditions to a receiving medical facility.

- U.S. Army Edgewood Chemical and Biological Forensic Analytical Center Modular On-Site Laboratory: Provides facilities with capabilities to analyze chemical agents.

- U.S. Army Radiological Control (RADCON): Supports the RTF to provide radiological monitoring.

- U.S. Army Radiological Advisory Medical Team (RAMT): Supports the RTF and local responders during radiological health situations.

- U.S. Army Technical Escort Unit (TEU): The U.S. Army unit that handles, dismantles, and disposes of chemical and biological weapons and munitions, and is based at Aberdeen Proving Ground, Maryland.

- U.S. Army Soldier and Biological Chemical Command (SBCCOM): Formerly the Chemical and Biological Defense Command, the SBCCOM has responsibility for training development and city training visits. The organization has established a chemical and biological hot line for expert assistance in an emergency, as well as a nonemergency help line.

- U.S. Navy Environmental and Preventive Medicine Unit: This is a Chemical, Biological, Radiological, and Environmental Defense Response Team. Its teams are created on an ad hoc basis suited to the situation, and they provided assistance to Chemical/Biological Rapid Response Teams (C/B–RRT) and local responders.

- U.S. Navy Environmental and Preventative Medicine Units (NEPMU): The NEPMU provides the occupational medicine technical expertise and assessment skills necessary to mitigate the long-term effects of a CBRN incident but do not provide individual patient medical treatment. NEPMU deployable teams, called Chemical, Biological, Radiological and Environmental Defense (CBRED) Teams, are on alert for rapid response. CBRED Teams are available to advise the C/B–RRT and public health authorities and to augment other C/B–RRT medical assets.

- U.S. Navy Explosive Ordnance Groups: These groups can be tasked to eliminate hazards from explosives that jeopardize operations conducted in support of the National Military Strategy. U.S. Navy Explosive Ordnance Disposal (EOD) detachments are structured for a relatively small footprint and rapid response in a variety of environments, afloat and ashore, and are capable of responding to underwater and surface ordnance, nuclear, biological, chemical, and improvised explosive device (IED) threats.

- U.S. Navy Medical Research Center Biological Defense Research Program (BDRP): This program defends members of the armed forces against a biological threat in a theater of operations. The BDRP has developed a capability that consists of a transportable biological field laboratory that is composed of four basic components that combine to provide a capability to identify bacteria, viruses, and toxins. Furthermore, the program conducts hand-held screening assays and immunoassays for clinical and environmental samples that can be deployed globally.

- Office of Naval Research (ONR) Naval Research Laboratory (NRL): is the U.S. Navy's corporate laboratory, which conducts multidisciplinary programs of scientific research and technology. The NRL is capable of providing uniformed microbiologists specifically trained in the use of U.S. Navy Medical Research Center (NMRC) laboratory equipment and tests in order to augment the NMRC. All NRL microbiologists are trained to work with chemical and biological threat agents.

- Marine Corps Chemical/Biological Incident Response Force (CBIRF): A U.S. Marine Corps unit that is developing the capacity to identify chemical and biological agents, "assess downwind hazards, conduct advanced lifesaving support, and decontaminate patients." Provide communications and enhance transportation capability. The CBIRF is a 373-man marine unit established to provide a chemical and biological incident capability. Funds were provided to stand it up in FY1999 and FY2000, and its equipment has been steadily improved. In FY1997, the DOD allocated $10 million for equipment to support the CBIRF. The DOD reports that the procurement for FY2001 is $1.9 million. Most funding, however, has gone for chemical warfare related equipment, and the CBIR only begins to acquire extensive amounts of biological warfare equipment in FY2001. Even then, most of its capability depends on the success of RDT&E activities described in the FY2001 program, which have no clear deployment date.[45] The CBIRF has limited technical expertise and manning and the DOD budget report has it sized as a medium incident chemical attack response force with limited biological incident capability.

- U.S. Air Force: For FY1999 the House appropriated $120 million for the provision of crisis response aviation support for critical national security, law enforcement, and emergency response agencies. This money was provisional, with the understanding that the president woul submit to Congress by March 15, 1999, an interagency agreement for the utilization of DOD assets to support the crisis response requirements of the FBI and FEMA.

- U.S. Air Force Radiation Assessment Team (AFRAT): The AFRAT is indirectly funded with operation and management funds from the Institute for Environment, Safety, and Occupational Health Risk Analysis (IERA), Radiation Protection Division. These funds go toward the equipment and training the AFRAT needs to respond to radiological incidents. The AFRAT is a small forty-three-person team funded with discretionary funding. It is one of the few teams with dedicated capabilities that could respond to a serious radiological incident.[46] AFRAT consists of three separate Unit Type Codes (UTCs): Nuclear Incident Response Force (NIRF) Team 1, NIRF 2, and the Radioanalytical Assessment Team (RAT). The teams are located at Brooks Air Force Base, Texas, and are assigned to the U.S. Air Force Material Command (AFMC). The AFRAT NIRF 1 and 2 provide rapid response to a wide range of radiological incidents and accidents and to the supported medical authority to ensure proper force protection. The RAT provides the supported medical authority with rapid and accurate evaluation of environmental and occupational samples. The generated data is analyzed and presented to provide the medical authority with expert guidance on effective force protection and consequence management. This UTC can deploy as a stand-alone team, or as a follow-on capability to the AFRAT NIRF teams.

- The U.S. Air Force provides the aircraft for the interagency Foreign Emergency Support Team (FEST). FEST assists with the management of terrorist attacks in foreign countries. The DOD needs funding to replace the thirty-eight-year-old aircraft. Seventy-three million dollars was appropriated in the FY Supplemental.[47] The DOD reports that there is no planned funding for FEST in FY2001. The replacement aircraft will be used.

- U.S. Air Force CBRNE-CM units include the following: Medical Biological Augmentation Teams, Bioenvironmental Engineering Nuclear, Biological, and Chemical Teams, Medical Patient Decontamination Teams, Medical Theater Epidemiology Teams, Medical Infectious Disease Teams with Augmentation, Medical Nuclear Incident Response Forces, Medical Radioanalytical Assessment Teams, and Medial Radiology Augmentation Teams.

- U.S. Air Force Institute for Environment, Safety and Occupational Health Analysis (AFIERA): maintains medical laboratory and technical capabilities, assets, and units at Brooks Air Force Base, Texas. Capabilities include a wide range of analytical, consultative, and monitoring services focused on the assessment of operational radiological, chemical, and biological risks to deployed populations. They also include laboratory support for the identification of biological agents of clinical concern; medical samples and select environmental samples; and analysis of numerous chemical compounds and radioactive elements in soil, vegetation, tissue, excreta, industrial materials, and air.

- National Guard: The Reserve Component Consequence Management Program Integration Office has been established under the command of the director of military support in order to integrate reserve and National Guard components into the national domestic preparedness strategy. This office will coordinate training, equipping, and exercising of reservists and National Guard components.

- Military Reserves: Reservists, like the National Guard, will be utilized to train first responders in their community and mobilized in the event of an attack. The DOD plans to establish 170 reconnaissance and decontamination teams, drawn mostly from existing chemical companies, to train and be equipped to support the Rapid Response Teams. The Reserve Component Consequence Management Program Integration Office has been established under the command of the director of military support in order to integrate Reserve and Guard components into the national domestic preparedness strategy. This office will coordinate training, equipping, and exercising of reservists and National Guard components.

- Defense Technical Response Group (DTRG): This group is a deployable team of civilian DOD scientists who provide specialized one-of-a-kind equipment and on-scene technical advice to EOD operators during a CBRN incident. The DTRG also provides support to military EOD technicians in the field at all command levels. Primary duties include providing safe access routes to suspect ordnance, training, and liaison support to other agencies.

- Special Operations Command: Special Mission Units are manned, equipped, and trained to deal with transnational threats, including WMD. The include members from the U.S. Army Delta Force, U.S. Navy SEAL Team 6, and U.S. Air Force Special Tactics Squadron 1. Also can include the U.S. Army's 75th Ranger Regiment and the 160th Special Operations Regiment. The Special Mission Units are under the command of the JSOC at Fort Bragg, North Carolina.

- Central Command: Central Command's area of responsibility extends to the Middle East and much of Africa. Within this area, this command must ensure the security of Americans and their property abroad from acts of terrorism. Central Command acts as the military's forward deployed eyes, ears, and arms to counter acts of terrorism within its area of responsibility.

Unfortunately, this list is far more impressive than the capabilities such teams and groups can provide. Most are small and have limited capability, and most have only a secondary mission in dealing with weapons of mass destruction. In some cases, overall funding is marginal at best.

### Research and Development

The DARPA is the core of the independent research and development funding identified in the DOD budget analysis for the Terrorism Consequence Management Program. The RDT&E activity in this category was funded at $89.0 million in FY1999, $134.7 in FY2000, and $164.7 million in FY2001. The DARPA portion was funded at $84.0 million in FY1999, $131.7 in FY2000, and $162.1 million in FY2001. This is a relatively robust effort and reflects a realistic emphasis on RDT&E in an area where the existing threat is limited, but major advances in technology are needed to defend against future threats like genetically engineered biological weapons.

The DARPA Biological Warfare Defense Program covers a wide range of efforts to create new characterization systems and defenses against bacterial, viral, and bioengineered organisms and toxins and to address full-scale and minor terrorist attacks. It involves major advances in detection and characterization technology to reduce the false alarm rate, increase speed, and deal with complex attacks. The program also involves consequence management and external protection technology, asymmetrical protocols for biological warfare defense, and genetic sequencing research.

It is important to note that this RDT&E program does not have strong service counterparts, and seems to be the only major U.S. government effort to seek major, new solutions to the threat posed by biological attacks. The military service and CDC efforts have an RDT&E component, but funding is comparatively limited and is concentrated on improving detection and response through the growth of existing technologies.

At the same time, the DARPA program is not described in ways that show any great consistency of effort from year-to-year or that give any evidence of a coherent future-year program. Such planning may exist, but it is not described in unclassified DOD or DARPA literature. No timelines or cost estimates seem to exist for deployment of most of the technologies involved, which generally are designed to fill critical ongoing gaps in the present U.S. government effort to deal with the threat posed by biological weapons.

### Intelligence

The broader problems in the U.S. intelligence effort were addressed in the discussion of the CIA. Virtually all funding in the intelligence category reported by the DOD goes to counterintelligence activity, with very limited funding for research and development. The counterintelligence effort is funded at $107 million in FY1999 and FY2000, and $106 million in FY2001. The RDT&E effort was funded at $4.1 million, $6.4 million, and $5.7 million, respectively. Total intelligence funding is $111.2 million in FY1999, $113.2 million in FY2000, and $111.7 million in FY2001.

In practice, the budget description of this activity indicates that virtually all of the intelligence activity involved is designed to support the force protection mission at the tactical level. None goes to developing new intelligence methods or broader intelligence efforts to deal with emerging threats or asymmetric warfare. Any funding of improved CIA, NSA, and DIA efforts is funded under other aspects of the national security budget. The independent RDT&E effort does, however, fund a limited program to support the Vice President's Task Force on Terrorism for preincident intelligence gathering and operations.

### Counterforce Capability against an Adversary's Nuclear, Biological, and Chemical Infrastructures

There are a number of other DOD activities that are not included in the department's reporting on homeland defense and that could play a major role in deterring, preempting, and defending against asymmetric attacks by foreign states and terrorist movements. These include DOD efforts to improve its capability to locate and strike against the headquarters, production facilities, weapons, and facilities used in such attacks.

The DOD's January 2001 report on counterproliferation noted that its combat forces have standing a mission need statement to be able to detect, characterize, and defeat nuclear, biological, and chemical facilities with minimal collateral effects. U.S. forces must be able to interdict an adversary's biological and chemical capability during each stage of an agent's employment. These counterforce operations include attacking agent production facilities, storage complexes, and deployed mobile weapon platforms. The DOD is developing a wide range of systems to improve its counterforce capabilities.

- The U.S. Air Force is conducting the Agent Defeat Weapon (ADW) program to develop the capability to destroy, neutralize, immobilize, or deny an adversary access to biological and chemical agents with little or no collateral damage. The effort is currently in concept exploration. Studies are being performed to identify and evaluate concepts to satisfy the mission need, with the goal of fielding an NBC-specific strike capability. All concepts must comply with relevant arms control treaties. Analysis tools are being developed to support ADW include agent release models, internal dispersion and venting models, and a lethality model to evaluate inventory and conceptual weapon effectiveness against NBC weapons and associated delivery systems.

- The Hard and Deeply Buried Target Defeat Capability (HDBTDC) program . . . is to develop intelligence and conventional weapons systems capable of denying access to, disrupting operations of, or destroying defended hard and deeply buried facilities. The HDBTDC effort is supported by Intelligence Community resources directed at finding and characterizing these facilities worldwide. Attaining the HDBTDC objective requires the organized efforts of the Services, DOD agencies, the Intelligence Community, and national laboratories. . . . Hardened targets are facilities that have been designed and constructed to make them difficult to defeat using current conventional weapons. Such facilities increasingly are being used to house NBC weapons, materials, and production capabilities. In some cases, these facilities might be used for other related support activities, e.g., command and control centers. Hardened, fixed targets fall into two broad categories. Many are hardened by using soil, concrete, and rock boulders atop the structure once it has been built. These cut and cover facilities are often built into an excavation and then covered. The second category includes tunnels and deep shafts, where the protection is provided by existing rock and soil. There is a depth threshold at which it becomes more economical to tunnel rather than to excavate and cover. Below this threshold, costs generally are constant regardless of the depth of the tunnel below the surface, so tunneled facilities can achieve functional depths of hundreds of meters. For this reason, tunnels often are referred to as deeply buried facilities.

- DTRA Hard Target Defeat projects are a key component of the DOD capability acquisition efforts and are an example of ongoing national technical efforts to develop the capability to defeat hard and deeply buried targets. Examples of research efforts within these projects include: Geomechanical modeling to identify the key aspects of geology impacting strike weapons penetration and damage propagation, advanced simulation and testing to improve understanding of weapons effects and effects-target coupling, and development of an operations-friendly automated target planning tool for tunnel defeat. Development of improved capabilities to understand target characteristics and functions, facilitating the identification of specific vulnerabilities that may be exploited.

- The Counterproliferation Advanced Concept Technology Demonstration (ACTD) develops, demonstrates, and delivers improved counterforce capabilities. DTRA serves as the lead for technology development, coordinating the contributions of multiple DOD components and the United States European Command serves as the primary operational sponsor. Priorities include improved capabilities for characterization and defeat of NBC targets, enhanced capabilities for forecasting and limiting collateral effects that might be associated with such attacks, and assisting the war fighter in the development of operational concepts. . . . In a conventional attack against an NBC facility, collateral effects may be due primarily to the response of the target, not the direct effects produced by the weapon; e.g., as might occur if a conventional bomb hits a chemical weapon storage bunker. Using the best experimental data available, plus lessons learned during the Gulf War, DTRA developed the munitions effectiveness assessment tool for weapons employment and combat assessments, and the hazard prediction assessment capability for prediction of collateral effects. These products have been transferred to multiple war fighting commands. The Joint Staff has recommended that they be accepted as the NATO standard for planning and assessing NBC facility attacks. A hard-target smart fuze is being evaluated which will optimize weapons detonation location to maximize lethality with minimum collateral effects. The fuze has had several successful tests of varying types, including live drops from Air Force and Navy aircraft against surrogate targets. An advanced unitary penetrator was demonstrated that will increase the penetration capability of a 2000-pound class warhead by a factor greater than two.

- Additional development and evaluation efforts involve a new inertial terrain-aided guidance capability, a weapon-borne sensor, and tactical unattended ground sensors. Improved sensors and guidance are important as enabling conditions for better characterization of targets and more effective and discriminate attacks against NBC facilities.

- Restorations of Operations (RestOps) ACTD Operations at fixed installations, including seaports and aerial ports of embarkation and debarkation and tactical airbases, are critical for U.S. strategic mobility and power projection. The consequences from a CB weapons attack on these essential fixed sites could seriously restrict the capability of U.S. forces to prosecute the war fighter. Forces at these sites must be able to mitigate the effects of such an attack and quickly restore operational capability. . . . The RestOps ACTD, which began in FY2000 and will continue through FY2003, will demonstrate those mitigating actions taken before, during and after an attack to protect against and immediately react to the consequences of a CB attack. These actions aim to restore operating tempo in mission execution and movement of individuals and material to support combat operations at a fixed site. . . . The objectives of the RestOps ACTD are (a) Integrate and demonstrate mature technologies and tools used to mitigate adverse effects and restore operations at a fixed site before, during, or after an attack of either chemical or biological weapons, (b) develop, improve, and integrate concepts of operations (CONOPS) and tactics, techniques, and procedures (TTPs) for executing RestOps contingencies at a fixed site, (c) capture lessons learned for incorporation into joint, multiservice, and service doctrine, and (d) evaluate the science and technologies available to support identification of potential improvements in current U.S. policy for CONUS and OCONUS RestOps scenarios.

## The Cooperative Threat Reduction Program

The Cooperative Threat Reduction (CTR) Program is another DOD program that is not counted as part of the DOD counterterrorism effort, even though it sharply reduces the threat that hostile states, terrorists, and extremists can obtain or build a nuclear weapon. The passage of the Soviet Nuclear Threat Reduction Act of 1991, which was sponsored by Senators Nunn and Lugar, established a program to respond to the threat of proliferation of the former Soviet Union arsenal of nuclear and chemical weapons and biological weapons materials and expertise that are in the territories of several New Independent States (NIS).[48]

The legislation designated the DOD as the executive agent for the program. Congress has authorized approximately $3.2 billion for the CTR Program as part of the annual DOD budget over the past nine years. The DOD uses these funds to help and encourage NIS states to dismantle strategic weapons and associated delivery systems; improve the security of thousands of WMD and weapons materials; prevent the proliferation of weapons technologies and technical experts; and facilitate defense and military contacts to encourage military reductions and reform.

The FY2000 budget submission initiated the Expanded Threat Reduction Initiative (ETRI), providing an additional $1.1 billion for CTR as well as additional funds for the State Department and DOE. Approximately 25 percent was identified for DOD CTR Program execution. The CTR Program is a mechanism through which a significant percentage of the president's ETRI will be funded and executed by the DOD. The president's budget through the Future Year Defense Plan included $4.5 billion for essential U.S. assistance programs under the ETRI. Future implementation of the ETRI program will build on the security cooperation and partnerships established by the DOD through the CTR Program.

A series of government-to-government umbrella agreements have been negotiated with NIS nations to establish the legal framework for CTR assistance activities and to provide a system of rights, exemptions, and protections for U.S. assistance personnel and for CTR Program activities. The agreements designate the DOD as the U.S. executive agent and various ministries in recipient states as executive agents for CTR program implementation. These agreements are in place for Russia, Ukraine, Kazakhstan, Georgia, Moldova, and Uzbekistan (Belarus has not been eligible to receive CTR assistance since 1997); others may be concluded with additional NIS states certified as eligible for CTR program assistance in the future.

The CTR Program has played an important role in deactivation of 5,014 nuclear warheads. CTR is actively enhancing security for dangerous biological agents. It helps to sustain the DOD's efforts to complete safety, security, and accounting improvements for Russian nuclear weapons at over one hundred nuclear weapons storage locations and to provide secure transport of the weapons to security-enhanced storage or dismantlement. The DOD is prepared to build a second wing for the Mayak fissile material storage facility, as well as support more directly the preparation of fissile material from weapons for long-term secure storage of up to fifty thousand containers of fissile material, and to eliminate weapons-grade plutonium production. CTR projects in Ukraine include the elimination of 14 SS-19 and 54 SS-24 missiles, 29 missile launchers, launch control centers, 23 bomber aircraft, and 493 air-launched cruise missiles. In addition, projects for nuclear and biological capabilities infrastructure elimination are planned in Ukraine and Kazakhstan.

CTR is focusing on three efforts to encourage the elimination of the chemical and biological weapons capabilities of the NIS. It is establishing an analytical monitoring capability to support Russia's chemical weapons destruction capability, developing security enhancements for chemical weapons stockpiles, and demilitarizing former chemical weapons facilities. It has proposed a fourth chemical weapons activity: the construction of a chemical weapons destruction facility at Shchuch'ye, which would be capable of destroying five hundred metric tons of nerve agent per year. It would also support the president's commitment to assist Russia in eliminating these weapons and to facilitate Russia's implementation of the CWC. In addition, CTR is prepared to significantly expand its biological weapons proliferation prevention program through collaborative research, securing dangerous pathogens at a number of facilities, and dismantling capacity that is not needed for peaceful purposes.

### Conclusions

The DOD has made progress in many areas. At the same time, there is clearly a major problem because the DOD has pushed hard to shift the homeland defense mission to civil departments and agencies. There is still a lack of focus and coherent organization of the DOD's efforts, at least as described in its public reporting. This is best exemplified by (1) the failure to tie together all of the key activities relating to homeland defense into a coherent plan, (2) the use of a narrow and often dysfunctional definition of counterterrorism, (3) the discrepancies in the DOD and OMB estimates of funding to combat terrorism, and (4) the lack of any apparent dedicate future year planning and programming effort. These problems point to obvious solutions. Counterterrorism is only a subset of a much broader problem that affects homeland defense in a world in which the risks of asymmetric conflicts and attacks force us to rethink our entire approach to national security. There is a clear need for a dedicated and more open PPB and FYP effort that covers all aspects of the problem. That also allows the president, Congress, and outside analysts to understand which programs and funding are moving forward, the current and planning capabilities, and the balance between the different kinds of defensive activity.

## DEPARTMENT OF ENERGY

The DOE plays a broad range of roles in defense against CBRN attacks. Table 7.1 provides a breakdown of the budget for DOE's activities relating directly to defense and response against terrorist attacks, and shows that its budget totaled $499 million in FY1998, $611 million in FY1999, $648 million in FY2000, and $664 million in FY2001.

DOE provides first responder training through established programs like the FBI's Hazardous Device School and loans pager-sized radiation detection instruments to FBI–accredited bomb technicians.[49] The DOE also maintains the Radiological Assistance Program, which provides twenty-four-hour access to personnel and equipment for radiological emergencies. It maintains the Radiation Emergency Assistance Center/Training Site, which provides around-the-clock direct and consultative assistance in the area of human health effects of radiological hazards. The program also trains emergency medical technicians, physicians, and nurses. This program works closely with DOD's Domestic Preparedness Program. Another element of DOE's antiterrorism effort is the Atmospheric Release Advisory Capability, which does computer-based predictive monitoring for tracking atmospheric dispersions of radiation and HAZMAT. Total FY1997 DOE spending for unclassified terrorism-related programs totaled approximately $1.42 billion.[50] There are a number of other important activities that the DOE oversees.

### Office of Nonproliferation and National Security

This office coordinates DOE activities in nonproliferation, nuclear safeguards and security, and emergency management.

### Office of Emergency Management

This office acts as single point of contact for all DOE emergency management and threat assessment–related activities. It operates the Headquarters Emergency Operations Center, the Communications Center, and the DOE Emergency Communications Network. It also ensures that a viable technical response is in place for any type of radiological or nuclear accident or incident including radiological releases, U.S. nuclear weapons accidents, or a malevolent event involving an improvised nuclear device or radiological dispersal device.

### Office of Defense Programs

This office ensures the safety, reliability, and performance of nuclear weapons without underground nuclear testing.

### Office of Emergency Response

This office is tasked with developing the ability to immediately respond to radiological accidents or incidents anywhere in the world. Directs seven emergency response capabilities, including Nuclear Emergency Search Teams (NEST).

### Nuclear Emergency Search Team

The DOE also provides NEST, which helps to resolve nuclear and radiological terrorist attacks. NEST consists of an advisory team to the LFA, search teams that can train and equip local and state responders, and joint technical operations teams that work with explosive ordnance disposal teams to neutralize a nuclear or radiological device. The FY2001 budget request for NEST is $44 million.[51] Its staff consists of engineers, scientists, and other technical specialists from the DOE's national laboratories and other contractors. It is deployable within four hours of notification with specially trained teams and equipment to assist the FBI in handling nuclear or radiological threats. NEST assets include intelligence, communications, search, assessment, access, diagnostics, disablement, operations, containment/damage limitations, logistics, and health physics capabilities.

### Radiological Assistance Program

Another program is the Radiological Assistance Program. The program is responsible for coordinating local bomb-squad responder plans with national response plans. The program divides the country into eight regions, and each region has a regional coordinating office, a federal response coordinator, and at least three response teams.[52]

## The Nuclear Safeguards, Security, and Emergency Operations Program

The Nuclear Safeguards, Security, and Emergency Operations Program is the primary DOE program to protect sensitive nuclear materials and assets. The Office of Security and Emergency Operations administers the program in a process involving updating threat assessments, security policy and implementation, and consequence management plans. Included in the Nuclear Safeguards, Security, and Emergency Operations Program is a technology development and applications program. The technology program has the responsibility of deploying security systems at DOE sites and for DOE security forces. The security systems defend against a variety of weapons, including explosives and chemical attacks. The FY2001 budget request included $25 million for the technology program.[53]

### Research and Development

The DOE requested $92 million for FY2001 for research and development. The research into chemical, materials, and biological sciences helps the DOE develop defenses against chemical and biological weapons attacks. The DOE's Chemical and Biological Nonproliferation Program (CBNP) plays an active part in combating the threat of chemical and biological weapons. The OMB states, "The strategy of the CBNP relies on close linkages between technology development and systems analysis and integration to systematically and comprehensively address the domestic chemical and biological terrorism threat."[54] CBNP's funding has grown from $17 million in FY1997 to a projected $63 million in FY2001.[55]

### ENVIRONMENTAL PROTECTION AGENCY

The OMB indicates that the EPA budgets $2 million to $3.2 million a year on combating terrorism and WMD preparedness. The EPA has several counterterrorism functions. These include:

- Responsibility over preparation and response to emergencies with oil, hazardous substances, and certain radiological materials
- Assist in the Domestic Preparedness Program on HAZMAT identification and with environmental cleanup
- Develop community response plans to deal with accidental or deliberate releases of HAZMAT substances and participate in the first responder training program[56]

The EPA's preparedness and response activities are exercised under the authority of the National Oil and Hazardous Substances Pollution Contingency Plan (NCP) and the Radiological Response Program. The EPA also provides technical assistance, response coordination and management, and resource assistance to local and state responders under the National Response System, which is the federal government's mechanism for emergency response to releases of HAZMAT contaminants that threaten human health or the environment.[57]

PDD-63 named the EPA the lead agency for the water supply sector. PDD-39 also directed the EPA to assist the FBI with HAZMAT and threat assessment in a terrorist attack and to assist FEMA with decontamination and cleanup. The directives allow the EPA to participate in crisis and consequence management phases of a terrorist attack.[58] The EPA also contributes to the DOD's Domestic Preparedness Program and provides HAZMAT training to areas not served by the Domestic Preparedness Program.[59]

### Office of Solid Waste and Emergency Response

The Chemical Emergency Preparedness and Prevention Office is the primary office within the Office of Solid Waste and Emergency Response that coordinates preparedness and prevention of chemical accidents and oil spills. It is responsible for the overall management and coordination of the EPA's activities involving accident prevention, preparedness, and response for natural and manmade disasters. It also oversees the EPA's Counter-Terrorism Planning Preparedness Program and the National Security Emergency Preparedness Program.

### On-Scene Coordinator

The federal on-scene coordinator (OSC) is the primary official under the National Response System. The EPA has approximately 215 OSCs for inland zones and the U.S. Coast Guard provides OSCs for coastal zones. OSCs are activated by the National Response Center, a first alert center for CBRN substances released into the environment. An OSC is the point of contact between federal and local officials and has the authority to manage all response efforts at the incident scene. An OSC can call on the Environment Response Team, the Radiological Emergency Response Team, and the U.S. Coast Guard National Strike Force.[60] The FY2001 budget request for these activities is $3.2 million.[61]

## FEDERAL EMERGENCY MANAGEMENT AGENCY

PDD-39 and PDD-62 designated FEMA as the lead federal consequence management agency if state and local officials request federal assistance.[62] Initially, the FBI maintains command until the attorney general transfers the lead agency role to FEMA.[63] The Bush Administration plans to further strengthen the role of FEMA. Although details of its plans are not yet clear, it must now react to the lessons learned from the attacks on the World Trade Center and the Pentagon.

FEMA plays a major role in defense against CBRN attacks. Table 7.1 provides a breakdown of the budget for FEMA's activities relating directly to defense and response against terrorist attacks, and shows that its budget totaled $5.9 million in FY1998, $17.6 million in FY1999, and $30.8 million in FY2000. FEMA's budget request for WMD preparedness in FY2001 was $34.5 million; $4 million will go toward the new Urban Search and Rescue Teams. Six teams will be created and these teams will operate in a CBRN–contaminated environment, and $24 million will go toward local and state assistance.[64] The Center for Nonproliferation, Monterey Institute of International Studies has summarized FEMA's counterterrorism efforts as follows:

- FEMA acts in support of the FBI in Washington, D.C., and on the scene of the crisis until the attorney general transfers the lead to FEMA.
- Though state and local officials bear primary responsibility for consequence management, FEMA is in charge of the federal aspects of consequence management to a terrorist act. Consequence management includes protecting public health and safety and providing emergency relief to state governments, businesses, and individuals.
- Chairs the Senior Interagency Coordination Group for consequence management policy issues and initiatives (includes representatives from DOD, DOJ, DOE, HHS, DOT, Agriculture, EPA, and General Services Administration).[65]

While FEMA's main role is to coordinate the federal response effort to a major attack or terrorist incident, it performs a number of ongoing planning and training activities.

### Response and Recovery Directorate

FEMA's Response and Recovery Directorate manages the Rapid Response Information System to inventory physical assets and equipment available to state and local officials and provides a database of chemical and biological agents and safety precautions.

### Preparedness, Training, and Exercises Directorate

FEMA's Preparedness, Training, and Exercises Directorate trains emergency managers, firefighters, and elected officials in consequence management through the Emergency Management Institute and the National Fire Academy at the National Emergency Training Center in Emmitsburg, Maryland. It also conducts exercises in WMD terrorism consequence management through the Comprehensive Exercise Program. These exercises provide the opportunity to investigate the capability of the Federal Response Plan to deal effectively with consequence management and to test the ability of different levels of response to interact.

FEMA also maintains the Rapid Response Information System, which can be used as a reference guide, training aid, and an overall planning and training resource for response to a chemical, biological, and/or nuclear terrorist incident. It is made up of several databases consisting of chemical and biological agents' and radiological materials' characteristics, first aid measures, federal response capabilities, help lines, hot lines, and other federal information sources concerning potential weapons of mass destruction. It is accessible on the Internet at <http://www.rris.fema.gov>.

### U.S. Fire Administration

The U.S. Fire Administration provides training to firefighters and other first responders through the National Fire Academy in conjunction with the Preparedness, Training, and Exercises Directorate.

### National Fire Academy and Emergency Management Institute

FEMA's Emergency Management Institute and National Fire Academy have both instituted new courses in first responder training. FEMA provides WMD and first responder training at its National Fire Academy and its Emergency Management Institute in Emmitsburg, Maryland. The academy and institute also provide materials to local and state officials to train responders. Some of these courses are "train the trainer" courses. About seventy-one thousand individuals have participated in the academy's training from October 1, 1997, through September 30, 1999.[66] A March 2000 GAO report provides a program description:

- FEMA provides WMD training to first responders through its National Fire Academy and its Emergency Management Institute. These organizations offer training at their combined residence campus in Emmitsburg, Maryland, and provide course materials to individuals for self-study or to state and local training organizations for their use. In addition, they offer courses that were not developed specifically for dealing with WMD incidents but would assist first responders with those incidents.

- The Fire Academy offers six courses to prepare first responders to manage the consequences of a terrorist WMD incident. It provides the training at its campus and also provides training materials for use by individuals and state and local training organizations. One course, its 6-day incident management course, is offered on campus and to state and local training organizations for their use. The other five courses are offered off campus using Academy-developed materials. These courses train individuals in emergency response to terrorism through (1) a self-paced, self-study course; (2) a basic concepts course, the same 16-hour course offered by Justice in its Metropolitan Firefighters program; (3) a two-day more advanced course for the first on-scene supervisor; (4) a two-day more advanced course for the first on-scene emergency medical services personnel; and (5) a two-day more advanced course for the first on-scene hazardous materials personnel. Many of these are train-the-trainer courses. About 71,000 students have participated in the Fire Academy's offerings from October 1, 1997, through September 30, 1999. This includes students trained by Academy instructors and by student instructors.

• The Emergency Management Institute also offers several courses related to the use of WMD. It offers a five-day course, integrated emergency management consequences of terrorism, on campus. Off campus, it offers a one-day course, senior officials workshop on terrorism, and a series of courses involving specific WMD scenarios, such as an anthrax incident, to aid senior officials to respond to and manage a WMD event.[67]

Both organizations offer courses on and off campus, which are not specifically WMD related but can help first responders deal with WMD incidents. For example, the institute has a five-and-a-half-day radiological emergency response operations course that provides training on response and management of radiological incidents.

Funding for FEMA's first responder training totaled $4 million in fiscal year 1998 and $3.6 million in fiscal year 1999 and is projected at about $6.4 million in fiscal year 2000. Included are small, antiterrorism training grants that FEMA makes available to the states, either directly or through its Fire Academy. FEMA's direct grants totaled about $1.2 million in fiscal years 1998 and 1999, or about $23,000 per state. The states can use these grants for a variety of purposes. For example, officials we met with in North Carolina and Virginia said that they have used FEMA grant money to help fund training in their community college and fire academy systems. The Academy's grants totaled about $2 million in fiscal year 1998 and $4 million in fiscal year 1999 and are budgeted for $4 million for fiscal year 2000. The states have to apply for the grants and can use the funds to pay for instructor travel, training equipment, and the use of facilities.

The Academy's and Institute's programs have been examples that critics like the GAO have cited in arguing for better federal integration of terrorism programs. DOD administers the Domestic Preparedness Program and DOJ administers the Metropolitan Firefighters program. The problem is the potential for and actual overlap in first responders' training among the DOJ, DOD, and FEMA programs. Furthermore, critics argue it is inefficient for responders in each city to attend three programs from three departments when an integrated program would save time and resources. However, DOJ and FEMA focus on slightly different populations. DOJ concentrates on the large metropolitan areas while FEMA makes its training available throughout the United States.[68]

As Table 7.1 shows, funding for FEMA's counterterrorism activities has increased tremendously from FY1998 to FY2001. Overall, it has increased 480 percent to $34.5 million, and all of the money goes toward WMD preparedness.[69]

## GENERAL SERVICES ADMINISTRATION

The GSA is involved in improving the defense of federal facilities against CBRN attacks. Table 7.1 provides a breakdown of the budget for GSA's activities relating directly to defense and response against terrorist attacks, and shows that its budget totaled $89.6 million in FY1998, $113.5 million in FY1999, $92.8 million in FY2000, and $116.9 million in FY2001. Most GSA money is spent on the physical protection of federal facilities. Table 7.1 also shows that GSA is not spending any money specifically on CBRN threats.[70]

## DEPARTMENT OF HEALTH AND HUMAN SERVICES

The HHS plays a critical role in responding to biological attacks. PDD-62 designated the HHS as the lead federal agency for medical emergency responses arising from WMD incidents. The HHS is also in charge of public health and medical consequence management of WMD attacks as mandated by Emergency Support Function 8 of the Federal Response Plan. Twelve agencies support the HHS in consequence management.[71] These include:

- U.S. Centers for Disease Control (CDC): The federal agency responsible for protecting the public health of the country through prevention and control of diseases and other preventable conditions and responding to public health emergencies. The CDC also works with national and international agencies to eradicate or control communicable diseases and other preventable conditions.

- Office of Emergency Preparedness: Coordinates the health and medical response of the federal government, in support of state and local governments, in the aftermath of terrorist acts involving chemical or biological agents. It was appropriated $2.5 million by the FY1999 Omnibus bill for a national medical disaster system.

- Metropolitan Medical Strike Teams (MMST): These teams provide initial on-site response and safe patient transportation to hospital emergency rooms and medical and mental health care to victims, and will move victims to other regions should local health care resources be overrun during a terrorist attack. Prototypes of the MMST were established in Washington, D.C., and in Atlanta, Georgia, during the 1996 Summer Olympic Games. Approximately twenty-five cities have been chosen to begin development of these teams.

- National Institutes of Health (NIH): Federal focal point for biomedical research, including extensive vaccine research. It was appropriated $10 million in the FY1999 Omnibus bill for vaccine research and development in support of bioterrorism preparedness.

Table 7.1 provides a breakdown of the budget for HHS activities relating directly to defense and response against terrorist attacks, and shows that the budget totaled $15.9 million in FY1998, $173.1 million in FY1999, $277.5 million in FY2000, and $265.3 million in FY2001. HHS' counterterrorism efforts are being exclusively focused on WMD preparedness. The FY2001 budget request of $265.3 million was slightly lower than the FY2000 budget, but funding still increased over sixteenfold from FY1998 to FY2000.[72]

The Bremer Commission has recommended that the HHS strengthen controls of pathogens and other biological materials at laboratories and during transport. The Bremer Commission observed that the current controls are designed for accident prevention, not to stop theft. The commission noted that biological controls are not rigorous nuclear controls. It also recommended regulation of sophisticated equipment necessary for the weaponization of pathogens to hinder the ability of terrorists to acquire the equipment.[73] Overall, capability requires money, and there is a concensus among experts, inside and outside these organizations, who believe the work they do is critical and that more resources are needed to do the job.

### Metropolitan Medical Response Systems

The HHS is responsible for aiding local authorities in dealing with the impact of a biological attack. Congress passed the Defense against Weapons of Mass Destruction Act of 1996, also known as the Nunn-Lugar-Domenici Act, after the Oklahoma City bombing. The act authorized funds for the DOD to help the secretary of HHS establish a program to enhance local medical response for a CBRN attack. Metropolitan Medical Response Systems (MMRSs) were created under HHS's Office of Emergency Preparedness. In 1999, MMRSs were in twenty-seven cities and consisted of trained and equipped local emergency teams. The systems also participate in DOD's Domestic Preparedness Program.[74] The president has requested $30 million for FY2001 for HHS's WMD preparedness and MMRS. The Office of Emergency Preparedness plans on developing twenty-five new systems for a total of ninety-seven systems by the end of FY2001.[75] The end goal of HHS is to have MMRSs in the 120 most populous cities.

The HHS released a fact sheet in May 2000 describing the MMRS:

> Because of the very rapid response time that would be required in countering the consequences of such terrorist acts, HHS's strategic plan includes developing partnerships with local jurisdictions to develop an enhanced Metropolitan Medical Response System (MMRS) as the primary local resource in responding to the health and medical consequences of a nuclear,

biological or chemical (NBC) terrorist incident. The MMRS plan serves to coordinate the public safety, public health and health services sector responses to an NBC terrorist incident. The MMRS is an enhanced local capability of the existing system. At the same time, HHS is improving the federal capability to rapidly augment state and local responses. The federal medical response component includes four national and geographically dispersed NMRT/ WMDs (National Medical Response Team/ Weapons of Mass Destruction).

The MMRS concept was generated by a group of state and local subject matter experts that met in July 1995 at the request of HHS's Office of Emergency Preparedness. The original concept of a Metropolitan Medical Strike Team soon expanded into the current systems approach. Pilot tested in the Washington, D.C. and Atlanta areas, systems development was initiated in fiscal year 1997 in the following 25 cities: New York, N.Y.; Los Angeles, Calif.; Chicago, Ill.; Houston, Texas; Philadelphia, Pa.; San Diego, Calif.; Detroit, Mich.; Dallas, Texas; Phoenix, Ariz.; San Antonio, Texas; San Jose, Calif.; Baltimore, Md.; Indianapolis, Ind.; San Francisco, Calif.; Jacksonville, Fla.; Columbus, Ohio; Milwaukee, Wis.; Memphis, Tenn.; Boston, Mass.; Seattle, Wash.; Denver, Colo.; Kansas City, Mo.; Honolulu, Hawaii; Miami, Fla.; and Anchorage, Alaska. The following 20 jurisdictions initiated systems development in fiscal year 1999: Pittsburgh, Pa.; Nashville, Tenn.; Charlotte, N.C.; Cleveland, Ohio; El Paso, Texas; New Orleans, La.; Albuquerque, N.M.; Ft. Worth, Texas; Oklahoma City, Okla.; Austin, Texas; St. Louis, Mo.; Salt Lake City, Utah; Long Beach, Calif.; Tucson, Ariz.; Oakland, Calif.; Portland, Ore.; Minneapolis/St. Paul, Minn.; Tulsa, Okla.; Sacramento, Calif.; and the Hampton Roads, Va. area. The goal is to develop Metropolitan Medical Response Systems for the 120 most populous metropolitan areas in the United States within five years. HHS is currently working to develop a "balance of the nation" strategy for those jurisdictions that would not be included in the list of 120 most populous cities.

The MMRS emphasizes enhancement of local planning and response system capability, tailored to each jurisdiction, to care for victims of a terrorist incident involving a weapon of mass destruction. These systems are characterized by: a concept of operations, specially trained responders, special pharmaceuticals, detection, personal protective equipment, decontamination, communication, and medical equipment and other supplies, and enhanced emergency medical transport and emergency room capabilities. The program includes a focus on biological response, including early warning and surveillance, mass casualty care and plans for mass fatality management. The concept of operations includes the local jurisdictions' plan regarding anticipated requirements federal health and medical augmentation assistance to include the forward movement of victims (when local healthcare systems become overloaded) via the National Disaster Medical System.

HHS recognizes that each city has its own unique, existing emergency medical system. Many have special HAZMAT response capabilities. Therefore, specific plans must be developed uniquely for each city that can build on existing systems and adapt them to meet a nuclear, biological or chemical challenge. Implementation of these plans will include special equipment, supplies, and pharmaceutical procurement and training. A "concept of operations" plan will also be developed with each city regarding federal health and medical augmentation assistance in response to a threatened or actual terrorist incident involving weapons of mass destruction.[76]

## National Pharmaceutical Stockpile Program

The HHS began to use the CDC to build a national stockpile of vaccines and medicines against potential biological and chemical agents in FY1999. The funding request for FY2001 is $52 million.[77] However, there has been criticism of the vaccine program. According to a June 1999 GAO report, the intelligence agencies disagree with the HHS on which vaccine stockpiles should be built, revealing a lack of coordination between agencies for medical countermeasures:

We have also observed a disconnect between intelligence agencies' judgments about the more likely terrorist threats particularly the chemical and biological terrorist threat and certain domestic preparedness program initiatives. For example, the Department of Health and Human Services' (HHS) fiscal year 1999 budget amendment proposal for its bioterrorism initiative included building for the first time a civilian stockpile of antidotes and vaccines to respond to a large-scale biological or chemical attack and expanding the National Institutes of Health's research into related vaccines and therapies. Specifically, the Omnibus Consolidated and Emergency Supplemental Appropriations Act (PL 105-277) included $51 million for the Centers of Disease Control and Prevention to begin developing a pharmaceutical and vaccine stockpile for civilian populations.

HHS's legislatively required operating plan discusses several chemical and biological agents selected for its stockpiling initiatives. These agents were selected because of their ability to affect large numbers of people (create mass casualties) and tax the medical system. We observed that several of the items in HHS's plan did not match individual intelligence agencies' judgments, as explained to us, on the more likely chemical or biological agents a terrorist group or individual might use. HHS had not documented its decision making process for selecting the specific vaccines, antidotes, and other medicines cited in its plan. Thus, it was unclear to us whether and to what extent intelligence agencies' official, written threat analyses were used in the process to develop the list of chemical and biological terrorist threat agents against which the nation should stockpile. Further, we have not seen any evidence that HHS's process incorporated the many disciplines of knowledge and expertise or divergent thinking that is warranted to establish sound requirements to prepare for such a threat and focus on appropriate medical preparedness countermeasures.[78]

An April 2000 GAO again highlighted the difference between the HHS and other agencies' judgments on which vaccines should be stockpiled:

Without the benefits that a threat and risk assessment provides, many agencies have been relying on worst case scenarios to generate countermeasures or establish their programs. Worst case scenarios are extreme situations and, as such, may be out of balance with the threat. In our view, by using worst case scenarios, the federal government is focusing on vulnerabilities (which are unlimited) rather than credible threats (which are limited). By targeting investments based on worst case scenarios, the government may be over funding some initiatives and programs and under funding the more likely threats the country will face. As an example, we have testified that the Department of Health and Human Services is establishing a national pharmaceutical and vaccine stockpile that does not match intelligence agencies' judgments of the more likely chemical and biological agents that terrorists might use. In some of our current work at other federal agencies, we are continuing to find that worst case scenarios are being used in planning efforts to develop programs and capabilities.[79]

These GAO comments understate a problem that permeates the federal government's response to the threat of biological attacks, and inevitably to the state, local, and private-sector response as well. First, there seems to be no systematic examination of lethality data and effects models to determine what data and models are credible and what level of uncertainty is involved. Second, there is no systematic effort to determine how the behavior of military agents might differ from the normal disease and what steps might have been taken to limit detection and defeat effective treatment. Third, there is no evidence of a systematic technical net assessment of the probable progress in defensive measures like vaccines versus progress in the offensive technologies necessary to defeat them. Finally, the entire concept of "cost to defeat" given measures like stockpiling by focusing on alternative agents seems to be alien to the biological sciences community.

There is, of course, no way to determine what level of classified activity is taking place. In general, however, the apparent tendency to treat biological weapons as if their effectiveness and treatment were a known quantity, and as if their use was an outbreak of disease rather than a carefully planned act of war is deeply disturbing. Such an approach may be valid in the near term for terrorists, but it is not valid for state actors, particularly because it often leads to the assumption that the United States will only have to deal with one kind of attack at a time, and that some sort of reliable detection and characterization system will be present.

### Public Health Surveillance System for WMD

The CDC is leading the effort to upgrade the public health surveillance system to detect WMD attacks on the homeland. The FY2001 budget request of $86.5 million stated it would allow the CDC to expand local and state preparedness efforts, improve WMD detection capabilities, and improve laboratory and medical capacity at the local, state, and national level.[80]

The Bremer Commission recommended that the HHS take further steps in enhancing surveillance capability by working with the State Department to develop an international surveillance system that would serve as an early warning system for infectious disease outbreaks as well as a monitoring system to detect potential terrorist experimentation. The commission noted that the United States has some domestic surveillance capabilities but said the international community is behind U.S. efforts.[81]

### Research and Development

The HHS research focuses on developing defenses against potential chemical and biological weapons attacks. The FY2001 funding request was $92 million: $45.2 million to the NIH for research and development on vaccines, therapeutics, diagnostics, and genomics; $30 million to the Office of the Secretary for research and development on improved civilian stockpiles of anthrax and smallpox vaccines; and $9 million to the Food and Drug Administration to develop rapid diagnostic tools and to expedite the pharmaceutical approval process of possible medicines against chemical and biological agents. The HHS research and development funding was also to go to the CDC for its rapid toxic screen project and to research equipment for first responders.

## DEPARTMENT OF THE INTERIOR

Department of the Interior counterterrorism spending now averages around $10 million.[82] The vast majority of the money goes to physical protection of government facilities and employees.

## DEPARTMENT OF JUSTICE AND FEDERAL BUREAU OF INVESTIGATION

The DOJ and FBI have steadily increased their activities in counterterrorism and WMD preparedness. Table 7.1 provides a breakdown of the budget for DOJ's activities relating directly to defense and response against terrorist attacks, and shows that its budget totaled $647.0 million in FY1998, $793.9 million in FY1999, $782.0 million in FY2000, and $949.2 million in FY2001. Overall spending increased over 45 percent from FY1998 to FY2001.[83]

PDD-39 and PDD-62 designated the DOJ, through the FBI, as the lead agency in domestic terrorism crisis management.[84] The FBI is responsible for preventing and responding to domestic terrorism.[85] It gathers and assesses intelligence on domestic threats.[86] Its Criminal Division is tasked with all criminal investigations not specifically given to another division. Its National Security Division manages the Awareness of National Security Issues and Response (ANSIR) Program, which is a means of distributing unclassified threat information on terrorism and other national security threats to corporate security workers, law enforcement, and other government agencies. The Criminal Investigative Division leads the FBI's Legal Attaché Program to conduct law enforcement investigations abroad, including those pertaining to terrorist acts. It has a broad mandate for conducting investigations into organized crimes, and it is responsible for contacts with other Executive Branch agencies; Interpol; foreign police and security officers based in Washington, D.C.; and national law enforcement associations.

According to a speech by President Clinton in 1995, a CIA official serves as the deputy chief of the International Terrorism Section at the FBI. This office works to investigate acts of international terrorism and foreign terrorists within the borders of the United States and abroad.

There is also an office for Domestic Terrorism/Counterterrorism Planning. This office contains the domestic terrorism operations unit, which monitors militias, the special events management unit, the WMD countermeasures unit, and the domestic terrorism analysis unit. It serves as the "program manager for WMD threats and incidents, including the coordination of the threat credibility assessment process," and provides a point of contact for assistance to the field and to other agencies. It helps staff the FBI HQ Strategic Information Operations Center during exercises and actual incidents, and works in conjunction with the DOE's Office of Safeguards and Security to ensure that FBI, DOE, and local elements know their responsibilities and roles during a terrorist incident at a DOE site.

This office also created Domestic Emergency Support Teams (DEST). The composition of a rapid deployment team will vary case-by-case and will include members of several agencies. Overall policy coordination rests with the Domestic Terrorism/Counterterrorism Planning office under the WMD unit. The role of the DEST is to provide expert advice and guidance to the FBI's OSC for the event, and to coordinate follow-on response assets.

The FBI also plays a role in reducing the threat that fissile material will be transferred to hostile states or terrorists. Congress provided authority in the FY1995 National Defense Authorization Act for up to $10 million in reprogrammed DOD funds to develop a joint program with the FBI to expand and improve efforts to deter, prevent, and investigate incidents involving the trafficking of nuclear, biological, and chemical weapons and related material. This created the DOD/FBI Counterproliferation Program. This program trains and equips the community of officials responsible for nuclear, biological, and chemical interdiction in Eastern Europe, the Baltic States, and the former Soviet Union.

The program's objectives are: (1) to assist in the continuing establishment of a professional cadre of law enforcement personnel and other officials capable of interdicting and investigating nuclear, biological, and chemical threats and incidents; (2) to assist in developing appropriate legislation, laws, regulations, and enforcement mechanisms for deterring, preventing, and investigating nuclear, biological, and chemical threats and incidents, and (3) to assist in building a solid, long-lasting bureaucratic and political framework in participating nations capable of implementing the above two objectives. The program consists of three basic elements: policy consultations and assessments, training and technical assistance, and equipment procurement.

The program initially focused on providing assistance to the community of officials responsible for nuclear, biological, and chemical interdiction in the southern tier of the former Soviet Union, particularly Kazakhstan, Uzbekistan, and Kyrgyzstan. The program has expanded to include the Caucasus and eastern and central Europe. Program activities include a two-week basic course for officials responsible for nuclear, biological, and chemical interdiction, usually held at the International Law Enforcement Academy (ILEA). Also planned are specialized WMD courses, WMD practical exercises, and WMD legal/legislative seminars in the participating countries. To date, the DOD/FBI Counterproliferation Program has conducted six large WMD basic training seminars at ILEA. This training has been provided to Kazakhstan, Uzbekistan, Kyrgyzstan, Georgia (two seminars), Moldova, and Slovenia. Additionally, a WMD legal dialog began with Kazakhstan and Uzbekistan through legal colloquia held in Washington, D.C. A follow-up legal workshop took place in Tashkent, Uzbekistan.

The Bremer Commission made many suggestions of how the DOJ and FBI could improve counterterrorism information collection and dissemination. The commission thought that the guidelines for opening an inquiry or investigation on terrorism need to be clarified. The Foreign Intelligence Collection and Foreign Counterintelligence Investigations guidelines cover international terrorism and the attorney general's guidelines on General Crimes, Racketeering Enterprise and Domestic Security/Terrorism Investigations cover domestic terrorism. The commission said field agents are hindered in their investigations because they were unsure if guidelines had been met. The Bremer Commission also recommended streamlining the process for obtaining a court order for electronic surveillance and physical searches of international terrorists. The Office of Intelligence Policy and Review (OIPR) reviews the FBI's application of a Foreign Intelligence Surveillance Act (FISA) before the FISA order is sent to a FISA court for approval. The commission recommended that OIPR work more efficiently with the FBI and require no more than what FISA statutes require before submitting an application to the FISA court. The commission supports the FBI's efforts to update information technology capabilities, including counterencryption equipment and data storage and retrieval systems. However, the commission recommended that the FBI establish reports officers similar to the ones in the CIA to determine what terrorist-related information would be useful to other agencies and policymakers. The commission said:

> Law enforcement agencies are traditionally reluctant to share information outside of their circles so as not to jeopardize any potential prosecution. The FBI does promptly share information warning about specific terrorist threats with the CIA and other agencies. But the FBI is far less likely to disseminate terrorist information that may not relate to an immediate threat even though this could be of immense long-term or cumulative value to the intelligence community, in part because investigators lack the training or time to make such assessments. The problem is particularly pronounced with respect to information collected in the FBI's field offices in the United States, most of which never reaches the FBI headquarters, let alone other U.S. government agencies or departments.[87]

The commission also recommended that the DOJ prosecute terrorists in an open court when possible and protect the rights of the accused:

> The 1993 World Trade Center bombing brought to light the problem of international terrorists entering and operating in the United States and illustrated the importance of removing suspected terrorists from the United States.
> In 1996, Congress established the Alien Terrorist Removal Court (ATRC). The legislation authorized use of classified information in cases involving the expulsion of suspected terrorists, but the law provided several protections for the accused, including the requirement that the alien be provided an unclassified summary of the classified evidence and appellate review by federal courts. For aliens legally admitted for permanent residence, the law allowed the use of special attorneys who hold security clearances (cleared counsel) who are permitted to review secret evidence on behalf of an alien and challenge its veracity.
> The ATRC has never been used. Rather, pursuant to other statutes and case law, the Immigration and Naturalization Service (INS) has acted to remove aliens based on classified evidence presented to an immigration judge without disclosure to the alien or defense counsel.
> The U.S. government should not be confronted with the dilemma of unconditionally disclosing classified evidence or allowing a suspected terrorist to remain at liberty in the United States. At the same time, resort to use of secret evidence without disclosure even to cleared counsel should be discontinued, especially when criminal prosecution through an open court proceeding is an option.[88]

The GAO has suggested that the FBI conduct a national threat and risk assessment. The FBI has begun these assessments, as reported in a July 2000 GAO report:

Regarding our recommendation for a national level threat and risk assessment, the FBI has agreed to lead such an assessment, using the following process: (1) identify initiatives that identify critical and high threat chemical and biological agents, (2) identify federal agencies and personnel to participate, (3) determine classification requirements, and (4) identify specific inquiries appropriate for participating experts, and compile responses and compare agents. The goal is to provide policy makers with "understandable and discriminatory" data to set funding priorities. The FBI has noted some limitations to its methodology. For example, as a law enforcement agency, it has strict legal limitations on the collection and use of intelligence data. FBI officials told us that the state and local assessments represent a thorough nationwide planning process that will compliment national-level threat and risk assessments and related policy making.[89]

### National Domestic Preparedness Office

There is a wide range of additional DOJ and FBI activities. The attorney general directed the FBI in October 1998 to lead an interagency coordination initiative to serve as the single point of contact and clearinghouse for WMD information for state and local emergency responders. Federal agencies involved include HHS, DOD, DOE, EPA, DOJ/Office of Justice Program (OJP), and FEMA. Other federal agencies interested in participating include the U.S. Coast Guard, Veteran's Administration, and the Nuclear Regulatory Commission.

The National Domestic Preparedness Office (NDPO) was set up in ways designed to ensure that it did not replace or usurp any agency's authority and that it would rather serve as a central coordinating entity with the goal of integrating and streamlining federal assistance:

The NDPO will be an interagency effort to enhance coordination among federal programs offering terrorism preparedness assistance to states and local communities. As such, it is intended to serve as the central coordinating office and information clearinghouse for federal assistance programs, with the goal of integrating and streamlining government assistance. As an information clearinghouse, the NDPO will provide details on federal assistance programs to state and local response agencies. The NDPO is not intended to be the creation of a new federal bureaucracy or to usurp the assistance programs under the management of other agencies, but rather to be a "one-stop shop" for state and local responders seeking information regarding federal domestic preparedness assistance and as a forum for federal domestic preparedness programs to coordinate policy affecting those programs.

The NDPO will be organized into six program areas to coordinate and share information related to federal domestic preparedness programs and to provide state and local first responders with a single, central point of contact for information about these programs. These program areas will provide an interagency forum in each area for coordination of federal policy and program assistance to state and local emergency responders. For instance, federal programs providing training will be assessed in this forum in order to eliminate duplication and to ensure that training programs adhere to minimum national standards. The NDPO will be staffed by federal, state and local program coordinators and experts, most of which are already engaged on a full- or part-time basis in domestic preparedness activities. In the coordination of federal programs, it is the NDPO's objective to ensure proper representation of experts from all disciplines responsible for domestic preparedness and emergency response. However, NDPO staff will not supplant the functions that are the responsibilities of its constituent departments and agencies, but rather serve as a forum to coordinate these programs.

The NDPO will not serve, nor is it intended to serve, as an operational entity. Response activities will remain with the various departments and agencies whose functions and responsibilities in a WMD event are described in the Federal Response Plan Terrorism Annex.

The NDPO describes its functions and activities as follows:[90]

A Vision for Working with First Responders to Enhance Domestic Preparedness: The NDPO will provide a forum to assess training needs at all levels and identify solutions as part of a national training strategy. The NDPO will act as a clearinghouse for information about federal WMD training, including the establishment and maintenance of a training catalog for first responders. The NDPO will not have "veto power" over any agency's programs, but rather, NDPO will work to avoid duplication among the federal programs by providing a forum to coordinate federal efforts.

Exercises: The NDPO will provide WMD exercise recommendations, assistance and technical support to federal, state or local agencies planning efforts. The NDPO, in its coordinating role, will facilitate the sharing of lessons learned through maintenance of databases, "after-action reports," and analyses. With the participation of all federal agencies involved in conducting WMD exercises, the NDPO will be able to facilitate the planning and coordination of WMD exercises between federal, state, and local officials.

Equipment/Research Development: The NDPO will coordinate federal efforts to provide the emergency response community with equipment necessary to prepare for, and respond to, a WMD terrorist incident. NDPO will help establish and maintain a Standardized Equipment List (SEL) to guide the responder community in identifying the types and models of equipment available which meet agreed on standards of performance and reliability. The NDPO will facilitate the dissemination of information about new and developing technologies through the member agencies of the NDPO. Existing technology review panels, such as the Interagency Board (IAB, co-chaired by FBI and DOD), will be leveraged to ensure interoperability, best performance, and reliability of equipment produced for the response communities.

Information Sharing and Outreach: State and local participation in the NDPO is a significant mission success factor. As such, personnel estimates are based on the goal of ensuring that state and local experts are well represented in each of the program areas. Therefore, the NDPO hopes to fill approximately one-third of its program staff, or 20 positions with state and local representatives, with approximately three state and local personnel per functional area. Participation from federal agencies involved in preparedness, planning, and response is essential to ensuring that federal programs meet the needs of state and local communities. The role of each of the federal partners is to assist state and local jurisdictions in enhancing their domestic preparedness capabilities by providing assistance in the areas of planning, equipment, technical assistance, training, exercise support, and information. Each federal partner will continue to provide its equipment, training, exercise, and technical assistance programs, but each will do so consistent with agreed on national WMD preparedness policy and guidelines. The EPA supports federal counterterrorism programs by using and building on the established hazardous materials response structure and mechanism at the federal, state, and local level.

Public Speaking Assistance: The NDPO will coordinate public speaking engagements relevant to domestic preparedness and its programs by maintaining a list of qualified speakers and topics. The NDPO will be able to provide public speaking assistance at the national, regional, state, and local levels. Through its information-sharing efforts, appropriate speakers will be recommended for upcoming speaking engagements. In addition to speakers representing NDPO itself, the NDPO will maintain a voluntary database for speakers with expertise in other areas. This data will be drawn from all of the participating agencies and regions nationwide.

Health and Medical Services: Specifically, the NDPO will serve as a "one-stop-shopping" point of information and referral for WMD-related health and medical preparedness issues and questions from stakeholders, states, and local jurisdictions. Second, it will serve as a mechanism for Health and Human Services to facilitate the coordination and review of health and medical issues with regard to domestic preparedness. Health care systems must have the ability to meet the unique challenges posed by a terrorist act involving a WMD. It will fall on the local jurisdiction's existing public health and medical systems to manage adequately and effectively the human health consequences of a WMD terrorist incident. Providing appropriate care for the affected population and obtaining critical health system assets, including health professionals, pharmaceuticals, equipment, and facilities, are crucial to a successful response. Health system response requirements are driven by the type of WMD incident encountered, and the setting in which it occurs (rural community, suburb, city, or major metropolitan area). A chemical incident will result in immediate effects at a known site, on-scene determination of the causative agent, and a timely response. The effects of the release of a biological weapon, however, may not be apparent for days or even weeks and would include response issues such as mass prophylaxis, mass patient care, mass fatality management and infection control.[91]

It may be too soon to appraise the NPDO's effectiveness, but the GAO noted the need for an agency such as the NDPO to coordinate federal assistance to local and state responders in testimony it gave in April 2000:

The federal government cannot prepare for CBRN incidents on its own. Several improvements are also warranted in intergovernmental relations between federal, state and local governments. For example, we found that federal agencies developed some of their assistance programs without coordinating them with existing state and local emergency management structures. In addition, the multitude of federal assistance programs has led to confusion on the part of state and local officials. One step to improve coordination and reduce confusion has been the creation of the National Domestic Preparedness Office within the Department of Justice to provide "one stop shopping" to state and local officials in need of assistance. This office has recently prepared a draft plan on how it will provide assistance.

There is still a need to better focus and coordinate federal programs to assist state and local governments prepare for terrorist CBRN attacks. For example, while local officials have praised federal CBRN training programs, some of the initial programs failed to leverage existing state and local response mechanisms. Further, some local officials have viewed the growing number of CBRN training programs as evidence of a fragmented and possibly wasteful federal approach toward combating terrorism. For example, at about the same time the Department of Defense was developing its Domestic Preparedness Program courses, FEMA and the Department of Justice were jointly developing a similar or potentially overlapping two-day basic concepts course on emergency response to terrorism. Similarly, multiple programs for equipment—such as the separate DOD and Public Health Service programs and the new Department of Justice equipment grant program—are causing frustration and confusion at the local level and are resulting in further complaints that the federal government is unfocused and has no coordinated plan or desired outcome for domestic preparedness.

A major federal initiative to provide better focus and to coordinate federal assistance programs is the National Domestic Preparedness Office. The Office, which was recently funded in the Consolidated Appropriations Act for Fiscal Year 2000, is just getting organized. The Office will function as an interagency forum to coordinate federal policy and program assistance for state and local emergency responders. For instance, the Office will assess federal training programs to eliminate duplication and ensure that the training adheres to minimum national standards. It is to coordinate and serve as an information clearinghouse for federal programs devoted to supporting state and local emergency responder communities in the area of CBRN–related domestic preparedness planning, training, exercises, and equipment research and development. However, the Office will not have veto power over any agency's programs, so its authorities to actually prevent or stop duplicate programs will be limited.

Since our last testimony before this Subcommittee, the National Domestic Preparedness Office has drafted an action plan. According to the plan, the Office will focus on (1) identifying existing needs assessment tools, (2) cataloging all federal domestic preparedness training, (3) verifying that federal domestic preparedness training initiatives meet the applicable standards, (4) identifying existing training delivery systems and coordinate among federal agencies, (5) coordinating the development of sustainment CBRN training for emergency responders, and (6) facilitating the incorporation of lessons learned into training curriculums.[92]

The Advisory Panel to Assess Domestic Response Capabilities for Terrorism Involving Weapons of Mass Destruction, also known as the Gilmore Commission, also recognized the need for a single agency to simplify the process for local and state responders seeking assistance and supports the concept of the NDPO:

> the federal bureaucratic structure is massive and complex. In various forums, state and local officials consistently express frustration in understanding where or how to enter this bureaucratic maze to obtain information, assistance, funding and support. In addition, federal programs, especially those involving grants for funding or other resources, may be overly complicated, time consuming, and repetitive.
>
> In recent months, the Federal Bureau of Investigation, pursuant to its "lead-agency" role (specified in the related Presidential Decision Directives) for crisis management for terrorism involving weapons of mass destruction, was directed by the Attorney General of the United States to organize, within its own resources, a National Domestic Preparedness Office (NDPO). The ostensible purpose of the NDPO is to serve as a focal point and "clearinghouse" for related preparedness information and for directing state and local entities to the appropriate agency of the Federal government for obtaining additional information, assistance, and support. There has been discussion about the issue of whether the FBI is the appropriate location or whether the NDPO structure and approach is the most effective way to address the complexities of the Federal organization and programs designed to enhance domestic response capabilities. The Panel is convinced that the *concept* behind the NDPO is sound, and notes with interest that the Congress has recently authorized and appropriated funds ($6 million) for the operation of the NDPO. While that authority will give the NDPO some wherewithal to operate and to hire persons from outside the FBI, the Panel has seen no specific direction to other Federal agencies to provide personnel or other resources to the NDPO, to assist in a concerted, well-coordinated effort.[93]

The NDPO said it is planning to develop a national counterterrorism strategy. However, the GAO has voiced concern that other agencies were creating a national strategy as well. The GAO reported in July 2000 that these multiple strategies could create more confusion in an already poorly coordinated program.

> Of additional concern to us is the potential development of additional national strategies by other organizations. In addition to the existing Attorney Generals' 5-year interagency plan, the National Security Council and the FBI's National Domestic Preparedness Office are each planning to develop national strategies. The danger in this proliferation of strategies is that state and local governments—which are already frustrated and confused about the multitude of federal domestic preparedness agencies and programs—may become further confused about the direction and priorities of federal programs to combat terrorism. In our view, there should be only one national strategy to

combat terrorism. Additional planning guidance (e.g., at more detailed levels for specific functions) should fall under the one national strategy in a clear hierarchy.[94]

## Office for State and Local Domestic Preparedness Support

"The Office of Justice Program's (OJP) Office for State and Local Domestic Preparedness Support (OSLDPS) was created to assist state and local response agencies throughout the United States prepare for incidents of domestic terrorism."[95] OSLDPS helps state and local officials in five ways.

### State Domestic Preparedness Equipment Program

One is the State Domestic Preparedness Equipment Program, which helps state and local jurisdictions to purchase first responder equipment and to fund state planning efforts. Equipment that can be bought with the grant money is stated on NDPO's Standardized Equipment List.[96] In FY1999, $51.8 million was available, $8 million for state planning and $43.8 million for equipment purchases. The FY2001 requested budget was $78 million.[97] The FBI also provided first responder training with bombs and WMD at its Hazardous Devices School. The training course teaches bomb identification, neutralization, and disposal. The FY2001 request for this program was $4.6 million.

Assistant Attorney General Laurie Robinson describes the program as:

> The threat of terrorist incidents in our Nation presents enormous challenges to the Federal Government and, more significantly, to State and local governments. To address these challenges, the Federal Government is committed to assisting State and local governments better prepare for and respond to terrorist incidents, should they occur. The role of the States in strategic planning—namely, the coordination of resources and responses—and in assessing overall State and local capabilities is a critical component of OJP's State and local domestic preparedness initiative. Indeed, the critical role of local government agencies as the Nation's primary first response groups must be reflected in any domestic preparedness plan the States develop. In recognition of the role local jurisdictions play in any weapons of mass destruction (WMD) response, it is expected that local police, fire, hazardous material, and emergency medical units will receive the majority of funds under this program.
>
> Receipt of funds under the program will be contingent on a State's development of two separate, but related, documents. The first is a State-based Needs Assessment, and the second is a Three-Year Statewide Domestic Preparedness Strategy. The Needs Assessment will require each State to assess its requirements for equipment, first responder training, and other resources involved in a WMD response. This Needs Assessment will form the basis of the Statewide Strategy. The Strategy will provide a "roadmap" of where each State will target grant funds received under the OJP equipment program and provide OJP a guide on how to target first responder training and other

resources available through OJP's Office for State and Local Domestic Preparedness Support. It is also important to understand that the Strategy is a multiyear document and will continue to guide deployment of these resources, by the states for equipment funds and OJP for other resources, over the next three years.

Through this effort, $51.8 million will be made available to the individual States under the Fiscal Year 1999 State Domestic Preparedness Equipment Program: $8 million will be distributed to support State planning efforts and $43.8 million will be available to support equipment purchases. The Attorney General and I believe that the best programs are those that reflect Federal, State, and local coordination and are built on an active partnership with State and local officials. Such partnerships are critical to the successful preparation of our Nation's communities to deal with terrorist threats. Further, such partnerships will strengthen our Nation's capacity to respond to terrorist acts.[98]

## Metropolitan Fire and Emergency Medical Services Training Program

The OSLDPS helps local and state responders through the Metropolitan Fire and Emergency Medical Services Training Program. This is DOJ's primary program to help first responders. DOJ established this program after the Antiterrorism and Effective Death Penalty Act of 1996 authorized the attorney general, in consultation with FEMA, to provide training for metropolitan fire and emergency service departments to respond to terrorist attacks. The Metropolitan Fire and Emergency Medical Services Training Program is designed to train the local responders who would then train other responders in the community, though DOJ also provides direct training. For the FY1998 and FY1999 total, the program received $10 million and trained forty-four thousand individuals in ninety-five cities and metropolitan areas. For FY2000, the program received $8 million plus another $2 million to work with DOD to create distance learning material.[99]

A March 2000 GAO report provides the following program description:

Justice provides WMD training to first responders primarily through its Metropolitan Firefighters and Emergency Medical Services Program but also uses the National Domestic Preparedness Consortium to provide such training. Justice, with assistance from FEMA's National Fire Academy, designed the metropolitan program to prepare first responders for terrorist incidents involving WMD. Justice designed the program to be presented in the largest 120 metropolitan municipalities, which includes cities and counties. In September 1999, Justice increased the number of jurisdictions targeted for the program from 120 to 255. According to Justice officials, the additions were to make the program more responsive to the needs of local responders by providing training to the 120 cities included in Defense's program as well as each state capital and/or the largest city in each state previously excluded from Justice's and Defense's training programs. Justice either trains-the-trainer or directly trains fire, emergency medical services, and hazardous materials personnel in local communities. Justice received $5 million in each year of fiscal years 1998 and 1999 to carry out the training segment of its program. For fiscal year 2000, Congress appropriated $8 million to Justice for training firefighters, emergency services personnel, and state and local law enforcement personnel. The fiscal year 2000 appropriation also provided $2 million for Justice to work with Defense in developing distance learning instructional tools such as interactive computer software and video transmission of WMD-related instructional materials.

The training lasts 16 hours and comprises five modules: understanding and recognizing terrorism, implementing self-protective measures, scene security, tactical considerations, and incident command overview. The overall objective of the course is to enable the participants to recognize the circumstances that indicate a potential terrorist act and to take precautionary measures. Through mid-November 1999, 44,000 participants in 95 cities and counties had received the training. This total includes those trained directly by Justice's instructors and the students later trained by the instructors.[100]

The Metropolitan Firefighters program has been an example that critics like the GAO have cited in arguing for better federal integration of terrorism programs. DOD administers the Domestic Preparedness Program and FEMA administers WMD courses at its National Fire Academy and Emergency Management Institute in Maryland. The problem is the potential and actual overlap in first responders' training among the DOJ, DOD, and FEMA programs. Furthermore, critics argue it is inefficient for responders in each city to attend three programs from three departments when an integrated program would save time and resources.[101]

### OSLDPS Technical Assistance Activities

The third way OSLDPS helps is with the six technical assistance activities that the it provides. The activities include risk/threat/vulnerability assessments, consequence management plan reviews, response plan development, grant application assistance, training, and conference design and support.

- **Risk/Threat/Vulnerability Assessments:** The threat of terrorism and mass casualties cannot be denied, nor should it be ignored. Preparation begins with an understanding of vulnerability and the development of a strategy for reducing it. OSLDPS Technical Assistance (TA) can assist local responders and emergency planners in identifying and evaluating those sites that represent the most attractive targets to would-be terrorists, whether government buildings, high-use commercial facilities, or infrequently used special event venues. Once identified, potential consequences can be estimated for a range of terrorism scenarios, involving local expertise in calculating the possible outcomes. This data can then be matched against local response capabilities to determine acceptable levels of risk and specific equipment, training, or other capability shortfalls.

- **Consequence Management Plan Reviews:** OSLDPS TA can assist local, city, and state government agencies with reviewing their plans for dealing with the consequences of acts of terrorism and can offer recommendations to enhance the effectiveness of emergency response to mass casualty events. The reviews are conducted by police, fire, and emergency medicine specialists from across the nation, with specialized training in dealing with the threat posed by chemical, biological, and nuclear/radiological WMD. Reviews are strictly for the purpose of identifying areas of possible improvement intended to enhance overall performance. The review process is professional-helping-professional and is conducted in a low-key, publicity-averse fashion. Results are provided to local officials on a close-hold basis, mirroring the confidentiality afforded all information provided to TA personnel during the review.

- **Response Plan Development:** OSLDPS TA can assist in the preparation of consequence/emergency management plans and can provide agencies in one jurisdiction with the experience gained from cities and states across the nation. Working with local experts from the emergency response communities, TA specialists can provide insight into WMD–driven strategic and tactical planning considerations, interface with other jurisdictions (including the role of federal assets), incident procedural flows, on-scene and command communications, and emergency medical response. TA is not a substitute for local-level planning, but an augmenting resource available to provide specialized knowledge and experience to a jurisdiction's existing planning team.

- **Grant Application Assistance:** OSLDPS TA is available to states involved in the preparation of OJP grant applications. Specialists can assist in all stages of the development, writing, and review of applications prior to submittal.

- **Training:** OSLDPS offers a broad spectrum of training to responders, ranging from Domestic Preparedness Program awareness and train the trainer courses to advanced specialist training, including courses offered through the National Domestic Preparedness Consortium. OSLDPS has also prepared "special topics" training for delivery to local jurisdictions, including the Senior Officials Seminar and the Responder Exercise Design Course. OSLDPS TA can also review existing training programs and materials employed at the jurisdiction-level and offer recommendations for enhancements.

- **Conference Design and Support:** OSLDPS TA can develop, conduct, and facilitate conferences and meetings addressing terrorism preparedness issues. It can assist in securing speakers, providing advice on agenda design, and supporting document preparation. Expert facilitation, whether of large gatherings or small working groups, can result in enhanced meeting effectiveness and focused, goal-oriented outcomes.[102]

### State Domestic Preparedness Equipment Program Needs Assessment and Strategy Development Initiative

OSLDPS's fourth method of helping first responders has been the State Domestic Preparedness Equipment Program Needs Assessment and Strategy Development Initiative. The initiative requires all fifty states to assess risks and needs, then use the information to develop strategies to counter WMD terrorism. These assessments are intended to provide a countrywide survey of WMD readiness as well as a basis for developing a three-year strategy for obtaining responder equipment as mandated by the OSLDPS State Domestic Preparedness Equipment Program.[103]

Assessments are essential means for gathering information, understanding the current state of readiness among states and localities, and for helping guide program direction and development, including decisions for prioritizing and allocating the resources (training, equipment, and exercises) intended to lessen the vulnerability of communities to terrorist use of WMD. Assessments ensure that measures taken to reduce vulnerabilities are justifiable and that resources are appropriately targeted to address identified risks and requirements. OSLDPS views assessments as the cornerstone of its state and local domestic preparedness efforts.

Formal assessments have been largely absent from most federal programs directed at addressing WMD terrorism. OSLDPS is changing that. During FY1999, OSLDPS undertook a major, two-phase, nationwide needs assessment aimed at providing a macro view of emergency response requirements across the nation. The first phase of this assessment, entitled "Responding to Incidents of Domestic Terrorism: Assessing the Needs of State and Local Jurisdictions," was released in June 1999. The second phase was released in March 2000.

While the June 1999 and March 2000 reports viewed the United States at the macro national level, OSLDPS is currently focusing in more detail at the state and local levels. As part of the OSLDPS "Fiscal Year 1999 State Domestic Preparedness Equipment Program," states will be required to conduct individual needs and risk assessments and, using the information gathered, develop individual state strategies addressing issues of training, equipment, and technical assistance in domestic preparedness support. These assessments, collectively known as OSLDPS State Domestic Preparedness Equipment Program Needs Assessment and Strategy Development Initiative, will result in detailed information for each of the fifty states. To assist states in completing this project, OSLDPS is providing planning grants and technical assistance, including assessment tools and instruments.

These OSLDPS state-based needs assessments are intended to provide a countrywide survey of the current WMD response environment. Working closely with other federal agencies, including the CDC and FBI, OSLDPS will engage city, county, and state emergency managers, law enforcement officers, and public health officials to help individual jurisdictions pinpoint vulnerabilities and develop plans for countering WMD terrorism. The assessment results will serve not only as a roadmap for program planning, but also as a benchmark for measuring program effectiveness.

A July 2000 GAO report noted OSLDPS's progress in developing local threat and risk assessments: "Regarding local threat and risk assessments, Justices' Office for State and Local Domestic Preparedness Support and the

FBI have worked together to provide a threat and risk assessment tool to state and local governments. This tool includes a step-by-step methodology for assessing threats, risks, and requirements. It also includes information on how to prioritize programs and project spending amounts."[104]

As part of its responsibilities under the OSLDPS's State Domestic Preparedness Equipment Program, each state will use the findings from the assessments as the basis for developing a three-year strategy. This strategy will serve as a roadmap for identifying where each state will target equipment grant funds and guide OSLDPS on how best to target first-responder training and other resources. These state assessments were carried out in the spring and summer of 2000. To facilitate the process, OSLDPS sponsored a series of Regional Workshops for invited state officials.

The practical problem with these activities is that they depend on valid threats and effects, neither of which seem to be available.

### TOPOFF Exercises

The fifth way OSLDPS helps is the situational exercises including top officials (TOPOFF) that are to be incorporated into training exercises. These situational exercises received $3.5 million for FY1999.

> As part of OJP's first responder training/domestic preparedness initiative, the Conference Report (H. Rpt. 105–825, p. 999) accompanying the Justice Department's Fiscal Year 1999 Appropriations Act provides $3.5 million for situational exercises for state and local emergency response personnel.
>
> The Conference language further directs that a portion of these funds be used to comply with language found in the Senate Report (S. Rpt. 105–235) requiring that a "TOPOFF" exercise be included under any exercise initiative. Under the Senate Report, two types of exercises are discussed. The first is a major national level "TOPOFF" exercise. The other is to incorporate situational exercises as part of OJP's efforts to improve the capabilities of state and local emergency personnel response to incidents of domestic terrorism.
>
> Similar language is found in the House Report (H. Rpt. 105–636) which directs the use of "confidence building exercises based on threat driven scenarios" be incorporated into OJP's training efforts.[105]

The Bremer Commission noted that funding for TOPOFF has been inadequate and the exercises are not required on a regular basis.[106]

### National Domestic Preparedness Consortium

The DOJ also administers first responder training through the National Domestic Preparedness Consortium. The consortium members consist of Fort McClellan, Alabama, New Mexico Institute of Mining and Technology, Texas A&M University, Nevada Test Site, and Louisiana State University. The WMD specialty training provided at Fort McClellan is for chemical explosive agents; at the New Mexico Institute of Mining and Technology, bombs and explosive devices; at Texas A&M, emergency medical services; at Nevada Test Site, radiological agents; and at Louisiana State University, law enforcement and biological events. The conference committee report for DOJ's FY1998 appropriation directed the attorney general to use the consortium for the DOJ's WMD training objectives and to provide funding for the consortium's first responder training in Fort McClellan and in New Mexico Institute of Mining and Technology. The conference committee report for FY1999 directed DOJ to use the consortium to the fullest possible extent and appropriated $24 million for consortium members. Fort McClellan received $2 million and $8 million, respectively, for FY1998 and FY1999, and received $13 million for FY2000. The FY2001 request for Fort McClellan was $15 million.[107] The other four consortium members received a total of $2 million and $12 million, respectively, for FY1998 and 1999, and received $14 million for FY2000. In FY1999, the consortium trained about three thousand individuals.[108]

### Awareness of National Security Issues and Response Program

ANSIR is a program within the National Security Division of the FBI that serves to disseminate unclassified security and threat information to corporate security directors, law enforcement, and other government agencies:

> The Awareness of National Security Issues and Response (ANSIR) Program is the FBI's National Security Awareness Program. It is the "public voice" of the FBI for espionage, counterintelligence, counterterrorism, economic espionage, cyber and physical infrastructure protection and all national security issues. The program is designed to provide unclassified national security threat and warning information to U.S. corporate security directors and executives, law enforcement, and other government agencies. It also focuses on the "response" capability unique to the FBI's jurisdiction in law enforcement and counterintelligence investigations.
>
> Information is disseminated nationwide via the ANSIR–Email and ANSIR–FAX networks. Each of the FBI's 56 field offices has an ANSIR coordinator and is equipped to provide national security threat and awareness information on a regular basis to corporate recipients within their jurisdiction. ANSIR–FAX was the first initiative by the U.S. government to provide this type of information to as many as 25,000 individual U.S. corporations with critical technologies or sensitive economic information targeted by foreign intelligence services or their agents. ANSIR–Email increases the capacity for the number of recipients to exceed 100,000 which should accommodate every U.S. corporation who wishes to receive information from the FBI. Interested U.S. corporations should provide their email address, position, company name and address as well as telephone and fax numbers to the national ANSIR–Email address at ansir@leo.gov. Individual ANSIR Coordinators in

the respective field divisions will verify contact with each prospective recipient of ANSIR–Email advisories.

The FBI is the lead agency for a variety of national security concerns. With regard to foreign counterintelligence activity, theft of U.S. technology and sensitive economic information by foreign intelligence services and competitors has been estimated by the White House and others to be valued up to a hundred billion dollars annually. It is therefore prudent and necessary that we provide information to those who are the targets of this activity. Critical infrastructure protection, cyber and physical, is also a major focus of the FBI and the ANSIR program helps to identify these infrastructures and ensure that communication with the FBI is established.

Each ANSIR coordinator in the FBI's 56 field offices is a member of the American Society for Industrial Security. This membership enhances public/private sector communication and cooperation for the mutual benefit of both. FBI ANSIR Coordinators meet regularly with industry leaders and security directors for updates on current national security issues.

The ANSIR program focuses on the "techniques of espionage" when relating national security awareness information to industry. Discussing techniques allows us to be very specific in giving industry representatives tangible information to help them decide their own vulnerabilities. These techniques include compromise of industry information through "dumpster diving," where Foreign Intelligence Services and competitors may try to obtain corporate proprietary information, or listening devices which may be as simple as using a police scanner to tune in the frequency of the wireless microphone being used in the corporate boardroom. Through the ANSIR program and the discussion of techniques of espionage corporations are able to learn from the experiences of others enabling them to avoid adverse results.

Along with awareness, the ANSIR program provides information about the FBI's unique "response" capability with regard to issues of national security. The FBI has primary jurisdiction for a variety of criminal and counterintelligence investigations that impact on national security. For instance, the recent passage of the Economic Espionage Act of 1996 opened up new areas of FBI response to the wrongful acquisition of intellectual property. It also encourages corporations to consider how best to protect their proprietary information or trade secrets from domestic and foreign theft.

The FBI ANSIR Coordinator in the local field office is the point of contact for information about the FBI's national security programs and also to receive initial information which may result in a response by the FBI. U.S. corporations should also contact the local ANSIR Coordinator to receive ANSIR–Email or ANSIR–FAX information.[109]

## National Institute of Justice

The National Institute of Justice is the lead agency in developing a standard for first responder equipment. It is working with the Technical Support Working group to develop wearable toxic agent detectors and easy access protective masks.[110]

## NATIONAL SECURITY COMMUNITY

The National Security Community is an OMB title for the DOD and the US intelligence community. Table 7.1 provides a breakdown of the OMB estimate of National Security Community activities relating directly to defense and response against terrorist attacks. OMB estimates that these activities were budgeted at $4,496.1 million in FY1998, $4,682.5 million in FY1999, $5,117.1 million in FY2000, and $5,124.0 million in FY2001.[111]

PDD-39 designated the national coordinator for security, infrastructure protection, and counterterrorism at the NSC the lead agency responsible for coordination of policies and programs dealing with CBRN terrorism.[112] The National Security Community requested $347 million for FY2001 for research and development to combat the CBRN threat. The research program was designed primarily for military needs but yields technologies useful for domestic preparedness.[113] The OMB report does not provide any additional data on non–DOD activities.

## NUCLEAR REGULATORY COMMISSION

The NRC spends roughly $6 million a year on counterterrorism. This spending, shown in Table 7.1, mostly goes to WMD preparedness, and specifically toward protecting the populace from attacks using nuclear and radiological materials, or strikes on nuclear facilities.[114]

## DEPARTMENT OF STATE

The State Department is the lead agency for international terrorism, and has steadily increased its expenditures in recent years. Table 7.1 provides a breakdown of the budget for its activities relating directly to defense and response against terrorist attacks. It shows that the department's budget totaled $186 million in FY1998, $1.579 billion in FY1999, $791 million in FY2000, and $1.312 billion in FY2001.[115]

Some of these activities involve direct efforts to aid foreign countries in counterterrorism and to improve international cooperation in dealing with such threats. For example, the department manages the Terrorist Interdiction Program, which helps selected vulnerable countries to stop terrorists from entering or using their territory. The FY2001 request for this activity is $4 million.[116]

### Embassy Protection

The bulk of State Department funds, however, go to the physical protection of facilities abroad and have little to do with homeland defense. The president's FY2001 budget requested $1.2 billion[117] and $3.4 billion in advance appropriations for FY2002 through FY2005. For FY2001, $500 million will go to new overseas facilities, $200 million above FY2000; $200 million will go to new protective measures for embassies such as alarms and perimeter barriers, an increase of $200 million from FY2000; $342 million will go to high security readiness, $74 million above FY2000; and $68 million will go to the State Department's Anti-Terrorism Assistance (ATA) Program, an increase of $35 million from FY2000. The ATA funding level provides $30 million to establish a center for antiterrorism and security training to meet the worldwide demand for ATA programs.

The White House press secretary released the following statement:

The president's FY2001 budget includes more than $1.1 billion to reduce further the risk of loss of life from terrorist attacks on our overseas diplomatic missions. This represents an increase of over $500 million in additional Federal funds to address enhanced security needs of diplomatic and consular facilities overseas. The request also includes $3.4 billion in advance appropriations for fiscal years 2002 through 2005 to provide a solid foundation for long-term building needs.

**New Construction**

- Invest $500 million in new overseas facilities in FY2001, an increase of $200 million above the FY2000 enacted level.

Consolidate the requirements of all foreign affairs agencies in new embassy construction.

- Establish a solid foundation for future years with $3.4 billion advance appropriation.

**Increase Protective Measures**

- Invest $200 million to begin a new series of increased protective measures such as perimeter barriers, alarms, and access control equipment for overseas facilities to meet applicable diplomatic security standards and address emergent needs as they are identified, an increase of $200 million over FY2000 enacted.

**Sustain and Improve Security Readiness**

- Maintain a high level of security readiness at a cost of $342 million in FY2001, an increase of $74 million above FY2000 enacted. This cost includes the recurring costs of additional security measures such as guards for overseas facilities and the operation and maintenance costs of security improvements already in place.
- Augment security personnel corps with an additional $16 million for 161 security professionals to create a surge capacity to respond quickly to evolving terrorist threats.

- Increase support for the Anti-Terrorism Assistance Program to $68 million, an increase of $35 million above the FY2000 enacted level, to provide a robust training component. This funding level includes $30 million to establish a center for anti-terrorism and security training to meet growing worldwide demand for ATA programs.[118]

### Office of the Coordinator for Counterterrorism

The Office of the Coordinator of Counterterrorism is the focus of counterterrorism efforts at the State Department, and leads interagency teams (FBI, DOJ, CIA, DOD, FAA, and so on) in consultations and cooperation with foreign countries and works with the intelligence community to identify state sponsors of terrorism. It also leads FEST teams and oversees the TSWG.

The State Department also designates foreign terrorist organizations (FTOs). The Antiterrorism and Effective Death Penalty Act of 1996 directed the secretary of state to designate groups that are a threat to the United States. The Bremer Commission asserted that FTO designations are not as credible as they could be because some terrorist organizations are left off the list.

> The FTO designation makes it a crime for a person in the United States to provide funds or other material support (including equipment, weapons, lodging, training, etc.) to such a group. There is no requirement that the contributor know that the specific resources provided will be used for terrorism. In addition, American financial institutions are required under the law to block funds of FTOs and their agents and report them to the government.
>
> The FTO designation process correctly recognizes that the current threat is increasingly from groups of terrorists rather than state sponsors. In addition to deterring contributions to terrorist organizations, FTO designation serves as a diplomatic tool. It provides the State Department with the ability to use a "carrot and stick" approach to these groups, providing public condemnation and a potential for redemption if the groups renounce terrorism.
>
> There is little doubt that all groups currently on the list belong there. But the exclusion, for example, of the Real Irish Republican Army, which carried out the Omagh car bombing in Northern Ireland in 1998 killing 29 people and injuring more than 200, raises questions about completeness of the list. This diminishes the credibility of the FTO list by giving the impression that political or ethnic considerations can keep a group off the list.[119]

However, Ambassador Michael Sheehan, then the coordinator for counterterrorism, testified before the Senate Foreign Relations Committee, explaining why more organizations were not designated FTO. The process of FTO designation is a long one requiring many resources, and the Office of the Coordinator for Counterterrorism is working hard to review more organizations. Ambassador Sheehan said:

The Commission observes that it is necessary to sustain credibility and dynamism in the Foreign Terrorist Organization (FTO) process, and I am committed to doing just that—not only with regard to FTOs, but with all of our counterterrorism policy tools. Congress has given us a very effective tool in the Secretary's authority to designate FTOs. Designations under the 1996 law criminalize financial support to a FTO, require U.S. financial institutions to block funds of FTOs and their agents, and render representatives and certain members of the FTO ineligible for visas and admission to the United States. State leads this work in consultation with the Departments of Justice and Treasury and with the intelligence community. In 1997, we designated 30 organizations as FTOs, allowing us to deter terrorist fund-raising more effectively. As important, the FTO list has proved invaluable as a diplomatic tool to stigmatize and punish terrorist groups and their supporters around the world.

In 1999, we re-designated 27 FTOs (designations expire after two years unless renewed), dropped three groups, and added Usama Bin Ladin's al-Qaida organization. Dropping three FTOs (the Democratic Front for the Liberation of Palestine, the Khmer Rouge, and the Manuel Rodriguez Patriotic Front of Chile) from the list sent an important signal that if you are out of the terrorism business by the standards of U.S. law, you will be dropped from the list.

Because of the significance of FTO designations and because they can be challenged in court, the designation process is painstaking and we are very careful about assembling the evidence that goes into making the case. A single designation consumes hundreds of hours of work carried out by my staff as well as by lawyers and analysts from Justice, Treasury, and the intelligence community. Because of the quality of this effort, we have won all court challenges (for example, from the MEK and LTTE) to our designations, thereby further bolstering the credibility of the FTO process.

But sustaining credibility and dynamism in the FTO process is an ongoing challenge, constrained mainly by limited personnel resources. We constantly review and assess various potential groups for addition to the list of FTOs—this can be done at anytime, not just every two years. I have directed my staff to review some 10 to 12 new groups before the year is out. We have already added a new officer for one year to work on this and would like to bolster our capabilities by adding another full-time lawyer. But undoubtedly there are some groups that will not be reviewed as soon as I would like. I am not satisfied with the pace of the FTO review process, and will continue to keep pushing my staff and the interagency team that processes these designations.[120]

This situation requires comprehensive review, given the new level of threat revealed in September 2001. The United States may have to be far more preemptive and inclusive than it has been in the past.

### Foreign Emergency Support Teams

FEST are emergency response teams led by an officer from the Office of the Coordinator for Counterterrorism and staffed by representatives of

DOD, CIA, FBI, and other agencies. A team may be dispatched within hours via a specially dedicated airplane (supplied by DOD) and is intended to be a small and flexible team of experts to assist an ambassador and a host government in resolving a terrorist crisis.

### Technical Support Working Group

The TSWG is an interagency team funded mostly by DOD. It conducts counterterrorism technology research and development and prototyping, focusing on explosives detection and technologies that will detect and protect against WMD terrorism, and coordinates and manages the National Counterterrorism Research and Development Program. The TSWG is made up of representatives from eight federal departments and over fifty agencies. It also has cooperative programs with Canada, the United Kingdom, and Israel to develop counterterrorism technologies.

### Bureau of Consular Affairs

The Bureau of Consular Affairs works with the S/CT, INR/TNC, DS, the intelligence community, and consulates abroad to maintain systems to deny suspected terrorists entry to the United States. It also issues warnings and travel advisories pertaining to terrorist threats.

### Bureau of Diplomatic Security

The Bureau of Diplomatic Security protects U.S. personnel and facilities abroad from terrorists. It investigates passport and visa fraud, which may accompany terrorist acts, and operates the Overseas Security Advisory Council, which maintains a security and terrorism-related electronic bulletin board for nonofficial U.S. citizens overseas. It also administers the ATA Program, which has trained over seventeen thousand officials from eighty-nine countries in counterterrorism. The program costs approximately $16 million annually.

### Anti-Terrorism Assistance Program

The State Department administers the ATA Program through the Bureau of Diplomatic Security. This program is directed at foreign countries, but has an indirect impact in reducing the terrorist threat to the United States.

ATA received $33 million in FY2000, and, according to the White House press secretary, the president requested $68 million for FY2001, including $30 million to establish a center for antiterrorism and security training to meet the worldwide demand for ATA programs.[121] The OMB reports the FY2001 request for ATA was $64 million. A State Department fact sheet describes the program as follows:

The United States is engaged in a vigorous campaign to promote by the year 2000 the universal adoption and ratification of all eleven existing international terrorist conventions. Every nation has the responsibility to arrest or expel terrorists, shut down their finances, and deny them safe haven. Our goal is to strengthen the rule of law against terrorism globally.

In June the Department hosted an important counterterrorism conference that included representatives from 22 nations in the Middle East, South Asia, Central Asia, Europe, and Canada. The conference promoted international cooperation against terrorism and the sharing of information on terrorist groups and countermeasures.

The United States conducts the successful Anti-terrorism Training Assistance program, which trains foreign law enforcement personnel in such areas as airport security, bomb detection, maritime security, VIP protection, hostage rescue, and crisis management. To date, we have trained more than 20,000 representatives from more than 100 countries.[122]

### Export Controls and Homeland Defense

As is the case with the DOD, the State Department also plays a major role in counterproliferation activities that have a major impact on homeland defense, but which are not included in the OMB and other analysis of narrowly defined counterterrorism programs. These include a variety of joint efforts with the DOC and DOD affecting export controls.

These efforts have two principal objectives. First, to stop—or at least retard—the transfer of those technologies, which could permit states of concern to design, manufacture, or acquire CBRN weapons, their delivery systems, or other dangerous armaments. Second, to monitor the flow of dual-use technologies that have legitimate commercial applications but that, if diverted or applied to military end uses, could have a negative impact on U.S. national security interests. A policy of denial involves carefully targeted export controls and the halting, where possible, of trade in weapons and technology transfers to countries of concern.

These efforts are intended to prevent the acquisition of dangerous and sensitive technologies by countries that pose threats to regional or global security. The State Department and other concerned US government agencies develop export control lists that try to identify and utilize "choke points" (goods and technologies important at critical stages of manufacture and application of military and dual-use items) as an effective means of control. The DOD, DOE, and the U.S. intelligence community actively support the export review process by identifying the key technologies that enable nuclear, biological, and chemical proliferation.

### Arms Control and Homeland Defense

The State Department, DOS, DOE, and U.S. intelligence community also play a major role in trying to block proliferation and the transfer of critical technologies through a wide range of arms control efforts. While these efforts apply largely to the actions of foreign states, they also affect any transfer of weapons, materials, or technology to terrorist and extremist groups. The treaties involved include the efforts shown in Table 7.5. Such efforts all have their limitations, but they are still an important tool in homeland defense, and again illustrate the fact that any effective effort to defend the United States against CBRN attack must look well beyond the borders of the United States.

## DEPARTMENT OF TRANSPORTATION

The Department of Transportation (DOT) has nearly doubled its spending on combating terrorism and WMD preparedness from FY1998 to FY2001. Table 7.1 provides a breakdown of the budget for DOT activities relating directly to defense and response against terrorist attacks. It also shows that its budget totaled $169.3 million in FY1998, $270.7 million in FY1999, $277.2 million in FY2000, and $298.1 million in FY2001.[123] Almost all of this money went to physical protection.

DOT's programs cannot be clearly separated into WMD and CIP components. One program that has WMD aspects is Transportation Infrastructure Assurance Research and Development, managed by the Research and Special Programs Administration. The program researches chemical and biological detection systems for major terminals such as subways, airports, and rail stations. The program also researches Intermodal Terminal Security for the intermodal freight transportation network. The FY2001 request was $3 million. Another DOT program is the Human Factors Analysis for Transportation Systems. The project analyzes the limitations of human preparedness, prediction, and response related to modes of transportation. The project's FY2001 request was $400,000.[124]

The DOT is continuing to acquire explosives-detection technologies to improve screening accuracy by requesting $100 million for FY2001. The DOT also wants further research and development into security to meet the growing and changing threat of terrorism. The FY2001 request for the program was $49.4 million. Security will also be improved at vital FAA facilities, and the FY2001 request was $18.6 million.[125] In cases of air piracy, the FAA is responsible for coordination of all law enforcement activity. In FY1997, total spending for unclassified terrorism-related programs totaled approximately $296.8 million. The DOT also has responsibility for the U.S. Coast Guard in peacetime. The Coast Guard could play a major role in intercepting suspected attackers and searching ships at sea for CBRN weapons.[126]

## DEPARTMENT OF TREASURY

The Treasury has responsibility for a number of counterterrorism functions. The U.S. Secret Service is developing chemical and biological

Table 7.5
Key Arms Control Efforts Relating to Asymmetric Warfare and Terrorism
Involving CBRN Weapons

- **Nuclear Nonproliferation Treaty (NPT)**
  - Nonnuclear weapon member states forswear the right to manufacture or acquire nuclear weapons. Exporting nuclear materials to nonnuclear weapon states is prohibited unless the material is safeguarded.
  - Nonnuclear weapon states that are NPT members agree to International Atomic Energy Agency (IAEA) safeguards at all nuclear sites.
- **Comprehensive Nuclear Test Ban Treaty (CTBT) (has not entered into the force)**
  - Signatories undertake not to carry out any nuclear weapons test explosions or other nuclear explosions.
- **Nuclear Suppliers Group (NSG)**
  - Members agree informally to control exports of nuclear materials and to establish tight controls on enrichment and reprocessing technologies.
- **Zangger Committee (ZC)**
  - Developed list of safeguarded trigger items that NPT members will export only to facilities under IAEA safeguards.
- **Australia Group (AG)**
  - Informal group whose members have adopted export controls on specific chemical precursors, microorganisms, and related production equipment with chemical and biological weapons applications.
- **Biological and Toxin Weapons Convention (BWC)**
  - Bans development, production, stockpiling, retention, or acquisition of biological agents or toxins that have no justification for peaceful purposes.
  - Treaty in force but has no verification or monitoring mechanisms.
- **Chemical Weapons Convention (CWC)**
  - Bans chemical weapons development, production, stockpiling, transfer, and use.
  - Requires adherents to declare and destroy stockpiles and production plants within ten years.
  - Entered into force in April 1997.
- **Missile Technology Control Regime (MTCR)**
  - Voluntary regime with thirty-two member states; no control over nonmembers; and no enforcement authority.
  - Main goal is to halt or slow the spread of missiles and UAVs that can deliver a five-hundred-kilogram or larger payload to three hundred or more kilometers.
  - Members agree to control two categories of exports related to missile development and production.
  - Category 1: whole missiles and UAVs with five-hundred- to three-hundred-kilometer payload/range, and complete subsystems.
  - Category 2: equipment and technology related to warheads and reentry vehicles, missile engines, guidance technology, propellants, and missiles and UAVs with a three-hundred-kilometer range but less than a three-hundred-kilometer payload.

detection, mitigation, and decontamination support for all presidential movements. The service is constructing a chemical and biological detection and protective program that combines multiple systems: fixed detectors, collective protection systems, and portable detection equipment.

The Bureau of Alcohol, Tobacco, and Firearms (ATF) is the lead federal agency in investigating armed violent crime, arson, and explosions. ATF has four National Response Teams that can arrive at major bombing and arson sites within twenty-four hours. The bureau is also researching the effects of large car bombs along with the U.S. Army Corps of Engineers and the Defense Technical Research Agency.

The Customs Service is responsible for stopping CBRN materials from entering the country, while the Secret Service is responsible for security at major events. These two services work together to prevent an airborne attack at major events. The Customs Air and Marine Interdiction Division will supply the air support to enforce temporary flight restricted areas, to survey the area, and to transport Secret Service assault teams and snipers. The FY2001 request for this joint program is $16 million. The funds will allow nineteen special agents to be trained and equipped for the air security counter-assault team.

The Bremer Commission suggested that the Treasury Department could be more effective in combating terrorism. The commission recommended that the Office of Foreign Assets Control (OFAC), which administers economic sanctions, create a unit dedicated to tracking terrorist assets. The commission recognized that the OFAC has the capabilities and expertise as well as resource constraints. The commission also suggested that the Customs and the Internal Revenue Service have information that could thwart terrorist fund-raising. However, the commission realized there is no agency that analyzes all the data available to the U.S. government to distribute to the relevant officials.[127]

Table 7.1 provided a breakdown of the Treasury Department budget for activities relating directly to defense and response against terrorist attacks. It shows that its budget totaled $341.3 million in FY1998, $368.0 million in FY1999, $348.0 million in FY2000, and $440.2 million in FY2001.[128] Unlike most federal civil departments and agencies, the bulk of the expenditure went to counterterrorism and response efforts, and not physical protection of federal facilities.[129]

## DEPARTMENT OF VETERANS AFFAIRS

PDD-62 instructs the Department of Veterans Affairs (VA) to assist the USPHS in maintaining an adequate national stockpile of pharmaceuticals. Four caches are maintained in strategic locations that would be dispatched to a scene of a WMD attack to help the capability of USPHS National Medical Response Teams.

The VA also assists the CDC in maintaining the National Pharmaceutical Stockpile, which is located in certain cities throughout the United States. It receives funds from the agencies it supports to maintain the stockpiles. It also trains medical personnel at National Disaster Medical System hospitals. It is working on constructing a counterterrorism training program to include with its training. The USPHS can transfer up to $1 million a year to the VA for the training.

The VA counterterrorism spending adapted from the 2000 OMB counterterrorism funding report shows that the VA supports its counterterrorism program from funding transferred by other agencies.[130] It should be noted that some experts have proposed significantly expanding the VA's contingency role in responding to biological attacks, in using its medical facilities for response purposes, and in playing a role in vaccine distribution and immunization.

## LOOKING BEYOND SEPTEMBER 2001

One thing is clear. This structure is the foundation the United States now has to build upon. But it is a loose structure indeed and one that is not yet adequate enough to deal with the threat of "conventional" terrorism that emerged in September 2001, much less the threat of CBRN attacks. It is equally clear that some control plan, program, and budget is needed to tie together those efforts; that more resources are needed to make each department effective; and that a new level of central control and direction is needed to reduce the current level of turf fights and focus departments and agencies on the actual mission.

## NOTES

1. Executive Office of the President, Office of Management and Budget, "Annual Report to Congress on Combating Terrorism, Including Defense against Weapons of Mass Destruction/Domestic Preparedness and Critical Infrastructure Protection," May 18, 2000.

2. Executive Office of the President, "Annual Report to Congress on Combating Terrorism."

3. Executive Office of the President, "Annual Report to Congress on Combating Terrorism."

4. "Standing Tall Overseas," *Washington Post*, August 17, 2000, A-28.

5. Center for Nonproliferation Studies, Monterey Institute of International Studies, "Agency Structures for Terrorism Response," 1999, <http://www.cns.miis.edu/research/cbw/response.htm>.

6. National Commission on Terrorism, *Countering the Changing Threat of International Terrorism* (June 2000).

7. Executive Office of the President, "Annual Report to Congress on Combating Terrorism."

8. First Annual Report of the Advisory Panel to Assess Domestic Response Capabilities for Terrorism Involving the Use of Weapons of Mass Destruction, *Assessing the Threat* (December 15, 1999), <http:www.rand.org/organization/nsrd/terrpanel.html>.

9. National Commission on Terrorism, *Countering the Changing Threat of International Terrorism.*

10. U.S. General Accounting Office, "Weapons of Mass Destruction: DOD's Actions to Combat Weapons Use Should Be More Integrated and Focused," GAO/NSIAD-00-97, May 26, 2000, <http://www.gao.gov/new.items/ns00097.pdf>.

11. Office of the Secretary of Defense, *Proliferation and Response, January 2001*, Internet ed. (Washington, D.C.: U.S. Department of Defense, January 2001), section 2, "Domestic Consequence Management."

12. Office of the Secretary of Defense, *Proliferation and Response.*

13. Office of the Secretary of Defense, *Proliferation and Response.*

14. See U.S. Department of Defense, Office of Combating Terrorism Policy and Support, Programs, Resources and Assessments Directorate, *Combating Terrorism Activities, FY2001* (Washington, D.C.: U.S. Department of Defense, January 14, 2000), 296–297.

15. U.S. Department of Defense, *Combating Terrorism Activities*, 193.

16. U.S. Department of Defense, *Combating Terrorism Activities*, 213.

17. U.S. General Accounting Office, "Combating Terrorism: Action Taken but Considerable Risks Remain for Forces Overseas," GAO/NSIAD-00-181, July 19, 2000, <http://www.gao.gov/new.items/ns00181.pdf>.

18. "Combating Terrorism," GAO/NSIAD-00-181.

19. "Combating Terrorism," GAO/NSIAD-00-181.

20. U.S. Department of Defense, *Combating Terrorism Activities*, 343–350.

21. U.S. Department of Defense, *Combating Terrorism Activities*, 394.

22. U.S. General Accounting Office, "Combating Terrorism: Need to Eliminate Duplicate Federal Weapons of Mass Destruction Training," GAO/NSIAD-00-64, March 21, 2000, <http://www.gao.gov/new.items/ns00064.pdf>.

23. Executive Office of the President, "Annual Report to Congress on Combating Terrorism."

24. U.S. Department of Defense, *Combating Terrorism Activities.*

25. "Combating Terrorism," GAO/NSIAD-00-64.

26. "Combating Terrorism," GAO/NSIAD-00-64.

27. "Combating Terrorism," GAO/NSIAD-00-64.

28. William S. Cohen, U.S. Department of Defense, "Annual Report to the President and the Congress" (2000), <http://www.dtic.mil/execsec/adr2000/chap7.html>.

29. U.S. General Accounting Office, "Chemical and Biological Defense: Program Planning and Evaluation Should Follow Results Act Framework," GAO/T-NSIAD-00-180, May 24, 2000, <http://www.gao.gov/new.items/ns00180t.pdf>.

30. U.S. General Accounting Office, "Future Years Defense Program: Comparison of Planned Funding Levels for the 2000 and 2001 Programs," GAO/NSIAD-00-179, June 14, 2000, <http://www.gao.gov/new.items/ns00179.pdf>.

31. "Chemical and Biological Defense," GAO/T-NSIAD-00-180.

32. U.S. Department of Defense, *Combating Terrorism Activities*, 325, 338.

33. U.S. Department of Defense, *Combating Terrorism Activities*, 361.

34. "Chemical and Biological Defense," GAO/T-NSIAD-00-180.

35. U.S. Department of Defense, *Combating Terrorism Activities*, 384.

36. "Chemical and Biological Defense," GAO/T-NSIAD-00-180.

37. U.S. General Accounting Office, "Chemical and Biological Defense: Observations on Non-medical Chemical and Biological R&D Programs," GAO/T-NSIAD-00-130, March 22, 2000, <http://www.gao.gov/new.items/ns00130t.pdf>.

38. U.S. Department of Defense Tiger Team, "Department of Defense Plan for Integrating National Guard and Reserve Component Support for Response to Attacks Using Weapons of Mass Destruction" (January 1998), <http://www.defenselink.mil/pubs/wmdresponse/chapter_5.html>.

39. Cohen, "Annual Report to the President and the Congress."

40. Charles Cragin, "Defense Leaders Commentary: The Facts on WMD Civil Support Teams" (March 31, 2000), <http://www.defenselink.mil/news/Mar2000/n0331200_20003311.html>.

41. Cragin, "Defense Leaders Commentary."

42. U.S. Department of Defense, *Combating Terrorism Activities*, 326.

43. U.S. Department of Defense, *Combating Terrorism Activities*, 382.

44. U.S. Department of Defense, *Combating Terrorism Activities*, 352.

45. U.S. Department of Defense, *Combating Terrorism Activities*, 369.

46. U.S. Department of Defense, *Combating Terrorism Activities*, 375.

47. Executive Office of the President, "Annual Report to Congress on Combating Terrorism."

48. This analysis is based on the Office of the Secretary of Defense, *Proliferation and Response*.

49. Executive Office of the President, "Annual Report to Congress on Combating Terrorism."

50. Center for Nonproliferation Studies, "Agency Structures for Terrorism Response."

51. Executive Office of the President, "Annual Report to Congress on Combating Terrorism."

52. Executive Office of the President, "Annual Report to Congress on Combating Terrorism."

53. Executive Office of the President, "Annual Report to Congress on Combating Terrorism."

54. Executive Office of the President, "Annual Report to Congress on Combating Terrorism."

55. "Chemical and Biological Defense," GAO/T-NSIAD-00-130.

56. Center for Nonproliferation Studies, "Agency Structures for Terrorism Response."

57. Environmental Protection Agency, "EPA Capabilities: Responding to Nuclear-Biological-Chemical (NBC) Terrorism," EPA 550-F-00-008, May 2000, <http://www.epa.gov/ceppo/pubs/brochurejune2000.pdf>.

58. Environmental Protection Agency, "EPA Capabilities," EPA 550-F-00-008.

59. Executive Office of the President, "Annual Report to Congress on Combating Terrorism."

60. Environmental Protection Agency, "EPA Capabilities," EPA 550-F-00-008.

61. Executive Office of the President, "Annual Report to Congress on Combating Terrorism."

62. U.S. General Accounting Office, "Combating Terrorism: Issues in Managing Counterterrorist Programs," GAO/T-NSIAD-00-145, April 6, 2000, <http://www.gao.gov/new.items/ns00145t.pdf>.

63. Federal Emergency Management Agency, "Federal Response Plan, Notice of Change," FEMA 229, Chg. 11, February 7, 1997, <http://www.fas.org/irp/offdocs/pdd39_frp.htm>.

64. Executive Office of the President, "Annual Report to Congress on Combating Terrorism."

65. Center for Nonproliferation Studies, "Agency Structures for Terrorism Response."

66. "Combating Terrorism," GAO/NSIAD-00-64.

67. "Combating Terrorism," GAO/NSIAD-00-64.

68. "Combating Terrorism," GAO/NSIAD-00-64.

69. Executive Office of the President, "Annual Report to Congress on Combating Terrorism."

70. Executive Office of the President, "Annual Report to Congress on Combating Terrorism."

71. Executive Office of the President, "Annual Report to Congress on Combating Terrorism."

72. Executive Office of the President, "Annual Report to Congress on Combating Terrorism."

73. National Commission on Terrorism, *Countering the Changing Threat of International Terrorism.*

74. U.S. General Accounting Office, "Combating Terrorism: Observations on Growth in Federal Programs," GAO/T-NSIAD-99-181, June 9, 1999, <http://frwebgate.access.gpo.gov/cgi-bin/useftp.cgi?IPaddress=162.140.64.21&filename=ns99181.pdf&directory=/diskb/wais/data/gao.html>.

75. Executive Office of the President, "Annual Report to Congress on Combating Terrorism."

76. Department of Health and Human Services, "Medical Response in Emergencies: HHS Role" (May 18, 2000), <http://www.hhs.gov/news/press/2000pres/20000518a.html>.

77. Executive Office of the President, "Annual Report to Congress on Combating Terrorism."

78. "Combating Terrorism," GAO/T-NSIAD-99-181.

79. "Combating Terrorism," GAO/T-NSIAD-00-145.

80. Executive Office of the President, "Annual Report to Congress on Combating Terrorism."

81. National Commission on Terrorism, *Countering the Changing Threat of International Terrorism.*

82. Executive Office of the President, "Annual Report to Congress on Combating Terrorism."

83. Executive Office of the President, "Annual Report to Congress on Combating Terrorism."

84. "Combating Terrorism," GAO/T-NSIAD-00-145.

85. Executive Office of the President, "Annual Report to Congress on Combating Terrorism."

86. "Combating Terrorism," GAO/T-NSIAD-99-181.

87. National Commission on Terrorism, *Countering the Changing Threat of International Terrorism.*

88. National Commission on Terrorism, *Countering the Changing Threat of International Terrorism.*

89. U.S. General Accounting Office, "Combating Terrorism: Linking Threats to Strategies and Resources," GAO/T-NSIAD-00-218, July 26, 2000, <http://www.gao.gov/new.items/ns00218t.pdf>.

90. National Domestic Preparedness Organization website, http://www.ndpo.gov/responders.htm.

91. National Domestic Preparedness Office, "Blueprint for the National Domestic Preparedness Office," <http://www.ndpo.gov/blueprint.pdf>.

92. "Combating Terrorism," GAO/T-NSIAD-00-145.

93. First Annual Report of the Advisory Panel, *Assessing the Threat.*

94. "Combating Terrorism," GAO/T-NSIAD-00-218.

95. U.S. Department of Justice, Office of Justice Program, Office for State and Local Domestic Preparedness Support, <http://www.ojp.usdoj.gov/osldps/html>.

96. Executive Office of the President, "Annual Report to Congress on Combating Terrorism."

97. U.S. Department of Justice, Office of Justice Program, Office for State and Local Domestic Preparedness Support, *FY1999 State Domestic Preparedness Equipment Program Application,* <http://www.ojp.usdoj.gov/osldps/docs/FY99StatePrepEQUIPMENTAppKit.doc>.

98. U.S. Department of Justice, *FY1999 State Domestic Preparedness Equipment Program Application.*

99. "Combating Terrorism," GAO/NSIAD-00-64.

100. "Combating Terrorism," GAO/NSIAD-00-64.

101. "Combating Terrorism," GAO/NSIAD-00-64.

102. U.S. Department of Justice, Office of Justice Program, Office for State and Local Domestic Preparedness Support, Technical Assistance Website, <http://www.ojp.usdoj.gov/osldps/ta.htm>.

103. U.S. Department of Justice, Office of Justice Program, Office for State and Local Domestic Preparedness Support, State Domestic Preparedness Equipment Program Needs Assessment and Strategy Development Initiative Web site, <http://www.ojp.usdoj.gov/osldps/assessments.htm>.

104. "Combating Terrorism," GAO/T-NSIAD-00-218.

105. U.S. Department of Justice, Office of Justice Program, Office for State and Local Domestic Preparedness Support, Exercises Web site, <http://www.ojp.usdoj.gov/osldps/exercises.htm>.

106. National Commission on Terrorism, *Countering the Changing Threat of International Terrorism.*

107. Executive Office of the President, "Annual Report to Congress on Combating Terrorism."

108. "Combating Terrorism," GAO/NSIAD-00-64.

109. Federal Bureau of Investigation, ANSIR Web site, <http://www.fbi.gov/programs/ansir/ansir.htm>.

110. Executive Office of the President, "Annual Report to Congress on Combating Terrorism."

111. Executive Office of the President, "Annual Report to Congress on Combating Terrorism."

112. "Combating Terrorism," GAO/T-NSIAD-99-181.

113. Executive Office of the President, "Annual Report to Congress on Combating Terrorism."

114. Executive Office of the President, "Annual Report to Congress on Combating Terrorism."

115. Executive Office of the President, "Annual Report to Congress on Combating Terrorism."

116. Executive Office of the President, "Annual Report to Congress on Combating Terrorism."

117. Executive Office of the President, "Annual Report to Congress on Combating Terrorism."

118. White House, Office of the Press Secretary, "Embassy Security Funding Fact Sheet" (February 10, 2000), <http://www.state.gov/www/global/terrorism/fs_000210_embsy.html>.

119. National Commission on Terrorism, *Countering the Changing Threat of International Terrorism*.

120. Ambassador Michael Sheehan, Office of the Coordinator for Counterterrorism, Testimony to the Senate Foreign Relations Committee (June 15, 2000), <http://www.state.gov/www/policy_remarks/2000/000615_sheehan_terrorism.html>.

121. White House, "Embassy Security Funding Fact Sheet."

122. U.S. Department of State, Office of the Spokesman, "U.S. Counterterrorism Efforts Fact Sheet" (August 4, 1999), <http://www.state.gov/www/regions/africa/fs_anniv_cterrorism.html>.

123. Executive Office of the President, "Annual Report to Congress on Combating Terrorism."

124. Executive Office of the President, "Annual Report to Congress on Combating Terrorism."

125. Executive Office of the President, "Annual Report to Congress on Combating Terrorism."

126. Executive Office of the President, "Annual Report to Congress on Combating Terrorism."

127. National Commission on Terrorism, *Countering the Changing Threat of International Terrorism*.

128. Executive Office of the President, "Annual Report to Congress on Combating Terrorism."

129. Executive Office of the President, "Annual Report to Congress on Combating Terrorism."

130. Executive Office of the President, "Annual Report to Congress on Combating Terrorism."

*Chapter 8*

# Federal, State, and Local Cooperation

Extensive work is already underway to improve coordination with state and local law enforcement agencies, emergency planning groups, and a wide range of different responders. A number of regional centers have been set up. Federal agencies and state and local governments have been involved in a range of exercises. There has also been an increasing effort to involve the private and civil sectors, particularly in areas like health care, the media, and utilities.

There are, however, no clear measures of the scope and effectiveness of these efforts to date, and state and local authorities and private-sector capabilities differ sharply even within major metropolitan areas. In many cases, the coordination effort has not gone beyond command post exercise—like activities whose main purpose has been to educate state and local actors in the generic risk of attacks.

No attempt has been made to create anything approaching an integrated analysis of federal, state, and local expenditures and activities. The problems created by a lack of coordinated federal planning, programming, and budgeting—and the lack of future year plans—are far greater in trying to analyze federal, state, and local efforts than they are within the federal government. What is not clear, however, is whether it is feasible to even attempt the creation of such a planning, programming, and budgeting effort. At this point, it is unclear whether it is possible to create and maintain more than a highly selective catalog of federal, state, and local capabilities in critical aspects of homeland defense.

## PLANNING FOR LOW- TO MID-LEVEL TERRORISM

Federal, state, and local exercises and activities now seem to be most effective in dealing with relatively low levels of attack, with effects limited to those that states and localities often have to deal with in emergencies caused by weather, accidents, low-level terrorism, or natural outbreaks of disease. Planning for large-scale, high-explosive attacks, and most chemical attacks, which may be similar in effect to major HAZMAT accidents, may be covered by such procedures. However, there was only a limited effort to determine critical vulnerabilities and to consider the broader impact of such attacks when they strike at utilities, key medical facilities, and so on. Certainly no one planned for "conventional" terrorism of the kind that struck the World Trade Center and the Pentagon.

Planning for nuclear and major biological attacks has been very limited, although some high-level exercises have been held. There is, as yet, little practical planning, organization, and training for major CBRN attacks of the kind that may occur in the future. Nuclear attacks have only been explored to a limited extent, and there is little detailed planning for response to the level of direct effects that can occur or to the long-term and secondary effects that may require a response over weeks, months, and years. Even the more sophisticated attack models and exercises being used assume that radioactive plumes and fallout are relatively predictable and that enough knowledge exists to predict the radiation thresholds that produce serious casualties that require prompt treatment and the areas that will be affected.

There is also a tendency to use highly structured approaches to modeling and exercising federal, state, and local cooperation that really do not stress the proposed systems involved enough to test their validity. Some federal plans and exercises seem to be a "feed forward" system that assumes that state and local needs are relatively predictable and that many capabilities will exist in all states and localities.

While an effort is underway to inventory current equipment and capabilities, it is not clear that this will always reveal the weakest or "critical" links limiting state and local capabilities. Or that either the federal government or the states will be able to deal with the complex problems created by the very different capabilities of given localities and jurisdictions. This problem is further complicated by interstate jurisdiction problems in the many target areas that involve more than one state and by the inability to predict and promptly characterize the nature and scale of the attack and its effect once it occurs.

There are still significant legal and jurisdictional problems in federal, state, and local cooperation in gathering intelligence—the most critical aspect of defense—and in law enforcement and defense. Grand jury and other laws limit full communication upwards from the local level, while there are severe limits on what intelligence and law enforcement agencies can do if there is even a risk that a U.S. citizen might be involved in surveillance and an investigation.

## WEST NILE OUTBREAK

The 1999 West Nile virus outbreak in New York City presents an example of the problems involved. It caused encephalitis in sixty-two people, killing seven of them. In spite of the fact that the outbreak was viewed by many as a test of bio-terrorism preparedness, the surveillance aspects of the investigation went well, as GAO stated in its report on the outbreak:

> We learned that many aspects of the surveillance network worked well, speeding the response to the outbreak. In many cases, such events might not be noticed until a number of physicians have reported the cases and the local health department identifies a cluster, or a number of victims seek care for similar conditions at the same location. Alert responses by the doctors and nurses who first see such victims are particularly crucial in alerting the public health community to the possibility of a wider problem.[1]

However, the outbreak also revealed many problems in bio-terrorism preparedness. The GAO reported that:

> *Uncertainty exists about what to report, when, and to whom.* While the West Nile outbreak was identified more quickly than otherwise might have been expected because an astute physician reported two unusual cases, it still provides evidence that the reporting system could be improved. The virus might have been identified earlier—perhaps by a week according to an involved official—if case reporting had been better and if good baseline data showing past trends of encephalitis and related diseases had been available. Similarly, a physician we interviewed who had treated West Nile patients said clinicians often do not know whom to call when a cluster of patients with a disease of unknown origins is noticed. Wildlife and zoo officials also indicated that within their fields there is a need for better information and guidance about whom to contact in the public health community when an outbreak is suspected.
>
> *Better communication is needed among public health agencies.* Experts consider rapid and reliable communication among public health agencies to be essential to bio-terrorism preparedness and coordination. Timely dissemination of information allows public health officials to make decisions with the most current information available. During the West Nile outbreak, however, officials indicated that the lack of leadership in the initial stages of the outbreak and the lack of sufficient and secure channels for communication among the large number of agencies involved prevented them from sharing information efficiently.
>
> *Links between public health and animal agencies are becoming more important.* Many infectious diseases, including West Nile, are zoonotic, that is,

capable of infecting animals and people. The West Nile outbreak shows how domestic, wild, and zoo animals can be considered "sentinels," providing an early warning device for diseases that can harm people. Animals may be the first victims, unintentionally or not, in a deliberate biological attack. Some key public health officials such as the city health department's Director of the Bureau of Communicable Disease, indicated that they were not aware of the similarities in clinical symptoms occurring in birds and humans until many days or weeks after the human outbreak began.

*Assessment of laboratory capacity and improvement of linkages among laboratories are needed.* Officials pointed out the need for more laboratory capacity for identifying and handling infectious agents of high concern to human health, particularly emerging or exotic ones. For example, they said at the time of the outbreak, only two or three laboratories in the country had the reagents necessary to identify the West Nile virus. Several officials commented on the declining capacity and expertise within the federal and state public health laboratory infrastructure, particularly as it relates to zoonotic and vector-borne diseases. The number of laboratories and extent of capacity have dropped, and the staffing, physical plant, and financial support of many remaining laboratories have also been affected. Testing for West Nile taxed those parts of the laboratory system that were dealing with the outbreak—and in some ways, affected what some of these laboratories were supposed to do. Due to the limited capacities of the New York laboratories, the CDC laboratory handled the bulk of the testing. Typically, the CDC laboratory's role would be to confirm test results rather than to perform diagnostic testing. Improving the laboratory network is key to improving the laboratory capacity to respond to surges in workload and to provide the new technologies, staff, and expertise to respond to outbreaks.

*Challenges in distinguishing between natural and unnatural events show common elements of preparedness.* The report of the possibility of a bioterrorist event, and the difficulties in correctly identifying the virus and its source, highlight how hard it can be to determine whether an outbreak has an unnatural origin. While the actual response to the West Nile virus outbreak might not have been significantly different had it been considered a potential bioterrorist act, such an event would require the involvement of additional organizations to carry out a criminal investigation. CDC's current recommended protocols are to notify the Federal Bureau of Investigation and law enforcement officials, who would also seek to determine whether terrorists had targeted additional locations for the release of the pathogen. An HHS Office of Emergency Preparedness Official indicated that an investigation of a real bioterrorist attack may start as an emerging infectious disease outbreak investigation that finds that the cause was terrorism. Bio-terrorism preparedness rests in large part on the soundness and preparedness of the public health infrastructure for detecting any disease and the causes of disease outbreaks.[2]

It should be noted that the GAO did not address the issue of the ability to characterize and treat a biological weapon as distinguished from a normal pattern of disease. Also ignored were the lessons learned from this experience if the attack occurred as the result of a large-scale attack by a state actor, proxy, or well-organized and efficient terrorist/extremists.

## THE LESSONS FROM "JOINTNESS"

The United States has learned over the years how to react to many kinds of emergencies, some at relatively a large scale by civil standards. In general, however, the burden of response falls first on local authorities and the local private sector, then on states, and then on the federal government. Existing capabilities are generally adequate and response can be improvised as needed. The same is true of law enforcement, although foreign and national counterterrorist and counterextremist activity has a higher element of federal involvement in intelligence and enforcement. The resulting capabilities to deal with low-level threats to the U.S. homeland are generally good for low-level threats and attacks and the effects of failure are highly localized. They will be tragic but not catastrophic.

The situation changes radically, as the level of attack escalates and changes in type. It can be argued that most practical chemical and radiological attacks will strain the existing structure of the local, state, and federal response. It will not be radically different in impact from a major chemical spill or HAZMAT incident if the public reaction can be contained and authorities make the limits of the attack clear. At the same time, even at this level of attack, a large number of private, state, local, and federal entities may be involved in unfamiliar activities where past experience and current plans are not adequate to the task.

The problem grows more severe as the threat escalates and becomes steadily more unfamiliar and unpredictable. Nuclear and biological attacks can reach levels where the priorities of detection and prevention force new and drastic approaches to intelligence and law enforcement, and where any effort to plan response becomes an exercise in managing chaos. Local capabilities of all kinds can be saturated and collapse. States will confront problems that they cannot anticipate, and the federal government may find that the first casualty in homeland defense, like war, is not truth but rather the plan of battle.

There is no way to validate such a conclusion with hard data, and the results are impressionistic. But neither the literature available nor practical experience in attending meetings and simulations indicate that federal, state, and local governments *as yet* understand the extent to which they will have to deal with unpredictable events, which they cannot properly characterize at any point in their defense and response activities and with the failure of their plans and organizational efforts. The events of September

2001 have certainly focused some efforts, but there is a "Task Force Smith" character to many such efforts. Capability is assumed either to exist or to be developed in the future. The ability to meet and discuss is confused with the ability to react. Federal, state, and local governments talk at each other, rather than fully communicate. Critical details are ignored, and real-world limits in capability are never discovered.

It is interesting to consider the experience of the U.S. military in this light. No amount of planning, coordination, organization, and designation of command authority ever created effective joint operations. Jointness was forced on the military by experience and by defeat. Every important lesson was learned the hard way. As a result, the need for true jointness only became fully clear years after all of the problems involved had supposedly been solved.

The U.S. military had to radically change its training and exercise doctrine. It learned that effective coordination can be helped with truly demanding command post exercises, but only if the participants are stressed to the point of defeat and are forced to be realistic. Exercises designed to produce success have been proven to be a failure ever since the breakdown in U.S. command at Kasserine Pass. Furthermore, the U.S. military learned that tactical execution required truly demanding field exercises and that every aspect of jointness that was not simulated and tested in the field failed. Meanwhile, the Persian Gulf War, Somalia, and Kosovo revealed that major problems still existed in jointness and coordination. At the same time, no one in the U.S. armed forces would argue that this effort is yet fully successful.

The problems in achieving effective jointness in homeland defense against CBRN attacks are likely to be far more daunting. Particularly because it is far from clear what attacks should be exercises, that realistic exercises are affordable, and that much of the experience from one exercise will apply to a different type of attack in a different area.

This is not a reason to give up on trying to deal with high levels of attack. It is, however, a reason not to confuse meetings, discussions cloaked as exercises, inventories, and creating new lines of authority as effective action. It is a good reason for the federal government to carry out as many realistic exercises as possible, and above all to firmly establish the limits of what it can do in mid- to high-level attacks and the operational limits of "jointness" at the state and local level. It is a good reason to question whether creating a new czar, lead agency, or cabinet member will accomplish any more in practice than the somewhat similar debate over how to conduct the war on drugs. It is also a good reason to assume that the capability to improvise will be more important than preexisting plans. Above all, it is a good reason at every level of government not to confuse assigning responsibility with creating capability.

## NOTES

1. U.S. General Accounting Office, "West Nile Virus: Lessons for Public Health Preparedness," GAO/HEHS-00-180, September 2000, <http://www.gao.gov>.

2. "West Nile Virus," GAO/HEHS-00-180.

## Chapter 9

# How Other Nations Deal with These Threats

Given the theater-driven nature of most threats, it is surprising that the United States is often ahead of its friends and allies in dealing with the CBRN threats posed by state actors, their proxies, and foreign and domestic terrorists/extremists. Indeed, many Europeans see the United States as overreacting to marginal threats in an almost paranoid fashion. This is partly a result of the fact that the United States does often overdramatize given threats and the need for given actions. It may also reflect the fact that not only does Europe not face the same scale of regional threats as the United States, but it also (and already) faces major problems in funding its existing security requirements.

The situation is different in the case of the United States' friends and allies in the Middle East, the Persian Gulf, and Asia. Most of its friends and allies are just beginning to understand just how different the threats they face can be if covert, state, terrorist, or extremist attacks use WMD. Even Israel and South Korea have done comparatively little to improve their deterrence and defense capabilities against such attacks or to improve their response capabilities beyond very limited, and largely symbolic, civil defense measures.

Many aspects of what the United States' friends and allies have done are classified or are not made public. The GAO did, however, publish a survey of the activities in five key friendly countries—Canada, France, Germany, Israel, and the United Kingdom—in April 2000. The GAO found striking similarities in their response:

The five countries we examined have similarities in how they are organized to combat terrorism.

- The countries generally have the majority of organizations used to combat terrorism under one lead government ministry. However, because many other ministries are also involved, the countries have created interagency coordination bodies to coordinate within and across ministries. For example, while many countries generally have their intelligence and law enforcement organizations under their ministries of interior or equivalent, they also need to coordinate with their ministries of foreign affairs, defense, and health or emergency services.

- The countries have clearly designated who is in charge during a terrorist incident—typically their national or local police.

- The countries have national policies that emphasize prevention of terrorism. To achieve their policies, the countries use a variety of strategies, including intelligence collection, police presence, and various security measures such as physical barriers at the entrances to public buildings.

- These countries primarily use their general criminal laws (e.g., those for murder or arson) to prosecute terrorists. The countries also have special terrorism-related laws that allow for special investigations or prosecution mechanisms and increased penalties.

- The countries' executive branches provide the primary oversight of organizations involved in combating terrorism. This oversight involves reviewing the programs and resources for effectiveness, efficiency, and legality.

The five countries we examined also had similarities in how they allocate resources to combat terrorism. Officials in the ministries involved said they make resource allocations based on the likelihood of threats taking place, as determined by intelligence assessments. While the officials we met with discussed resource levels in general, none of the five countries tracked overall spending on programs to combat terrorism.

Such spending was imbedded in other accounts for broad organizational or functional areas such as law enforcement, intelligence, and defense. Officials in all countries told us that because of limited resources, they made funding decisions for programs to combat terrorism based on the likelihood of terrorist activity actually taking place, not the countries' overall vulnerability to terrorist attack. They said their countries maximize their existing capabilities to address a wide array of threats, including emerging threats, before they create new capabilities or programs.[1]

The GAO also found, however, that countries differed in terms of the strength of their central governments and their perceptions of the threat. Officials in Canada, France, and Germany stated that the current threat from terrorism in their countries was low. This tracks with the State Department's report on global terrorism. It also states that terrorism in

Europe has declined, in part, because of the increased vigilance by security forces and the recognition by some terrorist groups that long-standing political and ethnic controversies should be addressed by negotiations. For example, the remnants of Germany's Red Army Faction, once among the world's deadliest, announced the dissolution of their organization.

At the same time, British officials said that terrorism related to Northern Ireland continues to take place and poses a real threat depending, in part, on developments in the peace process. They added that although activity is at historically low levels, the threat remains and is linked to developments in the peace process. Officials from all five countries cited the threat of terrorists using CBRN weapons as particularly unlikely. Israeli officials indicated that the level of terrorism fluctuated with the peace process— terrorism typically increased when the peace process was working, because those opposed to the peace process tried to derail it through violence.

## LEADERSHIP AND MANAGEMENT

The GAO found a common pattern of central leadership and coordination in dealing with the issues involved:

> Specifically, each country places the majority of resources for combating terrorism under one ministry, but each recognizes that it must coordinate its efforts to develop national policy on combating terrorism so it has interagency coordination bodies. Each country also has clearly designated leadership at the scene of terrorist incidents. The five countries have policies and strategies that emphasize the prevention of terrorism using resources such as intelligence collection, police presence, and security measures. In addition, each country uses its general criminal laws (e.g., those for murder or arson) to prosecute terrorists. The countries also have special terrorism-related laws that allow for special investigation or prosecution mechanisms, and increased penalties. In each of the five countries, the executive branch provides the primary oversight of organizations involved in combating terrorism.

### Lead Organization with Policy Coordination

In four countries, most of the resources to combat terrorism—law enforcement and intelligence services—are centralized under a lead agency, generally the countries' ministry of interior or equivalent. For example, the French Ministry of Interior includes the National Police and the two domestic intelligence agencies that have a primary role in combating terrorism. However, officials from all the countries said they view counterterrorism as an intergovernmental effort that requires coordination among law enforcement, intelligence, and other parts of the government that may be involved in combating terrorism, including foreign affairs, the military, and health and emergency services. Since they view combating terrorism as an interagency effort, officials in each country identified the prime minister or the chancellor as the one person in charge of combating terrorism. Below that level, the effort to combat terrorism requires an interagency body to formulate policy, coordinate activities, and provide recommendations to the prime minister or the chancellor. In Israel, for example, there is an interagency body called the Bureau for Counterterrorism that coordinates activities and provides advice to the prime minister regarding terrorism matters. . . .

### Clearly Designated Incident Leadership

All five countries have clearly designated who is to be in charge during a terrorist incident. For example, in the United Kingdom, the local Chief Constable (i.e., chief of police) has overall control of all aspects of handling a terrorist incident. For Israel, the National Police are in command within Israel, and the military are in command in the occupied territories. . . .

In Israel, the National Police are under one ministry; however, the main domestic and international intelligence services are not in the same ministry as the National Police and report directly to the prime minister.

Incident leadership is reinforced through written agreements and contingency plans or other agreements. For example, in Canada, the Royal Canadian Mounted Police has written agreements with major municipal police departments on who leads the incident response. The French government has written interagency contingency plans with command and control details for such terrorist situations as a heightened threat, aircraft hijacking, ship hijacking, or a chemical attack.

Officials in the five countries stated that they use the agreements or plans as the basis of their exercises to practice their response, which further reinforces who leads at the incident site. Clear incident command is also strengthened because the incident commander controls all response elements, including police, fire, medical, and other emergency services. Thus, there is one commander for police activities (e.g., assaults, arrest, and gathering evidence) as well as other emergency activities (e.g., evacuation, search and rescue, medical treatment, and decontamination). Officials in the United Kingdom cited the importance of having one person—the Chief Constable—in charge of the entire response. Officials in the other four countries made similar comments on the need for clear and unified leadership for the whole range of activities in a response to a terrorist attack.[2]

## POLICIES AND STRATEGIES

The GAO also found that all five countries had some strategies in common that emphasized prevention over response and that placed a heavy emphasis on intelligence in order to support the prevention effort:

Each country had developed policies to combat terrorism through their experience with various terrorist groups. The five countries' national policies to combat terrorism, which were not always written, emphasized prevention. Canadian officials were the only ones to provide us with their written policies on terrorism. Officials in the other countries told us they had no written policies. To implement their national policies, these countries had strategies that included intelligence collection, police presence, and other deterrent measures.

For example, the strategies in all five countries include domestic intelligence, and each has at least one security intelligence organization that gathers intelligence on domestic terrorist activities. Officials we spoke with said that an effective intelligence capability is essential for preventing acts of terrorism in their countries. In general, the role of their domestic security intelligence organizations is to prevent acts of terrorism by gathering information through a variety of sources and methods; assessing the threats to security; and monitoring and sometimes disrupting the activities of certain groups considered to be a threat within the country.

All of the countries' domestic intelligence organizations are separate from their law enforcement organizations. In Canada, France, and the United Kingdom, these organizations are under a single ministry. In Germany there are parallel federal and state intelligence and law enforcement organizations, and both are under their respective ministries of the interior. In Israel, the intelligence organizations report directly to the prime minister, and the national police are under the Ministry of Public Security. Cooperation between law enforcement and intelligence organizations was cited by officials in all five countries as important, in part, because the domestic intelligence organizations do not have powers of arrest. Law enforcement organizations become involved in combating terrorism when information from the intelligence services indicates that criminal activity has occurred, or is likely to occur, or when their own criminal intelligence sources indicate such.

. . . In addition to a strong intelligence capability, we found that the countries' strategies included using a visible police presence to prevent acts of terrorism. For example, in France, when there is a specific terrorist threat, law enforcement increases its public presence in a visible show of force. Likewise, the German Federal Border Police can provide additional manpower to supplement state police at events such as political demonstrations. In Israel, the National Police, as well as military personnel, is present at various locations throughout the metropolitan areas to respond to incidents as needed.

As part of their prevention strategies, the five countries use a variety of other techniques to deter terrorist attacks. For example, all five countries use physical barriers in certain critical areas and government buildings to deter direct attacks. Other techniques are as follows. In Israel, individuals and their belongings are often physically searched by police, defense personnel, or security contractors and pass through metal detectors before entering such places as shopping centers, airports, and local attractions. In the United Kingdom, police use video cameras to monitor daily events and watch for suspicious activity in London. In France, persons entering government buildings typically walk through metal detectors.[3]

## CLAIMED RELIANCE ON CRIMINAL PROSECUTION AS THE MAJOR RESPONSE AND DETERRENT

Rather than deterrence and retaliation, most countries relied largely on conventional criminal prosecution and punishment. Although Israel seems to have understated the linkage between the deterrent and offensive use of its military forces and counterterrorism, and Britain seems to have understated the role of its military forces and intelligence branches in performing direct operations against terrorist groups:

> All five countries use their general criminal laws to prosecute offenses committed during a terrorist act, such as the crimes of murder, arson, kidnapping, and hijacking. According to Canadian officials, treating terrorism as ordinary crime removes the political element and thereby dilutes the effectiveness of the terrorist act. The countries have also enacted a variety of special laws that relate to terrorism that may include a statutory definition or description of terrorism, or may invoke special investigation or prosecution procedures, or provide for increased penalties.
>
> Under French law, certain criminal offenses are considered terrorism when the acts are intentionally linked to an individual or group whose purpose is to cause a serious disruption of public order through intimidation or terror. Penalties may be increased if a criminal offense is related to such terrorism. France also has special judicial procedures to address terrorism such as special courts and prosecutors. Germany's criminal code has a special prohibition against the formation and support of a terrorist association.
>
> In addition to its general criminal laws, Israel has two principal laws that govern terrorism that contain a number of criminal offenses such as supporting terrorist organizations. The United Kingdom has two principal terrorism laws that designate a number of criminal offenses relating to membership in and support of terrorist organizations.[4]

## OVERSIGHT, PLANNING, PROGRAMMING, AND BUDGETING

None of the countries carried out oversight, planning, programming, and budgeting activities similar to those in the United States:

> Oversight reviews of programs and resources for effectiveness, efficiency, and legality are primarily the responsibility of those ministers in the executive branch that have a role in combating terrorism. Officials told us that in their parliamentary style of government, ministers are accountable for oversight and that this function is embedded in the ministers' responsibilities. They generally viewed oversight as an ongoing routine function of agency management, not an independent or separate review function. For example, in France, the Minister of the Interior, through their daily activities, reviews or oversees the activities of those resources within the Ministry.
>
> The legislatures in these countries do not hold oversight hearings or write reports that evaluate programs to combat terrorism. In these parliamentary style governments, the legislative branches do not provide ongoing independent oversight of efforts to combat terrorism. While the five countries do conduct some legislative review of national security activities (e.g., through designated legislative committees), these reviews generally have not focused

on activities to combat terrorism. At times, some members of the legislative branch are included in standing or ad hoc executive oversight bodies. In Canada and Israel, independent reviews of activities to combat terrorism are done by their national audit agencies. . . .

Officials in the ministries involved in combating terrorism within the five countries we visited said they made resource allocations based on the likelihood of threats taking place, as determined by intelligence assessments. While the officials we met with discussed resource levels in general, none of the five countries tracked overall spending on programs to combat terrorism. Such spending was imbedded in other accounts for broad organizational or functional areas such as law enforcement, intelligence, and defense. Due to resource constraints, they said their countries maximize their existing capabilities to address a wide array of threats, including emerging threats, before they create new capabilities or programs.[5]

## RESOURCE ALLOCATIONS ARE TARGETED AT LIKELY THREATS, NOT VULNERABILITIES: LIMITED CONCERN WITH WMD THREATS

The GAO also found that none of the countries shared threat perceptions similar to those that are now the focus of U.S. planning. Although part of the reason for this response is that the GAO only examined their response to conventional terrorism, rather than to the potential threat that state actors might carry out covert attacks:

The five countries we reviewed receive terrorist threat information from their civilian and military intelligence services and foreign sources. Using various means, each of the countries' intelligence services continuously assess these threats to determine which ones could result in terrorist activity and require countermeasures, which ones may be less likely to occur but may emerge later, and which ones are unlikely to occur.

Officials in all countries told us that because of limited resources, they made funding decisions for programs to combat terrorism based on the likelihood of terrorist activity actually taking place, not the countries' overall vulnerability to terrorist attack. For example, each of the countries may be vulnerable to a chemical, biological, radiological, or nuclear attack by terrorists, but officials believe that such attacks are unlikely to occur in the near future for a variety of reasons, including the current difficulty in producing and delivering these types of weapons.

Furthermore, officials in one country told us that the effects of these types of weapons would alienate the population from the political aim of the terrorist groups and therefore did not view this type of attack as likely. Officials we spoke with believed that conventional bombs and other traditional means, such as hijacking, are more likely to occur.

For less likely but emerging threats, officials in the five countries told us that they generally try to maximize their existing capabilities for responding to such threats, rather than create new programs or capabilities. For example, the same capabilities used to respond to a fire, industrial explosion, or chemical spill would be used for a terrorist incident involving chemical, biological, radiological, or nuclear weapons.

In addition, officials in each country said additional capabilities from neighboring states, provinces, cities, or national governments could be used by local authorities if the situation exceeded their capabilities. For example, Germany plans to rely on existing capabilities within the states rather than develop new federal capabilities.

Likewise, Israel has not developed new capabilities, but it has a nation-wide program that provides gas masks and training to its citizens for defense against chemical or biological attack in wartime that officials said has use for terrorist attacks.

The countries generally did not have major training programs in place to train emergency response personnel for chemical, biological, radiological, or nuclear attacks. However, the United Kingdom has a limited program to train selected police officials as incident commanders and is considering a training program for response personnel in selected locations. Also, Canada has launched a policy initiative to develop a strategy to strengthen national counterterrorism response capability, particularly the ability to respond to chemical, biological, radiological, and nuclear terrorist attacks.

Only France has created new capabilities to respond to chemical, biological, radiological, and nuclear terrorist attacks.[6]

## LEARNING FROM FOREIGN COUNTRIES

These conclusions imply that the United States has comparatively little to learn from the overall response its friends and allies are making to the emerging threats posed by mass terrorism, CBRN attacks, and new forms of covert state and terrorist/extremist attack, although there are certainly many areas where our allies are better prepared and we should do well to learn from them. This may reflect the fact that Israel sees such threats largely in military terms, and most European nations do not face the mix of global threats facing the United States. France is the only nation in Europe that has had enough recent experience with nations and movements that might use WMD to have some kind of contingency capability.

At the same time, it is clear that all five countries have seen the need for a single lead agency to emphasize prevention and to separate intelligence from police and related prevention and enforcement activity. They also have unified leadership in response to incidents. This tends to reinforce the conclusion that having a single lead agency or office to lead the United States may be an important reform, and that the United States might also benefit from having a unified leader for all forms of incident response.

## NOTES

1. U.S. General Accounting Office, United States General Accounting Office Report to Congressional Requesters, "Combating Terrorism: How Five Foreign

Countries Are Organized to Combat Terrorism," B-284585, GAO/NSIAD-00-85, April 2000.

2. "Combating Terrorism," B-284585, GAO/NSIAD-00-85.
3. "Combating Terrorism," B-284585, GAO/NSIAD-00-85.
4. "Combating Terrorism," B-284585, GAO/NSIAD-00-85.
5. "Combating Terrorism," B-284585, GAO/NSIAD-00-85.
6. "Combating Terrorism," B-284585, GAO/NSIAD-00-85.

*Chapter 10*

# Lessons from Recent Major Commissions on Terrorism

While the federal government has failed to provide either meaningful transparency or measures of effectiveness for its efforts, three major commissions have released reports with recommendations applying to federal counterterrorism efforts in 1999 and 2000. While these reports concentrated on counterterrorism within a relatively narrow definition of the term and largely ignored state threats and other forms of homeland defense, many of their recommendations are still of considerable importance in highlighting the improvements that are still needed in the U.S. homeland defense effort. These recommendations take on a new importance and priority in light of the attacks on the World Trade Center and the Pentagon.

## THE GILMORE, BREMER, AND HART-RUDMAN COMMISSIONS

The Advisory Panel to Assess Domestic Response Capabilities, also known as the Gilmore Commission, released its first report, *Assessing the Threat*, on December 15, 1999. The National Defense Authorization Act for FY1999 created the Gilmore Commission and directed it to assess federal domestic preparedness programs, including training for local responders, coordination and funding, and local equipment deficiencies and to release three annual reports. The commission gave eight recommendations on domestic preparedness in its first report.

The Gilmore Commission released its second report on December 15, 2000. In addition to supporting its conclusions of a year earlier, the advisory panel expanded its focus to assess national strategy and the organization of the federal government. Its second report recommended the creation of a "National Office for Combating Terrorism" with a director appointed by the president and confirmed by the Senate. This director would act as a point of contact for Congress. The office would develop national strategy to be approved by the president, have multidisciplinary staffing, formulate strategy and review plans and budgets, but not have operational control. It would be supported an Advisory Board for Domestic Programs.

The second report of the Gilmore Commission also recommended that Congress should create a "Special Committee for Combating Terrorism" with bipartisan membership and full-time staff from relevant committees. Furthermore, the report stated that this committee should have a direct link to the new "National Office for Combating Terrorism" and should also develop a consolidated legislative plan for authorization, budget, and appropriations and act as a clearinghouse and first referral for relevant legislation

Other recommendations were to:

Enhance intelligence, threat assessments, and information sharing

Improve human intelligence by rescinding CIA guidelines on certain foreign informants (DCI)

Improve measurement and signature intelligence through enhanced RDT&E (intelligence community)

Review/modify guidelines and procedures for domestic investigations (review panel/attorney general)

Review/modify authorities on certain CBRN precursors and equipment (executive branch and Congress)

Improve forensics technology/analysis and enhance indications and warnings systems (national office)

Provide security clearances and more information to designated state and local entities (national office)

Develop a single-source, protected, web-based, integrated information system (national office)

Foster better planning, coordination, and operations

Designate the Federal Response Plan as a single-source "all hazards" planning document (national office)

Develop a "model" state plan (National Emergency Management Association [NEMA] and FEMA)

Conduct inventories of state and local programs for nationwide application (national office)

Promote and/or facilitate the adoption of multijurisdiction and/or multistate mutual aid compacts (national office)

Promote and/or facilitate the adoption of a standard ICS, UCS, and EOC (national office)

Designate an agency other than DOD as the "lead federal agency" (president)

Enhance training, equipping, and exercising

Develop input to strategy and plans in close coordination with state and local entities (national office)

Restructure education and training opportunities to account for volunteers in critical response disciplines

Develop realistic exercise scenarios that meet state and local needs (national office)

Improve health and medical capabilities

Obtain strategy input and/or program advice from public health and medical care representatives (national office)

Promote certification programs for training and facilities (national office)

Clarify authorities and procedures for health and medical response (all jurisdictions)

Improve surge capacity and stockpiles (all jurisdictions)

Evaluate and test response capabilities (all public health and medical entities)

Establish standards for communications and for mandatory reporting (all public health and medical entities)

Establish laboratory standards and protocols (all public health and medical entities)

Promote better research and development and developing national standards

Develop, with the OSTP, equipment-testing protocols and long-range research plan (national office)

Establish a national standards program with the National Institute of Standards and Technology and NIOSH as co-leads (national office).

Enhance efforts to counter agroterrorism

Improve cyber security against terrorism[1]

A second commission called National Commission on Terrorism, also known as the Bremer Commission, released its report, *Countering the Changing Threat of International Terrorism*, in June 2000. The 1999 Foreign Operations, Export Financing, and Related Programs Act established the Bremer Commission and directed it to review federal counterterrorism policies regarding the prevention and punishment of international terrorism against the United States. The commission excluded domestic terrorism and consequence management from the scope of its study, and had a wide variety of recommendations ranging from intelligence to domestic preparedness.

Finally, a third commission, the U.S. Commission on National Security/ Twenty-first Century, also known as the Hart-Rudman Commission, was set up to examine and propose changes to the national security strategy to prepare for the twenty-first century. This commission released its strategy report, *Seeking a National Strategy: A Concert for Preserving Security and Promoting Freedom*, on April 15, 2000. Though the commission gave broad strategic recommendations, some apply to federal counterterrorism efforts.

## AREAS WHERE THE COMMISSIONS MADE SIMILAR RECOMMENDATIONS

Table 10.1 illustrates which of recommendations of these commissions coincide and which do not. Since each commission had a different area of focus, no identical recommendation came from all three commissions. However, there were many areas where the recommendations of two of the three commissions match.

### Gilmore and Bremer Commissions: Executive Coordination and Management

The Gilmore Commission had recommendations similar to those of the Bremer Commission in four areas: executive coordination, congressional coordination, information collection and dissemination, and authority roles. Both commissions concluded that the federal agencies were uncoordinated in regards to counterterrorism. To alleviate this problem, the Gilmore Commission supported the concept of an NDPO in its first report.

> The Federal bureaucratic structure is massive and complex. In various forums, state and local officials consistently express frustration in understanding where or how to enter this bureaucratic maze to obtain information, assistance, funding and support. In addition, Federal programs, especially those involving grants for funding or other resources, may be overly complicated, time consuming, and repetitive.
>
> In recent months, the Federal Bureau of Investigation, pursuant to its "lead-agency" role (specified in the related Presidential Decision Directives) for crisis management for terrorism involving weapons of mass destruction, was directed by the Attorney General of the United States to organize, within its own resources, a National Domestic Preparedness Office (NDPO). The ostensible purpose of the NDPO is to serve as a focal point and "clearing-house" for related preparedness information and for directing state and local entities to the appropriate agency of the Federal government for obtaining additional information, assistance, and support. There has been discussion about the issue of whether the FBI is the appropriate location or whether the NDPO structure and approach is the most effective way to address the complexities of the Federal organization and programs designed to enhance domestic response capabilities. The Panel is convinced that the *concept* behind

Table 10.1
Comparison of Commission Recommendations

|  | Gilmore | Bremer | Hart-Rudman |
|---|---|---|---|
| Executive coordination | x | x |  |
| Congressional coordination | x | x |  |
| Information collection and sharing | x | x |  |
| Authority roles | x | x |  |
| Control of pathogens |  | x | x |
| International consensus against terrorism |  | x | x |
| Biological surveillance |  | x | x |
| National plan | x |  |  |
| Threat assessments | x |  |  |
| Terms and definitions | x |  |  |
| Responder standards | x |  |  |
| Personal liability |  | x |  |
| State sponsorship |  | x |  |
| Terrorist organization designation |  | x |  |
| National fight against terrorism |  | x |  |
| Preparedness practice |  | x |  |
| Special forces |  |  | x |
| Detailed changes in role of federal departments and agencies |  |  | x |
| Detailed improvements in the integration of CBRN defense and CIP defense |  |  | x |

*Source*: Adapted by Steve Chu.

the NDPO is sound, and notes with interest that the Congress has recently authorized and appropriated funds ($6 million) for the operation of the NDPO. While that authority will give the NDPO some wherewithal to operate and to hire persons from outside the FBI, the Panel has seen no specific direction to other Federal agencies to provide personnel or other resources to the NDPO, to assist in a concerted, well-coordinated effort.[2]

In its second report, however, the Gilmore Commission found that the NDPO had not performed as expected.

Attempts to create a Federal focal point for coordination with State and local officials—such as the National Domestic Preparedness Office—have met with little success. Moreover, many State and local officials believe that Federal programs intended to assist at their levels are often created and implemented without consulting them. Confusion often exists even within the Federal bureaucracy. The current coordination structure does not possess the requisite authority or accountability to make policy changes and to impose the discipline necessary among the numerous Federal agencies involved.

We recommend the establishment of a senior level coordination entity in the Executive Office of the President, titled the "National Office for Combating Terrorism," with the responsibility for developing domestic and international policy and for coordinating the program and budget of the Federal government's activities for combating terrorism.

The principle task of the National Office for Combating Terrorism is to create a national strategy on combating terrorism to be approved by the President. The national strategy should be comprehensive covering international and domestic terrorism and inclusive of local, State, and Federal concerns. In addressing the shortcomings of the NDPO, the National Office for Combating Terrorism will be a stronger entity. It will have more control over its budget and programs, with the ability to coordinate intelligence and analysis, review local and State plans, propose changes, assist in Domestic Preparedness Programs, coordinated health and medical programs, and coordinate RDT&E to a national standard. It will also serve as a clearinghouse and act as a Federal point of contact for State and local officials.[3]

The Bremer Commission took a more direct approach to solving the coordination problem and recommended that the national counterterrorism coordinator participate in OMB budget decisions:

The United States does not have a single counterterrorism budget. Instead, counterterrorism programs exist in the individual budgets of 45 departments and agencies of the Federal Government. The National Coordinator for Security, Infrastructure, and Counterterrorism (currently a member of the President's staff) is responsible for ensuring that the counterterrorism programs in these departments and agencies meet the President's overall counterterrorism objectives. To discharge this responsibility, the National Coordinator established a process to set priorities, develop counterterrorism initiatives and review their funding in agency budgets. This process is an efficient means of balancing counterterrorism program requirements against other agency priorities, but it has a significant drawback. The National Coordinator has no role in the critical step when the Office of Management and Budget (OMB) decides what agency programs will be funded and at what levels. This decision is conveyed to the agencies when budget revisions are passed back to the agencies (called passbacks).

The Commission believes that whoever coordinates the national counterterrorism effort on behalf of the President should also have the authority to ensure that the President's counterterrorism objectives are reflected in agency budgets. That means the coordinator should participate with OMB in the passback of counterterrorism budget submissions, as well as in the final phase of the budget process when agencies appeal OMB's decisions.[4]

### Gilmore and Bremer Commissions: Congressional Oversight

The Gilmore and Bremer Commissions agreed that congressional coordination and oversight of counterterrorism programs need improvement. The Gilmore Commission recommended an ad hoc Joint Special or Select Committee to coordinate congressional involvement in counterterrorism:

> In much the same way that the complexity of the Federal bureaucratic structure is an obstacle—from a state and local perspective—to the provision of effective and efficient Federal assistance, it appears that the Congress has made most of its decisions for authority and funding to address domestic preparedness and response issues with little or no coordination. The various committees of the Congress continue to provide authority and money within the confines of each committee's jurisdiction over one or a limited number of Federal agencies and programs. The Panel recommends, therefore, that the Congress consider forming an *ad hoc* Joint Special or Select Committee, composed of representatives of the various committees with oversight and funding responsibilities for these issues, and give such an entity the authority to make determinations that will result in more coherent efforts at the Federal level.[5]

The Bremer Commission did not go as far as recommending a joint committee but did suggest joint hearings as a first step toward congressional coordination:

> Congress should develop mechanisms for coordinated review of the President's counterterrorism policy and budget, rather than having each of the many relevant committees moving in different directions without regard to the overall strategy.
> As a first step, the Commission urges Congress to consider holding joint hearings of two or more committees on counterterrorism matters. In addition, to facilitate executive-legislative discussion of terrorism budget issues, the House and Senate Appropriations committees should each assign to senior staff responsibility for cross-appropriations review of counterterrorism programs.
> Finally, the Commission notes the importance of bipartisanship in Congress and in the executive branch when considering counterterrorism policy and funding issues.[6]

The Gilmore Commission expanded its analysis of the need for congressional oversight in its second annual report. It proposed that Congress create a "Special Committee for Combating Terrorism" that would be a bipartisan effort with full-time staff members. It would either be a joint or separate house committee. Its main function would be to act as a clearinghouse for relevant legislative information. It would also coordinate with the executive branch by acting as a link to the National Office for Combating Terrorism.

### Gilmore and Bremer Commissions: Intelligence Gathering and Sharing

Both the Gilmore and Bremer Commissions highlighted the need for improved information collection and dissemination between counter-terrorism officials. The Gilmore Commission cited the Los Angeles area and New England as possible models for information sharing and suggested additional security clearances for state and local officials:

> State and local officials express the need for more "intelligence," and for better information sharing among entities at all levels on potential terrorist threats. While the Panel is acutely aware of the need to protect classified national security information, and the sources and methods by which it may have been obtained, the Panel believes that more can and must be done to provide timely information—up, down, and laterally, at all levels of government—to those who need the information to provide effective deterrence, interdiction, protection, or response to potential threats. This may entail granting security clearances to additional officials at the state and local level. And as noted, the FBI report on Project Megiddo, and the briefings of its findings to state and local officials, is salutary.
>
> The Panel is also aware of efforts in the Los Angeles area, in connection with the operational area terrorism working group (TWG) composed of LA county and municipal agencies, and the area's terrorism early warning (TEW) group; and of the multi-jurisdictional effort in New England aimed at collective information sharing of terrorist and other criminal threats. Those initiatives, as well as others that have been formed under the auspices of the FBI program to establish joint terrorism task forces, could be models for other regional programs, and for Federal interface with state and local jurisdictions, to improve and facilitate information sharing.
>
> The Panel is convinced that efforts in this area must be based on the use of the most modern information technology available.[7]

In its second report, the Gilmore Commission recommended that the National Office for Combating Terrorism take on much of the intelligence gathering and information sharing responsibilities. The panel suggested that the office should take on research and development in forensics technology and analysis, that it should be responsible for distributing information to the state and local level, and that it should create a Internet-based national database for combating terrorism information available for selected accessibility.

Another panel recommendation was that the National Office for Combating Terrorism should serve as a managing role for a "model" state plan for response to a terrorist act. This plan would be developed by NEMA with help from FEMA. The "model" state plan would serve as a flexible guideline for all states to follow.

The Bremer Commission provided a series of specific recommendations to improve intelligence gathering and sharing. The commission received much criticism for recommending the CIA recruitment of terrorist informants even if they have been involved in human rights violations. However, the commission said that the CIA had been creating an "overly risk averse" environment and needed to send a clear message that recruiting terrorists is a good thing.

The previous analysis indicates that there is reason to endorse this conclusion. Suspect informants are the sources of most civil law enforcement activity and much of the collection of human intelligence. If law enforcement and intelligence agencies were denied access to such sources on legal or humanitarian grounds, this would cripple their activities and produce immense additional human suffering. Terrorists are not usually criminals and often have strong ideological motives. They are harder to track and subvert and are potentially far more dangerous. In the case of terrorists associated with the risk of CBRN attacks, the threat is so great that it can literally be catastrophic. The Bremer Commission's recommendation is common sense, and opposing it means trying to live in a fantasy world that makes no sense at all.

The Bremer Commission also concluded that the FBI has a "risk-averse culture" and needs to clarify the guidelines for collecting information on possible international terrorists. Among the other recommendations of the Bremer Commission was the relaxation of DOJ scrutiny for approving electronic surveillance, the need for modern computer and communications technology to keep up with terrorists, the need for more linguists, and the need for the maximum dissemination of terrorist-related information as the law allows to relevant officials. There seems to be considerable truth in these comments as well, but it is unclear that the FBI has a risk-averse culture as distinguished from DOJ, and part of the problem seems to be the tacit assumption that the same procedures should be followed for all threats. There almost certainly is a strong case for treating the risk of CBRN attacks differently from lower-level threats and establishing review and authorization procedures to take more "risks" in detecting and preventing such attacks.

### Gilmore and Bremer Commissions: Clarify Authority, Command, and Control

The fourth and last area of agreement between the Gilmore and Bremer Commissions was the need to clarify authority and command and control when a terrorist act occurs. The Gilmore Commission believed that the issues of "who's in charge" and how command and control are transferred from local responders to federal officials need to be resolved. The Gilmore Commission said:

> Increasingly, the Panel and its supporting staff have heard the question raised, "When an incident occurs, who's in charge?" The Panel has initially concluded that there is no single answer to the question—a determination will likely have to be made on a case-by-case basis, taking into consideration, among other factors, the nature of the incident; the perpetrator source; the actual or potential consequences immediately and over time; and the then-current capabilities for effective response at various levels. In every actual terrorist incident, non-Federal local responders will always be in charge initially, unless of course the incident occurs on a military or other Federal reservation which has its own response capability. Even in the latter case, an incident may be of such proportions that non-Federal responders may be just as engaged, if not more so, as the Federal responders on the government enclave may be.
> . . . When an actual incident is or becomes one that requires a major Federal response, to the point that a Federal entity may have to "take command" of an operation, the issue of when and how an appropriate "hand-off" from local to Federal authorities takes place continues to be a significant one for resolution—sooner rather than later. While the Panel is aware that the issue is being addressed in inter-agency and inter-governmental agreements, and is being included in a number of exercises, efforts by entities at all levels must, in the opinion of the Panel, be accelerated to provide the necessary agreed-on templates for such hand-offs to take place. This issue, especially any specific agreements that may be reached between Federal and local officials, should always be included in related training, exercises, and other appropriate forums, to ensure that any such transition will be as smooth as possible in an actual operation.[8]

The Bremer Commission made two related recommendations about authority and command and control, one of which caused some controversy. The commission recommended the DOD create contingency plans to assume the lead in the case of a terrorist act so devastating that no other agency is capable of managing.

> The Department of Defense's ability to command and control vast resources for dangerous, unstructured situations is unmatched by any other department or agency. According to current plans, DOD involvement is limited to supporting the agencies that are currently designated as having the lead in a terrorism crisis, the FBI and the Federal Emergency Management Agency (FEMA). But, in extraordinary circumstances, when a catastrophe is beyond the capabilities of local, state, and other federal agencies, or is directly related to an armed conflict overseas, the President may want to designate DOD as a lead federal agency. This may become a critical operational consideration in planning for future conflicts. Current plans and exercises do not consider this possibility.

An expanded role for the DOD in a catastrophic terrorist attack will have policy and legal implications. Other federal agencies, the states, and local communities will have major concerns. In preparing for such a contingency, there will also be internal DOD issues on resources and possible conflicts with traditional military contingency plans. These issues should be addressed beforehand.

Effective preparation also requires effective organization. The DOD is not optimally organized to respond to the wide range of missions that would likely arise from the threat of a catastrophic terrorist attack. For example, within DOD several offices, departments, Unified Commands, the Army, and the National Guard have overlapping responsibilities to plan and execute operations in case of a catastrophic terrorist attack. These operations will require an unprecedented degree of interagency coordination and communication in order to be successful.

There are neither plans for the DOD to assume a lead agency role nor exercises rehearsing this capability. Hence, these demanding tasks would have to be accomplished on an ad hoc basis by the military.[9]

The recommendation was distorted by some to mean that the DOD should be the lead agency in all cases of terrorist acts, an assertion the commission has denied. The commission recognized that it is possible for a terrorist act to be so overwhelming that only the DOD would be capable of responding. It also recommended clarification of the legal authority that responders have in instances of catastrophic terrorism so no one hesitates or acts improperly.

The Constitution permits extraordinary measures in the face of extraordinary threats. To prevent or respond to catastrophic terrorism, law enforcement and public health officials have the authority to conduct investigations and implement measures that temporarily exceed measures applicable under non-emergency conditions. These may include cordoning off of areas, vehicle searches, certain medical measures, and sweep searches through areas believed to contain weapons or terrorists.

Determining whether a particular measure is reasonable requires balancing privacy and other rights against the public interest in coping with a terrorist threat which may lead to massive casualties. Advance preparation is the best way to deal successfully with a terrorist incident without jeopardizing individuals' Constitutional rights.[10]

These recommendations of the Bremer Commission seem valid when the attack involves response to a nuclear or biological attack of any significance. It is far less clear that such a response is needed to high-explosive or most chemical attacks. At the same time, it will be vital to ensure that biological attacks are properly characterized and that medical science shapes the response. This again illustrates the fact that extensive simulation is needed in order to determine how best to assign not only lead responsibility in the given types of attacks, but also how to ensure that all proper expertise is given a proper role in leading the response.

Similarly, the Gilmore Commission is almost certainly correct in assuming that someone must be in charge, but this could vary by type of attack and mid- to high-level attacks will inevitably directly involve the president and the NSC. Creating a peacetime czar or cabinet-level official is only one step in resolving the problem of operational authority.

### Bremer and Hart-Rudman Commissions: Biological Pathogens, International Consensus against Terrorism, and Strengthening of Public Health Systems

The Bremer Commission also had some recommendations that were similar to those of the Hart-Rudman Commission. The three common areas were: control of biological pathogens, international consensus against terrorism, and strengthening of public health systems. As part of a greater counterproliferation effort, the Hart-Rudman Commission recommended an international ban on the creation, transfer, trade, and weaponization of biological pathogens and supported programs to deal with existing stockpiles.

> The United States should seek enhanced international cooperation to combat the growing proliferation of weapons of mass destruction. This should include an effective and enforceable international ban on the creation, transfer, trade, and weaponization of biological pathogens, whether by states or non-state actors. Also, when available and implemented with rigor, cooperative programs to deal with existing stockpiles of nuclear, biological, and chemical weapons are cost-effective and politically attractive ways to reduce the dangers of weapons and weapons material proliferation.[11]

The Bremer Commission observed that the U.S. controls on the transfer of pathogens and related equipment are nonexistent and recommended HHS to strengthen security and Congress to create stricter controls of pathogens and related equipment.

> The Secretary of Health and Human Services should strengthen physical security standards applicable to the storage, creation, and transport of pathogens in research laboratories and other certified facilities in order to protect against theft or diversion. These standards should be as rigorous as the physical protection and security measures applicable to critical nuclear materials.
> The Congress should:
>
> - Make possession of designated critical pathogens illegal for anyone who is not properly certified.
> - Control domestic sale and transfer of equipment critical to the development or use of biological agents by certifying legitimate users of

critical equipment and prohibiting sales of such equipment to non-certified entities.

- Require tagging of critical equipment to enable law enforcement to identify its location.[12]

## Bremer and Hart-Rudman Commissions: Strengthening the International Consensus against Terrorism and the International Convention for the Suppression of the Financing of Terrorism

The Hart-Rudman Commission gave a broad recommendation that the United States strengthen the international consensus against terrorism: "The United States should also strive to deepen the international normative consensus against terrorism and state support of terrorism. It should work with others to strengthen cooperation among law enforcement agencies, intelligence services, and military forces to foil terrorist plots and deny sanctuary to terrorists by attacking their financial and logistical centers."[13]

The Bremer Commission was more specific in deepening the international consensus against terrorism by recommending that the United States ratify the International Convention for the Suppression of the Financing of Terrorism.

> In addition to domestic efforts, disrupting fundraising for terrorist groups requires international cooperation. A new United Nations convention, the International Convention for the Suppression of the Financing of Terrorism, provides a framework for improved cooperation. Each signing party is to enact domestic legislation to criminalize fundraising for terrorism and provide for the seizure and forfeiture of funds intended to support terrorism. The parties are to cooperate in the criminal investigation and prosecution of terrorism fundraising, and in extraditing suspects.
>
> . . . The Congress should promptly ratify the International Convention for the Suppression of the Financing of Terrorism and pass any legislation necessary for full implementation.[14]

The final common recommendation of the Bremer and Hart-Rudman Commissions was the need to strengthen public health capabilities. The Hart-Rudman Commission gave a general recommendation to augment U.S. capabilities, while the Bremer Commission specifically recommended an international surveillance program to monitor outbreaks and terrorist experimentation with pathogens.

## AREAS WHERE THE COMMISSIONS MADE DIFFERENT RECOMMENDATIONS

The Hart-Rudman Commission only had one counterterrorism recommendation different from the other commissions. The commission said that the United States should have specialized forces capable of dealing with threats and blackmail from terrorism and CBRN weapons.

### Gilmore Commission: Threat Assessments

The Gilmore Commission focused on domestic preparedness and gave four additional recommendations. One was on threat assessments. The commission felt that not enough attention was being given to higher-probability, lower-consequence threats and recommended more study of those threats in addition to the lower-probability, higher-consequence threats:

> The Panel has indicated its concern about a preoccupation with the "worst-case scenario," and the attendant assumption that any lesser incident can be addressed equally well by planning for the most catastrophic threat—ignoring the fact that higher-probability/lower-consequence attacks might present unique challenges of their own. As noted, this approach may not be the best means of setting budgetary priorities and allocating resources. The Panel is convinced, therefore, that more attention should be directed to assessments of the higher-probability, lower-consequence end of the potential terrorist threat spectrum—not at the expense of, but in addition to, assessments and analyses of the higher-consequence threat scenarios.[15]

It is not really clear that this is the case in the field or in much of the practical work being done at the agency and state and local levels. Many of the planning sessions, meetings, and simulations taking place outside the National Security area do focus on higher-probability, lower-consequence attacks even when they describe them as higher-level attacks. This, however, illustrates the need to plan for a spectrum of levels and means of attack, neither for the higher-probability, lower-consequence attacks nor for the worst case.

### Gilmore Commission: National Strategy for Domestic Preparedness and CBRN Terrorism Response

Another recommendation of the Gilmore Commission was the creation of a national strategy for domestic preparedness and CBRN terrorism response. The commission was aware that the NDPO plans on developing a national strategy for domestic preparedness issues but suggested that a true national strategy must be bottom up and have presidential direction.

> Based on the Panel's threat analysis, other relevant information that has come to its attention, and the knowledge and experience of its own members, the Panel is convinced that a national strategy to address the issues of domestic preparedness and response to terrorist incidents involving CBRN and other types of weapons is urgently needed.
>
> Combating terrorism is clearly a national issue, but the responsibility for the domestic response to a terrorist CBRN incident is not necessarily—and will almost never be exclusively—a Federal one. For a response to those

incidents described as "higher probability, lower consequence," the Federal role is essentially one of providing support to state and local responders, fundamentally in reaction to a request for assistance. It is at the local and state level where the task of the initial response and, in almost every case, the primary responsibilities lie. It is only in the case of a catastrophic event—certainly possible, but of the "lower probability, higher consequence" type—that major responsibilities will reside at the Federal level. Federal involvement in an incident, which could include numerous civilian departments and agencies as well as military entities, will be defined by the nature and severity of the incident. As an example, in any case where an incident may be a terrorist act, the FBI will have an initial involvement in an investigation; if the incident is determined to be terrorism, the FBI will assume a leading role. Nevertheless, the Federal role will, in most cases, be supportive of state and local authorities, which traditionally have the fundamental responsibility for responding.

At the same time, the Federal government can and must provide significant support and assistance, in preparation and in the event that such an incident actually occurs. There are considerable Federal resources that can be brought to bear in the areas of planning, training, standards, research and development, and equipment. Consequently, there needs to be a "Federal Government Strategy" component of the national strategy one which clearly articulates Federal responsibilities, roles, and missions, and distinguishes those from state and local ones. Federal funding, and the activities and programs of a number of Federal agencies, to address domestic preparedness and response to such incidents, have increased dramatically in recent years, especially in the wake of the [1993] New York World Trade Center and Oklahoma City bombings, and the Aum Shinrikyo attack in the Tokyo subway system. Despite good intentions, and recent improvements in coordination and implementation, Federal programs addressing the issue appear, in many cases, to be fragmented, overlapping, lacking focus, and uncoordinated. The Federal component of a national strategy can help to reduce the redundancy, confusion, and fragmentation of current Federal efforts.

Representatives of the National Domestic Preparedness Office (NDPO) . . . have stated that the NDPO will develop a "national strategy" to address domestic preparedness issues. Given the fact that the responsibility for the initial and, in large measure, continuing response to *any* such incident will likely fall most heavily on the backs of state and local responders, the Panel suggests that a true national strategy must have a "bottom-up" approach—that it be developed in close consultation and collaboration with state and local officials, and the law enforcement and emergency response communities from across the country. This Panel can help to forge that collaboration. Moreover, any such national strategy—despite its "bottom-up" structure—must have the direct leadership, guidance, and imprimatur of the President. Only that way can a strategy have a truly national tenor; but more importantly, it will contain a comprehensive, articulate expression by the nation's chief executive of the appropriateness of and distinctions between the Federal role and missions and those at state and local levels.

By focusing on higher-probability/lower-consequence threats, while recognizing and addressing concerns about lower-probability/higher-consequence events, a national strategy can lay the groundwork for assessing and monitoring the threat, and for making adjustments to response strategies as required. As has been argued elsewhere, too much of the Federal effort to date—even those programs that ostensibly are designed to enhance state and local response capabilities—has been predicated on the tacit assumption that preparing for the "worst case" will automatically encompass lesser threats. The foregoing analysis suggests otherwise, because the nature and scale of the consequences can vary so widely. This needs to be recognized and articulated at the national level.

The Panel is aware of the "Five-Year Interagency Counterterrorism and Technology Crime Plan"—recently released (September 1999) by the Attorney General of the United States, under the auspices of Department of Justice "lead agency" responsibility—as well as the interagency working group process dedicated to "WMD preparedness" within the National Security Council structure. Although significant steps in the right direction, the five-year plan does not equate to a comprehensive, fully coordinated national strategy—nor for that matter even the Federal government component of such a strategy—one with clear, concise, and unambiguous leadership and direction from the President in consultation with all who share responsibility for related Federal efforts.

The Panel also recommends that any such strategy include, within its purview, incidents involving more conventional weapons—such as conventional high-explosive or fabricated weapons (e.g., the type used in the Oklahoma City bombing)—that have the potential to cause significant casualties or physical damage; as well as incidents involving CBRN devices that may not be capable of producing "mass casualties" but that can, nevertheless, produce considerable fear, panic, or other major disruptions to the infrastructure or economy of the potential domestic target.

Considering the serious nature and potential consequences of any terrorist incident, the Panel is convinced that comprehensive public education and information programs must be developed, programs that will provide straightforward, timely information and advice both prior to any terrorist incident and in the immediate aftermath of any attack. The national strategy should lay the groundwork for those programs.[16]

In all frankness, this recommendation has only tenuous logic. It is certainly true that most of the burden of responding to low-level attacks and response will fall on local and state officials, but it is not clear that they need a national strategy as much as flexible national assistance that can supplement their activity when needed. Providing a flexible federal capability to deal with bottom-up demand is certainly necessary, but it is uncertain that this is a strategy in any normal sense of the term. Conversely, federal response is most needed to deal with mid- and high-level attacks, even if these are not the most probable near-term contingency.

This issue does, however, raise the broader issue of clearly distinguishing between risks where state and local authorities must have primary responsibility and the kind of CBRN attacks with which the federal government must deal. One problem with much of the current approach to counterterrorism is that it assumes that levels of threat that federal, state, and local authorities have dealt with for years deserve the same special attention as new and much more serious threats to the U.S. homeland. There seems no reason that this should be the case.

## Gilmore Commission: Standardization of Legal Terms

The final two recommendations by the Gilmore Commission deal with standardization. The commission recommended codification of terms and definitions related to terrorism. It cited the different definitions of "WMD" by the Nunn-Lugar-Domenici Act and the Posse Comitatus Act (18 USC, Section 2332a), the definitions of "terrorism" by the FBI and DOD, and the absence of a definition for mass casualties. There may well be a need for such action, but not at the cost of creating legislative inflexibility. Such legislation should also explicitly recognize the threats posed by proliferation and state actors, rather than simply "terrorism." If necessary, it should make clear that there are radically different levels and means of attacks and specify what differences—if any—are needed in the U.S. response.

## Gilmore Commission: National Standards for Equipment

The commission recommended the creation of national standards for equipment used by responders to a terrorist incident. It recognized that different response entities may have incompatible equipment that would greatly diminish responder capabilities. It was aware of DOJ's efforts through the National Institute of Justice to develop a list of equipment that meets certain standards, but the commission suggested that more research and development was needed to develop effective standards for compatibility and interoperability.

The Panel will devote significant attention during its current fiscal year activities to standards, especially for training and equipment. Given the likelihood that multiple jurisdictions in one or more states, as well as agencies of the Federal government, will be involved in any serious terrorist incident, it will be critical that every responder in a particular emergency function be trained to the same standard. The types of equipment used by response entities—detection devices, personal protective equipment, and communications equipment—must be compatible and inter-operable. The Panel commends the efforts being undertaken by the Interagency Board (IAB) for Equipment Standardization and InterOperability—composed of representatives of various federal, state, and local entities, as well as some nongovernmental professional organizations—in its attempt to develop a national "standardized equipment list," to provide responders at all levels with a resource with which to make better-informed decisions about the selection and acquisition of equipment. Such efforts are a positive step toward ensuring better compatibility and inter-operability of equipment among potential responders.

Local responders continue to express frustration at the vast array of devices and equipment available from industry that may have application for domestic preparedness for terrorist attacks. At the same time, some have expressed displeasure at the fact that certain items, previously purchased by local responders, do not measure up to the claims of manufacturers.

In order to develop and maintain operationally effective standards for equipment compatibility and inter-operability, the Panel has determined that more research and development is required to meet local responder needs. Given the significant costs associated with sophisticated equipment, such as certain chemical and biological detection devices, emphasis should be placed on the development of multi-purpose pieces of equipment, which can be used not only in the terrorism context, but which will also have application in other fields, such as the detection of naturally transmitted infectious diseases.

To help to reassure responders that the equipment that is being used is in fact capable of doing what it is designed to do, it is likely that an ambitious program of independent testing and evaluation will have to be undertaken. The Panel recognizes that any such program will likely have to be conducted—because of its national implications—under Federal sponsorship; and will require the addition or reallocation of significant resources. For reasons that are self-evident, local responders are insisting that testing be done with "live" agents.

The Panel is aware of a project being undertaken by the National Institute of Justice (NIJ), an agency the U.S. Department of Justice's Office of Justice Programs, which is ultimately designed to be a "consumer report" catalogue of available equipment that meets certain listed standards.[17]

The problem with this recommendation is that it assumes that federal, state, and local authorities already know the effects of CBRN attacks, what to stockpile in order to respond to them, where to put the stockpiles, and when and how to distribute them. This may be true in the case of lower levels of attack, although it is brutally clear in meeting after meeting that local and state officials, and elements of federal agencies, see such stockpiles as one more way of getting more federal money to solve long-standing problems or provide new capabilities that have little to do with terrorism. There is a real risk of creating a new federal entitlements program.

The problem is very different in dealing with more lethal levels of CBRN attacks. It is not clear that federal, state, and local authorities know what to buy, where to put it, or how to ensure it can get to the user. There are certainly some cases where the need is obvious, but in many cases—particularly in the event of biological and nuclear attacks—far more work needs to be done on requirements planning.

## Bremer Commission: Treatment of Former and Future States of Concern

The Bremer Commission focused on what could be improved to combat international terrorism. Its remaining recommendations were mainly related to designation of state sponsors and FTOs and to national counterterrorism efforts. For designations, the commission recommended that the United States keep Iran and Syria on the list of state sponsors:

> Iran remains the most active state supporter of terrorism. Despite the election of reformist President Khatami in 1997, the Iranian Revolutionary Guard Corps and Ministry of Intelligence and Security have continued to be involved in the planning and execution of terrorist acts. They also provide funding, training, weapons, logistical resources, and guidance to a variety of terrorist groups. In 1999, organizations in Tehran increased support to terrorist groups opposed to the Middle East peace process, including Lebanese Hizbollah and Palestinian rejectionist groups such as the Islamic Resistance Movement (HAMAS), the Palestine Islamic Jihad (PIJ), and the Popular Front for the Liberation of Palestine-General Command (PFLP-GC). Iran continues to assassinate political dissidents at home and abroad. The Iranians responsible for terrorism abroad are often also responsible for political oppression and violence against reformers within Iran. So a firm stance against Iranian-sponsored terrorism abroad could assist the reformers.
>
> There are indications of Iranian involvement in the 1996 Khobar Towers bombing in Saudi Arabia, in which 19 U.S. citizens were killed and more than 500 were injured. In October 1999, President Clinton officially requested cooperation from Iran in the investigation. Thus far, Iran has not responded.
>
> International pressure in the Pan Am 103 case ultimately succeeded in getting some degree of cooperation from Libya. The U.S. Government has not sought similar multilateral action to bring pressure on Iran to cooperate in the Khobar Towers bombing investigation.
>
> The Syrian Government still provides terrorists with safehaven, allows them to operate over a dozen terrorist training camps in the Syrian-controlled Bekaa Valley in Lebanon, and permits the Iranian Government to resupply these camps. Since its designation as a state sponsor of terrorism, Syria has expelled a few terrorist groups from Damascus, such as the Japanese Red Army, but these groups already were of marginal value to Syrian foreign policy. Meanwhile, Damascus continues to support terrorist groups opposed to the peace process. Although Syria recently made a show of "instructing" terrorists based in Damascus not to engage in certain types of attacks, it did not expel the groups or cease supporting them. This suggests Syria's determination to maintain rather than abandon terrorism.[18]

The Bremer Commission also recommended that the United States designate Afghanistan as a state sponsor and consider designating Pakistan or Greece as countries "not cooperating fully with U.S. antiterrorism efforts." On Pakistan, the commission said:

Pakistan has cooperated on counterterrorism at times, but not consistently. In 1995, for example, Pakistan arrested and extradited to the United States Ramzi Ahmed Yousef, who masterminded the World Trade Center bombing in 1993. In December 1999, Pakistan's cooperation was vital in warding off terrorist attacks planned for the millennium. Even so, Pakistan provides safehaven, transit, and moral, political, and diplomatic support to several groups engaged in terrorism including Harakat ul-Mujahidin (HUM), which has been designated by the United States as a Foreign Terrorist Organization (FTO). HUM is responsible for kidnapping and murdering tourists in Indian-controlled Kashmir. Moreover, as part of its support for Usama bin Ladin, HUM has threatened to kill U.S. citizens.[19]

The commission suggested that countries designated "not cooperating fully" should not be eligible for the State Department's Visa Waiver Program. For nonstate sponsored terrorist organizations, the commission recommended more frequent updating and inclusion of groups into the secretary of state's designation of FTO. The commission also recommended that Congress review the FTO statute to determine if changes need to be made.

### Bremer Commission: Targeting Terrorist Financial Resources

For national counterterrorism efforts, the commission recommended that the United States target terrorist financial resources. It suggested the creation of a joint task force of all relevant agencies that combat terrorist fundraising to develop and implement a plan to disrupt terrorist financial activities. It also suggested that the Office of Foreign Assets Control in the Treasury Department create a unit dedicated to enforcing economic sanctions against terrorist organizations.

Rather than relying heavily on the FTO process, the U.S. Government should take a broader approach to cutting off the flow of financial support for terrorism from within the United States. Anyone providing funds to terrorist organizations or activities should be investigated with the full vigor of the law and, where possible, prosecuted under relevant statutes, including those covering money laundering, conspiracy, tax or fraud violations. In such cases, assets may also be made subject to civil and criminal forfeiture.

In addition, the Department of the Treasury could use its Office of Foreign Assets Control (OFAC) more effectively. OFAC administers and enforces economic sanctions. For example, any U.S. financial institution holding funds belonging to a terrorist organization or one of its agents must report those assets to OFAC. Under OFAC's regulations, the transfer of such assets can be blocked. OFAC's capabilities and expertise are underutilized in part because of resource constraints.

Other government agencies, such as the Internal Revenue Service and Customs, also possess information and authority that could be used to thwart terrorist fundraising. For instance, the IRS has information on nongovernmental organizations that may be collecting donations to support terrorism, and Customs has data on large currency transactions. But there is no single entity that tracks and analyzes all the data available to the various agencies on terrorist fundraising in the United States.[20]

These recommendations make excellent sense, provided that they are carried out under sufficient review to ensure that the selection of groups and individuals to be monitored does not become an abuse of civil liberties or lead to surveillance of groups that are politically undesirable or who criticize the United States without posing a threat of violence.

## Bremer Commission: Liability Insurance

The Bremer Commission recommended that the FBI and CIA reimburse their agents for the full cost of personal liability insurance so that agents could be more aggressive in combating terrorism and not fear lawsuits for officially sanctioned activities. Providing such insurance seems valid and providing it would not affect adequate supervision or discipline or the right to sue and seek legal redress with all of the attendant public scrutiny.

## Bremer Commission: Realistic Exercises

The commission also recommended more federal preparedness exercises and more funding for TOPOFF, the senior management exercise administered by the DOJ and FEMA.

In addition to DoD exercises, a realistic interagency exercise program, with full participation by all relevant federal agencies and their leaders, is essential for national preparedness to counter a catastrophic terrorist attack. In June 1995, the President established an interagency counterterrorist Exercise Subgroup and program which included preparation for a catastrophic terrorist attack. However, not all federal agencies have participated in or budgeted for these exercises.

Additionally, in September 1998, Congress funded and mandated the Department of Justice and the Federal Emergency Management Agency to conduct a counterterrorism and consequence management exercise, called TOPOFF, involving relevant federal agencies and their senior leadership, with select state and local governments participating, to evaluate the U.S. Government's preparedness for a catastrophic terrorist incident. However, sufficient funding was not provided and there is no requirement to exercise on a regular schedule.

The President should direct (1) the Exercise Subgroup, under the direction of the national coordinator for counterterrorism, to exercise annually the government's response to a catastrophic terrorism crisis, including consequence management; and (2) all relevant federal agencies to plan, budget and participate in counterterrorism and consequence management exercises coordinated by the Exercise Subgroup and ensure senior officer level participation, particularly in the annual exercises.[21]

As has been noted earlier, it is far more important that federal, state, and local authorities understand what they really need to do and how to do it than to establish new lines of authority, fund the wrong program, and focus efficiently on the wrong set of contingencies and requirements.

## NOTES

1. Rand Corporation, *Second Annual Report List of Key Recommendations* (December 15, 2000), <http://www.rand.org/organization/nsrd/terrpanel/recommendations.html>.

2. First Annual Report of the Advisory Panel to Assess Domestic Response Capabilities for Terrorism Involving the Use of Weapons of Mass Destruction, *I. Assessing the Threat* (December 15, 1999), <http://www.rand.org/organization/nsrd/terrpanel/html>.

3. Second Annual Report of the Advisory Panel to Assess Domestic Response Capabilities (December 15, 2000).

4. National Commission on Terrorism, *Countering the Changing Threat of International Terrorism* (June 2000), <http://www.fas.org/irp/threat/commission.html>.

5. First Annual Report of the Advisory Panel, *Assessing the Threat*.

6. National Commission on Terrorism, *Countering the Changing Threat of International Terrorism*.

7. First Annual Report of the Advisory Panel, *Assessing the Threat*.

8. First/Second Annual Report of the Advisory Panel.

9. National Commission on Terrorism, *Countering the Changing Threat of International Terrorism*.

10. National Commission on Terrorism, *Countering the Changing Threat of International Terrorism*.

11. U.S. Commission on National Security/Twenty-first Century, *Seeking a National Strategy: A Concert for Preserving Security and Promoting Freedom* (April 15, 2000).

12. National Commission on Terrorism, *Countering the Changing Threat of International Terrorism*.

13. U.S. Commission on National Security, *Seeking a National Strategy*.

14. National Commission on Terrorism, *Countering the Changing Threat of International Terrorism*.

15. First/Second Annual Report of the Advisory Panel.

16. First/Second Annual Report of the Advisory Panel.

17. First/Second Annual Report of the Advisory Panel.

18. National Commission on Terrorism, *Countering the Changing Threat of International Terrorism*.

19. National Commission on Terrorism, *Countering the Changing Threat of International Terrorism*.

20. National Commission on Terrorism, *Countering the Changing Threat of International Terrorism*.

21. National Commission on Terrorism, *Countering the Changing Threat of International Terrorism*.

*Chapter 11*

# Conclusions and Recommendations

The United States faces growing potential threats from state actors, their proxies, and independent extremists and terrorists. While various analysts may have tended to exaggerate the immediate threat or the current threat posed by given actors, the events of September 2001 show this scarcely means that the threat is not real or that the nation does not need to improve its defense and response capabilities. The United States must plan to defend against such threats not only to defend its own homeland, but also to protect its ability to deploy forces overseas and its allies.

The practical problem is to decide exactly how to be deal with highly uncertain emerging threats in a world where the United States has limited resources and many other priorities. The United States cannot bet the lives and well being of its citizens on today's threats and probabilities. There are many potentially hostile foreign and domestic sources of such threats, and some key threats like biological weapons involve rapidly changing technologies that will pose a steadily growing threat to the U.S. homeland. U.S. involvement in the world, the strength of U.S. conventional and nuclear forces, and vulnerability at home are a dangerous combination, and unless the United States acts to improve deterrence and defense, the risk of major asymmetric and terrorist attacks involving CBRN weapons is likely to grow.

Finding the right mix of defense and response is extremely difficult, however, and it is far easier to call for dramatic action than to determine what actions will really succeed and be cost-effective and then execute them. It is clear from the preceding chapters that the federal government is making progress in many areas and is laying the groundwork for improved co-operation with states, localities, the private sector, and the public. Indeed, by the standards of many governments that face far more clear threats than the United States, the United States has already made significant progress in beginning to address these issues. In many cases, it is already well ahead of its friends and allies.

## CORRECTING THE STRATEGIC GAPS IN THE U.S. APPROACH TO HOMELAND DEFENSE

At the same time, there is still much to be done, and the Bush Administration faces massive challenges in developing a truly effective federal program. There are basic conceptual and strategic gaps in the way the United States is approaching the problem. The most serious gap is the one between the DOD's growing focus on the threats posed by asymmetric warfare and by states and well-organized nonstate actors and the focus of civil departments on lower levels of foreign and domestic terrorism. At the same time, defining "homeland defense" in terms of defense and response against attacks inside the United States understates the importance of looking at the link between theater threats and conflicts and attacks on the United States, and the threats to our allies and military forces.

An effective approach to homeland defense also means understanding that the range of threats is sufficiently great so that the United States cannot plan to deal with just one attack at a time. Attacks may be coupled to ongoing theater conflicts. If missile threats against the United States are serious enough to deploy WMD, then defense must consider the threat of mixes of missile and covert attacks and response must consider the risk that a missile attack will penetrate any WMD defense. Multiple attacks are possible, as are sequential attacks. The United States must also deal with the "morning after." The first major covert or terrorist WMD attack on the United States or its major allies may change the strategic environment fundamentally. The United States must already begin to think and act in response to such risks, but with the foresight that its defense and response to the first attack will set the precedent in a world in which many similar threats may occur in the future.

The United States must broaden the way it deals with homeland defense to address all of the tools it has at hand. Approaches to improving homeland defense that arbitrarily exclude U.S. offensive and deterrent capabilities and the ability to defend by identifying and striking at hostile foreign governments and terrorists ignore an important part of homeland defense. So do definitions that understate or ignore the broad spectrum of U.S. counterproliferation efforts, including arms control. Finally, putting a new emphasis on homeland defense is not a reason for creating a new form of isolationism. Cooperation with our allies and friendly governments can be critical in defending against and deterring asymmetric attacks by foreign states and counterterrorism. Such actions cannot defend against domestic terrorists and extremists, but they can have a major impact in reducing what may well be the most serious source of potential attacks with nuclear and effective biological weapons.

## FOCUSING LESS ON WHO'S IN CHARGE AND MORE ON WHAT THEY SHOULD BE IN CHARGE OF

The U.S. government needs to be less focused on chains of command and be more objective about the need to accept uncertainty and carry out the necessary research, development, and improved planning to reduce that uncertainty. Far too many studies of homeland defense worry about the issues of "who's in charge" in the federal government, rather than the details of which senior official should be in charge of what. In many cases, there seems to be an assumption that creating the right organization chart and set of federal responsibilities can create a mix of federal authority, capabilities, and liaison efforts with state and local governments that can deal with the problem.

One does not have to be a believer in chaos theory to realize that such an approach is almost certainly wrong. No federal approach to a highly uncertain range of threats, particularly ones with consequences as devastating as attacks with nuclear and biological weapons, can hope to develop a system that will be truly ready to deal with such threats and attacks when they actually emerge. The U.S. government cannot and should not pay the money today to try to deal with the worst case threats that may emerge in the future, and it cannot require state, local, and private entities to assume more than limited additional burdens.

There are many areas where basic research and planning activity is needed to resolve grave uncertainties, and others where special interest pleading threatens to waste vast amounts of public money on the wrong priorities or measures that may either be ineffective or easy to counter. There have been far more attempts to define broad strategies or to issue broad directives than to come to grips with the need for detailed planning, adequate programs and program budgets, and meaningful ways to review and coordinate annual budgets and programs.

Many proposed and ongoing programs probably cannot meet the most basic tests of intellectual validity and federal responsibility. There is no long-term plan, program, or program budget. There is no supporting analysis of the balance of offense and defense, the countermeasures that could defeat a given program, and the cost to defeat it. There is nothing approaching an adequate ongoing national threat analysis of domestic and foreign threats, no net assessment of the overall balance of defense and offense, and no net technical assessment of the trends in offensive and defensive capability.

There is a sharp decoupling in dealing with major asymmetric threats, which can involve states, their proxies, and more sophisticated terrorist and extremist groups in nuclear and major biological attacks, from the lower-level forms of CBRN attacks that are the "worst cases" today's terrorists seem to pose, and that form the focus of most of today's efforts to improve defense and response. These problems are compounded by major legal issues that limit key aspects of intelligence and law enforcement activities and by efforts to improve response that are often linked to other goals like improving health services or emergency response capabilities.

Effective planning and action cannot be based on vague calls for improved strategy, exercising and training based on today's threat analyses and techniques, or altering organization charts at the top. It will take years of effort to create a coordinated and effective plan for federal, state, and local action. In most cases, it is the willingness and ability to address detailed issues and to make hands-on efforts to create and implement a wide range of cost-effective programs that will determine the success of the U.S. effort in homeland defense and not the effort to find a few major recommendations. The devil really does lie in the details, and "bumper sticker" or one-issue approaches to policy are a recommendation for disaster.

Effective research and development efforts are needed in virtually every key area of defense and response activity to improve the United States' ability to use political, economic, and military actions outside the United States to deter and defend foreign asymmetric and terrorist attacks. At the same time, effective research and development efforts require certain key tools that are sadly lacking in many, if not most, such programs. There must be a comprehensive and regularly updated net technical assessment of the trends in defensive and offensive technology to establish priorities and the probable cost-effectiveness of given programs. Basic advances are needed in estimating and modeling the CBRN threat to determine what research and development activities are most needed. Each research and development program requires a clear analysis of how the end result would be deployed and of the procurement and life cycle costs of deploying effective national programs. There must be an end to pleading about the merits of a program against today's threat, and the lack of program-by-program justification based on analysis of the trends in offense and defense, countermeasures to the proposed or ongoing research and development activity, and the cost to defeat a deployed system.

## PLANNING FOR HIGHER-PROBABILITY, LOWER-CONSEQUENCE, AND LOWER-PROBABILITY, HIGHER-CONSEQUENCE EVENTS

The events of September 2001 has shown that the United States must come firmly to grips with the fact it does not exist at the end of history and has not forged a kinder and gentler world:

- Unchecked vulnerability is an unacceptable danger for "the world's only super-power." Nature may abhor a vacuum, but enemies do not, and the evolution of more effective homeland defense is almost certainly essential to deterrence. At the same time, the very term "homeland defense" can be misleading. There are no boundaries that separate U.S. counterproliferation and counterterrorist activity in defense of the U.S. homeland from defense of its allies, military forces, and citizens overseas.

- The threat involves asymmetric warfare as well as terrorism, and response must also deal with threats such as the failure of a national missile defense system to intercept more orthodox methods of attack. An adequate homeland defense program cannot be based on defending and responding to terrorism, extremism, or the kind of limited CBRN attacks that now seem most prob-able. States, their proxies, and more sophisticated nonstate groups may at-tack as well. Advances in biotechnology may give individuals or smaller groups far more lethal weapons in the future.

- Deterrence, counterproliferation, counterterrorism, and law enforcement must be closely linked in dealing with these new threats, and it is clear that United States must rethink many of its current security concepts. Even the strongest advocates of homeland defense must recognize that a better offense may of-ten be more effective than improved defense. Improving the offensive threat of retaliation overseas may often be the best way of defending U.S. interests overseas and U.S. territory. A given investment in strengthening its allies may often be a better defense against proliferation and terrorism than investing in domestic counterterrorism programs. Hard trade-offs may have to be made between investments in the intelligence needed to intimidate and deter foreign states and terrorist groups, and the law enforcement capabilities needed to intercept attackers once they enter the United States.

- The United States cannot afford to rely on rethinking the offense as a substi-tute for improved defense anymore than it can use defense as a substitute for deterrence, offense, and retaliation. The United States cannot prepare itself for the new threats posed by asymmetric warfare, foreign proliferation and terrorism, and domestic violence using new means like chemical, biological, and information warfare without much stronger programs to prevent such attacks in the United States and to respond to them if they succeed. The world of the twenty-first century will not be a repetition of the mutual ensured de-struction of the Cold War. Radical states, regimes acting under extreme pres-sure, terrorists, and American citizens can turn threats like CBRN weapons into grim realities in ways the United States will never be able to deter with complete confidence.

- The United States must act now if it is to prepare for the future. Developing an effective program means thinking at least twenty-five years into the future. It will take at least a decade for federal, state, and local authorities to develop the organization they need to deal with these threats. There are massive or-ganizational problems that federal, state, and local authorities must solve in order to cooperate efficiently. The role of the federal government must be redefined in ways that are compatible with a free society and that can pre-serve one when it is under attack and when attacks are successful. It will take years of exercises, tests, and training to determine what courses of action can be made to work and are most effective. Investing in such a process of change means that it must be flexible and modular enough to react to the fact that no one can predict the nature of future attacks. But any meaningful improvement in capability will be so expensive that it can only be justified if it can cope with uncertainty.

- The United States must now decide whether it will begin to fund effective defenses against attacks on a scale far different from any form of covert or serious attack than it has planned to deal with since the end of its efforts to provide civil defense against nuclear attack. Marginal changes in federal, state, and local efforts, and in the relationships between federal, state, and local agencies, can do much to cope with the threat posed by attacks using large amounts of high explosives, chemical weapons, and low-lethality biological and radiological attacks. While the level varies by state and locality, attacks involving one thousand to ten thousand casualties do not require radical changes in response capabilities. Nuclear and high-lethality biological attacks can, however, easily produce casualties in excess of ten thousand to one hundred thousand Americans. To date, most studies and exercises indicate that existing programs and capabilities would not be adequate to deal with such attacks and that they would require far more decisive federal action and intervention than is currently feasible. There are those who strongly argue that no such threat currently exists and those who argue with equal force that they are inevitable. The present reaction of the federal government seems to be to try to improve near-term response capabilities to deal with lower levels of attack, while at the same time conducting research and development in the higher levels of attack. But the policies involved remain unclear and the actions of federal agencies reflect very different perceptions of these threats.

- The United States must take a new approach to research and development and technology. There are many areas of new technologies that must be moved off the drawing board, tested, deployed, and modified if the United States is to have defensive tools that begin to match its offensive capabilities. At the same time, the United States needs careful net assessments of the trends in the threat and how these impact new approaches to defense and response. Effective planning means that the United States cannot afford to mix the myth of technology with reality. The past track record of U.S. efforts to create and use new technologies in its defense is one of amazing eventual success. At the same time, it is one of almost universal evidence that even the best technologists cannot be trusted to create successful and deployable tools with anything like the promised effectiveness at the promised cost and time.

The development of such a complex approach to threat assessment and program development—particularly one that is based on a frank admission of the vast uncertainties involved—goes against the basic grain of the American character and forces far more demanding criteria for program justification than is normally required. The United States cannot, however, deal effectively with threats posed by state actors, their proxies, or independent extremists and terrorists unless it adopts such an approach.

Even if the United States adopts such an approach, it will still have to concentrate limited resources on making limited improvements in current capabilities to deal with current threats, while evolving a far larger and more comprehensive program to deal with more serious and emerging threats. As a result, any U.S. program is likely to be in a state of flux and evolution for at least the next half-decade.

## PLANNING FOR TERRORISM AND ASYMMETRIC WARFARE

No one can predict that the U.S. homeland will be subject to major asymmetric attacks using WMD. At the same time, this book has indicated that there is a clear incentive for such attacks and that there are states and movements that could emerge as potential attackers. There is no firm way to assign priorities to the need to fill the gap between "terrorism" and the concern with overt threats like ballistic missiles, but the following factors must be considered:

- Low-level terrorist attacks are indeed more probable and are in fact constantly occurring at the cyber and false-alarm level. Seen over a twenty-five-year period, however, the probability of some sophisticated form of major asymmetric attack is high. This probability not only affects the United States, but its allies.
- The United States faces a "non-Gaussian" reality in trying to predict and characterize the nature of such threats. There is no "standard distribution curve" of past events that can be used to predict the future.
- The cumulative probability over time for a higher-probability, lower-consequence event may actually be the highest priority for planning, rather than for the lower-probability, higher-consequence events.
- The United States cannot deal with the problem by adding analytic and technological elegance to the classic American solution to all critical problems: "Simple, quick, and wrong."
- Crisis- and/or war-driven intentions and escalation are extremely difficult to predict.
- History is irrational and is often made out of worst cases. Intelligent, prudent, business-as-usual intentions usually mean crisis never occurs in the first place.
- Asymmetric values and perceptions are very real, but extremely difficult to assess and transform into meaningful predictions of future hostile action against the U.S. homeland.

In reacting to the higher levels of threat posed by asymmetric warfare, the United States must consider the following factors:

- The problems of warning, defense, and response differ sharply by level of attack and threat.

- The rules change for all responders as attacks escalate from conventional low-level terrorism ("crooks and crazies") to major levels of damage and casualties.
- A true national emergency involving a nuclear and/or major biological attack will probably force the DOD into a critical lead role.
- Law enforcement must operate in a state of national emergency, rather than on a business-as-usual basis. The issue of having to retask law enforcement to operate in an undeclared state of war becomes a very real prospect.
- Public health and emergency services will be saturated and face realities they can only half-anticipate.
- Possible threats can put at risk the basic structure of America's commerce, economic infrastructure, and continuity of government.
- Any nuclear and/or major biological attack on the U.S. homeland will be linked to a serious theater-driven crisis or war. If so, the threat will not be directed at the United States per se, but at the United States as extension of regional/theater/foreign nation objectives.
- Allied targets, U.S. forces and businesses overseas, and critical economic facilities can be targeted, not just the U.S. homeland.
- Multiple and sequential attacks become more likely, as are mixes of methods of attack.
- The availability of sophisticated biological and nuclear weapons more likely.
- The possibility of simultaneous attacks on information systems and critical infrastructure will offer asymmetric attackers a low-cost adjunct to virtually all forms of asymmetric and theater warfare.

Within this context, it is important to consider what asymmetric threats and terrorism have in common and some of the critical differences. The common areas include:

- All threats relate to a wide range of different national security activities as well as a wide range of domestic defense and response efforts.
- All efforts to improve homeland defense compete for limited resources and federal emergency management capabilities.
- All U.S. response risks "squeezing the balloon"—that is, defending in one area while failing in the others allows attackers to attack the less defended area.
- There are many common problems in law enforcement.
- There are many common problems in public health and emergency services.
- Effective defense and response depends on an accurate assessment of the relative vulnerability of commerce, economic infrastructure, and continuity of government.
- At the same time, there are critical basic differences between the impact of most forms of terrorism and state-sponsored or proxy asymmetric warfare.
- All attacks are not created equal. Limited chemical, biological, and radiological attacks at the terrorist and extremist level are fundamentally different from nuclear and highly lethal nuclear and biological attacks.

- Covert and proxy attacks by foreign governments are acts of war. Truly sophisticated terrorists will not operate under the limits currently assumed in most studies.

- Such attacks sharply raise the probability of "cocktails" of different agents, mixes of CBRN and cyber attacks, and the use of such attacks to supplement theater conflicts. In such cases, WMD plus CBRN weapons plus CIP are then credible.

- The current and perhaps any affordable response effort will collapse at finite and limited levels, forcing federal, state, and local governments and the private sector to improvise radically.

- Sophisticated attackers will respond to U.S. defensive measures by shifting their methods of attack to strike at the least defended areas and by developing countermeasures to exploit the weaknesses in any defense.

- This makes "cost to defeat" and net technical assessment of all defensive programs and options critical.

- There does not seem to be any current prospect of dramatic changes in the ability to build a nuclear bomb in the basement and in domestic or foreign terrorist ability to acquire nuclear weapons.

- The situation with biological technology *may* be radically different. Bioattacks with immune or genetically engineered strains that have unpredictable delays, persistence, symptoms, ability to defeat treatment and vaccines, and lethality are a real possibility.

- The are major and natural differences in priority between defenders and law enforcement/responder communities. Each focuses on business as usual:

  - Responders/defenders do not focus on levels of attack so different from their experience that they are regarded as "mission impossible."

  - The linkage to foreign threats and wars is largely ignored outside the DOD and the national security community.

- Intelligence and law enforcement efforts are now decoupled in ways that pose serious legal barriers to effective action in dealing with asymmetric warfare and the threat of nuclear and major biological attacks.

- Asymmetric warfare can push the United States rapidly toward presidential state of emergency, while most terrorism can be dealt with as "business as usual":

  - Defense/response may have to be given high priority relative to normal legal procedures and civil rights. This, however, requires a clear and present danger as a justification, and clear safeguards to minimize any interference with civil liberties.

  - Federal, regional, and state efforts to cope with the breakdown and/or collapse of local defense and response efforts must have a much higher priority.

  - The risk of attacks with effects so costly in damage and casualties that response may prove unaffordable is much higher, and there is a very real uncertainty that the technology and response systems are now available for effective response.

## REACTING TO THE UNCERTAIN NATURE
## OF THE THREAT

There are many "true believers" who feel that a given threat will or will not materialize in a given form. Given the inherently uncertain nature of predictions as to who will be a threat, the means of attack they will use, and the effectiveness of the means of attack they will use, it is almost certain that some of these "true believers" will eventually prove to be right. The problem is that there is no sufficient evidence to say which threats are most important or to predict the means of attack and level of effectiveness.

The events of September 2001 have shown that federal programs are now forced to deal with an extremely broad spectrum of potential threats that individually have low probability, but where there is high probability that some of these threats will emerge as threats to the U.S. homeland. As a result, each agency and department tends to treat the threat in terms of its own mission and institutional bias, and this problem cannot be resolved by central direction. Having the NSC, a "terrorism" czar, or an interagency forum agree on a given threat or threats will not affect the laws of probability. Uncertainty is simply uncertainty.

There is also an inherent danger in attempting to create a truly coherent program. When a truly high degree of uncertainty exists regarding the need for specific forms of federal action, enforcing a high degree of coherence from the center may actually interfere with the efficient use of resources. In many cases, individual agencies will achieve a higher capability to deal with uncertainty if they suboptimize to improve their existing capabilities to deal with a wide range of threats. This is particularly true in a sharply resource-constrained environment where many potentially desirable actions will remain unfunded until a much clearer pattern of threats emerges.

Resource constraints can be particularly critical when the threats at issue involve a wide spectrum of extremely lethal biological and nuclear weapons. Large amounts of high-explosive, chemical weapons and less lethal biological weapons can produce truly tragic consequences. However, the level of deterrence, defense, and response pales in terms of cost in comparison with the ability to deter, defend, and respond to the kind of attacks that could involve casualties far in excess of ten thousand Americans and billions of dollars worth of damage.

We now know all too well that the United States may not get strategic warning that the risk of such attacks has increased and of the form they will take. If it does not, it may benefit from the fact the first such attacks come against its allies or other nations. It is far from clear whether the intelligence and analytic tools that exist are capable of warning that a possibility is becoming a probability, of providing a certainty in time to react, and of giving sufficient clarity to make the United States react. As a result, the United States must be prepared to see increasing "possibility" and not just increasing "probability" as strategic warning, and recognize that it needs contingency plans to change its defense and response plans and programs the moment an attack is successful or a pattern of attack is probable.

The United States cannot afford to focus on dealing with one successful attack or mix of attacks. It must consider the risk of an emerging pattern of asymmetric warfare and highly lethal terrorism, and plan for the "morning after." A mentality that treats any catastrophic attack as a strategic defeat and that does not prepare for immediate action to deal with follow-on attacks is a recipe for strategic disaster and an incentive for further attack. U.S. response plans must explicitly recognize these risks and the need to ensure the nation, its allies, and its enemies that it will not be paralyzed or panic even if a nuclear or major biological attack succeeds.

There are more problems involved in such threat analyses that badly need to be dealt with to further U.S. efforts in planning and executing effective programs:

- Most of the lethality and effects data for CBRN weapons involve major uncertainties that badly need to be resolved, and the federal government is just beginning to develop effective models and simulations of such effects. There is no lack of effects data or models per se, simply an immense lack of credibility and parametric modeling of uncertainty in a form that goes from dramatizing the problem to being useful in developing specific lessons for federal, state, and local responses. These problems have also been compounded by a natural tendency to build models to justify given policy recommendations or programs. To be blunt, agencies in the federal government, FCRCs, contractors, and nongovernmental organizations are far better at using analysis to market given policies and programs than to perform analysis per se. There is a striking lack of intellectual rigor and analytic integrity in many of today's efforts that must be remedied if the United States is to prioritize federal actions and funding.

- Programs shaped around today's threats, or some prioritization based on current assessments, will not solve any of the key problems in planning and programming. Democracies do not suddenly develop solutions they can then keep secret from their enemies. U.S. programs take time to implement and must be publicly funded and implemented in an open society. As a result, potential attackers can adopt new methods of attack and respond to any remaining gaps in U.S. capability. This makes it absolutely essential to explicitly analyze the cost of defeating any given federal program over time and the probable impact of improving any U.S. capability in driving attackers to use other means.

- New methods of analysis must be developed that examine the present and future balance of offensive, defensive, and response capabilities. They must be supported by adequate net technological assessments and by analysis of countermeasures and costs to defeat all ongoing and proposed federal activities. It is difficult enough to analyze current or near-term risks, but such analysis simply is not adequate. Effective U.S. programs can take a decade or more to fully implement, while the technology shaping current threats is constantly changing. This is not simply a matter of basic advances like biotechnology; rather, it is a matter of the steadily growing dissemination of the technology equipment needed to produce and deliver large amounts of high-explosive, chemical, and biological weapons. Much of the description of potential threats does not explicitly analyze the potential growth or changes in threat technology even when it proposes the adoption of new deterrent, defensive, and response technologies over a period of many years. There is a lack of technological net assessment that is a key not only to identifying and prioritizing effective programs, but also to managing them so they counter technology growth.

- The United States must fundamentally reexamine its assessments of the effects of CBRN weapons in the event of various types of asymmetric and terrorist attacks. Far to often the United States attempts to address the evolving threat and consequence of each type of CBRN attack by using dated research and modeling that has been designed for the needs of the Cold War, or that has been developed to deal with selected generic threats. Rather than conduct a zero-based examination of the current and potential future consequences of CBRN attacks. The modeling of nuclear and major biological attacks that underpins federal planning seems particularly weak, especially in dealing with the impact of attacks in specific major urban areas, fallout and ecological effects from a nuclear attack, and biological attacks involving multiple agents, infectious agents, and tailored or genetically enhanced weapons. It is unclear that any major effort is underway to give local, state, and regional responders the ability to model or simulate a range of attacks that apply to specific areas and cities in ways that support improved defense and response planning. The efforts of the DTRA are a major first step toward such efforts; however, they are now acutely limited in terms of resources, scale, and comprehensiveness.

- There is little real analysis of the impact of multiple, sequential, and longer-term consequences of attacks. The focus is often almost exclusively on deterring, defending, or responding to the first attack. The U.S. focus on terrorism, rather than asymmetric warfare, has left a major gap in the planning and analysis of homeland defense between relatively limited terrorist use of CBRN weapons and the far more drastic threat from ballistic missile attacks. Ironically, there is almost no practical response planning for a missile attack or any other kind of easily attributable biological or nuclear attack, although the United States is considering spending tens of billions of dollars on a missile defense system that is almost certain to remain imperfect. As a result, most "worst cases" fall fatally short of being real worst cases. There is far too little analysis of the longer-term physical, psychological, economic, political, and strategic impacts of a major successful attack or of contingencies involving multiple and sequential attacks. Truly new methods of long-term attack like agricultural or ecological attacks receive limited attention.

## THE LACK OF "TRANSPARENCY" IN FEDERAL PROGRAMS

There is nothing unique about the lack of transparency in federal programs to deal with the threats posed by state actors, their proxies, and foreign and domestic extremists and the use of CBRN weapons. The U.S. budget and agency program and budget descriptions often fail to describe their budgets, the nature of their programs, and measures of effectiveness in any detail. Aside from the DOD, there are virtually no future year spending projections, and the DOD classifies the breakouts of its future year spending projections that provide any useful description of how money is to be spent.

Far too much of the federal literature on "terrorism," however, is threat-driven. It does not describe and justify the program, it simply describes the threat. There is no description of exactly what program activities are involved or of past, current, and projected costs. There are no measures of effectiveness and total spending and procurement are confused with such measure. As a result, it becomes extremely difficult to understand what the federal government is doing and why it should do it. Many of the descriptions that agencies do provide raise real questions about the extent to which given agencies have simply reshaped existing activities to take account of the fact that Congress is providing new incremental funding and that counterterrorism has become fashionable.

These problems are compounded in part by the fact that the OMB is required to report to Congress, but there is no central agency charged with creating a plan, program, and budget. As a result, there is a large pool of federal reporting on individual problems and issues, but little effort to appraise the overall program.

There are those who would argue that part of the reason for the lack of transparency is security. There are certainly areas like intelligence where detailed program descriptions could compromise security. There are other areas where too detailed a description of U.S. investigative and response capabilities could aid an attacker in planning an attack. In broad terms, however, there is little reason to classify most of the information needed to allow outside analysts to fully understand the nature of federal efforts, and there are good reasons to require federal agencies to provide such data.

To put it bluntly, far too many existing federal activities seem to have limited substantive value, raise major uncertainties, reflect the reshaping of existing programs to obtain incremental funding, or raise questions about duplication. Furthermore, there is a tendency to imply that short-term solutions to long-term problems can be found or to fund minor palliatives simply for sake of seeming to act. Few, if any, programs provide any picture of what it will cost to fully implement the activities agencies are now beginning. None seem to provide meaningful measures of effectiveness or any analysis of the current and future costs of "defeating" the capabilities being funded.

- While there are sharp limits as to how much transparency and coordination can be given tp a wide range of federal activities, the federal effort would almost certainly benefit from a requirement for a comprehensive annual report, similar to the one the Secretary of Defense provides on the national security activities of the DOD. And for including a net assessment of the threats and U.S. capabilities and the future year budget implications of given federal activities as well as a description of the current budget request.

- Regions, state, local governments, and private entities cannot prepare in a closed environment, and there is little opportunity for feedback from outside the federal government. Equally, there are few practicalities in determining the best trade-offs between federal, regional, state, and local efforts. There cannot be an effective national partnership in dealing with homeland defense or basis for popular support without a high degree of transparency as to federal efforts and ongoing discussion and debate over what needs to be done. The federal government lacks every conceivable element of the capability to plan and impose effective homeland defense on state and local governments and the private sector. It needs constant feedback and commentary, and federal officials need to be exposed to constant challenge from state and local officials and experts, as well as analysts outside the federal government.

- Regardless of how the issue of congressional jurisdiction is resolved, there is also a clear case for requiring the federal government to submit an annual budget justification document and future year budget plan that covers all related federal activities at the same time the president submits the federal budget. Such a document could be both unclassified and classified. It would thus ensure that the executive branch coordinate its programs fully, as part of the budget process. That whoever is in charge of the federal government has real review authority. That all elements of Congress review a common plan, which may be far more important than creating a single new committee; and that state and local officials have full public review and access to the overall federal plan. It is easy to talk about "reinventing government"; it would be nice, however, to actually provide some degree of functional transparency in a critical new mission area.

## EFFECTIVE ACTION MUST BE BROAD-BASED AND SUBOPTIMIZE EFFICIENTLY

At the same time, there are limits to how much coordination is practical and how much central direction can be applied. The federal government, individual agencies, and state and local governments will often have to suboptimize changes to their current programs in those areas where they can do the most in the near term with the least money. While the Clinton administration sought to create a cohesive federal program and made progress toward this end, there are still no models, analytic methods, or simulations that can hope to integrate all of the elements of homeland defense into some master analysis or set of priorities based on a common model.

The problem is not specialization and compartmentation per se. It is that it must be the result of central management and oversight, particularly given the severe limits on what any foreseeable combination of allied, federal, state, and local efforts can do. Cost constraints will be tight, trade-offs will be made whether or not they are made openly and explicitly, and the result will be anything but leakproof. Most importantly, central direction is needed to ensure that the capabilities the United States creates evolve to respond to reality and not to established bureaucratic priorities.

It is also far from clear that threat and risk assessments can be used to create a set of scenarios that focus the defense effort or that prioritize it around a select and well-defined group of scenarios. Once again, the problem is to determine the range of low-probability events the United States may have to react to and what this means for deterrence, offense, defense, and response. While it is most likely that the United States will have to react to a series of relatively low-level events in the near term, the cumulative probability that the United States may have to react to a few much more serious events over the mid to long term may be equally as high. As a result, threat and risk assessments must consider nuclear and highly lethal biological attacks.

Furthermore, there are deep conceptual problems. As has already been discussed in depth, the range of threats simply are not predictable enough for given agencies to attempt more than a constantly evolving and uncertain process of suboptimization. Put differently, departments and agencies must often do what they can to improve their capabilities at the margin, rather than seek to create building blocks in some kind of coherent homeland defense.

Such efforts may not, however, have great impact on the United States' ability to defend against nuclear and highly lethal biological attacks. They may give the impression of defense and response capability, but the end result might not be able to cope with high levels of attack, which may well force all levels of government to improvise radically with little warning and under intense pressure. Marginal improvements in resources may fail to deal with response requirements or be impossible to allocate efficiently within the time windows required. This is particularly true because there currently seems to be little practical understanding of what a worst case or high-level attack would really do and how uncertain its effects now are.

Finally, the present coordination effort often focuses either on worst cases or on those federal programs identified as being directly designed to defend or respond to the threat state actors, their proxies, or independent extremists and terrorists pose to the U.S. homeland. This is almost certainly *not* the right way to create the most effective overall program to actually improve homeland defense. Such a program must explicitly consider the offensive, deterrent, and retaliatory capabilities of the U.S. military and intelligence agencies and the role their activities overseas can play in creating an effective deterrent to foreign attacks on the United States.

As a result, the United States needs to rethink its approach to develop a program that constantly evolves and that is based on the dilemma that it must try to manage chaos.

> Effective homeland defense must be based on responding to the patterns of threats that actually emerge and to shifts in the most likely contingency requirements. It is virtually an iron law that any effort will fail if it is based on the current theories of what threats may emerge in a given area. Once again, a guiding principle is that there is a timeline of at least a quarter of a century of uncertain risk. No program or analysis made today can possibly be based on the correct priorities. The issue is rather how quickly and effectively programs can anticipate change and react to it.

> The key to a successful result is that suboptimization must be deliberate and subject to broad review, rather than simply evolve by accident. Whatever the federal government does, it must involve an explicit and well-reasoned balance between:

> offense and defense

> actions overseas that are in concert with its friends and allies and measures actually taken in the United States

> counterproliferation and counterterrorism

> defense and response

> threats in the spectrum of threats requiring special action by the federal government as part of homeland defense and the role played by conventional law enforcement.

## FOCUSING ON PRIORITIES, PROGRAMS, AND TRADE-OFFS: CREATING EFFECTIVE PLANNING, PROGRAMMING, AND BUDGETING

The United States would face serious resource allocation problems even if CBRN threats were less uncertain and ambiguous. The threat posed by covert, terrorist, or extremist use of WMD is only one of the new threats the United States must react to. Homeland defense includes "conventional" terrorism, covert attacks, direct threats such as missile attack, and other evolving threats like information warfare. There are other transnational threats like narcotics, organized crime, and illegal immigration that pose a serious threat to American society even if they are not military or paramilitary in character. At the same time, the United States faces major problems in funding its existing future year defense program and its civil discretionary and entitlements budget. Money is, and will remain, a critical factor and will force hard trade-offs on all government action.

This book focuses on the threats to the U.S. homeland posed by state actors, the use of proxies, terrorist and extremist attacks by foreign groups or individuals, and terrorist and extremist attacks by residents of the United States using conventional weapons and WMD. Other books focus on the threat posed by direct attacks by foreign states using weapons like ballistic missiles and the threat of information and economic warfare.

This focus is not intended to imply that the emerging threats to the U.S. homeland can be neatly compartmented or do not interact. The spectrum of threats foreign governments can pose includes all of these methods of attack. Well-organized foreign and domestic terrorist/extremist groups have the *potential* to pose a wide range of high-explosive, chemical, biological, and information warfare threats. There are no rules that say foreign governments and foreign and domestic terrorist/extremist groups cannot cooperate or piggyback on each other's activities. In broad terms, however, the threats to the U.S. homeland posed by state actors, the use of proxies, terrorist and extremist attacks by foreign groups or individuals, and terrorist and extremist attacks by residents of the United States using conventional weapons and WMD require a different mix of responses. These responses can only be discussed in terms of practical alternatives if they are narrowed down to the point where the major relevant homeland defense options can be analyzed in depth.

As is the case with national missile defense, this book deals with issues that are highly politicized. Preparing to deal with the spectrum of threats posed by foreign states and terrorists using WMD is currently fashionable and "politically correct." This has had major benefits in many ways. The president and high-level officials have set forth clear policies for dealing with many aspects of the problem; Congress has passed dramatic new legislation; and major changes are well underway to improve federal, state, and local preparation to deal with the threat. There is new money available to federal agencies at a time when severe budget constraints exist on virtually every form of government spending.

Unfortunately, the very popularity of the issue of terrorism and WMD also means that there has been a rush to react to potential threats without developing a common definition of the combined threat posed by covert attacks by state actors, state use of proxies, terrorist and extremist attacks by foreign groups or individuals, and terrorist and extremist attacks by residents of the United States. There is still insufficient definition of the different kinds of threats that different kinds of WMD pose and how these relate to threats using conventional explosives and other means of conventional attack. In many cases, departments and agencies are defining the nature and intensity of the threat to meet their own internal needs and perceptions or are acting on assumptions that imply a far better ability to predict the future than can possibly exist.

As yet, there is only limited coordination in many federal, state, and local efforts except at the organization chart level. Departments and agencies struggle for resources and influence, and there are good reasons for the resulting "feeding frenzy." Even if one ignores all federal funding for CIP, the funding for counterterrorism has risen from $6.5 billion in FY1998 to $8.3 billion in FY2001. The funding for new efforts such as dealing with the threat posed by WMD has risen from approximately $645 million in FY1998 to $1.6 billion in FY2001. The attacks on the World Trade Center and the Pentagon have also led to a virtual flood of additional money.

Under these conditions, old programs are being recast to suit new policy priorities and rhetoric, while agencies compete to create new programs and assume lead responsibility. In some ways, homeland defense has replaced the Strategic Defense Initiative as the "next best thing." As the GAO and Congressional Budget Office have pointed out, the sharp rise in spending has not yet led to tight central management of the homeland defense effort, although there is a growing and steadily more effective effort to develop balanced and coordinated capabilities. There also has been little success in estimating the mid- and long-term budget implications of program growth and new responsibilities at the federal level, much less at the state and local level. Many RDT&E efforts have been started without clear deployment and life cycle implementation plans, and there are few meaningful measures of effectiveness for federal spending.

The eventual, real-world limits on how much money and human resources can be allocated to this aspect of homeland defense will, however, soon force the United States to be much more selective in choosing the programs it can continue to expand or sustain. Even today, the government needs to make every effort to coordinate its efforts and prioritize them. Regardless of partisan rhetoric, it is clear that United States is not yet prepared to pay for its existing military forces and capabilities. Furthermore, there are other major transnational problems like drugs, immigration, and cybercrime. There are many unrelated shortfalls in law enforcement and emergency response capabilities. For example, the United States faces a major crisis in medical spending even without considering the impact of responding to biological, chemical, and nuclear attacks and is sharply reducing the size of its emergency medical facilities and hospital intensive treatment capabilities.

It is only possible to ignore these realities at the start of a homeland defense program, at a time when planning is largely threat-driven and the cost of major new activities is relatively limited. As long as there is a crisis atmosphere and current outlays are limited, it is all too easy to find a credible potential threat, issue warnings, make a speech, issue an executive order, or pass a law. Any competent analyst, contractor, research firm, nongovernmental organization, or advisory group can find a new way to focus on potential threats and merits of uncosted and poorly defined solutions. The end result we risk is starting far more activities than can be finished, failing to consider the future trade-offs that must be made to deploy effective capabilities, duplicating other efforts, or refashioning existing programs under new labels.

- The United States needs to realize that improvements in policy and strategy are no substitute for effective management, programming, budgeting, and measures of the effectiveness. The practical challenge is to use more management information systems and planning, programming, and budgeting methods to tie the efforts of government together to develop clear priorities, ensure that cost estimates are provided to bring programs to maturity and sustain them, tightly manage where the money goes on an ongoing basis, ensure that the risk of countermeasures and cost to defeat is assessed on a continuing basis, find suitable measures of effectiveness, and make suitable iterative trade-offs. In fact, one recommendation of this book is that there be one central point in the federal government charged with developing a budget overview of current programs, an analysis of their future year and deployment costs, relevance to the threat, and measures of effectiveness.

- The United States must develop future year plans and coordinated program budgets. It must develop five-year plans for ongoing programs and long-term RDT&E plans that include deployment plans and cost and supporting net threat assessments for each federal department and agency. It must coordinate them at the White House level, where it will also be necessary to carry out review of relevant annual budget submissions to ensure the continued execution of federal efforts.

- The United States needs to carry out net technical assessments of the changing CBRN threat and of the technological options to improve defense and response capabilities. It also needs to examine the threat and federal RDT&E efforts in ways that support coordinated efforts to use technology to improve homeland defense and response in order to ensure that the uncertainties in threat effects are reduced, that RDT&E efforts are tied to practical deployment plans, and that risk assessments examine the cost to defeat new programs and RDT&E efforts.

- The United States must immediately undertake efforts that are nonresource intensive, such as contingency planning on legal, psychosocial, and even military issues. This planing should extend to worst case scenarios involving asymmetric state attacks, nuclear attacks, and major biological attacks, and involving the use of mixes of agents, multiple attacks, attacks against multiple cities or targets, and sequential and copy-cat attacks.

Unless the proper level of transparency and improved planning and programming is ruthlessly forced on the federal government—in the executive branch and Congress—no amount of organizational changes, committees, legislation, and directives will create the proper focus. The creation of lead agencies will be a bureaucratic farce, and state and local authorities will be confronted with conflicting demands and will often have little impact on federal bureaucratic infighting.

Equally important, congressional oversight and effective outside review and constructive criticism will be impossible. The constant misuse of security classification will create large areas of "black programs" that encourage departmental empire building and a lack of management. Programs with limited relevance will be recast as part of the homeland defense effort, and areas that really need funding will be ignored.

## MANAGING RESEARCH AND DEVELOPMENT, RATHER THAN TREATING ASYMMETRIC ATTACKS, TERRORISM, AND THE CBRN THREAT AS AN EXCUSE FOR A "WISH LIST" AND "SLUSH FUND"

Research and development programs receive little detailed description and the description that is provided often concentrates on the threat with which is being dealt. No agency provides a meaningful description of its future program, future costs, milestones, or measures of effectiveness. Cooperation with state and local agencies is often ignored, and when it is not, it tends to be discussed in anecdotal terms.

There is no evidence that any department or agency has provided a technology net assessment to examine whether its programs will provide defensive capabilities that outpace advances in offensive capability. There is virtually no discussion of the risk posed by countermeasures or the cost to defeat current and planned programs. There is no discussion of the outyear costs of research and development activity or of estimated deployment schedules and measures of effectiveness and life cycle costs. Almost without exception, there is no way to be certain to what degree which given programs in given departments or agencies are actually focused on CBRN and other counterterrorism activities, or have simply recast ongoing or desired programs to compete for such funds.

- RDT&E is not a magic bullet that should be exempt from adequate planning, programming, and threat validation. Federal research and development efforts have a poor to dismal record of effective management. It is time to reverse this situation.

- Threat analysis needs to be improved by joint efforts within the intelligence and federal RDT&E communities to create annual national threat assessments that evaluate the overall trends in threat technology and methods of attack and to provide RDT&E planners with better and more technologically oriented threat forecasts. This should probably take the form of an annual NIE with outside support from a task force composed of cleared RDT&E experts. It should explicitly consider the risk of asymmetric state, as well as terrorist and extremist attacks, and the linkage between the growing risk of biological attacks, the problems created by changes in the pattern of natural disease, and the changes in biotechnology. Two key goals behind such an effort will be to educate the intelligence community in the impact of changes in technology and to improve strategic warning.

- The United States must develop and conduct ongoing annual net threat assessments of the foreign and domestic threat of CBRN attacks and terrorism. Threat assessments are not adequate to establish the balance of evolving trends in offensive and defensive technology and the formulation, prioritization, and execution of successful RDT&E programs.

- RDT&E program planning and justification needs fundamental improvement at the individual program level. As has been discussed earlier, programs should not be justified or executed without regularly update plans that examine how the technology would be deployed, the systems and training required, estimated life cycle costs, and the required test and evaluation program and measures of effectiveness. Programs should only be carried out after examination of the probable and possible trends in the threat, the availability of countermeasures to defeat them, and the cost to defeat them. Where possible, there should be independent assessments of the probability of success and the validity of the cost analysis and test and evaluation program.

It should be obvious that basic research programs require a different level of justification, planning, and programming from research and development efforts that are moving toward deployment. The basic problem, however, is that these improvements either do not now take place as programs mature, or often take the form of internally managed efforts that are more designed to sell the program involved than prioritize and manage it.

## LOOKING BEYOND CBRN THREATS: DEALING WITH ALL MEDICAL RISKS AND COSTS, THE NEED FOR A COMPREHENSIVE PUBLIC INFORMATION CAPABILITY, AND THE LINKAGE TO IMPROVED STRATEGIC DETERRENCE AND RESPONSE CAPABILITIES

The previous analysis indicates that there is a need for a zero-based review of the current data on the lethality of biological weapons and for a comprehensive net technical assessment of current and future trends in biological offense and defense. Biological warfare defense and response efforts cannot, however, be separated from the need for an effective national health program.

Response measures against biological and nuclear attacks can require truly massive increases in public health efforts and emergency services at a time when the United States already faces major problems in funding medical entitlement programs and growing cost constraints are being placed on investments in medical capabilities that normally have high utilization rates. The response capabilities required in dealing with large biological and nuclear "incidents" may simply be unaffordable without far more evidence that such attacks are likely, and effective treatment may simply be impossible. One grim result is that "triage" may have to be performed in ways that deliberately allow a high number of casualties to die.

The risk of attacks on the U.S. homeland that have massive medical consequences requires that homeland defense measures deal with two major interrelated problems in public health policy and spending.

- The key limiting factor in terms of response capability and expense will be medical treatment. This requires nationally distributed capabilities, but it is unclear that they are technically credible and can be made cost effective. It is far from clear that today's defense and response training really prepares anyone for threats other than relatively small and easily characterized events. Much of the nonmedical response effort seems to be focused around obtaining equipment and facilities to "get well" from past underfunding or to provide equipment for small events. It is unclear that creating standard packages of such equipment, or responding to responder's priorities, really deals with the problem of homeland defense. The question is what kinds of training and equipment really help and what can really be done locally on a nation-wide basis.

- There is a significant amount of medical literature—including a recent report by the National Intelligence Council—that indicates that the United States is under significant cumulative threat of the outbreak of some disease for which current medical treatment is not adequate. In short, the United States may face a serious threat from nature as well as from foreign attackers and domestic extremists.[1]

- However, U.S. medical spending has already reached the point where it dominates much of the end use of the entitlements in the federal budget and where drastic efforts are being made to down-size medical spending. These facts are largely ignored in much of the current discussion of homeland defense, which (1) focuses on threats and on research and development measures that do not have a deployment cost, and (2) often involves response efforts so limited in estimated casualties that the list of equipment is "affordable" largely because it is assumed that the existing infrastructure can deal with the casualties and that the medical impact is treatable and involves noninfectious threats. These assumptions, however, are only valid as long as the most serious threats are defined away and the eventual need to pay for facilities and a full spectrum of response measures is ignored.

- The United States should not invest in more stockpiling of vaccines and medicine, improved public health measures, or other major new response efforts without far better planning, programming, and justification than it currently possesses. Similarly, no measures should be taken to suggest or require improvements in federal and military health and medical capabilities, private health care, or medical education without such an effort. Major improvements may well be needed in all of these areas, but rushing forward in individual areas without coordinated programs can waste federal money and potentially impose massive waste on state, local, and private-sector efforts. This is particularly true because many efforts are vulnerable to simple countermeasures.

- Such as using a disease for which there is no stockpile, a mix of diseases, or tailored diseases with new symptoms or effects that make timely response extremely difficult, make the improved facility a target, or prove to be of marginal value in a limited attack or be overwhelmed in a major attack. To put it bluntly, the U.S. medical, biosciences, and emergency responses communities have an alarming tendency to demand that federal money be thrown at problems without adequate overall planning and justification—often with motives that seem to be focused more on other priorities than homeland defense. Focusing narrowly on the highest-priority programs will almost certainly stress available funding beyond its limits. There is no room for hobby shops and technical adventures.

- There are fundamental problems in medical ethics and civil rights that must be addressed at higher levels of attack. No one really wants to address the fact that quarantines may be necessary in ways that threaten civil rights. Overwhelming medical and response services with suspected, curable, and fatal cases will require decisions as to who lives, suffers, and/or dies, and who receives limited treatment resources, which can challenge every current practice and aspect of medical ethics. It is fundamentally unrealistic, however, not to explicitly address these issues and unethical to place the burden without real warning on state, local, and private responders and medical practitioners.

- A similar problem must be addressed in terms of the psychological impact of attacks, on a short- and long-term basis. There is an unresolved and critically important debate over the extent to which attacks will produce local, regional, and national panic and a host of related psychosomatic problems that may or may not be related to physical problems. Some argue for intensive treatment and care. Others argue that such careful may be unaffordable in terms of resources and that exaggerating the threat may become a self-fulfilling prophecy. Far too often, those who focus on the psychological dimension ignore the strategic priorities of the United States. It have to minimize the broader national impact of an attack and/or ignore the collateral problem of dealing with the long-term physical problems created by radiation and exposure to disease, toxins, and chemical poisons. This aspect of response needs a major research effort and should not be ignored simply because it is difficult and unfamiliar.

- Practical real-time information may often be more cost-effective and save more lives than investments in medical services, biosciences, and physical response efforts. Much of the current response effort is built around comprehensive rescue and treatment. It fails to focus on the need to provide real-time data to all of those in the area under attack, and nearby, as to what to do to minimize exposure. There is no plan to use the national broadcast information system to create a single, reliable source of data or to educate national and local media as to the need to be ready to provide help in the event of warning or execution of an attack. There are no plans to characterize attacks precisely with real-time detection and characterization and to communicate specific information about whether to stay (and what physical measures should be taken), whether and how to flee, and whether to seek treatment. At high levels of attack, such measures may be far more effective and affordable than any practical investment in improved medical care and other physical response capabilities.

- The United States must address the issue of deterrence and defensive response against foreign threats, as well as the issue of aiding its allies if they come under such attack. The United States cannot afford to rely purely on internal defense and response. Attacks on the United States may well escalate out of theater- or regional-driven conflicts and tensions. Foreign movements and governments need to be deterred and the United States must have plans to respond to prevent attacks and limit or respond to follow on attacks. This creates new dilemmas in international law in an era of undeclared wars, as well as highlights the gap in U.S. strategic offensive planning between counterterrorism efforts overseas, conventional warfare, and nuclear retaliation. Creating an effective political, economic, and military capability to respond to an asymmetric nuclear or major biological asymmetric or foreign terrorist may again do far more to reduce casualties than any practical investment in improved medical care and other physical response capabilities. At the same time, it raises critical issues about attribution, targeting, collateral damage, international law, and international politics that the United States has only begun to address.

It should also be noted in this context that much of the current planning for medical and response treatment focuses on attacks on human beings, rather than on livestock, agriculture, or the ecology. This focus probably is valid in reflecting current probabilities, but it ignores critical possible vectors of attack, especially those where hostile states or terrorists may develop steadily greater expertise and capability. Attacks on agriculture and the ecology may offer a subtle form of attack, further compound the problems in attribution and response, and be conducted as either a long-term form of anonymous attack or silent revenge long after a crisis seems to be over.

## HOMELAND DEFENSE AND/OR LAW ENFORCEMENT

The United States also faces major problems in defining the point at which federal intervention in some form of a homeland defense program is needed, as distinguished from a reliance on normal federal, state, and local law enforcement. Many of the definitions now used for terrorism include virtually any threat of violence by an individual or small group with a political or ideological agenda. In practice, however, most such threats are dealt with as normal law enforcement activities unless some foreign element is involved. Even in the cases where foreigners are involved, many are dealt with through normal law enforcement means.

It does not make sense to change these arrangements without clear cause, and the previous statistics on terrorism in the United States need to be kept in perspective in allocating law enforcement resources, as well as the new level of risk that was demonstrated by the attacks on the World Trade Center and the Pentagon. Horrible as the resulting casualties were, there are other risks and other violent threats. According to the FBI's uniform crime statistics, there were ten cities in the United States with populations of one hundred thousand or more that had more than one hundred murders in the first six months of 1999, and three with over two hundred murders. If rapes and assaults are counted, there were forty-seven cities in the United States with populations of one hundred thousand or more that had more than one thousand "casualties" in the first six months of 1999, and nine with over three thousand.[2]

There is a reason why it now takes forty thousand armed men and women to try to secure the greater New York metropolitan area alone. There is also a reason why law enforcement activity cannot be centered around counterterrorism or dealing with low-probability covert attacks until there is a far clearer and more dangerous threat than that which now appears to exist. At the same time, it is inconceivable that the United States could develop an effective approach to homeland defense that did not attempt to make use of these resources at every level of law enforcement.

- The task is to find the right trade-offs between reliance on normal law enforcement and specialized homeland defense activity, and between using existing resources with other primary missions and creating new dedicated homeland defense components.

- It may be that the United States will require a more decentralized and distributed defense and response effort than the federal government now realizes. Most forms of federal response, and a great deal of state and regional response, could come too late to fit the critical time windows for biotreatment and to deal with the prompt effects of nuclear explosions and fallout. Some form of decentralized and distributed local and/or civil defense may be the only answer. The concerns then become prompt attack characterization, instructions to flee or stay, proper guidance to responders, and options for low-cost distributed defensive aids like masks, medicines, and so on.

- The United States needs to rethink civil defense. It must look beyond asymmetric warfare and terrorism, consider broader national public health priorities, and WMD "leakage" problems. Real-time warning and threat and attack characterization allow federal, state, and local defenders and responders to provide the widest area of coverage with the most cost-effective methods. The effective use of media to warn and advise citizens at risk will often help people avoid the effects of attack. Flee or stay advice will be critical, as will detailed advice on what to do in the office, home, or car. There must be a real-time linkage between defender, responder, and media. At the same time, the United States should analyze whether there are credible and affordable low-cost civil defense options and examine what citizens, corporations, local, state, and federal governments might really be able to afford. Options like gas and biological defense masks, home shelters, and so on need examination.

- At a different level, the United States again needs to establish its ecological and agricultural defense requirements. The risk posed by biotechnology cannot be evaluated solely in terms of threats to human beings.

## THE ROLE OF THE INTELLIGENCE COMMUNITY AND THE NEED FOR IMPROVED INTELLIGENCE

The previous recommendations have touched on many aspects of intelligence and the need for improved threat assessment, linkage between intelligence and law enforcement and response, intelligence for deterrence and military response, and net assessments in which the intelligence community plays a major role. At the same time, there is a need for caution.

When federal planners deal with uncertainty, they tend to make impossible demands on the intelligence community for strategic warning, detection, characterization, attribution, targeting, and damage assessment. There is an almost ritual tendency to round up the usual suspects and call for yet another strategic warning study or effort to expand human intelligence. In far too many cases, there is an effort to make impossible demands on intelligence and/or shift responsibility. Without providing a net assessment of capabilities and responsibilities, the necessary resources, and/or the tasking necessary to either maintain such efforts or execute painful trade-offs between existing tasking and new tasking. Under these conditions, it is hardly surprising that experienced intelligence officers find it difficult to take such efforts seriously and are forced to silently accept what they privately regard as an irresponsible allocation of responsibility by policymakers.

No one can quarrel with the fact that virtually every commission, study group, and analyst that has examined homeland defense calls for improved intelligence. There is broad agreement among most of the experts in the field, and they are almost certainly right. There are, however, important warnings about each of the efforts to improve intelligence that are recommended by various experts.

- Delegating "mission impossible" is not a solution. There will almost certainly be serious shortfalls in warning, defense, detection, characterization, attribution, targeting, and damage assessment regardless of what is done to improve intelligence resources, capabilities, and technology. The United States must not repeat the critical mistake it made in its planning for the revolution in military affairs by placing an impossible burden on the intelligence community. It must accept the fact that the fog of war will be a key problem in asymmetric conflicts and terrorism, and plan accordingly.

- Political, economic, and military response planning must explicitly be based on the high risk that no improvement in defense, detection, characterization, attribution, and targeting can meet peacetime legal standards in many contingencies, and the United States will still have to respond immediately to a critical threat to its strategic interests. Intelligence cannot eliminate risk and uncertainty, and is very unlikely to meet all of the criteria for an idealized approach to international law. This is no excuse for reckless action or a homeland defense strategy based on "ready, fire, aim." It also, however, is no excuse for a political, economic, and military response plan based on intelligence and law enforcement's ability to perform "mission impossible."

- Isolated intelligence efforts are no substitute for the fusion of intelligence, planning, and operations into a single integrated effort. As is touched on in more depth shortly, it has been clear since the Vietnam War that efforts to segregate intelligence, operations, and planning are not practical whenever joint operations are needed and the stakes demand the most quick and effective response possible.

- Strategic warning can be improved. However, it is as much a problem in decision making as intelligence, and it can never be relied on or be a substitute for real-time intelligence in a crisis. The intelligence community has been tasked with improving strategic warning for nearly forty years, and virtually every time a new strategic problem arises or the nation has not prepared for a new crisis or event. In case after case, however, the problem remains that decisive and unambiguous warning is impossible and that decision makers tend to ignore any warning with honest caveats and uncertainties. The reality that intelligence may also not have better access to indicators and decision makers is ignored, sometimes in ways that try to shift the blame for failing to foresee a given crisis or event onto the intelligence community. In the real world, strategic warning is a net assessment activity, the added data available to the intelligence community does not give it the gift of prophecy or a crystal ball, and no amount of warning can compensate for the policymakers refusal or inability to act.

- Human intelligence (Humint) can help, but it is not a solution to warning or uncertainty. Intelligence resource managers have every reason to cringe when outsiders call for added resources for human intelligence. Such recommendations have been made for decades and the result is almost invariably to increase intelligence tasking without providing the resources. Often, such recommendations are made without an adequate understanding of just how difficult it is to improve human intelligence and make it reliable, the level of effort and resources required, and the need to become deeply involved with terrorists and officials in some of the world's most repressive governments. Furthermore, no improvement in collection has meaning without an improvement in analysis.

- Major challenges will also exist in improving the National Technical Means (NTM) and the work of the NSA and National Reconnaissance Office (NRO). The idea that resources can be freed to improve Humint by taking them from NTM requires far more validation than simple policy-level assertions. The United States faces massive technical and resource challenges in maintaining the current level of NSA and NRO activity in the face of changes in technology, and these challenges will be compounded by shifts toward asymmetric warfare, improvements in terrorist operations, and changes in CBRN technology and means of delivery. The Cold War is over, but the fact remains that there is still the same ongoing average of twenty-five to thirty conflicts in the world that has existed during every day since the end of World War II. Unless far better analysis and programming becomes available, there is no reason to assume that NTM can be preserved even with its current coverage and resources.

- Technology is unlikely to be a magic bullet for improving intelligence, law enforcement, or operations. Technology can greatly improve U.S. detection, characterization, attribution, and targeting capabilities. However, far more promises are being made than can possibly be kept, and many are repetitions of promises about the same use of new sensors, detection, and characterization equipment during the height of efforts to improve technology for the war on drugs, or even in the Vietnam War. Far too often, promises are made about devices and new analytic techniques like data mining that bear little relation to their real-world capability, availability, and cost. In some cases, the technology is being developed as a device or technique without any practical plan to deploy a system to use it or to examination such an effort's cost-effectiveness. This is as true of technology for defense, response, and military operations as for intelligence. However, the compartmentation of intelligence, and the need to protect sources and means, often exacerbates these problems.

The events of September 2001 have shown that America faces real threats that are so costly and dangerous that it must hunt down and kill those involved if no other means are available. At a minimum, it needs a strong operations capability in the intelligence community to assist in capturing and/or targeting such individuals. This means rebuilding operations capabilities and finding a way to give a "license to kill" when this is necessary. It also means adding new operational capabilities such as financial and information warfare.

Once again, it must be stressed that improving intelligence is a vital aspect of effective homeland defense. However, predelegating the blame for the failure to create effective defense is not. Neither is making promises that cannot be kept.

## THE CHALLENGE OF OPERATIONS

As yet, there are no clear plans provided for effective command, control, communications, computer support, intelligence, and "battle management" ($C^4I$/BM) capability to defend and respond to asymmetric state and large-scale CBRN terrorist attacks of the kind that would saturate and/or destroy local capabilities to use law enforcement and emergency response techniques. There is also a tendency within the federal government to assume that agency-level coordination in Washington could substitute for the deployment of a $C^4I$/BM capability to the area or areas of attack and for the fusion of all capabilities into a single operations and crisis management center.

This approach tacitly relies on precrisis exercises and coordination methods within the federal government—between federal, state, and local governments—to create an effective operational capability to deal with events that require on-scene expertise in the field, the fusion of information and operations, and decision making and response in real-time. It may well be adequate in dealing with low- to medium-level threats and attacks, but it goes against all of the painful lessons the U.S. military has learned about jointness, fusion, and the need to put operations firmly on the scene. It relies heavily on the assumption that FEMA can be restructured to improvise the needed crisis management authority in Washington and in the field.

Often on the assumption that the reaction times and focus of Washington-based federal coordination, coupled to federal activities elsewhere in the country, are adequate to meet regional, state, and local needs in a true mass emergency.

These are exceedingly dangerous assumptions, and state and local responders have already raised challenging questions about how well federal programs can be managed that are remote from the scene and the reactions times for federal decision making and response in a wide range of fields. There is no way to provide firm recommendations without a great deal more planning and exercise data, however, some things are clear:

- An operations center may be needed at the federal level with an integrated command and on-scene fusion of all the necessary expertise and decision-making authority. Serious study is needed of exactly what kind of operations center, authority, expertise, and facilities will be needed and how to immediately tailor this federal effort to specific contingency conditions.

- Similar examination is needed of what kind of operations center will be needed in the field, what role the federal government should play, and how to allocate federal, state, and local levels of authority and jurisdiction at different levels of attack. Today, there is far too great a gap between planning to use state and local authority and vague discussions of what would happen if the president should declare a state of national emergency. There is far too little study of real-world time-line and reaction requirements. Coordination is generally used as a substitute for fusion and too many assumptions are made about what can be improvised in Washington and what needs to be immediately deployable in the field.

## RULE OF LAW, HUMAN RIGHTS, ASYMMETRIC WARFARE, HIGH LEVELS OF ATTACK, AND "NEW PARADIGMS"

Homeland defense impacts heavily on legal and human rights issues. Until now, the threats to the United States have been limited enough so that the United States can afford to shape its response on the basis of strict observance of civil law and human rights. There is also ample emergency authority for the president, governors, and local officials to use virtually all of the assets of government to deal with homeland defense emergencies if they arise. Even restrictions on the use of the military, such as the Posse Comitatus Act (18 USC 1385), have so many exceptions that the problem is much more likely to get sufficient warning to act than any practical legal barrier to effective action.

As has been touched on earlier, however, much of the present discussion of legal and human rights issues, however, ignores what would happen if the threat of the use of biological or nuclear weapons against the U.S. homeland became more tangible and immediate. It also ignores the real-world effects of state actors or terrorists/extremists carrying out highly lethal attacks. These effects include the problems in human rights created by the need to deal with mass triage in the face of saturated medical facilities and/ or to contain a civil population with force in the event of an attack using a highly infectious agent.

- U.S. intelligence efforts and law enforcement must reorganize to deal with the risk of a "paradigm" shift in the willingness and ability to use WMD in unconventional attacks on the U.S. homeland and be given the proper legislation and regulations. Many states are now involved in a process of proliferation that will change their capabilities to carry out such attacks. Advances in manufacturing, petrochemicals, and the biological sciences are making it steadily easier for state and non-state actors to build lethal chemical and biological weapons. The technology and components to develop every aspect of nuclear weapons other than weapons-grade uranium and plutonium are becoming more available.

- At the same time, there is a need for new basic safeguards to the rule of law and human rights. No change should be made to the protection of civil and individual rights that does not require extraordinary due process and carefully defined levels of threat and potential risk. Virtually all attacks and threats to date have not posed a level of risk that justifies any change in current legal restrictions or protections of civil liberties. Such threats may emerge in the future, but they also may not. The risks posed by WMD and asymmetric warfare must be defined in ways where changes in the role of U.S. intelligence, defense, and response are clearly linked to outside judicial review and where only the most serious risks involve changes in the way in which government deals with such threats. There must be clear plans for possible states of emergency that do more than enable effective governmental defense and response. The United States must define how it will act to protect civil rights and liberties even under worst case defense and response conditions and provide a clearly defined set of reviewing authorities for any action in a state of emergency.

- The issue of "live or let die" triage in the event of an actual attack where casualties saturate response capability poses the greatest single threat to human rights. It must be addressed to guide local responders and to determine whether new diagnostic and detection technology can reduce the medical burden. The United States should not wait for the event to come to grips with the critical issue of how triage can be provided in response activities in ways that best protect individual rights as well as allow the most effective use of limited response resources.

## THE NEED FOR CENTRAL COORDINATION AND MANAGEMENT OF THE FEDERAL EFFORT

There is broad agreement that some central office is needed to coordinate the federal effort, to ensure proper program and budget review, to coordinate auditing of capability, and to coordinate emergency response capability. There is also broad agreement that such a coordinator needs sufficient rank and authority to speak for the president on these issues and to ensure that agency budget submissions include adequate programs and funding. Some have proposed an independent office similar to the Year 2000 Program, some a new form of drug czar, and some a cabinet-level officer. The Bush Administration has tentatively chosen to expand the roles of the vice president and FEMA, although its plans remain somewhat vague.

- These issues need far more careful study and have to clarify who is in charge of what and what planning and management tools will be provided. Similar arguments are being made about providing a coordinator to deal with critical infrastructure attacks and all of homeland defense. At the same time, many of the prevention and response skills involved are highly specialized and duplicate the activity needed to respond to many other forms of emergency, such as accidents, weather, and so on. At this point in time, what really seems to be needed is a presidential task force to review the broad need to deal with all of the emerging threats to the U.S. homeland and to draft recommendations and a PDD for the next president.

- There are fundamental differences in the response needed at given levels of attack and threat. Coordinating counterterrorism, civil law enforcement, and response to relatively limited attacks does not involve a state of national emergency, an undeclared war, or the kind of defense and response efforts needed to deal with major nuclear and biological attacks. It is not clear that an office focused on "peacetime" threats will have the staffing, contingency planning capability, and crisis management capability to deal with the kind of threats posed by asymmetric warfare.

- Nuclear, large-scale biological attacks, and/or infectious biological attacks require very different levels of skills. Regardless of the federal direction of homeland defense efforts, the technology and effects of the most lethal forms of attack are so different that any effort to manage the response must include different mixes of skills and federal departments and agencies.

- No change in management or direction can be effective unless it resolves how to integrate the DOD and U.S. intelligence community into a homeland defense effort designed to deal with asymmetric threats or state and proxy attacks using nuclear weapons or effective biological weapons. Scale is a critical issue, as is the potential need to integrate the response to attacks on the U.S. homeland with U.S. action in theater or regional conflicts.

- Effective coordination and management means effective review of budgets and future year programs. No change in leadership or management can be effective if it is not based on review authority over the budgets of federal departments and agencies. The development and review of an integrated future-year program that includes a rolling program budget that projects expenditures at least five years into the future and allows mission-oriented assessment of the overall federal effort.

- Similarly, effective coordination and management requires full review of all federal RDT&E efforts and sufficient net technical capability to make risk assessments and to carry out net technical assessments. Technology offers major potential improvements in homeland defense, but it must be applied as a system or systems, rather than as a series of uncoordinated increments, and analysis of the cost to deploy technology and means of defeating it needs far more explicit analysis than it currently receives.

- Crisis and operations management can be required at radically different levels and involve radically different levels of planning assistance. Anyone can be called a crisis manager. Actual crisis management is extremely difficult. The moment a crisis escalates from "conventional" terrorism to a major threat or response to major uses of WMD, an effective operations command or management capability must be in place.

## BROADER SOLUTIONS AND NEW APPROACHES TO NATIONAL STRATEGY: REACTING TO ASYMMETRIC WARFARE

Finally, the United States needs to close the current gap between counterterrorism and asymmetric warfare in ways that go beyond narrowly defined defense and response efforts. Homeland defense should not be defined purely in terms of reactions within the U.S. homeland. The United States must examine ways it can use its offensive capabilities to deter such attacks and respond to them in ways that will ensure such attacks are limited in scope or do not occur in the future.

There is a need to revise U.S. strategic offensive doctrine to deal with these issues. The Cold War may be over, but the threat of CBRN attacks is not. Homeland defense should not mean that the United States drifts toward a response-oriented approach or a Maginot Line–like emphasis on defense. Major asymmetric attacks must be firmly deterred, preempted or reduced in size, and firmly retaliated against. It must be clear that attacking states, and states that deliberately host terrorist movements, will be the target of U.S. strikes directed at the nation and not simply at the leadership, and the United States needs to give its theater and strategic forces this option. As part of this effort, the United States must answer the following questions:

- What changes to deterrence, offensive strike capability, and retaliation really matter if states and foreign movements are involved?
- What can be done to aid defenders in securing U.S. borders and territory?
- What can be done in terms of intelligence and technology to rapidly and conclusively identify the attacker?
- What can be done to accelerate and improve warning time for offensive, counterattack, and deterrent purposes?
- When is the threat and/or attack one that justifies "war"? When does a civil emergency become a de facto conflict?
- What should the retaliatory doctrine be? How lethal should the escalatory action be? How can the United States best halt or punish the attacker? How can it prevent follow-on attacks? How can it deter future attackers?

- What strategic linkage is needed between homeland defense and theater defense? What will act best to defend the U.S. homeland and enhance force protection? What will protect our allies? What will deter third-party adventures and copycats? What is needed to cope with multiple, mixed (cocktail), and sequential attacks?

Responding to the threats posed by asymmetric warfare also means revisions to intelligence, threat assessment efforts, arms control, and counterproliferation efforts. Once again, effective U.S. efforts raise key issues that go beyond the scope of this book:

Establishing opportunities and limits for intelligence capability is critical to effective action.

How much can targeting, precision strike, weapons effects, and battle damage assessment really be improved?

Limiting asymmetric capability and peacetime improvements in threat characterization are critical, and limiting and monitoring technology transfer and RDT&E efforts is the first line of defense.

What can be done to improve or replace Humint? Can data-mining and artificial intelligence provide a new technological approach?

The myth that expanding Humint efforts will help needs to be transformed into a reality or be dismissed.

How can cooperation with U.S. allies' intelligence services and international law enforcement agencies be used as a first line of defense?

Detection of efforts to proliferate is not enough. Homeland defense requires U.S. intelligence to improve its capability to characterize the nature of possible attacks as precisely as possible to reduce burden on defender and responder, and to help prioritize and define options for offensive and/or counteroffensive action.

Nunn-Lugar is extremely cost-effective homeland defense and needs to be fully extended to biological weapons.

Sanctions, arms control, and export control regimes like the Nuclear Nonproliferation Treaty, the Missile Technology Control Regime, the Australia List, the Wassener Convention, the CWC, and so on are vital parts of an effective homeland defense effort. They all have limits, and these limits generally are far more serious in detecting and preventing the development of small asymmetric threats and terrorism than the deployment of large war fighting capabilities. Existing arms control inspection and verification regimes can also act to license the transfer of key nuclear and chemical technologies to suspect countries or countries where terrorists and extremists operate. Even though they have little impact on the threat of internal terrorism and extremism in a sophisticated industrial power like the United States. Nevertheless, they can be useful tools in creating a more effective approach to homeland defense.

The problem of controlling biological threats in the form of asymmetric warfare and terrorist attacks requires a zero-based reexamination of efforts to create an inspection regime for the BWC, develop effective export and supply control regimes, and improve the detection and characterization capability of world medical facilities and the WHO. Far more open debate and net technical assessment is needed of what can and cannot be done to control the spread of biotechnology, the use of convertible pharmaceutical and food processing equipment, and the access to this kind of equipment. The ongoing debate between those who say control regimes are feasible and those who deny this needs to be resolved with far more objective analysis and explicit attention to the new threats that may emerge to the U.S. homeland.

As has been stressed at the beginning of this chapter, and throughout the whole book, the United States must take an all-inclusive approach to homeland defense and rethink what is sometimes a near isolationist approach to homeland defense. Much of the literature assumes that the United States will be the primary target of attacks and the only scene of attacks. One classic argument is that the generic nature of the U.S. role as the "world's only super power" makes it the primary target of foreign action. Similarly, there is a tendency to assume that U.S. deterrence, defense, response, and political and economic action can occur as part of a two-person, zero-sum game.

In actual practice, the United States is a target of foreign movements largely as an extension of theater-driven conflicts and tensions where it is often a secondary target for state and terrorist attacks. This is certainly true today in Northeast Asia, the Persian Gulf, and the Middle East. In many, if not most cases involving state, proxy, and large-scale terrorist attacks, attacks on the U.S. homeland will be an extension of theater-driven conflicts by other means. The United States will be linked to its allies, coalitions, regional peacemaking efforts, or other critical foreign involvements. Even where this is not the case, the United States will often badly need the support of its allies and international law enforcement agencies. Homeland defense is not an exercise in isolationism, and if the United States does try to play a two-person, zero-sum game it will probably lose or pay an extraordinarily high price for its conceptual and practical failure to deal with the world it lives in.

## NOTES

1. National Intelligence Council, "The Global Infectious Disease Threat and Its Implications for the United States," CIA NIE-99-17D (January 2000), <http://www.cia.gov/cia/publications/nie/report/nie99-17d.htm>.

2. Federal Bureau of Investigation, *Uniform Crime Reports* (January–June 1999, and November 21, 1999), Table 4.

## About the Author

ANTHONY H. CORDESMAN is the Arleigh A. Burke Chair in Strategy at the Center for Strategic and International Studies, and a military analyst for ABC News. The author of numerous books on Middle Eastern security issues, he has served in senior positions for the Secretary of Defense, NATO, the Department of Energy, State Department, and the U.S. Senate.